PETER GATRELL

The Unsettling of Europe

*The Great Migration,
1945 to the Present*

ALLEN LANE
an imprint of
PENGUIN BOOKS

ALLEN LANE

UK | USA | Canada | Ireland | Australia
India | New Zealand | South Africa

Allen Lane is part of the Penguin Random House group of companies whose addresses
can be found at global.penguinrandomhouse.com.

First published in the United States of America by Basic Books, an imprint
of Perseus Books, LLC, a subsidiary of Hachette
Book Group, Inc. 2019
First published in Great Britain by Allen Lane 2019
001

Printed in Great Britain by Clays Ltd, Elcograf S.p.A.

A CIP catalogue record for this book is available from the British Library

ISBN: 978-0-241-29045-3

www.greenpenguin.co.uk

MIX
Paper from
responsible sources
FSC® C018179

Penguin Random House is committed to a
sustainable future for our business, our readers
and our planet. This book is made from Forest
Stewardship Council® certified paper.

Contents

Contents

Abbreviations

AfD	Alternative für Deutschland (Alternative for Germany)
BAMF	Bundesamt für Migration und Flüchtlinge (Federal Office for Migration and Refugees)
DOMiD	Dokumentationszentrum und Museum über die Migration in Deutschland (Documentation Centre and Museum of Migration in Germany)
DP	Displaced Person
EEC	European Economic Community
EEU	Eurasian Economic Union
EU	European Union
Eurodac	European Data Archive Convention
Eurosur	European Border Surveillance System
EVW	European Volunteer Worker
FAS	Fonds d'action sociale (Social Action Funds)
FLN	Front de libération nationale (National Liberation Front)
FRG	Federal Republic of Germany
Frontex	European Border and Coast Guard Agency (Frontières extérieures)
GDR	German Democratic Republic
ICEM	Intergovernmental Committee for European Migration

Abbreviations

INED	Institut national d'études démographiques (Institute for Demographic Studies)
IOM	International Organisation for Migration
IRO	International Refugee Organisation
MSF	Médecins sans Frontières (Doctors Without Borders)
NATO	North Atlantic Treaty Organization
NGO	Nongovernmental organisation
ONI	Office national d'immigration (National Immigration Office, France)
SBZ	*Sowjetische Besatzungszone* (Soviet zone of occupation)
SIS	Schengen Information System
SONACOTRAL	Société nationale de construction de logements pour les travailleurs Algériens (National Housing Construction Company for Algerian Workers)
SPD	Sozialdemokratische Partei Deutschlands (Social Democratic Party, Germany)
UNHCR	(Office of the) United Nations High Commissioner for Refugees
UNRRA	United Nations Relief and Rehabilitation Administration
USEP	US Escapee Program
WCC	World Council of Churches
WRY	World Refugee Year

Acknowledgements

First and foremost, my thanks go to Simon Winder at Penguin Books and Lara Heimert at Basic Books for inviting me to write a book about European migration since 1945, and to Felicity Bryan for being a staunch advocate from the outset. They have all offered much-needed encouragement along the way. I should also like to mention Paul Betts, who originally recommended me to the Felicity Bryan Agency.

Katie Lambright at Basic Books sent me numerous comments on a first draft: she knows how much her careful and perceptive reading improved what was originally a sprawling manuscript. As copyeditor, Kathy Streckfus helped me to put my ideas across more clearly. I am enormously grateful to them both for their advice. I would also like to thank Ellen Davies, Stephanie Summerhays, and others on the team at Penguin and Basic Books, and George Lucas at Inkwell Management in New York. I found it very inspiring at a late stage to work with my picture editor, Cecilia Mackay. Her advice on images and layout was much appreciated.

I am grateful to the Faculty of Humanities and the School of Arts, Languages and Cultures at the University of Manchester for granting me research leave that enabled me to work on this book and to manage all my other commitments.

Acknowledgements

Much of what I have to say in this book relies heavily on the work of specialists in the field, as well as the published testimony of migrants. I hope the endnotes reflect how much I owe to them. Colleagues at the ever-helpful staff in the Document Supply Unit at the University of Manchester Library kept me supplied with books. I should also like to thank staff at Cambridge University Library and the Library of the London School of Economics and Political Science, where browsing the stacks regularly threw up all sorts of surprises. This is also an opportunity to acknowledge once again the many archivists whose expertise enabled me to carry out research for this and other books of mine.

Given the scope of this book, I needed to consult with people who could advise me on my areas of ignorance. In naming them and expressing my gratitude, I should emphasise that none of them should be held responsible for any errors or misinterpretation on my part.

Katia Chornik, Hans Wallage, and Gustav Ängeby contributed valuable research assistance at an early stage, and I am grateful to them for placing at my disposal their knowledge of the literature in Spanish, Dutch, and Swedish, respectively.

A number of colleagues at the University of Manchester offered advice on specific issues and encouraged me along the way. They include Ana Carden-Coyne, Eleanor Davey, Alex Dowdall, Pierre Fuller, Yoram Gorlizki, Sasha Handley, Laure Humbert, Jo Laycock, Margaret Littler, Yaron Matras, Frank Mort, Tanja Müller, Kasia Nowak, Sarah Roddy, Julie-Marie Strange, Bertrand Taithe, Vera Tolz, and Alexia Yates, together with Jackie Ould and Hannah Niblett at the Ahmed Iqbal Ullah Race Relations Resource Centre. I also profited from discussions with Ria Sunga and Becky Viney-Wood, as well as with successive cohorts of undergraduate students.

Elsewhere in the UK, many friends and colleagues provided useful leads and encouragement. They include Naures Atto, Nick Baron, Mateja Celestina, Kelly Hignett, Shirin Hirsch, Susan Hodgett, Aaron Moore, Máiréad Nic Craith, Stavroula Pipyrou, Pedro Ramos Pinto, Rosie Rickett, Lyndsey Stonebridge, and Roseanna Webster.

I have incurred many debts to colleagues beyond the UK. In Germany, I particularly appreciated support and information from J. Olaf

Kleist, Patrice Poutrus, Margit Wunsch-Gaarmann, Frank Wolff, and Beate Fieseler, as well as Eva Völker and Joachim Baur, both at the Museum Friedland, and Klaus Magnus and Jürgen Bast. I received helpful advice from Francesca Rolandi about Italy and from Pär Frohnert, Norbert Götz, Anu Mai Köll, Erik Olsson, Admir Skodo, and Johan Svanberg about Sweden. In Finland, Seija Jelagin and Merja Paksuniemi made valuable suggestions, as did Tomas Balkelis about Lithuania. From the Netherlands, I benefited from brief discussions with Nadia Bouras, Irial Glynn, Leo Lucassen, and Marlou Schrouver, while Frank Caestecker and Jozefien De Bock offered advice on Belgium. Danilo Sarenac helped me out with information about Serbia, and Emilia Salvanou did the same for Greece. Beata Halicka gave helpful advice about Poland after the Second World War. Farther afield, I enjoyed stimulating conversations in Australia with Joy Damousi, Klaus Neumann, Sarah Green, Jordy Silverstein, Alexandra Dellios, May Tomsic, and Jayne Persian, not forgetting my former colleague Laurence Brown. In the United States, I learned a lot about aspects of European migration from Theodora Dragostinova, Anna Holian, Andrew Janco, Michael Kozakowski, Aldis Purs, Karl Qualls, Lewis Siegelbaum, and, above all, Pamela Ballinger, whose work continues to be a source of inspiration and whose friendship I value greatly. I apologise if I have inadvertently overlooked anyone.

I have been sustained throughout by friends and family who have shown an interest in my work. They include Martha Katz, Erika Drucker, Elizabeth Price and David Denison, Anthea and Gordon Millar, Karen and John Churcher, Julia and Nick Mansfield, Lisa and Nick Fletcher, Zhenia and Peter Shoenberg, Caroline Gatrell, and my beloved brother, Tony Gatrell.

Jane Gatrell did a much better job than I could have translating the Russian doggerel verses discussed in Chapter 10. But this is only a tiny fraction of what she has contributed. She has listened to my ideas, pointed out items I might have overlooked, and offered support and constructive advice during the entire writing process. More than that, being with her makes everything worthwhile. Together, we treasure the company of

Acknowledgements

Dave and Chloé Gatrell and Lizzy and Andrew Winstone. This book is for our much-loved grandchildren, Rosa, Evie, and Ollie, in the hope that they will one day understand why I wanted to write it.

Manchester, March 2019

Maps

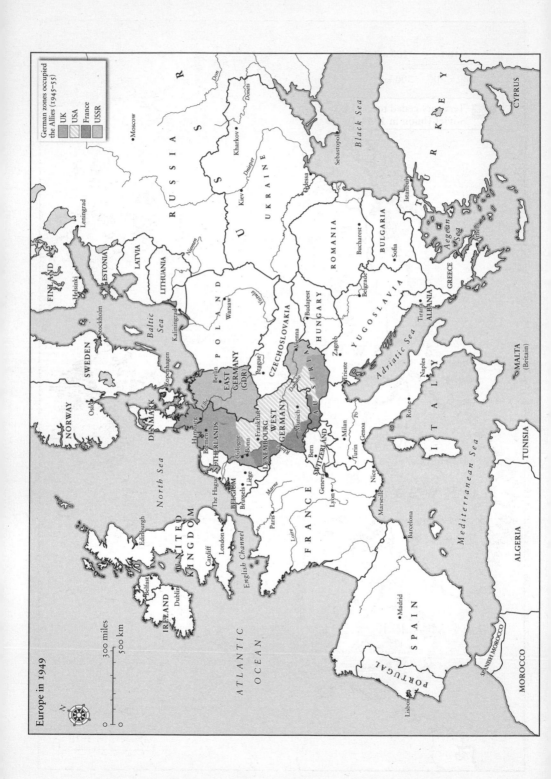

Europe in 1949

German zones occupied
the Allies (1945–55)

UK
USA
France
USSR

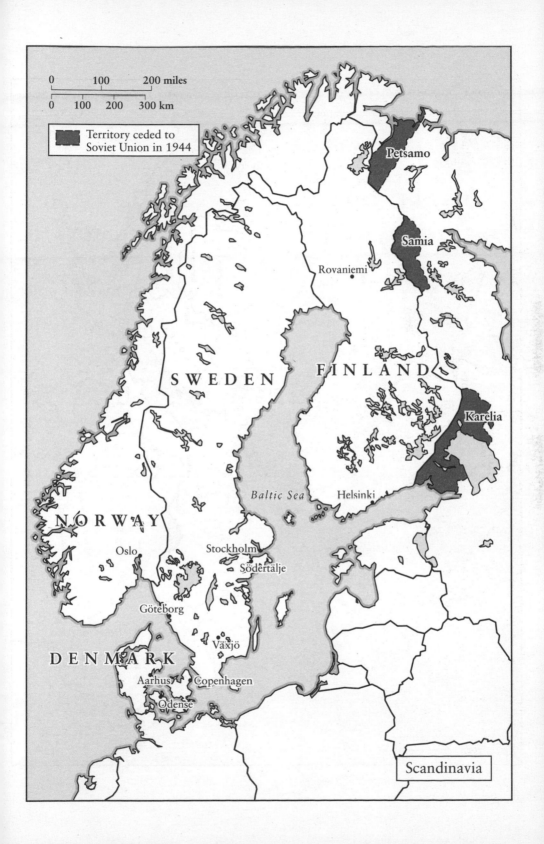

0   100   200 miles

0   100   200   300 km

Territory ceded to
Soviet Union in 1944

Petsamo

Samia

Rovaniemi

SWEDEN

FINLAND

Karelia

Baltic Sea

Helsinki

NORWAY

Oslo

Stockholm

Södertälje

Göteborg

Växjö

DENMARK

Aarhus

Copenhagen

Odense

Scandinavia

SCOTLAND

Edinburgh

UNITED
KINGDOM

North Sea

Belfast

Mosney

Dublin

IRELAND

Morecambe Bay

Bradford Hull
Oldham
Liverpool
Manchester

Nottingham

Birmingham • Leicester

WALES

Luton

Cardiff

London

Bristol

Southampton

Dover

NETHERLANDS

Amsterdam
Utrecht

The Hague

Antwerp
Ghent
Molenbeek
Calais
Roubaix

Maastricht

Brussels
Marcinelle
BELGIUM

Amiens Hauts-
de-France

Creil

Normandie Paris

Île-de-
France

Grand Est

Bretagne

Pays
de la
Loire

Orléans

Centre-
Val de Loire

Bourgogne-
Franche-Comte

Lyon

Nouvelle-
Aquitaine

Auvergne-
Rhône Alpes

Bordeaux

Aveyron

Toulouse

Occitanie

Montpellier Arles

Provence-
Alpes-
Côte d'Azur

Avignon
Nice

Carnoux

Marseille

Toulon

0   100   200 miles
0   100   200   300 km

Northwestern
Europe

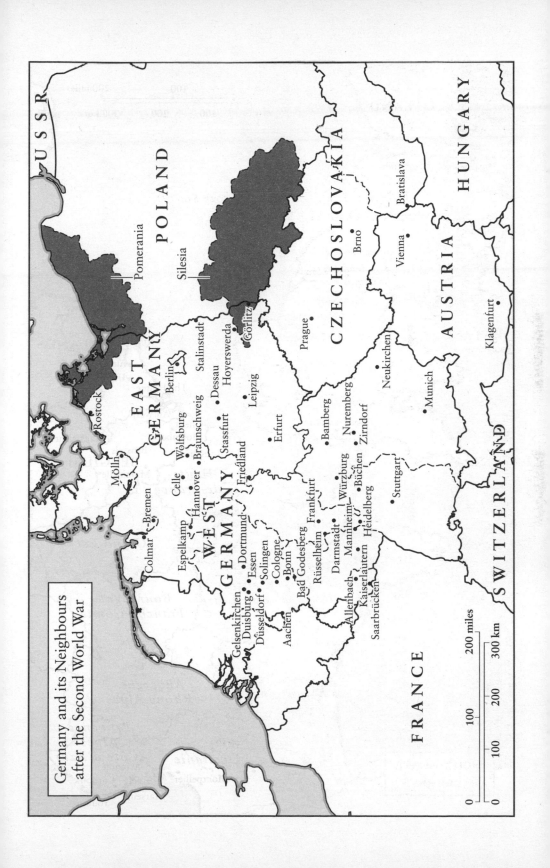

Germany and its Neighbours
after the Second World War

USSR

POLAND

Pomerania

Silesia

EAST GERMANY

Rostock
Mölln
Bremen
Celle
Hannover
Braunschweig
Wolfsburg
Berlin
Stalinstadt
Dessau
Hoyerswerda
Görlitz
Leipzig
Erfurt
Stassfurt
Friedland

CZECHOSLOVAKIA

Prague
Brno
Bratislava

Vienna

AUSTRIA

HUNGARY

Klagenfurt

Neukirchen
Munich
Nuremberg
Bamberg
Zirndorf
Würzburg
Büchen
Heidelberg
Stuttgart
Mannheim
Darmstadt
Frankfurt
Rüsselheim
Bad Godesberg
Bonn
Cologne
Solingen
Essen
Dortmund
Düsseldorf
Duisburg
Gelsenkirchen
Aachen
Kaiserlautern
Allenbach
Saarbrücken

WEST GERMANY

Colmar
Espelkamp

FRANCE

SWITZERLAND

0   100   200 miles
0   100   200   300 km

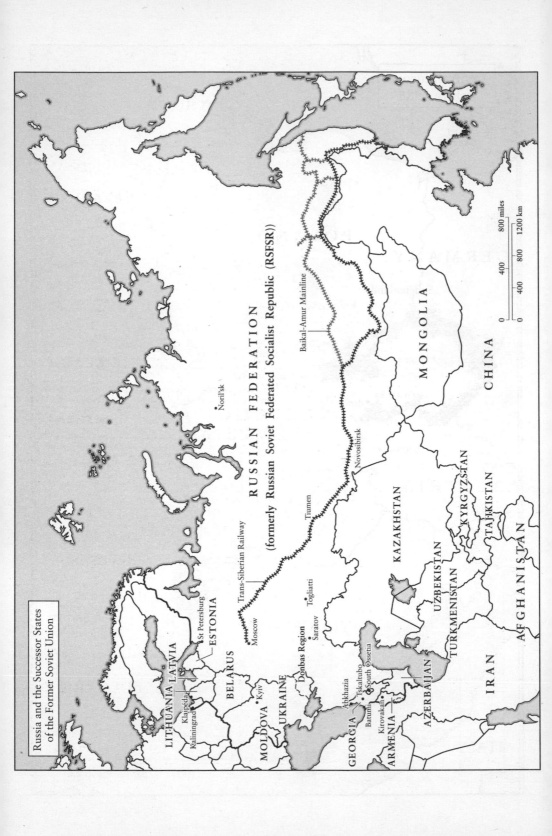

Russia and the Successor States of the Former Soviet Union

LITHUANIA LATVIA
ESTONIA
St Petersburg
Klaipėda
Kaliningrad
BELARUS
Kyiv
MOLDOVA
UKRAINE
Donbas Region
GEORGIA Abkhazia Tskaltubo
Batumi South Ossetia
ARMENIA Kirovakan
AZERBAIJAN

Moscow
Saratov
Togliatti
Trans-Siberian Railway
Tiumen

Noril'sk

RUSSIAN FEDERATION
(formerly Russian Soviet Federated Socialist Republic (RSFSR))

Baikal-Amur Mainline

Novosibirsk

KAZAKHSTAN

UZBEKISTAN
TURKMENISTAN
KYRGYZSTAN
TAJIKISTAN

MONGOLIA

CHINA

IRAN

AFGHANISTAN

800 miles
1200 km
800
400
400
0
0

Central Europe
Before 1989

LITHUANIA
Kaunas
Vilnius
Minsk
Gdańsk
Szczecin
BELARUS
POLAND
GERMANY
Warsaw
Łódź
Lublin
Sudetenland
Wrocław
Kielce
Chelm
U S S R
Olovi
Katowice
Kraków
Rzeszów
Prague
Lubomierz
Lvov
UKRAINE
Zastávka
Brno
C Z E C H O -
Ivano-Frankivsk
S L O V A K I A
Vienna
AUSTRIA
Budapest
H U N G A R Y
Dunaújváros
Banat region
ROMANIA
YUGOSLAVIA
Bucharest
BULGARIA
Sofia
ITALY
ALBANIA

| 0 | | 100 | | 200 miles |
| 0 | 100 | 200 | 300 km | |

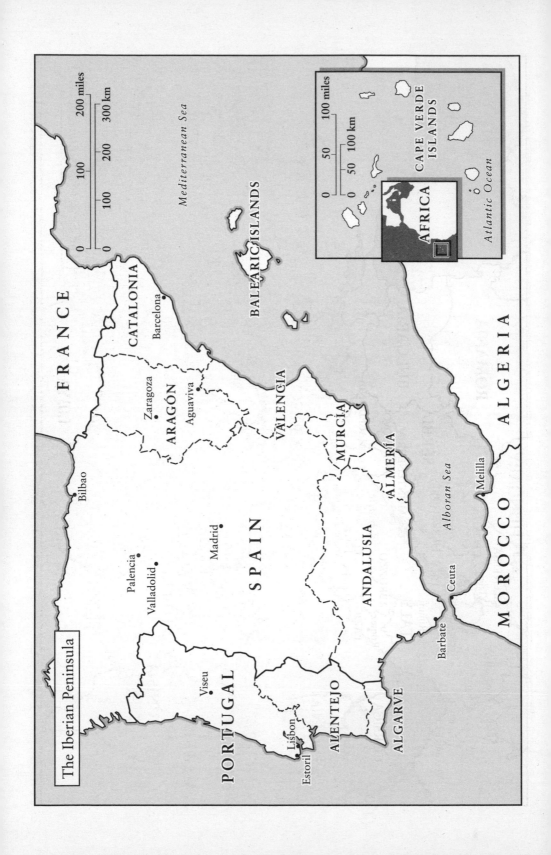

The Iberian Peninsula

FRANCE

Mediterranean Sea

Bilbao

CATALONIA
Barcelona

Zaragoza
ARAGÓN
Aguaviva

BALEARIC ISLANDS

VALENCIA

MURCIA

ALMERÍA

Palencia
Valladolid

Madrid

SPAIN

ANDALUSIA

Alboran Sea

Melilla

Ceuta

MOROCCO

ALGERIA

Viseu

PORTUGAL

ALENTEJO

ALGARVE

Barbate

Lisbon
Estoril

200 miles

300 km

200

100

100

100

0

0

100 miles

100 km

50

50

100 km

0

0

CAPE VERDE ISLANDS

AFRICA

Atlantic Ocean

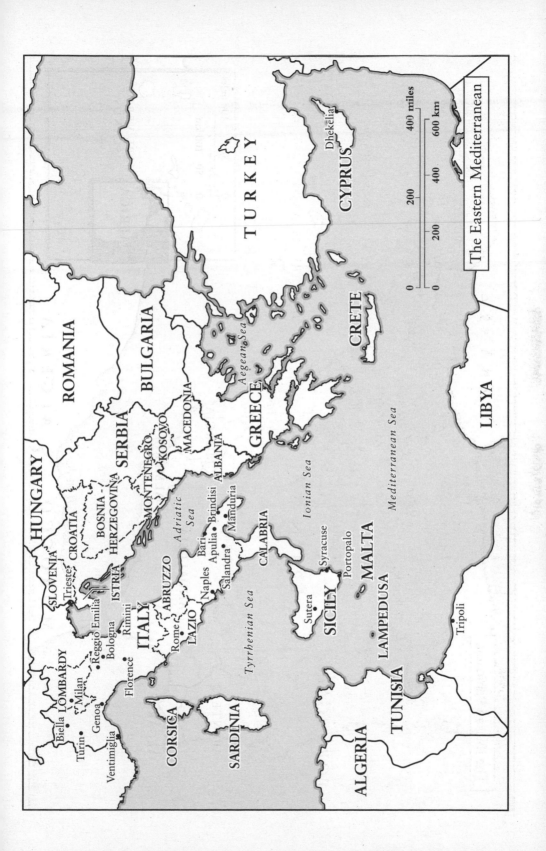

The Eastern Mediterranean

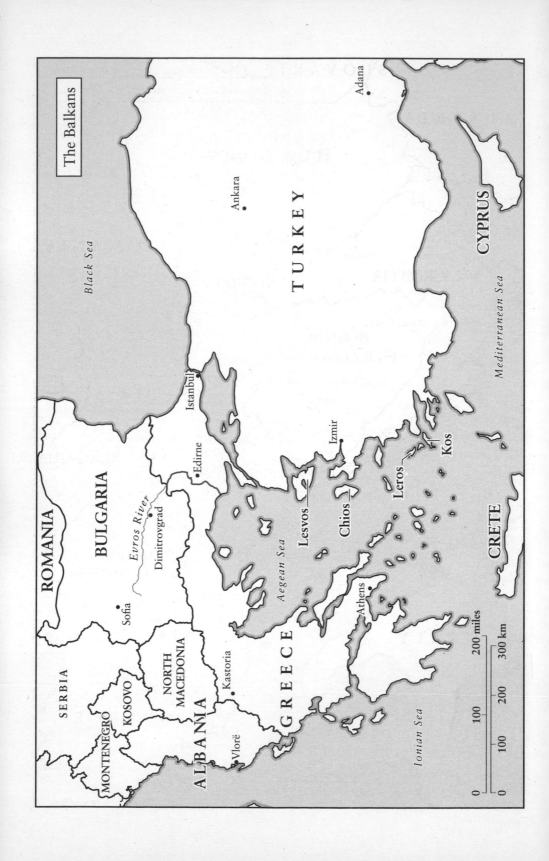

The Balkans

ROMANIA

BULGARIA

Black Sea

Sofia

Euros River

Dimitrovgrad

Edirne

Istanbul

TURKEY

Ankara

Adana

SERBIA

MONTENEGRO

KOSOVO

NORTH
MACEDONIA

ALBANIA

Kastoria

Vlorë

GREECE

Athens

Aegean Sea

Lesvos

Chios

Izmir

Leros

Kos

CYPRUS

Mediterranean Sea

CRETE

Ionian Sea

0   100   200   300 km

0   100   200 miles

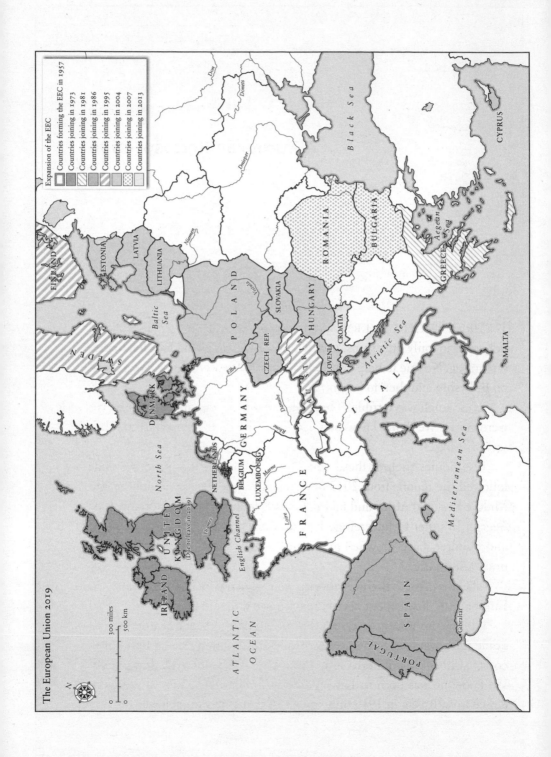

The European Union 2019

Expansion of the EEC

Countries forming the EEC in 1957
Countries joining in 1973
Countries joining in 1981
Countries joining in 1986
Countries joining in 1995
Countries joining in 2004
Countries joining in 2007
Countries joining in 2013

N

300 miles
500 km

FINLAND

ESTONIA

LATVIA

LITHUANIA

SWEDEN

Baltic Sea

POLAND

Vistula

ROMANIA

BULGARIA

Black Sea

GREECE

Aegean Sea

CYPRUS

SLOVAKIA

HUNGARY

CZECH REP.

AUSTRIA

CROATIA

SLOVENIA

Adriatic Sea

MALTA

DENMARK

North Sea

GERMANY

Elbe

Danube

Rhine

Po

ITALY

NETHERLANDS

BELGIUM

LUXEMBOURG

Marne

UNITED KINGDOM
(De to leave in 2019)

IRELAND

Thames

English Channel

FRANCE

Loire

ATLANTIC OCEAN

SPAIN

PORTUGAL

Gibraltar

Mediterranean Sea

Don

Donets

Dnieper

Niemen

ATLANTIC OCEAN

A European Retrospective

PEOPLE TRYING EVERY WAY to get out in boats. Bigger ships could not come in, only little ships. I remember there was an old lady left to die, screaming. No one to help her. Left to herself. We were lucky. We get out on little ship and then to big ship.'

'The stench was terrible. There was no air. We didn't know where we were going. We didn't know how long we'd be on the ship. We couldn't see anything.'

Testimonies such as these will strike a chord with anyone who has followed the reports from 2015 onwards of people fleeing conflict in the Middle East and Africa and taking to boats to cross the Mediterranean or Aegean in order to find refuge in Europe. Thousands of men, women, and children have drowned at sea in the attempt. Many more face an uncertain future.

Like them, these two eyewitnesses were looking for a place of safety in Europe. But their experiences belong to two different eras.

The first testimony describes the strenuous efforts of a young man to evade the advancing Soviet Red Army by crossing from the eastern Baltic coast to Lübeck in northern Germany in 1944. His name was not recorded. We know he was born in Latvia, a country that had achieved independence from Russia in 1918 only to be invaded and occupied successively by Soviet and German forces during the Second World War; it came under Soviet control at war's end, a decision confirmed at the Yalta Conference. Keen to avoid living under Soviet rule, this young man had followed numerous other refugees in fleeing westwards. After a brief spell in Germany, and having given up hope of being able to return to a free Latvia, he settled in the UK, where he picked fruit and vegetables in East Anglia before finding work in a brick-making factory. Eventually he became a restaurant chef. Tantalisingly, he remains otherwise unidentifiable in the historical record.[1]

In the second fragment, an Algerian woman (she, too, is anonymous) recalls being hurriedly transported to France in 1962 along with hundreds of other *harkis*, mainly Muslims who had backed the French state during Algeria's fight for independence. More than 130 years of French rule came to an end in that year. Eyewitnesses to brutality perpetrated by both sides to the conflict, and vulnerable to retaliation by the new rulers of Algeria, they had little choice but to flee. These refugees, who came in cargo vessels that ferried entire families across the Mediterranean, also eventually had to accept that a return to the country of their birth was unlikely. But unforeseen difficulties lay ahead after their journey to the European mainland. They have continued to live on the margins of French society — many of their children grew up without any contact with their French neighbours. And rather than decreasing in intensity, anti-Algerian racism in France appears to have only increased in recent years.[2]

Europe's past discloses many stories in the same vein, telling of distressed people being engaged in the struggle for survival, and sometimes literally engulfed by the sea itself, as they seek to move to a place of safety. But it is one thing to describe or read about their suffering, and quite another to understand what has driven such mass migrations into and within Europe throughout history, and particularly over the past century.[3]

Stories such as this are not just of passing interest. They connect the experiences of individual migrants to the transformation of an entire continent. This book is about the questions that migration has posed to Europe and what migrants have asked of Europe. The answers form an integral part of European history. Without putting migration and migrants at its heart, the history of Europe since the end of the Second World War is incomplete.[4]

Indeed, every major development in postwar Europe is connected to migration. Think of the recovery and reconstruction of the continent in the aftermath of world war; the closer alignment of states that formed an economic community and then the European Union; the creation of a rival political and economic bloc in Eastern Europe; the shedding of Europe's overseas empires and the legacies of colonial rule; the collapse of communism and the redrawing of the map of Europe. At the time of writing, another major development is taking place as the vision of closer European cooperation is threatened by disagreements over migration and asylum.

The Unsettling of Europe reinterprets the big events in postwar Europe and reconnects them with the history of people on the move. It is a story of migrants, many of them Europeans, escaping from violence or being relocated against their will. But not all migrants have been buffeted by war or other torments. This book is also about people moving in search of greater opportunities.

For both types of migrants, we have rich documentation. These sources show a wide variety of reasons for migration. During the 1950s, for example, Irish nurses took the ferry across the Irish Sea to support Britain's new National Health Service. Throughout the twentieth century, and even earlier, ocean liners brought migrants to the UK in search of economic betterment or to gain professional qualifications. Their testimony emerges in diaries, oral histories, and semiautobiographical accounts. In 1956, Sam Selvon, a major figure in West Indian literature, published *The Lonely Londoners*, a novel vividly depicting the everyday life of migrants from Trinidad and Jamaica: his protagonist, Moses, describes in creolised English how men who had settled in London much earlier continued to flock to Waterloo Station, where they recalled their own arrival in the capital on the boat train from Southampton: 'Sometimes tears come to his eyes and he don't know why really, if is homesickness or if is just that life in general beginning to get too hard.' It is a reminder of the complex emotional charge of migration.[5]

These voices belong to people whose migration to European shores took place within living memory. Their experiences of migration and those of millions of others are not remote from us either in time or in geographical distance. They resonate in ways that speak to their descendants and to migrants who arrived afterwards. They deserve to be heard by anyone who believes that migration has only now begun to alter the landscape of Europe.

These stories often have similar motifs. For example, they often, though not always, involve boats. Boats do not in themselves explain anything, but they have a powerful resonance, no matter the culture of origin. They make us think about the risk of capsizing and drowning, and of capture and captivity. But they also carry connotations of adventure and escape, of enterprise and even liberation.

Despite such common themes, however, migrants describe very different experiences and trajectories, stories of migration as ordeal, for example, and stories of migration as opportunity. For those fleeing violence, further torment might be in store, as happened when the harkis were placed in camps in provincial France. Migration might, as in the case of the Latvian refugees, hold out the hope of resettlement and employment, and the possibility of gaining new friends, or becoming naturalised. There might be opportunities to make visits back home, perhaps to return permanently, but not for everyone: sometimes migration is irreversible.

In speaking of 'migration' rather than 'immigration', I have taken a deliberate decision: the two missing letters make all the difference. Dropping them conveys the various strands of mobility. 'Immigration' implies that people buy a one-way ticket, whereas 'migration' takes account of regular return journeys—the decision not to burn bridges with one's place of birth. 'Migration' speaks of interrupted journeys, and travel between different destinations. It acknowledges that migrants may have a stake in more than one place simultaneously.

The optimistic version of European history is a story of liberation, democratisation, economic reconstruction, and enhanced social welfare, particularly in the postwar years. Most soldiers and civilians returned to their homes in 1945 or shortly afterwards. Across Europe, villagers moved to the city or to another country in order to take new jobs, aspiring to a higher standard of living. Although not all migrants attained that goal, migration is nonetheless viewed as both the cause and the consequence of increased prosperity. Freedom of movement between the member states of the European Economic Community, the forerunner of the European Union, was a sign of the efforts to bring about closer European cooperation. Furthermore, the collapse of communism in Eastern Europe in 1989 was soon followed by the demise of the Soviet Union, and this development appeared to herald the triumph of democracy across the entire continent. When exit restrictions in the Soviet bloc ended, ordinary citizens from those countries took advantage of this change. All of these developments buttressed a positive narrative of postwar Europe.

There is substantial truth in this rosy picture. Europe welcomed people from near and far who relished the opportunity to get ahead and make new lives for themselves. Many made a permanent home in a strange land and raised families; their children and grandchildren put down roots. Opportunity migration was central to the history of postwar Europe. West Germany led the way by reaching bilateral agreements with Italy, Turkey, and Yugoslavia to recruit 'guest workers', many of them excited at the prospect of earning money to support family members back home. Cahit, a Turkish man who arrived in West Germany in 1964, recalled his aspirations in an interview many years later: 'As I was looking out of the window of the train, noticing that we were crossing the border from Turkey into Bulgaria, I thought, I will return in five to ten years a millionaire.' It is easy to write this off as a hopeless fantasy, but it deserves to be taken seriously. Countless men and women who arrived as guest workers in France, Switzerland, the Low Countries, and Scandinavia shared his aspiration.[6]

Internal migration was equally significant. Urbanisation enabled men and women to move from low-wage agricultural jobs to manufacturing sectors where labour productivity was higher, thereby helping to advance overall economic progress. In Italy, more than half the population lived in rural areas in 1950, but by 2000 this had fallen to one-third; in Spain, the relative decline in the rural population was even greater. The story was much the same in Sweden. Like many of his compatriots, Ingvar Kamprad, the founder of the legendary Swedish firm IKEA, who was the son of a German immigrant, embraced the opportunities of industrialisation and left his native village. More than 1 million apartments were built in Sweden in the 1950s and 1960s to accommodate this internal exodus.

Flat-pack furniture, invented by a migrant, made the lives of migrants easier.[7]

Another positive sign in Europe was a commitment in many countries to offer hospitality and protection to refugees. In the course of the 1950s, so-called 'escapees' made their way across the Iron Curtain and were welcomed as witnesses to communist oppression. Stories of flight from communism abounded during the Cold War, as in the case of a forty-five-year-old, Albanian-born Haki F., who arrived in Greece via Yugoslavia in 1953. He stated that the 'people in Albania are only waiting for the moment they will be assisted to start a revolution against the present regime; war has never been over for them. Misery, terrorism and uncertainty of life have constituted the daily routine since 1945.' The sympathetic official who assessed his claim described him as 'brave and conscientious', and he was duly allowed in.[8]

Other refugees benefited from the landmark Refugee Convention adopted by the United Nations in 1951. Western government signatories acknowledged a responsibility towards individuals who were victims of persecution on grounds of race, nationality, religion, or membership in a particular social or political group and who had crossed an international frontier. Initially, the mandate of the United Nations High Commissioner for Refugees (UNHCR) applied only to those who had been displaced as a result of events in Europe before 1951, but the UNHCR's reach gradually extended to other recognised refugees in other parts of the world. European states also devised and implemented ad hoc programmes of assistance — these enabled Ugandan Asians, for example, who had been kicked out of their country to settle in the UK in 1972, and for thousands of refugees from war-torn Vietnam to be admitted to France, Sweden, the UK, and other countries later in that decade.

This optimistic story of economic betterment, improved welfare, and expanded consumption acknowledges that migrants made a notable contribution, shared in the benefits of growth and welfare, and enriched European social and cultural life, making Western Europe more diverse and cosmopolitan. Even grander vistas appeared to open up. As early as 1964, a Catholic writer, Georges Rochau, went so far as to suggest that migration contributed to the creation of 'a United Europe under our eyes'. Influential European movers and shakers shared that vision. Momentous political transformations towards the end of the twentieth century supported the idea of freedom in Europe. The Schengen Agreement of 1985 and subsequent legal instruments were designed to facilitate intra-European migration among EU nationals. Freedom of movement became a cornerstone of European cooperation.[9]

Other parts of the picture can be filled in by pointing to a shared commitment on the other side of the Iron Curtain to economic transformation in which migration would play an equally important role. During the third quarter of the twentieth century, the countries of Eastern Europe enjoyed their own economic boom. New communist governments in the region promoted rapid urbanisation: towns and cities grew, partly thanks to natural increase, but also through mass migration. In the Soviet Union, workers continued to move in huge numbers to new sites of industry, just as they had before the Second World War; the government simultaneously encouraged migration to underdeveloped parts of the country, such as in Central Asia, where jobs were available in agriculture as well as in manufacturing and services. Living standards improved. Other socialist countries, including Cuba and Vietnam, sent guest workers to Eastern Europe, where they added to the industrial labour force. At the turn of the century, Vietnamese were still the third-largest migrant group in the Czech Republic (after Ukrainians and Slovaks), making up around 15 percent of the immigrant population. Thus, on both sides of the Iron Curtain, the economic miracle that took place in the third quarter of the twentieth century rested on the promise of abundance, but was realised by migrant labour.[10]

Not everything can be written as a history of progress, and not all these instances of the loosening of the ties that bound people to their particular places of origin were beneficial. There is an alternative and more sombre version of the history of postwar Europe. To see what this picture looks like, it is necessary to retrace our steps.

In 1945, the continent of Europe was at its lowest ebb since the First World War. I think of it as an era of 'violent peacetime' to draw attention to the many reasons for the continuation of involuntary migration in the postwar years. The numbers of Europeans on the move—perhaps as many as 17 million people—beggared belief.

Part of this upheaval resulted from ordinary people seeking to escape Soviet domination. But this more sinister dimension to migration in Europe had many faces. At the Potsdam Conference in July 1945, the Allied powers, Western and Soviet alike, agreed to a massive transfer of ethnic Germans from Eastern Europe to the divided state of Germany. These so-called 'expellees' had no choice but to comply, and the language was as uncompromising as the procedure. With the agreement of the Allies, Poland enlarged its territory westwards at Germany's expense. In a speech later that year in the newly acquired 'Polish' city of Wrocław (formerly Breslau), the Polish minister of industry, Hilary Minc, spoke in uncompromising terms: 'We acquired territory with some remnants of the German population, which we have the moral and international right to liquidate in such time and by such means as we shall deem proper.' This statement gave local troops and civilians licence to use brute force against innocent European civilians.[11]

Subsequent developments appeared to suggest that violence on this scale and intensity was a thing of the past. Even the revolution against communist rule in Hungary in 1956, which propelled thousands of Hungarians to seek refuge abroad, and the conflict in Cyprus following the Turkish invasion in 1974, which divided the island and caused widespread internal displacement, failed to lessen the new sense of confidence that Europe understood how to live in peace.

However, no one anticipated the upheaval in Yugoslavia, whose implosion in the 1990s brought about the greatest catastrophe in Europe since the end of the Second World War. Each of the constituent republics declared independence, and nationalist leaders encouraged paramilitary groups to launch attacks on the minorities in their midst. The protracted conflict caught other European governments by surprise and shattered their optimism about the collapse of communism ushering in an era of democracy and stability. It represented a failure of European leaders to prevent ethnic cleansing and exposed their inability to devise an agreed policy for accepting refugees in search of a place of safety. Multiethnic Yugoslavia gave way to new nation-states founded on the principle of ethnic homogeneity.

Other elements of Europe's postwar history presented difficulties for migrants even where no overt compulsion was involved. Those who had high expectations could easily be disappointed by the realities of life in their chosen destinations. Substandard accommodation was the norm. Most migrants who worked did menial tasks and were paid poorly in return, often with little prospect of advancement. Workers encountered prejudice, including the assumption that workers from particular ethnic backgrounds should be relegated to particular jobs. Adjusting to a new life was especially challenging for migrant women, whether they were planning to work or came with their husbands and expected to be housewives. The term 'guest workers' indicated that migrants were not expected to remain permanently. Many did return to their countries of origin, not out of choice, but because they were no longer needed when the Western European economy ran out of steam in the early 1970s. That was not true for everyone: West German employers, for example, were in no hurry to lose workers and then to have to replace them with fresh migrants who would have to be trained. Those who had left family members behind in their home countries benefited from new programmes designed to facilitate family reunification in accordance with states' obligations under international human rights law.[12]

Migration was an integral part of the history of European empire and decolonisation. Colonisation not only involved European settlement to buttress colonial rule and exploit overseas possessions but also entailed the violent displacement of indigenous people, particularly when they challenged imperial rule. But decolonisation was no less unsettling. Migrants from Europe's former colonies who had spent their entire lives overseas, whether as settlers, civil servants, or soldiers, now came 'home'. It was a difficult homecoming: many ex-colonials faced a cool reception, because their presence pointed to the abandonment of empire. And non-white migrants had a much tougher time than whites—such as Zahia Rahmani, the daughter of a harki, who described being spat upon, kicked, and humiliated by her new neighbours.

At the same time, colonial subjects, such as Moroccans who went to France and Indians who went to Britain, looked to Europe as a place of opportunity. These ties encouraged migrants to make the journey to Europe after the curtain came down on empire. Colonial subjects could freely enter the UK under the 1948 Nationality Act, and Algerians could enter France. In both cases, the migrants bolstered the domestic labour force at a time when labour was in high demand.

Decolonisation led some groups to regard Europe as a place of refuge. When the Dutch state renounced its empire in the East Indies, for example, thousands of Moluccans who sided with the Dutch against the Indonesian nationalist movement joined the flow of men, women, and children returning to Europe. Like many newcomers, Moluccans did not ask for special treatment and instead wanted to be accepted: as one man put it, 'I've adapted, I wear western clothes and go to a Dutch school. Did you ever think to adapt to me? Did you ever try to come to me? I always come to you. I speak your language; I work for you. What more do you expect of us?'[13]

In Eastern Europe, another kind of decolonisation took place. The collapse of communism in 1989 reversed decades-long restrictions on exit from countries in the former Soviet bloc. In the early 1990s, the *Financial Times* predicted that 7 million people would leave the former Soviet Union. Other estimates suggested the total would be closer to 25 million. None of these predictions came true; what happened instead was that migration took place mainly within the former USSR—for example, when ethnic Russians moved from Central Asia to Russia. These upheavals were no less unsettling than events in Western Europe had been a generation earlier.[14]

Europe's history of migration betrayed a recurrent anxiety about newcomers. Some depicted migrants as strangers who imported a different language and religion. Cultural and ethnic differences challenged expectations of integration or assimilation and exposed hierarchies of acceptability. This was true of guest workers and colonial migrants alike. Would mass migration from overseas lead to 'ghettoes' in European cities, or would migrants 'integrate', and if so, how? Would they impose too great a burden on the welfare state, or would they contribute to society through their work and through the taxes they paid? Would the arrival of entire families undermine the principle that guest workers were expected to return home, or did families help migrants adjust to a new culture?

Yet the stranger came in many guises. In his book *Pig Earth*, John Berger recalled the remark made by a Parisian resident to a domestic servant from Savoy: 'Go back to your goat shit.' The comment showed that French natives could suffer the same kind of insults and humiliation as non-French migrants. Internal migrants were not immune from discrimination and were often regarded with disdain or suspicion.[15]

With the end of the Cold War, migration gave rise to other misgivings, too—for example, about people being smuggled in and trafficked to or within Europe. These preoccupations were not new, but they intensified with the greater freedom of movement after 1989, and they helped ratchet up support for action to be taken against 'illegal' or unauthorised migration. Nevertheless, the growing alarm that governments and commentators expressed about irregular migration had antecedents in postwar Europe. From the 1950s onwards, migrants from Spain and Portugal had sought to escape not only from poverty but also from the iron grip of authoritarian rule. They relied upon well-disposed helpers to cross the Pyrenees in the 1960s, where European employers and liberal-minded governments had welcomed them. This gives the lie to the notion that people-smuggling is a recent phenomenon.

As some barriers came down, however, so others were erected in their place. The disintegration of the Soviet bloc in 1989 created new divisions and challenges—what to do with ethnic Russians in non-Russian parts of the former Soviet Union, for example, and how to manage migrants from East-Central Europe into the European Union. EU expansion created new internal and external borders. The enlargement of the European Union in 2004 brought Cyprus and Malta into the fold along with the Czech Republic, Hungary, Poland, Slovakia and Slovenia, and three former Soviet republics, Estonia, Latvia, and Lithuania, followed by Bulgaria and Romania in 2007 and Croatia in 2013. Enlargement made a big difference. Non-EU countries looked on, like neighbours uncertain of their place. Their citizens did not enjoy the same freedom of movement as their counterparts in the European Union.

The sombre and distressing features of post-1945 migration thus appear to have been compounded by recent changes. In the European Union, freedom of movement has been much trumpeted, but member states could still resort to the imposition of tough controls, limiting migration on grounds of public policy, public security, and public health. Thus, freedom of movement was always conditional: national self-interest meant that safeguards were available to states that wanted to curb migration from within the European Union, not to mention the arrival of third-country nationals. There is now much talk of 'fortress Europe'—and of how to prevent its walls being breached.

Another cloud has appeared on the horizon as Europe approaches the third decade of the new millennium. European politicians have bickered over migration and asylum, agreeing only about the need to shift responsibility for deterring refugees to other countries: by asking Turkey, for example, to keep Syrian refugees, and expecting Libya to detain and—where possible—deport migrants looking to cross the Mediterranean. Policy makers have spoken of the 'externalisation' of control, in effect relocating the borders of Europe and giving short shrift to the human rights of migrants. Even the international refugee regime no longer seems secure. The shift was visible back in 2004, when former British prime minister Tony Blair argued that the Refugee Convention had 'started to show its age'. A London-based barrister concurred: 'It's time to tear up the Refugee Convention, and begin a proper debate about immigration that is premised on the state's right to control its borders.' The elision demonstrated how easy it was to shift from a discussion of obligations towards recognised refugees to a discussion of 'immigration' more broadly, culminating in what Prime Minister Theresa May has described as the need to create a more 'hostile environment' for migrants.[16]

Whenever mention is made of the 'threat' that migrants are believed to pose, including the threat of perpetrating terrorist attacks, I think of the insecurity and outright terror that migrants have faced by virtue of their perceived strangeness. Part of the sombre picture of migration is the violence inflicted by resident groups and individuals on newcomers. To take just one instance among many: In November 1992, in a racially motivated arson attack in Mölln, close to Lübeck, far-right extremists killed two teenage Turkish girls and their grandmother. Twenty years later, a Turkish community group complained that the town council had refused its request for a street to be renamed in commemoration of these deaths. The murder speaks of migration as ordeal, whilst the subsequent debate makes it clear that memory has remained a battlefield. The official rebuff compounded the original hurt.[17]

So this is not a straightforward history. There are abundant instances of generosity on the part of host communities, whose local efforts have sometimes intensified at the most difficult times for migrants. Yet hospitality appears to have been badly compromised. Europe's relationship with migration and migrants is conflicted. The political unease spreads far and wide: 'Today everything is immigration', complained Donald Tusk, president of the European Council, in a speech he delivered in September 2015. Nothing has happened since to lessen the force of his statement, which seems to speak of migration as a curse rather than a blessing. Yet there is a sense in which 'everything' in Europe has always, not just today, been about migration and migrants.[18]

Migrants, including refugees, face bureaucratic, economic, and social hurdles. They are rarely described as 'intrepid'—a word usually reserved for European or American explorers of remote regions—but in fact this is a good way of describing how they negotiate obstacles, try to stay safe, support themselves, and realise their dreams in new settings, without necessarily severing ties to the place of their birth. They draw on networks and resources of different kinds in their destination countries, including community associations, labour unions, and faith groups that provide them with succour and solace.

I began this Introduction with a reference to migration by boat, but today these boats wash up on different shores, where migrants encounter a wide range of political interests and public reactions. From the vantage point of 2019, we can see just how much these public reactions matter. In Germany, the anti-immigration political party Alternative für Deutschland (AfD, Alternative for Germany) gained seats in the Bundestag in 2017, having already secured a toehold in most state parliaments as well as seats in the European Parliament. At the end of 2017, the far-right Freedom Party in Austria took the key foreign, interior, and defence posts in a new coalition government, and the Italian general election in March 2018 brought major gains for right-wing, anti-immigration parties, campaigning on a platform of targeting vulnerable migrants and turning back asylum seekers. Spanish politics has become more febrile, even though the number of migrants has declined considerably since 2016. To persist with the nautical metaphor, demagogues can whip up a storm.

Migration has become a battleground, a source of angry exchanges among nationalist and liberal political leaders and a source of disharmony within the European Union. Periodic jeremiads warn that, as historian Walter Laqueur put it, 'the native population [are] becoming strangers in their own homelands' who resent the changes wrought since 1945; in his view, 'new immigrants' have proved unwilling to 'adapt' or 'integrate'.[19]

I take a different view, which is that migration in Europe today is another iteration of the continuous convulsions and opportunities, brought about by pressures and rivalries not only from beyond Europe but also from within Europe, that have characterised European history for decades. I offer neither an optimistic nor a purely pessimistic account. I argue that migration cannot be reduced to a simple formula of cause and effect, and that people move for all sorts of reasons. Some people migrate in order to save their skin ('refugees'), others to improve their economic prospects ('economic migrants'). Many people migrate, but many also do not—or cannot. People's motives are often difficult to disentangle in any straightforward way, and migration can make a mockery of attempts to draw a clear distinction between them.[20]

Disagreements and difficulties over policy and practice are not new. They have been an integral part of Europe's history of migration, and by extension, of European history itself. It behoves us to think about that history and what it implies: migration cannot be undone, except in the dangerous fantasy world of the far right. It is far better to confront animosity and division by becoming better informed about how migrants have negotiated the difficulties and opportunities to which they have been exposed.

This book, then, is an unfinished history of migration within and to Europe over seven decades. It deals with transformation and disruption in the lives of individuals, in society at large, and on a continental scale. It treats migrants as flesh-and-blood people, with their own motives, aspirations, and anxieties, not an abstract entity. Some migrants live in the shadows, and others are keen to advertise their presence. This book also examines the ideas of European cooperation and integration whilst also paying proper attention to national histories of migration. Its extensive coverage sheds light on different episodes, enabling us to understand the unfamiliar and hidden dimensions of migration that provide a different perspective on current preoccupations and policies. At moments of what appears to be frenetic and unparalleled change, this richer history allows us to take stock, to think about the policies that have been devised and the postures struck by those for and against migration. When fewer than two in five Europeans describe themselves as 'well informed about immigration and integration related matters', insights from history cannot be more timely.[21]

It is often said by opponents of migration that 'Europe is full', as if a continent or a country is a fragile vessel at risk of capsizing under the weight of migrants. The metaphor is a powerful one. But it can be turned on its head. Migrants have made all kinds of contributions to Europe. Indeed, they helped to build the boat.

PART 1

Violent Peacetime, Cold War Rivalry, Rebuilding Europe

1945–1956

CHAPTER 1

Forced Migration in Europe: Changing Places

THE SECOND WORLD WAR in Europe came to an end in May 1945. The final defeat of Nazism was understandably a cause for celebration, but it also brought sorrow and uncertainty. Partly, this was because of the enormous loss of life. The Soviet Union lost around 20 million soldiers and civilians. Poland and Yugoslavia each lost 10 percent of their prewar population. Much of the Jewish population of Eastern Europe perished in the Holocaust, leaving around 1.5 million survivors. Partly, it reflected the fact that bringing back home millions of prisoners of war and civilians who had been wrenched from their homes to work for the Nazi war economy posed administrative and logistical problems, to say nothing of the mental and physical damage inflicted on those who had been forcibly uprooted and incarcerated.

It fell to the victorious Allied powers, Britain, France, the United States, and the Soviet Union, to arrange the return of prisoners and forced labourers. With one exception, they committed to carry out repatriation with maximum speed—the exception being that Soviet leaders refused to release captured German soldiers until they had extracted every last ounce of work from them. All governments needed labour to sustain economic recovery, hence the Soviet claim that exploiting German prisoners would help offset the loss of able-bodied men and women.

Barring this important exception, postwar plans entailed mass repatriation for both economic and psychological reasons. In the United States, the former first lady, Eleanor Roosevelt—a key figure in postwar debates around a new world order—spoke of the need to find ways, 'in the interest of humanity and social stability, to return people who had been uprooted from their homes and their country to a settled way of life'. Many civilian forced labourers and military personnel could not wait to go home. A flurry of bureaucratic activity ensured that they were quickly repatriated. American, British, French, and Soviet military forces in Germany, each of them responsible for a zone of occupation, took charge of this organised endeavour.[1]

This picture of a gradual return to normality was nevertheless highly deceptive, on two fundamental counts. The first is that millions of civilians decided to flee from their homes. Even before hostilities ceased, refugees fled for various reasons, including those on the Eastern Front escaping from the advancing Red Army as it retook Soviet territory and then projected communist power into Poland and Germany. The second is that the victorious Allies embarked on mass population expulsions as part of an orchestrated programme to create ethnically more uniform nation-states. Forced migration in peacetime became the means whereby Europe would be transformed along national lines.

The epicentres of forced migration were to be found in East-Central Europe and Southeast Europe. Here, above all, Europeans were on the run from other Europeans. What had existed in 1939 no longer existed. The prolonged conflict between 1939 and 1945 made it impossible to entertain a return to 'normality'. The aftermath of war reinforced the sense that there was no going back, either literally or figuratively.[2]

Something of this extraordinary upheaval emerged in an account by the Canadian historian Modris Eksteins, in which he set the odyssey of his Latvian family against the backdrop of war and forced migration in the twentieth century:

> Beyond the corpses, beneath the rubble, there *was* life, more intense than
> ever, a human anthill, mad with commotion. A veritable bazaar. People
> going, coming, pushing, selling, sighing—above all scurrying. Scurrying

to survive. Never had so many people been on the move at once. Prisoners of war, slave labourers, concentration camp survivors, ex-soldiers, Germans expelled from Eastern Europe, and refugees who had fled the Russian advance....A frenzy.[3]

Eksteins had been born to middle-class parents in Latvia, a state created in 1918 as a result of the dissolution of the Russian Empire, but occupied by the Soviet Union at the outbreak of war in 1939, and then by Nazi Germany after Hitler declared war on Russia in 1941. By the end of the war, ordinary Latvians faced a difficult decision: whether to remain in their homes in the certain knowledge that they would again become subject to Soviet power, or to flee. The Eksteins family avoided the fate of becoming trapped in communist Latvia, fleeing first to a camp in liberated Germany for so-called Displaced Persons (DPs) and then to Canada. Their odyssey is but one fragment of the widespread postwar displacement of populations. But they were able to exercise a choice of sorts. The experiences of other civilians revealed just how brutal the postwar reckoning could be.

Refugees did not take long to decide to save their skin and moved westwards in order to escape the onward march of the Red Army. Some 4 million ethnic Germans from East Prussia, Silesia, and Pomerania took to the road in the first months of 1945 or were evacuated by boat from ports on the Baltic Sea. The distinguished Polish author Tadeusz Borowski, who had survived Auschwitz, described postwar Germany as 'swarming with starved, frightened, suspicious, stupefied hordes of people who did not know where to turn and who were driven from town to town, from camp to camp, from barracks to barracks by young American boys, equally stupefied and equally shocked by what they had found in Europe'. Other contemporaries, too, favoured the image of a 'swarming mass'. But a 'swarm' implied that people moved without reason or direction, and this was simply untrue. Although described as 'spontaneous', nevertheless some degree of deliberation lay behind their decision to flee, albeit often in hazardous conditions.[4]

Personal accounts conveyed something of the mixed emotions of these refugees. The Latvian American author Agate Nesaule was seven years old when she arrived with her parents and older sister at the first of a long succession of camps in Germany, having already witnessed the beatings, rapes, and executions of Latvians at the hands of Red Army soldiers as they retook territory from the retreating Nazi forces in 1944. Writing in middle age, Nesaule recalled the safety provided by a Displaced Persons camp in the British zone of Germany, but this did not lessen her sense of despair about what the future would hold.[5]

Much later, fictional accounts of wartime displacement would add to the sense of ordeal. Hans-Ulrich Treichel's novella *Der Verlorene* (The lost one), first published in 1998, and published in English translation as *Lost*, tells the story of a young boy whose older brother, Arnold, goes missing towards the end of the war when the family flees westwards from East Prussia in order to escape Red Army soldiers. Initially the boy is led to believe that his brother starved to death in his mother's arms, but this story turns out to be untrue; instead, his mother had hurriedly handed him over to a stranger in order to save his life. Treichel concentrates on the shadow that this ordeal—and the mother's rape at the hands of Soviet soldiers—casts over the surviving family members. The parents do not give up hope of being reunited with their older son, and they jump through endless hoops in order to establish whether a particular boy in a children's home is in fact Arnold. Treichel paints a picture of the bureaucratic process to which the family is subjected. In the denouement, the father's business, which he has carefully built up over several years, is destroyed in an arson attack—Germany itself was no guarantee of economic security. Ultimately, however, this is a story of emotional restraint and repression. In this bleak family scenario, the author asks his readers to consider who and what is in fact 'lost'.[6]

The postwar turmoil suggested that the main problems to address revolved around people who had either been forced from their homes by the Nazi war machine or were seeking to escape Soviet revenge and the communist takeover. Yet this summation gives a very partial and misleading impression of the contours of mass population displacement. The situation was further complicated by the decision of the victorious Allies to agree to a series of territorial adjustments and population expulsions.

The agreement reached at the Potsdam Conference in July 1945 sanctioned the punitive expulsion of millions of ethnic Germans from farms and businesses in Poland, Czechoslovakia, and Romania. In the worst cases, the order for expulsion gave Germans only minutes to pack their bags. The postwar Czech government also expelled the Hungarian minority, 'to solve the problem once and for all'. Other expulsions and deportations, affecting Poles, Ukrainians, Karelians, Turks, and others, were accompanied by the expropriation of land and other assets. People who had lived quietly for generations alongside their neighbours were unceremoniously kicked out of their homes.[7]

In a speech to the British House of Commons in December 1944, Winston Churchill spoke of the need for a 'clean sweep' of ethnic Germans from Poland. Forced migration was motivated by revenge and the desire to punish all Germans, regardless of age or conduct. But influential decision-makers among the victorious Allies also held that peace was best assured if ethnic groups were separated in order to create more homogeneous nation-states, denying any revival of the sort of irredentism which Hitler had manipulated so effectively. In this spirit, but with a firm eye on retaliation as well, Władysław Gomułka, already a dominant force in Polish politics, stated categorically that 'we must expel all the Germans, because countries are built on national lines and not on multinational ones'.[8]

The Potsdam Agreement in July 1945 gave notice that the Allies agreed to the 'humane and orderly transfer' of Germans from Central and Eastern Europe, the emphasis on 'order' reflecting a concern that the transfer should not 'increase the burden already existing on the occupying authorities'. Yet although the crucial decisions were taken at Potsdam, discussions between the Allies had already begun during the war about addressing the status of minorities in Czechoslovakia. Philip Nichols, British minister to the Czech government-in-exile, offered his support to the Czech desire to make the country after the war 'as homogeneous a country as possible from the standpoint of nationality', in other words, a state in which Czechs would prevail over other groups. The Czech leader Eduard Beneš envisaged a five-year period of organised resettlement, with the seizure of German property in the Sudetenland as recompense for the harm inflicted on Czechoslovakia during the war. As Czechoslovakia proceeded to expel its Sudeten German population, Beneš spoke of transfer as being consistent with 'civilised' norms of conduct, although this was a fig leaf to cover naked aggression against people regardless of age, gender, political persuasion, or behaviour. In the words of one of his associates, the 'ulcer' had to be cut out.[9]

In truth, so-called 'wild' expulsions had already been under way before the ink was dry at Potsdam. Stalin casually claimed that 'all the Germans had run away' from Poland, and Churchill agreed. This concealed the fact that throughout the summer of 1945 Czechs took matters into their own hands, forcing 800,000 Sudeten Germans from their homes in a manner that one British eyewitness likened to Nazi persecution. One illustration was the decision to require ethnic Germans in Czechoslovakia to wear armbands with the letter N (for Němec, or 'German') and to give up their ration cards. The death rate reached alarming proportions. Losing any remaining inhibitions, Beneš urged Czech citizens to 'definitively liquidate the German problem'. The total number of expellees (*Vertriebene*) eventually reached around 10 million, including 2.7 million Germans from Czechoslovakia (more than 600,000 of them children below the age of twelve), and 6 million Germans from Poland. An additional 340,000 Germans were expelled from Yugoslavia, 178,000 from Hungary, and 100,000 from Romania.[10]

This was a reckoning on a grand and terrible scale whereby the 'victim' nations, Poland and Czechoslovakia, turned on resident Germans, for whom they harboured an overwhelming antipathy. Paul Merker, a leading figure in the German Communist Party who later headed the East German Labour and Social Welfare Administration, described their expulsion as the 'boomerang' that Germany necessarily faced as a consequence of Nazi aggression. No one was spared, and women, children, and the elderly made up the greatest share of the total. They were almost equally split between Protestant and Catholic, much like the total German population; remarkably, the expellees included 4,000 Jews.[11]

Forced migration was even greater on Poland's eastern borders. In 1944 the Red Army pushed across the River Bug. Stalin and his Ukrainian associates, such as Nikita Khrushchev, were determined to 'cleanse' Ukraine (particularly Volhynia) of its Polish population—the bald term 'repatriation', needless to say, overlooked the fact that these men and women had never lived in Poland—and to extend Ukrainian territory westwards at Poland's expense. An additional aim was to move the Ukrainian minority in Chełm (Kholm) into western Ukrainian territory to help rebuild the shattered collective farm economy. Far from welcoming the newcomers, however, the Ukrainian newcomers faced a hostile reception from locals who labelled them 'Polaks' (a derogatory term for people of Polish descent) and 'kulaks' (the pejorative Russian word for wealthy peasants).[12]

One particularly brutal episode of population redistribution went by the name of 'Operation Vistula' (*Akcja Wisła*) in the spring of 1947, when Communist Polish authorities deported 150,000 Ukrainians and Łemkos from southeastern Poland and dispersed them throughout the western borderlands, partly in order to neutralise the threat from the Ukrainian Insurgent Army (the UPA), and more broadly to weaken the appeal of Ukrainian nationalism as part of a strategy of securing Poland for the Poles. The boundary between Poland and the Soviet Union was confirmed in July 1948 and then declared 'final' in May 1951. The aim was clear: as a Polish official put it when the war ended, 'having reached an understanding with the Soviet Union to establish an ethnographic frontier, we have a tendency to be a national state, and not a state of nationalities'.[13]

Something similar happened in Lithuania, where Soviet Lithuanian authorities deported to Poland large numbers of local Poles from the area around Vilnius. On the one hand, Moscow gave the project its blessing as part of the postwar settlement to repopulate devastated parts of Poland. On the other hand, it was also connected to the emergence of 'national communists' in Lithuania led by the head of the local Communist Party, Antanas Sniečkus, who believed that reconstructed Lithuania should give pride of place to ethnic Lithuanians. He wanted to 'cleanse' the social body of the ethnically mixed eastern part of the country. When the Polish residents of Vilnius insisted that 'we Poles don't want to leave for Poland', their complaints fell on deaf ears.[14]

Other new states in Eastern and Central Europe followed suit. In May 1947, in a move designed in part to appease impoverished Czech and

Slovak farmers by giving them more land, the government in Prague proceeded to expel its minority Hungarian population. Implementing this deal was fraught with difficulties, since the size of the ethnic Magyar population in Czechoslovakia was variously estimated at 500,000 and 650,000, and Hungary resisted taking these numbers at such short notice. There was even talk of giving Hungary part of Czech territory where the Magyar population was most heavily concentrated, but nothing came of this. Instead, the Slovak authorities embarked on a so-called 'orderly' process. Whereas Sudeten Germans were permitted to take no more than fifty kilos of luggage per person, Hungarians could take twice as much, although this represented only a fraction of their movable property. The Hungarian government set up a dedicated Relocation Committee, which was deluged with complaints from the Magyar newcomers about the poor conditions they faced in Hungary compared to the fertile soil of Slovakia they had left behind. Being included in a national 'homeland' turned out to be a bitter experience.[15]

This merry-go-round of forced migration flourished in Romania, Yugoslavia, and Ukraine as well. Romania persuaded Czechoslovakia to accept ethnic Czechs and Slovaks. Around 100,000 Czechs and Slovaks were also transferred from Yugoslavia. Under an agreement between the Soviet Union and Czechoslovakia, around 30,000 Czechs and Slovaks left the territory of Carpatho-Ukraine, which was transferred to the USSR in 1945. It was supposed to be a mutual exchange of population, but thousands of Ukrainians living in Carpatho-Ukraine also managed to make their way into Czechoslovakia. Another deal provided for the move to Czechoslovakia of some 29,000 ethnic Czechs who had been living in Volhynia since the late nineteenth century. All of this contributed to a widespread enthusiasm on the part of these states for what was euphemistically called 'repatriation', a word that carried connotations of homecoming but which concealed the extent of brute force used on people who were not consulted about their fate.[16]

Elsewhere, the postwar settlement took a more convoluted path. In Bulgaria and Turkey, ethnic divisions contributed to mass migration between the two world wars. An agreement signed in 1925 provided for the organised emigration of ethnic Turks from Bulgaria, and more than

125,000 Turks left Bulgaria between 1928 and 1939. The new communist government that came to power after the Second World War imposed tough restrictions on emigration and took steps to improve the status of Bulgaria's ethnic minorities, in a sign of the need to conserve reserves of labour for reconstruction. However, reconstruction meant expropriation by the state, and Turkish peasants and merchants in Bulgaria accordingly looked for the means of escape from collectivisation and nationalisation policies. In 1950, some 250,000 Turks (one-third of those living in Bulgaria) applied to be 'repatriated' to Turkey. The Bulgarian government insisted that the process be completed within ninety days and allowed people to take just a handful of belongings. Turks who lacked entry visas to Turkey were held at the border without food for days on end until their identity could be verified. In the bitter winter of 1950, thousands of Turks congregated in an overcrowded former military barracks at Edirne close to the Turkish border, at which point the Turkish government understood that it could make political capital out of people it described as 'unfortunate victims of communism'. A sign at the camp entrance read: 'Welcome, immigrants, to your homeland: we take you back with love, back to our breast.'[17]

No sooner was the transfer under way than it came to an abrupt halt in January 1952. Bulgaria wanted to stem the loss of its workforce and disliked the anti-communist propaganda being peddled by its neighbour. This decision went down well in Turkey, where local authorities were already complaining about the burden. In order to help its ally in the region, the United States stepped in to cover one-quarter of the costs of resettlement. Turkey itself established a Committee to Aid the Refugees, part of its commitment to link their 'repatriation' with investment in new infrastructure. The government inspected refugees for signs of infectious disease and to ensure that no communist 'spies' had infiltrated. Those who settled in rural areas complained that they received insufficient land on which to farm and were therefore obliged to look for work as agricultural labourers, a sign of their downward social mobility. This did not stop the Turkish government from advertising the success of resettlement and 'its love for the Turkish refugees', a sign of its readiness to make political capital out of their misery.[18]

The story of postwar displacement was told in northern Europe as well. Again, it was related to the emerging Cold War. Finland had been at virtually uninterrupted war with the Soviet Union since 1939, and its collaboration with Germany after 1941 ensured that the might of Soviet arms was brought to bear on the country. The Lapland War in 1944–1945 displaced around 100,000 civilians from Rovaniemi and other areas; they ended up in temporary accommodation elsewhere in Finland, or in Sweden. As a result of the Soviet-Finnish armistice in September 1944 that ceded the eastern part of Finland to the Soviet Union, some 430,000 Karelians and others were 'evacuated' to Finland. (Some Karelians had already been evacuated following the Winter War in 1939–1940.) The 'evacuees' represented more than 10 percent of the population of postwar Finland, so this was no minor matter.[19]

Their arrival in Finland was equally unplanned and unsettling, and created problems not unlike those confronting German expellees. Culturally, the Karelians were perceived as different, by virtue of dialect and religion—many of them were Russian Orthodox rather than Lutheran Protestant, and locals sometimes described them as 'gypsies' or 'Slavs'.[20] Like the expellees, Karelians were excluded from international protection. But the Finnish government rose to the challenge. It agreed to compensate refugees for the property they had lost, by providing them with cash or farmland belonging to the state or to large landowners. The money was found by imposing high taxes on the capital assets of Finns. Finnish sociologist Heikki Waris later conducted research into their social adaptation and concluded that they had adjusted quickly, thanks to timely government intervention. A study of their subsequent economic status confirmed this finding, explaining that they moved from low-income to higher-income occupations. So forced migration did not necessarily imply permanent misfortune, provided the necessary institutional support was put in place and provided migrants were willing to do their bit.[21]

Population movements in this part of Europe did not all lead in one direction. The peace treaty between Finland and the USSR also contained a key proviso whereby 55,000 Ingrians (recognised by the Soviet state as a distinct ethnic group) were to be repatriated to the Soviet Union—since 1940 they had been under Finnish jurisdiction and treated with suspicion as a potential fifth column: 'infected by the Bolshevik poison', as one newspaper had it. Sweden colluded by secretly extraditing Ingrians to the Soviet Union in 1945–1946. Many of them ended up in remote parts of the USSR, such as Komi and Siberia, only being permitted to return to Karelia in the late 1950s and 1960s. When Soviet rule collapsed in 1991, some of their descendants returned to Finland, but they received a lukewarm reception as 'Russians' rather than 'authentic' Finns. It was another chapter in a prolonged and sorry saga of migration tied to the postwar settlement and to the Cold War.[22]

Other pathways and trajectories emerge from the historical record. Around 70,000 Finnish children had been evacuated to foster homes in Sweden in 1942. Later in life, they described a painful dislocation in their lives. Toini Gustafsson, a six-year-old at the time, recollected that her new home in Sweden contrasted with 'backward' Finland: 'In Haapovaara you'd get water from the well and the evenings meant carrying the slop pail outside and making sure the paraffin lamp was burning.' Returning to an impoverished Finland after the war, one evacuee said, 'I came back to a family where no one spoke Swedish. I didn't understand Finnish when I returned and I was always being beaten on account of it. My mother was ashamed of me and sent me to live at relatives' every summer.' Ann-Maj Danielsen returned to Finland together with her younger sister in August 1946 and recalled the profound sense of loss at having been kept apart from her family: 'I was sent with an address label around my neck to another world', she said, echoing the painful sentiments expressed by Jewish children sent to Britain on the Kindertransport in 1938–1939. Jean Cronstedt remembered one incident from the new Finnish world into which she was thrust as a child migrant: 'One dark evening, as I walked from my gymnastics class, three youths attacked me, making it very clear in Finnish that my school uniform gave me away as a "hurri", the commonest derogatory name for Finnish-Swedish people at this time.'[23]

Others nevertheless took something positive from their experiences. Aira Bengtson wrote that:

> What I brought back to Finland was what I would like to call a comparative or contrasting knowledge, regarding the two countries' different living

conditions. My whole life I've made use of this comparative thinking, being able to see and analyse problems from very different viewpoints. I brought a lot of joy back from Sweden. The language was my most precious thing that I gathered, and it wasn't even heavy to carry.

There was another side to forced migration.[24]

The Swedish government meanwhile pursued ambitious economic objectives, advertising job vacancies and admitting hundreds of refugees from northern Germany and from among German expellees. Like the Karelians in Finland, their experiences were usually wretched. As if the trauma of escaping the Red Army were not enough, they had a torrid time in towns where they were sent to work, as local residents blamed them for shortages of food and housing. Refugees were accused of having spread infectious diseases and of launching a crime wave. As one of them recalled, 'When we lived in the refugee camp, I only owned one dress. When my mother washed it, I had to stay in bed until the dress was dry.' In Sweden, however, where her mother worked long hours in the garment industry, she managed to put some money in their pockets: 'We would live in style, buy clothes and all that.' Ultimately, migration was her passport to a higher standard of living.[25]

The link between postwar migration, the redrawing of frontiers, and the Cold War emerged in a lethal form at the other end of the continent, in the region known as the Julian March, sandwiched between Italy and Slovenia and comprising Venezia Giulia and Istria, the peninsula between Italy, Slovenia, and Croatia. German troops had occupied Italy following its withdrawal from the Axis in 1943. Italy's capitulation simultaneously provided an opportunity for communist partisans to advance in the entire region. Partisans had gained confidence from their success in resisting the German occupation of Yugoslavia that began in 1941. Under the leadership of Josip Broz Tito, they secured the backing of the Western Allies. The war in Yugoslavia was characterised by great brutality on both sides, not least because it turned into a civil war in which communists fought pro-German fascists, notably the Croatian Ustashi. This brutality carried over into the Julian March. By 1954, when the Allies' military administration of the region finally came to an end and Tito's Yugoslavia was granted control of part of Istria, a total of 300,000 Italians and 50,000 Croats and Slovenes had fled westwards to evade the retribution meted out by partisans, who often threw their fascist opponents into the numerous karst pits (*foibe*) that are a feature of the Istrian landscape.[26]

The Italians who left the region after 1947, when Italy signed a peace treaty with the Allies, were officially classified as refugees (*profughi*). But they did not fall within the remit of the intergovernmental organisations established to protect refugees, and instead became the responsibility of the Italian government. They were sent to makeshift accommodation, including former concentration camps, and thence to transit camps, before eventually settling into government-built apartments in Trieste (Trieste was governed by the Allies until being returned to Italy in 1954) or in more distant locations in Italy, and even abroad. Luckier ones found lodgings with friends or relatives. Peasants struggled to adjust to urban life in Trieste. Many other refugees were still living in camps in various parts of the country a decade or more after their displacement, rubbing shoulders with other Italians who had left Italy's former colonial possessions in Libya, Eritrea, and the Dodecanese. Finding work was an additional problem, given the high levels of unemployment in postwar Italy. To complicate matters further, most 'refugees' left Yugoslavia not during the height of Tito's attacks on fascist sympathisers in 1944, but in the late 1940s and early 1950s, when the communist authorities made life difficult for otherwise comfortable private property owners and peasant farmers. In other words, they could just as easily have been regarded as 'economic migrants', not as refugees who were victims of persecution.[27]

Not all Italians joined this exodus. Others stayed put out of political sympathy with the anti-fascist partisans in the new Yugoslavia. Italians who stayed in Istria after 1943, who became known as *rimasti* (those who remained), articulated feelings of suffering born of persecution during the fascist era. Nevertheless, their ethnicity exposed them to taunts by local Croats and Slovenes that they were 'fascist'; some ended up in Tito's prison camps. But a more complex political and cultural process was also at work. Rejecting the claims of the *esuli* (the exiled, those Italians who left the Julian March) that they were 'contaminated' by virtue of their association with the Slovenes and Croats in Yugoslavia—'there are no

Italians left in Istria', as one exile put it—the *rimasti* expressed pride in the affirmation of a mixed Latin-Slav identity. Those who did not, or could not, migrate had to adjust to the new political realities in Yugoslavia, a state whose leaders were keen to retain able-bodied workers.[28]

Other dramatic migrations in the region were also directly linked to Cold War rivalries. During the Greek Civil War between 1944 and 1949, the Greek Communist Party arranged (in 1948) for the organised relocation of children from the northern part of Greece to Eastern Europe in order to avoid having them brought up by the 'fascists', who eventually came out on top. Queen Frederica of Greece described this decision as 'genocide'; so, too, did a voluble right-wing diaspora organisation of Greek Macedonians, the Pan-Macedonian Association, Inc. The Greek government urged the United Nations in 1950 to recognise that the evacuation of children was tantamount to 'hostage-taking' by 'Slavo-communists', since no responsible mother would give up her child voluntarily. There was an element of truth in this, since the Greek communists exerted pressure on parents to entrust their children to strangers: there was a fuzzy distinction between child abduction and 'rescue'.

For its part, the left-wing League for Democracy in Greece, a short-lived body based in London, argued that the evacuation offered Greek and Macedonian children the possibility of a life of 'peace and prosperity' and maintained that the Greek Communist Party had undertaken 'a vast humanitarian enterprise'. This was not a one-sided enterprise: royalist forces behaved in a similar manner during the civil war, abducting around 12,000 children from communist strongholds and placing them in camps. Around 28,000 children ended up in Romania, Yugoslavia, Bulgaria, Poland, Hungary, and Czechoslovakia; nor were siblings necessarily kept together. Some of them ended up in the territory that Poland had 'recovered' from Germany after 1945.[29]

One tale of 'abduction' was recounted by Risto Donovski, who was born in Greece, close to the border with Yugoslavia. In 1948, at the age of ten, the local communist partisans arranged for him and other children from his village to be sent across the border to Bitola with the assistance of the Red Cross. In an interview, he said: 'From Bitola, a train, full of children. Among all the countries, you could end up in Albania, Bulgaria, Rumania, Hungary, Czech Republic, Poland or East Germany. At that time, I was not aware of this. I found out this later. They sent us to Hungary.' Donovski recalled that, 'as time passed, we could speak Greek, Hungarian and Macedonian. We couldn't speak Croatian or Serbian.' He had to wait until 1955 before being reunited with his family, who had fled to Macedonia. Although other children likewise returned to Greece in the 1950s, often helped by the Red Cross, others continued to live in Eastern Europe and only returned as adults after the collapse of communism in 1989. There are some fascinating as well as heart-breaking stories of parents who tried unsuccessfully to establish contact with their children.[30]

Adults, too, were caught up in the maelstrom of the Greek Civil War. Left-wingers went into permanent exile. The distinguished composer Iannis Xenakis left Greece in 1947, having narrowly escaped execution at the hands of Greek royalists who were busy rounding up their communist opponents. From his new home in Paris he reflected on the pain of exile and on his sense of obligation to the people and places he had left behind: 'For years I was tormented by guilt at having left the country for which I'd fought. I left my friends—some were in prison, others were dead, some managed to escape. I felt I was in debt to them and that I had to repay that debt. And I felt I had a mission. I had to do something important to regain the right to live. It wasn't just a question of music—it was something much more significant.' His testimony reiterated the emotional as well as the political significance of migration for people who had little or no choice but to leave their homeland.[31]

By these various means, the extraordinary demographic turbulence of the Second World War was replicated in what we can think of as violent peacetime. Migration manifested itself in uncontrolled expulsions and state-sanctioned deportations, a settling of scores and a concerted refashioning of the map of Eastern Europe. Internecine warfare erupted in Eastern and southeastern Europe, forcing people from their homes, sometimes at a moment's notice. Concerted attempts simultaneously to redraw frontiers and to transfer or expel people reflected a belief that Europe stood a better chance of avoiding future conflicts if populations could be rear-ranged according to nationality. The settling of old scores—as well as the mass extermination of European Jews—meant that states in East-Central Europe became ethnically more homogeneous in a way that was new to the people of these countries.[32]

European powers bore their share of responsibility for forced migra-tion. As the World Council of Churches put it, 'the homelessness of the vast majority was caused directly by the post-war actions of the victorious Powers'. The rights of millions of people had been abrogated, and they now lived an uncertain existence, unwelcome migrants in their new home. The unsettling of Europe—a combination of postwar retaliation and demographic engineering—disrupted the lives of millions of people and bequeathed a troubling and long-lasting legacy.[33]

CHAPTER 2

Migrants in Limbo:
Displaced Persons in Postwar Europe

IN SEPTEMBER 1946, THE prime minister of Poland, Edward Osóbka-Morawski, made a heartfelt appeal to the large number of Polish men and women who remained in Western Europe a year after the end of the war: 'What kind of future awaits you abroad? Here your nearest and dearest are waiting for you. There is a job for you that will benefit you and your country. Everyone who comes back will be given work and land.' He was speaking on behalf of the new Provisional Government of National Unity which had recently taken power. His words were directed in part at Poles who had been wrenched from their homes and forced to work for the Nazi war economy in what Hitler described as 'compulsory labour service'. They were paid a pittance and given no choice as to where they would be sent. With the defeat of Germany, these Displaced Persons, or DPs, found themselves in one or other of the four occupation zones under American, British, French, or Soviet control.[1]

The Polish state, under the increasing influence of communists, had other Poles in its sights, including Polish military personnel and their families who had come to Britain after a lengthy and arduous odyssey via the Soviet Union, the Middle East, and liberated Europe; some were temporarily living in Italy. Making no direct mention of the power now increasingly wielded by the communist regime in Poland which he led,

Osóbka-Morawski claimed that all Poles had a patriotic duty to rebuild their liberated country, where they would all be welcomed home 'like brothers', and where every month that passed represented a loss of able-bodied persons for the country and a deprivation for individual Poles. His speech reflected the fact that not everyone had responded to the call to return.

More than twelve months had passed since the end of the war, and a great deal had happened in the interim. No one spoke of Displaced Persons until the war in Europe neared its end. But by the summer of 1945 the Allied military forces in Germany could speak of little else other than these 'civilians outside the national boundaries of their country by reason of the war, who are desirous but are unable to return to their home or find homes without assistance'. DPs—not just from Eastern but also from Western Europe—were expected to return to their homes, although no one was under any illusions about the magnitude of the logistical challenge.

The Allied military authorities hoped to reduce the financial and administrative costs of supporting DPs by getting them to leave Germany and Austria. By the end of 1945 an agreement was in place whereby the United Nations Relief and Rehabilitation Administration (UNRRA) would cooperate with the military to arrange for their repatriation, initially by assembling DPs in holding centres. The easiest way of doing this was to organise DPs in existing camps according to nationality. In the summer months of 1945, dedicated reception centres became congested, although officials in Mulhouse, on the French-German border, proudly noted that 'the interior of the building is decorated with paintings of French home life'. A film made with the cooperation of the US military, *Le Retour* (*Reunion*, 1946), offered scenes of men and women, civilians and prisoners of war, being transported from German camps to French soil, which they greeted in a mood of unalloyed joy, signalling what appeared to be a restoration of normal life. At this point, French nationals were being repatriated at an average rate of 32,000 per day.[2]

Matters were more complicated where DPs from Eastern Europe were concerned. Not only were the numbers far larger than in the West, but the wartime destruction of transport infrastructure on the Eastern

Front now made organised repatriation virtually impossible. In these circumstances, DPs took matters into their own hands, either making their way home by foot or hitching a ride on military vehicles. This kind of 'self-repatriation' met with disapproval on the part of the Allied military, because it threatened to undermine arrangements for monitoring the health of the returnees. As transport difficulties eased, the Allied military began the complex task of registering Soviet and other DPs according to nationality. This project was relatively straightforward in the case of former Soviet citizens of Ukraine, Belarus, and Russia. In the space of just twelve months, more than 5 million Soviet nationals were repatriated, mainly to the three Soviet republics.[3]

Repatriation necessitated cooperation between the British, French, US, and Soviet authorities in occupied Germany. Soviet agents combed DP camps in an attempt to convince DPs to return. From a Soviet point of view, repatriation offered the opportunity to punish war criminals who concealed themselves among civilian DPs. But an important additional consideration was the need to mobilise reserves of labour to help rebuild the badly damaged infrastructure. It helped that many DPs were keen to return to their homes: one Russian-born woman, Aleksandra Abramova, told a Dutch boyfriend, whom she had met in Dresden, 'I want home and only home, nowhere else' (a decision she later came to regret).[4]

Reinstating men and women in communist society was not straightforward. Forced labourers had suffered physically and psychologically. There were added political complications. Soviet officials convinced themselves that DPs who had tasted a different kind of life should be investigated to ensure that they would not be importing anti-Soviet ideas. The chosen method was 'filtration', involving careful scrutiny of their political views and war records: as the head of the repatriation administration in Lithuania noted, 'hostile elements could arrive under the guise of a repatriate'. However, the more challenging issue derived not from official suspicion—the Soviet state lacked the resources to scrutinise millions of repatriates—but from local animosity towards people who had, so it was thought, avoided the hardships of war on the Soviet home front, and who had (astonishing as it now seems) even become 'wealthy' during their time in Germany.[5]

What would happen to those who had no wish to go home? These DPs, whatever their nationality, gave everyone a headache—the Allied occupation forces, repatriation officials, aid workers, German civilians who were their neighbours, and one another. They became part of what a US congressman called the 'venomous postscript' to the Second World War. By the end of 1946, a full eighteen months after the end of the war in Europe, at least 660,000 DPs of various nationalities remained in Germany, refusing to repatriate. They certainly included people who had collaborated with Hitler in order to fight Bolshevism and now wished to evade Soviet justice. But others were not war criminals and objected to repatriation on the grounds that the land of their birth had been transformed by a communist takeover.[6]

This was clearly the case with Latvia and Lithuania, independent states incorporated into the Soviet Union in 1939 and reoccupied (or 'liberated') by the Soviets in the latter stages of the Second World War. A tug-of-war took place over some 180,000 Baltic DPs remaining in Germany. The Kremlin claimed that these were Soviet citizens who should be returned to the Soviet Union, whereas Britain maintained it had good legal grounds for refusing repatriation from the zone it administered. In Latvia, the new Soviet leadership instructed the relatives of Latvian DPs to write letters pleading with them to return from Germany. At the same time, DPs were bombarded with information by diasporic groups in the United States, France, and elsewhere, imploring them not to be beguiled by promises of a warm welcome in the homeland.

Ukraine had a different status, having been a Soviet socialist republic since 1922. Besides, Ukrainian DPs included former residents of Galicia, land that had historically been part of Poland, Austria, and Poland again but was now divided between Poland and the USSR. They had no wish to live under Soviet rule, or indeed, to see any Ukrainian obliged to do so. Some of them counted on a dramatic military reckoning between the Western Allies and Stalin that would overturn Soviet power in Eastern Europe. But these hopes were soon dashed. Ukrainians adopted various strategies to avoid detection, included marrying a foreigner, attempting to find relatives abroad, or, in several cases, enlisting in the French Foreign Legion. Others moved from camp to camp, staying one step ahead of

UNRRA officials and the Soviet repatriation officers. Mostly they tried to pass themselves off as Poles because, as one senior Allied officer put it, 'there really is no such nationality [as Ukrainian]—a Ukrainian is a Pole, or a Soviet citizen, or stateless according to his origin'.[7]

More than 1 million Polish DPs, who made up more than two-thirds of the total DP population at the end of 1945, posed a particular challenge. Arrangements began to be made for their repatriation to Poland, but many DPs objected to the presence of the Red Army on Polish soil and to the growing influence of communists in Polish political life. The ever-tightening grip of the Communist Party signalled that DPs would return to a very different country from the one Hitler had forced them to leave. The new regime in Warsaw kept up the pressure on DPs who showed no sign of accepting the offer of repatriation. The head of the communist-controlled Polish repatriation mission maintained that 'Poland was like the mother who loves her children and has forgiven them. The country calls upon you to return to your work and to be rehabilitated.' His reference to rehabilitation implied that the DPs would have to atone for their displacement: this was hardly the message that DPs wished to hear.[8]

UNRRA officials made every effort to persuade Polish DPs that it was in their interests to return to Poland, where they would 'find there familiar patterns and a way of life more in keeping with their national culture than if they were to seek resettlement in strange lands'. UNRRA insisted that Polish DPs should contribute to the task of 'building a new home in which everyone will feel happy...an enormous task [to be undertaken by] a nation whose spirit was never broken'. This argument anticipated the kind of rhetoric that Osóbka-Morawski and his colleagues would deploy a few months later. UNRRA threatened to reduce the rations of those who refused to return. Its 'Operation Carrot' duly led 50,000 Poles in the American occupation zone to repatriate in the last three months of 1946. But this still left 120,000 Polish DPs behind.[9]

The situation was further complicated by the presence of a significant number of Jewish refugees, whose status was even less clear. Up to 230,000 of them had escaped from Poland before the Nazi occupation in 1939 and had found sanctuary in the Soviet Union. Stalin repatriated most of them to Poland in the first six months of 1946. But Jews were made to feel unwelcome, and the terrible pogrom in the provincial town of Kielce in July 1946 persuaded more than half of them to leave Poland by the end of that year. The rest followed soon afterwards. Some moved to Germany, where they sought protection in the American zone of occupation. By 1947–1948, the total of these 'infiltrees', as the Allies dismissively termed them, stood at 250,000. Their main aim was to get to the United States or Palestine, although they had to overcome obstacles from the US State Department and from the British government, which controlled admission to Palestine prior to the formation of the state of Israel in May 1948. Both the Americans and the British believed that Jewish refugees were potential troublemakers who refused to return to their homes for economic rather than political reasons.[10]

Meanwhile, tens of thousands of Jews also spent time in DP camps. They complained of being housed in former army barracks, converted hotels, apartment blocks, schools, and hospitals, a situation created by Allied foot-dragging and a mark of the failure of American Jewish organisations to make the case for their resettlement strongly enough. Some demanded that Germans be forced to give up their homes, but American officers insisted that 'two wrongs don't make a right...they must help rehabilitate themselves'. Irving Heymont, the American commandant of the DP camp at Landsberg am Lech, near Munich, recognised that what DPs most wanted was a degree of autonomy ('the word they use over and over'): 'After their sacrifices and sufferings...they must surely find it rankling to have their private lives regulated and subjected to constant inspection while the Germans live a relatively free life.' But he added that many DPs were 'demoralised beyond hope of rehabilitation' and would need to 'relearn the habits of work and industry: you can't live in the shadow of the past forever'. Polish Jews did not want to live in the shadow of the past, but they remained in limbo until their resettlement was agreed. Meanwhile, they were left to follow the orders of people like Heymont, who appeared to equate rehabilitation with following his orders.[11]

An even more distressing instance of the ways in which the Allies dealt with wartime displacement emerged with respect to around 440,000 people of Yugoslav origin. Some of them were civilians, dragooned into becoming forced labourers and mostly repatriated rapidly in the autumn of 1945 along with other DPs. But, in what had become a familiar story, not everyone wished to return home. It was a different story for soldiers captured in Austria by the Western Allies, who were handed over to Tito or to the Red Army, according to nationality. They included Croats and Slovenes, along with pro-German Russian Cossacks, Ukrainians, and others. There were confirmed reports of suicides and of a swift retribution meted out to those who were forcibly repatriated.[12]

The issue of what to do with the large number of non-repatriated Displaced Persons—in the words of one British diplomat, Thomas Brimelow, their 'ultimate disposal'—subsequently landed on the desk of the newly created International Refugee Organisation (IRO), which replaced UNRRA in December 1946. The IRO constitution spoke of encouraging and assisting DPs to return to their country of origin, while 'genuine refugees and displaced persons should be assisted by international action, either to return to their countries of nationality or former habitual residence, or to find new homes elsewhere'. Its directorate calculated that it had a responsibility towards some 2 million people, namely, 'pre-war refugees' who had come under the aegis of the now defunct League of Nations (who received only legal assistance), Jewish survivors of Nazism, and 'displaced persons' awaiting repatriation. But the term 'genuine refugees' held open the possibility that individual DPs could refuse repatriation, on the grounds that they had 'valid objections' to being returned to a country where they faced likely persecution. On these grounds, the Soviet Union refused to have anything to do with the new body.[13]

The IRO needed to determine who came under its mandate. Not for the first or last time, migrants had to prove their credentials. Anyone who lacked documentation automatically attracted the attention of the IRO's eligibility officers. DPs sometimes curried favour with officials by denouncing fellow DPs for having collaborated willingly with the Nazi regime. Its eligibility officers screened thousands of cases, such as that of Erwin T., a DP living in a camp in Pavia, Italy, reporting: 'He doesn't wish to return to Poland, because he lost his parents during the war. He has no other relatives in Poland, whereas here in Italy he is living with his wife-to-be. He likes Italy more than his home country. Poland is under

Russian influence now, and he doesn't like the Russians. Two of his brothers have been killed in Russia [fighting in the German army]. He fears that the communists could make his life difficult or persecute him if they get to know that he has been fighting side by side with the Germans.' But his claim to be a refugee and request for resettlement in the United States was rejected, on the grounds that in 1942 he had been conscripted into the German army as *Volksdeutsch*, that is, a member of the 'German race'. It is not known what became of him. What we do know is that his story is consistent with IRO practice, which sought to identify anyone who might be an imposter or a security threat.[14]

Humanitarian aid organisations that worked alongside UNRRA, and later the IRO, spoke of supporting the 'rehabilitation' of DPs. No one was very certain what this term meant. In one formulation, it encouraged DPs 'to make a new start as happy, well-adjusted human beings'. 'Adjustment' was another term of uncertain meaning but considerable vintage, and it would continue to find favour among policy makers. In the postwar era, it had a very clear political resonance, but it also concerned the impact of war and displacement on the mental world of the DPs. Difficult questions arose as to how their displacement—and their subsequent containment in the refugee camp—affected their potential to become productive and active citizens.[15]

All of this drew attention to the fact that Europe's refugees were trapped. This immobility posed a serious dilemma for refugees, aid workers, and governments alike. As decisions were yet to be made about their future, the continued confinement of DPs encouraged a sense among some observers that their wartime experiences might influence their conduct in peacetime in ways that made their future resettlement problematic. The American author Kathryn Hulme, who worked on UNRRA's behalf in the DP camp at Wildflecken in West Germany, spoke of the 'ruin in the human soul'.[16]

The Chicago-based sociologist Edward Shils, who served with the US Army in Europe, wrote about the social and psychological consequences of the war, describing the loss of community and family ties. The remaining DPs, he said, suffered 'a widespread psychological regression, a collapse of adult norms and standards in speech, behaviour and attitude, and a reversion to less mature patterns'. He was particularly alarmed at the number of children who had been orphaned or separated from their parents, who lived 'in hordes...by marauding': 'They promise to become the new gypsies, undisciplined, untrained, ready for any political disorder and without any sense of communal responsibility.' In his view, the mind of the migrant, especially the young migrant, was at least as important as the body. DPs spent much of their time waiting. Waiting led to boredom, boredom led to accusations from aid workers that DPs were merely 'apathetic'. The concept of 'DP apathy' prompted considerable debate. Shils suggested that DPs remained apathetic, 'cantankerous', and incapable of 'rational political thought'. He called upon the DP camps to become 'experiments in group therapy', designed to prepare the displaced for resettlement in a third country or, failing that, to allow them to settle in West Germany.[17]

Group therapy did not solve the problem of idleness. Already in March 1946, Brimelow spoke of the need to promote 'welfare work' among DPs, 'in order that they should not go to pieces as a result of forced inactivity'. Useful labour would also be a means of discouraging criminal behaviour, such as black market transactions (although DPs were less involved in criminal activity than the Germans). The IRO insisted on the need to put them 'to useful employment in order to avoid the evil and anti-social consequences of continued idleness'. Middle-class DPs found work as interpreters and teachers. Those from a working-class or peasant background took jobs on building sites and farms. Everyone was encouraged to become more self-reliant, as the best possible passport to local integration or resettlement.[18]

Yet economic deprivation was never far from the surface. The IRO was keen to avoid the charge from German civilians that they were being treated less favourably than DPs by offering them generous rations. A lack of sufficient means encouraged DPs to resort to desperate measures, and those who were caught trying to make ends meet, by falsifying ration cards or trading on the black market, forfeited their right to assistance.[19]

A closer look at the DP camps revealed a more mixed picture—of boredom, certainly, but also of activism. Apathy only captured part of the DP experience. In the view of UNRRA and IRO aid workers, it was important to enable DPs to develop a sense of belonging—the question, however, was to what entity they would belong. Aid worker Joyce Biddell praised the way in which young boys in a DP camp in Austria formed part of an international community: 'There are all sorts here: Russians, Serbs, Yugoslavs, *Volksdeutsche*, as happy as larks together. It's a real education in international friendship, just what everyone is praying for.'[20]

Yet this was to see things through rose-tinted spectacles. Instead of a new cosmopolitanism, Allied policies had actually encouraged the revival of 'competitive nationalism', at least according to British Quakers who worked in the camps. The segregation of groups by nationality made this all but inevitable in their view. One aid worker commented, 'Perhaps we shouldn't have been quite so keen on keeping them as Poles or Ukrainians or whatever, but it was so important to them, they had lost everything and they wanted to keep that bit of their being.'[21]

All DPs who refused repatriation, whatever their nationality, shared a common commitment to anti-communism, but there the similarity ended. DPs insisted on their exclusive national identity. History gave them a strong sense that their own displacement was connected to the suffering of the 'nation' in years gone by. Polish DPs maintained that they could be regarded as exiles (*wygnańcy*), with echoes of nineteenth-century nationalist martyrs, or as nomads or wanderers (*tułacze*), with similar romantic overtones. They named camps after national heroes from the distant past. They enlisted Catholic priests to remind them of the need for solidarity to confront the challenges of displacement. One thing was clear above all others: they wished to use the experience of their current confinement as a means to construct a Polish community beyond communist Poland. They called this 'Polonia', an idea that required Polish DPs to 'fight the enemies of Poland to your last breath'.[22]

Ukrainian DPs likewise cultivated a strong sense of national identity, based around language and faith, and Ukrainians already living in North America supported these endeavours. Ukrainians portrayed themselves as the heirs to a political struggle in the tradition of the eighteenth-century Cossack leader Ivan Mazepa. They served the cause of the 'fatherland' by dint of committing themselves to exile 'until the time of a free and joyful return home'. But returning to Ukraine under communist rule was unthinkable. In these circumstances, Ukrainians would need to stick together. As a leading Ukrainian political activist, Roman Ilnytzkyj, put it: 'We must face the fact that our people will be scattered in small groups around the globe. These small Ukrainian islands will be washed by foreign seas until the seas cover them and swallow them up. Will we allow this to happen? Is there any hope of resisting that process without a country of our own?' His answer was that the Ukrainians would need to rely upon their literature and sense of national pride.[23]

Distinctions operated not just between DPs of different ethnic backgrounds, but also between DPs and the 'host' populations, for whom the DPs had become a nuisance (and a reminder of Nazism). The Russian-born author Natascha Wodin, who wrote in German but grew up surrounded by Russian DPs in a camp in Nuremberg, recalled that the local school she attended exposed her to the contempt of her German classmates, for whom she represented Russian 'barbarity'. She added, 'Everything was German as far as you could see and hear, but only outside. Inside, everything was Russian.' Ironically, it was the camp that protected her from bullying. Yet the suffering she endured as a Russian DP was nothing compared to the disdain that everyone felt towards the Roma who lived nearby. Wodin was 'fascinated by whatever secret thing it was that made them even bigger social outcasts than my parents and I. They stole and cheated, said our neighbours, and they were dirty and dangerous—they chucked their garbage out of the window. We ourselves had shiny silver garbage cans that stood in the basement.' There was a hierarchy in displacement, and even a Russian DP did not belong at the bottom of the pile.[24]

Mobility and immobility became key themes of one of the masterpieces of postwar European cinema. Roberto Rossellini's neglected classic, *Stromboli* (1949), presented a psychological study of displacement and resettlement. It addressed the soul-searching of a young DP (played by Ingrid Bergman) who marries a Sicilian fisherman—revealingly, Rossellini could not make up his mind whether she was supposed to be Czech or Lithuanian, as if it were her 'DP-ness' in general that drove the narrative forward. The central highlight of the film was a breathtaking extended scene of tuna fishing, which embodied the 'traditional' way of life she had found so oppressive. In the final shot, Ingrid Bergman is shown climbing towards a threatening volcano, as if to suggest that her wartime torment at the hands of the Nazis, and then the stifling oppression of a closed society, could only be resolved by succumbing to an unstoppable force of nature.[25]

Other films, too, provided a means of personalising and dramatising the plight of DPs and camp life. The American film star Henry Fonda supplied the voice-over to a 1949 American film, *The Homeless*, that presented life in a German camp for displaced Baltic citizens. It trod a cautious line by making little of their anti-communism and stressing instead their miserable conditions. A more notable example was *The Search* (1948), whose Austrian American director, Fred Zinnemann, visited DP camps, where he was shocked by the 'remnants of various decimated nationalities', in 1947. He shot his film among the ruins of German cities, with Montgomery Clift in an early screen role as an American GI who befriends a young Czech refugee boy, Karel, whom he hopes to take back to the United States. These plans come unstuck when the boy is eventually reunited with his mother, thanks to the energetic efforts of an UNRRA aid worker. Together, mother and son make plans for their repatriation to Czechoslovakia.[26]

The Search made a broader point about the problem of unaccompanied child refugees and how best to address it, whether through schemes of international adoption or repatriation, preferably the latter. (Jewish children were depicted as imminently being taken to Palestine.) But the film also posed questions about the world in which children were growing up: certainly, they were victims of the war that had just ended, and that had inflicted physical and psychological damage on them. Now, in addition, they might become victims of a tug-of-war between rival political blocs.

As relations between West and East turned frosty, Western governments began to look more favourably on resettlement. Support for repatriation dwindled on the grounds that DPs would suffer persecution, and diasporic organisations duly fed often accurate horror stories about the harsh treatment that returnees suffered at the hands of the Soviet state. Between 1947 and 1952, the IRO (known in some quarters as 'an international employment agency') resettled more than 1 million DPs and refugees, the majority to Australia, Canada, and the United States. In the

United States, the 1948 DP Act granted permanent residence to around 200,000 refugees, initially from Czechoslovakia, although this did not signal an open door policy, because it was strictly time-limited, and the numbers admitted were subtracted from existing immigration quotas. Some 132,000 Jewish DPs went to Israel with the assistance of the Jewish Agency for Palestine and the American Joint Distribution Committee. Britain accepted around 87,000 Jewish DPs, and France and Belgium agreed to take 38,000 and 23,000, respectively.[27]

Economic and political interests coincided. Countries of prospective resettlement planned to rescue DPs from Soviet clutches, but also regarded DPs as a valuable labour resource. A census conducted by the IRO in 1948 indicated that four-fifths of them were under forty-five years of age, and three-quarters of the men were skilled or semiskilled. For countries facing a shortage of labour, this was a dream come true, as in the case of France, which planned to resettle DPs to help revive abandoned villages.[28]

Resettlement entailed selection and rejection. Selection required a demonstration of one's physical strength and a clean bill of health. Refugees experienced intimate health inspections and X-rays as humiliating, the more so as the health checks were designed to expose infectious diseases (particularly tuberculosis), bodily ailments, and poor teeth. Inmates complained of a complete lack of privacy. It also helped to be from the Baltic states—there was an unspoken ethnic hierarchy that had Latvians and Lithuanians at the top and Ukrainians at the bottom, with Poles in the middle. One British official suggested that 'Ukrainians are not particularly suited for employment', and recommended that they be sent to the United States, Bolivia, or Iran, anywhere but Britain. Applicants with any kind of disability or infectious disease were excluded from resettlement, and this affected family members, who had to decide whether to leave the afflicted person behind. French officials emphasised 'professional ability, physical shape, social background and behaviour'.[29]

Western governments were not immune from criticism on the grounds that the selection of prospective migrants seemed tantamount to a 'slave auction', according to the Quaker relief worker Grigor McClelland. French critics described the actions of IRO eligibility officers as those of 'animal dealers'. An American critic spoke of a 'catalogue' in which IRO officers 'prowl in the camps as if in department-store bargain basements, where the marked-down price tags feature race, size, family status, age, skill and muscles'. In this feverish marketplace, professional people reinvented themselves as plumbers or farm labourers to maximise their chances of success at the selection board.[30]

Most DPs were eventually able to get out. Jonas Matulionis, born into a prosperous family in interwar Lithuania, managed to get out of a DP camp in 1947 and make a new life in England. He wrote in his diary that 'emigration ended our nomadic period of life. It was temporary, challenging and exhausting. We lived on the mercy of others.' But he wondered if the well of mercy would dry up: 'Thank God, the western world did not leave us alone, but how difficult it is to live on the mercy of others! Will we be happy in our new countries...? I doubt it.' Many DPs shared this sense of uncertainty. Resettlement held out the possibility of becoming a citizen—or rather, earning citizenship—in the resurgent West through purposeful work, something that the DP camp could easily stifle, but finding a place of safety in a democratic country followed a tortuous course.[31]

The prospect of a better life was nevertheless also tinged with sadness. A female DP, who ended up in Bristol after the Second World War and was rescued from a camp, wanted to convey something of her gratitude: 'We begin to feel that we belong somewhere and hope that we shall not remain refugees for ever, because after nine years we hate being refugees. You are leading us into a new world and you are making us live again.' Yet she also insisted: 'We lost seven precious years and we got older. We lost a great deal of our moral values, our will, faith and hope, also a great deal of our physical strength. The vegetative character of our life in these years left ineradicable marks on our spirit and body.' Her words conveyed hope for the future, but they also underlined a sense of wasted years, not only under Nazi rule but also during the time she spent in the camp.[32]

Deliverance from the camps reflected the growing demand for labour. In October 1951, the IRO celebrated the resettlement of the one millionth DP, Slovak refugee Alexander Razenay, who had spent six years in a DP camp. The fanfare signalled the IRO's commitment to solving the 'DP problem' once and for all, part of a growing preoccupation with the perceived problem of overpopulation in Europe, which the IRO director, J. Donald Kingsley, called 'an excess of people in Europe whose very presence constitutes a threat to political and economic stability'. Kingsley pointed to the 'vast and growing demand in other parts of the world for the labour, the skill and the political and cultural assets possessed by these fretfully idle men and women'. The language reflected a helpful global economic environment, enabling refugees to be portrayed as capable and productive assets.[33]

When the IRO wound up its operations, it left unresolved the question of what to do with the 'hard core'. This demeaning term had been in circulation since 1946. It referred to those whose claims for resettlement had been turned down on grounds of physical or mental disability, for having a criminal record, or for other reasons. Since many families chose to stay together, any fault found with one member had serious consequences for the rest. Irrespective of its achievements in resettling other refugees and DPs, the IRO failed to address the needs of these individuals. The United States regarded these needs as best met through economic growth and 'integration' in West Germany and Austria. As we shall see, a small but significant minority were recruited to work on farms or in factories, hospitals, and care homes in Britain and other countries. But five years after the end of the war in Europe, the IRO admitted that some 175,000 individuals still belonged to this 'hard core', an indication that Western countries refused to offer them a lifeline.[34]

Mass migration in its various forms meant that numerous governments and UNRRA, and later the IRO, spent endless hours debating and deciding who was eligible for rehabilitation and resettlement, and where. DPs had to present themselves as liable to political persecution: to present oneself as merely an 'economic migrant' risked exclusion. It helped that persecution came to be seen in a more expansive light. By 1949, the IRO had begun to look favourably on applicants who could demonstrate that they had forfeited their property in the wave of communist expropriation; this, too, qualified as persecution.[35]

Resettlement gave migrants the prospect of new opportunities, but on terms set by the prospective host country, which retained the right to decide whom to admit. Often these states looked upon DPs as a reservoir of labour to be tapped, provided they were healthy and able-bodied. Communist countries condemned the West not just for failing to arrange for the repatriation of DPs, but also for using them as a source of cheap labour to stoke the capitalist economy.

For thousands of others left behind in West Germany and Austria, the 'hard core', the DP camp symbolised their abandonment by Western countries. In Espelkamp, north Westphalia, a former ammunition dump became a thriving city of refugees in 1948, complete with street plans, water mains along with a drainage system, schools, children's homes, and workshops, supported by Swedish and Norwegian churches. It was just as well that they had all this activity to show for their incarceration: eight years later, more than 5,000 people were still living there. Stranded in conditions of uncertainty, their difficulties were compounded by the fact that DPs and refugees of non-German origin lived alongside Germans, not only locals but also newly arrived ethnic German expellees and refugees. As we shall see, this made for difficult encounters and confrontations.

Postwar migration could not be separated from Cold War rivalry. For the Soviet bloc, resettlement schemes amounted to organised slavery, turning DPs into unwilling servants of the capitalist system. Western politicians and business leaders took a diametrically opposed view. Work would provide them with a purpose in life, a means of achieving dignity and integration in Western Europe. Neither perspective, however, acknowledged the reality of the lives of those DPs in the refugee camp who had nowhere to go. The 'hard core' simultaneously epitomised communist oppression and the failure of the West to offer a decent future to all who asked. In a world of resurgent nation-states, those assigned to this category belonged nowhere.

CHAPTER 3

People Adrift: Expellees and Refugees

THE LATE 1940S AND early 1950s were formative years in Europe's migration history. Millions of uprooted people looked for somewhere to live where they could be safe. They included ethnic Germans who had been kicked out of their homes in countries such as Poland, Czechoslovakia, Hungary, and Romania. Their misfortune barely registered beyond Germany. In addition to these expellees, all of whom were dumped— there is no other word—in Germany, refugees continued to flee westwards in order to escape the strengthening grip of communist rule. Given its location at the edge of the Iron Curtain, West Germany was the first destination they reached. By 1950, around 17 percent of the population of the three Western zones that eventually became the Federal Republic of Germany (FRG) were still classified either as expellees or refugees, 8 million people out of a total population of less than 48 million. The percentage was even higher in the Soviet zone of occupation (*Sowjetische Besatzungszone*, SBZ), which in 1949 became the German Democratic Republic (GDR).

Unlike the expellees, refugees gained international attention. Who, though, was a 'refugee'? The International Refugee Organisation in 1947 stipulated that a person qualified as a recognised refugee if he or she could make a credible claim to have suffered from or be at risk of political

51

persecution. The emphasis on persecution carried over to the 1951 United Nations Convention Relating to the Status of Refugees, a document that remains a cornerstone of international refugee law. The signatories agreed that persecution could only be claimed where it had taken place in Europe as a result of events from before January 1951. Anyone who gained refugee status could not be returned to their country of origin against their will.

The flight of refugees did not stop in 1951. People fleeing East Germany or other countries in the Soviet bloc crossed into West Germany. Regular reports appeared in the news media of artists, scholars, and others who fled communism by whatever means. Until the building of the Berlin Wall in 1961, there was a steady stream of these so-called escapees, who were welcomed as victims of communism, and even celebrated as heroic figures who had an important part to play in securing the West's claims to moral superiority in the Cold War.

Nevertheless, whatever international law had to say, European governments were faced with the practical problems of how to accommodate the millions of new migrants who fled to the West. Sir John Hope Simpson, an acknowledged expert on refugees, stressed that a laisser-faire approach would exacerbate political instability across the continent: 'Nor is peace safe while masses of people live in conditions intolerable in a civilised era. In Central Europe the ground lies ready prepared for the seed of revolutionary propaganda.' The dilemmas also emerged in a wide-ranging article published in 1953 by the newly appointed UN High Commissioner for Refugees, the Dutch diplomat G. J. van Heuven Goedhart, in which he spoke of his responsibility to protect Europe's 'stateless wanderers' engaged on a 'perilous journey'. Resettlement, in his view, offered only a partial solution to the problem: if countries in northwestern Europe were willing to open their doors, well and good, but the most promising outcome would be the integration of refugees in West Germany, Austria, Italy, and Greece.[1]

Certainly, for German expellees, local integration remained the only option. They did not fall within the mandate of the UNHCR, because member states did not consider them to have been persecuted and they had German nationality. Church leaders, such as those who spearheaded the World Council of Churches, denounced the decision to exclude the expellees from international legal protection and assistance, a policy that did not accord with 'Christian principles'. But so far as the Allies were concerned, the expellees were Germany's problem.[2]

German expellees became highly important figures in postwar social life and politics in the Western and Eastern zones of occupation. What they found in their new destinations, and how they coped with this abrupt change in their lives, requires us to consider not one Germany, but two, although both states, however great their political differences, confronted immense challenges in integrating expellees, who reached Germany with little advance notice.

The West German government laid down the legal framework and underwrote the costs of resettlement. The legal position was determined by the Basic Law of 1949, Article 116, which gave German citizenship to descendants of people living in Germany as of December 1937. Citizenship was one thing; securing an adequate livelihood was another matter altogether. There was a significant regional dimension to this forced migration. Expellees were expected to move to rural areas, where the housing stock had suffered relatively less damage than in urban centres. Most expellees ended up in Bavaria (in the American occupation zone) and in Lower Saxony, North Rhine–Westphalia, and Schleswig-Holstein (all in the British zone). In Bavaria they made up more than 20 percent of the total population, and in Lower Saxony expellees and newly arrived refugees made up more than 27 percent of the population.[3]

The Allied occupation authorities attempted to ease the problem by insisting that private homeowners give up rooms to accommodate the newcomers, with penalties for noncompliance, although these were difficult to enforce. Some expellees found temporary accommodation in disused air-raid shelters; others were sent to hotels. Local government officials frowned upon extended stays in camps, lest this create a new category of humanity, '*Homo barackensis*', a breeding ground of despair and radicalism. But it was not easy to dismantle camps, which held some attraction for those unable to afford the rent on an apartment. In any case, camps were needed for refugees from East Germany, who continued to arrive throughout the 1950s. Camps remained for years a feature of the German landscape.[4]

Expellees struggled to find jobs. Those with a professional or clerical background had to set their sights lower or risk unemployment. Some Sudeten Germans with skills in various trades and services managed to set up in business on their own account, particularly if they were bakers, butchers, or hairdressers, for example, or if they could work as bricklayers, carpenters, or electricians. Cottage industry made a comeback, as in the new town of Neugablonz in Bavaria, where glass and jewellery makers were rehoused from Gablonz (now Jablonec) in Czechoslovakia. Other expellees commuted from villages into nearby towns and cities in search of work. But no one could do much more than just scrape by, and life was particularly tough for those who could not find work and for the elderly and disabled.[5]

With the Allies having rapidly washed their hands of any further responsibility towards German expellees in the West, nongovernmental organisations (NGOs), including church groups and charities, worked to plug the gap. Food shortages meant that expellees bartered what few belongings they had in order to obtain food, or else simply appealed to local parishioners to take pity on them and spare some scraps. Finally, local authorities stepped in to insist that local parishes provide allotments. In 1949, the Lutheran World Federation established more permanent settlements, such as at Espelkamp in North Rhine–Westphalia, in order to provide 'a bulwark against communism' and a place for 'Christian reconstruction'. Homes for expellees came with strings attached, however: only those with a guaranteed job were assured of a place to live. The emphasis was on self-help.[6]

Knowing the dramatic circumstances of their enforced expulsion did not make local Germans any more sympathetic to the newcomers. Sympathy soon gave way to suspicion and outright contempt, particularly in rural areas or small towns that had escaped relatively unscathed from the war and where expellees were more conspicuous (bigger cities generally offered a warmer welcome). Farmers complained that expellees were lazy and arrogant—farmers from the East, they maintained, had employed Poles to do the hard work on their farms—and sometimes even claimed they were dishonest. One Schleswig-Holstein farmer reported: 'The children steal so much fruit that I might as well cut down the trees.' As it became clear that the expellees were there to stay, villagers began to speak of them as a 'Slav element', or, in one particularly odious formulation, 'mulattoes'. These characterisations were a racialised depiction of the expellees, as if their 'German blood' had been tainted by long years living in Eastern Europe.[7]

Much later, the historian Rainer Schulze interviewed middle-aged expellees who settled in Celle, a rural district in northwestern Germany. He found that they had to adjust to a sense of estrangement. Herr O., who arrived as a seven-year-old expellee in 1945, became a champion marksman but relinquished his status in order that locals would not resent him. Expellees described being isolated, a direct consequence of the Allies' decision to disperse them: families might be allowed to stay together, but communities were deliberately dismantled, lest they form 'a state within a state' and support revanchist claims, or, in other words, campaign for a reversal of the postwar territorial settlement. There was more than an element of truth in this concern: to begin with, at least, many expellees felt that any attempt on their part to 'integrate' into West German society was tantamount to accepting the *fait accompli* of postwar borders.[8]

The Basic Law provided expellees with the opportunity to create formal associations, known as *Landsmannschaften*, or 'homeland societies'. By 1955 there were twenty of these with a total membership of more than 1.3 million. They provided a degree of mutual aid but also served as a focal point for annual political rallies, in which they demanded to be allowed to reclaim the land from which they had been expelled. A major political pressure group appeared on the scene in the shape of the Bund der Heimatvertriebenen und Entrechteten (BHE, League of Expellees and Those Deprived of Rights) in 1950, renamed the Bund der vertriebenen Deutschen (BvD, League of Expelled Germans) in 1954, whose leaders pressed for the recovery of territory from Germany's eastern neighbours and a return to the 1937 borders—but excluded the Sudeten Germans. West German politicians responded in more temperate fashion. The Charter of the German Expellees, adopted by the West German government in August 1950, rejected 'all thought of revenge and retaliation', pinning its hopes instead on European unity 'as the only permanent solution to the continent's minority problems'.[9]

In 1952 the federal government in Bonn passed the Equalisation of Burdens Law, which was designed to facilitate the political incorporation of expellees by agreeing that West Germans would foot the bill. This decision helped to neutralise the more extreme claims mounted by expellee organisations, particularly the BvD. Expellees could claim compensation on a sliding scale for property they had been forced to abandon; they also became eligible for a pension under social insurance legislation that afforded them the same rights as other citizens. By some accounts, one-tenth of German taxation went to support expellees between 1945 and 1960, although this figure included money earmarked for refugees. The importance of this commitment cannot be exaggerated: a fragile German state, badly damaged by long years of war, demonstrated its support for millions of newcomers who had been punished for being ethnically German. The government of West Germany acknowledged that their expulsion was the price it had to pay for the crimes of Nazism.

In a move designed to curry favour with the expellee leadership, the Federal Republic launched a massive exercise to collect the testimony of expellees. The project came under the leadership of Theodor Schieder, who had worked for the Nazi regime to devise plans for the large-scale settlement of Germans on Polish soil. Far from treating expulsion as an indirect consequence of Nazi policies of expansion and consolidation of German settlement, Schieder's aim was to portray Germans as victims. Nevertheless, the prevailing mood in Germany in the 1960s and after was that expellees had no grounds on which to complain, and if they did express any discontent, no one in a position of political authority was of a mind to do anything about it. Attendance progressively dwindled at the meetings organised by 'homeland societies'.[10]

The policy of rapprochement with Eastern Europe, *Ostpolitik*, was the final nail in the coffin of expellees' hopes. In 1973, a treaty between the Federal Republic and Czechoslovakia confirmed the existing border, pulling the rug from under the feet of the remaining expellee activists, such as those from the Sudetenland, who could no longer entertain any hope that it might be regained by Germany.

The impact of expulsion in the longer term emerged in a study that found that first- and second-generation expellees remained at an economic disadvantage in West Germany. (No equivalent study exists for their counterparts in the East.) By 1971, they had significantly lower income levels and higher risks of unemployment compared to those who had not been expelled. Many expellees had been obliged to take manual jobs, even though they were highly qualified. From this point of view, the government's attempt to integrate the expellees did not achieve its objectives.[11]

Overall, however, the expellees supported the economic miracle by enabling employers to keep wages low and generating profits for investment. Besides, their pay was higher in the industrial economy than it would have been had they remained in agriculture. Working-class expellees from towns and cities such as Breslau (Wrocław) managed to secure better-paid jobs than many of the others. Economic benefits were not evenly distributed among individuals, but some expellees certainly achieved wealth and status. This success helped deliver an unexpected degree of political stability.

East Germany, too, had to take responsibility for expellees on its own territory, some 4.3 million of whom arrived between 1945 and 1949, equivalent to 24 percent of the total postwar population. In Mecklenburg and West Pomerania, every second person was an expellee. The authorities struggled to cope, not only because of the scale of displacement but also because resources were diverted to sustain the Red Army and to pay reparations to the Soviet Union. Hundreds of thousands of expellees were assigned to makeshift barracks and camps—600 such camps were dotted around the Soviet zone of occupation by the end of 1945—where they could be interrogated and given 'political instruction'. As the camps were gradually closed, German officials began the complicated task of moving men, women, and children out of camps and onto land that had been socialised. But this was far from a smooth process. Although government statistics spoke of providing 'housing units', in practice the expellees were forced to live for months in attics, cellars, or stables. Attempts to get locals to share their living space with expellees yielded few results.[12]

As in the Western zones, many expellees had no other option than to become labourers, although some of them found jobs as accountants, farm managers, and the like. Others contributed to the reconstruction of coal and copper mines, or iron works and shipyards. Expellees who settled in towns and cities had a relatively easier life than their counterparts in the countryside, partly because of higher pay and a degree of prestige associated with being proletarian. Women, especially, found it difficult to get jobs, and had to rely on modest welfare payments. Legislation in 1950 eased some of the pressure by providing workers with access to credit and state benefits, but the settlement was less generous financially than in the West.[13]

The East German authorities favoured the euphemism *Umsiedler*, 'resettlers', because their presence was deemed to be irreversible. The term was meant as a positive government endorsement of the contribution they could make to the new society. State-sponsored 'resettler committees' and 'resettler weeks' (*Umsiedler Wochen*) encouraged other citizens to donate money, but the main effort came from the government, either directly, through spending on new housing projects, or indirectly, through social reforms. By the beginning of the 1950s, the official coinage of 'former resettled' implied that they had been fully integrated in the 'new homeland' (*die Neue Heimat*). Relations between the newcomers and locals were no less fraught than they were in West Germany. One woman wrote that her new neighbours treated her 'like an unwanted intruder and alien element'. Although in principle they enjoyed equal status with the local population, the newcomers were demonised as 'gypsies', 'Polacks', and 'vermin'. Religious differences—most resettlers were Catholic, most locals were Protestant—compounded the problem.[14]

Many expellees, particularly younger ones, acknowledged that over the long term the GDR provided them with a good education and promoted upward social mobility—in return for their political loyalty. Skilled workers, in particular, stood to benefit from the state's overarching commitment to economic, social, and political transformation. Others found jobs in the expanding civil service or in educational institutions.[15]

Meanwhile, the experiences of expellees emerged in films, memoirs, and novels. One in five films produced in Germany in the 1950s belonged to the genre of *Heimatfilme*, 'homeland films', that conveyed how expellees had made a new home for themselves even as they expressed a degree of nostalgia for the homes they had been forced to renounce. In the GDR, the government sponsored a film in 1968 titled *Wege übers Land* (Paths across the country) which implied that expellees had now been 'returned' to their original home in Germany. Nothing was said about forced expulsion.[16]

Alongside expellees, West Germany faced another major challenge, the result not of a decision forced upon it by Potsdam but by the decision of ordinary people to flee from communist countries and seek sanctuary in the West. Around 130,000 people left the SBZ (that is, East Germany) in 1949 alone, and this number climbed to more than 330,000 by 1953. The entire decade saw an exodus of 3 million German refugees to West Germany. Most of them were unskilled or semiskilled workers, but they also included nearly 5,000 doctors and dentists, 1,000 pharmacists, 700 lawyers, 17,000 teachers, and 17,000 engineers, imposing a significant drain on the professions. Refugees continued to cross to the West until the Soviets put a stop to this by building the Berlin Wall in 1961.[17]

Although under Section 16.2 of the 1949 Basic Law only those who could demonstrate political persecution or a risk to life and limb were legally recognised as refugees, in practice the West German government eventually turned a blind eye to the significant numbers of people, many of them young adults, fleeing from East Germany for 'economic' reasons. Refugees argued that at home they were forced to live a 'collective' existence in a totalitarian state, and should be admitted on these grounds.[18]

Legal changes alleviated some of the difficulties that new refugees faced in Germany. In April 1951, the government of the Federal Republic passed a Homeless Foreigners Act protecting them from being repatriated against their will. It provided them with the same rights as German citizens relating to place of residence and freedom of movement, social security, the right to work, and the right to public education. Nevertheless, official support did not easily translate into being made welcome by one's new neighbours. One pastor instructed refugees not to take a seat in church until all his regular attendees had found a pew, since refugees were, in his words, 'only guests in Lower Saxony', an odd way of describing people who had few options as to where to go. There were even instances where West Berliners alerted the Stasi when they knew of an East German's plans to escape, justifying this betrayal on the grounds that refugees would otherwise take jobs that rightfully belonged to West Germans.[19]

Matters were further complicated by the concurrent arrival of ethnic German refugees from other parts of the Soviet bloc. Following Chancellor Konrad Adenauer's historic visit to the USSR in September 1955, at which point the Soviet leadership agreed to treat these refugees as a 'human' rather than a 'legal-political' issue, several thousand ethnic Germans who remained in the Baltic republics were allowed to leave in the late 1950s. (This visit also paved the way for the release of the last POWs in Soviet captivity.) These refugees were immediately granted citizenship in West Germany. Just like the expellees, they continued to insist that their 'homeland' was under communist 'occupation'.

Migration also took place in the reverse direction, albeit on a much smaller scale. Refugees from West Germany, some of them prominent cultural figures, arrived in the East and denounced politicians in West Germany as 'fascists'—one new arrival in 1958 spoke of having left 'the country of lies' for 'the land of freedom'. They were joined by a handful of Americans escaping McCarthyism and by others who were ideologically sympathetic to the communist cause or who simply looked upon East Germany as a place where they could be guaranteed a job and an apartment. However, the communist authorities offered a heavily qualified welcome, deeming the newcomers a potentially disruptive presence. The chance for them to make a fresh start in East Germany rarely turned out as intended.[20]

Beyond Germany, the classic case of refugees who were sidelined by the international refugee regime was that of the displaced Turks. In August 1950, the Bulgarian government announced that a quarter of a million refugees of Turkish heritage had 'volunteered' to leave for Turkey. Turkey's first reaction was to close its border with Bulgaria, but it relented after reaching an agreement with its neighbour to issue visas in an orderly fashion and to send back illegal immigrants. By the summer of the following year, 140,000 had been admitted, half of them children under fifteen years of age. They were practically destitute, 'having been almost totally dispossessed before their departure'. Attempts were made to have them recognised as refugees under the 1951 Convention Relating to the Status of Refugees, but they did not qualify, because they were already deemed to have Turkish citizenship.[21]

The Turkish Red Crescent and other organisations, including the World Health Organisation, offered assistance to refugees. The Turkish Ministry of Agriculture settled them on uncultivated land abandoned by Greeks in the 1920s during the massive population exchange between Greece and Turkey. The government provided refugees with loans, farm equipment, seed, and livestock, supplemented by a contribution from the US aid budget, as part of a programme for rural modernisation. The programme pointed to two significant developments: one was the importance of Turkey to the United States, which regarded it as a frontline state in the Cold War. The second was the connection that Turkey made between migration and the potential for long-term economic development, not dissimilar to the situation in West Germany.[22]

The question as to who qualified as a 'refugee' by virtue of having been persecuted continued to bedevil European politics in the 1950s. The respected international lawyer Jacques Vernant opened his mammoth study of refugees in the postwar world by saying that '"refugees" turn up, sometimes in large numbers, at the frontiers of the countries of asylum, and partly in order to secure a more advantageous status and partly, but mainly, to avoid exclusion, seize any favourable opportunity to invoke political reasons as a cloak for their search for a better life'.[23] A recurrent difficulty concerned Yugoslav asylum seekers who fled to Italy, seeking to persuade the Italian authorities that they had suffered persecution and should therefore be given refugee status. One Yugoslav refugee articulated his case before a dubious official in this way:

> Your question proves to me that the West understands very little of the real nature of the Communist system. If by persecution you mean a term of imprisonment then I must confess that I have not been persecuted. But there are a thousand little pressures in the everyday life of every person which, taken together, might make life unbearable....Like the great majority of the people in Yugoslavia, I have suffered *oppression*. It is from this that I am a refugee, it is because of this that I do not wish to return.[24]

In practice, very few non-Italian refugees were allowed to settle permanently in Italy in the years following the Second World War. But this man's eloquent plea—we do not know if it had the desired effect—pointed to the problem of how to determine refugee status. It is a problem that has never gone away.

Western governments exercised a good deal of discretion. They did so by making provision for people who escaped from communist rule after 1951, namely, those who could not be legally recognised as refugees under the terms of the Refugee Convention. The key figure here was the 'escapee'. The US Escapee Program (USEP), created in March 1952, reflected Cold War concerns about the 'emergence of a young generation who have grown up under communism and have no experience or concept of conditions outside the orbit of Soviet domination'. Its officials argued that 'each refugee from the Soviet orbit represents a denial of the inevitability of the communist system'. One interpretation of USEP is that it actually encouraged people to flee rather than responding to those who fled.[25]

The US administration trod a careful line, portraying itself as a country that held the door open to 'escapees' for reasons of political calculation, but also as wanting to keep them in check. As President Harry S. Truman explained in a speech to the US Congress in 1952: 'Italy is struggling with very serious problems of overpopulation and is urgently trying to resettle large numbers of its people overseas. Greece faces great difficulty in absorbing the refugees of Greek origin who are being driven out of the Balkan satellites by the communists. The brutal policies of Soviet tyranny are aggravating overcrowded conditions which are already a danger to the stability of these free nations.'

A year earlier, when establishing a Provisional Inter-Governmental Committee for the Movement of Migrants from Europe (PICMME being the mischievous acronym), Truman indicated that the objective was to provide 'specific aid and assistance . . . for the people who are fleeing at the risk of their lives from Southern and Eastern Europe'. He emphasised that 'a substantial number of them want to stay in Europe [that is, Western Europe] and should have the chance to do so'. Seventeen countries joined PICMME, which was renamed the Intergovernmental Committee for European Migration (ICEM), in October 1952, and became the forerunner of the International Organisation for Migration (IOM). Member states, including Argentina, Brazil, Chile, Australia, and Israel, were free to select migrants in accordance with their own national interests, with transport costs being met from the ICEM budget.[26]

The US State Department channelled funds to NGOs to address what were described as 'creeping challenges to our humanitarian task'. Staff provided new refugees with a 'welcome kit' before screening them to confirm their eligibility and to make sure they did not pose a security threat. Resettlement centres, such as Wels and Glasenbach (Austria), Zirndorf (Germany), and Lavrion (Greece), offered counselling, helped with visas and transportation, provided vocational training and language courses, and offered legal and other assistance. Where resettlement ceased to be feasible—for example, because of the growth in numbers—USEP explored the possibilities of local integration.[27]

NGOs such as the World Council of Churches actively sought 'human-interest' stories from escapees 'on the doorstep' of Western Europe, such as those of ethnic Greek or Albanian origin who had recently fled to Greece from communist Albania or Romania. New arrivals who might be able to provide 'interesting information about conditions in the homeland' were particularly sought after. They recounted tales of starvation, police harassment and torture, pressure to demonstrate Communist Party loyalty, and dispossession of farmers and small businessmen. For example, Evangelos N., who escaped from Romania in 1951, simply stated, 'I am grateful to God that I and my family have been able to escape into the free world. Poverty and misery is what prevails in life there.' A Bulgarian, Demetrius G., maintained that 'only 30 percent of the Bulgarian people believe in Communism. The remainder simply accept and suffer the consequences of a totalitarian regime waiting for the time of their liberation.' It helped if these escapees had 'photogenic' qualities that confirmed their look of determination—but it was unclear if they were isolated escapees or the heralds of a much larger exodus from the Soviet bloc.[28]

Such disavowals of communism seemed ostensibly to be music to the ears of Western diplomats. But expressions of hatred for communism did not always translate into a positive welcome for escapees. Asylum seekers from Eastern Europe might find themselves being treated as a potential fifth column. In 1953, authorities locked up dozens of Polish sailors who had docked their boats in Holland and claimed asylum. The rigorous security checks that ensued took months to complete. In private, Western officials acknowledged that they frequently sold escapees short by denying them visas. Some escapees had no choice but to stay in former Nazi concentration camps, where they were 'repeatedly interrogated by overlapping agencies who sought to strip new arrivals of usable intelligence'. Confined in intolerable conditions, they were then 'turned loose to shift for themselves after being squeezed dry of information'.[29]

To be sure, celebrity escapees, such as dancers, musicians, scientists, and diplomats, secured a sympathetic reception in the West. Ivan Pluhar, a Czech who managed to tunnel out of a prison camp near the uranium mines where he had been sentenced for anti-communist activity, was subsequently admitted into Yale Law School 'with much fanfare'. Undoubtedly the most famous Soviet defector was the ballet dancer Rudolf Nureyev in 1961. Nureyev continued dancing in the West, to great acclaim. But others found themselves in the spotlight only in death. Peter Fechter, a young bricklayer who attempted to cross the border between West and East Berlin on 17 August 1962, was shot by East German border guards and left to bleed to death in the so-called death strip, or no-man's-land. His friend Helmut Kulbeik managed to escape. The West German media turned Fechter's death into a symbol of the GDR dictatorship, and the memorial erected in 1990 after the Berlin Wall was pulled down can be seen on Zimmerstrasse. It reads, 'Er wollte nur die Freiheit' (He only wanted freedom). Kulbeik himself appears to have settled into a life of anonymity, becoming a footnote in the history of those who aspired to migrate but instead were murdered.[30]

The total number of Berlin Wall victims has been put at 140 people, and Fechter came to symbolise the heroic and tragic escapee. But not everyone conformed to the image of the freedom-loving escapee. As historian Ned Richardson-Little observed, 'many fatal escape attempts were prompted by breakups, arguments at work, or just plain loneliness.' From a vantage point in 2019, it is possible to remember their fate whilst also reflecting on the loss of life at the new walls that European states have recently built to deter migrants.[31]

The first major test in Europe for the UNHCR came in 1956, when the outbreak of revolution in Hungary gave rise to the most dramatic refugee-generating crisis in continental Europe between the end of the Second World War and the collapse of Yugoslavia in 1991. The turning point came when Hungary took the fateful decision to leave the Warsaw Pact, prompting the Soviet leadership to send in the Red Army in order to preserve Hungary's position in the communist bloc. By early 1957, in the aftermath of the 1956 uprising, nearly 190,000 people crossed the border to neighbouring Austria. Another 20,000 refugees made their way to Yugoslavia, but the difficult conditions in refugee camps caused them to leave for Austria as well.

The UNHCR's original mandate appeared to confirm that these refugees did not qualify for international protection under the terms on which it had been established, since their flight clearly took place after 1 January 1951. With legal advice from Paul Weis, who had arrived in the UK in 1939 as a refugee from Nazi Germany and who worked on protection issues for the International Refugee Organisation before joining its successor body, the UNHCR decided that the Hungarians were eligible for temporary assistance on the grounds that their 'persecution' could be traced back to the communist revolution. Soviet bloc countries, unsurprisingly, expressed outrage, but the Hungarian refugee crisis gave a powerful impetus to the international refugee regime, even if it did nothing to weaken the sovereign power of the nation-state to be the final arbiter of the claims made by asylum seekers.[32]

The West's response was governed not only by ideas of rescuing Hungarians from persecution, but also by the fear that social instability in Austria—a country on the front line of the Cold War by virtue of its geographical location, and which had only seen the end of Allied occupation a year earlier—could encourage a renewed political radicalism. Refugees were portrayed as victims of communist tyranny who had escaped 'carnage and deportations' in order to find 'liberty and justice', although only a minority took part in the uprising. Having deftly incorporated Hungarian refugees within its mandate, the UNHCR in practice devolved much of the day-to-day support for refugees onto the Austrian government.

Austria housed the refugees in more than 200 makeshift facilities and appealed to its citizens to donate money.[33]

Before long, however, Austria was complaining about the strain that the refugees—equivalent to 5 percent of the total population—placed upon the public purse. They were increasingly described as economic migrants rather than political refugees, and a 'flood' that threatened to 'inundate' Austria, demeaning language that denied these migrants dignity. According to one account, once Hungarians entered coffee bars or tried to set up a small business, and no longer played the prescribed role of poor and helpless refugees, public opinion turned against them. But this was not the end of the story. Other problems arose because, as a contributor to the bulletin of the International Catholic Migration Commission put it in 1958, 'some Hungarians also told lies to the authorities, to members of relief organizations; how could they know—trained as they were in dissimulation during the years of terror—that here evasions and lies were no longer necessary?' Austrian psychologists reported that refugees lacked the character to become full citizens. Here, too, a tension emerged between the valorisation of refugees as heroic escapees and their 'confused' psychology, to which the long and awkward relationship between Austrians and Hungarians added a further complication.[34]

Hungarian refugees were admitted to other countries besides Austria as well, including the United States (which took around one-fifth of the total), Canada, Australia, West Germany, Switzerland, and the UK. Some contemporaries who were otherwise sympathetic to the plight of Hungarian refugees held that Western propaganda was perhaps to blame for the fact that many of them expected far too much of the country of asylum. Those who had fought against Soviet domination were treated as heroes in the worldwide struggle against communism, but others (it was said) 'had merely taken the opportunity of emigrating'. One UK journalist remarked, without offering any evidence, that 'enterprising' DPs from among the 'residue' had surreptitiously returned to Hungary in 1956 from DP camps in Austria in order to secure fresh status as refugees. Critics on the British left suggested that politically undesirable individuals, such as 'Horthyites' (meaning those sympathetic to the fascist regime in wartime Hungary), took advantage of unrestricted entry to gain admission to the West.[35]

NGOs did not hesitate to advertise their effectiveness or to affirm the gratitude of Hungarian refugees. The British Council for Aid to Refugees (BCAR) gave grants of food and other basic necessities, provided writing paper and stamps for refugees in Neukirchen and other temporary camps, and arranged sponsorship and adoptions. Refugees were encouraged to feel at home by setting up shoe repair shops, sewing rooms, barber shops, recreational opportunities, and reading rooms inside the camp. BCAR published news sheets 'helping to calm the wild excitement of families having no news and hearing every kind of extraordinary story and rumour'. The British Red Cross pronounced newcomers 'pathetically grateful for the gifts they received'. Although some refugees were repatriated to Hungary following protracted negotiations, the Hungarian 'brain drain' brought economic benefits to host countries in the West.[36]

The Dutch government scoured the refugee camps in Austria to select workers who were willing to labour in the coal mines. Professional men and women found their way to Britain and West Germany, and the Rockefeller Foundation gave grants to enable Hungarian students to take up places in European universities. More than 115,000 refugees were eventually admitted to the United States and Canada. Having initially agreed to admit 2,500 Hungarians, the British government eventually opened its doors to ten times that number. It helped that many refugees were portrayed as healthy, energetic, and able to contribute intellectual capital, although some were accused of having 'inflated ideas of Western prosperity' and 'not really expecting to have to work hard for a living'.[37]

If the Hungarian refugee crisis exposed both the generosity of countries that offered temporary asylum and the limits of such generosity, other episodes suggested that governments could tie themselves into knots when confronted by people who were desperate to escape communist rule. A striking illustration was the arrival from Poland of the final trainload of ethnic German expellees in Schleswig-Holstein in February 1959. The fanfare quickly turned into a fiasco when it emerged that several wagons contained a contingent of Roma refugees. The local police in the small town of Büchen attempted to collect them prior to deporting them back to the Soviet zone. Eventually the government of Schleswig-Holstein allowed them to remain in Germany, not least because of the negative publicity that the entire affair had generated. The presence of the national and international news media resulted in photographs of men in German uniforms standing guard over a bedraggled group of terrified people. The historian Ari Joskowicz writes, 'Even observers unfamiliar with the full repertoire of Holocaust iconography could not miss the uncomfortable parallels to Nazi deportations of, among others, Romani detainees.'[38]

So far as refugees were concerned—'left-over people', as they were called at the time—the prevailing political atmosphere was relatively propitious, because it encouraged the idea of rescuing people from the clutches of communism in Western Europe. Germany occupied a crucial place by virtue of being at the epicentre of Cold War confrontation.[39]

From his position as the deputy high commissioner of the UNHCR, and thus responsible for ensuring that signatories abided by the 1951 Refugee Convention, James Read drew an important lesson from the Hungarian refugee crisis: that Westerners could 'almost speak of a new concept, that of considering the whole of Western Europe as territory of first asylum'. He invited European governments to deliver on this promise, although he knew better than anyone that states jealously guarded their right to decide whom to admit. Subsequent developments would do nothing to weaken that determination.[40]

CHAPTER 4

Rebuilding Western Europe:
Adventures in Migration

IN OCTOBER 1946 A small group of young Latvian women arrived in London, the vanguard of a much larger contingent of around 20,000 women from the Baltic states and Eastern Europe who were recruited to work in Britain between 1945 and 1950. The boat dropped them off at Tilbury Dock, where the famous HMT *Empire Windrush* would berth less than two years later, bringing new migrants from the West Indies. Unlike their Caribbean counterparts, however, these women had no prior connection with Britain, and they came to the UK via a circuitous route.

One of the Latvian women, known as Ilona (not her real name), interviewed in 2000 by the geographer Linda McDowell, recalled being snatched from her home and taken to Nazi Germany as a forced labourer. Ilona ended up in a DP camp at war's end. Like so many of her compatriots in 1945, she resisted the call to return to her home in what now formed part of the Soviet Union. Instead she took the chance to come to the UK under one of the many schemes of organised recruitment undertaken by the British government. Ilona described being instructed by the British to work in a mental hospital, where she had to scrub the floors, light the coal fires, and wash the dishes. It seemed like a dead end, but chance encounter changed everything. Ilona said: 'There was an old German doctor and he kept talking to me and he saw that I had all the education. I showed him my papers and so on and he said that he would try to help me, that I could do nurses' training. So I, before my time, before a year was out, I was already a student nurse.'[1]

Ilona's story can be read in various ways. It was a dual deliverance, from forced labour in Nazi Germany and from the unwelcome prospect of life in Soviet Latvia. She now had to submit to a different authority and take the first job she was offered. Nevertheless, looking back on her experiences from a distance of nearly half a decade, Ilona expressed pride in having contributed to Britain's new National Health Service. She seized the opportunity to get ahead by gaining new qualifications.

Ilona's personal account forms part of a much broader history of postwar European reconstruction and the associated demand for labour. Part of that demand could be satisfied by getting people out of military uniform and back into civilian jobs. But there were never enough domestic workers to satisfy the need for labour. Countries had to look beyond their own borders for men and women to add to the workforce. Peacetime dictated economic migration.

Schemes of organised migration to boost the labour supply began immediately after the war. In a series of initiatives designed to meet economic objectives, rather than to pursue humanitarian motives, Britain, Belgium, and Norway energetically recruited 'alien' workers such as Ilona from DP camps. Belgium promoted a scheme called 'Black Diamond' whereby DPs were recruited to work in industry. Norway's equivalent was called 'Northern Lights'. DPs were not the only source of imported labour. Under the so-called North Sea Scheme, Britain recruited German women for menial work in British hospitals. Various other schemes brought Italians to the UK—men as foundry workers, women for textiles and the pottery trade. Sweden granted residence permits to tens of thousands of Baltic refugees who had entered illegally after the war but had found jobs. Indeed, Sweden briefly recruited workers from Hungary in 1945–1947, by which point migrant workers from Greece and Yugoslavia began to take their place. National economic priorities mattered more than humanitarian rescue operations.[2]

Without people like Ilona, the rebuilding of Western Europe would have taken much longer to complete. Economic reconstruction meant not only repairing war-damaged houses, factories, transport installations, and other infrastructure, but also new investment. It required people to work in industry, agriculture, construction, energy, and transport as well as in health care, education, and retailing. The seeds of economic reconstruction were sown by migrant men and women, many of whom had travelled relatively short distances but had to adapt to an unfamiliar environment and new routines.

In a major study of the postwar economic boom, the American economist Charles Kindleberger argued that economic growth in West Germany was secured by an abundant supply of labour, which kept down costs of production; the resulting profits could be reinvested in technological improvements. Part of the addition to the labour force derived from the natural increase in population and from drawing on reserves of the unemployed, but the contribution of expellees, new refugees, and foreign workers was decisive. In the immediate postwar period, the labour participation rate among migrants was relatively low, as the expellee population included many dependents, but this profile changed when young adult refugees began to arrive from East Germany in significant numbers. Throughout Western Europe, orchestrated recruitment ensured a steady labour supply.[3]

Under the name 'Westward Ho!', beginning in February 1947, the British Ministry of Labour despatched officials to the DP camps to identify suitable workers in order to satisfy the demand for labour in key occupations, such as cotton textiles, agriculture, and other essential industries. The scheme was aimed in the first instance at Balts and Ukrainians in the British zone but was then extended to the American and French zones. By the time it ended in 1950, even a handful of German expellees were included. Between 1946 and 1949, a total of around 90,000 men and women were recruited by these means. British officials dubbed them European Volunteer Workers (EVWs), in the belief that calling them simply 'foreign workers' would expose them to animosity. The designation 'workers' clearly mattered: the programmes did not offer opportunities for middle-class professionals to gain a foothold in the occupations for which they were qualified.[4]

There was a barely disguised element of discrimination in these schemes, as governments and employers decided who was healthy and able-bodied and who was not. No employer was interested in the so-called residuum, individuals who could not be resettled in third countries on grounds of old age, prolonged health issues (such as tuberculosis or mental illness), or disability. Pregnant women were also excluded. Anyone over the age of thirty-five, particularly if they had a higher education, was normally ruled out from resettlement. 'Balt Cygnets' (the unofficial name for Latvian EVWs) who were pregnant but slipped through the net could be returned to the DP camp, although this rarely happened.[5]

Discrimination was also about ethnic differentiation and ethnic hierarchy. The Balt Cygnet scheme targeted young unattached women from the Baltic states who were deemed to be of 'sound stock' and 'scrupulously clean in their persons and habits', which made them suitable to be employed in hospitals and TB sanatoria. Ukrainians, on the other hand, were regarded as better suited to work as hospital cleaners, laundry maids, and kitchen staff, where they were less likely to come into contact with British patients.[6]

Economic considerations prevailed: the British government viewed these DPs as economic migrants, not as refugees entitled to humanitarian assistance. None of this went down well with the Latvian DPs and others, who regarded themselves as indeed refugees and erstwhile citizens of a vanished state who might yet return to a 'free country'.[7]

Male EVWs were assigned to physically demanding jobs in mining, agriculture, forestry, and construction. (There was even a suggestion from miners that some pits should be reserved for foreigners.) One Latvian described arriving in Hull after living for two years in a DP camp in Hamburg. Taken to Cambridge, his first job was to pick fruit. He reported: 'Next we went to jam factory, picking plums.... Now we must make choice of place to work. Steel, cotton mills, coal mines or agriculture. I like fresh air, so I decide agriculture. I was sent [to] Ely camp. Many nationalities there, Ukrainians, Poles, Hungarians, all kinds. Sleep dozen in a room. It was harvesting time. The first job was potato picking.' He struggled to learn English, but resolved to stay in England 'because it is near Europe.... [T]hose first years we were always hoping to go back to our own country.'[8]

DPs and EVWs who settled in the UK encountered hostility as well as material hardship. In a 1948 article with the headline 'Let Them Be Displaced', the *Daily Mirror* encapsulated the backlash against EVWs in highly dismissive terms: 'Other countries had taken the cream and left us most of the scum. Some no doubt are in the Black Market. They add to our discomfort and swell the crime wave. This cannot be tolerated. They must now be rounded up and sent back.' In 1949 the *New Statesman* called for a rigid selection of Ukrainians in order 'to exclude the illiterate, the mentally deficient, the sick, the aged, the politically suspect, and the behaviourally disruptive'. The BBC, however, retorted that most EVWs were hardworking and, far from being 'fascists' or 'collaborators', were entitled to an opportunity to begin a new life in Britain. In some areas, local people gained a reputation for generosity—for example, Bradford came to be regarded as a safe and welcoming town for migrants because of hospitality schemes for Poles that the locals developed.[9]

Migrant workers, especially women, had little bargaining power. One worker, Lina, seventeen years old at the time, later said:

> I didn't know anything. I didn't know the laws, I didn't know my rights, I didn't know anything and also in domestic service in those days there were no trade unions. People could ask you to work any hours they liked and they did. You can't say I am going to my room for 15 minutes, you couldn't do that; it wasn't done. If you didn't like it you left and tried to find a better place. But you couldn't say I am not going to do it, because you are there and that's it. So when I finished there, I thought never again because basically you really do have no life of your own really.[10]

For some migrants, their arrival in a foreign country signalled fresh oppression rather than freedom. Other stories of personal suffering made for even more painful reading. A young Polish woman, anonymised in the sources as 'Maria', who had been deported to Germany before ending up in an UNRRA camp in Allenbach, volunteered under the 'Westward Ho!' scheme in 1947, after being abandoned by a suitor. In Britain she wrote to the Federation of Polish Women in 1949 that she worked as a maid for fourteen hours a day for a family that treated her like a slave—'These people live like pagans.' The Ministry of Labour eventually agreed to her request for a transfer and she was assigned to a cotton mill in Oldham, where she lived in a hostel with three other Polish girls and eighteen EVWs of various nationalities. There she was ostracised for working over-time in order to save up the money to join her sister, the sole surviving member of her family, in Klagenfurt. Lonely and frantic, she attempted suicide; as a result she found herself before a magistrate, who ordered her immediate deportation to West Germany on the grounds that she was of unsound mind. Her subsequent fate is not recorded.[11]

The British government also launched a Polish resettlement scheme in 1946. Its stated purpose was 'to effect as speedily as possible the orderly disbandment of the Polish armed forces and to facilitate their repatriation to Poland, emigration to other countries, or resettlement in civilian life here [in the UK] according to the individual wishes of the members of those forces'. Some 250,000 people were involved. Most chose to stay in Britain, where they were joined by Poles who, having been allowed to leave the Soviet Union, had spent the war years in India. The emphasis on 'individual wishes' signalled that they would not be returned to Poland against their will. In practice, the British government treated them as political refugees and offered them full citizenship.[12]

Under the terms of the Polish Resettlement Act of March 1947, thou-sands of Polish soldiers and airmen and their dependents were accommo-dated in more than 260 designated resettlement camps or hostels. The government intended that these adult Poles, now civilians, would make a contribution to Britain by filling job vacancies. Trade unions initially opposed the employment of Poles in coal mines: Emanuel Shinwell, the minister of fuel and power, reportedly said it would happen 'over my dead body'. But opposition evaporated when other cabinet ministers agreed to offer sweeteners to the deal, such as better housing for British workers. A government White Paper made the point that everyone stood to benefit: recruiting overseas workers would help address the severe labour short-age, which posed 'a standing threat to the employment of workers in other industries and services, who may find themselves without the fuel or raw materials on which their jobs depend'.[13]

Newcomers to Britain faced other difficulties. The families of members of the Polish armed forces sometimes met with an unsympathetic response from civil servants. A government education committee offered a patronising view of the prospects of integrating Polish children whose early years had been badly disrupted: 'They had lived in the Tower of Babel. Their native Polish was often imperfect and the scraps of tongues, ranging from Russian to Swahili, which they had picked up during their transcontinental wanderings could hardly be regarded as suitable entrance qualifications for schools in the public education systems of England and Scotland.' It would be best, in other words, to get them to learn English at the earliest opportunity. A more constructive approach held that the government should support collective organisations such as Polish community groups, lest 'the Poles sink into being a helpless, miserable, discontented flock of homeless tramps'.[14]

DPs, EVWs, and members of the Polish armed forces had been offered a lifeline in Britain. In a parliamentary debate in November 1948, George Isaacs, the minister of labour and national service, acknowledged with respect to EVWs that 'this is a settlement of a permanent character; these people came here working their passage to British citizenship'. It remained a matter of debate whether their integration and that of others was best achieved by encouraging ethnic particularism or by ignoring ethnic identity. Certainly, the EVWs who came to Britain retained a strong sense of dual belonging: to a country that had provided them with a degree of freedom, but also to a national homeland that had changed out of all recognition but still exerted an emotional pull.[15]

Other Western European governments followed suit with policies described as 'active immigration'. More was at stake than purely economic requirements, however. As in the UK, migrants encountered deep-seated cultural attitudes and assumptions that made for a difficult adjustment. In the case of Sweden, for example, Estonian refugees who found work in the engineering industry after 1945 adopted a much more conservative stance than their Swedish counterparts. Many of the newcomers were from rural backgrounds, and industrial relations in Sweden—involving consultation between the government, employers, and the powerful metalworkers' union—conflicted with their ideas of independence. Trade union solidarity sometimes came up against the intransigence of these migrants, as an Estonian refugee recalled many years later: 'We did not want to have anything to do with the trade union. We said immediately that we could take care of ourselves, and that the union at that early stage did not have to interfere with us. Finally they started to force us, [and said] that we who did not join the union could not stay and work there.' He deemed his personal autonomy to be incompatible with membership in a union. The result was that, to begin with, at least, migration reinforced ethnic differences in the workplace.[16]

In the short term, France also followed in the footsteps of the UK and Scandinavian countries by recruiting foreign DPs. Although the French Communist Party opposed the policy, complaining inter alia about the recruitment of 'war collaborators' and demanding that employers prioritise returning POWs, deportees, and demobilised soldiers, nevertheless a motley group of more than 80,000 DPs and refugees entered the country between 1947 and 1949. They included 37,000 Jews, 15,000 Polish DPs, 4,500 Hungarians, who were all expected to work on construction and railway repair, and 7,000 Banatais from Romania, who were encouraged to settle on abandoned or underutilised land. German POWs were also put to work. But this was not a feasible long-term strategy. France had to look elsewhere to plug the gap.[17]

In March 1945, the president of the Provisional Government, Charles de Gaulle, advocated the recruitment of 'good immigrant elements methodically and intelligently into the French nation'. A newly created Office national d'immigration (ONI, National Immigration Office), formed later that year, envisaged recruiting foreign workers carefully, partly to ensure that they did not drive down the wages of domestic workers, but also to protect the 'national community'. ONI helped set the terms of the national debate. Its objectives were supported by the French Institut national d'études démographiques (INED, Institute for Demographic Studies), established in October 1945, which served as the main source of research to support policies that would 'promote the familial and demographic politics of France'. INED drew heavily upon the expertise of social scientists such as Alfred Sauvy and Georges Mauco, whose careers had taken off during the Second World War under the pro-

German Vichy regime. Like de Gaulle, they spoke of the need for new blood (there was talk of admitting perhaps up to 5 million newcomers), but recognised that the infusion had to be carefully monitored. Mauco controversially recommended an assessment of the cultural and economic 'desirability' of migrants according to age, gender, occupation, class, and ethnicity, some groups being deemed more culturally 'French' than others. He envisaged a strict ratio, with 50 percent of new immigrants to be admitted from northern Europe, 30 percent from Mediterranean countries, and 20 percent from Slavic countries, although this crude arithmetic found no favour with either government or employers. Sauvy was more relaxed about the admission within reason of 'Arabs' and Turks, but he shared Mauco's view that, in addition to monitoring the health of all migrants, careful attention should be paid to their 'moral character'. Perhaps not surprisingly, given the language in which this debate was framed, migrants encountered an intimidating environment: an opinion poll in 1949 found that two-thirds of the French population answered no to the question, 'Are you in favour of a number of foreigners being settled in France?'[18]

The Belgian government, determined to rebuild the country's coal industry, tried to attract domestic workers but had only limited success, and therefore turned to Italy, with whom it signed an agreement in June 1946. The aim was to recruit up to 50,000 Italian workers in exchange for supplying Italy with coal. In a sign of things to come, Belgian employers set up an office in the basement of the train station in Milan, where they examined the health status and political opinions of prospective miners. Italian workers were concentrated in the heavily industrialised provinces of Hainaut and Liège. Anyone who took up the offer of a job but then refused to go down the pit was arrested and held at a military barracks in Brussels that had been a prison for wartime collaborators before being repatriated. When Italy complained about the lack of deliveries of coal in accordance with the original agreement, the Belgian government threatened to look elsewhere, and the Italians backed down. It was an inauspicious start to international cooperation.[19]

The war left the Italian economy severely damaged. Unemployment stood at around 10 percent in 1945. Wages were low. A succession of postwar governments expressed concern about 'overpopulation' and tried to promote the migration of 'surplus population' to the United States and Argentina. Large-scale emigration resumed after 1945, reflecting a wish on the part of migrants to pursue economic opportunities abroad. In the immediate aftermath of the war, annual net emigration stood at around 150,000, but the number of men and women who expressed a wish to emigrate was far greater. Extraordinarily, a survey carried out in 1946 by a public opinion institute found that as many as half of all Italian men wanted to leave their homes. The proportion fell to 28 percent by 1953, but this still equated to 1:8 million prospective emigrants.[20]

Faced with American doubts about large-scale migration, the Italian government insisted to the US State Department in 1951 that 'unused manpower in Italy must be viewed as a weakness and a danger for the whole Atlantic community while, used wherever favourable conditions exist, it becomes an important asset'. The Italian prime minister, Alcide De Gasperi, nevertheless failed to persuade the Truman administration to relax its restrictions. As a result, towards the end of the decade Italy increasingly looked to European destinations to ensure that these so-called 'communists of the stomach', 'starving and discontented people', as De Gasperi described them, whom he deemed liable to be radicalised by their impoverishment, would be given an alternative diet.[21]

Italy signed a series of bilateral schemes with European governments to promote what was termed 'authorised migration'. The first agreement, signed with France in February 1946, required Italian workers to undergo medical checks and meet 'occupational, moral, political and civic standards'—this was partly to address extensive 'illegal' immigration. An agreement between Italy and Belgium in 1946 included provision for insurance against accidents at work. It was in Belgium that the risks of working in dangerous occupations emerged most dramatically. In 1956, a terrible mining disaster in Belgium, in the coalfield at Marcinelle, led to the deaths of 256 miners, of whom 136 were Italians. Germans, Poles, French, and Dutch workers also lost their lives. Marcinelle is now an industrial heritage site. In 2013, at a ceremony to commemorate their deaths, the Italian parliamentarian Laura Boldrini drew a parallel between this disaster and the denial of rights to migrants from North Africa: 'We neglect to see that migrants arriving at Lampedusa have the same eyes as our fathers who arrived at Marcinelle.' This striking analogy served as a reminder that ordinary Italians had also suffered in the pursuit of a better life abroad.[22]

Ireland also emerged as a country where migration offered the prospect of overcoming poverty. Each year between 1946 and 1962, more than 50,000 Irish men and women crossed the Irish Channel in order to take up jobs in mainland Britain or to look for work. The Catholic Church lamented mass emigration but, as one migrant put it, 'you got the feeling there was something wrong if you didn't leave Ireland'. Tens of thousands of Irish men and women had come to the UK during the Second World War, but migration gathered pace after the war. Half a million left Ireland in the 1950s alone. As historian Enda Delaney wrote, 'no other western European society experienced mass migration at the same rate as the independent Irish state after 1945 and few western countries were so profoundly shaped by the departure of such a large proportion of its citizens'. For all intents and purposes, the Irish continued to be treated as British subjects and were free to come and go as they wished.[23]

Irish migrants often spoke of being forced to leave their homes, and whilst there is an element of truth in this, it misses the importance of individual decision-making and the influence of family and friends who returned intermittently with stories of opportunities to earn more money or to achieve greater recognition than was available in Ireland. Without such information, it was easier to stay put, as many Irish politicians hoped they would. The *Taoiseach*, or prime minister, of Ireland, Éamon de Valera, bemoaned the materialistic motives of those of his fellow countrymen who made for the English Midlands when 'work is available at home, and in conditions infinitely better from the point of view of health and morals'—a recurring theme in the contemporary literature. The Irish government-appointed Commission on Emigration and Other Population Problems issued a series of reports between 1948 and 1954 that provided insights into the motives of migrants to the UK, as in the following example from County Longford: 'Male, 36 years old, married with one child; from rural area; wife working in cigarette factory in Britain earning

£3 15s per week. He is going to tile-making plant and will earn £7 per week; stated that he had worked casually dealing in horses and cutting timber for sale. Intends to stay in Britain.'[24]

Managed migration was not entirely the preserve of individual governments. In July 1951, French foreign minister Robert Schuman argued that 'a solution to the problem of refugees and population surplus is a precondition to the success of European integration policies'. Only by addressing the 'excess', and better managing the distribution of population, could the projected community succeed. Schuman's vision of closer international cooperation culminated in the decision in May 1953 to create the European Coal and Steel Community (ECSC). The founding members—Belgium, France, Italy, Luxembourg, the Netherlands, and West Germany—agreed to harmonise supply and demand for labour through national and local labour exchanges. Member states agreed on procedures to notify one another of job vacancies that foreigners were entitled to fill. The ECSC also played an important part in encouraging members to recognise qualifications earned in one country and to standardise social security benefits. But it was essentially an agreement to promote Franco-German collaboration in two key sectors of industry, and hardly anyone regarded it as a blueprint for broader economic, still less political, integration.[25]

The new coal and steel community was not the only game in town. From its inception in 1947, the Organisation for European Economic Cooperation (OEEC) debated the mobility of labour. It was a potentially significant moment, because the OEEC had a larger membership than the coal and steel community, and included the UK, Ireland, Austria, Portugal, and Turkey, among others. There was little to show for its debates in the first few years save for general agreement on the need to establish procedures to enable movement across national boundaries. One fundamental difficulty concerned the disparity between countries in northwestern Europe, which were keen to maintain relatively high levels of employment, and their southern counterparts, where economic opportunities remained relatively limited. Governments in France, the Benelux countries (Belgium, Netherlands, and Luxembourg), and West Germany did not want to encourage uncontrolled migration from the south.

Eventually, however, in October 1953, the Council of Ministers of the OEEC agreed upon a code for the liberalisation of the movement of labour stipulating that 'member countries must allow nationals of another member country to take employment in their territory if: an employer wants him; no suitable "home" worker can be found for the job in question within a month; there is no undercutting of wages and conditions of employment; and industrial peace is not endangered'. The code also made it easier for workers to have their permits extended where they had already been working in the country for several years. The effect was by no means a free-for-all: the obligation to issue a permit in the circumstances set out above did not apply in cases where a member state 'considers that for imperative reasons of national economic policy it is against its interest to increase, or even to maintain at its existing level, the number of workers, in particular industries or occupations by the admission of foreign workers'. Individual workers thus still needed (and could be denied) a work permit. The agreement applied to all member states except Portugal and Turkey, because of their 'special geographic, cultural and governmental situations', a reference to the dictatorship in the former and political instability in the latter. But it paved the way for growth in the number of guest workers who arrived in the following years.[26]

Much of the most important intergovernmental initiative was realised in 1957, with the Treaty of Rome launching the European Economic Community As with the ECSC, bread-and-butter issues were paramount. At the same time, the treaty included a key provision to enable the free movement of labour among member states: France, West Germany, Italy, Belgium, the Netherlands, and Luxembourg. Articles 48 and 49, inserted into the Treaty of Rome at the insistence of the Italian government, set out the basis of freedom of movement. Although the text did not specify citizens of member states, the treaty was widely understood to apply to them and not to anyone else. Article 48 stipulated that 'freedom of movement for workers shall be secured within the Community by the end of the transitional period at the latest', although the transitional period would only come to an end in 1970. No discrimination would be allowed as regards employment and conditions of work. Those workers who accepted job offers were free to move within the territory of member states. Provision was made under the second article for national employment services to cooperate in order to ensure liberalisation of procedures and to maintain 'a balance between supply and demand in the employment market'.[27]

This was a landmark decision, extending by some distance the provisions of the Treaty of Paris that created the ECSC. But the Treaty of Rome provided some important caveats regarding freedom of movement. It specifically applied to blue-collar and white-collar workers, not to public servants, seasonal workers, the self-employed, or those providing other services, and so the right of free movement was not universal. In addition, anyone not gainfully employed had no right of residence. Member states could impose restrictions where issues of public policy, public security, or public health were concerned, something that found its way into future international agreements on migration. The treaty did not, therefore, promote complete freedom of movement; rather, it supported freedom of migration for workers in accordance with the prevailing doctrine of a common market in labour, capital, and goods. No one batted an eyelid when, in endorsing the freedom-of-movement clause, the European Commissioner for Social Affairs delivered a speech in 1961 that stressed the need 'to limit maximally the possibility of uncontrolled and useless movements'.[28]

Other international agreements enabled refugees and other migrants to settle in North America, Latin America, and Australia, a process overseen by the Intergovernmental Committee for European Migration. Whereas the UNHCR worked on behalf of refugees, and the International Labour Organization (ILO) focused on labour migration, ICEM concentrated on permanent resettlement by supporting assisted passage schemes, processing and transporting workers and their families, and arranging for family reunification. The initiative was the result of an international conference convened in Brussels in 1951 'to find some way of moving the large number of persons who remain homeless, dispossessed and disinherited'. Communist countries were not invited: at the behest of the United States, membership was restricted to 'governments with a demonstrated interest in the principle of free movement of persons'.[29]

Discussions broadened to include the planned redistribution of Europe's 'population surplus'. Under the auspices of ICEM, Italian workers and their families were sent to Brazil and Greek families were despatched to Australia, creating durable communities in both countries. ICEM officials also looked at resettlement opportunities in Paraguay and Southern Rhodesia. They collaborated with the UNHCR in assisting refugees to relocate. Between 1952 and 1960 ICEM assisted more than 1 million people, including 280,000 Italians, 214,000 Germans, 150,000 people from Austria (some of them Hungarian refugees), 82,000 people from the Netherlands, and 66,000 Greeks.[30]

Initiatives such as these to enable international migration were nevertheless an uncomfortable reminder that one group remained in limbo, unable by virtue of disability or a criminal record to be resettled in a third country. This so-called 'hard core' of Displaced Persons, living in camps or ramshackle accommodation in West Germany, Austria, Italy, and Greece, finally attracted serious international attention when the United Nations agreed to support a World Refugee Year (WRY) in 1959–1960. Described as a campaign 'to save the world's refugees' from neglect, WRY was an attempt to atone for the selective policies Western governments had adopted in the late 1940s and 1950s, when religious leaders and liberal critics had accused them of having 'skimmed the cream' and left others 'to rot in unofficial camps, garrets, attics, cellars and shanties'.[31]

Although it extended beyond Europe, the campaign raised substantial funds (some $620 million in 2019 prices) to help improve the accommodation and prospects of elderly and disabled DPs (and their relatives who chose to remain with them) rather than abandoning them. Most of the money went to tearing down wooden huts and building modern apartments complete with running water, electricity, and modern kitchen equipment. WRY thus claimed, with some justification, to have helped clear the remaining refugee camps in Europe. Some refugees also received loans enabling them to start new businesses. Resettlement was a subsidiary aim and secondary outcome, although countries such as Canada and Australia agreed to take some of the 'hard core' as a humanitarian gesture.[32]

The British government preferred to offer money to improve the lives of DPs in situ rather than to provide them with a ticket to a new life in the UK. Commenting on the inspection teams it sent to West Germany, a British civil servant said languidly that 'the position had now arisen where it was a handicap for a refugee not to be handicapped enough for immigration schemes'. An official who went to Italy to sift through applicants in the camp at Latina could scarcely conceal his irritation at the task he was being asked to do. He rejected a Yugoslav woman who was 'so fractious as to be an embarrassment', adding that she 'would be virtually unemployable in the sort of work open to her in the UK'. Likewise, he described a sixty-five-year-old Yugoslav man as a 'tiresome old man, whom the medical officer considers mental': '[He is] quite incapable of supporting himself, and is quarrelsome and pugnacious with his fellow camp-dwellers. Has a tendency to violence, and is prepared to denounce as a communist everybody who does not share his maniac enthusiasm for the Karageorgevic dynasty.' Evidently it paid to be anti-communist, but not to excess.[33]

In 1960, the British filmmaker John Krish, whose father and grandparents had come to the UK as refugees from Eastern Europe, wrote and directed a short film, *Return to Life*, to enlist public support for WRY. The film explored the difficulties a family of European refugees faced while trying to negotiate a new life in Britain after their rescue from a DP camp. At first, the character Josef is suspicious of charity workers and government officials, but he and his wife, Anna, together with his elderly mother, gradually accept that decisions about housing and work are being made in their best interests. He hopes to find a white-collar job, but is resigned to becoming a general labourer. His lack of English means that it is difficult to make friends. His clothes are cast-offs. The voice-over tells the viewer that Josef has 'lost his identity'. The only crumb of comfort is that he is able to keep his family together. Their small boy, Mirko, is beginning to make new friends. There is the prospect that he, at least, will be able to integrate in British society. To that extent, *Return to Life* ends on an upbeat note.

In reality, things were more complicated. Krish told subsequently of how, in looking for someone to play the part of Josef, he had 'wanted somebody who would not instantly be sympathetic to an audience'. He chose a Serb living in Brighton who had been imprisoned by the Soviets. The woman who played his wife was Croatian and, according to Krish, a fascist sympathiser. When the filming ended, the actress spat in her 'husband's' face. Worse still, Krish made a throwaway remark to the refugee who played the part of the mother that she was 'no longer needed'. He later learned that she had apparently taken this literally, and killed herself. It was a devastating reminder that, no matter how good the intention, enlisting refugees to tell the story of forced migration could have traumatic consequences.[34]

World Refugee Year was only partly about the needs of refugees. It reflected the preoccupations of Western governments, whose leaders dutifully lined up to proclaim their support for refugees. Prime Minister Michel Debré of France struck a positive note, observing that 'the majority of the 300,000 refugees living in France have become integrated into French life'. And yet, he added, the government had to acknowledge that a significant minority, 'mostly old or sick people, still lead a very wretched existence'. West Germany advertised its support for WRY, which a West German diplomat said was 'due mainly to the fact that the German people themselves have experienced the problems of homeless and displaced people and they know that everything possible must be done to bring material and spiritual relief to these unfortunate people'.[35]

The British government insisted that it could not entertain any significant resettlement of refugees. Prime Minister Harold Macmillan launched the British contribution by immediately putting a dampener on proceedings at the official opening for WRY:

> Some people may think that the best contribution that we can make is to take in a large number of the refugees ourselves. They may say that the life of our country has been enriched because 80,000 refugees, the majority of whom were Jewish, came here before the war, and because we have taken in about a quarter of a million other refugees since then. But precisely because in our small country we have welcomed so many, we cannot raise further hopes in this direction.[36]

Even more dismissively, an Irish government official told the UNHCR that 'Ireland, not waiting on a WRY, has absorbed into her national citizenship all the lame ducks, the tubercular and mental defectives, discarded and refused visas for entry into larger and more prosperous countries'. Her remarks implied that Ireland had imported the dregs of Europe while simultaneously exporting its brightest and best.[37]

The campaign for World Refugee Year also helped to advance the idea that refugees had something to offer in return for resettlement. As campaigners insisted, 'the positive aspect of the contribution of the refugee is generally unrecognised; greater efforts should be made in all countries to inform the public that although refugees may at first be a burden on the community they progressively become an economic asset themselves or through their descendants'. Hard work was construed as a passport to integration. But the suggestion that refugees had the potential to make an enduring contribution to European societies would be challenged by opponents of migration in years to come.[38]

CHAPTER 5

Building Communism in Eastern Europe

THE MAP OF EASTERN Europe looked very different following Germany's defeat in the Second World War. Germany itself was divided in two. New borders were drawn. Poland gained territory in the west at Germany's expense, but it was also obliged to hand over territory in the east to the Soviet Union. The formerly independent Baltic states had been incorporated into the USSR. Soviet power extended across the entirety of Eastern Europe, which now became enveloped by communist rule. An Iron Curtain separated the Soviet bloc from countries in Western Europe. Fundamental differences in political ideology and the conduct of political life reinforced a sense that the citizens of Eastern Europe inhabited a separate universe.

Economic reconstruction in the Soviet bloc meant modernisation on socialist foundations. Communist governments embarked on mass nationalisation of industry and large estates, part of a programme for the transformation of the economy and society under state control. The mechanisms of central economic planning—detailed targets covering all aspects of production and consumption—that had taken shape in the Soviet Union during the 1930s were now rolled out across Eastern Europe. The state controlled the allocation of resources, including labour. Migration took place within a very different political and economic framework compared to the prewar arrangements in Eastern Europe.

The imposition of political control in the Soviet bloc extended to emigration. At one extreme, the Albanian dictator Enver Hoxha equated unauthorised emigration with treason. The Polish communist government adopted a slightly softer tone, asking Poles who were contemplating emigration if they wished to be domestic servants and dishwashers or would rather contribute honest toil to the economic reconstruction of their homeland, a reminder that Western governments were scouring the refugee camps in West Germany and Austria for able-bodied workers. These economic imperatives mattered: in 1945, even before the communists took over, the Czech government imposed restrictions on emigration in order to deter an outflow of skilled workers.[1]

Migration was an integral part of economic improvement. It brought men and women from low-wage agricultural areas to better-paid jobs in industry and services, and from relatively backward regions to areas where opportunities were greater. Programmes of education and vocational training enabled the next generation of workers to contribute to reconstruction and building a new socialist society that would—so its leaders hoped—demolish the claims of governments in the West to economic supremacy and political legitimacy. Overall responsibility for realising these ambitions lay with Communist Party leadership across the Soviet bloc. A decade after the end of the war, the Soviet bloc looked more stable and prosperous than ever. To be sure, communist rule did not go unchallenged, notably in Hungary in 1956, but political leaders were by and large able to count on the acquiescence of people who craved a greater degree of stability. Economic recovery and growth convinced most citizens that their prospects looked much brighter than they had for a generation.

Yet it would be unwise to assume that migration in Eastern Europe followed a wholly distinctive path. Economic imperatives and migration in the Soviet bloc went hand in hand in ways that paralleled developments in Western Europe. Central planning might dictate overall economic objectives, but no communist society could eliminate individual ambition or freedom of manoeuvre. Migrant workers grabbed the chance to get ahead. The Iron Curtain was hugely significant, but it should not obscure similarities in the way that European states behaved or how migrants experienced mobility.

Migration had already played an important part in Eastern Europe before the Second World War. In the Soviet Union, in addition to the well-known deportation of 'class enemies' during the 1930s, a series of state-led measures in support of rapid industrialisation had steered young men and women to towns and cities in European Russia. New factory sites offered some peasants an escape from the turmoil of Stalin's collectivisation of agriculture. Russian workers moved to Siberia and Central Asia to seize new economic opportunities. Rural life in independent Eastern Europe was not turned upside-down to the same extent, but villages were regularly emptied in Romania, Bulgaria, and Yugoslavia as impoverished peasants moved to the towns or emigrated in search of a better life.

The hard, physical work of construction and factory work frequently fell to women and the elderly, as well as to German prisoners of war, the last of them only repatriated from Russia to the Federal Republic of Germany in 1955, under an agreement signed by German chancellor Konrad Adenauer and Soviet premier Nikolai Bulganin. Prisoners of war were regarded as war criminals, and therefore not subject to the Geneva Convention. German, Hungarian, and Romanian POWs were put to work on construction projects. Horst Howler, then aged just seventeen, for example, described being captured in Kaliningrad at the very end of the war and being sent on a lengthy train journey to Kirovakan in Armenia, where he built roads and bridges. He was not released until 1949. His experience underlines the extent to which the retention of men against their will contributed to economic reconstruction in the USSR long after the war was over.[2]

The recruitment, training, and distribution of the labour force formed an integral part of the system of central economic planning. At one extreme, as happened in the late 1930s, this meant establishing rigorous controls over the freedom of Soviet workers to move from one job to another without permission. These controls were eventually relaxed after Stalin's death in 1953, when the state accepted that workers should have the right to choose their place of work and to leave after giving due notice.

Officials instead adopted other instruments to encourage workers to take up jobs in less attractive and distant locations. Under the scheme called 'organised labour recruitment' (*orgnabor*), Russian peasants signed contracts under which they agreed to work in distant coal mines. Wage inducements played an increased role: skilled workers, in particular, were much sought after and suitably rewarded. The managers of Soviet enterprises used a variety of informal arrangements to ensure that they had the right number and mix of workers to meet production targets. Factory scouts looked far and wide for workers, and this, too, encouraged mass migration, including seasonal migration to construction sites and to remote forestry enterprises. Seasonal workers were offered scarce and desirable consumer goods, or supplied with timber to build a family dacha back home. All of this suggested that the Soviet planners did not entirely control migration.[3]

In remote parts of the Soviet Union, forced labour continued to be a significant feature of the system: the 'Gulag archipelago' stretched across vast swathes of northern Russia, Siberia, and the Far East, making use of prisoners to cut timber, build railways, and dig for coal and precious metals. The release of 4 million prisoners from the Gulag between 1953 and 1958 provided a boost to ordinary enterprises. Many of the former prisoners failed to find jobs, however, and a minority enjoyed an itinerant lifestyle that flew in the face of Soviet claims that vagrancy had become a thing of the past. By the middle of the decade, the only way to replenish the labour force in remote locations north of the Arctic Circle and in Eastern Siberia was to encourage ordinary workers to move there by offering wage incentives and the promise of better housing.[4]

The political and economic significance of migration emerged with particular clarity in the case of the sovietised Baltic republics. Immigration helped offset the loss of deportees and refugees—close to 10 percent of all Estonians departed for Sweden or for more distant shores in 1945, leaving a large gap in people of working age. (The three Baltic republics lost 3 percent of their populations in just ten days at the end of March 1949.) In 1945 the population of Estonia stood at 0.85 million; by 1989, thanks to internal Soviet migration, it had increased to 1.6 million, of whom first-generation immigrants, mainly from Russia, made up one-quarter of the total. Ethnic Latvians comprised 83 percent of the population of Soviet Latvia in 1945, but their share had fallen to 60 percent by 1953. Half a million Russians and people of other nationalities arrived in Latvia between 1945 and 1959. Soviet officials praised their economic contributions, but they gave the game away by recommending 'political educational work' in order to combat 'bourgeois nationalist propaganda', the legacy of years of Baltic independence before 1939. Baltic exiles in the West kept the nationalist flame alive by denouncing what they regarded as Soviet occupation and Russian colonisation.[5]

Russians also moved to Ukraine in great numbers. Demobilised soldiers were joined by as many as 1 million newcomers between 1959 (the year of the first postwar census) and 1970, at which point ethnic Russians made up close to one-third of the population of Soviet Ukraine. Workers were attracted by the relatively high wages in heavy industry and by better schools and hospitals. The growing Russian presence in the industrial heartlands of the Donbas and Dnipropetrovsk—a presence that stretched back to before the Russian Revolution of 1917—underpinned a thriving heavy industry that contributed substantially to Soviet growth. But it also stored up problems for the future.[6]

These developments formed part of a broader demographic transformation. In a fundamental study of population displacement, Eugene Kulischer, who fled the Russian Revolution and eventually settled in the United States, wrote that 'a flood of migrants is moving westward into all the marches between the Arctic and the Black Sea'. A Moscow radio broadcast applauded this migration to 'the Soviet far west'. Kulischer mentioned a short story, 'Uncle Vanya', by an obscure author, in which an officer moves from Kazakhstan to live on a kolkhoz, or collective farm, in his native Ukraine, 'where apples, pears, peaches and melons abound'. New settlements in Soviet Karelia were populated not only with local villagers but with workers imported from Belarus, Ukraine, and other republics to work in forestry.[7]

The Soviet state cast the net even wider in its search for suitable workers, including those who had fled after the 1917 revolution and lived beyond the Iron Curtain. In a desperate attempt to coax them to return, Stalin sent a captured German transport ship to Shanghai in 1947, where the Russian refugees listened to speeches from Soviet consular officials and an orchestra that played patriotic tunes. At least 4,000 refugees decided to try their luck, but their unpleasant experiences in Russia quickly discouraged their compatriots from following suit. Those who stayed in China ended up being trapped by the communist revolution there two years later.[8]

Something similar happened to ethnically Armenian 'repatriates', most of whom, as the descendants of survivors of the Ottoman genocide during the First World War, had never set foot on Armenian soil. Soviet Armenian leaders suggested to Stalin that 360,000 Armenians in the diaspora, including the families of refugees in Bulgaria, Romania, and Greece, might be tempted to settle in the small Soviet republic of Armenia, particularly if (as the Soviet leadership intended) territory could be taken from Turkey. Around 90,000 Armenians, mainly poor families from Greece, Syria, and Lebanon, countries in the midst of civil war or experiencing the end of colonial rule, opted to 'repatriate'. In a little-known episode in September 1948, 42 passengers being taken from Egypt to the port of Batumi on the coast of Georgia on board the Soviet vessel *Pobeda* (Victory) died when a fire broke out. Stalin blamed the disaster on Armenian spies working for the US State Department.[9]

The repatriates were met with a mixture of indifference and hostility: although the official rhetoric welcomed them as *ahbar* (brothers), many local residents looked upon them as snooty and demanding newcomers. These attitudes, together with economic hardship, led many of them to leave for good: only a minority felt able to make a life for themselves under communist rule. Those who remained were largely left to their own devices, and any residual sense of Soviet obligation towards the global Armenian diaspora soon evaporated. But the abortive history of repatriation left its mark on established communities in Armenia, where 130,000 Azeris were ordered to leave their homes and 'return' to neighbouring Azerbaijan to make way for the Armenian repatriates. Their forced resettlement had another objective, namely, to contribute to the revival of cotton growing in Azerbaijan. Their complaints ('Better to die in one's native village than to move to another place', said one villager) fell on deaf ears. Visions of Soviet economic transformation meant uprooting people for what was described as the greater good, but they did little to contribute to social harmony.[10]

All of this supports the view that migration was driven by a mixture of motives. Central planners regarded the Soviet Union as a single economic space in which workers could be induced to move to support the goals of the state. Economic reconstruction required the mobilisation of all available sources of labour by various means, including, but not restricted to, compulsion. Political imperatives meant the despatch of dedicated Russian communists to the Baltic republics to consolidate Soviet power. The consequences were equally mixed: migration enabled economic growth, but non-Russians began to ask whether planned migration translated into Russification.

This potentially unsettling combination of politics and economics emerged in Central Asia. The Communist Party of the Soviet Union, with the new general secretary, Nikita Khrushchev, at the helm, sought to enhance its legitimacy by promising improvements in social welfare. One component of this strategy was the famous Virgin Lands Campaign, which was designed to plough up as much as 15 million hectares of pastureland in Central Asia, the Urals, and Western Siberia in order to feed the demand for grain of the growing population in the Russian heartland. The campaign lasted for a full decade, from 1954 to 1964. Much of the effort was concentrated in northern Kazakhstan, the lands known in Russian as *tselina*. After a disastrous harvest in 1955, the following year witnessed a bumper crop; it appeared that the policy had been vindicated. Subsequent harvests, however, yielded erratic results. More seriously still, the entire programme posed a challenge to the traditional way of life of Kazakh nomads, some of whom retained memories of the brutal suppression of a revolt against tsarist rule on the eve of the Russian Revolution. Put bluntly, they wondered whether this would be another instance of local interests being subordinated to those of Moscow.[11]

In the first year alone, in an enthusiastic response to Khrushchev's invitation to contribute to socialist achievements in the region, more than 300,000 Russians headed east. The earliest volunteers, chiefly from the Soviet Komsomol (the party's youth organisation), were joined by soldiers and workers who were given seasonal contracts to work on the new state farms (*sovkhozy*), some of which were created by transferring indigenous households to other parts of Kazakhstan. Other Kazakhs moved north to the *tselina*. They were joined by members of ethnic minorities who had been deported during the Second World War, including Chechens, Ingush, Kalmyks, Crimean Tatars, Poles, and Volga Germans, who were officially designated 'special settlers'. This aspect of the programme introduced an additional complication. The newcomers tended to deride these deportees as 'enemies' and 'parasites'.[12]

Although observers in the West portrayed the entire campaign as a form of Soviet compulsory labour, there was a good deal of enthusiasm for it among the migrants themselves, particularly on the part of young people who wanted to escape the deprivation in Russia's western borderlands that had suffered so severely from the Nazi occupation. One Russian student, interviewed in later life by the historian Michaela Pohl, touted 'living under the open sky' as an alluring opportunity. Soviet filmmakers did their bit, too: in 1958, Ivan Lukinskii directed *Ivan Brovkin na tseline* (Ivan Brovkin in the Virgin Lands), which became a hit in the late Khrushchev era.[13]

Meanwhile, reports reached Khrushchev's desk of poor relations between Kazakh locals and the Russian newcomers, who expected some creature comforts but instead found a wasteland. Some of the first settlers were petty criminals who had been dumped in Central Asia by Russian officials. Yet, whatever their social origin, everyone faced acute shortages of housing until the early 1960s—in a familiar pattern, new arrivals regularly had to make do with huts (*zemlianki*) and barracks. Thereafter, new investment provided the funds for reasonable apartment blocks, along with schools, kindergartens, and leisure facilities, and the local authorities managed to import consumer goods from Eastern Europe.[14]

The Virgin Lands represented a vision of socialist modernisation in a relatively underdeveloped part of the Soviet Union. It provided opportunities for social mobility and adventure. Over time, the Virgin Landers came to think of themselves as part of a new socialist collective. Russian settlers expressed pride in what they had managed to achieve: 'We opened the new lands, we really did have a great life', reminisced Antonina Azeeva in 1996. The settlers invested their presence in Kazakhstan—a land which had often been called a 'planet of a hundred languages'—with a sense of contributing in important ways to Soviet prosperity. Relations between the different groups were in fact surprisingly good: mixed marriages, for example, took place between Russians and Kazakhs. Soviet officials made an effort to support religious festivals and preserve 'traditional' cultural events. Signs of trouble sometimes rose to the surface, however, as when Kazakh nationalists complained about the closure of Kazakh-language schools. Chechen settlers supported Sufi brotherhoods that over the long term helped sustain Chechen identity, and although many Chechen and other deportees were allowed to return to their former homes during the 'thaw', others opted to remain in Kazakhstan, where they put down new roots.[15]

Whatever its mainsprings, migration meant the arrival of newcomers. This basic fact and its consequences were evident in other parts of the Soviet bloc as well, where people were often moved around like pieces on a chessboard. Migrant workers were called upon to rebuild war-torn countries, but they were also expected to contribute to the creation of new national entities.

Postwar Poland lost territory in the east but gained (or, in official parlance, 'recovered') lands in the west that had belonged to Germany. The contemporary Polish linguist Mikołaj Rudnicki put the nationalist case succinctly when he declared, 'We are not newcomers to this land, we are instead returning to it.' The expulsion of ethnic German residents went hand in hand with the settlement of families from central Poland, who made up just under half of the population of the recovered lands. Settlers from the territory lost to the Soviet Union made up a further 28 percent, with the so-called autochthons, those Poles already residing in the recovered lands, making up the remainder, together with a small percentage of those who returned to Poland from abroad after the war.[16]

Many of the properties of Germans and others deemed to be 'non-Polish' in the recovered lands were taken over by Poles who had been transferred from Soviet Ukraine. Poles moved into apartments in Wrocław and hung flags from the windows to mark their territory. The overwhelming course of government policy favoured the 'repatriates'. Władysław Gomułka, subsequently first secretary of the Polish Workers' Party, described the settlement of Poles in the 'recovered territories' (*ziemie odzyskane*) as their 'repatriation' from the east, and the term stuck. Its implication was that the areas concerned were inherently and historically Polish and that ethnic Germans had no legitimate claim on them. Gomułka encouraged the mass settlement of 'pioneers', 'a new type of Pole' in the western borderlands. Some of these 'repatriates' quickly took advantage of the new dispensation to make careers in Communist Party politics, and behaved as if they were untouchable—as indeed they were. The whole process of resettlement was infused with an unpleasant rhetoric: a leading historian and arch-nationalist, Zygmunt Wojciechowski, applauded 'the possibility to cut out the Prussian-Nazi cancer which had been leading Poland to complete annihilation', adding, 'In place of the German "Drang nach Osten" [drive to the east] comes the era of the renewed Slavic march towards the west.'[17]

The Polonisation of cities under the auspices of the new Ministry of Recovered Lands (Gomułka's bailiwick) did not proceed smoothly. Germans were still needed to work on public transport and in the postal service, and were given special certificates exempting them from being replaced. Considerable efforts went into distinguishing ethnic Poles from Germans, but, as one official remarked in 1947, 'there is no objective criterion that would differentiate a German from an autochthon'. Newcomers baulked at the way in which natives in Silesia spoke, failing to understand how they could be considered 'Polish', given the Germanic influence: 'What kind of Poles are these who do not speak Polish, know nothing of Polish history, culture, literature?' According to the Polish Repatriation Commission, 'the deportee [from the east] saw in every autochthon a German or a Nazi.... [T]he first colonists treated these territories as an occupied territory inhabited by Germans.' Non-German nationals, such as Silesians, Pomeranians, and Kashubians, were equally demonised and unceremoniously turfed out of Poland. Children were taught a patriotic version of the history of the 'recovered lands' in which Germans played a minor part. 'Reading German books in public places, tending the graves of German soldiers [and] retaining German inscriptions in private homes' also exposed people to denunciation and expulsion.[18]

In short, population resettlement was designed to make the 'recovered lands' as 'Polish' as possible. Like other frontier towns in Silesia, Wrocław was repopulated by newcomers from the countryside. They took pride in using modern forms of transport for the first time, but established residents complained that their ramshackle buildings for goats, cows, and pigeons were turning the old town into a farmyard. The city's residents took a long time to get used to one another. As one of their number put it, the resettlers felt 'they had lost what they had in the East and did not feel like the owners of what they had obtained in the West'.[19]

Something similar happened in Lubomierz (previously Liebenthal, and briefly the Slavic-sounding Miłosna), where the locals taunted newcomers for being unable to identify the names of saints in the church, or to read signs in German. This mutual incomprehension worked both ways. Germans prided themselves on animal husbandry and maintaining fish ponds, whereas Poles from the east were more familiar with root vegetables, and reportedly baffled by modern farm equipment. One Polish resettler lamented that 'our world remained over there, in the east. Here we are only waiting for death. We have nowhere to which we can return, so we are stuck here, but it is not our land.' The first generation of resettlers experienced a collective sense of alienation, insecurity, and apathy, mixed with nostalgia for the lands they had to leave.[20]

The victorious Polish Workers' Party legitimised a sense of belonging, at least in principle. But the first people to arrive relied heavily on their own resources and sometimes by pilfering and looting—the Polish word *szaber* described 'appropriating' goods that had been abandoned by their owners, a common practice in the recovered territories, where the local administration had yet to impose any kind of order. The black market and bartering of goods replaced normal transactions. Such individualism was at odds with the new communist system. Many workers depended on the factory canteen, since state rations were virtually nonexistent in the immediate aftermath of war. This was a rather bizarre introduction to the new pioneering way of life that the government had planned.[21]

In 1956 an institute in Poznan launched a competition for the best memoirs written by Polish resettlers. More than 200 people submitted entries, spurred on in many instances by the relative political liberalisation in Poland and the opportunity to make their feelings known. They spoke of a 'wild west' where homes were assigned and then reassigned in a chaotic and often arbitrary fashion. Other things could not so easily be shared in public, such as an intense nostalgia for the homes in Ukraine they had been obliged to abandon. Parents, however, took pride in fostering a sense of ambition among their children, to give them some protection against further upheaval. As one resettler put it, 'in a new life situation, the cult of new values emerged, values that are indestructible, that cannot be lost, and that die with the man—the cult of knowledge, of skills that can resist cataclysms'.[22]

The cultural significance attached to resettlement emerged in a series of notable Polish films. Stanisław Rózewicz's 1956 film *Trzy kobiety* (Three women) tells the story of Helena, Maria, and Celina, who make their way to Warsaw after being liberated from a German concentration camp. Finding the city in ruins and with no sign of family or friends, they decide to try their luck in the recovered lands. Helena starts a school, Celina works as a librarian, and Maria eventually moves to Kraków. Only the friendship forged in the camp enables them to survive this fresh displacement. In 1964, Jerzy Hoffman directed *Prawo i pięść* (The law and the fist), the account of another concentration camp survivor, who is sent to a fictional town as a government official. He and the other government representatives he encounters are interested only in looting property, confirming what personal memoirs had already indicated.[23]

Other films, by contrast, supported the official view that resettlement contributed to the country's modernisation through the dedication of hardworking Poles arriving from the east. By far the most popular film came out in 1967, under the title *Sami Swoi* (All friends here). Part of a trilogy directed by Sylwester Chęciński, it offered a comical account of a long-standing quarrel between two Polish families who move from the east to Silesia, where they once more find themselves as neighbours. They are reconciled by the marriage between the son of one family and the daughter of the other. 'She is one of us, a *repatriańka*' [repatriated woman], says her prospective father-in-law, hinting at a difference between resettlers and other Poles. Chęciński's approach offered a gentle counterpoint to the overly patriotic communist depictions of resettlement, and this probably explains why it touched a chord with Polish audiences.[24]

Elsewhere in the Soviet bloc, expelling Germans created economic opportunities for those who took their place. In Romania and Yugoslavia, the property of Germans who had dominated economic activity in the Banat region was redistributed among the local peasantry. The expulsion of Germans from Czechoslovakia meant that employers lost much of their labour force. In the Sudetenland, Czech workers took over positions formerly held by Germans and occupied German farms. The main story here was the arrival of Czechs and Slovaks from the interior to settle frontier areas in the late 1940s. So-called gold diggers seized farms and businesses from Germans, but they looked in vain for suitable workers to employ. The government filled the gap in one key sector by recruiting Czech and Slovak miners from France, Belgium, and Germany. But the 're-emigrants' were treated with disdain by their new neighbours, on the grounds that their long association with German-speakers made them doubtful members of the Czech nation.[25]

The Czech government was undeterred by these local misgivings. In addition to the thousands who came from Carpatho-Ukraine to work in Czechoslovakia, the government encouraged 15,000 coal miners of Czech origin to leave France and Belgium and resettle in Czechoslovakia; another 5,000 came from the Rhineland and Westphalia. Their numbers were swollen by 10,000 Czechs and Slovaks from Poland as well as 6,000 from Yugoslavia. More came from Romania and Bulgaria. The border region of Oloví, in the old Sudetenland, famous for its glassworks, became a centre for many of these repatriates. According to an American journalist writing in May 1947, 'On the streets of Oloví, one may hear French, German, Hungarian, Serbo-Croat and Romanian from the lips of children who are now having to learn Czech', another reminder that postwar migration was bound up with fostering a more exclusively national identity in East-Central Europe.[26]

Not everything was about this kind of voluntary immigration: the wives and children of jailed Czech political prisoners were unceremoniously told to vacate their apartments in the centre of Prague or Bratislava and move to run-down outskirts of the city, or to border regions, where the facilities were primitive but where they were expected to contribute to agricultural production. The communist authorities called this 'Akcion B' (Action B). The more fortunate and resilient of the individuals in this group turned it into a positive experience, but others found it dispiriting and demeaning to have been singled out.[27]

Across Eastern Europe, the newly installed governments embarked on ambitious schemes of economic reconstruction. As in Western Europe, the outcome was mass urbanisation, albeit with a distinctive communist tinge. Demonstrating political zeal, if not much imagination, East Germany created Stalinstadt. In 1947 Bulgaria launched Dimitrovgrad as a 'model socialist city'; many people moved there to take up jobs in coal mining, and a decade later it was home to 40,000 inhabitants. In Hungary, the foundations of a new city named 'Stalin City', Sztálinváros, were laid in 1950, although by the time construction finished it had become politically expedient to give it another name, Dunaújváros (New City by the Danube). The Hungarian government regarded it as a model city that would generate high volumes of industrial output while improving the health and even the personalities of its inhabitants. Newcomers in search of economic betterment included construction workers, factory workers, and itinerant peddlers from rural areas. Their lifestyle marked them out: there were complaints that rural migrants kept livestock in their apartments and factory barracks. Moreover, their religious devotion was at odds with the society the communist regime wished to create. The state wanted to make migration relatively painless and trouble-free for the newcomers, but it discouraged religious tradition in favor of new patriotic norms.[28]

In Poland, the famous Nowa Huta steelworks, on the outskirts of Kraków, recruited workers from Rzeszów, Kielce, and Lublin to participate in socialist industrialisation. Up to three-quarters of them had a rural background. Millions of these migrant workers were popularly described as having been 'cowherds' before their migration; their labour contributed to factory construction and industrial production and laid the foundations for the city itself. Indeed, socialist reconstruction offered them the chance to become skilled workers. One memoirist, Edmund Chmieliński, could not wait to leave his former village, where he felt he was treated 'like an animal': Nowa Huta offered him the chance of a new life. Another man described how the effort he contributed to the collective work brigade gave him 'satisfaction and a tremendous zest for life'.[29]

This enthusiasm translated into demands that planners should meet the newcomers' expectations of decent facilities. The authorities themselves bemoaned the fact that many workers 'lived wild' or had to share rooms until new housing became available. Nowa Huta and its inhabitants—who also included Roma, forcibly resettled by the communist government, along with Greek refugees from the civil war—were defined by migration, industrialisation, and a vision of a viable socialist future. As in Hungary, the migrants were regarded as backward and unhygienic in their habits. Isolated from the centre of Kraków, the Nowohucians were made to feel unwelcome when they ventured out; they suffered the indignity of being called *Hutasy*, a word that combined *huta* and *kutas* (a farm implement) but was also a slang term for penis.[30]

In 1955, the Polish poet Adam Ważyk published "Poemat dla dorosłych" (Poem for adults), which became famous for its depiction of the social turmoil associated with migration and industrialisation under late Stalinism:

> *From villages and little towns, they come in carts*
> *to build a foundry and dream out a city,*
> *dig out of the earth a new Eldorado.*
> *With an army of pioneers, a gathered crowd,*
> *they jam in barns, barracks, and hostels,*
> *walk heavily and whistle loudly in the muddy streets:*
> *the great migration, the twisted ambition,*
> *with a string on their necks—the Czestochowa cross,*
> *three floors of swear-words, a feather pillow,*
> *a gallon of vodka, and the lust for girls.*[31]

Ważyk suggested that Nowa Huta's migrants were 'thrust suddenly from medieval gloom'. Free from family and other constraints, they embarked on orgies and criminal escapades. It was not a great advert for socialist industrialisation and the 'new socialist man'. By the 1970s, however, Nowa Huta had become an enormous factory town with its own hospital, schools, kindergartens, clubs, and cinemas—in other words, a place defined by production rather than by migration.

The 1960s and 1970s also witnessed an ambitious project in Czechoslovakia, where the government turned the town of Most, located in the former Sudetenland, into a leading centre of the coal mining industry. In fact, the town had already begun to expand after the war, as thousands of Roma and other settlers flocked from Slovakia to northern Bohemia to replace the expelled German population, whose property was confiscated by the state. As the planners contemplated enormous new investment to extract coal, they began to think of 'gypsy nomads' as an unwelcome embodiment of precisely the kind of backwardness the government hoped to supplant. Removing the Roma and other residents from the old city centre (together with the Gothic church) went hand in hand with an offer to build new apartments (*paneláky*) on behalf of the newly arriving Czech proletariat.[32]

Governments across the region had a problem with 'gypsy nomadism' and sought to curb it through legislation that criminalised 'vagrancy', a broad term that drew attention to petty crime but that also effaced the rich history of horse-dealing, fortune-telling, and knife-grinding that kept the Roma in business. The Soviet state formally banned nomadism in 1956, and Czechoslovakia followed suit two years later. Before long, Poland, Bulgaria, and Hungary added laws on 'permanent settlement' to the statute book. The basic principle was that welfare should be linked to settled wage labour, and that gypsies should not benefit without fulfilling their duties as socialist citizens. Local government authorities deported gypsy nomads to keep them from becoming a charge on the public purse, although Slovak gypsies continued to migrate seasonally to work on distant construction sites. As they did so, they were accused of importing bad habits: according to Czech ethnographers, gypsy families treated apartments in a cavalier manner, tearing up beds to use as firewood and sleeping on straw mattresses 'next to piles of potatoes'. It was not difficult to portray the Roma as the antithesis of socialist modernity, as awkward migrants who followed their own customs and practices, and as a minority that was not easily accommodated within the nation-state.[33]

Yugoslavia belonged in a category of its own by virtue of its complex ethnic relations. A relatively new state, it had already been ravaged by internecine ethnic and political conflicts, such as the massacre of Serbs by Croat fascists during the Second World War. The peace settlement at the end of the war provided for the creation of ethno-territorial units along Soviet lines; these were to be held together by the apparatus of communism and the promise of greater prosperity. These arrangements directly affected the course of migration within Yugoslavia and indirectly affected migrants who moved beyond the borders of the state. One instance of interethnic conflict that propelled citizens of Yugoslavia across the frontier was the organised resettlement of around 150,000 Bosniaks (Muslims living in the Sandžak region of Yugoslavia) from Yugoslavia to Turkey between 1953 and 1960. Typically, the motives for migration were a mixture of economic and political: poor living conditions in Sandžak combined with religious discrimination in the new communist state. But the travails of the migrants did not end with their arrival in Turkey: locals reviled them as 'unbelievers' (*gavur*) who were required to demonstrate that they had renounced communism. This hostility rubbed off on the Bosniaks, some of whom were made to feel 'mute and illiterate' because of their inability to speak Turkish. What looked like an escape from persecution and poverty turned into a fresh ordeal.[34]

The widespread violence associated with forced migration was only one manifestation of migration in Eastern Europe, but it should not be minimised. It coincided with a rhetoric that humiliated and demonised political opponents and other social and ethnic outcasts, such as Roma. Particularly in Poland, migration supported the view that the postwar state had succeeded in regaining territory that was inalienably Polish and that had now been restored to the nation. In practice, however, resettlement meant a chaotic free-for-all.

As in Western Europe, migration had implications for established communities, particularly when ethnic Russians descended on the Baltic republics and the Virgin Lands in Central Asia, and when Poles muscled their way into formerly German towns and villages in Silesia. The Russian presence in non-Russian republics stored up problems for the future, particularly when self-appointed nationalists took up the cudgels on behalf of a 'threatened' indigenous population.

Migration in the postwar Soviet Union and Eastern Europe was both cause and consequence of economic modernisation and cultural change. New communist governments encouraged peasants to move to towns and cities to help rebuild shattered foundations and to invest in the future. Industrialisation also supported industriousness—in other words, governments and town planners believed that exposure to an urban environment would help to forge a 'new person', one committed to socialist values. It would be wrong to overlook the enthusiasm with which some migrants embraced this ambition—not only to move to the city but also to settle in the Virgin Lands, even when it meant living in tents and out of a suitcase for months on end. There was an important pioneering dimension to migration.

On both sides of the Iron Curtain, migrants were often left to their own devices. They were expected to contribute to postwar reconstruction without getting much in return for their labour. Their predicament reflected badly on European governments, none of which provided adequate assistance, except in the case of expellees in Germany. Refugees, repatriates, resettlers, expellees, and other migrants all faced a chilly reception even when, as in the case of the expellees, they found themselves living among co-ethnics.

Although there were exceptions, the era of recovery and reconstruction in Eastern and Western Europe was primarily one of permanent migration and resettlement. Resettlers in Poland and Ukraine, like German expellees, understood that there was no turning back. Even in the face of adversity, whether it derived from challenging material conditions or the ostracism of new neighbours, migrants did not give up hope of making a better life for themselves.

PART 2

Decolonisation, Guest Workers, and Economic Growth

1956–1973

CHAPTER 6

Migrants of Decolonisation

THE GOLDEN AGE OF economic growth from the 1950s to the early 1970s was also the era in which European colonial powers shed their overseas possessions in Africa and Asia. Decolonisation had political, social, and economic dimensions, but it also carried powerful cultural meanings. In the apt words of historian Jordanna Bailkin, migrants were 'bearers not only of the colonial past, but also of the decolonising present'. The presence of migrant workers in Britain, France, the Netherlands, and Portugal reflected decades or even centuries of colonial rule and the two-way traffic that it had enabled. Whether unfettered entry to the metropole should or would continue after countries gained their independence remained to be determined.[1]

Decolonisation largely reversed the direction of movement associated with the growth and consolidation of European empires. When the curtain came down on these empires, the stage was set for a mass exodus of elites who had been instrumental in governing overseas colonial possessions. Colonial officials, soldiers, and settlers moved from former colonies to the European metropolitan 'core', a process characterised at the time as 'repatriation' or 'return'. These were misleading terms, since many of those who were 'returning' were the descendants of landowners and businesspeople who had never before set foot in Europe but who, like colonial officers, believed they had an unbreakable bond with the nations whose interests they had represented overseas. 'Repatriation' also suggested something relatively straightforward and benign. Nothing could be further from the truth. Many repatriates faced an inhospitable reception.

Decolonisation brought other groups to Europe as well, in the form of those who had cooperated with or worked for the colonial powers. Their position was understandably precarious. The abrupt and substantial movements of these colonial accomplices and auxiliaries had more in common with forced migration than with economic migration, although there were elements of both. They, too, had little or no connection with the 'homeland'. Their skin colour also made them far more visible. These nonwhite groups expected some acknowledgement or compensation for the support they had given colonial rule in holding the forces of independence at bay. In what amounted to enforced exile, they had to negotiate racism and discrimination in European society.

At the same time, the process of return and repatriation embodied the failure of the colonial project. Its implications were expressed most dramatically by the Dutch colonial lobby in response to the independence of Indonesia in 1949: 'Indie verloren, rampspoed geboren' (The East Indies lost, a disaster is born). Later on, when Portugal renounced its overseas empire in 1974, defenders of colonial tradition posed a question: What was the undivided body of the nation without its 'limbs'? As these colonial diehards finally yielded to the forces of independence, a second question arose: What was to be the fate of people in the severed parts of the body politic?[2]

To be sure, the results were not hugely significant in relation to the populations of the countries in which they arrived. In France, Britain, and the Netherlands, the migrants of decolonisation only amounted to around 4 percent of the population, although the proportion was higher in Portugal by virtue of its smaller size. The absolute numbers—between 6 million and 8 million repatriates in total—were nevertheless considerable. Furthermore, these migrations caught European governments largely by surprise. The consequences were immense, both for the receiving societies and for the 'returnees' themselves, not least in France (discussed further in Chapter 7).[3]

The significance of colonial connections stretches beyond imperial retreat and migration. The loss of empire forced a reconsideration of what it meant to be European and a postcolonial nation-state — looking inwards, so to speak, rather than outwards to parts of the globe that had been dominated by the exercise of force.

These questions first arose in Italy at the end of the Second World War. The victorious Allies obliged defeated Italy to renounce its empire in Ethiopia, Eritrea, Somaliland (collectively known as 'Africa Orientale Italiana'), and Libya, as well as in Albania and the Dodecanese islands, and the seal was set on this decolonisation by the peace treaty in 1947. Somewhere between 480,000 and 580,000 Italian nationals made their way to the Italian Peninsula as a result. They included government officials, soldiers, engineers, colonists, workers, and teachers. As part of his colonial ambitions, Mussolini had sent nearly 60,000 Italian farmers, teachers, and others to Albania. By 1945, the United Nations Relief and Rehabilitation Administration began to organise their repatriation, although the new communist government in Albania insisted on retaining Italian technical specialists to contribute to the country's reconstruction. Other Italians had married into Albanian families and decided to stay on, as outposts of the nation, so to speak.[4]

In Libya, under British supervision following Italy's defeat, the process was less straightforward. The Italian government delayed approving requests from colonial settlers to repatriate, on the grounds that they would struggle to find work. Meanwhile, other Italians made their way without authorisation from Sicily to Libya in the late 1940s, some to rejoin family members, others to gain an economic advantage they believed would be denied them on the impoverished Italian mainland. As historian Pamela Ballinger has written, with an eye on developments in the Mediterranean, particularly since 2015, 'it is an irony lost on almost all Italians that not so long ago [these Italians] constituted the "illegals"'. For a generation, they managed to hold out in Libya, and then, in 1970, Colonel Muammar al-Gaddafi, who had seized power the previous year, expropriated their land and expelled them. His abrupt decision directly affected some 20,000 Italians.[5]

Italian returnees acquired the label of 'national refugees' (*profughi nazionali*), a status conferring citizenship and entitling them to support from the Italian government, although not to any international assistance. Some of them were able to afford private accommodation or to find a place to live in the homes of relatives, but for many others the only option was to be housed in refugee camps. During World Refugee Year in 1960, Italy stipulated that the funds raised by Italian citizens during the campaign should be spent to clear these camps, as well as to support those who had newly arrived from Somalia, after Italy's supervision of the UN trusteeship came to an end in the same year. Italy eventually provided them with purpose-built homes. But the relationship between national refugees and other Italians remained uneasy. It was not uncommon for residents to deem newcomers from Libya or Ethiopia as 'africano', an indication that their formal status as citizens did not constitute full inclusion in the Italian nation.[6]

The situation in the Netherlands, with its extensive overseas empire, was even more fraught. Indonesia's independence in 1949 convinced white settlers and colonial officials, together with people of mixed Dutch and Indonesian descent (often amalgamated into a category of so-called Indisch Dutch), of the need to move to the Netherlands. Although they had lived a life of relative privilege before the Second World War, they endured great hardship as a result of the Japanese wartime occupation. In official parlance, they were 'repatriates', not immigrants. Between 1949 and 1960, the year in which Indonesia nationalised all Dutch-owned enterprises, the total number of repatriates amounted to between 250,000 and 300,000 people.[7]

The adaptation of these repatriates was not a foregone conclusion. A contemporary account of the Indisch Dutch suggested that 'Dutch society as a whole shows little awareness of the presence of this group of repatriated persons and of their singular adaptation problems'. Their appeals for compensation for the loss of property (and for an acknowledgement of the suffering they endured at the hands of the Japanese in occupied Indonesia) fell on deaf ears. A government minister suggested that their interests would be better served 'by their remaining in Indonesia'. Dutch progressives regarded them as a reactionary presence, and Dutch conservatives viewed them as symbols of national humiliation: they were pejoratively described as 'regretters' (*spijtoptanten*).[8]

With few contacts in the Netherlands, the returnees had to rely upon local philanthropy to get by. Faced with limited job prospects, many of them pinned their hopes on emigration. The difficulties emerged in the petitions made by Dutch nationals to the World Council of Churches and the American Friends Service Committee (AFSC) in the hope of being allowed to migrate from the Netherlands to the United States. Jacques L., born in Bandung in 1938, explained that he had been employed as a welder by an oil company in Indonesia before arriving in the Netherlands in April 1958; there, he had taken up a job as a car mechanic. Jacques requested the chance to move to the United States 'to seek a way of life that offers more possibilities and is less restricted than here in the Netherlands'. He was described as a 'nice boy, serious purposed, conscientious'. Ultimately, however, he decided not to emigrate because his hospitalised sister needed his help. Another petitioner, Franciscus L., along with his wife, Johanna, and their seven children, also petitioned to be allowed to leave for the United States, where they had distant relatives. Franciscus had been taken prisoner by the Japanese; after the war, he had served in the air force and as a mechanic before coming to Holland, where six of his children were born. He, too, had worked as a car mechanic following his move to the Netherlands. The interviewing officer described them as 'a fine family unit' and noted that the parents 'wish[ed] to immigrate to give their children better future opportunities than they are liable to have here in little overcrowded Holland'. However, they fell out with their relatives in America and decided to stay in the Netherlands.[9]

So not all those who desired to emigrate were able to do so. Other families, however, found the prospect of a passage to the United States — or to some other country, such as Australia — not only alluring, but practicable. A family of three — Willem (born in Tandjungkarang, Indonesia, in 1924) and his wife and baby son were forced to leave Indonesia in 1958 when the new government took over the sugarcane factory he managed. They entered a Dutch hostel for repatriates, where Willem took a job as a qualified machinist. As an American immigration officer explained, the family still lived in a reception centre, and there was 'no chance of private living quarters in view of the housing shortage'. American Quakers in the AFSC agreed to sponsor the family, and they left the Netherlands. In the long run, many repatriates seem to have been successfully integrated in the Netherlands, where municipal authorities made housing available to them at controlled rents—although this did not stop the government from seeking to offload them elsewhere, in order to alleviate pressure on the housing stock.[10]

Alongside this 'repatriation' there was a significant influx of Moluccan (Ambonese) migrants who, having first fought for the Dutch against the Japanese occupation, and then, in 1945–1949, against the Indonesian nationalist forces led by Sukarno, looked upon the Netherlands as a temporary abode to spare them revenge from the new, unitary Indonesian state. The Dutch government had promised to support the predominantly Christian Moluccan population in securing a state of their own. When it reneged on this promise, the Moluccans' options narrowed. The new Indonesian state regarded them as traitors to the cause of independence, and they opted for what they envisaged as temporary refuge in the Netherlands.[11]

In 1951, around 15,000 Moluccan fighters and their dependents moved to the Netherlands, where they were hurriedly demobilised. The Dutch government initially held them in temporary accommodation, including in former German concentration camps such as Westerbork. As it became clear that they could not return to Indonesia, they became stateless: as late as 1968, only one in five of them had Dutch citizenship. Many of them were unemployed. Moluccan neighbourhoods were located on the outskirts of Dutch towns. The walls of their freezing apartments ('we can never get the cold out of our bones', recorded one resident) were decorated with pictures of the tropical beaches to which they hoped eventually to return. They rejected the paternalist view of Dutch politicians and others who told them to integrate—they regarded this as a kind of colonial mentality. 'We want to go back to our own free fatherland and we are against integration', stated a spokesperson of the Front Pemuda Maluku (Moluccan Youth Front) in 1959.[12]

Over time, Moluccan youth experienced displacement in a dual fashion: as a loss of homeland and as a weakening of paternal authority: 'When I went to the Christian college in Westerbork I encountered another world', one recalled. 'My fellow Dutch students were much more direct and freer in expressing their opinion. In the camp where we lived, my father's will was law. You always obeyed.' Yet, far from remaining passive in the face of the expectation that they would maintain a low profile, young radicals went on the offensive during the 1960s and 1970s. In response to the execution in 1966 of a Moluccan separatist leader by the Indonesian state, Moluccan activists set fire to the Indonesian embassy in The Hague. In 1975 and 1977, a series of occupations and train hijackings drew attention to the Moluccan cause. A 1977 train hijacking and the occupation of a primary school at the same time only ended with the intervention of Dutch marines, whose role remained murky. The episode raised difficult questions for the Netherlands: Might not the Moluccans have a reasonable case to return to the East Indies and create a state of their own?[13]

The decolonisation of the Dutch Empire on the other side of the world also had implications for migration. Under an agreement reached in 1954 between the Dutch government and the governments of Surinam and the Dutch Antilles, the inhabitants of the Dutch West Indies were eligible as overseas citizens to enter, work, and live in the Netherlands. Several thousand of them seized this opportunity. As in the Italian case, colonial connections brought Surinamese women to the Netherlands to work in care homes for the elderly, often claiming that their traditional upbringing qualified them to undertake this role. However, the main surge in migration did not take place until 1974–1975, when 30,000 Surinamese arrived in anticipation of the end of free movement between Surinam and the Netherlands in 1980. (These numbers were considerable in relation to the total population of around 400,000 in Surinam.) The government funded Surinamese support organisations and made affordable housing available. The Netherlands admitted tens of thousands more from Surinam during the era of dictatorship between 1980 and 1987.[14]

By this stage, Dutch politicians had come around to the view that the Netherlands was, after all, a country of immigration. New initiatives led to the creation of national minority organisations to represent each group. This policy went hand in hand with measures to restrict further immigration by imposing visa requirements on countries with what officials termed a 'high immigration potential', including countries such as Morocco that had for some years supplied seasonal workers in large numbers. It was relatively easier to control extra-European immigration where no colonial legacy existed.[15]

The legacies of colonialism were at least as marked elsewhere in the Low Countries. The Belgian colonial presence in the Congo had amounted to around 110,000 people, a mixture of officials, private-sector employees, settlers, and missionaries. The numbers in Rwanda and Burundi (formerly Ruanda-Urundi) were smaller, and the proportion of missionaries somewhat larger. But identifying who was 'Belgian' and who was not was not always a straightforward matter. Mixed marriages and their offspring complicated the picture; some of the children of interracial marriages had been shunted off into mission schools. As late as 1958, the Belgian presence in the Congo appeared secure—Expo 58, the Brussels World's Fair, advertised the colonial contribution to its 'civilisation', and Congolese were brought over to Brussels for the amusement of visitors. But a revolt in Leopoldville in 1960 precipitated independence, and the crisis quickly became internationalised when the United Nations agreed to deploy troops. Belgian authority collapsed. More than 22,000 Belgians were quickly and ignominiously airlifted out of the country in July 1960, many of them replaced by Belgian troops seeking to protect Belgian interests in the wealthy, mineral-mining region of Katanga.[16]

Belgium's panicked withdrawal from the Congo in 1960 was followed by the mass flight of colonial settlers and officials from Ruanda-Urundi in 1962. The exodus gave rise to stories of harassment and physical violence, including graphic details of gruesome murders by Congolese soldiers and civilians wreaking revenge on their former masters. Some ex-colonials moved to South Africa, but the majority 'returned' to Belgium with the assistance of government money channelled via the Catholic charity Caritas, the World Council of Churches, and the Hebrew Immigrant Aid

Society. The Belgian government offered some support to former colonial officials, but other returnees were left to their own devices. (It helped that the domestic economy offered the prospect of jobs in Belgium, at least in the short term.) Several thousand Belgians remained in the Congo, as the government hoped they would, until the nationalisation of their companies and political turbulence forced them to leave in the 1970s.[17]

There are at least two reasons why this mattered. First, the arrival in Belgium of former colonial officials and others revived disturbing memories of the country's collapse in 1940: significantly, the Belgian press referred to the repatriates as 'refugees'. Second, the end of colonial rule did not mean an end to colonial connections. Indigenous Congolese men and women made their way to the metropole, but attitudes towards their presence were coloured by stories of rape and murder in 1960. If white women embodied a beleaguered Belgian nation, black Congolese men stood for colonial violence and its potential to cause havoc in Belgium itself.[18]

Colonial unrest also had repercussions in the British Empire and closer to home. In Cyprus, regarded by the British as a strategically important island in the eastern Mediterranean, opposition to British rule during the 1950s was expressed as a movement to unite the colony with Greece, a campaign that led the colonial power to impose a state of emergency. Postwar migrants from Cyprus, like their forebears, had freedom of entry as 'citizens of the UK and colonies', but they were closely watched for signs of political subversion by Cypriot communists and right-wing nationalists. The situation became even more difficult after Cyprus gained its independence in 1960, when long-standing antagonisms between the Greek and Turkish communities flared up with renewed intensity. An outbreak of violence in 1964 prompted Turkish Cypriots to flee after being targeted by their Greek neighbours. For example, the family of Argun Ismet Imamzade was caught up in the fighting in his home town of Limassol. His parents moved to England, leaving him behind with his grandparents, his brother, and his three stepbrothers. But after their home was bombed, and after spending months in a refugee camp, he and his older brother sailed to England. Greek Cypriots who already had jobs in Britain also decided to remain rather than to return, because in Britain 'there is no wars, there is no earthquakes [*sic*]'.[19]

The end of British colonial rule had even more profound implications for 'return' migration. Unlike in France, the Netherlands, or Portugal, in Britain the numbers were not large: perhaps as few as 15,000 white British settlers returned to Britain from sub-Saharan Africa by 1980, although twice as many had left the Indian subcontinent in the wake of Partition in 1947. Those who stayed on considered the options available to them. A decade after Indian independence, the World Council of Churches suggested that the 'Anglo-Indian remains in his own country [sic] but conditions around him have so changed that he finds himself as much in need of rehabilitation as any refugee'. Those who carved out a niche in India had to think of the options available to their children, whose sights might be set on 'dress-making, child-care, stenographer, nursing etc. for girls and carpentry and mechanics for boys'.[20]

For those who did return, the end of empire brought down the curtain on a comfortable way of life. A newly created Overseas Services Resettlement Bureau helped some men to find suitable employment, although one official suggested that although these returnees 'might be good at dealing with a tribal riot [they were] most unlikely to be of much use in modern industry'. Having returned to the UK, their wives were now expected to perform tasks that native workers had previously done for them.[21]

Many years later, the documentary filmmaker Molly Dineen interviewed Hilary Hook, a lieutenant colonel who had lived the life of a colonial army officer and settler, most recently in Kenya, before returning to Britain. Her film contrasted his privileged life running a game lodge in Kenya with the difficulty of adjusting to life in a country that had changed out of all recognition. Hook's disillusionment may explain why not everyone regarded Britain as a magnet: many colonial expatriates moved to Canada, Australia, South Africa, or Southern Rhodesia, following in the footsteps of people who left Britain after the Second World War in search of sun, swimming pools, and servants.[22]

The reference to Kenya directs attention to the significance of the British settler presence in East Africa, which was much larger than in the colonies of West Africa, such as Nigeria. Britain's reluctance to hold onto Kenya was exposed in the 1950s when colonial forces used brutal means to try and suppress the struggle launched by indigenous Kikuyu in support of independence. The war against the so-called Mau Mau insurgency lasted as long as the French war in Algeria. It regularly surfaced in the British press and in newsreel films that cultivated an image of 'native savagery', whilst carefully avoiding any reference to the mass displacement of Kikuyu or the African victims of mass violence, including British brutality. The war ended and the British finally renounced control of Kenya in 1963, prompting the 'return' or relocation of white settlers such as Hook. However, unlike indigenous forces loyal to the colonial powers in places such as Algeria and Indonesia, many of whom took refuge in their host countries after independence, the Kikuyu who had served in the King's African Rifles remained in Kenya. The difference seems to have been that many ordinary Kikuyu tolerated the choices these loyalists had made in serving the status quo, particularly when Mau Mau leaders had inflicted harm on Africans as well as whites. Kenya's new leaders did not regard the Mau Mau as the authors of Kenyan independence, so those who helped the British to defeat the insurgency did not face the wrath of the postcolonial state.[23]

Mau Mau nevertheless left a powerful cultural legacy that sometimes surfaced in surprising places. The distinguished educationist Beryl Gilroy, who arrived in the UK in the 1950s, recalled being asked: 'Are you a Mau Mau lady?' The fact that she came from Guyana, rather than Kenya, revealed the powerful resonance of colonial wars in British culture and implied a deep-rooted assumption of a relationship between violence and people of colour. With even more hostile intent, a black teenage girl out shopping in Liverpool in 1955 was told to 'go back to Mau Mau land'. She was British-born, a descendant of migrants. Her colour exposed her to everyday racist ignorance, perhaps reinforced by the realisation that Britain's hold on its overseas empire was growing weaker with each passing year.[24]

This kind of knee-jerk racism eventually met its match in the writings of cultural critics of West Indian heritage, such as Stuart Hall. In a memoir published after his death, Hall wrote: 'People like me who came to England in the 1950s have been there for centuries; symbolically, we have been there for centuries. I was coming home. I am the sugar at the

bottom of the English cup of tea. I am the sweet tooth, the sugar planta-
tions that rotted generations of English children's teeth. There is no
English history without that other history.' Hall's analysis was not just a
comment about amnesia, however. It underlined the connection between
colonial rule and postcolonial migration, making the outsider into an
insider.[25]

One part of the former British Empire decided to go it alone and to
preempt the imposition of black majority rule. In Southern Rhodesia
(Zimbabwe), the white minority, led by Ian Smith, unilaterally declared
independence in 1965 in order to preserve its power. Some of the British
colonial officials who no longer had a job in Tanganyika (Tanzania) or
Kenya opted to move to Rhodesia or South Africa in the hope of maintaining the kinds of benefits to which they had been accustomed. The
government in Salisbury (now Harare) ruled with an iron fist, imprison-
ing its opponents and forcing others into exile. But it remained a pariah
state, backed only by the apartheid regime in South Africa, until a negotiated settlement created an independent Zimbabwe in 1979.[26]

This troubled history was reflected in the arrival of black Zimbabwean
student activists in the UK. Although they were unwilling exiles, they
looked back on their stay in the imperial metropolis as a time of excitement that gave them the chance to interact with left-wing supporters as
well as black British groups. They thought of themselves as being temporarily displaced, supporting the freedom struggle until such time as they
could return to Zimbabwe after independence, becoming prominent lawyers, academics, civil servants, politicians, businesspeople, and journalists. 'We were in the imperialist den but we found there were some friendly
lions inside', said one former activist. The Marlborough Arms on Gower
Street, London, became known as 'the Zimbabwean pub'. There, exiles
rubbed shoulders with freedom fighters from North Vietnam, Cuba,
South Africa, and Palestine.[27]

Some ex-colonials opted for Portugal, and the attraction of the Algarve
in the southwest of the country was said to be that you could 'live the kind
of life you used to live in the Colonies'. It was no accident that Portugal
was an authoritarian state that at this juncture retained its colonial posses-

sions. British newcomers who spoke nostalgically of the loss of empire felt more at home there than in the UK. One expatriate recalled that in the 1960s the Algarve was 'a bit like the days of the Raj—servants were aplenty, booze was cheap and the climate was good'.[28]

The Portuguese dictator Antonio Salazar, who held power from 1932 to 1968, insisted that Portugal was an 'undivided and multiracial nation' with 'overseas provinces', not colonies. The main 'provinces' were Angola, Mozambique, Cape Verde, Guinea-Bissau, and the islands of São Tomé and Príncipe in the Gulf of Guinea. An undivided nation placed no restrictions on Portuguese migration. Well into the 1950s, Salazar encouraged impoverished peasants on the mainland to settle overseas, a policy designed in part to weaken the lure of the city, which he regarded as a potential hotbed of working-class radicalism.

One early exodus followed the loss of Goa, an enclave that had been in Portuguese hands for four and a half centuries. Goans had protested against Portuguese rule throughout the 1950s. Following an invasion by Indian forces in December 1961 in support of India's claim to Goa, the European residents rushed to evacuate their families. Contrary to the wishes of the government in Lisbon, some 700 people clambered aboard the merchant vessel *India*, which had room for only half that number. The captain reported that the evacuees slept in the ship's toilets. Other European residents who were entitled to Portuguese citizenship after India's annexation of Goa opted instead to make their way to Mozambique, following in the familiar footsteps of previous generations of colonial migrants.[29]

After the restoration of Portuguese democracy in 1974, the new government finally renounced its hold on its colonial possessions. A total of 800,000 *retornados* (returnees) arrived from Angola and Mozambique, equivalent to around 15 percent of the total population of Portugal. Some of them then headed for Brazil, the United States, or South Africa. Repatriation took place in a hasty and chaotic fashion, and it did not help that Portugal was going through a recession. It is important to add that under a decree issued in 1975, the right to settle in Portugal was mainly reserved to 'whites'. Exceptions were made for Goans, for some Indians who settled in Portuguese territory in Africa, and for some African military personnel who served in the Portuguese army. But generally speaking, the whites were privileged in a way that nonwhite and mixed-race returnees were not. The 'undivided and multiracial nation' proved to be a hoax.[30]

The difficulties and dilemmas are captured in a semiautobiographical book called *The Return* by Dulce Maria Cardoso, one of whose characters observes that 'we'll never be here again [in] our Angola'. Cardoso's characters feel nostalgic about the scents of flowers and the cooking aromas of Angola, but not the indigenous Angolan population. The returnees accuse the post-Salazar political elite of having sold them out by abandoning Angola. The narrator's family leaves its departure until the last moment, and their reluctance to abandon their property means they must take a hastily arranged flight, leaving the father behind to an uncertain fate. Neighbours who take a boat to Portugal in a more timely fashion are more fortunate, as they can load their belongings onto ship containers. Upon the family's arrival in Lisbon, the Institute for the Support of Returnee Nationals (IARN) provides basic support, but the predominant experience is one of uncertainty and endless queues for food. In an ironic observation, the narrator says that IARN is 'more important and generous than God'. Even IARN, however, can do little to lessen the sense of humiliation the returnees experience as they realise how little their money is worth. They have to make do with hand-me-down clothes, for example. In writing this story, Cardoso drew upon her firsthand experience of having been displaced.[31]

'Returnees' and residents of metropolitan Portugal regarded each other with mutual incomprehension. Although a significant number of the *retornados* had been born in Portugal, many of them spoke a distinct kind of Portuguese. They dressed differently. One described how, 'when I arrived in Portugal, people would say that we had gone to Africa to exploit "blacks" and now we were in Portugal to exploit them [the Portuguese]'. Another experienced the 'shock' of arriving in Lisbon: 'They all thought we were reactionaries.' Media representations of their repatriation regularly likened it to an 'invasion'. As in Cardoso's fictional portrait, the returnees hoped to be treated as something other than second-class citizens of the 'motherland', but were quickly disabused of this notion. The narrator, fifteen-year-old Rui, describes his maths teacher's habit of calling him 'Returnee' rather than using his name.

The passage of time did not appear to have lessened the *retornados'* sense of being marginalised. The very term implied a distinction between them and mainstream Portuguese society. In 1993, a group of Portuguese friends attended a fundraising event in Lisbon on behalf of people suffering from leprosy. One of those present asked pointedly: 'Leprosy, is there still leprosy in Portugal?', to which another partygoer gave a brisk reply: 'Oh yes, the *retornados* brought it', meaning that they had imported the disease from Lusophone (Portuguese-speaking) Africa. As returnees recalled, 'everything was our fault, everything'. They had citizenship, but were nevertheless an unwelcome presence: legal, but not, so to say, legitimate.[32]

The Portuguese economy in the 1970s was in the doldrums. Jobs were in short supply, although the demise of the Salazar regime left some vacancies at the upper echelons of the civil service. Added to the lack of employment opportunities was the housing crisis. Most of the *retornados* ended up in makeshift accommodation until the government finally arranged for more permanent social housing. Returnees gradually began to organise and demand compensation for the loss of property, but organisations such as the Alliance of Portuguese Returnees from Overseas did not boast a large membership. Not until 1996 did the government create a high commissioner for immigration and ethnic minorities.[33]

Nevertheless, repatriation did not preclude other kinds of initiatives. Some returnees were able to capitalise on family connections to ease their integration into the domestic economy and to contribute to its modernisation: Cardoso has one of her characters say that 'if we can build nations in the lands we were forced to abandon we'll certainly be able to improve the backward life of the Motherland'. Rui's father makes it to Lisbon with plans to invest in breeze-block housing, although IARN levied high interest rates on its loans.[34]

Existing economic links between former colonies and the metropole were maintained. Migrants from Cape Verde, a few hundred miles from the coast of West Africa, populated Portuguese shantytowns (known as *bairros*) such as Cova da Moura, which became a familiar sight in and around Lisbon during the 1980s. Men from these areas took low-paid jobs on construction projects, and women found work as domestic cleaners. Their remittances helped to sustain the impoverished Cape Verdean economy, and migrants sometimes pointedly affirmed that they were 'going to work there [in Portugal] in order to come back and have a better life here'. Here, again, migration was not a one-way street.[35]

Some migrants made a spectacular name for themselves by virtue of their skills and talents in particular fields, particularly sports and entertainment. Sports offered a route to fame, fortune, and acceptance for a select few, and the leading Portuguese football clubs scoured Mozambique and Angola for potential players. Their greatest find, Eusébio da Silva Ferreira, had been born to a white Angolan railway worker and a black Mozambican mother and raised in a modest home on the outskirts of Lourenço Marques (now Maputo). His footballing prowess brought him to Lisbon in 1960. Eusébio had a glittering career with Benfica, where he was acclaimed for refusing to sign for an Italian club ('because his mother wanted him to stay in Lisbon'). As captain of the national team, he was regarded as a role model for Portuguese youth because of his work ethic and modest lifestyle. After his death in 2014, his ashes were interred in the National Pantheon in a ceremony attended by the Portuguese president.[36]

One final flurry of formal decolonisation in Europe occurred when Spain renounced its overseas possessions. Until 1975, some 20,000 Spanish men and women maintained the country's colonial presence in the Spanish Sahara. A similar number of Spanish citizens lived in Tangier, until Morocco regained control in 1959, but their numbers were dwarfed by residents in Morocco itself. Spain also occupied the small territory of Ifni, which it returned to Morocco in 1969. Officials and businesspeople also lived in Equatorial Guinea, which gained its independence in 1968. Much of the remaining Spanish population of Morocco left between 1973 and 1975, following the nationalisation of the enterprises they owned or in which they were employed. In each instance Spanish officials were speedily evacuated. Around 6,000 who arrived in Spain from Equatorial Guinea garnered a great deal of publicity: the government created an emergency facility at Madrid Airport and took steps to provide the 'repatriates' with loans and other forms of assistance, including partial compensation for the loss of property. Other repatriates also claimed compensation. There were other strands to decolonisation, too: some of the native troops who served the colonial regime in the Sahara, for example, opted to move to the remaining North African Spanish enclaves of Ceuta and Melilla.[37]

Migrants from former colonial possessions thus managed to make a living of sorts, but many of them were repudiated by the 'homeland'. Only in exceptional circumstances did they achieve the stature of Eusébio. All too often, they suffered hardship and discrimination. White returnees and migrants of colour alike occupied a marginal position in the postcolonial nation-state. The unsettling of empire translated into personal uncertainty.

CHAPTER 7

French Revolution: Decolonisation, Migration, Modernisation

IN 1962, THE FRENCH director Jean-Luc Léridon made a documentary, *Travailleurs Africains* (African workers), giving workers from North Africa and sub-Saharan Africa a platform to talk about their aspirations and experiences, a remarkable approach. A Senegalese man spoke of the need to set the record straight: 'We've arrived and others will come. We must tell what brought us here because besides the truth, there are only lies. We did not come here to stay and settle down; we came for work, we'll return home. Some will stay because they are happy here, others may just encounter death. If people want to help us, fine. If they don't want to help us, they should leave us alone.'[1]

For their part, French scholars were slow to engage with the experiences of migrant newcomers, who struggled to be accepted in French society. Until the 1980s, French historians wrote very little about migration. Leaving them alone, so to speak, contributed to a wider public perception that France relied on foreign workers only to a limited extent. Nothing could be further from the truth. In fact, migration from beyond France helped provide a labour force in mining, construction, and manufacturing from the later nineteenth century onwards. Employers in the private sector as well as state-owned enterprises recruited men from French colonial territories; most of them worked for a few months or years at a time before returning to their homes. In addition, after the First World War, Armenian and Russian refugees settled in major towns and cities such as Paris and Marseille, where they found jobs in manufacturing. After 1945, migrants from North and sub-Saharan Africa arrived in considerable numbers, joining pockets of people from the French colonies who were already living and working in France.[2]

Migration on this scale sustained what became known as the *trente glorieuses*, or 'thirty glorious years'. French society in the later 1950s bore all the hallmarks of modernisation: accelerated urbanisation and town planning; government investment in industry and in the transport infrastructure; growing prosperity, associated with manufacturing and services, including tourism; and the growth of a consumer society. Skilled and unskilled migrants from overseas contributed their labour, paid their share of taxes, sometimes invested in businesses, and sustained the French economy as consumers of goods and services. They shared in the economic glory, having played their part in making it possible.

The dynamics of migration were heavily influenced by decolonisation. Syria and Lebanon, both French protectorates, gained independence in 1946. France withdrew from Indochina (Vietnam, Laos, and Cambodia) in 1954. Tunisia and Morocco became independent in 1956, followed by Senegal in 1960 and much of French West Africa in 1962. The implications of this transformation were profound. In the late colonial era, governed by an elite that was metropolitan and white, and supported by indigenous (and French-educated) leaders who both embodied and were expected to sustain the principles of the French republic, France could conceive of itself as a multicultural empire. By the early 1960s, as colonies gained their independence, the country could reconfigure itself as a nation-state that demanded of its citizens a commitment to core values, including secularism (*laïcité*). Whatever their origin or background, migrants who wished to make their home in France were expected to assimilate on terms laid down by the metropole.[3]

In the light of postwar decolonisation, it is important to recognise that France had a long history of immigration from the nineteenth century onwards. In the nineteenth century this manifested itself in the recurrent seasonal migration of labourers from Belgium and Italy who worked in fields and factories. Belgian workers were a common sight in the mines and textile factories of northern France. Italians were heavily concentrated in the rural south, but they, too, laboured in the mines of the north. They were joined by Polish miners as well as Kabyle labourers from North Africa. All of them maintained a close affiliation with their families, who remained behind in their countries of origin. Movement between France and their home countries was more or less uninterrupted. Migration to France revived after the First World War, which had itself drawn large numbers of Algerian and Moroccan men to work in French munitions factories and to fight on the Western Front. Although the Great Depression prompted an exodus of foreign workers—spurred in part by a wave of popular xenophobia—the presence of foreigners in France was sustained by the arrival of refugees from the Spanish Civil War. Migrants, not all of them white, were a familiar part of the landscape of France.[4]

Before the First World War and in its immediate aftermath, racist and eugenicist attitudes prevailed. The leading demographer Alfred Sauvy supported ethno-racial categorisation as a criterion of selection for migrants (along with age and professional skills). He presented Arabs as 'fatalist and credulous', and Jews from Central Europe as 'industrious [and] haunted by the desire of upward social mobility'. Sauvy argued that 'waves of Slavic people', by whom he meant Czechs, Serbs, Poles, and Hungarians, assimilated quite well in French society. Polish newcomers, in particular, he said, supported conservative family values and rejected birth control, giving them an affinity with French culture. In general Sauvy represented migration as a pool in which French officials and employers needed to fish with care if economic objectives were not to clash with cultural norms.[5]

Sauvy's rigid hierarchy yielded to forces beyond his control. Vietnam, for example, provided a regular source of migrants to metropolitan France. One group of French settlers and officials who returned with their families following France's military defeat in Indochina in 1954 numbered 70,000. Vietnamese factory workers, along with a sprinkling of merchant seamen, merchants, and restaurant owners, also made their way to France, following in the footsteps of Vietnamese students and intellectuals who had already settled in Paris before the Second World War. They included as many as 35,000 Vietnamese 'repatriates' who had sided with France during the independence struggle. Successive generations came from different social backgrounds; variously practised Buddhism, Caodaism, or Catholicism; and embraced different political views, so it would be misleading to speak of a Vietnamese 'community'. By 1990, around 72,000 Vietnamese were living in France, half of them with French citizenship, including elderly men and women living in small towns in the Auvergne, where the Vietnamese reinvigorated a settlement that declined following the closure of the coal mine.[6]

Decolonisation gave rise to 'return' migration from North and sub-Saharan Africa. Although significant numbers of French expatriates remained behind in Senegal, Guinea, and other former colonies, around 1.5 million people were 'repatriated', a term that included the offspring born to French parents living overseas. Along with 170,000 'repatriates' from Tunisia and 230,000 from Morocco, around 1 million people 'returned' from Algeria. Indeed, the situation was particularly fraught in Algeria, the site of a bitter war between those committed to maintaining its status as part of France and those who campaigned for its independence. Algeria was part of France, however, so Algerians were free to come and go. Migration took off after the Second World War, with the number of Algerians registered on the mainland increasing from 20,000 in 1946 to 210,000 eight years later. By 1954, as violence intensified, large numbers of Algerians continued to cross the Mediterranean to look for work.[7]

The war in Algeria changed everything. It lasted for eight years, from 1954 to 1962, and was marked by extreme brutality on both sides and by an unrelenting war of words. It was fought not only on Algerian soil but also in mainland France, turning Algerians into objects of suspicion. The French government poured troops into Algeria in a military migration of 512,000 soldiers by 1956. Around 1 million civilians were rounded up and incarcerated, and 250,000 more fled to neighbouring Tunisia and Morocco. These refugees, who did not come under the aegis of the 1951 UN Refugee Convention, relied upon local and international charities for basic subsistence. Freedom fighters and their supporters moved abroad to continue the struggle. Keen to make political capital out of the situation in Algeria by staking a claim to support the 'Third World' in its struggle to throw off colonial shackles, the Soviet Union invited young Algerian refugees to complete their education in Moscow, drawing attention to the 'thousands of refugees fleeing from punitive expeditions and bombings'. Some Algerian nationalists made their way to the Federal Republic of Germany to take jobs in towns such as Saarbrücken and Kaiserslautern, where they could—if they were lucky—avoid the unwanted attention of the French security forces.[8]

Confrontations between Algerian freedom fighters in the Front de libération nationale (FLN, National Liberation Front) and French loyalists had bitter consequences in metropolitan France, where both sides engaged in mutual recrimination and violent conduct. However, elements of the French state perpetrated the biggest atrocity. On 17 October 1961, members of the Paris police force massacred close to 200 French Algerians who had gathered to protest the curfew imposed by the notorious prefect of police Maurice Papon (others too, including Tunisians, Moroccans, and even Italians, were caught up in the bloodbath). 'Ici on noie les Algériens' (Here we drown Algerians) was the terrible slogan scrawled on the bridges over the Seine. Subsequent investigations revealed the involvement of army veterans in the massacre, men who had served in Vietnam or in Algeria itself as members of the Organisation armée secrète (OAS, Secret Armed Organisation), the notorious far-right group whose members never accepted the renunciation of French rule in Algeria. This was a reminder that decolonisation had the capacity to bring migrants to the metropole who had their own murderous agenda.[9]

The eventual success of the liberation movement and the declaration of Algerian independence in July 1962 culminated in the abrupt exodus of French settlers of long standing (so-called *pieds-noirs*) and members of the former colonial administration, together with 200,000 Muslim soldiers (known as *harkis*) who had served with the French army. Henceforth, Algeria was no longer part of the French republic. An independent Algeria meant that any Algerian who wished to enter metropolitan France was now deemed to be an 'immigrant'. The French government had already established a Secretariat for Repatriation in 1959; it now set aside the equivalent of $330 million to assist with the integration of the settlers and civil servants from Algeria, who bemoaned their loss of status when they returned to France: one former administrator later said: 'Imagine a man having ruled millions of people for ten years without supervision suddenly finding himself piling up files in a tiny office.'[10]

What would become of the pieds-noirs, whose numbers were put at 984,000? In metropolitan areas, many of the French looked upon them with disdain, rather as happened in Britain, where the 'settlers' were thought to have failed 'over there' but were not welcome 'over here'. By the summer of 1962, almost all of them had hurriedly made their way to the 'Hexagon', shorthand for mainland France. The French state struggled to come to terms with their status: Were they 'repatriates' (since Algeria was no longer an integral part of the *patrie*), were they 'retreating' (as defeat implied), or were they 'refugees'? Might they be 'bandits' who posed a terrorist threat to France, the country that had unceremoniously abandoned them to their fate? Were they, as one dismissive report suggested, merely 'holidaymakers'? Newspapers described families who were desperate to flee, but who also held out the possibility—a forlorn hope, indeed—that they might return to Algeria.[11]

The preferred solution to the 'problem' was eventually found in the Gaullist project for planned economic growth, which, among other things, meant to absorb them into the expanding labour force. The economy would come to the rescue. French journalists expressed the hope that they would not only contribute 'abundant manpower' but also become 'solvent consumers', rather than constituting a continual burden on society and drain on the state budget.[12]

In the short term, the sudden arrival of the so-called repatriates (*rapatriés*) created immense difficulties. Remarkably, the French government had made no plans in advance. More than 100,000 repatriates arrived in Marseille in May 1962, and 350,000 followed in June. They spent days and weeks camping on the docks and in public squares. The overcrowded city was already struggling to cope with other migrants, who had little option but to find what shelter they could in the city's mushrooming shantytowns, or *bidonvilles*. Local charities, church groups, and residents did what they could at this stage. Contemporaries accused the newcomers of adopting a haughty and disdainful attitude towards the locals. As the local mayor put it, it would require 'extraordinary measures to confront this exceptional situation', including the need to reassure local residents, who blamed a series of robberies on the repatriates.[13]

Before long, the French state mobilised resources to support the pieds-noirs. In August 1962 it launched a large programme of relief, including an initial payment and a monthly allowance for those with insufficient funds, in order to help people find housing and work. They were given social security benefits, an allowance for furniture and other needed items, and funds or low-interest loans to help with job retraining or to open a business. The government issued identity cards to them as well where these had gone missing, provided temporary tax relief, and organised a range of other loans and tax exemptions. Elderly repatriates received benefits including a pension supplement. According to one estimate, the repatriation policy cost the state around 16 billion francs between 1962 and 1970. The government encouraged the pieds-noirs to move to areas where jobs were available, and it withdrew benefits from those who refused. Most of them opted to remain in the south of France, congregating in cities such as Marseille, Avignon, Toulon, and Nice. New towns, such as Carnoux, sprang up virtually overnight.[14]

Pieds-noirs did not take long to organise on their own behalf. Temporary settlements promoted a kind of 'brotherhood of misfortune', but this did not translate into an integrated or single community. The largest organisation of Algeria's former settlers was the Association nationale des français d'Afrique du Nord, d'outre-mer et de leurs amis (ANFANOMA, National Association of the French from North Africa, from Overseas, and Their Friends), which had formed in 1956 but after 1962 became dedicated to lobbying the French government on behalf of the pieds-noirs, particularly in order to secure compensation for property losses and to seek decent housing and jobs. By 1962 its membership stood at a quarter of a million, although internal divisions led to a succession of splits. In the late 1970s, Jacques Roseau established the political lobby organisation RECOURS-France to encourage pieds-noirs to vote tactically in municipal and national elections. In 1987, their support for the conservative Jacques Chirac paid off when his new government passed legislation to compensate them for losses incurred as a result of Algerian independence. This did not, however, satisfy some of the more outspoken pieds-noirs, who came close to commending the OAS for its actions during the war. Roseau himself was killed in 1993 by uncompromising pieds-noirs, who denounced him as a 'pro-Arab traitor' for having sought a rapprochement with the Algerian government. The Algerian war cast a very long shadow.[15]

Local politicians rewarded the pieds-noirs for their support by investing in new housing, such as the Petit Bard in Montpellier and tower blocks in other parts of the city. As the historian Émile Chabal noted, 'a large majority of these flats were classed as social housing (*habitations à loyers modérées*, HLM) and therefore available at preferential rates. By offering them to the pieds-noirs, [Mayor François] Delmas made an astute political calculation. He was genuinely concerned about the *rapatriés*, but he also knew that he would be guaranteed re-election with such a devoted support base.'[16]

Employment told only one side of the story. Migrants also contributed to economic life as entrepreneurs of various kinds. In Montpellier, the pieds-noirs transformed the fortunes of failing businesses in the city centre and opened restaurants that simultaneously generated new income and provided a space for people to meet. They restored local vineyards and farms that had been badly affected by the tough winter of 1956. Longtime residents initially resented the subsidies that were handed out to the pieds-noirs, but eventually acknowledged that they had helped to revive a moribund local economy and society.[17]

One curious feature of the 'repatriation' of settlers from Algeria is that around half of the French citizens living in Algeria had originated from Malta, Gibraltar, Spain, and Italy. For some of them, although memories of Algeria had begun to recede, France remained a foreign land. As one migrant of Maltese heritage put it after being forced to abandon Algeria, 'in France, nothing reminds me of my country....I don't find the same smells, colours....I get the feeling that I'm always *en voyage* to France, I'm floating.' Some of these first- and second-generation pieds-noirs now cultivated and maintained a stronger affiliation to Malta than to Algeria and participated in associations that celebrated their Maltese background — the island's history, its language, and its cuisine — as a means of transcending their otherwise marginal position in modern France. Being of Maltese rather than Algerian heritage seemed to hold out the promise of a more secure foothold in France.[18]

In the 1970s, as the historian Jean-Jacques Jordi has shown, the pieds-noirs devoted more time to the preservation of their cultural heritage through organisations such as the Cercle Algérianiste (Algerianist Circle), which dedicated itself to collecting personal testimony in order 'to express the collective conscience of our scorned, exiled, and dispersed community in order to save from oblivion and nothingness the little that remains to us of our magnificent and cruel past'. Its monthly publication, L'Algérianiste, rehearsed the argument about retaining 'pride in our past' and cultivating a sense of fraternity. The pieds-noirs established amicales (associations) that brought together people from the same part of Algeria or the same professional background. Part of the purpose was to commemorate those who had died during the war in Algeria and to preserve cemeteries in Algeria.[19]

In 1978 the French novelist Daniel Saint-Hamont published Le Coup de Sirocco (When the Sirocco blows), devoted to the exodus of the pieds-noirs. It was subsequently made into a film by the same name (directed by Alexandre Arcady, 1979). The lead actor described it as 'more than a film, but a chance to take part in a collective sentimental adventure', and, somewhat grandiosely, as 'an opportunity for the pieds-noirs to reconcile themselves to one another and to the metropolitans'. But—taking a stance unlikely to commend itself to the intended audience—he also insisted that the history of French colonisation was one of brutal occupation.[20]

None of this altered the diminished status of Algerians who had fought for the French in Algeria, the harkis, whose situation encapsulated the postcolonial dilemma of what to do with people who collaborated with the colonial state. 'Will there be sun in France? I didn't know where I was', said a female harki regarding her arrival. Her entry into metropolitan France, like that of all other harkis, was closely controlled, and immigration officials took an instant dislike to anyone who was elderly, sick, or unlikely to 'assimilate'. Tellingly, the French president in those years, General de Gaulle, quickly ditched the terms citoyens (citizens) and rapatriés (repatriates) in favour of harkis and réfugiés (refugees), underlining the popular perception that no Algerian Muslim could be regarded as French: 'The term repatriates', he insisted, 'obviously does not apply to the Muslims. In their case, we are dealing only with refugees.'[21]

The Algerian Muslim 'refugee' had become a distinct category, a foreigner rather than a citizen. The war in Algeria raised the stakes by associating Islam with terrorism, or at least with ineradicable difference. In March 1959, de Gaulle famously defined France as a country 'of the white race, of Greek and Latin culture and the Christian religion.... The Muslims, have you seen them, with their turbans and their djellabas. You can see clearly that they are not French!' He entertained the alarming possibility that, in the absence of restrictions on entry, 'my village would no longer be Colombey-les-Deux-Egliscs, but Colombey-les-Deux-Mosquées', in which twin mosques would replace the two churches. Those on the right of the political spectrum quoted the speech approvingly.[22]

In a further demonstration of their diminished status, and in contrast to the pieds-noirs, the harkis and their families were brought to France surreptitiously, often at the dead of night in overcrowded boats. Some managed to arrive clandestinely and find their own accommodation; most were despatched to 'temporary' camps, to small hamlets, or to dedicated social housing in remote parts of France. The French minister of the interior, Roger Frey, spoke of the need to exercise 'vigilant surveillance'. The official justification for internment in camps was threefold: to separate them initially in order to prepare them for 'integration', to safeguard them from retaliation by members of the FLN or recruitment into the OAS, and to prevent them from overwhelming the limited housing stock in the country at large.[23]

One notorious facility was the Larzac military camp in Aveyron, which had housed German prisoners of war and FLN internees. By the summer of 1962 it had become a 'temporary' home for more than 3,000 harkis and their families. Another internment camp, Saint-Maurice-l'Ardoise, had likewise originated as a military camp, but for housing Spanish republican refugees, German prisoners of war, and DPs. New prefabricated buildings were hurriedly erected. The appalling conditions contributed to high rates of infant mortality from preventable causes. Some 43,000 people passed through these overcrowded camps between 1962 and 1969. As late as 1974, 16,000 harkis were still living in camps, the last of which only closed at the end of the decade.[24]

The government also took advantage of their arrival to settle harkis in abandoned or depopulated villages, giving a boost to the local economies, and used the new arrivals as unpaid construction workers. Others were accommodated in out-of-town housing blocks in the south of France or much farther north in Amiens and Roubaix. There were constant reminders of the colonial past: army officers from among the pieds-noirs were entrusted with the administration of camps and other settlements, where they treated the harkis like 'natives', lumping them together irrespective of the differences in terms of region of origin.[25]

Colonial power relations were perpetuated by other legacies. The Muslim notable Saïd Boualam left behind extensive property in Algeria when he was evacuated to France along with his entourage of sixty-seven dependents, who were all installed in the village of Mas Thibert in Bouches-du-Rhône, close to Arles. By 1964 an entire estate had grown up, complete with school and café. Boualam became a celebrity among his fellow harkis and perpetuated his status as a man of prestige (bachaga), both locally and within the National Assembly, where he sat from 1958 until the mid-1970s and cultivated contacts with sympathetic leaders among the pieds-noirs.[26]

Although ANFANOMA lobbied on behalf of the harkis, on the grounds that they were French by nationality and by virtue of the loyalty they had demonstrated to the French state, in fact their misfortune attracted little public attention. Isolated and segregated, and speaking little French, they had few opportunities to express themselves on a public platform. Men suffered from a sense that their authority within the household had diminished, and those who protested in public might face further incarceration in mental hospitals or be threatened with deportation to Algeria. Women who fled their abusive husbands had no option but to take on numerous cleaning jobs, with little prospect of improvement in income. Migration for many harkis thus meant multiple kinds of deprivation and uncertainty.[27]

The difficulties facing the harkis emerged in a powerful memoir published by Zahia Rahmani in 2006, *France: Récit d'une enfance* (*France: Story of a Childhood*). Rahmani left Algeria as a small child with her parents in 1967, after her father was released from prison by Algeria's new rulers. She described the taunts she suffered at the hands of fellow pupils (and her stunning academic success), as well as her complicated relationship with her father, who eventually committed suicide. Her autobiography expressed her ambivalence towards Algeria, a country she visited periodically as an adult: 'I no longer believed in the romantic, comforting illusion of a faraway land. I gave up on the idea of ever going back.' At the same time, 'France wasn't the right place for me. In no way did this country, still overly reliant on its precepts of universalism, want to support me.' In France's eyes, she added, she 'contributed nothing'. An unnamed Algerian woman who lived in Paris responded to this kind of lament by accusing the harkis of self-indulgence: 'They say they cannot go back to Algeria because they know that their life is better here.' Reminded by her husband that Algeria would not welcome them, she retorted, 'They—and their children—have to recognise the harm they did to their country.' In these circumstances, as Rahmani put it, 'beyond their political cannibalisation and ignoble treatment in France [i.e., of the harkis], our first responsibility was to live'.[28]

France was slow to acknowledge the sacrifice and losses of the harkis who had fought to stem the tide of Algerian independence. Interviewed years later, fifty-year-old Mabrouk, who had been a young boy at the time, complained bitterly about their abandonment: 'What I can't understand is why, after all these years, the French state has not recognised what we did for France and give us compensation and jobs for the children, for example. Those who were the enemy are now treated better than we are.' The sense of having been deserted by the state reached its apogee in their enforced immobility in the internment camp. In 1991 the children of the harkis protested their insubordinate status. One young adult explained that the protests 'broke the wall of silence. We had nothing to lose. Our lives had been fucked up.' The sit-ins and street protests drew attention to legal disabilities, such as the lack of freedom of movement and the benefits available to Algerian immigrants. At the same time, one adult harki said: 'It was on the barricades that I discovered that I was really French.'[29]

In the mid-1990s, the government responded to calls from second-generation harkis for recognition. Leading voices, such as the writer Fatima Besnaci-Lancou, likened their suffering to that of France's Jewish population when it had been rounded up during the Second World War. The French state had a duty to accept responsibility for having (in her words) 'abandoned' the harkis. In 2001, Chirac acknowledged that they were 'victims of a terrible tragedy' and that the state had not done enough to recognise their loyalty. A survey in 2003 found that more than two-thirds of the French believed that the harkis had been treated badly. In 2012, an imposing national memorial was inaugurated, but in a remote corner of the Bouches-du-Rhône. Well-meaning French people speak of having treated them shamefully, yet at the same time often still think 'they were after all traitors to their people'. Views such as these reinforced a sense of the harkis as a group apart from mainstream French society. Although they had French citizenship, their descendants were—and still are—to be found disproportionately among the unemployed. They live on the margins of society among immigrants who arrived later and who lack citizenship rights. The harkis experienced a double migration, arriving in France, and then, after lengthy incarceration, being sent to the north of the country to contribute to industrialisation, as well as a double segregation, first in the bidonvilles and then in the *banlieus*, or suburbs of French cities.[30]

Migrants from former French colonial possessions, particularly from Morocco and Senegal, came to France without having been driven from their homes by the kind of protracted conflict that affected those from Algeria. They supported themselves by finding work in low-paid occupations and constantly had to negotiate prejudice at work and on the street, but also seized new opportunities to get ahead where they could. African migrants from Senegal were to be found in large numbers as dock labourers in Marseille and on the factory floors of Renault and other car plants in Paris. French trade unions fought for equal wages and social rights, although they prioritised migrants from Spain and Portugal, who were present in greater numbers. Africans also faced prejudice of various kinds, including from French trade unionists, who doubted their 'work ethic' and their willingness to engage in the workers' struggle against capitalism.[31]

In support of migration from the Caribbean, the French government created a dedicated office, the Bureau pour le développement des migrations dans les départements d'outre-mer (BUMIDOM, Office for the Development of Migrations Within Overseas Departments). Established in 1963 against the backdrop of rising unemployment in the overseas departments of France, BUMIDOM prepared migrants from French Guiana and the Antilles (as well as Réunion in the Indian Ocean) by giving them lessons in how they should conduct themselves. Although it envisaged the dispersal of the migrants around France, most migrants bypassed it altogether as they made their way to Paris to fill vacancies in the expanding telecommunications sector and the health service. Despite suffering discrimination in the workplace and harassment outside of work, Antillean migrants had French citizenship, and so were at least protected from deportation. Women gravitated towards domestic work, where their services were much in demand among middle-class households, but they also found work in hospitals, and later in administrative positions. They mobilised themselves in support of better wages and living conditions, and joined students in campaigning against racism in France, in order to hold the country to account in its supposed commitment to equality.[32]

As in the case of migrants from Algeria, for these migrants housing became a touchstone of the state's readiness to contribute to their welfare. Initially, they were left much to their own devices. The very first bidonvilles (from the French word for the metal oil drums they used in makeshift construction) appeared in Morocco in the 1920s, when Arab migrant workers cobbled together improvised dwellings to live in when they moved to Casablanca to serve the expanding European urban elite. In postwar France the dwellings took the form of modest huts tacked onto the back of North African–run café-hotels. Additions were made to accommodate new arrivals. The design of these areas resembled the villages of North Africa, with rooms laid out to create a sense of household privacy, high windowless external walls, and a courtyard (as on the Rue des Près in Nanterre). Beyond this sense of familiarity, migrants also looked to the bidonvilles to provide an autonomous space or 'refuge' from the prying eyes of French officials and the police. Outsiders dismissed the villages as places of degradation, disease, and danger, and as a 'problem' caused specifically by Algerian immigration. There was a degree of truth in the official view, insofar as the pro-independence FLN maintained a significant presence in the bidonvilles during the 1950s and collected money for the armed struggle in Algeria.[33]

The French state adopted a dual approach to the assimilation of Algerian migrants. In the first stage, the police and municipal authorities demolished the shantytowns and invested in improved social housing via the Fonds d'action sociale (FAS, Social Action Funds), established in 1958, and a housing corporation, the Société nationale de construction de logements pour les travailleurs Algériens (SONACOTRAL, National Housing Construction Company for Algerian Workers). They built hostels and dormitories (*foyers*) for Algerian single men, along with *cités de transit* (transitional housing) and rent-controlled HLM flats. In Marseille, the FAS funded the Aide aux travailleurs d'outre mer (ATOM, Aid for Overseas Workers) and similar bodies in Paris and Lyon. SONACOTRAL also provided jobs for some of the engineers and architects who fled Algeria during France's war against the FLN. A second strand of government policy had a more transformative and long-term purpose. Even before the loss of Algeria, preparations were under way. In 1959 the French government launched the Constantine Plan to support welfare programmes with the aim of 'eliminating terrorism' as well as 'to promote cultural and psychological social education for migrants and their families, to act to promote public opinion and separate agitators from the mass of migrants that can be welcomed comprehensively and fraternally'. This top-down approach signalled the willingness of the state to commit resources to support Algerian newcomers and to secure political stability.[34]

As more and more migrants from North Africa entered the country, urban redevelopment aimed not only to improve living conditions but also to transform cultural practices. Change proceeded in fits and starts throughout the 1960s. The Ministry of the Interior bemoaned the fact that 'mediocre living standards pose innumerable problems of a social order', and that migrants struggled to 'adapt' in the bidonvilles. Employers were invited to do more to stump up funds for new housing. Meanwhile, municipal authorities in Paris invested heavily in housing estates and tower blocks in suburbs designated as 'zones à urbaniser en priorité' (priority areas for urbanisation). The population of La Courneuve, for example, just outside the capital, doubled between 1962 and 1968. Some municipalities pursued an enlightened policy. In the large Parisian suburb of Saint-Denis, the left-wing authority supported public housing as an integral part of its policy of absorbing newcomers in the 1950s and recognising their rights, whereas the neighbouring conservative authority in Asnières, best known for the Louis Vuitton atelier, undertook schemes to rehouse Algerian and 'French' migrant families without consulting them. North African men were sent to distant hostels. The local mayor spoke tellingly of 'liquidation', a phrase that turned human beings into a social 'problem' and that carried unfortunate connotations of totalitarian practice.[35]

Changes in the living conditions of migrants were thus quite uneven. Some of them lived in furnished lodging houses where it was common to sleep six or ten to a room. This did not stop French residents in cities such as Marseille from complaining that the municipal authority favoured Algerian newcomers over the needs of locals. Disaster sometimes struck, as during the early hours of 2 January 1970, when five Mauritanian workers died of carbon monoxide poisoning in an overcrowded hostel owned by an exploitative Mauritanian landlord in the Paris suburb of Aubervilliers. The residents merely wanted to keep warm, but because the owner had switched off the electricity, they turned on a car engine to provide a little heat. For a brief moment, the French labour movement got behind African workers, but this support soon evaporated as trade union leaders insisted that acknowledging the exploitation of a specific group only served to divide the working class. This looked suspiciously like a recipe for inaction.[36]

Writers and filmmakers did not shy away from confronting the issues raised by migration. One of the most notable contributions was a semiautobiographical novel by Claire Etcherelli, *Élise ou la vraie vie* (Elise or the real life), which appeared in 1967. Set in the late 1950s, it tells of the struggle of a young woman to adjust to life in Paris. She moves there from the provinces to join her brother, where both find work on the assembly line at the Citroën plant. Her discreet love affair with a young Algerian man, Arezki, opens her eyes to prejudice. The novel, which was turned into a film by Michel Drach in 1970, offered a meditation on different themes, including those of internal migration, colonialism, working-class life, police surveillance of Algerian migrants, and everyday racism. Etcherelli's juxtaposition made for a very powerful statement. Not surprisingly, her book was reviled by the French right. No less remarkable was a 1966 film by Ousmane Sembène, *La Noire de*... (called *Black Girl* in English-speaking countries). It starred Mbissine Thérèse Diop, whose character arrives in Paris with the promise of becoming a nanny but is instead expected to perform the most menial tasks. Seeing no way out of her everyday humiliation and the isolation she endures at the hands of her employers, she kills herself.[37]

Overall, the growth of industry and the broader modernisation of French society after 1945 would have been inconceivable without the supply of labour from France's colonial possessions and from post-independence migration. Migrants were expected to contribute their labour power, and they did indeed perform backbreaking work. Algerians, particularly the harkis, were regarded as part of the vanguard of a new labour force once they had undergone suitable 'preparation'. Hard work by itself was not enough.[38]

Preparation meant more than physical labour combined with vocational training. The French state invested in educational and cultural programmes to enable migrants to adjust. Women were expected to abandon the hijab, to learn to sew European clothes and cook French dishes, and to know how to use domestic appliances as part of what one journalist termed their 'apprenticeship for citizenship and French culture'. A government-sponsored film in 1963 showed two harki children, named Gisèle and Jacques, living with their parents in a small village near Carcassonne. They must come to terms with the French language—implying, in the words of the historian Claire Eldridge, that 'for this family at least, the seeds of successful assimilation had been sown'.[39]

Racist portrayals showed how difficult it was for migrants to assimilate, particularly if they had black skin. *La France étrangère* (Unfamiliar France, 1968), a book by Banine, the nom de plume of a wealthy émigré from Azerbaijan who arrived in France after the Russian Revolution, includes the author's caustic observation of African refuse collectors:

These men were tall, lean and black as shoe polish. It was surreal: in the heart of a beautiful Parisian neighbourhood, a black tribe and a horde of roaring mastodons were looking for garbage. But where are the bows and arrows? They must be rusting in the abandoned villages. In Paris, however, the tribe uses brooms, shovels, wheelbarrows, spades and trowels. They cannot even consult their sorcerers who have been replaced by doctors. So how are they adapting to their new life? We can guess: poorly.[40]

Colonial-era stereotypes were shocking enough, but to see them reproduced in a widely read treatise indicated just how little had changed in public attitudes.

Migration on the scale witnessed in France during these golden years of sustained economic growth posed questions that have not lost their importance in French society. Arguments continued to rage around French citizenship, assimilation, the rights of migrants, and the inculcation of what are deemed to be 'French' values and conduct, areas in which the state intervened emphatically. But the rhetoric of belonging obscured the plight of migrants, many of whom were vulnerable to exploitation. It took little to expose the bedrock of anti-migrant sentiment, or the deeply entrenched discrimination they faced. It also effaced the violence that brought many of them to the metropolis in the first place.

CHAPTER 8

Guest Workers in West Germany: Migration, Miracles, and Missing Out

MIGRATION TO THE NEW Federal Republic of Germany was remarkable. West Germany had admitted millions of German expellees in the 1940s and continued to admit refugees through the 1950s, many of whom were absorbed into the labour market. But its unquenchable thirst for labour resulted in the organised recruitment of foreign workers from the late 1950s until the early 1970s. The arrival of migrant workers from countries in southern and southeastern Europe stood out. Government and employers alike described them as 'guest workers' (*Gastarbeiter*), and the label stuck, because it indicated that their contribution to the host society would be temporary and that they would return home, to be replaced by a fresh supply of labour.

Bilateral agreements between countries were the main instrument for hiring guest workers in what a leading German newspaper described as 'that perennially restless search through Europe's economic hinterlands', areas deemed ripe for the recruitment of 'surplus' labour. Germany recruited guest workers from Italy (with which it concluded a labour recruitment treaty in 1955), Spain and Greece (similar treaties were signed with both countries in 1960), Turkey (the 1961 treaty was revised in 1964), Yugoslavia, Morocco (1963, revised in 1966), Portugal (1964),

Tunisia (1965), and other countries. The prevailing assumption was that workers would not have the right to settle permanently.[1]

It is important to add that Germany was not the only destination country in Europe. As early as 1946, Belgium signed an agreement with Italy. Switzerland, outside the European Economic Community, relied extensively on foreign workers and recorded 1 million foreigners (*Fremdarbeiter*, 'resident aliens'), equivalent to 17 percent of its total population and a third of its labour force. By the end of the 1950s, three-quarters of these foreigners had lived in Switzerland for more than ten years; the remainder held work permits that were subject to annual renewal.[2]

Demand for labour was only half the equation. The question of supply presented a different set of issues for Germany as compared to Britain, France, and the Netherlands, where colonial affiliations gave migrants a claim to citizenship or the right of residence in the 'mother country'. By the same token, there was no colonial 'return' migration; Germany had to go looking for workers abroad. There were, of course, connections with countries from which it sourced labour, notably Italy and Greece, countries that Nazi Germany had invaded and occupied during the Second World War. In the case of Turkey, Germany's economic and commercial ties stretched back to the late nineteenth century. Cultural connections were a different matter: an Algerian or Senegalese worker in Paris or Marseille was able to communicate in French, whereas an Italian or Turkish migrant worker confronted a foreign language. Hence, no discussion of migrant workers can be confined to economics. There were broader questions about their potential contributions to the host society—in other words, what was meant by their 'acceptability' in cultural as well as economic terms.

The term 'guest worker' turned migration into something all too mechanical, as if guest workers were no more than inputs into the production process. What considerations brought these workers to Germany, apart from the needs of employers keen to sustain production and profitability? Politicians and business leaders in West Germany spoke of an 'economic miracle' and acknowledged that guest workers played their part in bringing it about. But alongside this economic transformation, huge social changes were afoot, and migrants were part of this story, too, in ways that were initially unpredictable. What kind of reception were they given in Germany, and how did they negotiate a new environment in which the language was unfamiliar to them?

Debates about policy obscured the fact that guest workers had their own perspectives on migration. Migrants expressed the hope that their lives would take a turn for the better: they might aim to accumulate savings, for example, or to earn enough money for decent clothes or even a car. Debates around the desirability of labour migration were also conducted almost entirely as if it were 'men who migrate, women who wait'. John Berger's famous book, A Seventh Man, gave the impression that guest workers were mainly young men, but this was deceptive: one-third of Italian labour migrants to Switzerland were female, for example, and they felt doubly marginalised, as women and as migrant workers.[3]

Asked in 1965 for his thoughts on the 'problems' posed by guest workers, specifically Italian workers in Switzerland, the Swiss author Max Frisch replied with a brisk observation: 'We asked for hands, but we got people instead.' He was referring to the fact that migrants deliberated about their conditions of work and weighed up the pros and cons of staying put, and of bringing their families to join them. Frisch added that no one should feel threatened and that guest workers made a net contribution to the economy: 'They don't consume prosperity, on the contrary, they are indispensable to it.' This was a remarkably astute and prescient observation, and it was equally true of West Germany.[4]

Between 1955 and 1973, around 14 million guest workers came to West Germany, of whom 11 million, mainly Italian, Greek, and Spanish workers, eventually returned to their countries of origin. By the end of this period, Germany had a foreign population of around 4 million, or around 10 percent of the active labour force. The total number of Turkish workers and their dependents reached 470,000 in 1970, not far short of the other main countries that supplied foreign workers—the number of Italians stood at 574,000, and there were 515,000 Yugoslavs. In the following year, the Turkish population increased by nearly 200,000, whilst the number of other foreign residents remained constant. The upsurge came to an abrupt end in 1973, when the sudden hike in international oil prices sent the global economy into a tailspin. But for more than twenty years the West German economy and society were synonymous with the arrival of workers from other parts of Europe.[5]

Beyond the interests of sovereign states such as West Germany and the interests of migrants themselves, other impulses were at work. Closer economic and political cooperation between European states became something of a mantra. The German minister of labour, Theodor Blank, maintained in 1964 that labour migration not only promoted 'international understanding' but also held out the possibility of closer European integration. He harkened back to the establishment of the European Economic Community through the Treaty of Rome (1957), a key provision of which was an agreement between the six signatories— France, Germany, Italy, Belgium, the Netherlands, and Luxembourg—to enable the free movement of labour among member states over the course of the following decade. Closer integration envisaged intra-community mobility, but the pursuit of economic growth required migration from other sources as well. By the 1970s three-quarters of all foreign workers in the European community hailed from non-EEC countries, particularly Turkish and Greek migrants in Germany and North African migrants in France, raising questions about their long-term presence in Western Europe.[6]

One way of looking at the guest worker phenomenon was to portray it as being in the interests of both the country of prospective emigration and the country that wanted to recruit foreign workers. The former could off-load its surplus workers whilst receiving part of their income in the form of remittances. The latter gained workers without having to pay the costs of their upbringing. But the interests of exporting and importing countries did not necessarily coincide. Countries such as Italy and Turkey did not wish to lose valuable skilled workers, but German firms often sought these qualified workers—whose training had been paid for by the country of origin. Partly for this reason, Germany explored avenues other than formal bilateral agreements, allowing its foreign consulates to issue work permits or tourist visas to individuals with desirable skills.[7]

In 1954 the German foreign minister, Ludwig Erhard, met with his Italian counterpart to negotiate an agreement on behalf of the ruling

Christian Democratic Union (CDU) for the recruitment of between 100,000 and 200,000 Italians to satisfy the demand for labour in German agriculture, where shortages had arisen. The reason for the shortages was that many young men and women preferred moving to towns and cities over working for relatively low wages doing backbreaking farmwork. Those in favour of the deal argued that the regional labour and housing markets were too tight to give unemployed Germans the vacant jobs: according to the historian Ulrich Herbert, 'there were many unemployed in Schleswig-Holstein, for example, but they were needed in the Ruhr region and in Stuttgart, where suitable housing for them was unavailable'; Italian workers, unlike German ones, could be placed in barracks. The German Social Democratic Party (SPD), trade unions and the Ministry of Labour, and the Federal Institute of Labour expressed outrage at Erhard's proposal. Several CDU politicians followed suit, proclaiming that the last German worker should be given a job 'before we can give thought to such matters'. Their objections fell on deaf ears, and Erhard got his way, sweetening the pill by indicating that the recruitment of unskilled foreign workers would go hand in hand with efforts to improve the skills of German workers.[8]

The preamble to this first bilateral agreement spoke of the two countries being 'guided by the desire to promote and deepen relations between their peoples in the spirit of European solidarity...in the endeavour to achieve a high employment rate and to utilise productive potential to the fullest'. The signatories added their 'conviction that these efforts [would] serve the common interests of their peoples and promote their economic and social progress'. A model labour contract was drawn up in cooperation with German trade unions, guaranteeing that wages would be governed by existing agreements. Organised labour remained lukewarm about foreign workers and argued that an increase in domestic wages would attract hidden reserves of German labour. There was no indication at this point that Erhard's agreement would be the first of many more recruitment drives, in Germany and elsewhere.[9]

By the beginning of the 1960s, however, Germany faced a severe labour shortage, with the number of registered job vacancies exceeding the number of those seeking work. Several factors were at work, including the abrupt reversal of refugee arrivals with the building of the Berlin Wall in 1961; the small cohort of young adults who were 'war babies'; improved pensions and retirement provisions, leading to early retirement; expanding educational and training opportunities, which kept young people out of the job market; and a decline in the average number of working hours per week. With no obvious reserves of German labour to plug the gap, employers recruited Italian workers on similar terms and conditions to those of their German counterparts.[10]

The ink was not yet dry on the bilateral agreement with Yugoslavia when the Federal Office for Labour Recruitment (Bundesanstalt für Arbeitsvermittlung) opened new offices in Verona, Athens, Madrid, Istanbul, Lisbon, Tunis, and Casablanca. As the historian Christoph Rass pointed out, 'many of the bilateral agreements allowed officials from labour-sending countries to monitor the treatment of their compatriots working abroad, to set up agencies intended to provide certain social services, and to monitor the migration process. They were intended not only to protect a nation's own citizens but, in many cases, it was hoped that cultural and social links could be kept alive in order to foster labour migration that would turn out to be temporary rather than permanent.'[11]

Germany's recruitment of guest workers from Turkey meant a change of political as well as geographical direction, because it indicated that the German government was prepared to look beyond the frontiers of the European Economic Community. Turkish workers had made their way to Germany in the 1950s—Germany had established an employment agency in Turkey as early as 1946. Guest workers particularly resented the intimate medical examinations they were forced to undergo before being allowed to board the train for Germany—this was a way of 'weeding out' pregnant women and anyone with tuberculosis. Sometimes the grounds for rejection could be entirely arbitrary: a woman from Anatolia who had a scar on her leg was rejected without further ado. Men were instructed to undress in the presence of a female nurse, who translated for the benefit of the male doctor. Years later, the humiliation still rankled with elderly male and female guest workers, particularly because the authorities seemed much less interested in their vocational skills and qualifications than in their medical records. It was not an auspicious start.[12]

Opponents of mass economic migration feared that guest workers might attempt to convert fellow workers to communism. What better way, they asked, for communist secret services to undermine democracy in Western Europe than by infiltrating fifth-columnists in the guise of *Gastarbeiter*? The question went unanswered, and no one appears to have taken it seriously. Instead, and more convincingly, some German business leaders, perhaps with Greece in mind, argued that their presence increased income per capita in the countries of origin, thus indirectly helping to nip any sympathy for communism in the bud. By the same token, the SPD and trade union leaders believed that sustained immigration would strengthen the capitalist class in Germany. Other opinion formers, particularly left-liberals, maintained that Germany had a duty to admit non-Germans to demonstrate that it had buried all vestiges of its Nazi past.[13]

German politicians were also wont to say that the presence of guest workers contributed to 'international understanding', 'friendship', and even 'European integration'. Theodor Blank, the minister of labour, spoke in 1964 of 'the merging together of Europe and the rapprochement between persons of highly diverse backgrounds and cultures in a spirit of friendship'. But how far this was a rhetorical fig leaf is difficult to say: certainly he lost no opportunity to put distance between the 'new' and the 'old' Germany. Whatever Blank's intention, there was not much *public* debate about the merits or otherwise of recruiting guest workers, largely because their presence was expected to be seasonal or at least short-lived.[14]

Who, exactly, were these guest workers? German employers and members of the public regarded migrants from Turkey as simply 'Turks', but although many of them originated from Anatolia, this did not make them ethnically Turkish. Some were ethnic Kurds and Albanians who had been expelled from or had chosen to leave Montenegro, Kosovo, or Macedonia in the interwar period, as a result of 'repatriation' treaties signed between Yugoslavia, Greece, and Turkey. They tended to be literate, semiskilled workers with some experience of heavy-duty work in Turkey: only a minority could be thought of as 'peasants', and many of them had only recently left their villages in central and southern Anatolia after the war.[15]

Although German car manufacturers tended to employ men, other sectors of industry had a more diverse mix. By 1966 more than a quarter of all foreign workers were female (around one-third, in the case of Yugoslav guest workers), and in some companies, such as the pharmaceutical firm Merck, based in Darmstadt, more than a third of the workforce was female. Married women sometimes left prior to their husbands and later helped them learn to cope in Germany. The distinguished Turkish sociologist Nermin Abadan-Unat explained that women were better placed to make this adjustment, because marriage had often already exposed them to a different environment from the one in which they had been raised. Occasionally, Turkish women joined the exodus in their own name. Filiz Y. described how she lost her job in Istanbul in 1964 but immediately applied to the German firm Telefunken in Berlin and was taken on. She told her distraught parents that it was no big deal: she was simply following in the footsteps of other women.[16]

Entire families arrived from Italy and Greece, suggesting that migration was seen as a long-term commitment. There were good reasons to encourage women to join their husbands. Tadeusz Stark, general secretary of the International Catholic Migration Commission and a staunch supporter of international migration, wrote that 'it is only legitimate for a man to try to emigrate in order to assure himself and his children of a better future'. He added that 'the situation may be more difficult if the migrant remains a long time without his family which is left behind in the country of origin'. This was a familiar refrain: workers with families were thought to be not only more productive than single workers but also better 'adjusted' and more 'content'.[17]

The West German employment liaison officers in Istanbul 'painstakingly debated every aspect of worker transportation to West Germany — from calories in the travel provisions to the number of train seats'. Pamphlets stipulated in minute detail what provisions were allowed on board: 150–200 grams of cooked mutton, 150–200 grams of meatballs, 100 grams of liver, 1 kilo Turkish bread, vine leaves, two tomatoes, and so forth. But the best-laid plans were often frustrated by delays in issuing transit visas in Belgrade and Sofia, and no one planned for the lack of fresh water and adequate toilet and washing facilities. The situation was complicated by the fact that Greek and Yugoslav workers also clambered aboard to get back to West Germany after visiting their relatives. The German railway authorities blamed 'backward Mediterraneans' for the poor sanitary conditions of the trains, omitting that many of them were not equipped with the necessary facilities for overnight travel.[18]

German newspapers described the fast trains that brought migrants from Turkey to Germany. Writing in 1969, one journalist made much of the overcrowded compartments and likened his journey to a 'safari'. His remit was to address questions posed by members of the German public: 'Does the "guest worker express train" really resemble a cattle transport for the civilized people of the twentieth century?' 'Is it true in all honesty that no "normal" traveller would dare to travel on this train?' His observations appeared to confirm that conditions left a lot to be desired. What stuck in the memory of Alfredo Giordano, an Italian who took the train to Germany in 1965, was that passengers could not get to the toilet and had to relieve themselves in the corridor.[19]

Italians from the south who took the overnight train to Milan commented on the noise of the city once they arrived, the street lighting, and the billboards advertising consumer goods. Those who had no relatives to stay with ended up in cheap lodgings close to the railway station. The peasant migrants were easily identifiable from their dialects. Instead of asking for the names of workers who had appointments, one worker recalled, a man with a megaphone shouted out company names: 'To the Bremen something factory... to the dockyards... to Opel in Rüsselheim, to Volkswagen in Wolfsburg, to Mercedes and so on.' It didn't help that the German bureaucracy spoke of 'transport lists', a dehumanising phrase that carried negative connotations, reminding some of the Nazi administration of the railways in carrying out the Holocaust during the Second World War.[20]

First impressions definitely mattered. The leading German newspaper, *Handelsblatt*, in an article in September 1955, pointed to the main difference between forced labourers in the Third Reich and guest workers: whereas the former were coerced, the latter arrived voluntarily and could quit if conditions no longer suited them. But this was to see the situation of guest workers in a much-too-favorable light. They could also be dismissed without fanfare. Like many forced labourers, non-German workers lived in barracks or hostels and usually had to obey a curfew. Tellingly, at this early stage the *Handelsblatt* author advised employers to 'put together the necessary information on character, industriousness, family situation, political views, possible criminal record, if any'. As late as 1974, a sign in Braunschweig atop a barbed-wire entrance read '*Gastarbeiterlager*' (camp for guest workers), with a fierce notice in Serbo-Croat warning visitors to obey the rules.[21]

The legal framework itself contained awkward connotations from the Nazi past. In 1951, the German government reintroduced a statute from 1938 that began by stating: 'The residence of foreigners will only be permitted if their character and reason for residence in the Reich guarantees that they are worthy of the hospitality extended towards them.' In 1965, a fresh law omitted the phrase about 'worthiness', substituting the point that a residence permit could be issued to a foreigner provided his or her presence 'does not compromise the interests of the FRG'. This clause put the German state firmly in the driving seat.[22]

Germany's 1965 Law on Foreigners distinguished the rights of citizens from Common Market countries such as Italy from others, making it easier to dismiss the latter when conditions demanded. It also codified the concept of non-permanency, insofar as foreign workers received a residence permit for one year, renewable at the discretion of federal German authorities, and tied to a specific place of work.[23]

Meanwhile, economic critiques of the guest worker phenomenon gathered ground. In an article published in 1967, the economist Carl Föhl argued that the employment of guest workers acted as a deterrent to investing in more modern equipment, and thereby improving labour productivity. Besides, extra resources would need to be found for social overhead spending, to support the growing numbers of guest workers who were likely to remain in Germany. There was the added risk that a failure to improve productivity would have an adverse impact on overall tax revenues.[24]

Men were concentrated overwhelmingly in construction, metalworking, and mining, mostly in the lower-paid jobs requiring heavy lifting, shift work, or assembly-line tasks. Women migrants began to be employed in greater numbers in light industry, such as confectionary and canning, and in the growing service sector, such as hotels and restaurants. Stories soon circulated of the discrimination and humiliation they encountered. German employers refused to take on expectant women, and women who became pregnant were subsequently denied proper health and safety protections. In one extraordinary episode in 1971, a company in Aachen forced migrant women to give up their newborn babies for adoption under the threat of evicting them from company housing.[25]

Women who joined their husbands initially described living 'in the shadows', afraid to step out of the home in case they encountered strange men or had to make conversation with German speakers. Speaking to the anthropologist Werner Schiffauer many years later, Suleika U., who arrived to join her husband in 1972, welcomed the gradual increase in the number of Turkish stores that not only provided familiar goods and services but also offered a place to socialise. As her German improved, so did her self-confidence, and she was able to venture farther afield. Protestant churches helped to some extent, by supporting women workers who faced particular difficulties in making the transition from 'traditional' to 'modern' society and had to negotiate an unfamiliar world.[26]

Oftentimes, however, women were left to their own devices. Turkish mothers in Germany described their struggle to combine child-rearing responsibilities with work outside the home. One mother spoke of having to leave her three-year-old daughter on her own for more than an hour before her shift finished, in the hope that she would stay asleep. She did manage to enlist the help of a sympathetic neighbour, who could let herself into the flat to make sure the toddler was safe. In another instance, a young child was placed with her grandmother, then in a nursery, followed by a spell with an elderly German couple, and finally a Turkish residential home.[27]

Like the ethnic German expellees who had arrived after 1945, guest workers in Germany had to negotiate their relationship with the host population. Psychologist Giacomo Maturi spoke in the early 1960s of the 'eccentricities and differentness of these southern people' who prized 'a more contemplative life'. He elaborated: 'Difficulties arise primarily when one tries to handle these people like Germans.' It was important to offer encouragement and a kind word, he said: 'Equality of rights and compensation is not sufficient for [the guest worker]; he is receptive and looks for a smile from his boss or employer.' Only by taking cultural differences into account could German society foster the 'adaptation' of the workers. Other commentators also focused on questions of personality: Tadeusz Stark, for example, argued that employment planning was all very well, but that governments should allow for the individual migrant's 'desires' as well. This looked remarkably like the attitudes of a colonial power, keen to demonstrate its benevolence whilst keeping migrants in their place.[28]

German newspapers pandered to readers' prejudice and began to comment adversely on the behaviour of foreigners, portraying them as 'noisy', 'unclean', and 'immoral'. Journalists wrote of posters in German factories explaining to Turkish guest workers that they should sit on the toilet seat rather than squat, thereby managing to offend the newcomers, who were in most cases perfectly familiar with modern sanitation. *Handelsblatt* reported on the squalid living conditions of Turkish, Greek, and Moroccan workers in Düsseldorf in February 1967: 'All the men are already in bed, though it's only 8.30 in the evening. What else should they do in this hole?' In the basement of another apartment, there were 'six North Africans, crowded into a tiny room', the paper said: 'The toilet is filthy and so cramped that you can hardly turn around inside.' For this each person paid sixty-five marks in rent per month. These views were inflected by a sense of ethnic hierarchy, as reflected in a cartoon published in 1973 showing two German officials standing in a room of the barracks for guest workers. It depicted just a bunk bed, a chair, three mugs, a pail for slopping out, and a single lightbulb. The caption read: 'Here we can either integrate three Italians, six Greeks or twelve Turks.' Some guest workers were more equal, or 'acceptable', than others.[29]

Officials and employers in Western Europe made a fanfare of new arrivals, and this turned into something of a circus in September 1964, when German employers and government officials decided to celebrate the arrival of the one-millionth guest worker in Germany. The person in question, Armando Rodrigues de Sá, a Portuguese carpenter from Viseu, had left his family behind to take up a job in the Federal Republic. In an

153

ostentatious welcome, devoid of any sense of the difficulties most guest workers faced, Rodrigues received a moped and a bunch of carnations on his arrival in Cologne. A local band played the national anthems of Germany and Portugal. The event was orchestrated by Werner Mühlbradt, the press officer of the BDA (Bundesvereinigung der Deutschen Arbeitgeberverbände), the Confederation of German Employers' Associations. But the point was not just to advertise the prospects for guest workers: Rodrigues was presented as strong, healthy, and determined.[30]

The exercise was repeated in November 1969, when Ismail Babader, a Turkish worker, took the spotlight. The president of the BDA, Josef Stingl, presented him with a television set to celebrate the fact that he was the millionth Turkish guest worker to have arrived since 1957. Yet another flourish followed less than five years later, when Vera Rimski arrived in Munich, having taken the train from Yugoslavia. At the railway station she found the Bavarian minister of labour affairs waiting to greet her as the 'two millionth' guest worker. She, too, received flowers, along with a portable TV. The minister 'thanked the Yugoslav woman and all other *Gastarbeiter* for their significant contribution to the Gross National Product, which had made possible the high standard of living in the Federal Republic'. His statement said nothing about the social or cultural assets that guest workers generated, let alone their own plans and expectations.[31]

Yugoslav filmmakers did more than their Turkish counterparts to address the emotional impact of migration, even if they, too, tended to appropriate migrants' experiences. Krsto Papić made a documentary titled *Specijalni vlakovi* (Special trains, 1971) that drew attention to the humiliation migrant workers endured and the pain of being separated from their families for long stretches of time. On arriving in Munich, the workers he depicts are initially accommodated in the basement of the main railway station, formerly a Second World War air-raid shelter, and given a number to which they have to answer. In his 1982 feature film *Suton*, Goran Paskaljević introduces the audience to a migrant worker who scarcely visits his children; he finally discloses the fact that he has run off with a German woman. The children, who work long hours on the family farm, have to come to terms with the fact that he is unlikely to return to Yugoslavia. Other films treated migration in even more poignant terms. In

Ratko Orozović's short film *Čizme broj 46* (Size 46 boots, 1984), the protagonist pays a short visit to his village, where he is surprised to see a large
pair of boots on the porch. Believing them to have been left outside by his
wife's lover, he leaves his suitcase outside and returns to Germany—not
realising that they belong to his son, who has quickly grown into adoles-
cence during his father's absence.[32]

Labour-exporting countries were not mere onlookers. Italy and Greece
provided prospective guest workers with information about conditions in
Germany. Turkey's political leaders urged migrant workers to be on their
guard against local Germans who might tempt them with 'poisonous
ideas' about the country of their birth: 'They will attempt to alienate our
workers from the work they are doing with promises of money and women,
and try to deceive them by saying that they will find them better jobs. But
more importantly, if encouraged, they will defame our homeland, our
government, our state, our regime, and our glorious army, and will
attempt to lure you away from your straight path.' To this end, the Turkish
government appointed social and cultural attachés as well as religious
'commissioners' to keep an eye on the guest workers. This kind of scrutiny
remained in place, which pointed once again to the way in which migration became entangled with questions of national identity.[33]

Turkey expected that migrant workers would return after a suitable
sojourn in order to contribute to their home country's economic development. In the meantime, the government in Istanbul encouraged guest
workers to put their savings into Turkish banks in Germany, to facilitate
the transfer of remittances to invest in local enterprises. Guest work was
therefore not a one-way street. Remittances by Turkish workers increased
from $45 million in 1964 to $273 million in 1970. By the time new migration came to an abrupt halt in 1973, remittances were thought to be four
times the 1970 amount. Early expectations that returnees would bring
with them a portfolio of new skills and a sense of enterprise when they
returned proved to be overly optimistic, although some of those who
returned later in the 1970s did create small businesses in Turkey.[34]

For their part, guest workers were not passive, either during the hiring
process or once they entered the labour force. Certainly, recruitment officers pursued an aggressive advertising strategy, but guest workers were

equally canny. For example, Italian workers registered with several employment agencies simultaneously, planning to choose the most attractive offer. Some of the Turkish men and women who were rejected following the medical inspection managed to travel to Germany on tourist visas and then to find jobs. Turnover of foreign workers was relatively high, as some employers, such as the chemical conglomerate Merck in Darmstadt, found when they wanted to retain guest workers who had been trained on the job. But firms could not prevent them from looking for better jobs elsewhere, or indeed, from giving up and going home.[35]

Defending the economic interests of guest workers in Germany was another matter. Many guest workers belonged to trade unions, often at the behest of employers who saw this as a means to improve communications between management and workers. However, native German workers did not always welcome the presence of the guest workers on the shop floor: only in 1992 did a Turkish trade unionist succeed in being elected to the executive council of the powerful metalworkers' union.[36]

A desire to ensure that employers abided by hiring agreements provoked migrant workers into taking action. There were several protests in the early 1960s, including a noteworthy stoppage by Italian workers at the Volkswagen plant in Wolfsburg in 1962. In April 1970, Italian and Spanish migrant workers employed by the Geneva-based construction company Murer protested the failure of management to honour the terms on which they had been hired, claiming they were being forced to sleep in huts or former air-raid shelters. Before the unofficial dispute came to an end, some 5,000 mainly foreign workers took part in a massive street demonstration. Guest workers elsewhere organised wildcat strikes protesting summary dismissals and in disputes over labour contracts, as well as over work conditions such as the quality of canteen food and poor medical facilities. A particular bone of contention concerned holiday entitlement and the deductions in pay when workers returned late from visits home. The most famous strike took place at the Ford plant in Cologne in 1973.[37]

Migrant workers who took industrial action risked being dismissed and deported for their 'communist' sympathies. Three hundred Spanish women workers at the Bahlsen biscuit factory in Hannover ('Carmen in the Biscuit Factory' was a common phrase), the first of whom had been recruited in May 1960, were dismissed in April 1967 when they went on strike to protest higher work norms and in support of fellow workers who had been transferred to lower-paid jobs. The factory manager reportedly slapped one woman in the face. As in the Murer dispute, the German trade unions refused to get involved. The ringleaders were dismissed and lost their housing as a result. Many of them went back to Valladolid and Palencia and to the villages around Castile.[38]

What would happen to those who committed to working in Germany for the foreseeable future? As one Turkish guest worker, Fuat Bultan, recalled, the newcomers initially found individual Germans willing to welcome them into German homes. But this did not last long: Turkish guest workers occupied an uncertain position in German society—they were 'wanted but not welcome'. The press carried lurid stories of misconduct towards German women, and although the impact of these charges might be offset by the expectation that the offenders would only be in Germany for a short while, their place would be taken by others who were deemed to be similarly uncouth and unrestrained. In July 1973, *Der Spiegel* carried an article that spoke of 'invasion' and of 'ghettoes' emerging in Berlin, Munich, and Frankfurt. The headline read, 'The Turks Are Coming—Run for Your Lives'.[39]

Turkish guest workers nevertheless portrayed themselves as people with lives beyond the workplace. Those lives extended to the homeland: As consumers, they purchased items to send back home, including kitchen goods, such as meat mincers and pasta makers, and even fashionable undergarments. They advertised the economic advantages that accrued back home, keeping photos of the new homes they built in Turkey, in which they posed on the doorsteps with their children. The Turkish state welcomed this sense of affiliation, believing that it heralded their eventual return to the homeland.[40]

For those who did return, economic pressures in Germany and personal motives were the primary factors. Elderly parents sometimes insisted that their children return home to look after them. Abadan-Unat, the Turkish sociologist, also detected a change in the attitudes of the returning migrants, particularly towards the state: namely, they had a new reluctance to be treated as mere objects and insisted instead that they were active citizens. Migration had broadened their political horizons.[41]

The economic miracle provided growth in terms of both production and consumption: it thrived on a relatively abundant supply of labour that included foreign workers who had been educated and often trained abroad, rather than at German taxpayers' expense. Guest workers helped to sustain this production whilst restricting the unfettered growth of domestic wages. The jobs assigned to them were often arduous and poorly paid by German standards. German workers found it much easier to move into white-collar work, whereas their Turkish counterparts remained trapped. Guest workers were also consumers, but they were not expected to exercise the same kind of consumer power as German households. They paid taxes, but unlike elderly Germans they were not expected to make demands on the state budget, because they would be going home once they were too old to work, if not sooner. Yet these expectations were confounded to the extent that Turkish guest workers were joined by family members.

From a conservative standpoint, the growth in the number of Turkish guest workers amounted to cultural colonisation. They undoubtedly transformed daily life and spending habits by introducing food, music, and other cultural imports that made a permanent mark on Germany. These cultural imports were regarded as 'exotic', at best. To be sure, this did not tell the whole story when it came to cultural imports in Germany during the era. As the historian Karen Schönwälder put it, 'when almost half of the population in 1967 insisted that German cultural life should be kept clean of foreign influence, they most probably had America, Coke and pop music in mind'. Nevertheless, culture could all too easily become a source of mistrust and conflict—'Bockwurst statt Döner', as the right-wing slogan in Germany had it: 'Sausages, not kebabs.'[42]

It was a sign that the presence of guest workers in Germany had the potential to sharpen antagonisms along ethnic lines.

CHAPTER 9

Unsettling the European Periphery:
Migration to the UK

BRITAIN, TOO, HAD GUEST workers—before the 1950s, particularly from Ireland. Although the Irish and the British spoke a common language, the labourers who took the ferry across the Irish Sea were not that different from the guest workers arriving in Germany. They were expected to leave in due course and to be replaced by a fresh cohort. In the 1950s and 1960s, the Irish presence in Britain steadily began to yield in significance to migration from other parts of the world. Many of these migrants expected to stay for a few months or years before returning to their countries of origin, but others planned to make a permanent home in Britain.

There were important differences between guest workers and the steady stream of newcomers from the Caribbean and the Indian subcontinent, many of whom arrived without any firm promise of a job. These men and women came to the UK by virtue of the imperial connections forged between Britain and their countries of origin, connections expressed institutionally in the shape of the British Commonwealth, an association of independent and equal member states that shared a common history of being colonised by Britain and that accepted the British monarch as their figurehead. In keeping with the idea of a multiracial 'family', citizens of the Commonwealth were free to settle temporarily or permanently in the UK. The legacy of colonialism meant that migration of this type to Britain had more in common with what was happening in France at the same time. Like their counterparts in Paris or Marseille, people who arrived from the Commonwealth, and particularly from the Caribbean, spoke the language of the host country, but stood out by virtue of their skin colour.

Stories of migration to Britain spoke of excitement and anticipation. 'London is the place for me'—so sang Aldwyn Roberts, aka 'Lord Kitchener', in a calypso he wrote on board the HMT *Empire Windrush* that docked in Tilbury in June 1948, bringing 492 West Indian passengers to the UK. The event was sufficiently noteworthy for cameras to record their arrival for the newsreels, and Roberts played to the camera by giving an impromptu performance of his new song, complete with an invocation of Britain as the 'mother country'. As if to reinforce the point, the *London Evening Standard* ran the headline 'Welcome Home'. But to allay any suspicion as to their motives, the voiceover on the newsreel made a point of saying that the newcomers had arrived 'with good intent'. Within a few days they were taking tea with the mayor of Lambeth at the Astoria Cinema in Brixton, just south of the River Thames, a sign not only of official approval of their arrival, but also of the gratitude they were expected to show for being able to escape a life of poverty.[1]

As Kitchener's song emphasised, they felt a close attachment to Britain. What this meant in practice was another matter. An unnamed Montserrat-born migrant voiced the uncertainty of migration when he observed that 'the English are a tolerant people for now. But it might go the other way.' Others framed migration as temporary sojourn. 'Don't get too comfortable', the Jamaican-born parents of the writer Colin Grant told him when he was growing up: 'We're only passing through.'[2]

The *Windrush* story is important, but it was only one of many strands of migration to the UK before and after 1945. Britain had long been home to people from all over the world. Liverpool, for example, boasted sizeable communities of Chinese, Irish, Yemeni, and West African migrants, first-generation dockhands and seamen and their descendants. This diversity was evident in the passenger list of the *Empire Windrush*, which included 100 Polish DPs.[3]

To be sure, migrants put down roots in the UK. However, the long history of migration did not betoken any lessening of anxiety on the part of British-born whites about 'newcomers'. Although Displaced Persons and European Volunteer Workers faced a hostile environment when they arrived in the UK in the late 1940s, the situation was different where it concerned 'dark strangers', a phrase the sociologist Sheila Patterson used for the title of her study on West Indian migrants in London. (She was also familiar, through a brief marriage to a Polish officer, with the Polish exile community in Britain.) *Dark Strangers*, in which she anticipated the eventual acceptance of West Indians into British society, belonged to the emerging field of 'race relations', in which race was defined not in terms of biological difference but as a question of social and cultural distinctiveness, a distinctiveness that manifested itself in the behaviour of Caribbean migrants, men in particular. In pursuit of improved race relations, British whites might be encouraged to learn about the 'dark strangers', but the latter were still expected to adapt, and their behaviour became the terrain on which the battle lines of migration were drawn.[4]

Yet the issues around postwar migration first surfaced in relation to Italians and Irish newcomers, not West Indians. Britain had little difficulty recruiting workers from either country. Astonishingly, when their numbers peaked in 1961, Italians made up one-quarter of the foreign migrant labour force in Britain. In the late 1940s, the Ministry of Labour sponsored a series of dedicated 'emigration centres' in Naples and other cities, where prospective migrant workers underwent a medical check. British officials also weeded out those deemed to be politically subversive. Not for the first or last time, migration prompted anxieties about health and public order.[5]

Many of those who obtained work permits found jobs as hospital auxiliaries or as farm labourers, following in the footsteps of Italian POWs who had stayed in Britain after the war. Some joined relatives in the expanding ice-cream business. Bedford—where road signs appeared in Italian as well as English—was a magnet for Italians from Calabria and Sicily, often from the same village. They became the mainstay of the local brick-making industry.[6]

Women, in particular, took advantage of the opportunities provided by organised recruitment schemes to escape. Interviewed by a historical geographer, Kathy Burrell, nearly half a century later, Marietta, a first-generation Italian migrant, explained how as a young teenager she could not wait to leave behind her village in the south of Italy, the Mezzogiorno, although her compatriots in Florence, Milan, and Turin regarded migrants from areas like hers as country bumpkins. Eventually, she and her parents settled in Leicester, and although this kind of prejudice followed them to Britain, emigration opened up new horizons and afforded an opportunity to get ahead.[7]

In an unfamiliar setting, other differences emerged. Migration upset existing gender norms, for example. Italian men recalled how 'in Italy you didn't see any girls going out in the night, to a disco or anything like that, especially on their own, obviously'. This observation could be read as a lament on the part of those who felt that standards of behaviour were declining. But the relaxation in expectations of acceptable conduct also held out new possibilities for socialising, helped by the fact that the cost of entertainment was relatively cheap. Where relations between the sexes were concerned, migration had the potential to change the ground rules.[8]

The most enterprising migrants opened cafés and restaurants and set up new businesses as hairdressers and the like, helped by greater spending power on the part of British consumers. Italians were quick to spot opportunities. The photographer Romano Cagnoni, who joined his English wife in London in 1957, found himself in demand as a wedding photographer for Afro-Caribbean migrants in London's East End; he was taking advantage of the fact that existing studios regularly refused commissions from black customers, who were keen to have high-quality photos to send to family members in the West Indies to communicate their new status. Small firms such as this one became magnets for family members, who joined their relatives in the UK to help out.[9]

Irish migration to the UK stretched back generations. The Common Travel Area, negotiated following the creation of an independent Ireland in 1922, enabled people to travel between the two countries unhindered, although it had been suspended during the Second World War. Between 1946 and 1971, the net outflow of people from Ireland was estimated at

670,000, but more than twice as many men and women left the country at some stage in search of greater opportunities. The UK's Irish-born population stood at just under 1 million, according to the 1971 census, twice as high as it had been twenty years earlier.[10]

Irish migrants did not have to face the challenge of learning a new language. Nevertheless, the palpable shock that migration could still induce among newcomers was reflected in a film by Philip Donnellan, *The Irishmen: An Impression of Exile* (1965), a hard-hitting account of the experience of Irish workers in London. Donnellan focuses on a young fisherman from Connemara who migrates to Britain to work on the excavations for the Victoria Line Underground. 'Where were all the cows?' asks one worker. 'Nothing in sight, all I could see was buildings and tracks. Where were they all leading to?' The normal answer for Irish labourers was penury.[11]

Although many Irish migrants worked in low-wage jobs, as bricklayers or porters in hotels and hospitals, by early 1951 around one in four of them were employed in white-collar work, including engineering and medicine. Irish women, too, arrived in large numbers, working as nurses, midwives, and teachers. Nevertheless, they confronted stereotypes about class differences. Female Irish professionals were quick to assert that 'we weren't all navvies and chambermaids'. It hardly helped that the Irish middle class in places such as London inhabited a different world from that of the migrant newcomers.[12]

The author Brian Keaney recalled that his Irish-born parents viewed their time in Great Britain as only temporary, even after some thirty years: 'As far as they were concerned they weren't living in England at all, just visiting.' One woman described 'a terrible longing to go back to Ireland', even after spending forty years in Britain. Others had a different outlook, such as the newcomer who spoke of having 'a better life in Croydon than in Sligo', referring to a commuter town close to London and a county town on the northwest coast of Ireland, respectively. In one study of nurses and midwives, one of the women interviewed, explaining her decision to leave Ireland years earlier, said: 'I wouldn't marry a farmer, not on your life. You'd have to battle the old mother.' Many of the respondents said they did not like the isolation of small rural communities in Ireland with 'everybody knowing your business'. Common responses were: 'I just couldn't stick that now', and 'I like being *near* home, but not *at* home'. Migration was thus both escape and opportunity. The new National Health Service (NHS) subsidised holiday visits and allowed nurses to accumulate holiday entitlement so that they could make extended trips back to Ireland.[13]

The intense emotional pull that Ireland still exerted on migrants reflected a degree of discomfort in Britain, where, in the words of one sociologist, John Archer Jackson, they were 'in it, but not of it'. If anything, migration reinforced their sense of Irishness, which migrants cultivated through Irish social clubs and other community organisations, rather than weakening it. There was more than a residue in British society of colonial attitudes towards the Irish. At one extreme, Conservative Member of Parliament (MP) Robin Turton declared in 1961 that the Irish were 'far more likely to cause danger of infection to other people'. They were not 'dark strangers', and they were certainly free to come and go, but they nevertheless stood apart from mainstream British society.[14]

The demarcation of migrants according to skin colour was sharp and contentious. It was contentious by virtue of the right of every citizen of the British Commonwealth to settle and work in the UK, as enshrined in the 1948 British Nationality Act. Henry Hopkinson, the minister of state for colonial affairs, confirmed as much in 1954: 'In a world in which restrictions on personal movement and immigration have increased, we still take pride in the fact that a man can say *civis Britannicus sum* ["I am a British citizen", to spin an ancient Latin phrase] whatever his colour may be, and we can take pride in the fact that he wants and can come to the Mother country.' Migrants took advantage of this right and also benefited from the cheap forms of travel made possible by shipping companies, which, to fill empty places on passenger steamers returning from South America, stopped in the Caribbean after taking Spanish and Italian migrants overseas.[15]

The 1951 census recorded 15,300 West Indians in Britain; two decades later, this figure had climbed to 446,200, of whom half had been born in the UK. Many men worked in the postal service or on the London Underground, where London Transport Executive struck a deal with the Barbados Immigrant Liaison Service whereby migrants received a loan to cover the cost of passage, repaying the debt out of their wages. Caribbean women followed their Irish counterparts into nursing, and in 1968, Sislin Fay Allen, originally from Jamaica, became the first black female police officer to join the Metropolitan Police, prompting the inevitable barrage of hate mail.[16]

Almost all the Caribbean migrants maintained strong ties with their family members back home, sending back remittances on a regular basis. (Sislin Allen briefly returned to Jamaica, to join the local police force there, but then resettled in the UK.) Parents often left their younger children behind to be looked after by grandparents, but some of the money they sent enabled family and friends to join them in the UK. The musician and entrepreneur Levi Roots, one of six children, described how his parents came to Britain from Jamaica in 1962: 'The plan was to work hard, buy a house and send for us. Every year, a suitcase would arrive and we would know which one of us was leaving to join them. I was last. I didn't see them again until I was 11. My mum cleaned toilets, worked in hospitals, on the buses, doing menial jobs nobody else would want. My father worked as a pest controller for Lambeth council.' This emphasis on hard work and getting ahead recurs in other migrant testimonies, and sometimes in the well-intentioned but patronising words of white British observers—such as Joyce Egginton, who described West Indians as 'cheerful workers' who wanted to stay out of trouble, a reminder that their conduct was always under scrutiny.[17]

A separate stream carried migrants from the Indian subcontinent to the UK. The 1961 census established that the population of South Asian origin (that is, both immigrant and UK-born) stood at 106,000. Ten years later, the figure had tripled, and by 1981 it reached more than 1 million. This was a very mixed group: it included students, businesspeople, servants, and others. Sylheti migrants, for example, found a niche in the rapidly expanding restaurant and takeaway sector; others were likewise self-employed—for example, as taxi drivers. Sikhs and Muslims from Punjab managed to get ahead by capitalising on higher levels of educational attainment. In Newcastle, Muslim migrants succeeded in setting up their own businesses with the help of family members and friends who provided capital.[18]

Popular attitudes ran counter to the legal position. Opponents of migration made much of 'overcrowded' Britain and its limited 'capacity'. In 1957, in a rhetorical flourish that anticipated the remarks of continental European conservatives, Dame Patricia Hornsby-Smith insisted that 'we are not a country of immigration'. Granted, she conceded that exceptions might need to be made in an emergency, as with the sudden arrival of Anglo-Egyptians who were expelled from Egypt in the wake of the Suez crisis. After all, the crisis had been brought about by the invasion of British, French, and Israeli troops seeking to regain control of the Suez Canal, following its nationalisation by the Egyptian government. They, too, were British subjects, many of them of Maltese heritage, and they had enjoyed a relatively privileged life in Egypt. Some 8,000 were placed in hostels before the government established a Resettlement Board to arrange accommodation and relief payments. More than one in ten subsequently emigrated to a third country. They entered and left with little fanfare, but their odyssey was another manifestation of the residues of empire.[19]

One strand in the emerging restrictionist discourse was that higher rates of immigration would place an intolerable load on the welfare state and the health service, a view that was given additional support by the belief that Commonwealth immigration led to an increase in the incidence of tuberculosis. The British Medical Association spoke of 'a pool of ill-health which is constantly being replenished from abroad', and added that this group was vulnerable to TB by virtue of 'congestion and substandard hygiene' or 'primitive' practices. The irony was that migrant nurses, not only from the Caribbean and Ireland but also from Hong Kong and Malaysia, helped to keep the NHS afloat.[20]

The very idea of a 'national' health service posed questions as to who belonged to the nation. Racialised discourse in the 1950s insisted that black and Asian immigrants were distinct and subordinate groups. In a class-based society, white British workers were expected to do menial tasks, something that was unthinkable in colonial society. The adjustment could be unsettling. A Jamaican migrant who came to the UK in 1955 recalled the lesson she learned upon her arrival: 'I had never hoped to challenge the whites in Jamaica for a job. [But in Britain] if the white man was sweeping the street, then any job I asked for would mean a challenge for him. I was not one of the "mother country's children". I was one of her black children.' She understood that in the UK it was possible to be white and socially inferior to other whites. But her blackness meant that she was always going to be defined by the colour of her skin. She was not part of the effort to build the nation. From this point of view, mass migration from the 'new Commonwealth'—a euphemism for nonwhite migrants—came to be regarded as a 'problem' in and beyond the workplace.[21]

A flurry of strikes in the West Midlands in 1955 came about because officials of the Transport and General Workers Union objected to the employment of an Indian bus conductor. The demands of workers included the call for a tiny quota on 'coloured' workers, partly because of racial prejudice, but also because an increase in the workforce threatened their earnings from working overtime. Civil rights campaigners fought on the other side, however, In a famous bus boycott in 1963 led by the activist Paul Stephenson, Bristolians protested the Bristol Omnibus Company's refusal to employ black or Asian bus crews; the boycott lasted two months, but the firm finally gave in. It showed that collective action by consumers could have a greater impact than working-class solidarity.[22]

Something of the dynamics on the shop floor emerged in a report in 1968 by Sheila Patterson based on her survey of immigrants in British industry. It included an interview with the superintendent of a railway workshop in Croydon, whom she described as 'lively, enthusiastic, tough, well-read and travelled, an ex-naval officer, a Fabian, and a member of many and diverse communities'. Given the opportunity to characterise his role, he said, 'Some of the local lads call me the "Patron Saint of Poland" and "Jesus Christ for the Negroes". I'm a mixture of Irish and Jew myself so I'm more inter-racially minded than the locals.' Speaking of Polish workers, he suggested that 'the local men know the Poles can lick them hands down at the job but this doesn't mean any of them are fully accepted. You might say they're "with us" but not "of us".' In his view, Polish workers were 'clannish', although the ex-officers kept aloof from working-class Poles. Most of them felt threatened by Afro-Caribbean newcomers, who, as Commonwealth subjects, had a prior claim on jobs, but whom the Poles regarded as culturally inferior.[23]

Yet the most significant manifestation of how migration contributed to unsettling Britain was to be found not in the workplace but on the street. Social tensions culminated in race riots in the St Ann's district of Nottingham and in Notting Hill, London, in 1958. The sentences handed down to white assailants provoked claims that they were the real victims. This grotesque fiction became apparent with the racist murder of an Antigua-born man, Kelso Cochrane, in Notting Hill in May 1959. Cochrane, thirty-two years old, was stabbed to death on his way to a hospital appointment. He left behind his fiancée, Olivia Ellington, a trainee nurse from Jamaica. His death immediately prompted speculation that the assailants just wanted money, and that his death had 'absolutely nothing to do with racial conflict'. Black activists responded that the reaction to his murder showed just how systematic the disenfranchisement of black British subjects was. In a speech at the memorial service, Carl La Corbiniere, deputy prime minister of the West Indian Federation, reaffirmed the importance of a Commonwealth 'community' in which everyone enjoyed equal rights. But the atmosphere remained toxic. The Ku Klux Klan tried to inflame public opinion, calling for a 'rally of anti-colour forces', and the notorious fascist politician, Oswald Mosley, stood in the 1959 General Election on a platform to 'keep Britain white'. Amidst the discussion of teenage hooligans ('Teddy boys') and vice, there was even talk of 'communist influence', a reminder that issues of race were often bound up with other anxieties. Despite his mother's wishes that her son's body be taken to Antigua, Cochrane was quietly buried in Kensal Green Cemetery in West London, because the Home Office feared further public demonstrations if his body were removed.[24]

Notting Hill was also the stamping ground of the infamous landlord and racketeer Peter (Perec) Rachman, a Polish Jewish refugee who had endured captivity first by the Germans, and then the Russians, before finding his way to the UK in 1946. Once there, he began to exploit loopholes in the market for rented property, and by 1960 he owned around 150 houses. He used tactics of intimidation to get rid of tenants and bring in others prepared to pay a higher rent. At the time of his death in 1962, he 'still hoarded bread-crusts under his bed as security against starvation'—the kind of behaviour that the anti-immigration brigade

Official from the United Nations Relief and Rehabilitation Administration (UNRRA) in Klagenfurt, Germany. *Haywood Magee / Getty Images.*

Estonian farmworker, Sweden, 1946.
Otto Ohm / Heritage Images / TopFoto.

Latvian farmworker, England, 1948.
Kurt Hutton / Getty Images.

European Volunteer Workers from
Lithuania in England, 1949. *TopFoto.*

Metropolitan police officer from Jamaica in
England, 1968. *TopFoto.*

'Come with us to the Virgin Lands!', Soviet poster, 1954. Russian State Library, Moscow. *Heritage Images / TopFoto.*

Muscovite migrant worker on a state farm in Kazakhstan, 1961. *Sputnik / TopFoto.*

Polish family in Nowa Huta, Silesia, 1956. © *Erich Lessing / Magnum Photos.*

Housing for North African migrants, Nanterre, France, 1955. *AP / Rex / Shutterstock.*

Housing for North African migrants, Nanterre, France, 1979.
© *Ferdinando Scianna / Magnum Photos.*

Italian guest workers, Munich, West Germany, 1960. *Süddeutsche Zeitung Photo / Mary Evans.*

The 'millionth guest worker', Cologne, Germany, 1964. *Picture Alliance / TopFoto.*

Turkish guest worker in West Germany using a compass and qibla indicator to determine the direction of Mecca. *Picture Alliance / TopFoto.*

Language class for Arab-speaking workers, France, 1980s. *Roger-Viollet / TopFoto.*

West German workers,
Stuttgart, Germany, 1966.
Picture Alliance / TopFoto.

Guest workers from Mozambique in
East Germany, 1980s. *Matthias Hiekel /
Bundesarchiv.*

Guest workers from Vietnam in
East Germany, 1980s. *Süddeutsche
Zeitung Photo / Mary Evans.*

Pieds-noirs leave Algeria for France, 1962. *Gamma-Rapho / Getty Images.*

Harki family in Marseille, France, early 1960s. *Gamma-Rapho / Getty Images.*

Asian families from Uganda arrive in Britain, 1972. *AP / TopFoto.*

Riso amaro (Bitter rice), Italy, 1949.
Photo12 / Alamy.

Trzy kobiety (Three women), Poland,
1956. *Filmoteka Narodowa, Warsaw.*

Angst Essen Seele Auf (Fear eats the soul), West
Germany, 1974. *PictureLux / The Hollywood
Archive / Alamy.*

Dirty Pretty Things, United Kingdom,
2002. *Photo12 / Alamy.*

would presumably have found intolerable if it were manifested by a person of colour. At the same time, Notting Hill was also the site of counterprotests in which black and white Londoners came together in a show of solidarity against the far right.[25]

'Rachmanism' became a byword for rogue landlords, but it also drew attention to the importance of housing as a touchstone of 'race relations'. Attempts to address overcrowded dwellings through redevelopment schemes sometimes backfired on established multicultural communities. In Cardiff, a thriving port city in years gone by, the community of Tiger Bay was redeveloped in the 1960s without consultation with its residents. Olive Salaman, who had married a Yemeni in 1937, opened the Cairo Café, which became the hub of the community in the 1950s, as she explained in an interview for a government information film in 1961 about 'Moslems in Cardiff' that painted a positive portrait of the city. Forty years later, she recalled the demolition of her home and her family's forced relocation to a suburb. Slum clearances such as this led working-class residents to speak of 'wholesale emigration', something to be endured rather than celebrated.[26]

Housing was certainly the touchstone of prejudice and of deprivation. It was not just a question of the quality of the housing, but also a question of the availability, affordability, and accessibility of housing. Signs on rental property sometimes specified that people of colour need not apply. Letters to MPs complained about the shortage of housing and jobs, as well as the demands placed on the welfare state, but blamed the government for keeping the door open rather than for its failure to invest in public services. Some politicians argued that improvements to the housing stock would only encourage more immigration.[27]

Amidst all the talk of migration from the new Commonwealth, it was easy to overlook people who arrived from elsewhere. Cypriot migrants had come to the UK in search of work before the Second World War and traditionally worked long hours in dead-end jobs, but the postwar generation instead sought a measure of independence by setting up small businesses. Corner stores, fish and chip shops, and kebab outlets became a familiar sight on the British high street. Women worked as tailors and hairdressers, serving mainly Cypriot customers. In 1961, the Cyprus-born population in the UK numbered close to 100,000, a tenfold increase on its size in 1951. Variously described both as 'white Commonwealth immigrants' and as 'coloured Commonwealth citizens', they encountered prejudicial comments in the media and government circles to the effect that they engaged in criminal activity or were only interested in social security benefits. Moves were made to restrict their right of entry: by 1960, when Cyprus became independent, they had to provide evidence of ability to speak English, along with an affidavit of support in the UK and an agreement to cover the costs of return passage if they could not find a job. Thus unfettered admission was being undermined even before everything changed with the passage of legislation in 1962 doing away with the existing Nationality Act.[28]

At the turn of the decade, the British government decided that enough was enough. A briefing paper prepared by the Home Office justified a shift in the government's position:

> The UK has not been a country of free immigration since 1905. It is generally recognised that in the modern world a State may have to restrict immigration not only for security reasons but on social and economic grounds as well. The UK is a small and densely populated country, with high social standards secured in the Welfare State. The maintenance of these standards is an objective of policy and would not be compatible with allowing anyone to come and settle here who felt inclined to do so.

The unnamed official added that job vacancies were limited and that 'in any case, British subjects from overseas have a prior claim upon our hospitality'. This became the new sticking point: what to do about those with such a claim.[29]

Parliament debated a Commonwealth immigrants bill towards the end of 1961. The context was the growing concern about migration from the 'new Commonwealth', but the immediate backdrop was an outbreak of infectious disease in London and Cardiff. A recently arrived migrant from Pakistan who had contracted smallpox prompted a rapid vaccination campaign to prevent its spread. This campaign, however, was hampered by the reluctance of some of his contacts to come forward, because by doing so they might expose their association with illegal gambling. In a message designed to reassure the population, the Ministry of Health stressed that 'smallpox is not a disease peculiar to immigrants', but others were less measured in their response. A much more serious outbreak in the Yorkshire city of Bradford poisoned the atmosphere in a place that hitherto had a reputation for hospitality towards migrants. The local newspaper bemoaned the absence of border health checks, while the local Tory MP added that 'the Pakistani thought to have brought the disease in stopped in Paris—he could have contaminated the whole of Europe', implying that stricter controls were needed across the continent.[30]

The main point of principle concerned 'primary immigration' from Commonwealth countries. The Conservative backbench MP Cyril Osborne spoke of the 'cancer' of immigration and (happily mixing his metaphors) described the welfare state as a 'honeypot' to those of a 'different standard of civilisation'. Osborne was something of a maverick: he was widely derided as belonging to 'the lunatic fringe', and many politicians and civil servants defended a more liberal approach to immigration. The leader of the opposition, the Labour MP Hugh Gaitskell, described prospective immigrants as 'part of us', whilst Tory MPs, such as Nigel Fisher, pointed out that the proposed bill directly challenged the idea of a 'multi-racial Commonwealth'. Endorsing the legislation, one Conservative MP, Hugh Lucas-Tooth, began by stating that 'all arbitrary control of human movement is repugnant to us. We feel that such control derogates from a man's freedom and from his dignity, whatever the colour of his skin.' However, he went on to say that the present situation discriminated in favour of what he called 'the black people'. In his view, it was intolerable to limit the entry of migrants from continental Europe ('Italy, Spain, where you will') whilst allowing free access to those coming from much farther afield. This approach anticipated a reorientation in British migration policy towards the European Economic Community.[31]

The 1962 legislation imposed immigration controls on anyone other than Commonwealth citizens who had been born in the UK or who held passports issued in the UK. Crucially, it did not apply to citizens of Ireland. Although the act enabled dependents of those already living in Britain to enter the country freely, any adult migrant who intended to work in

Britain could now only do so with a voucher of employment. These permits were to be issued according to the individual's skills and qualifications. The bill also included a clause providing for the deportation of immigrants convicted of an offence where it had taken place within five years of their arrival. Liberal opinion backed this measure as a means of improving race relations, on the grounds that it would remove the 'bad' immigrants while drawing attention to the law-abiding majority. It nevertheless affected people such as Carmen Bryan, a young Jamaican woman who had been living in the UK for two years, and who pleaded guilty to a minor shoplifting charge. She was held in Holloway Prison before being deported, just one casualty of the new politics of migration.[32]

Whereas between 1955 and 1962 around 260,000 West Indians entered Britain, just 64,000 entered between 1962 and 1968. The number fell to a trickle in the 1970s. Meanwhile, the percentage of Britons favouring unlimited entry for 'new Commonwealth' workers declined from 37 percent in 1956 to 10 percent in 1964, and to just 1 percent in 1968. The trend supported the view that intolerant opinion was less the cause than the consequence of restrictionist legislation. Certainly, those in favour of restriction formed 'Immigrant Control Associations' in towns and cities such as Birmingham, where opposition to 'coloured immigration' was accompanied by weasel words about the importance of maintaining good 'race relations'.[33]

Debates around migration were none too subtle. Generalisations about migrants ignored the differences in their background and motivation. An American sociologist, Nancy Foner, found that Jamaican women improved their position relative to men by taking jobs that gave them not only a wage but also a greater degree of control over household resources: 'I have my own pay packet and don't wait on my husband for money', said one. Some of her informants learned to drive and expressed their independence by joining their husbands in the pub and taking up smoking, something that would have been frowned upon in Jamaica. They believed that they had secured better lives for themselves than would have been possible back home.[34]

Serious investigations about how to improve 'race relations' continued to appear, but arguably at least as important was the role of new popular culture in enabling Britain to get to know migrants from the Caribbean. Music was one such conduit. Calypso music connected immigrants from the West Indies with friends and families back home, but it also introduced a white British public to a vigorous musical tradition. Trinidad-born Boscoe Holder was credited with introducing the steel band to Britain through his TV programme, *Bal Creole*. Other well-known figures undermined the stereotype of Afro-Caribbean musicians. Trinidad-born Winifred Atwell moved to the UK in 1946, where she found fame playing popular tunes on the piano for an enthusiastic TV audience. Ironically, she had been trained as a classical pianist, but her husband convinced her that she had a more promising future playing ragtime rather than Ravel.[35]

Like music, film became a means of introducing white audiences to black migrants. Philip Donnellan, mentioned above, made a remarkable film titled *The Colony* (1964). Filmed on location in Birmingham, it represented West Indian immigrants as people from different countries with different backgrounds and motives, rather than as a uniform population. Among others, Victor Williams, a bus conductor from Jamaica; Stan Crooke, a railway signalman from St Kitts; and Polly Perkins, a nurse from Barbados, offered a range of experiences of work as well as trenchant opinions. One unidentified speaker contrasted the curiosity that brought many migrants to the UK with the absence among British people of an 'open mind' towards people of colour. He spoke pointedly of the terms on which he had been enticed to the UK: 'Sometimes we think we shouldn't blame the people because it's we who have come to your country and troubled them. On the other hand, we think if they in the first place had not come to our country and spread the false propaganda, we would never have come to theirs. If we had not come, we would not be the wiser. We would still have the good image of England, thinking that they are what they are not.' *The Colony* thus stood the conventional interrogation of 'newcomers' on its head by asking questions about English national identity and its relation to empire.[36]

Meanwhile, the government attempted to promote greater tolerance. In particular, a series of Race Relations Acts passed beginning in 1965 made discrimination unlawful. But these initiatives were accompanied by fresh restrictions on entry. The 1968 Commonwealth Immigrants Act had devastating consequences for prospective migrants to the UK who had otherwise faced relatively few restrictions on entry, making it incumbent on migrants to demonstrate that they had 'patrial' ties to Britain or at least one grandparent born in Britain. It was a device to discriminate in favour of white Commonwealth citizens, because they could more easily demonstrate a 'close connection' to the UK, either through birth or through parentage. In keeping with a consensus on both left and right in British politics, the Labour home secretary, James Callaghan, argued in favour of restriction as 'our best hope of developing in these islands a multi-racial society'.[37]

The debate over new legislation reflected specific concerns over the right of entry of 200,000 Kenyan Asians who had been expelled from Kenya that year. After attempting to offload them elsewhere, the UK government admitted them and allowed them to work. In public, much was made of their business acumen, the very qualities that exposed them to persecution in the country of their birth. The image of the enterprising migrant only corresponded to part of their experience: most Kenyan Asians struggled to make a living in low-wage jobs. But the fundamental damage had been done. The aim was to limit the entry of any more such migrants to a few thousand persons each year. Although Kenyan Asians rushed to beat the deadline before the 1968 act came into force, it was a further nail in the coffin of Commonwealth migration, hammered home still more by the 1971 Immigration Act.[38]

The other defining moment in the history of postwar migration also came in 1968, in the form of the infamous 'Rivers of Blood' speech by the maverick Conservative MP Enoch Powell. A verbal missile directed in part at the new race relations legislation, Powell's speech was calculated to reassert a vision of Britain, or, in his words, what it meant to be 'a decent, ordinary fellow Englishman', in the light of nonwhite migration. In particular, he targeted the new generation, the children of immigrants: those who were 'native-born' but still 'alien', in his opinion, by virtue of culture and behaviour (he was careful not to talk of biological difference). Legislation that outlawed discrimination protected the status of immigrants, he said, but did nothing to satisfy the English, who now found that 'their wives [were] unable to obtain hospital beds in childbirth, their children unable to obtain school places'. Powell gained an enthusiastic following among dockworkers and the porters in London's Smithfield Market, who considered themselves the embodiment of Englishness. His ideas continued to be recycled by those insisting that migration was the source of social problems. They advocated further restriction rather than investment to build more and better homes, schools, and hospitals, institutions to which, theoretically, migrants had equal access, and to which in practice they contributed as taxpayers and workers.[39]

Four years after he arrived in Britain, Aldwyn Roberts, or 'Kitchener', composed 'Sweet Jamaica', which spoke of the suffering and regret of West Indians who journeyed to the UK, especially the lack of job opportunities. Many of those who stayed on contributed to the growth of the British economy, but they often experienced the effects of racism: inequality, poverty, unemployment, and discrimination, such as the notorious 'stop and search' policy of London's Metropolitan Police. They built the houses, but often had to live in squalid and dangerous accommodation. In January 1981 a terrible house fire in New Cross in southeast London, an area in which the far-right National Front was active, led to the death of thirteen black youths in circumstances that have never been satisfactorily explained. For many newcomers, the hopes they had invested in Britain as 'the place for me', and by extension for their children, were not realised, but betrayed.[40]

For anyone who wanted to loosen the ties between Britain and the 'new Commonwealth', Europe was the obvious place to look for a different relationship. The Conservative government applied to join the European Economic Community in 1961. It was a long, drawn-out, and convoluted process, reflecting, in part, the importance that many politicians and members of the public attached to the Commonwealth. But their objections to closer ties with Europe made less and less sense as trade with the UK's closest neighbours became more and more important.

Prospective membership in the EEC posed important questions about migration, given that the foundational Treaty of Rome (1957) provided for freedom of movement within the Community. This provision raised the political temperature in Britain. A Romanian-born journalist, Paul Einzig, argued that 'the removal of barriers to the immigration of continental labour might induce the worst type of foreign workers to come to Britain'. The eminent Hungarian economist Nicholas Kaldor, a leading figure in the British establishment, struck a similar pose: 'Every inhabitant of the Common Market Area, from Sicily to the Baltic, including also labour from the French West Indies and Guiana, could come to Britain without permit or entry visa, and many would do so for the sake of social-security benefits.' Once again, protecting the existing welfare system served as a mantra to justify controls on migration.[41]

Neither Einzig nor Kaldor had their way, at least not entirely. When the UK did finally join the EEC, on 1 January 1973, the British government declared that it would not countenance freedom of movement for non-patrials, a measure designed to restrict the right of people from the 'new Commonwealth' and to assuage the anxiety of some member states, such as the Netherlands, that black Commonwealth citizens would migrate in large numbers. This stipulation, a core element of the 1971 legislation that came into force on the same date as entry to the EEC, was clearly discriminatory: as was pointed out at the time, 'white citizens of the UK and Colonies who have never settled in this country' enjoyed that right as 'UK nationals'.[42]

Whether Britain's accession to the EEC implied that workers from other member states would cross the English Channel in large numbers remained to be seen. W. R. Böhning, a leading authority on European migration, said that most continental Europeans who came to Britain did so in order to learn the language, not to work. So far as British workers were concerned, the relatively low wages in Europe in the 1960s made it unlikely, in his view, that unskilled workers would be tempted to move in the opposite direction. Rather, those who looked overseas favoured South Africa, Canada, and Australia—a sign of the attraction that countries of white settlement held for people wedded to an imaginary ethnic homogeneity that they believed was being undermined by postcolonial migration to Britain.[43]

CHAPTER 10

Migrants Under Communism

ON EITHER SIDE OF the Iron Curtain, economic modernisation was both cause and consequence of the migration of millions of people from country to city. The results in Eastern Europe were spectacular. Although official statistics tended to exaggerate communist economic achievements, the period from the late 1950s to the early 1970s was one of sustained economic growth in Soviet bloc countries: the Soviet Union, Bulgaria, Czechoslovakia, the German Democratic Republic, Hungary, Poland, and Romania, all of them members of the Warsaw Pact and Comecon, the Council for Mutual Economic Assistance (Albania withdrew from both organisations in 1961). Annual average rates of growth stood at between 4 and 7 percent, higher than in many Western European economies. Communist Yugoslavia, which maintained a nonaligned status and was not part of the Soviet bloc, also made rapid strides. Eastern European countries, most of them a byword for economic backwardness in the first half of the twentieth century, now began to close the gap with the West.[1]

Economic progress in all communist countries depended heavily on substantial and sustained internal migration. With the important exception of Yugoslavia, cross-border migration was virtually impossible. The routes taken by internal migrants, the opportunities available to men and women, and the associated social and economic transformations were enormously significant.

Throughout the Soviet bloc, the overarching framework was determined by the ruling communist parties and by the centrally planned economy. Communist rule was unquestioned except for a small number of dissidents, and the party dictated the overall course in each country. Central planning was somewhat less sclerotic than the political system. By the 1960s, the traditional methods of central economic planning—nonnegotiable targets imposed on state-owned factories and collective farms—were being questioned by reform-minded economists, who also understood that opportunities to transfer labour from low-productivity agriculture to higher-productivity sectors were finite. In other words, the traditional mechanisms whereby rapid economic growth depended upon migration from country to town no longer applied to the same extent as hitherto. But this did not reduce the significance of day-to-day migration.

There was an added dimension to migration, with political implications for the Soviet Union in particular. The Soviet Union was a federation comprising fifteen constituent republics, each of which bore the name of a titular nationality—Russian, Ukrainian, Kazakh, Armenian, and so forth. Each of these ethno-territorial units enjoyed an equal status, at least in theory. Political unity was guaranteed through the dominant role played by the Communist Party at union and republican level. Economic unity was cemented by central plans, also at union and republican level. Political and economic union removed legal obstacles to migration between the republics. Indeed, migration was expected to contribute to the erosion of national consciousness and to cultivate a more cosmopolitan outlook, although most migration took the form of intra- rather than inter-republican mobility.[2]

Soviet-era migration tended to magnify ethnic differences, notably in republics where the growing number of Russians meant a 'dilution' of the titular nationality. Insofar as the settlement of Russians evoked memories of the policies pursued by the tsarist empire, this migration sounded alarm bells among non-Russians in the Soviet Union. The fact that such migration took place ostensibly in support of all-Union economic development did not convince them that it was politically or culturally desirable.

A central tenet of the Communist Party of the Soviet Union was to manage migration by 'scientific' means: that is, identifying sectors and regions where labour was most needed and setting targets for employment, wages, and training programmes accordingly. In practice, incentives were given to workers and technical specialists to move to far-flung parts of the country, particularly to the most inhospitable regions of Russia. Generous wage differentials, accelerated pensions, and other benefits formed part of this package. These practices often had the desired effect — for example, when migrants arrived in new boomtowns associated with rapidly expanding oil and gas production. It did not mean that they stayed to see out their contracts: labour turnover was a constant bugbear for factory managers.[3]

Planners thus had to accept that people needed to be able to exercise a degree of choice, and thus had to offer inducements to get them to work where they were most needed. Not everything could be administratively planned. Stalin had attempted to do so in the late 1930s, by making it a criminal offence to leave one's place of work without permission, but terrorising workers in this way was no longer acceptable in the relatively more relaxed post-Stalin era. Ordinarily, managers of large industrial enterprises, wherever they were located, found informal ways to entice new workers, particularly skilled workers, in order to fulfil the all-important output targets. Migration, whether long-distance or not, seasonal or semipermanent, therefore reflected a degree of competition for workers.

Since one purpose of central economic planning was to redirect part of the rural labour force to areas of greater need, especially in industry and construction, Soviet planners sought to avoid putting intolerable pressure on the urban infrastructure. Two administrative instruments were the internal Soviet passport and the residence permit (*propiska*), although the overall influence of the passport system is debatable. Their chief purpose was to curb overcrowding in Russia's two largest cities, Moscow and Leningrad, partly to monitor the movement of former deportees and convicts, and partly to remove 'socially undesirable elements' such as vagrants and 'parasites' who made no contribution to Soviet society. Inevitably, this did not put a stop to clandestine migration among these migrants and others who wanted to head to the bright lights.[4]

Unhappily for Soviet planners, by the 1960s evidence began to accumulate showing that some parts of the country (such as Uzbekistan) contained pockets of hidden unemployment, whilst factories in other parts (as in Russia's industrial heartland) struggled to find qualified workers to fill the jobs that were available. Little could be done, except to hope that incentives would solve the problem. Meanwhile, rural depopulation was not susceptible to central planning: migration seemed to be running out of control as people opted to migrate 'spontaneously'. Anxieties were expressed that the countryside was bleeding to death as a result of migration to towns and cities.[5]

Between 1956 and 1959 the urban population of the USSR increased by 13 million, and during the 1960s it grew by 36 million. In the Russian Soviet Federated Socialist Republic (RSFSR), the rural population fell from 48 percent of the total in 1959 to just 31 percent by 1979. A natural increase in towns and cities explained only a small part of these changes: overall, some 25 million people moved from the countryside to the cities between 1956 and 1963 alone. The population of Moscow grew by 2 million in the 1970s and 1980s, mainly on account of migration. The fastest rate of increase occurred in the Urals, in Siberia (where peasants left for cities such as Novosibirsk, or Noril'sk in the Far North), and in Central Asia, although population growth was also rapid in the countryside of Kazakhstan because of a high birth rate. Flight from the countryside was also marked in Belarus, Lithuania, and Estonia.[6]

Managed migration entailed addressing the social, economic, and cultural differences between town and country so as to limit uncontrolled rural depopulation, although these efforts did not always succeed. With the relaxation of Stalinism, fresh attempts were made to highlight the causes and costs of rural depopulation, or what was called the 'disappearing' village, a term coined before the Russian Revolution of 1917 and revived during the 1930s before gaining extra currency in the post-Stalin era. The Soviet censuses of 1959 and 1970 put statistical flesh on the bones of debate, demonstrating the decline in the rural population throughout the Soviet Union and the growth of the urban population, partly as a result of natural increase, but even more as a consequence of the flight from the countryside that left behind an ageing population. As the Russian historian Liubov Denisova put it, 'there was no one left to migrate'. A questionnaire issued in the late 1960s to 400,000 migrants in Ukraine detected a wish to improve their wages, living standards, and access to cultural amenities, shops, schools, and clinics. In the country-side, wrote a group of correspondents from Voronezh, 'vodka is the only form of "entertainment".'[7]

Already in the 1950s Khrushchev had attempted to stem the tide of rural depopulation by improving rural living conditions and encouraging the consolidation of villages in order to create economies of scale. The Virgin Lands Campaign drew tractor drivers, mechanics, and skilled workers from other Soviet republics to Kazakhstan in numbers that reached into the thousands in 1967 alone. Efforts intensified in the fol-lowing decade to provide these 'village towns' (*agrogoroda*), with better housing, services, and other amenities. However, they still did not prove popular with Russian peasants, who resented the related decision to aban-don so-called *neperspektivnye*, or 'futureless' villages, some 143,000 of which vanished from the Soviet map. Older peasants remained attached to their homes and expected their children to return in due course. Mikhail Gorbachev, general secretary of the Communist Party of the Soviet Union from 1985 until its dissolution in 1991, revived the policy of consolidation in the late 1980s. Adverts in Soviet newspapers encouraged city dwellers to think of the village as an attractive place to live, with abundant plots of land, animals, and (for young men) a favourable male-to-female ratio. However, anyone whose heart was set on moving to a city, such as Moscow, Kyiv, or Leningrad, only had to find an official to bribe — or at least to persuade to turn a blind eye in situations where the applicant had made a fictitious marriage with a person who already had a right of residence. So the decline in the rural population continued, and the grim reaper completed what industrialisation had begun.[8]

During the 1960s the disappearing or 'dying village' became a recur-rent theme in the literary output of the 'village prose authors' (*derevenshchiki*), chief among them Fedor Abramov and Vasilii Belov. Abramov produced a string of novels that painted prewar collectivisation and late Stalinism in very sombre colours. Belov denounced the corrupting influence of the city on an 'authentic' Russian tradition, suggesting that urbanisation deprived ordinary Russians of a spiritual connection with nature and turned them into a 'rootless' mass; the problem could only be reversed, he said, by reconnecting them to the land. In that sense, migration epitomised a disastrous cultural and religious dismemberment, not just a social and economic rupture. The lament for a lost pastoral world went hand in hand with a belief that urban temptations fostered harmful and antisocial behaviour on the part of migrants, a view particularly associated with the Siberian author and environmental activist Valentin Rasputin. This strand of opinion, not surprisingly, helped animate Russian nationalist politics following the collapse of the Soviet Union.[9]

Russian ditties drew attention to the emotional impact of the loss of young men to the city or the remote construction site:

> *Once there were guys a-plenty*
> *Anywhere you cared to look*
> *But now without some vodka*
> *You won't find one to hook.*
> *I did a lot of singing*
> *But my singing cost me dear*
> *I bid my love farewell, and now*
> *He's far away from here.*

Other witticisms also spoke of the consequences of the unfavourable ratio of women to men:

> *There's loads of girls 'round here*
> *Too many, it's been said*
> *Now word has come from Moscow*
> *It's girls with girls must wed.*

Equally, women spoke of their unwillingness to remain passive in these circumstances, challenging the administration of the collective farm to improve their lot:

I've told the kolkhoz chairman
And the secretary too
If you don't find a guy for me
I'm out of here, I'm through.

Against this backdrop it is perhaps not surprising that women tended to outnumber men among out-migrants during the 1960s and 1970s. In addition, the city afforded an escape from the triple burden of paid work, unpaid housework, and looking after the village plot.[10]

Although a brief lull in urbanisation occurred during the late 1950s, when many Baltic deportees returned from Siberia to the Baltic country-side, the general trend was a drift from the village to the city. The population of Lithuania's three largest cities, Vilnius, Kaunas, and Klaipeda, virtually doubled between 1950 and 1965, leading to a boom in the construction of new housing. One result was that many collective farms were left with few men of working age. Another was the complaint that Russian newcomers jumped the queue in securing apartments. The accusation of Russification began to be heard, not least when compulsory Russian-language teaching was imposed on rural schools virtually devoid of Russian pupils. However, teaching in Russian was not unreasonable, given the need to equip rural students with skills they would need if they were to make their way in the Soviet system.[11]

In Moscow, the new arrivals were colloquially known as *limitchiki*, not to convey a temporary sojourn in the city or to indicate the strain migrants put on the available housing stock, but to confirm the ceiling, or 'limits', that the factory management agreed upon with the planners. Just as during the breakneck industrialisation drive in the 1930s, in later decades Soviet planners put these young, mainly ethnically Russian men to work on the most physically demanding jobs in industry and construction. They lived in dingy hostels in remote suburbs and commuted into the city. Although the planners thought of them as a temporary presence (three years was regarded as the norm), and although the city authorities resisted allowing permanent settlement, many young migrants settled down nonetheless, either by overstaying the visas stamped in their passports, by paying bribes to local officials, or by marrying people with permanent residence rights. This suited employers, who recruited young men in the hope that they would commit to the medium or long term and repay the investment the employer would be making in their education and training. By the late 1980s the total number of migrant workers was put at 11.5 million. Beyond work and training, they were expected to learn about proletarian solidarity—although, unsurprisingly, the most popular leisure activities were participating in organised sports and watching films. It is easy to dismiss this as Soviet propaganda, except that cultural projects designed to introduce migrants to a new lifestyle were part and parcel of a common modernising goal shared by socialist and capitalist countries alike.[12]

Most *limitchiki* came from surrounding regions, but there was also long-distance 'internal immigration'. This sort of migration gave rise to the image of the Soviet *shabashniki* (from the Russian verb *shabashnit*, meaning to have a break from work), seasonal labourers—many of them peasants—who worked in collective brigades, particularly on construction projects and in forestry in the Far North and in Eastern Siberia, as well as in European Russia, where they bypassed the planning system. Their numbers are hard to come by: estimates of the annual total range from half a million to more than 2 million in the 1970s. *Shabashniki* were thought to contribute close to 10 percent of all construction work in the Soviet Union, and even more on the collective farm. Here was another indication of the ways in which official efforts to plan the allocation of Soviet labour could be subverted by personal initiatives that might take workers hundreds or even thousands of miles from home.[13]

As used by Soviet politicians, the term *shabashnik* had pejorative overtones, implying that the individual lacked a proper job or lived dishonestly, securing an income by private negotiation with the factory boss or the foreman on the construction site. Sometimes Russian speakers substituted the word *kalymshik* (from the Russian word for 'dowry') to describe income from dubious sources. In the 1970s, for example, Chechens were lambasted as 'economic migrants', men who were infected by the 'bacillus of acquisitiveness'. According to one observer, they were 'depressingly vain [and] their houses are palaces with swimming pools, wine cellars and garages'. This ostentation did not fit with official ideology, and yet, without the intensive work ethic of migrants in the semiformal economy, the state would not have fulfilled its construction targets.[14]

In the final years of the Soviet Union, the *shabashniki* began to emerge from the shadows. The political and economic reforms Gorbachev introduced, known as *perestroika* (restructuring), relaxed the constraints on Soviet journalism. In 1987, an article titled 'The Life of a *Shabashnik*' appeared in print. The worker in question, given the pseudonym Viktor Gal'chenko, described making—in less than two months on construction sites in Tiumen (Eastern Siberia)—what it would have taken him a year to make in the city. He organised his own work team (*kollektiv*), and they 'worked like madmen'. Gal'chenko explained that, 'of course, we didn't go just to smell the taiga, but we also didn't go only for the money'. He described a sense of adventure and a desire for his fellow workers to test the limits of their endurance. The dramatic economic slump in the 1990s following the disintegration of the Soviet Union largely put an end to this path of migration, thereby limiting the earnings of migrant workers, men in particular.[15]

Housing was a perennial problem. Khrushchev pinned many of his hopes on the construction of mass-produced prefabricated buildings, which were popularly known as *Krushcheby*, a play on his surname and the Russian word for 'slum'. A showpiece development took shape in the Moscow suburb of Cheremushki, immortalised in a musical extravaganza by composer Dmitrii Shostakovich. In 1961 the party promised that 'during the first decade of the building of communism the housing shortage will be eliminated', but this vision did not come to pass. Many city dwellers sought an intermittent escape to the dacha, where they could breathe cleaner air and pick mushrooms to their heart's content. Nevertheless, those families (and there were many of them) that moved from communal apartments to newly built flats of their own welcomed the opportunity to 'migrate'. (In 2017 the Moscow municipality embarked on a controversial consultation exercise which is expected to lead to the demolition of most of the old apartments in favour of more luxury accommodation that can be sold to the new rich, with the prospect of forcing longtime residents to move to new districts where they will have to rebuild social networks.)[16]

The best-known post-Stalinist example of a new, purpose-built Soviet city was the automaking factory town of Togliatti, home of the Volga Automobile Plant in the Samara region. Its population grew from 72,000 in 1959 to 250,000 in 1970, climbing to 630,000 in 1989. Most of this growth was the result of migration. It became a showpiece, partly because of its association with Fiat, but also because of the availability of modern sporting facilities. Closed cities such as Saratov could boast something similar, but this did not lessen the need for residents to make frequent trips to Moscow, where they could be sure of obtaining supplies of fresh meat and sausages—including (thanks to the vagaries of the planned economy) sausages produced in Saratov itself.[17]

In the 1970s the Soviet leadership embarked on yet another campaign, with the same kind of fanfare and bold expectations that had accompanied Khrushchev's Virgin Lands programme twenty-five years earlier. The aim this time was to construct a 2,500 kilometre railway, known as the Baikal-Amur Mainline (BAM), that would cross Siberia and the Far East, supplementing the Trans-Siberian Railway. Leonid Brezhnev included it in the Tenth Five-Year Plan (1976–1980), calling it 'the construction project of the century'. (Earlier efforts to work on the BAM took place after the Second World War employing German and Japanese prisoners of war.) The party offered various inducements to workers to move 'from sunny Moldavia' and other republics to this inhospitable region, including the promise of foreign travel permits and even cars. It was another sign of the Soviet state's appeal to proletarian duty.[18]

As a showcase project, BAM was expected to cement 'family' solidarity between Soviet nationalities. In addition, foreign workers—East Germans, Cubans, and members of other 'fraternal nations'—were invited to participate. Individual voices spoke of a sense of adventure, but the overall experience left the majority disillusioned. In one particularly frank observation, an East German worker complained about the mosquitoes and the mud. To cap it all, the settlements along the length of the railway suffered a drastic decline in population and in some instances became ghost towns after the project had been completed.[19]

Contrary to popular perceptions of communist rule, Soviet-bloc countries did not always create impermeable borders. The Polish historian

Dariusz Stola has questioned the portrayal of communist Poland as 'a country with no exit'. To be sure, with some exceptions, very little emigration occurred in the early phase of communist rule (the exceptions included the expulsion of ethnic Germans and the emigration of elderly Germans in the 'recovered territories' as well as the emigration of Polish Jews, whose exit the government encouraged because it brought scarce foreign exchange from Israel). As in the Soviet Union, travel abroad was deemed by the authorities to be a privilege, not a right. The application process was very cumbersome and often resulted in intensive scrutiny of the individual applicant. In 1954, the passport office of the People's Republic of Poland approved a grand total of fifty-two visits by private citizens who wished to visit Western countries. Virtually all cross-border movements consisted of Soviet military personnel. But this picture changed abruptly following the death of Stalin and during the political thaw that then took place throughout the Soviet bloc. Some migration represented a continuation of postwar policy rather than a departure from it: for example, the West German government negotiated a series of broader agreements for family reunification of ethnic Germans seizing the opportunity created by the economic and political crisis in Poland in 1956. The porous frontier between Poland and the two Germanys contributed to the emigration of Germans from Silesia to North Rhine–Westphalia. In the three decades after 1956, more than 1.2 million ethnic Germans relocated from Poland to the FRG.[20]

De-Stalinisation loosened the controls hitherto imposed by the passport bureau. Poles managed to travel more freely within the Soviet bloc and even to Western countries. Stola talks of 'mobile pioneers' who had been refused visas, but who now took advantage of the more liberal climate in Poland to travel abroad; their success encouraged others to be bolder in making similar requests. The procedures remained bureaucratic, but they no longer reflected the direct control of the Polish secret police. Legislation in 1959 codified the 'right to a passport' and specified the grounds on which a passport could be denied. Passport offices proliferated. Restrictions were eased on trips for business purposes ('socialist cooperation') and for tourism in the Soviet bloc and in Yugoslavia — although some of this 'tourism' was actually a device to engage in petty trade. In 1972 Poland and the GDR signed an agreement relaxing travel restrictions for ordinary citizens in order 'to deepen the strength of fraternal relations'. More than 15 million visits were recorded in the first nine months—and several thousand marriages resulted—although this went only some way to offsetting the lingering tensions caused by the postwar expulsion of Germans by the Polish state. Travel to the West became easier thanks to the Helsinki Accords in 1975.[21]

Applications for permanent departure from Poland continued to attract the attention of government officials. According to Stola, 'the elderly, disabled or those otherwise a burden for the state had the greatest chance for an emigration permit', and applications from young and highly skilled people were less likely to succeed. Family reunification contributed to a spurt in emigration after 1976, the result of a rapprochement between Poland and the Federal Republic of Germany. Around half a million people left Poland for good between 1960 and 1980, at least half of them from three provinces (*voevodships*)—Katowice, Opole, and Olsztyn—that had a substantial residual German population.[22]

Other frontiers were heavily policed, including within the Soviet bloc. A Ukrainian woman spoke of the problems she faced visiting her relatives in Poland before the border opened in 1991: 'It wasn't possible....[Y]ou could pretend that you were going *turystychno* (as a tourist), on your annual vacation....God forbid you said anything [to the Polish border force] about relatives. But if you wanted to see the sights..., they would sometimes let you go.' Generally speaking, however, there was one rule for officials and another for ordinary Ukrainians. On the border between Bulgaria and Turkey, or between Bulgaria and Greece, news occasionally filtered out of young men and women from East Germany, or from Bulgaria itself, who masqueraded as tourists but were sometimes arrested or even shot on sight. According to the writer Kapka Kassabova, 'one of them was a young DJ from Leipzig called Thomas who was mauled by dogs and shot in the leg in 1981. The army took him to Burgas hospital, where his leg was amputated before he was repatriated [to the GDR].' What she described as an opportunistic 'tourism of escape' was a high-risk enterprise.[23]

None of this prevented communist states from trumpeting the doctrine of internationalism. These ideas, circulated widely, promoted the benefits of diverting economic assistance from more developed parts of the Soviet Union to less developed parts, and of enabling Third World migrants and refugees to work and study in the USSR. The Council for Mutual Economic Assistance, Comecon, supported multilateral trade (mainly barter trade) as well as the exchange of ideas and technical specialists between member states, so there was some travel involved. Albanian officials welcomed East German advisers in the 1950s, contrasting them with the Italian colonial experts who were despatched to Albania before the war, or the 'scheming' Yugoslav engineers who came in the late 1940s. But not all experts from elsewhere in the Soviet bloc were treated equally, and some visitors complained about the poor quality of their accommodation and other facilities. They did not stay for very long.[24]

The recruitment of migrant workers to socialist countries was portrayed in part as a 'gift' from the 'Second World' to the 'Third World'. Czechoslovakia devised a programme in the late 1960s to admit and train a new generation of Vietnamese workers. In 1981, the government adopted something more akin to a classic labour recruitment programme, offering four-year contracts to thousands of Vietnamese, who were provided with language courses and a clothing allowance. Three-quarters of the migrants were men, and they were employed in engineering and construction. The same happened in the GDR and Hungary. In a sense, the Soviet bloc not only imported cheap labour but also reproduced a kind of colonial exploitation.[25]

Recent research has uncovered hidden histories of Vietnamese women workers who came to Czechoslovakia to work in textiles. They were not supposed to become pregnant; those who did were expected to return to Vietnam. In general, however, the state ensured that guest workers received the same kinds of benefits that were available to their Czech counterparts. By 1989, as a more liberal economic model gained ground— at which point 30,000 Vietnamese workers were living in Czechoslovakia (along with several thousand Cubans)—Czech enterprises, rather than the state, were made to pay the travel and other costs incurred by guest workers. These workers were employed in small shops and open-air markets, often leaving their children in the care of Czech nannies.[26]

No matter how committed communist regimes were to internationalism, the everyday experience of migrants proved deeply troubling, particularly where people of African and East Asian origin were concerned. Mozambican apprentices in the GDR encountered prejudice on a daily basis, which East German officials blamed on a mixture of youthful exuberance and alcohol. This did not stop them from trotting out stereotypes of African sexual prowess. In June 1986, a twenty-three-year-old Mozambican working at a sawmill in Dessau was thrown off a train and killed by a gang of neo-Nazis. When another young Mozambican man, Carlos Conceicao, was murdered in Stassfurt in 1987, the government told his friends to be more careful; to add insult to injury, they built a sports centre for the exclusive use of local German youth.[27]

Soviet internationalism and education constituted a kind of soft power for communism, enabling hundreds of thousands of students from Eastern Europe and the 'Third World' to pass through Soviet institutions of higher education. During the 1960s and 1970s, under bilateral agreements, students from Vietnam, the USSR, and Cuba flocked by the hundreds to Hungary to attend university. The programme was supposed to demonstrate socialist solidarity, but there were language problems and political differences. The students complained about the weather and said that Hungarian cheese reminded them of the soap in Vietnam. There were stories of discrimination, and interracial marriages took place, which met with disapproval from parents and university authorities. In the 1980s, guest workers arrived from Cuba under bilateral agreements to work in industry, but they were deemed too 'impulsive' and not 'rational'. Socially isolated, they were also targets of violence.[28]

In some instances, students from abroad died while attending university in the Soviet Union, and there was evidence of foul play with racism at the root of the crimes. The deaths provoked mass demonstrations in Soviet university towns and cities. A Ghanaian student, Edmund Assare-Addo, died in Moscow in December 1963, and the death remained unexplained. Two years later, another student from Ghana was murdered, this time in Baku in Azerbaijan. His death provoked anti-Soviet protests and the abrupt departure of Kenyan students. In 1975, Rwandan students in Lviv complained of the taunts they endured from Soviet students. The students at fault maintained that Soviet workers were being denied a place at university and 'consigned to factory work'. This view was shared widely among Soviet citizens, who also felt that educational resources were being invested in people from comfortable backgrounds who contributed nothing of benefit to Soviet society.[29]

Like the Soviet Union, Yugoslavia was divided into constituent republics, each of them ruled by the Communist Party but retaining a degree of independence. Given that they were identified according to nationality, this tended to instil a strong degree of national particularism, such as on the part of Serbian and Croatian leaders. Although the country's leadership under Josip Broz Tito kept the lid on separatist challenges to the Yugoslav federalist structure, the potential remained for division. Here, too, migration could potentially destabilise the political system. The country's readiness to promote emigration, however, meant that migrants could generate earnings from working abroad, and these remittances could strengthen Yugoslavia's overall wealth.

Yugoslavia did not follow the same pattern as other communist countries. Tito rejected the intricate features of central planning in favour of a lighter touch in economic administration. Yugoslavia also adopted a more open stance towards non-communist states. This included its policy towards the mass migration of guest workers to capitalist countries: when Tito relaxed the ban on emigration in 1962, a substantial flow of workers to capitalist countries ensued. Temporary emigration served to minimise unemployment and sustain a flow of hard currency through migrants' remittances. Substantial increases in the number of Yugoslav workers in Germany in the 1960s and early 1970s followed the rapprochement between German chancellor Willy Brandt and Tito. The 1971 census in Yugoslavia recorded 790,000 Yugoslav workers as 'temporarily' employed abroad, one-third of them from Croatia, along with a small but significant group of Roma migrants. They contributed to an upsurge in economic growth, sending millions of deutschmarks back to Yugoslavia and helping the country to offset its trade deficit with Germany.[30]

The authorities in Belgrade nevertheless had some misgivings. They understood that guest workers would be exposed to a capitalist lifestyle, and so it proved: workers returned for brief winter visits often bearing lavish gifts for friends and family. Party leaders continued to hope that the guest workers would be cultural ambassadors for the Yugoslav version of socialism, but the views of the workers themselves were more ambivalent. A forty-year-old bricklayer who had spent four years on building sites in Germany, for example, drew on socialist ideas to complain about the circumstances that compelled him to seek work abroad without adequate recognition or recompense. Blame attached to Yugoslavia for exporting workers and to capitalist countries for taking advantage of their presence. Questioned in 1971, he commented that 'it is a large-scale national shame that foreign states exploit our workforce, which loves to work and gets excellent recognition....I don't know what use this is to our Homeland. And we've become foreign slave labour?'[31]

Any hopes that Yugoslav workers would fly the flag for socialism were soon dashed. A series of surveys in 1972 and 1973 found that Yugoslav workers would not participate in strikes—French trade unions hoped the Yugoslav workers 'would teach [the trade unions] something [about labour militancy]', but instead they were prepared to cross the picket lines. Croatian guest workers spent more time at church services than at union meetings. They also came home with enthusiastic reports of modern enterprises in Germany, Austria, and Sweden, where employers adopted a more rational investment strategy than they had seen at work in Yugoslavia and encouraged greater work discipline than their Yugoslav counterparts, under whose auspices workers' self-management had turned into a byword for corruption. Sometimes migrant workers returned home to face taunts that they had developed a taste for foreign consumer goods.[32]

Often guest workers' education and skills were wasted in their work assignments. A trained pharmacist from the Croatian coastal town of Senj, for example, was obliged to find work in a Mercedes factory in Germany. As he later pointed out, he had 'spent the best years of his life building CAPITALISM'. Ultimately, when many guest workers returned to Yugoslavia, they often proved to be more subversive than supportive of communism. This was just what the communist critics of a lax migration regime had feared. Yugoslavia's economic stagnation in the 1960s and 1970s only reinforced the negative attitudes of the workers. They had to draw on savings, while seeing evidence that members of the Communist Party elite enjoyed unfettered privileges.[33]

Swedish recruitment of workers from Yugoslavia in the late 1960s and 1970s followed consultation with the trade unions. One such agreement concerned the Svenska Fläktfabriken in Växjö (the Swedish fan factory). By 1975, some 37,000 Yugoslav men and women were living in Sweden. One of them, Ivan Stanković, was employed as a sheet-metal worker when the Swedish agents came looking for recruits. Stanković fit the bill perfectly, having been qualified for more than three years. Being recently married and with a young child made him even more desirable, because the 'family man' was regarded as more reliable and responsible: 'I was young and a bit interested in travelling and seeing other countries, people and cultures', he later said. 'I planned in those days [on] staying [abroad] a couple of years, to make some money and go back again. I dreamt about starting my own business.' He was duly summoned for a medical examination and an aptitude test; having satisfied the firm's agents, he then travelled to Sweden, and his family joined him soon afterwards. Young married women had high hopes of finding gainful employment, too, but their travel costs had to be met by deductions from their husbands' wages. Married women gravitated towards textile factories, and by hiring spouses of workers already in the country, the management saved on the costs of labour recruitment abroad. Some guest workers found the housing situation in Växjö difficult and returned to Yugoslavia, but most remained for a few years and sent money back home on a regular basis.[34]

One Serbian villager, Predrag Ilić, arrived with his wife and three children in the Swedish industrial town of Södertälje on the Baltic coast, where he worked on an assembly line for the automaker Saab. He was trying to earn enough money to finish building a new house in his home village, and drove back to the village for a month each summer to add a bit more to it. By 1976, he had already been 'commuting' for eight years, and he expected to do the same for at least five more years. His take-home pay was around five times what he could earn in Yugoslavia. The family kept in touch with Serbia by listening on a secondhand shortwave radio.

After interviewing him, the journalist Jane Kramer wrote: 'Predrag says that no one in Sweden treats him badly. The problem, he says, is that no one seems willing to admit that he is really there'. In Sweden, he and his fellow guest workers were simply known as *invandrare*, immigrants. In 2018, Södertälje reported that two-fifths of its population was foreign-born or had a foreign background, including a significant number of Assyrians. Assyrians first arrived in 1967 as refugees from Turkey and were invited to work in the area. The small community expanded rapidly as a result of the war between Kurdish freedom fighters and the Turkish government during the 1980s.[35]

The presence of Yugoslav guest workers and exiles in Sweden and Germany had political as well as economic implications. In addition to working on the shop floor, they had the potential to raise the political temperature. The increase in numbers led to fears in Western Europe that the communist government in Belgrade could attempt to smuggle political subversives in among the guest workers. Ironically, however, the real threat came from elsewhere. In 1962, a group of anti-communist Croat exiles blew up the Yugoslav mission in Bad Godesberg, and in 1966 the Croatian Revolutionary Brotherhood (Hrvatsko revolucionarno bratstvo) murdered the Yugoslav consul in Stuttgart. Ethno-political rivalries spilled over onto the other side of the Iron Curtain.[36]

Soviet leaders expressed pride in the heterogeneity of the Soviet Union, but other countries in the Soviet bloc did not necessarily follow this example. Poland, Bulgaria, and Hungary were more committed to ethnic homogeneity. Only in the USSR did the political leaders try to give substance to the idea of a friendship of peoples whose intermingling could be sustained by internal migration between the different republics. Beyond the Soviet bloc, Yugoslavia supported a similar doctrine. However, national self-consciousness always lay close to the surface. The communist-era migrant was portrayed as the heroic emblem of economic progress, but could all too easily become the embodiment of cultural and national difference. From this point of view, migration had the potential to destabilise society and the state throughout communist Europe.

PART 3

European Odysseys

1973–1989

CHAPTER 11

A Dual Challenge: Recession and Asylum in Europe

NEARLY TWO DECADES IN which Western European states actively promoted migration came to an abrupt end in 1973. The fundamental cause was the unexpected decision by oil-producing countries in the Middle East to place an embargo on petroleum exports to Western countries that supported Israel during the Arab-Israeli War in October 1973. Oil prices quadrupled within the space of a few months. Economic activity was badly affected: economic growth slowed down and unemployment began to rise inexorably. The European recession lasted longer than a decade, and the economies of Western Europe only began to recover in the mid- to late 1980s. Average unemployment in the European Economic Community stood at below 3 percent in 1973, but rose to nearly 11 percent in 1987.[1]

The crisis had uncomfortable echoes of the Great Depression of the 1930s, when Western governments had reacted in part by imposing tough restrictions on immigration. The question now was whether history would repeat itself. The signs did not look good. In many places, foreign workers were the first to feel the brunt of the recession. The Dutch government imposed visa requirements on migrants from Turkey and Morocco, for example, with the aim of closing the door to new guest workers. A so-called *Anwerbestopp*, or 'recruitment ban', brought an end to the sustained and organised migration of guest workers that had been a feature of German life for two decades. The size of the foreign labour force in the FRG fell from 2.6 million in 1973 to 1.9 million in 1976. The total number of registered seasonal workers plummeted in Switzerland, falling from 188,000 in 1974 to just 90,000 in 1976, although the numbers began to climb again by the end of the decade.[2]

The prolonged recession prompted calls across the German political spectrum to limit new migration. In January 1973, German chancellor Willy Brandt told the Bundestag: 'We should carefully consider where the ability of our society to absorb has been exhausted and where social common sense and responsibility dictate that the process be halted.' Steps were taken to increase the fees for permits issued to workers from outside the EEC. Other German politicians were less circumspect in their choice of words. In 1976, Wolfgang Bodenbender, an adviser to Brandt's German Social Democrat Party, which renewed its coalition government with the liberal Free Democrats, caught something of the mood when he spoke of a 'social time bomb' in the shape of a high birth rate among migrants and the creation of urban ghettos. The explosion could only be prevented by slamming the door shut.[3]

The public mood in Germany did not improve in the short and medium term. Between 1979 and 1982, the proportion of West Germans who supported the return of guest workers to their countries of origin increased from under 40 percent to over 65 percent. Trade unions did little to stand in the way of those who opted to return. The German government encouraged them to return to Turkey, dangling as an incentive the right of immediate access to their accumulated pension contributions. In 1983, Chancellor Helmut Kohl felt able to trumpet the success of what the government termed 'remigration'. However, rather than a dramatic increase, what took place was simply a modest upturn in the rate at which guest workers went back home. In 1985, 213,000 Turkish migrants left for Turkey, but this was not much of an increase on the normal rate of return. Nor did the policy free up jobs for German workers; this outcome was prevented by the depth of the recession, which persisted into the early 1980s, when unemployment reached even higher levels.[4]

Another clear sign of the higher temperature of political rhetoric and the hardening of public attitudes could be detected in Sweden, where the percentage (although not the absolute number) of migrants from non-European countries climbed in the 1970s as the recession discouraged West European migrants from arriving. In 1976, border guards were reportedly instructed to identify non-Nordic citizens 'by observing the hair, shoes, and clothing of tourists'. According to the sociologist Tomas Hammar, suspected persons were stopped and asked to identify themselves, and two thousand people were refused entry. Hammar wrote: 'This procedure thus has had results, but at the cost of embarrassing Nordic citizens with the "wrong" appearance.'[5]

There were other similar straws in the wind, notably in France, where economic woes underlined the determination of the government to be seen to do something.[6] President Valéry Giscard d'Estaing issued a decree on 3 July 1974 'temporarily' banning the recruitment of workers from abroad. (At this stage, foreign workers represented around 7 percent of the French labour force.) It hit younger workers from Morocco and Yugoslavia particularly hard. The ban did not prevent existing workers from bringing immediate family members to join them, nor did it apply to refugees. Needless to say, it could not prevent illegal immigration, either. Nevertheless, it added France to the Europe-wide drive to restrict primary immigration, and the government created a fund to encourage migrant workers to return to their countries of origin.

Further measures followed in 1977, when Jacques Chirac's appointee as secretary of state for the condition of manual labourers, Lionel Stoléru, announced a scheme to give 10,000 francs to immigrants who would return to their home countries. The proposal was aimed primarily at North Africans, in the hope that a million or so of them would agree to the deal. Mass protests in Paris briefly brought together a range of unions and socialist groups under the banner of working-class unity. In a delicious irony, fewer than 58,000 African migrants took up the government's offer, a far cry from 'le million Stoléru'. Instead, Portuguese and Spanish families decided this was too good an offer to miss, and returned to countries that had by then thrown off the shackles of authoritarian rule.[7]

Worse was to come during the 1980s, when the far-right politician Jean-Marie Le Pen whipped up his supporters by claiming that 'increased unemployment, delinquency and insecurity [are] in large measure connected to the constant increase in immigrants'. In September 1986, in order to appeal to voters who were likely to back Le Pen, Minister of the Interior Charles Pasqua (who had nailed his colours to the past ten years earlier, when suggesting that the government would pursue a policy of 'zero immigration') invited foreigners to prove that they could support themselves or else risk deportation. He went further by presenting a bill to Parliament designed to change the automatic right of children born in France to foreign parents to gain French nationality, and to replace this with a 'voluntary request', which might or might not be approved. Mass demonstrations again resulted, and in the light of legal advice, Pasqua chose to retreat. His initiative nevertheless inspired the mayor of the small town of Hautmont in the Nord Pas de Calais region to organise a referendum on asylum and immigration to call for tougher restrictions. In the referendum, nearly nine out of ten people voted in favour. When the courts ruled the referendum invalid on a technicality, the citizens of Hautmont voiced their outrage.[8]

These measures as well as public attitudes appeared to bear out the analysis of political scientist James Hollifield, who identified a 'liberal paradox', by which he meant that firms in Western Europe endorsed minimal barriers to trade, investment, and labour, but a majority of the domestic electorate favoured closure in order to protect their entitlements to welfare and other benefits conferred by citizenship. Countries needed migrant workers, but nation-states did not want to extend citizenship to newcomers.[9]

There was accordingly a gap between rhetoric and practice. Governments might publicly endorse restrictions to reassure nervous domestic electorates, but they did not want to discourage foreign workers from coming, because they would be needed when the economy improved. Nor did democratic politicians endorse compulsory expulsion of guest workers who had legitimate grounds for having arrived. Employers were in no hurry to lose workers and then to have to replace them with new migrants, whose training would impose additional costs. Migrants, for their part, had plenty of incentives to remain in Europe, including emotional and family ties as well as the benefits to which they were entitled, having contributed directly to social insurance schemes and indirectly to economic prosperity. Many decided to stay put and to weather the storm, calculating that if they returned to their countries of origin for short-term respite, they might forfeit the possibility of being allowed back in. With this in mind, and to forestall any future restrictions, they increasingly called upon their dependents to join them under organised schemes of family reunification, such as happened across Western Europe.[10]

It would thus be a mistake to think that the recession changed everything. Notwithstanding the colder economic climate, migration was not a tap that could be turned on and off at a moment's notice. Furthermore, migrants who expected to stay for a few years now decided to settle for good. The refrain of 'rotation migration' was quietly forgotten, and migrants were in Europe to stay. Governments and public opinion took some time to digest the implications.

In any case, measures to restrict mass migration had to be accompanied by efforts to improve the prospects of those migrants who had made a home in Europe. This challenge was not confined to any one country. France, Britain, and the Netherlands had a residual obligation to postcolonial migrants, for example. Germany acknowledged a clear commitment to ethnic Germans. Host countries also understood that it was important for social stability that families should be allowed to stay together, something that had been recognised long before the recession took hold. It was therefore not surprising that in 1979, three years after Bodenbender's speech, Heinz Kühn, a newly appointed commissioner for foreigner affairs, wrote a memorandum in which he sought to calm rather than inflame German public opinion, speaking of the need to integrate migrants who were already settled in Germany. Mainstream politicians increasingly argued that countries of immigration should safeguard the entitlements of those who had already made their home in Western Europe, and who had contributed their labour, sustained domestic consumption, and paid their taxes. Whatever the economic conditions, and notwithstanding the 'liberal paradox', migrants began to attain civil and legal rights.[11]

As the recession began to abate, much more attention focused on the prospects for collective European action, particularly to streamline migration. The basis for cooperation and coordination among members of the European Economic Community had already been established by the Treaty of Rome in 1957, with its vision of 'an ever closer union among the peoples of Europe'. As before, the debates centred on the collective interests of member states, and whether they could be reconciled with the views and objectives of individual states. Ideas of closer economic integration continued to gain traction. Already in 1968, the members of the EEC stipulated that nationals of another member state should be given equal treatment with respect to employment vacancies as nationals of that state. Workers who were injured, who became sick and unable to work, or who lost their jobs retained their residence permits. They had the right to remain in the country when they reached retirement age, provided they had worked there for a minimum of three years. By the end of the decade, therefore, a fairly comprehensive system was in place, including arrangements for family reunification.

As W. R. Böhning, the author of an informative study of the subject, concluded in 1972, freedom of movement represented 'a truly remarkable advance into one of the most sensitive areas of the modern nation-state'. EEC enlargement in 1981, with the admission of Greece, and in 1986, when Portugal and Spain joined, extended the number of countries to which internal freedom of movement applied.[12]

Another major turning point took place in 1985, with the decision reached at Schengen. In essence, the Schengen Agreement epitomised the direction in which the member states of the EEC wished to travel. It created a single area, enabling citizens to cross internal borders without being subjected to border checks. Five states signed up—Belgium, France, Germany, Luxembourg, and the Netherlands—followed by Italy in 1990, and Spain and Portugal in 1991.[13]

Closer European cooperation helped to alter at least some rules of the game, although individual countries continued to insist on the need to safeguard their sovereignty over migration and asylum. Thus, although Schengen was designed to keep border checks for citizens of signatory states to a minimum, it permitted any state to reintroduce border controls for such citizens if deemed necessary to safeguard 'public policy or internal security', much the same provisions as applied in the original Treaty of Rome. There was considerable latitude to interpret this provision in ways that suited national self-interest. In times of emergency, efforts at further harmonisation of policy were likely to take a back seat to the management of migration by the nation-state. Members of the European club decided to put guards on the entrance.[14]

Schengen also instituted common visa arrangements among signatory states to determine the eligibility of third-country nationals (TCNs) for admission. Applicants had to jump through a lot of hoops. Obtaining a Schengen visa was deliberately complicated: it required a valid passport, proof that applicants could support themselves, a contract of employment, salary slips, social security details, travel insurance, and a confirmed reservation for a return trip. Under Article 21, backed by a new Schengen Information System (SIS), officials sought to judge whether the applicant presented 'a risk of illegal immigration or a risk to the security of Member States' as well as to assess whether the applicant demonstrated an intention to leave once the visa had expired.[15]

British prime minister Margaret Thatcher's speech in Bruges in 1988 set the tone for much of the discussion of European migration policy in the years that followed: 'Of course, we want to make it easier for goods to pass through frontiers. Of course, we must make it easier for people to travel throughout the Community', she conceded. 'But it is a matter of plain common sense that we cannot totally abolish frontier controls if we are also to protect our citizens from crime and stop the movement of drugs, of terrorists and of illegal immigrants.' Thatcher was not alone in insisting that each member state should reserve the ultimate right to decide whom to admit, including, where necessary, citizens of other EEC countries.[16]

The new agreements created a stronger political and administrative membrane between the EEC countries and everyone else. As Thatcher pointed out, frontier controls became more, not less, imperative. Coinciding with her Bruges speech, Massimo Pacini, the director of the Agnelli Foundation in Turin, acknowledged that 'it is necessary to have controls at the frontier in order to be in accord with the legislation of the European

Community. Even the Mediterranean can be controlled. If we do not do this, we risk remaining outside of Europe.'[17]

At the same time, Thatcher's words also amounted to a clear statement of what the European Economic Community had already achieved in dismantling restrictions on the movement of goods and people. Her use of the first-person plural, though typical of her rhetorical stance, was in this instance unexceptional. The EEC had committed its members to freedom of movement between member states without limiting their power to restrict such movement where circumstances dictated, let alone encroaching on their right to determine the admission of those seeking asylum from persecution.

Debates in Western Europe around migration were accompanied by a collective concern about how best to manage unauthorised entry. Some of those who hoped to find work in Europe presented themselves as asylum seekers in order to stand a chance of being admitted. It did not take long for the mass media to latch on to this phenomenon. The hitherto widely held belief that the 'deserving' refugee embodied opposition to communism now gave way to the image of the 'illegal immigrant' and the 'bogus' asylum seeker who sought to enter via the back door. This shift had obvious implications for refugees and opened up intense debates as to how states could monitor claims to asylum. West European governments continued to adhere to their obligations under international refugee law, namely, the principle of non-refoulement, which was designed to protect refugees from being returned to their countries of origin against their will. But the asylum seeker still had to prove the validity of his or her claim to recognition, and each state reserved the right to reach a decision. Even if granted asylum, individuals had no guarantee as to the kind of support to expect. So the state held most of the cards.

The process of being granted asylum in West Germany as a political refugee was protracted, partly because of uncertainty in the minds of asylum seekers and their lawyers as to whether it was better to appeal to the Basic Law or to apply under the terms of the UN Refugee Convention, which enlarged the scope of 'persecution', but included temporal and geographical restrictions. Existing legislation maintained the issue of residence permits, subject to the proviso that the foreigner 'does not harm the interests of the Federal Republic of Germany'. The government operated quite generously in continuing its policy of not returning asylum seekers from Eastern Europe whose applications had been turned down, and there had been no complaints in 1968 when the West German government admitted refugees from Czechoslovakia. A new Office for the Recognition of Foreign Refugees, in Zirndorf, determined asylum claims. But the government also needed to reckon with the interests of individual German states. The government of Bavaria, for example, wanted to reserve its position in order not to be 'flooded' by refugees from the Eastern bloc, as it claimed had happened in 1956.[18]

Germany witnessed a rapid increase in applications for asylum from the mid-1970s onwards. The government admitted left-wing activists from Chile after the coup of 1973 but made it clear that these refugees were expected to conduct themselves discreetly and not conduct their political struggle on German soil. Turks, too, claimed asylum, after the military coup in 1980. There was also a rise in applications from Iraq and Vietnam. Vietnamese refugees published graphic accounts of their ordeal, including in refugee camps in Thailand, and when the government of Malaysia threatened to shoot any boat that approached its shores, German public opinion immediately thought of East German border guards. The Christian Democrats (CDU) eventually accepted that Vietnamese refugees should be admitted in addition to existing asylum quotas, on the grounds that this was consistent with its historical support of the victims of communism.[19]

Asylum seekers were nevertheless kept in limbo. The office in Zirndorf became the site of protests by asylum seekers who were kept there for years whilst officials considered their claims. In 1974, the federal government decided that claimants should lodge their claims in the state (i.e., *Land*) where they had arrived, one aim being the need to alleviate the overcrowding in Zirndorf. As pressure increased on state budgets, the well of sympathy dried up. The federal government continued to interpret political persecution in very partisan terms, such that refugees from communism got a much easier ride than refugees from Turkey, a fellow member of NATO, whose government tortured its political opponents. In June 1980, *Der Spiegel* carried an article that castigated Turkish and other migrants who tried to get into Germany by the back door: 'Most asylum seekers throng to the Federal Republic not because of political persecution but rather because they want to earn money.' *Die Zeit* added: 'All of a sudden everyone is talking about the fact that we could be flooded and crushed in our own country by foreign guest workers and their families, by false—and even real—asylum seekers.'[20]

The admission of more 'deserving' refugees to Germany did not happen without objection and even bloodshed. In the early hours of 22 August 1980, a neo-Nazi group attacked a hostel in the Billbrook district of Hamburg, killing two young Vietnamese refugees. It received little publicity. Elsewhere, extremists burned down a building on the outskirts of Stuttgart that housed Ethiopian refugees. Asylum seekers were threatened in other provincial towns as well. At the same time, German asylum policy became more restrictive. The number of claimants dropped after 1980, procedures for screening became faster, and the government was able to take greater recourse to deportation. Against the backdrop of rising domestic unemployment, in 1982 the Federal Republic of Germany passed a Law on Asylum Procedure (*Gesetz über das Asylverfahren*), which introduced restrictions on the employment, residence, and movement of refugees. A decade later, in a constitutional amendment in July 1993, the government introduced various deterrent measures, such as turning down claims for asylum from anyone arriving at the frontier via Poland and the Czech Republic, because these were 'safe third countries'. The government also speeded up the processing of asylum applications.[21]

The stakes involved in determining who was and who was not 'genuine' also became higher in the Netherlands during the 1970s and early 1980s. Few asylum seekers entered the Netherlands prior to that time, apart from a handful of Portuguese war resisters, who quickly found paid work. By 1980, around 3,000 Christian Turks, mainly Syrian Orthodox Christians, but also Armenians, claimed asylum with the backing of churches and secular lobby groups. These supporters publicised dramatic stories of persecution in Turkey and wrote letters stressing the need to adhere to the Dutch tradition of hospitality. But they were countered by local opposition on the grounds that Holland had a 'limited absorption capacity', not least because of rising unemployment. To reinforce the point, opponents maintained that 100,000 Christian Turks were waiting to come to Europe. Many asylum claims were complex, insofar as they included complaints of economic discrimination and loss of income as well as evidence of religious persecution, and only the latter made them eligible under the UN Refugee Convention. To a hard-nosed official, these Christian Turks looked like economic migrants. Only when evidence mounted that the prolonged wait for a decision contributed to—and amounted to—psychological distress did the government finally relent. Even then, the arguments advanced on behalf of Christian Turkish asylum seekers included the suggestion that in their country they had been targeted by 'backward, barbarian and fanatic Mohammedans'. The offer of asylum came with a message about the cultural backwardness and religious extremism of people of Islamic faith, something that was hardly reassuring to the substantial numbers of first- and second-generation Muslim migrants in the Netherlands.[22]

Refugees also made their way to other European countries. Sweden, one of the initial signatories to the 1951 Refugee Convention, had developed a reputation for treating refugees with relative generosity. It adopted an Aliens Act in 1954 that provided information about jobs and offered preliminary lessons in Swedish. Refugees were expected to be (or to become) self-sufficient, but where this was not possible the state stepped in with training courses and financial benefits. Officials prided themselves in the fact that, as was said at the time, 'most of the refugees get integrated in the Swedish economic life after a short time'.[23]

Sweden admitted several thousand refugees from Chile arriving in the wake of the 1973 coup and faced a substantial increase in the number of asylum seekers later in the 1970s and in the 1980s from Bosnia, Eritrea, Ethiopia, Somalia, and Vietnam, as well as in Kurdish refugees from Turkey. The government maintained 9 reception centres in 1985, but this number mushroomed to 135 by 1991. In 1985, taking a leaf out of Germany's book, the Swedish government decided to disperse refugees under the rubric of the 'Whole of Sweden Strategy'. The goal was to distribute the 'burden' of hosting refugees among various municipalities, reversing the previous policy that offered refugees a degree of choice. The policy boosted the population and thus the labour force of municipalities that had suffered an exodus to other parts of the country.[24]

By the late 1980s, however, the tide began to turn. The government expressed concern about the arrival of even small numbers of Afghan refugees: according to a diplomat based in Kabul, 'Swedish border control must improve. One wonders how the [twenty-five] asylum seekers could come all the way to a Swedish airport without having a visa for any country along the way.' The government devoted its efforts to ensuring that Afghan refugees stayed in Pakistan rather than arriving in Europe. In 1989, Sweden adopted a more restrictive policy on refugees, arguing that only a small proportion of asylum seekers now strictly satisfied the criteria of the Refugee Convention. Here, as elsewhere in Europe, the search for ways to deter 'economic migrants' reflected a view that controlled migration was necessary in order to sustain integration and to nip xenophobia in the bud. The government decided to limit the admission of refugees and made refugees wait for up to a year to hear whether they had been granted permission to remain in the country. Swedish policy also insisted that refugees should 'respect the fundamental human-rights values embraced by Swedish society'. But even this was not enough to satisfy the far right: 'How long will it be before our Swedish children will have to turn their faces toward Mecca?', demanded Vivianne Franzén, the leader of the New Democracy Party. As in other Western European countries, mainstream politicians weighed in, complaining that 'bogus' refugees had entered the country.[25]

Britain regularly pointed to a 'proud tradition of asylum', but this claim came unstuck when it played a direct role in displacing civilians whom it had a responsibility to protect. Between 1965 and 1973, thousands of Chagossians were forced to leave the Chagos Archipelago, a remote group of islands in the Indian Ocean that was a British territory. Most of them were relocated in 1966, when the British government handed over the largest island, Diego Garcia, to the United States as part of an agreement between the two countries that enabled the United States to create a naval base in the Indian Ocean. The Chagossians were relocated in Mauritius, which until 1968 was part of the British Empire, but lay some 2,000 kilometres from their homes. They struggled to make ends meet. They were finally granted British citizenship in 2002 and allowed to settle in the UK, where they continued to live on the margins. As one Chagossian put it, 'I don't want to spend the rest of my life in England. I don't feel at home, I can't adapt. I miss my native country—not Mauritius, but my own country.' The prevailing view among those who settled in Britain was that they had exercised a choice to leave Mauritius, but that their initial uprooting from the Chagos Islands had turned them into refugees. Given the British government's refusal to countenance compensation, let alone the return of the Chagossians, this sorry episode not only illustrated how the end of empire displaced civilians but also highlighted the exercise of sovereignty over a powerless population.[26]

The legacy of empire emerged much more dramatically in East Africa, where the British government was taken completely by surprise by Idi Amin's decision in 1972 to expel 'Ugandan Asians' as part of his attempt to redistribute their wealth and 'Africanise' the country. (Amin referred to them as 'British Asians'; mainly from South Asia, they were originally brought in by the British to build railways when Uganda was a British protectorate. Many of them subsequently became successful businesspeople.) Hundreds of these expellees spent months in transit camps in Europe. With no automatic right of entry, some 28,000 of them waiting to get into Britain were finally issued vouchers of admission—others had already anticipated Uganda's measures and moved to the UK as British passport holders. Public opinion came round to the view that Britain had an obligation towards them, particularly as news circulated of Amin's brutal rule. The Asians themselves advertised their affiliation to the UK by virtue of the schooling they had received. As one put it, 'I did Macbeth, Dickens, and Tennyson. I wasn't taught Indian history, but the history of the British Empire.'[27]

Caught up in this frenzy, Mahmood Mamdani, a historian specialising in African history who was himself a Ugandan of Indian descent, concluded that the British 'seemed to be getting ready for us as one prepares for a swarm of locusts'. The government decided to send the Ugandan Asians to resettlement centres—a term that Ugandan Asians themselves had less trouble accepting, because it avoided labelling them as 'refugees'.

The Ugandan Resettlement Board (URB) earmarked places in former army camps, such as Tonfanau in Wales and Greenham Common in Berkshire. Mamdani ended up in a camp at Kensington Barracks in London, which, with its strict hierarchical administration and its emphasis on discipline, provided him with his 'first experience in what it would be like to live in a totalitarian society'. The inmates, Mamdani included, protested at the proposal to move them to a different camp, which would mean unnecessary disruption and an interruption in their children's education. No one he spoke to in the URB could understand their objections, which smacked (he was told) of their 'ingratitude' and 'insubordination'. The British government intended to disperse the Ugandan Asians in towns and cities across the UK, but this only increased the refugees' resolve to settle in cities such as Leicester, where there was already a sizeable community of their compatriots. In the end, their decisions won out over government policy. The local authorities in Leicester acknowledged that the arrival of Ugandan Asians eventually helped revitalise run-down parts of the city.[28]

With the economy in the doldrums, the British government decided it would take in only around half of the Ugandan Asians, the remainder to be dispersed to India, Canada, Sweden, and elsewhere. Community leaders believed that the British media could have done more to advertise their plight, with one telling an interviewer: 'So many of our people are still struggling to make ends meet, they're living in council houses, and their families have broken up, the daughters have run off and left all of this because of the struggles they have faced over here, but you never see that in the paper.' Yet, over time, the dominant image of victimhood was—as in the aforementioned case of Kenyan Asians—replaced by that of the successful, self-made entrepreneur, a kind of model Thatcherite.[29]

The end of US intervention in 1975 and the mass departure of Vietnamese from a country that had been reunited under communist rule created another challenge, one that the British government could not dismiss, because of what it regarded as a clear duty to assist anti-communist refugees. There was another aspect to the crisis caused by the fact that many refugees sought sanctuary in the British colony of Hong Kong, where they were held in appalling conditions to await a decision on their future. British officials, following a steer from Prime Minister Margaret Thatcher, flirted with resettling Vietnamese refugees either on the Solomon Islands or the Falkland Islands. But they yielded in the face of a media campaign designed to highlight the persecution to which the so-called boat people had been exposed. The *Daily Mail* wrote: 'Because we have closed the door to mass immigration — and rightly so — it does not mean we need be deaf to the knocking of some of those whose claim to help requires no passport or birth certificate to establish its piteous authenticity.' In the House of Lords, the Labour peer Lord Elton urged the admission of 'reasonable proportions' of Vietnamese, although he was keen to make the point that 'we are an overcrowded island, and it is vital not to make the mistake that Governments did in the fifties and sixties of contemptuously ignoring public opinion, as they did over the mass New Commonwealth immigration'. Others intervened to stress that Vietnamese refugees were likely to be a 'steady, hard-working labour force, especially if recruited to work in our hospitals, where I am sure they would never go on strike'. The refugees thus benefited from barely disguised racism directed at Afro-Caribbean and South Asian migrants and from a Conservative government drive to defeat trade union militancy.[30]

Fewer than 20,000 Vietnamese refugees were eventually admitted. They met with a mixed response. Kensington Barracks was once more turned into a reception facility. One of these refugees, a boy named Hung Nguyen, remembered being sent off to a school nearby where a teacher named Elizabeth tried to help them make the transition to British life. 'She taught us to use a fork', he recalled. 'We'd never seen one. It looked dangerous. Why would you stick it in your mouth? So we used spoons. After that they hid all the spoons. We stuck the knives in our mouths quite happily, but not forks.' His memory of forced migration was not of a dangerous journey to a place of safety but the cavalier British assumption that along with demonstrating gratitude they needed to be taught a lesson in handling cutlery.[31]

The admission of Vietnamese refugees in Britain, France, and Germany, albeit on nothing like the same scale as their admission to the United States, was turned into a story of official generosity, particularly in providing them with basic accommodation, but also one of self-help and individual success. Granted that governments and voluntary organisations provided support of various kinds, Vietnamese welfare associations and faith-based organisations, such as the Hamburg Vietnamese Refugee Association and the Võ-Việt-Nam Martial Arts Association, played a key role. Not unlike the Ugandan Asians, the refugees themselves figured as authors of their own triumph over adversity, particularly where they could make use of their social capital.[32]

The war in Syria brought memories flooding back for the now elderly Vietnamese who had settled in the UK. 'I cried when I saw the news about Germany taking all those refugees', said one of them. 'I was quite surprised they were that open to that many people. I was really moved by what the Germans did. I think the British could have done more.' In due course, however, the admission of Vietnamese refugees was transformed into a sugarcoated myth of British generosity, part of the constant refrain that the UK had always done its bit, and so it was now up to others to step in.[33]

This depressing picture of individual suffering emerges in a slightly different light when we take account of humanitarian concern. Alongside animosity, it was not difficult to find evidence of local support for refugees, for example, in Britain and Germany. Globally, too, the Vietnamese refugee crisis gave rise to an initiative undertaken by the German journalist Rupert Neudeck, who formed a committee under the title 'A Ship for Vietnam'. In 1979, the group chartered a commercial freighter, *Cap Anamur*, and embarked on a rescue mission in Southeast Asia which claimed to have rescued 10,000 refugees and provided medical treatment for thousands more. Government officials emphasised the need to exercise discretion and caution as individual humanitarians stepped up to do their bit. For Neudeck, the mission evoked memories of events close to home, as he was the son of German expellees from West Prussia. Even those who are sceptical of gestures such as this could acknowledge his contribution to alleviating the suffering of others—the empathy shown by one person with a migrant background towards others in distress.[34]

Meanwhile, individual stories of hazardous escapes from communist Eastern Europe gained less publicity in the 1970s and 1980s than in earlier decades of the Cold War, although one episode bucked the trend, and it briefly turned the international spotlight on Sweden. In 1985, two Polish brothers, fifteen-year-old Adam Zieliński and twelve-year-old Krzysztof Zieliński, sneaked onto a Polish truck that was leaving the port of Świnoujście to head for Sweden. The Polish government attempted to have them brought back, but their parents refused to give permission for their extradition. Adam and Krzysztof spent three months in a Swedish 'integration camp'. They were refused asylum twice, but because the Polish authorities revoked the parents' rights over their children, the boys were allowed to stay in Sweden, where they were adopted by a foster family. A feature film recounting their journey, *300 mil do nieba* (300 miles to heaven, directed by Maciej Dejczer), appeared in 1989 and proved very popular with Polish audiences. In a 2015 interview, Krzysztof Zieliński, by then in his early forties, stated, 'Today I know that I don't fit in either in Poland or in Sweden. I am in between these two countries.'[35]

Dramatic escapes such as this grabbed headlines, but other kinds of upheaval emerged in the testimony of ordinary people who had to negotiate complicated circumstances not of their own choosing. Consider, for example, the life story of Kamilla, who was born in Germany in 1945 but raised in Hungary. At the age of sixteen she learned that she was the illegitimate daughter of a German couple who had abandoned her at a clinic, where she was rescued by a Hungarian doctor. Later she was adopted by a Hungarian couple. As a young adult with a talent for singing, she joined a dance company that performed in the West and sought asylum in Italy. At that point, she unwittingly became ensnared in a tax fraud case in Hungary. Kamilla continued to live in Italy following her brief marriage to an Italian, but she also lived intermittently in Germany and South Africa. She felt guilty at having severed personal contact with her parents. Little in her life suggested stability: 'Since I left Hungary I've been fighting to overcome the difficulties of life. Nothing worked out the way it should have.' It was a poignant admission that, although refugees from communism might find a place to live, this was no guarantee that they felt they belonged anywhere.[36]

CHAPTER 12

Unsettling Southern Europe

POVERTY AND BACKWARDNESS IN Europe's Mediterranean countries had for decades prompted people to leave in search of a brighter
future elsewhere. Emigration was traditionally seen as a route out of poverty, swelling the numbers of Spaniards and Italians in the Americas, for
example, and Greeks in Australia. Politics exerted a significant effect as
well, as the opponents of authoritarian regimes in Spain, Portugal, and
Greece sought a means of escape from oppression. In Cyprus, political
and economic motives led Greek and Turkish Cypriots to seek out new
opportunities overseas, and the Turkish invasion of 1974 convulsed the
entire island.

But the picture is more nuanced than this. Internal migration played
a big part in unsettling southern Europe. In Italy, for example, people
moved from the south to the north of the country in hopes of earning
higher wages and boosting their standard of living, sometimes bringing
family members with them, and sometimes leaving them behind and
sending money back to support them. The modernisation of urban infrastructure and better access to education and health services encouraged
people to raise their sights. Once a few of these pioneers made their way
to the towns, they fed information back to the village, encouraging others
to follow in their footsteps.[1]

Internal migration provided the necessary labour force for Italy's steel industry, automobile production, and construction. Peasants moved to the city; people from the south moved to the north. After the Second World War the Italian south remained predominantly a country of subsistence farming alongside a rural proletariat that struggled to make ends meet on low wages. Peasant farmers made up the bulk of those who migrated. Entire villages and towns came to be known as 'Paesi Fiat', sending young men to work in the car factories in and around Turin. The hilly countryside of Piedmont also supplied part of the growing labour force in nearby Turin. The population of Turin doubled between 1950 and 1970, mainly owing to the migration of around 700,000 people from the south, as well as others from the northeast. Not for nothing did contemporaries speak of Turin as Italy's 'third southern city'.[2]

One of the most important results was a reduction in economic disparities between north and south: in the early 1950s output per person in the south was only half what it was in the north, and by the early 1970s the gap had narrowed to two-thirds. But this came at a cost. Migrants who left Sicily for Turin and Genoa lamented that their villages had been decimated, claiming that it was mostly old men who were left behind, propping up the bar.[3]

The first generation faced miserable living conditions as they made the transition from countryside to city. Migrants from the south lived in ramshackle dwellings in Turin and Milan, and by 1960 the number had reached 100,000 in Rome. To its credit, the Italian government created new infrastructure, including schools and hospitals, to cope with the new urban population. The Catholic Church also paid for child care and free schooling, as well as offering other financial help, in order to protect migrants from destitution and with an eye to preventing their political radicalisation.[4]

Internal migration thus enabled Italian enterprises to capitalise on cheap supplies of labour, just like their counterparts in Germany and elsewhere. This economic transformation found its greatest expression in the manufacturing centres in the north of the country. The impact on individual families was captured in the memoir of Antonio Antonuzzo, who moved from a village in Tuscany to take a job at the Alfa Romeo factory in Milan. He described feeling as if he were 'in a forest where there was not a single living being'. However, factory life was also his introduction to trade union activism, and thus to solidarity of a very different kind from what he had known in rural Italy.[5]

The consequences manifested themselves in the behaviour of factory workers, particularly during episodes of industrial unrest, such as in 1969 in the Fiat factories and other locations. In his memoirs, Mario Mosca, one of the leaders of the unofficial trade union at Pirelli in the Milan suburb of Bicocca in 1968, recounted the public shaming of workers who refused to join the strike. This behaviour reminded him of a *tamplà*, or charivari, with which he was familiar from his village in the Polesine region, a poor area with a tradition of rural radicalism. His own father, a farmworker, was a staunch communist. Following the dramatic floods that hit the Po Valley in 1951, the entire family decided to leave, and in 1955 Mosca found his first job at a furniture factory near Milan.[6]

Migrant workers in Milan decided to build cheap houses on land they bought with their savings, but without planning consent: these dwellings were called *coree*, since they first made an appearance during the Korean War. Others, such as a worker named Vito from the village of Cavarzere in the Veneto, who migrated to Milan, ended up sleeping in the cellars of the houses they were building on construction sites. Vito cooked his meals on a camping stove in one of the homes under construction while at the same time building a place for his own family to live on a small plot of land he was able to purchase. He hoped his wife and three daughters would be able to join him, and that the daughters would also be able to work in Milan. After twenty-four years of marriage, perhaps he and his wife would finally be able to swap their straw mattress for a proper bed. But they faced other challenges, too. There was little in the way of a decent health service, and there was mutual incomprehension between immigrant children and the northerners in the school system. Other accounts also pointed to the cultural obstacles migrant children faced. The Italian author Gino Chiellino described how his parents sent him to a Christian boarding school 500 kilometres from his home in Calabria. At home he had spoken the local language, to which he was deeply attached, but in his new school he 'made the full transition to Italian overnight, almost without noticing it.... [S]peaking in our mother tongue was defined as a sin which one had to confess in the confessional.'[7]

Meanwhile, some of the classics of European cinema captured the cultural dimensions of migration. The lives of successive generations of migrant women from the south, known as *mondine*, who laboured in the rice fields of the Po Valley in Piedmont—and whose songs became an important part of the repertoire of Italian performers in Italy and beyond—emerged in *Riso Amaro* (Bitter rice, 1949), directed by Giuseppe de Santis. The film portrays something of their lives in a neo-realist style, with a strong dose of melodrama that turns upon the female protagonist's encounter with a petty criminal. Likewise, Luchino Visconti's film *Rocco e i suoi Fratelli* (Rocco and his brothers, 1960) tells of the Parondi family—a widow and her four sons—migrating from southern Italy to Milan to join another son. Visconti depicts the harsh realities of migration, including its potential to corrode the relationship between siblings in an environment that is no longer governed by the rules of peasant society. Among many other remarkable elements is Visconti's decision to show the limited options available to this family, which has to rely on the uncertain income of one of the sons, who takes up boxing. The brothers yearn for the life they have left behind, a 'land of olives, moonlight and rainbows'.[8]

Internal migration in Spain likewise reflected a growing demand for labour in manufacturing, construction, and the service sector. Spanish farmers adopted labour-saving devices, and the industrial sector offered the prospect of higher wages. The proportion of people living in rural areas fell from one-half in 1950 to one-quarter by the end of the century. Catalonia absorbed peasants from impoverished Andalusia in the 1950s and early 1960s. Young people were more likely than older ones to leave the countryside (women, in particular, relished the chance of a different lifestyle), and this contributed to a fall in the crude birth rate. The reasons for the drift from country to town were not hard to detect.

Rural depopulation in Spain and Portugal gathered pace even under the dictatorships of Franco and Salazar, although both of them praised rural life as the bedrock of the nation. A leading member of the Franco regime urged resistance to the 'turbulent, proletarian city of the masses', adding that 'if we do not stop even in an artificial and provisional way this tremendous rural exodus we will end up ruining the countryside'. But neither dictator was able to stop the tide of urbanisation even as they lamented its supposedly corrosive consequences. Migrants, needless to say, felt the consequences of upheaval directly. A Spanish woman who migrated from the north of the country to Andalusia 'felt like crying when she came here because she couldn't understand a word. It was like a different language to her.'[9]

Shantytowns (*chabolas*) became a familiar feature of the urban landscape of Spain. These included Orcasitas in Madrid, Otxarkoaga in Bilbao, and Somorrostro and el Camp de la Bota in Barcelona. This trend began under Franco. Orcasitas grew rapidly between 1955 and 1962, but it was only the tip of a large iceberg. A series of government enquiries uncovered a lack of basic amenities in these areas, such as running water, but new migrants privately described a preference for the anonymity of a large city, where they were less likely to suffer the intrusive presence of the Catholic priest or the local policeman. They could also live in close proximity to their place of work. Neighbourhood associations sprang up to support new arrivals. Bars and cafés served traditional drinks and dishes from Andalusia, Asturias, and Extremadura, sustaining a sense of sociability and solidarity. Ultimately, these experiments in local self-government and entrepreneurship on the part of migrants from the Spanish countryside, and their claims for recognition, contributed to the struggle for democracy. As the leader of one neighbourhood association put it in 1975, 'when he returns from the factory the worker turns into a citizen'. Discussions about the need for urban reconstruction and renewal became a lesson in democratisation.[10]

The same pattern can be observed in Portugal. The population of Lisbon and its environs grew from around 600,000 to 800,000 in the space of two decades. This growth was largely due to migrants abandoning the backward villages of Alentejo for shantytowns and prefabricated housing close to Lisbon. The new arrivals joined protest movements, denouncing property speculators, seizing empty apartments (particularly during the

1974–1975 political transition), and eventually extracting concessions from local and central government at a time of great political uncertainty. Internal migration was no less momentous than the more visible manifestations of emigration.[11]

Nevertheless, southern Europe remained a cauldron of emigration. Seven million Italians left Italy between 1945 and 1975, some of them opting to emigrate permanently to South America, Australia, or North America under the auspices of the Intergovernmental Committee for European Migration. But the migration of Italians within Europe was even more impressive than this overseas migration, as workers looked to opportunities in Switzerland, France, Germany, and Austria. In the 1950s, the French government handed out short-term, renewable residence permits, and after five years the migrants who received them could move to jobs anywhere in the country. The momentum continued in the 1960s, when 490,000 Italian newcomers arrived in France. The French census in 1971 counted 700,000 Italians, although Italian migrants were by then beginning to favour Germany and Switzerland instead. Germany provided Italian apprentices with on-the-job training in construction, mining, or metallurgy, and the Italian government hoped they would in due course return home. Female migrants moved for a variety of reasons: some to earn money, others to escape parental control or simply to embark on an adventure. Hopes of greater independence led Italian women to seek work in a range of occupations, including in factories, in hotels and catering, and in domestic service.[12]

A study by the Italian demographer Massimo Livi-Bacci in 1972 pointed to the economic and social significance of emigration from southern Europe. In particular, the remittances of migrant workers helped to offset a negative balance of payments in the labour-exporting countries. In the case of Portugal, remittances helped the country to cover the costs of its colonial wars.[13]

The size of these transfers, organised by an extensive banking system, reflected the fact that workers had left family members behind. Migrants were prepared to make sacrifices in terms of their own living standards, forgoing consumption in order to sustain their dependents, with whom they hoped to reunite in due course. Some of their earnings, of course, stayed in the host economy. Young single men, in particular, wanted to buy furniture, bicycles, and record players. But it was different for married couples: an Italian woman working in Switzerland spoke for many others when she said, 'We make sacrifices, we don't go out much.'[14]

The right-wing regimes that prevailed in southern Europe for much of this period looked on emigration with some dismay. The presence of so many migrants in capitalist countries appeared to reflect economic failure on the part of their own countries. As Livi-Bacci pointed out, 'the emigrant never helps to embellish the social and economic image of the country of origin'. Nevertheless, emigration did yield economic benefits for the exporting country. Livi-Bacci noted, 'The potential emigrant who is unemployed or underemployed in his home country has to be regarded as a machine lying idle while having to be kept and repaired. It is only too obvious, also, that renting the machine to somebody, who can use it and pay a price for it, is a good business.'[15]

The depopulation of Portugal and Spain reflected not only their impoverishment but also their harsh political climate. The exodus from Portugal peaked between 1963 and 1973, when around 1.5 million people left for France, Germany, and the Benelux countries, a figure not far short of one-fifth of Portugal's total population. Spain officially recorded 1.6 million migrants to Western Europe between 1959 and 1971, although the regular return of migrants brought the net exodus down to 950,000. The province of Andalusia alone contributed one-third of the total migration from Spain to other European countries, with Valencia and Murcia making up another one-third.[16]

Up to a point, Franco encouraged emigration from Spain, entrusting its management to the Instituto Español de Emigración (IEE, Spanish Emigration Institute), founded in 1956, which issued approved workers with a so-called 'E-Pass'. Prospective migrants had to undergo a medical examination, which weeded out one in ten applicants. Not everything was tightly controlled, however. Many Spanish migrants arrived in Western Europe without a work contract or residence permit. In Portugal, the countryside was emptied as young men moved to other countries in order to evade conscription; they thus avoided being sent to fight in Salazar's colonial wars. Some 80,000 Portuguese war resisters sought refuge in France. Thousands more were permitted to stay in the Netherlands, albeit without the formal status of refugees. Artists and intellectuals likewise opted for a freer life elsewhere. Smugglers took migrants across the Pyrenees to France and unceremoniously dumped them in places where they could avoid detection.[17]

Workers from Spain and Portugal found clandestine means of escape from poverty or political oppression. Anti-fascists supported migrants who sought to cross into France. In the late 1960s, France was home to 600,000 immigrants from Spain and 480,000 from Portugal. A French amnesty for illegal migrants in 1981 revealed that the Portuguese constituted the third-largest group after Moroccans and Tunisians. In the 1967 film *O Salto* (The leap, directed by Christian de Chalonge), the protagonist, Antonio, is a Portuguese carpenter who emigrates to France. He manages to evade the clutches of Franco's police in Spain and finally reaches Paris, where his comrades look after him. He exemplifies the working-class men and women of his generation who did the same, and the title refers to the 'leap' they took in leaving the country.[18]

In the short term, emigration brought some economic relief to the Salazar regime, but migration on this scale exposed its political shortcomings and lack of legitimacy. Portuguese workers and students became the symbolic embodiment of political opposition and an effective conduit of opposition activity, although they supported a moderate political platform. Ultimately, they helped to weaken the prospects of communist and far-right parties alike.[19]

Putting their fate in the hands of people-smugglers brought its own risks to opponents of fascist regimes. But the migrants developed survival tactics. John Berger described the tactics that Portuguese migrant workers adopted to keep from being fleeced by the smugglers:

> Before leaving they had their photographs taken. They tore the photograph in half, giving one half to their 'guide' and keeping the other themselves. When they reached France they sent their half of the photograph back to their family in Portugal to show that they had been safely escorted across the frontier; the 'guide' came to the family to prove that it was

he who had escorted them, and it was only then that the family paid
the $350.

This sum may appear modest, but it was equivalent to an average annual
income in Portugal.[20]

French hosts also had to prepare themselves, as a semi-humorous conduct manual pointed out. A guide published in 1964 for French households planning to employ Spanish maids carried a warning: 'If you don't
know Spaniards or Spain, if you do not like that land, or if you don't feel
a natural sympathy for the Spanish soul, if finally you are a French person
too reasonable, logical, or with a sad nature, do not hire a Spanish maid!'
For those who did engage a maid, it was important not to assume that 'all
Spaniards are dark-haired, bullfighters, or flamenco singers'. Nevertheless, 'almost all have a happy nature, and are intense and cheerful . . . . [T]hey
tend to obey and not to make demands, as French do. In general they do
not complain, and they accept their fate as a destiny inherited from the
Arabic occupation of the country.' The guide not only fed stereotypes to
potential employers but also underlined the fact that the employer ultimately wielded control over domestic workers.[21]

As elsewhere in southern Europe, the history of Greece was one of
urbanisation, abandoned villages, and emigration. The population of
Greece increased from 7.6 million in 1951 to 8.4 million in 1961. During
the decade, some 270,000 Greeks moved abroad to work. Between 1961
and 1971, the population increased at a slower rate than in the 1950s,
reaching a total of 8.8 million. During the same period 830,000 people
left Greece, mainly for destinations in Europe, particularly Germany and
Belgium, citing a wish to take advantage of economic opportunities
abroad.[22]

Emigration was accompanied by a drift from rural to urban areas—
which was described as *astyphilia*, or 'runaway urbanisation', the result in
part of a lack of health and social services in the countryside. In the 1960s
the Greek government welcomed emigration on the grounds that it
reduced domestic unemployment; enhanced the skills of the migrants,
who would contribute to the revival of the Greek economy when they
returned; and increased the level of savings among the population by

means of remittances, which amounted to $6 billion between 1960 and 1975. Much of the cash went into house construction, which boosted overall economic activity. And yet Greece could ill afford to lose the skilled and productive workers who were the first to leave. Half of those surveyed in 1964 gave no indication as to how long they were likely to remain overseas. Those who did return cited family pressures rather than having achieved the goals that had propelled them to depart in the first place.[23]

Greece also produced refugees in the shape of political opponents of the military junta that seized power in 1967. Politicians from different parties, along with students and young professionals, fled to Britain, France, Italy, West Germany, and Switzerland. Sweden, Norway, and the Netherlands formally recognised them as refugees. Among the most prominent exiles was the composer Mikis Theodorakis, a staunch opponent of the colonels who had imprisoned him and banned his music before permitting him to leave the country and settle in France. Less well-known people relied on the kindness of friends and neighbours, particularly when the junta prevented family members in Greece from sending money abroad. In one tragic case, a twenty-two-year-old student, Kostas Georgakis, set himself alight on a square in Genoa in 1970 to protest the regime in his home country. Many exiles returned to Greece when the colonels renounced power in 1974.[24]

In spite of the stranglehold of right-wing regimes—or perhaps because of it—Portuguese and Spanish migrant workers retained an intense attachment to their countries of origin. Although many of them lived abroad for several decades, they spoke of someday returning, even if that return was being deferred for years longer than they had planned. But returning to Spain frequently brought disappointment: half of all Spanish migrants who returned to their villages in Andalusia in the 1970s felt that local conditions had not improved since they left, citing, in particular, the results of the fascist repression of trade unions.[25]

Migration in Portugal reflected the history of colonisation. Portugal's colonial possessions in sub-Saharan Africa brought hundreds of thousands of white settlers to Angola and Mozambique. Migrants from sub-Saharan Africa and Brazil, in turn, flocked to Lisbon, where there was also a thriving diasporic community from Cape Verde. A fifty-two-year-old man who arrived in Portugal in the early 1960s from Cape Verde, a group of islands in the mid-Atlantic that had been colonised since the late fifteenth century, expressed his dismay at what he experienced on the mainland: 'I was not allowed to use the kitchen or the toilet and had to do my bodily functions in a shack outside in the yard. I think they treated me like that because I was black and did not speak Portuguese, and they thought that where I came from people did not know how to live in houses. But I think that my life was not much different from the life of any Portuguese peasant newly arrived from the backwoods.'[26]

Cape Verde became an overseas department of Portugal in 1951. The islands finally achieved independence in 1975. Before and after that date, thousands of men and women travelled long distances to take up jobs in the colonial metropolis, especially during the boom years of the 1960s. The recollections of this man, who was interviewed in 2000, are a compelling reminder of the everyday discrimination people of colour faced when they migrated to Europe and to other areas of the world. But his words also draw attention to deep-rooted antipathies towards all newcomers, whether they originated from colonial possessions or were internal migrants.[27]

Migrants from the Cape Verde islands built roads and hotels and worked in shipbuilding and manufacturing. With few other opportunities available to them, women peddled fish on the city streets until in the mid-1980s the Portuguese police and the municipal authorities revoked their licences. By the 1990s many of them became domestic cleaners for the expanding Portuguese middle class. Cape Verdean migrants, in particular, played an important role in substituting for Portuguese workers who had taken jobs in France and Germany. The government did not stand idly by, establishing an Aid Centre for Overseas Workers (Centro de Apoio aos Trabalhadores Ultramarinos). This indicated official willingness to support migrant workers, but the government was powerless in the face of widespread prejudice from employers who deemed Cape Verdeans 'hot-blooded' and 'unstable troublemakers'.[28]

Portuguese associations in France grew from around two dozen in 1971 to nearly a thousand by the 1980s. Some had been established after the First World War, by Portuguese soldiers who fought for France and stayed on afterwards. Others acted as recruiting agencies, going in search of workers from their native villages. Sympathetic groups helped to smuggle Portuguese anti-fascists across the border; many ended up in the Portuguese 'colony' in the department of Puy de Dôme. At the same time, the Salazar regime expected local Catholic priests to keep a close watch on migrants, lest they engage in 'subversive' activities. When democracy was restored in Portugal, new commercial organisations began to flourish, including banks to assist with remittances. Meanwhile, cafés, dance groups, festivals, sports clubs, and after-hours Portuguese language classes gained new adherents. Political activity was only one dimension of this vibrant scene. One activist lamented that 'the majority of people come here to dance, to enjoy themselves. I would like them to come to cultivate their minds.' But singing, sports, and festivals sustained old and young alike throughout the migrant experience.[29]

Being part of a larger diasporic group contributed to a sense that one was not alone as a migrant. Solidarity, however, was in short supply. The Cape Verdean diaspora in Portugal was divided between elite mixed-race Portuguese Cape Verdeans and black labour migrants. The former regarded themselves as honorary whites with a middle-class status in mainstream Portuguese society, whereas the latter tended to identify as African and took low-paid jobs.[30]

Where did this leave the complex question of migrants' sense of identity? Kiluange Liberdade, a young Angolan video artist who moved to Lisbon, drew on his knowledge of second-generation black youths to make observations about the community:

In Portugal there are boys and girls who do not have a fatherland. They are neither Cape Verdean, for they have never been to Cape Verde, nor Portuguese, for they speak another language [Creole] and their families do not follow the customs of the Portuguese. They do not want to be Portuguese. Maybe they will want to be Cape Verdean someday. As to now, they just belong to their neighbourhood, be it Pontinha, Pedreira, Arrentela, Miratejo, or Cova da Moura. They have their own frontiers, laws, languages, ideas and codes.[31]

Their identities were linked quite precisely to the localities to which they felt the closest attachment, and where their parents had reproduced a familiar social world.

Staying on was partly a financial calculation. Older Portuguese workers in West Germany hoped to wait until they could collect their German pensions before returning. They opted not to buy property in Germany, and still less would they contemplate being buried on German soil. Portuguese migrants in France, in contrast, gradually put down stronger roots, and many of them—particularly those in the younger generation—came to think of Portugal as a place to spend a pleasant vacation, rather than as a country to which they were deeply attached. Often they opted for dual citizenship, which became possible through a change in Portuguese law in 1982. But it had been a hard slog, and migrants told of being discriminated against in the early years.[32]

Colonial connections continued to exercise a strong grip on the pattern of migration. When Portugal abandoned its colonial possessions, and as a result of ongoing conflict, thousands of migrant workers arrived from Angola and Mozambique, either through legal channels or as illegal workers circumventing the restrictions imposed in 1981. Mozambicans reportedly had an advantage over Angolans thanks to being better educated. Family members joined them in the 1990s. Unlike the *retornados* discussed above, they did not have Portuguese citizenship.[33]

Other important developments were a harbinger of things to come. The decline in economic opportunities in northwestern Europe for migrants from the Third World in the 1970s encouraged them to look at other options. Growing prosperity in Italy, for example, attracted many non-European migrants to take jobs in the service sector, construction, and agriculture. They faced a hostile environment, however. In one particularly tragic instance, the denigration of foreign workers led to a man's murder by a band of Italian robbers in August 1989. The victim, Jerry Masslo, had arrived in Italy via a roundabout route that had taken him by boat from apartheid South Africa to Nigeria, and then, by plane, to Rome. When his claim for asylum was turned down, Masslo decided to seek work picking tomatoes on a farm near Naples. Like his fellow migrant workers, he received a pittance and lived in substandard accommodation. He spoke publicly of the racism he encountered in Italy: 'I thought that in Italy I would find a space to live, a breath of civilisation, and a reception that would allow me to live in peace and to cultivate the dream of a future without barriers or prejudices. But I am disappointed. We in the Third World are contributing to the development of your country, but it seems that this has no weight. Sooner or later one of us will be killed, and then you will know that we exist.' Masslo's murder sparked mass demonstrations in support of migrant workers (100,000 people took to the streets in Rome in October). It also helped inspire a film, *Pummarò* (directed by Michele Placido, 1990). It was the first Italian feature film to portray—albeit by a white director—the lives of black migrant workers and the violence to which they were exposed by mafia bosses and unscrupulous employers.[34]

Greece, too, became home to sizeable and well-established communities of migrants from Africa, in particular Eritrea, Ethiopia, and Somalia, and later on from Egypt, Sudan, and Pakistan, although they were far outnumbered by first- and second-generation migrants from Eastern Europe. This history complicated notions of a stable 'Greek identity'. Declining birth rates in rural Greece created a demand for migrant workers who arrived from Poland, Romania, Bulgaria, and especially Albania; many of them came illegally and therefore were paid a relative pittance. They helped collect the olive and orange harvests in the peak summer months, and the Greek government treated them as seasonal labourers. (Demand for these products increased after markets in Eastern Europe opened up.) Their presence became something of a fixture as key sectors came to rely on a regular supply of labour. Only in 1997 did the state introduce a system of residence permits that enabled migrant workers to be recognised legally, partly to enable the government to collect untaxed income. Even then, they were in a precarious position. Migrant workers received few benefits and remained socially and politically marginalised. At best they were left to their own devices—literally so, as most of them came to rely on mobile phones to keep in touch with family members and with one another—and for safety's sake they stuck close to fellow migrants who came from the same district in Albania.[35]

One young migrant described his arrival in Greece in 1990 at the age of fifteen, having hitchhiked and walked from his village in Albania. He 'had heard good things about Greece, easy money, a rich place'. But he was quickly disabused of this notion: 'We were sleeping in abandoned buildings and eating wild greens', he later said:

> Finally I made it to Kastoria and was able to find work harvesting peaches. I stayed there for a while then got a bus ticket further south, to Larissa. I worked there for a while but then the police caught me and sent me back to the border. I had only managed to work for two months, but I saved a little money, took a bus home from the border. My parents were happy to see me, they didn't know if I was alive or dead! The next year I came back, but this time I knew what to expect.[36]

This remarkable testimony points not only to the different kinds of uncertainty that migrants and their family members endured, but also to the determination they displayed in the face of harassment, recurrent deportation, and exploitation. In other contexts this would be celebrated as a kind of pioneering spirit.

The presence in Greece of migrants from abroad—whatever their background, they were collectively known as 'the Albanians'—sent some villagers into panic mode. They laid any crime at their door, believing that Albanian migrants had crossed the border in order to escape the criminal justice system in Albania. Those migrants who claimed Greek heritage were treated with disdain. 'These ones who came, they are not Greeks', said one villager. 'You can tell by how they act.' Another villager spoke of a 'crazy situation' in the 1980s when Albanians arrived in large numbers but 'didn't appreciate our hospitality.... [T]hey would murder you for ten euros. These people have no civilisation, they are like animals.'[37]

In another part of the Mediterranean, the issue was about a war, one that pitted the residents of Cyprus against one another and created a crisis of internal displacement. Turkey's invasion of Cyprus in 1974 created shockwaves both on the island and farther afield. Around 200,000 Greek Cypriots (two-fifths of the total population) and 50,000 Turkish Cypriots fled their homes in search of sanctuary. Many left within twenty-four hours of being confronted by the occupation and found temporary shelter with relatives or in makeshift accommodation, expecting to return to their own homes before long. One refugee described how his hasty and furtive departure, and the need to grab what belongings he could, made him feel 'as if we were thieving from our own houses'.[38]

The crisis was largely contained within Cyprus itself, although the United Nations monitored the 'Green Line' between the two halves of the island. According to international law, those who fled were classified as internally displaced persons. The label of refugee quickly stuck, although Greek Cypriots resented it, because it implied that they were unlikely to be able to return in the near future to what they termed the 'occupied areas' (*ta katexomena*). Some refugees worked in the booming construction industry or the growing tourist sector. Enterprising refugees established new businesses, which they named, for example, 'Refugee Kebabs' or 'Refugee Taxis', terms that suggested a determination to trade on their status. The overwhelming majority of the villagers found the move to towns in the south hugely disconcerting. It did not help that they met with barely disguised contempt from locals. One refugee recalled, 'You could rarely see discrimination [but] there were people who used to say to their children "eat your food or else the refugee will come and eat it", or pointed their finger at us saying "these are refugees".'[39]

On the north of the island, settlers arrived from Turkey with promises of land, jobs, and free housing in the Turkish-administered north. They were joined by migrants in search of temporary employment. As a result, the long-standing Turkish Cypriot population complained of being 'outnumbered' by newcomers from Anatolia. One resident complained that his friends had all left for Britain and Canada to avoid being made strangers in their own home: 'We are the last of the Mohicans.... [T]hey got rid of a whole culture. At least there are people who still remember the Indians, but who will remember us?'[40]

The partition of Cyprus turned what refugees believed would be a temporary sojourn into a lengthy internal exile. Ideas of return and restitution were difficult to realise. When they spoke of 'no going back', refugees employed the phrase in a dual manner, meaning a determination to complete their journey to a place of safety and their despair at the diminishing likelihood of returning for good to their original village. Notices placed by refugees ('temporarily residing in Limassol') only served to draw attention to the fact that desire did not easily translate into repatriation. In 2003, the Turkish Cypriot authorities allowed refugees to make short visits to the north of the island. Others refused the offer of a visit, regarding it as offensive that they were being asked to show their passports at the frontier. One refugee eloquently described feeling 'tied like another Odysseus who could not accept this degrading process'. Nevertheless, although something might trigger painful memories—the death of a loved one, a newspaper headline, or another screening of the well-known documentary film *Attila '74* (directed by Mihalis Kakogiannis, 1974)—refugees from both communities displayed an impressive capacity to get on with their lives, whether in Cyprus or in the wider diaspora. It helped, too, that the economy in the Greek half of the island proved remarkably dynamic, not least because of the productive potential of the refugees. Events in Cyprus were a reminder that forced migration was not only an extra-European problem, but an intra-European problem.[41]

The history of migration in Spain, Portugal, and Greece reflected the juxtaposition of prolonged authoritarian rule with relative economic backwardness, a combination that provided an inducement for migrants to escape. It took the peaceful overthrow of fascism for these states to begin to look outwards and explore the possibility of joining the European Economic Community. Migrants, meanwhile, had already looked outwards: some of the best and brightest opted to live a freer and economically more enticing life, and attempts by the government to control migration had relatively little effect. To be sure, migrants' remittances helped Greece, Spain, and Portugal climb out of the bottom of the league table of economic development, and to that extent they helped right-wing regimes to survive. Italy made faster economic progress than these countries, however, thanks in part to the rapid pace of internal migration and in part to its history as a founding member of the EEC, which enabled a smoother path for those Italians who wanted to work in other member states.

There was thus a bigger story to tell, in which each country eventually took the route of European economic integration: Greece joined the

EEC in 1981 (six years after applying), Spain and Portugal in 1986, and Cyprus (its southern half) joined the European Union in 2004. Unhappily, the European Union was saddled with the problem of a divided Cyprus and its refugee population. But Cyprus, fortunately, was uniquely problematic, and even Cyprus, over time, developed into a thriving economy. Elsewhere in southern Europe, Greek, Spanish, and Portuguese migrants, whether as workers or as political exiles, helped blaze the trail for those countries to become part of the European mainstream.

Unhappily, the countries of southern Europe, including their Mediterranean islands, would in the new millennium become the focus of migration on a larger scale, putting this other history in the shade.

CHAPTER 13

'Melting Pot' or 'Salad Bowl'? Public Opinion and Government Policy

INTERVIEWED IN 1997 FOR a French documentary, Philippe Deforges, technical adviser to the French secretary of state for migrant workers, offered a vivid analogy: 'When it came to the North Africans, the lump of sugar didn't dissolve in the way it should.' The general idea was clear enough. Like the metaphor of the 'melting pot', more familiar to American than to European readers, this was about belonging to a common political project and subscribing to common values. But it also entertained the possibility of failure: in other words, it embraced notions of 'backward' migrants who allegedly could not assimilate because of unbridgeable differences, whether expressed in religion, race, or the fuzzy term 'culture'. If the 'lump of sugar' failed to dissolve, as Deforges feared, European societies would become divided. They might be left with urban 'ghettoes', whether in Brussels, Hamburg, Bradford, or Paris.[1]

Given that democratic governments were strongly opposed to the expulsion of people who had been encouraged to work and allowed to settle in Europe, the emphasis shifted to programmes of integration or assimilation. Assimilation required that migrants adjust to the host society on its terms by forfeiting cultural attributes that stood in its way. Sensible integration, on the other hand, meant accepting migrants and providing them with legal status and political rights—in other words, giving them a proper foothold in the host society and ensuring adequate social and economic security without discrimination. Integration meant tolerating and enabling cultural difference and diversity. Integration was about gain, but, to all intents and purposes, assimilation was about loss.[2]

The response among European progressives was to consider the merits of a multicultural approach to migration, that is, allowing and enabling migrants to maintain their own cultures in the countries where they lived and worked. Diversity suggested that it was time to ditch the metaphor of the melting pot in favour of the 'salad bowl'. Multiculturalism was part of this integration strategy, not its antithesis.[3]

By the late 1960s, expressing this political and cultural shift, Roy Jenkins, the British home secretary in the 1964–1970 Labour government, maintained that there was no longer any need in Britain for a 'melting pot'. In his view, integration should not mean 'the loss by immigrants of their own national characteristics and culture'. The chief purpose of government was to ensure a level playing field for everyone—above all, by outlawing discrimination, a purpose embodied in the 1968 Race Relations Act, and updated in legislation creating the Commission for Racial Equality in 1976. The contrasting view, making strenuous claims for 'assimilation or else', came from the political right. It was encapsulated in the famous suggestion by British Tory cabinet minister Norman Tebbit in 1990 that immigrants would find a place in British society once they passed the 'cricket test', by which he meant that they should support the national team rather than opposing teams from the West Indies or the Indian subcontinent. Less remembered now is that Tebbit also told a parliamentary colleague that he did not think certain immigrant communities could or would assimilate, 'because some of them insist on sticking to their own culture, like the Muslims in Bradford and so forth, and they are extremely dangerous'.[4]

In very broad terms, integration meant how people were socialised, but it had specific meanings—and contested meanings—in relation to migration, particularly given that migrants had already been socialised elsewhere. Was integration a chimera, and if so, was this because of the attitudes of the host society towards newcomers? Or was the challenge of integration related to structural conditions, whereby migrant workers tended to be concentrated in economically insecure and poorly paid jobs?

In other words, did those conditions condemn them to remain 'outsiders', whatever efforts they made or that were made on their behalf? Migrants were admitted conditionally, their purpose being to work, often in isolation. Hidden from sight, their role as migrant workers both qualified them for admission and disqualified them from full integration.[5]

Integration took different forms. It included a strong whiff of moral approval of migrants who embraced government programmes for integration, the corollary being disapproval of those who went their own way, particularly where they seemed to favour seclusion. It was partly about finding a 'common language'. Some countries went about integration without too much fuss. Denmark gradually introduced Danish language classes for migrants, along with classes in how to get around town on a bicycle— adaptation meant also learning the rules of the road. The language and practices of integration were clear-cut in the Netherlands, where government policy aimed to support migrants through education and job training and to couple these programmes with measures to prevent discrimination.[6]

There was a darker side to integration and to multiculturalism. According to the historian Rita Chin, multiculturalism was designed to keep migration off the political agenda, but if this was its aim, it failed. Support for 'controlled migration' gathered momentum. A recurrent thread of discrimination and periodic expressions of outright racism also emerged. Disguised in some cases as a wish to defend 'indigenous culture', European electorates had, at best, a love-hate relationship with migrants. It took only a slight shift in political leadership to feed an appetite for repatriation, as the 'million Stoléru' campaign had indicated.[7]

Particularly in France, assimilation went hand in hand with naturalisation, on the assumption (established in practice and in law since the late nineteenth century) that sufficient willingness and motivation on the part of immigrants, together with sufficient energy on the part of the state, could 'make migrants French'. (However, assimilation did not lead directly to naturalisation.) France adhered to the long-established 'Republican' policy of equality, opposing institutionalised ethnic difference. The aim was to promote civic incorporation for those immigrants who had permission to stay. If not necessarily supporting assimilation, France nevertheless had plenty of experience of integration on which to draw. From the early 1950s, the Ministry of Public Health and Population had sponsored and coordinated programmes on behalf of foreign workers, particularly Poles and Italians who did not wish to return to their homes after the war. The Service social d'aide aux émigrants (Social Service Support for Emigrants) provided 'help in all the [migrants'] material and moral difficulties', particularly language instruction. Holiday camps for the children of migrants provided opportunities for them to make friends with French children, and it was hoped that these friendships would 'affect all the later stages of their cultural integration'.[8]

A clearer emphasis on assimilation could be detected during the 1960s and 1970s, when the emphasis was on promoting family life and French 'habits'. Married men who wanted to bring their wives to join them had to go through elaborate procedures involving social workers, the police, the local administration, and the National Immigration Office (ONI), including its officers on the ground in the country concerned. The mayor considered the documents that the applicant submitted and passed his opinion further up the decision-making chain. Questions would be asked about the 'professional stability' of the migrant and the 'adaptive capacity' of his family. Women were expected to demonstrate that they could make the home 'agreeable'. Social workers spoke of the difficulties they sometimes perceived: 'Three or four years ago we had an influx of young Moroccan wives who stay in their own homes and are completely isolated.' It was important to nip cultural difference in the bud, if migrants were to become French.[9]

The consequences of failing in this grand ambition emerged in dramatic fashion in 1973. In August, a thirty-six-year-old Algerian man by the name of Salah Bougrine boarded a bus in Marseille and began to stab the driver and his fellow passengers. The driver, Désiré-Emile Gerlache, died at the scene. Bougrine was nearly lynched and went into a coma after being attacked with an iron bar by a former boxing champion who happened to be driving past. A subsequent investigation discovered that, four years earlier, Bougrine had been badly injured (reportedly by a harki) while working in a factory, and that this event had triggered his acute mental disturbance. His murderous attack was soon followed by anti-immigrant violence whipped up by right-wing newspapers: 'Enough of these stealing Algerians [wrote the conservative Le Meridional], enough of these swaggering, troublemaking, syphilitic, raping, pimping, insane, murdering Algerians.' The British novelist Bruce Chatwin wrote a moving piece about Bougrine, albeit laced with an exotic depiction of 'the Kasbah [where] Senegalese dandies with soulful fingers were dipping their brioches into bowls of café au lait'. In the shantytowns of Marseille, Chatwin found among Algerians 'the kind of sight you expect in Calcutta'. The main bidonville had been a prisoner-of-war camp and was then turned into a centre for Jewish refugees. In 1974 a Gaullist politician likened it to 'gangrene', and like gangrene, said it had to be cut out.[10]

Chatwin painted a disturbing picture of racist incidents and hate crimes in Toulon and Grasse, as well as in Marseille, where a thirteen-year-old boy, Ladj Lounès, was shot and killed—the police accused him of being a car thief, when in fact he had been playing football with friends. One immediate consequence was that Algeria suspended the migration of its citizens to France. As the renowned Moroccan-born commentator Tahar Ben Jelloun pointed out, this did nothing to reassure the Algerians on French soil, who felt vulnerable and exposed. 'French hospitality is wrecked', Ben Jelloun wrote. Why, he asked, had French 'civilisation gone off the rails'? Ben Jelloun denounced the tendency to blame the victim rather than addressing the limitations of government policy and tackling racist behaviour.[11]

One stark manifestation of the more hostile atmosphere emerged in the shape of an appalling fantasy, Le Camp des Saints (The Camp of the Saints), a 1973 novel by Jean Raspail. Raspail gave his readers a grotesque dystopian account of the mass arrival of migrants on Europe's shores, suggesting that they threaten to trample Europe underfoot. Thousands of 'children from the Ganges', having circumnavigated the globe in a 'refugee fleet', arrive in France: 'Can a door protect a world that has lived too long?' he asks. In his book, the characters who favour allowing the migrants into the country speak a kind of hippie language; in one early episode, the 'elderly professor' who observes the scene from his nearby house despatches one of the French hippies with a single shot: 'a victory, Western style, as complete as it was absurd and useless'. The book ends with an apocalyptic vision in which only Switzerland holds out against the mass 'invasion' of Europe.[12]

Efforts at *intégration* also portrayed migration as a 'problem'. Not surprisingly, therefore, a report by Alain Girard and Jean Stoetzel in 1975 on attitudes towards immigrants in Lyon, Paris, and Marseille found that public opinion simultaneously exaggerated the size of the foreign-born population in France and demanded a reduction in their number. Responses varied according to the ethnic minority on which French nationals were being asked to form a view. Italians could integrate easily, they responded, followed by Spanish and Portuguese, but only one in three people interviewed thought that North Africans could integrate. The issue came down to one of 'irreducible differences, race, language, mores, culture', with only 3 percent of respondents suggesting that living conditions or the nature of work contributed to difficulties in integrating. The phrase 'irreducible differences' was another way of saying that some migrants had no place in France.[13]

Even well-meaning contributions to the debate adopted a patronising tone and had a depressing feel. A TV programme called *Mosaique* was broadcast on Sunday mornings on channel FR3. It was financed by the Social Action Funds (FAS)—in other words, from funds earmarked for immigrants. As Ben Jelloun put it, 'in a sense the immigrants pay a double television licence, yet all they get in return is a programme that is quaint rather than cultural and chiefly concerned to avoid giving offence'.[14]

The French state had more sinister weapons up its sleeve. There was a tension between the universalism of the mental health services in France, on the one hand, and the readiness among many French psychiatrists to make assumptions about the mind of the migrant newcomers. Immigrants stood accused of inventing or exaggerating their mental afflictions as a pretext to obtain financial compensation. One social psychologist, Sylvie Jarry, made assumptions about the psychological consequences of displacement 'from a Muslim to a Judeo-Christian civilisation', suggesting that 'the immigrant is like a sailor lost in an unknown sea, without map or compass. This inability to express himself renders him as vulnerable as a child.' It was another case of blaming the victims.[15]

The emotional consequences for the host population were neatly encapsulated by Ben Jelloun: 'The individual feels threatened by change, and senses it may soon leave him high and dry. [This] places the individual on the defensive and makes rejection of strangers almost instinctive, a gut feeling. It is not the moment to ask him to be tolerant and welcoming.'[16]

In Switzerland, there was no official or public appetite for integration, and Italian migrants in Switzerland, in particular, confronted xenophobia. The Swiss politician James Schwarzenbach sponsored a movement that gathered pace under the banner 'National action against the over-foreignisation [Überfremdung] of people and homeland'. In 1965, Swiss voters rejected a government recommendation to liberalise the rules for Italian migrants to be joined by their wives and to reduce the waiting time for permanent residency. Although a national referendum to reduce the numbers of foreign-born people failed to gain majority support, new regulations nevertheless came into force whereby the number of foreign workers was to be reduced by 5 percent, reversing the successive annual increases since 1960. Even so, the proportion of foreign-born residents (16 percent by 1975, but an even higher proportion of the labour force) was much higher than anywhere else, with the exception of Luxembourg.[17]

Ultimately, the economic downturn in the 1970s went some way to meeting xenophobic concerns by encouraging migrant workers to return to Italy. Unsurprisingly, a report on Swiss attitudes towards Italian migrant workers revealed a spectrum of opinion. Italians were thought to be hard-working and thrifty, but also 'backward'. A Swiss paediatrician said that 'we learn from one another, and Switzerland is in any case a heterogeneous society'. But others spoke of the 'danger' of feeling like 'guests in one's own country'. As the author of the report pointed out, class differences mattered in framing attitudes towards Italians: Swiss who travelled first class, ate in expensive restaurants, and sent their children to private schools would scarcely set eyes on migrant workers, whereas parents on a modest income might well find that migrant families needed to take up places at their local day nursery. But this suggested more resources should be found for such services, rather than providing any affirmation that attitudes should give way to xenophobia. When it came to offering citizenship, most respondents recommended a lengthy period of prior residence. In Switzerland, naturalisation was particularly difficult to attain and conditional on votes by the communal parliament or the communal assembly. Foreign workers continued to be classified as 'resident aliens', enabling the Swiss to insist that their country, like Germany, was 'not a country of immigration'.[18]

With a less extensive history of immigration than Switzerland, Sweden remained to a large extent ethnically homogeneous; as late as 1975, less than 7 percent of the total population was foreign-born. Post-1970 patterns of migration changed the profile, however: by the mid-1990s, migrants, refugees, and their Swedish-born children accounted for close to 16 percent of a total population of 8.7 million. Successive governments made the case for integration, providing Swedish language instruction but simultaneously supporting a raft of migrant associations. The management of migration to Sweden came within the mandate of the Statens utlänningskommission (National Alien Commission), established in 1949, and in 1969 the Statens invandrarverket (National Immigration Board). In 1975, the Swedish government passed legislation whereby any migrant who had lived in Sweden for more than three years could vote in municipal elections and stand for public office. This law was part of a broader package of measures designed to support integration by offering immigrants equal treatment and the option of pursuing fuller assimilation or retaining cultural distinctiveness.[19]

Dutch government restrictions on migration went hand in hand with policies designed to improve relations between native Dutch and newcomers. But not all newcomers were deemed to be alike. Thus, attempts to cultivate Dutch 'habits' among Indisch Dutch from Indonesia were regarded as successful, but the members of this group could simultaneously maintain their cultural identity: by the late twentieth century, strenuous efforts were being made to support the Tong Tong Fair as a celebration of traditional 'Indo' culture and enterprise. Moluccans, in contrast, were considered temporary residents, a belief that became increasingly untenable as the strength of the Moluccan claim for an independent state in the south of the Moluccan archipelago progressively diminished. Only in the late 1970s did the government shift its stance by providing education and training as part of an official integration policy that gave the Moluccan immigrants full rights of residence. Most of these Moluccans eventually gained Dutch citizenship. The grant of citizenship did not presuppose that they had assimilated, but they had to acquire 'a reasonable knowledge of Dutch' and 'sufficient acceptance by Dutch society'.[20]

It was a different matter with regard to Turkish and Moroccan migrant families, who professed a different faith from most postcolonial migrants and often struggled with the Dutch language. Voices on the far left came out with strong denunciations of Islam. In 1983 the Dutch Socialist Party reported that its 'research' underlined the fact that these immigrants 'will not stand a chance in our society' because of their 'consistent convictions pertaining to their religion' and 'the arrears in development' of their countries of origin. In other words, the party laid the failure of integration firmly at the feet of the migrants, rather than attributing it to any fault on the part of government, business, or society at large, and in ways that marked out Muslim migrants as particularly problematic.

A more positive answer, according to the anthropologist Lotty van den Berg, writing in the 1970s, was that the Dutch government should provide bicultural schools for foreign children: 'I believe that an exclusively Dutch education is very dangerous for a Moroccan child, because in that case the Moroccan child will feel completely Dutch. Consequentially, he would not be accepted any more in Moroccan society. Without education in their own language and culture they are obliged to assimilate with Dutch society, at the expense of the attachment with their own group.' The government listened. The Dutch Nationality Act in 1985 illustrated that stricter controls over immigration were to be combined with a liberal naturalisation regime and a commitment to 'mutual adaptation in a multicultural society'. The legislation granted citizenship at birth to third-generation migrants provided their parents and grandparents lived in the Netherlands. New migrants could apply for and be granted naturalisation if they had lived in the country for at least five years, provided they spoke Dutch to a reasonable standard and renounced their foreign nationality. In the following year, non-Dutch residents were given the right to vote in local elections. But the sting in the tail was that toleration for existing migrants and entry restrictions went hand in hand.[21]

The support of the government for multiculturalism antagonised other elements in Dutch society. In the wake of the Salman Rushdie affair in 1988–1989, when the novelist was attacked for blasphemy against

Islam, a journalist writing for the leading Dutch newspaper *NRC Handelsblad* launched a blistering attack:

> All our manpower and time was spent on multilingual education and youth work for cultural, religious and ethnic marginal groups. And what are the consequences? The Muslim society is walking in masses through the streets, and shouting like savages: Rushdie dead, Allah is great. We are civilizing them. They are coming from undeveloped areas. They are not used to anything. We spoiled them in the beginning with plush chairs, but in short time they demolished them. I visited Morocco once. I don't want to generalise. But over there, they cannot soil the carpet or demolish the toilet because they have a hole in the floor.[22]

Attitudes such as 'I don't want to generalise, but...' paved the way for emerging far-right demagogues in the 1990s.

Germany pursued a different path. The prevailing view was that any foreigner who wished to become a citizen had to demonstrate 'a voluntary and lasting orientation towards Germany'. Successive West German governments repeated the mantra that Germany was 'not a country of immigrants'. An official statement issued in 1977 read that 'West Germany is a country in which foreigners reside for varying lengths of time before they decide *on their own accord* to return to their home country'. The Bonn government made naturalisation very difficult to obtain for anyone not of ethnic German descent. Although noncitizens (particularly Turks) were able to enjoy a range of civil rights, they were rarely able to attain full citizenship. In any case, some scholars have argued that, because foreigners already enjoyed significant rights, the option of seeking naturalisation, abandoning one's existing citizenship, and having to pay a high fee for the privilege did not necessarily hold much appeal for Turkish workers. Furthermore, the Basic Law of 1974 offered protection, particularly from forcible repatriation.[23]

These considerations acted as a brake on further initiatives, although a landmark decision in 1978 introduced a 'permanence regulation' (*Verfestigungsregelung*) giving foreigners the legal right to an unlimited residence permit after five years of continuous presence in Germany.

However, the permits were issued at the discretion of the authorities in each state (*Land*), and this resulted in a kind of lottery. Migrants working in Bavaria or Baden-Württemberg, which were dominated by the Christian Democratic Union (CDU), found themselves at a particular disadvantage.[24]

Debates over a new foreigner law being considered by a coalition between the CDU and the Freie Demokratische Partei (FDP, Free Democratic Party) in 1982 soon came up against a 'crusade' led by the minister of the interior against family reunification. The minister restated the 'no immigration' view, according to which guest workers were only ever 'temporary' migrants. But liberal political parties, church leaders, NGOs, and trade unions led an opposition to this stance. In January 1991, a new Foreigner Law came into being, with no mantra and no reference to return migration. This legislation conferred rights on migrants and settled the argument over family reunification for good. (The Catholic Church had been arguing for this in the 1950s, partly because it would prevent 'moral' temptation and 'spiritual' degradation.) Germany accepted its obligations towards people who had been 'brought into this country' rather than arriving 'spontaneously'. This inevitably influenced the debate about integration, since it was now understood that many migrants intended to stay.[25]

The German government, meanwhile, encouraged social scientists to carry out research on integration, particularly on the children of guest workers and the need to support teachers who wished to promote students' awareness of foreign cultures. Political parties jumped on board. The CDU favoured a policy that would improve German understanding of cultural differences without requiring the assimilation of foreigners who were expected to return to their countries of origin. The Social Democratic Party insisted that foreigners were there to stay, and Germans needed to find out more about them. In parallel, civic organisations, including Catholic and Protestant charities together with informal associations of citizens, contributed resources to support the families of guest workers. The Arbeiterwohlfahrt (AWO, Workers Welfare Association) assumed responsibility for Turks, Moroccans, and Tunisians, while the Catholic charity Caritas looked after those from Spain, Portugal, and

Italy; the Protestant charity Diakonisches Werk supported guest workers from Greece. In 1978, Protestants organised a nationwide event with the slogan 'Day of the Foreign Fellow Citizen' (*Tag des ausländischen Mitbürgers*); it was designed to showcase foreign cultural traditions. The term 'foreign fellow citizen' was an attempt to move away from the terminology of 'guest worker', although it maintained the distinction between German and non-German.[26]

In 1982, a group of conservative German university professors dropped a bombshell by writing what became known as the 'Heidelberg Manifesto'. It began by expressing 'concern' about the consequences of 'a euphorically optimistic economic policy' that had resulted in the presence of 5 million guest workers and their families in Germany, followed by a further 'influx'. The authors denounced the failure, as they put it, to consult the German people, and the fact that public discussion was stifled in order to avoid 'accusations of Nazism'. Nevertheless, they went on to suggest that the task of reunification was endangered by the current 'foreigner policy', which damaged the interests of 'active and viable German families'. Specifically, they asked, 'how is reunification to remain a possibility when many regions of Germany are becoming ethnically foreign?' The statement was leaked to the press and published in the *Frankfurter Rundschau* in May, prompting a flurry of commentary about the growing hostility towards migrants among the population. The Heidelberg Manifesto provoked a counterstatement from the liberal media, but the damage had been done. It was no longer necessary to treat any expression of xenophobia as a revival of Nazi doctrine. Instead of the Nazi fixation with 'racial purity', conservative politicians could focus on cultural difference, typified by a resilient Turkish presence in German cities.[27]

In addition to its focus on culture as a signifier of difference, the Heidelberg Manifesto also deserved attention because the authors insisted that technological change, environmental challenges, and the needs of less industrial countries were all part of the mix. Technological advances suggested that 'machines must be brought to people, not people to machines'. Reducing the number of foreigners ('on a voluntary basis, of course') would help alleviate damage to the environment of 'our over-industrialised country'. Lastly, the federal government should concentrate instead on 'targeted development assistance', in order to discourage foreign migrants from looking to Germany as a land of economic opportunity. All of this seemed to suggest that the authors sought to appeal to a number of constituencies, including people on the left of the political spectrum.[28]

Yet, remaining in Germany gave Turkish migrants access to social and residential rights that they had built up over many years of hard labour—rights that trade unions had insisted upon on the grounds that all workers should enjoy similar benefits. In other words, the longer they stayed, the longer they felt entitled to the same rights as established citizens, and the more they secured them.

The emergence of a second generation, children of guest workers and other migrants, gave rise to further anxieties, about a deprived and alienated underclass. Broadly speaking, the first generation of European and non-European migrants arrived with offers of work. They were subsequently likely to be joined by dependents or to form attachments and raise a family. Those who made a permanent home in their new environment were determined to ensure that their children would receive at least as good an education there as they would have in the country of their parents' birth. In due course, however, this second generation, whether Turks in Germany, West Indians in the UK, Algerians and Moroccans in France, or Indo-Surinamese in the Netherlands, frequently struggled to get off to a strong start in life.[29]

Numerous reports in Germany on this issue failed to reach a consensus. One common finding pointed to discriminatory and racist assumptions on the part of teachers and education officials, sometimes coupled with the observation that central and local government agencies were unprepared to meet the challenge of mass migration and lacked the resources to do so. Other commentators sought to pin the blame on low expectations on the part of parents, who they said wanted nothing more than for their children to find the same kinds of jobs as themselves, as a study of the children of Turkish guest workers in Bremen concluded. (The same study suggested that parents keep their children out of school if they feared the discrimination and intimidation to which they would be subjected.)[30]

The education gap was thus connected to the generation gap. This link revealed itself in a variety of ways. One manifestation was the kind of behaviour among the children of migrants that their parents deemed to be appropriate or otherwise. One parent, Ayhan G., complained that the teenage children of German Turks had developed bad habits, 'becoming alcoholics and spending too much time on slot machines'. A common refrain within the Turkish community in Germany was that children no longer respected their parents, although parents also had to acknowledge that without their children's help, navigating Germany's bureaucratic procedures would have been a struggle. Gender differences complicated the picture still further: a study of North African adolescent girls in Lyon indicated that their fathers expected them to marry at a young age and abandon their education.[31]

Needless to say, education could create a gap between parents and their children, who rapidly attained fluency in the new language. Over time, this gap transformed family dynamics. The author Natascha Wodin reported that she was able to keep secrets from her father—such as her poor school grades—because she knew he lacked the ability to make enquiries of the school in the German language. In his old age, when he went into a nursing home, Natascha had to communicate with the staff on his behalf.[32]

The generation gap also manifested itself in the attitudes of children towards the land of their parents' birth. Something of the challenges emerged with respect to German Turks, among whom the number of children under the age of seventeen increased from 160,000 to 420,000 during the 1970s. Notwithstanding ideas around 'guest work' and 'rotation', these children now became the responsibility of the German state. Second- and third-generation Turkish young adults expressed a wish to stay in Germany, regarding Turkey as remote, a place they visited only occasionally and had left behind psychologically. The corollary was that they sought to make a reasonable life for themselves in the country where their parents or grandparents had settled.[33]

Finding schools for their children spoke volumes about their parents' wish that they should be enabled to negotiate their new surroundings and eventually get ahead. Young Italians, for example, preferred to send their children to establishments teaching in one of the languages spoken in Switzerland (primarily German and French); they thought their educational

245

prospects would be enhanced by being forced to learn a foreign language. The results could be mixed. A later study of Italian migrants found that the French emphasis on assimilation did indeed provide children with a good education, whereas Italians in Switzerland struggled. Here, Italian children were overrepresented in schools for children with special educational needs. The situation in Belgium was no better. In Germany and Belgium, the children of Italian migrants often had to repeat a year.[34]

Opinions varied as to whether the explanation for differences in the educational attainment of the children of migrants was to be found in the 'cultural' shortcomings of migrant families or in the lack of adequate provision. In the UK, for example, the Swann Report in 1985, titled *Education for All*, emphasised, among other things, the need for more ethnic minority classroom teachers. In Newcastle the local authority adopted its recommendation and sought to give migrant children the opportunity to develop proficiency both in English and in their mother tongue. Whatever the explanation or the extent of sensible initiatives such as these, the education gap did not go away: that is to say, the children of migrants might have gained a better education than their parents, but they did not necessarily narrow the gap with native children. There was also a gender gap. Evidence suggested that girls did better at school than boys, and among the older children it was because they were more likely to stay at home and concentrate on their studies rather than go out in the evening. Furthermore, they used this education to secure better jobs. However, a study of Italian migrants conducted in the 1990s found that those who acquired new skills were at something of a disadvantage in a competitive job market, because their training steered them away from specialised 'ethnic niches'.[35]

Other kinds of prejudice emerged in the xenophobic attitudes of parents who tried to dissuade their children from socialising with migrant youth. In Switzerland, for example, Swiss girls faced the wrath of parents and friends if they went out with Italian boys. One young woman reported: 'There are people who refused to say hello, my mother didn't want to know me for a time. My boss asked if I had no taste [*ob ich eine Geschmacksverirrung habe*].' A farmer made the point in explicit racist fashion: 'I won't tolerate Italians in my home, we must keep Swiss blood pure.' The younger generation had fewer qualms.[36]

The counterpart of migration to Western Europe was the return to one's place of birth—a kind of reintegration. For some migrants, such as Moluccans who settled in the Netherlands, it was virtually impossible to visit, although by the 1990s the children of wealthier Moluccan families had begun to do so. Guest workers were more likely than permanent settlers to make the effort to travel to and from their homes. They wanted to maintain contact with family members, and often to make improvements to the family home. Staying abroad for good could be an entirely rational decision, even when economic conditions might have dictated one's departure. Migrants could count on welfare benefits or on support from family members to cushion the effect of unemployment or other unforeseen events. Besides, they had invested in the host society, often learning a new language and acquiring new skills and contacts.[37]

Parents, of course, had to consider the needs of their children who were born abroad. Ayhan G. told an interviewer, 'We began to give up on the idea of returning to Turkey when our children started school in Germany.' In her work on migration in Europe, the historian Yvonne Rieker found that in 1989 only one in three Italians in the fifteen- to twenty-five-year-old age group living in West Germany intended to remain permanently, and they expressed uncertainty about their future. In Switzerland, the proportion was higher, although their intentions were vague. In France at the end of the 1970s, just over half of all Italian nationals insisted that they wanted to stay for good. Perhaps, as Rieker suggested, the close proximity between France and Germany, as well as their membership in the European Union, enabled migrants to keep their options open.[38]

What did it mean to return home? A study in 1981 of returning Spanish guest workers found that the time they had spent abroad made them more willing to take risks. This kind of finding was very much in line with prevailing theories of modernisation, according to which migrants were able to leave 'traditional' society behind. A more nuanced approach was taken by Barbara Wolbert, who carried out ethnographic research in Izmir and Istanbul in the late 1980s. Returning migrants were known as *Almancılar* and *Almanyalılari* ('the Germans', and 'those from Germany'). Some of them returned to Turkey but left again, making use of the German work permits they retained. These migrants lived between two worlds, keeping one foot in Germany without rupturing ties in Turkey. Return, in other words, was part of the process of mobility, not necessarily an irreversible decision. Female Turkish migrants returning to Izmir and Istanbul in the 1980s in particular had a hard time adjusting to life in the country of their birth, not least because of price inflation in Turkey. They reported episodes of depression. Alongside individual stories of adventure and self-discovery, there were accounts of ruptures in family relations. One woman expressed the distance between Turkey and Germany in terms of emotional distress rather than kilometres: 'If only I were a bird and could fly to see my son.'[39]

Staying put was a calculated decision that had enormous implications in terms of the prospects of the second generation and the ageing first generation. The decision to stay was heavily influenced by current or anticipated economic opportunities and by the possibility of family reunification, not forgetting the prospect of broadening one's horizons. The key issue was less about integration as such than about the multiplicity of relations that migrants sustained and in which they were embedded.

Where did this leave the image of the melting pot? Some social theorists maintained that modern migration encouraged a kind of hybridity, rather than a straightforward assimilation, on the one hand, or an assertive ethnic identity, on the other. Others suggested that identity is always provisional and incomplete. Much ink was spilled on government policies of integration and assimilation, and rather less on what migrants understood by these vexatious terms and their social and cultural implications. At the very least, it is wise to heed the words of a French activist, Madjiguène Cissé, who insisted that integration works both ways: whilst migrants learned how to get by in the host society, 'there must be a minimum of respect for our cultures of origin'. The Swiss author Max Frisch put it even better: rather than expect migrants to assimilate, Europe should learn to accept them for who they are—in his words, 'assimilate reality'.[40]

CHAPTER 14

Migrants in Western Europe:
Living in a Cold Climate

IN THE 1970S, THE Algerian-born sociologist Abdelmalek Sayad, exploring the meaning of migration in modern France, asked where migrants belonged. He gave his answer in a series of essays that were collected into a book published posthumously, later translated into English as *The Suffering of the Immigrant*: it was that migrants belonged neither in the host nation nor in their country of origin. They had to learn how to conduct themselves in order to get by in the new country, and they had to relearn how to behave when they returned for a home visit. As far as Sayad was concerned, the real issue was not 'integration' but 'disintegration', the severing of long-standing social relations in one's birthplace. Inevitably, this was a dynamic process. The migration of entire families helped to overcome the alienation the pioneer migrants felt upon first arriving in France. Migrants came to understand that they were not just wage-earners, but people who had a responsibility to support the dependents who joined them. Connections among migrants created a sense of community. Ultimately, integration should be compatible with the chance to be with loved ones and to enjoy the company of one's compatriots. And even in the most demanding situations, this was already happening: migrants, so to speak, were making integration happen for themselves, from the bottom up.[1]

Whether in the workplace, on the street, or in the home, migrant lives in Europe came in various forms. Many migrants arrived without a clear vision of what lay ahead; others knew what awaited them, because they had already been alerted by family and friends. Refugees, who often had to escape at a moment's notice, were unlikely to have made advance preparations. Ordinary migrants were disadvantaged in some ways, too, such as being assigned the most wretched and poorly paid jobs, which economic necessity made it impossible to refuse. But there was another side to the picture: some migrants left their homes seeking adventure, and this potential for self-realisation gave additional meaning to their lives. The focus on policies as outlined in the previous chapter does not, there- fore, tell the whole story: an accurate account of migration must be leavened with a discussion of the cultural and social life of migrants.

Perhaps no one demonstrates more vividly this kind of forging of con- nections following migration than the South African artist Gavin Jantjes. An opponent of apartheid, Jantjes left South Africa to study in Germany at the age of twenty-two, in 1970, and was granted asylum there in 1973. He later moved to London before eventually settling in Oslo. From Ger- many Jantjes became a vocal critic of apartheid, and he served as a con- sultant for the United Nations High Commissioner for Refugees. Over the past several decades he has had a highly successful career, not only as an artist exhibiting his own works, but also as a curator for exhibitions of the works of others, as a member of various councils and boards of trust- ees, and as a lecturer and writer. Speaking in 1994, he insisted, 'I haven't come here to disappear.' He added: 'I am the new European. I am here to alter the conception of nations and national cultures.' Certainly, Jantjes spoke from a position of relative privilege—he has now been able to divide his time between Norway, South Africa, and the UK. As a migrant, however, Jantjes drew attention to something fundamental about migra- tion. To not 'disappear' was to make a difference in two important ways: first, he contributed to the society that had become his home, and sec- ond, he did it while 'being different'. Migration, for Jantjes, was about making his mark, and doing so without losing his sense of identity—an identity that came from having different attitudes and beliefs, not by blending in.[2]

Contrast this with the prevailing view in the final quarter of the twentieth century, when European politicians of all stripes believed that the goal for permanent migrants was essentially to make them vanish through concerted programmes of integration and assimilation. Among other things, this objective ignored the fact that migrants of colour found it impossible to disappear. They could not avoid being visible.

As Sayad recognised, migrants forged a meaningful life by drawing upon their own resources, including support networks, whether these were informal kinship groups or more formal associations. Rather than waiting for trade unions or other existing bodies to come to their aid — which was unlikely to occur — working-class migrants created their own organisations. Migrant associations played an especially important role in migrant life, providing a cultural and psychological sanctuary from the rigours of work and from an unfamiliar and often hostile environment. They protected migrants from isolation and provided a degree of insurance against exploitation, and they were a source of advice and assistance with housing and other practical matters. They helped migrants negotiate with landlords and government officials, particularly where important paperwork required knowledge of a language the new migrant did not yet possess. They supplemented, but did not replace, host welfare organisations, which often had good intentions but sometimes lacked familiarity with the culture and needs of the newcomers.[3]

By the early 1970s, migrant self-help was common in Western Europe, and scholars and other observers recognised its importance. Forming their own groups ensured acceptance for migrants in a variety of activities and gave them a means of avoiding the activities of mainstream society where they felt unwelcome. In the UK, for example, one well-informed writer on the subject of migration noted that West Indians were reluctant to join what he termed 'locally provided general activity clubs' — that is, clubs not specifically for West Indians — lest they be rejected. Like many other migrants, they felt that until they had 'earned' acceptance it was incumbent upon them to keep together.[4]

Of course, for migrant workers the first priority was to find work and adjust to their new jobs. Workers often took up jobs in heavy industry and construction, where the work was arduous, often unhealthy, and sometimes dangerous. Not everyone worked on the factory floor or in construction, however. Significant numbers of Italians were self-employed—for example, owning small businesses such as hairdressing salons, ice-cream parlours, or restaurants. In the Belgian city of Ghent, Algerians, Moroccans, Turks, and Spaniards who had arrived in the 1960s to work in textiles or construction borrowed money from family members or from the bank to establish cafés, restaurants, and corner shops in the 1960s and 1970s, working long hours and making modest profits, but maintaining a degree of economic independence. It was the factory workers, however, who typically drew the most attention from the broader society. The aspiring shopkeeper was relatively uncontroversial, whereas the collective strength of workers received constant scrutiny at a time when union activity was an important issue in many countries in the West. Union activity sometimes took a dramatic form, with strikes, rallies, and the like becoming frequent themes. There was a consensus among outside observers that the 'problem' of migration would be solved or become further inflamed by what happened to the proletariat.[5]

Sure enough, labour militancy in the early 1970s seemed to bear this theory out. Italian guest workers joined the famous unofficial strike at the Ford plant in Cologne in 1973, which employed 12,000 Turkish workers, more than one-third of the factory's total labour force. A smaller strike had taken place three years earlier, resulting in the dismissal of Turkish and Italian workers who protested the lack of representation on trade union bodies. In 1973, a much bigger protest surfaced around demands for improvements in work conditions and housing—nearly half of these workers lived in unsanitary, prewar company buildings ('the sun hardly makes its way into the backyard', one worker complained). They were shunned by other local residents. Guest workers were expected to do the dirtiest, most monotonous, and least well-paid work on the assembly line. A radical newsletter, Devrimci Motor (Revolutionary motor) incited unrest.[6]

The tipping point came when 300 Turkish workers at the Ford factory lost their jobs when they tried to return to work in Germany in August 1973 after briefly overstaying their annual vacation. News reports described street demonstrations in which those who had been dismissed were joined by strikers from the Turkish workforce. A spokesman for the strikers, Baha Targün, claimed that ethnic solidarity should outweigh political and religious differences, announcing: 'We include Muslims, Christians, socialists, fascists, democrats and communists.' The outcome of the protests left no one happy. The leading German trade union refused to lend its support to the Turkish workers. Some German and Turkish officials accused communist 'agitators' at Ford of being behind the strike, although at least one Turkish diplomat sympathised with the workers' complaints. The whole incident ended in summary fashion when police stormed the factory gates. The strikers made only limited gains in terms of workplace representation and a small pay raise, and the workers whose predicament caused the strike in the first place lost their jobs and were deported.[7]

Ultimately, the events came to be portrayed as the product of purely Turkish grievances. Journalists said the workers' distress had been accentuated by their life in the 'ghetto', rather than explaining it as an expression of working-class discontent more generally. Much ink was spilled on the concentration of Turkish families in the suburbs of cities such as Berlin, where Turks comprised nearly one-fifth of the population of Kreuzberg in the mid-1970s. The fact that it was traditionally a working-class neighbourhood made for a less interesting story than one about ghettoisation.[8]

Something of the difficulties of earning a living emerged in the first part of Aras Ören's Berlin trilogy, 'Was will Niyazi?' (What does Niyazi want?). Written in Turkish in 1973, the Berlin trilogy, a cycle of poems, was immediately translated into German. The aspirations of the protagonist, Niyazi, are not so different from those of his working-class German neighbours in Kreuzberg: they have cars, modern apartments, fall in love. Nevertheless, Ören paints a bleak picture of exploitation and unrealised dreams among the Turks, and this picture was at odds with the self-congratulatory stance of liberal German politicians. Forced to work overtime in order to survive, Niyazi incurs the wrath of German workers on the shop floor.[9]

Guest workers made their voices heard in other ways, too. Soon after becoming German chancellor in 1974, Helmut Schmidt regularly received letters asking for his help in finding work for people whose ill-health or disability prevented them from working in physically arduous occupations: 'I have no more strength, no money, no savings and no inner reserves....I am in a hopeless situation', wrote one worker, Ismail Y., in July 1974. These requests usually languished in official files. Turkish associations began to spring up in cities such as Düsseldorf to defend the interests of workers, but this did nothing to assist those who were unemployed. Helmut Schmidt himself believed that too many Turkish migrants were only interested in welfare benefits, declaring: 'We cannot handle a further wave of foreigners into this country.' The workers sometimes contrasted their capacity for hard work with the 'laziness' of native workers.[10]

Migration aroused anxieties not only in Germany but also in Turkey. The notion of 'alienation' surfaced among Turkish politicians, who urged guest workers to focus on their work and not be sidetracked by 'promises of money and women'. In February 1972, the editor of a right-wing Turkish-language newspaper, *Tercümen*, denounced 'hippie culture' in Germany, and, disturbingly, ascribed the threat to Turkish customs as the result of 'Jewish capital'. Guest workers were doubly exposed, on the one hand to German antagonism, and on the other to Turkish cultural nationalism. Suspicion all round seemed to be the norm.[11]

Sometimes guest workers were rebuffed when they tried to make new friends. Deniz, a successful Turkish professional woman who had arrived in Germany as a child in the 1960s, recalled attending a party with two Turkish friends, one a doctor, the other a businesswoman. At the party, they met up with German acquaintances. But they decided to leave early, having been made to feel uncomfortable. As Deniz told an interviewer much later: 'These German women have no problem if we are oppressed, beaten by our husbands or fathers, headscarved; then they run to our side to save and emancipate us. But if we are uncovered, independent, successful professional women, free, and even single, they can't cope with us and they resent us.' Another woman threw down the gauntlet to her interviewer: 'Come with me to see the authorities, and I'll show you who you are. And if I go to the disco and say that I'm a German, they'll laugh me off the stage.'[12]

In March 1983, Ali Levent Sinirlioglu, a Turkish man living in Germany, placed an advert in several newspapers asking about opportunities for work of any kind. There was no shortage of job offers. However, Ali's credentials were bogus. His real name was Günter Wallraff, a forty-year-old undercover journalist. Wallraff prepared for his deception by asking an optician to provide him with dark contact lenses—the optician expressed surprise, because most of his customers asked for blue eyes. Wallraff learned to speak like a 'foreigner' by dropping syllables from words and speaking a kind of Cologne dialect. He passed himself off as the slightly dimwitted son of a Kurdish father and a Greek mother who had grown up in Greece speaking no Turkish. Whenever he was asked to communicate in Greek, he offered a few lines from Homer's *Odyssey*.[13]

In his famous 1985 book *Ganz Unten* (At the bottom, translated into English as *Lowest of the Low*), dedicated to the memory of Semra Ertan, a young writer who set fire to herself in 1982 to protest growing xenophobia in Germany, Wallraff exposed the living conditions of Turkish guest workers. While living and working alongside them, he had observed and conversed with many of them, including farmworkers who laboured for a pittance, some of them on the farms of refugees who had arrived from the East; clerks serving at fast-food restaurants, including McDonald's; and others who cleared drains and cleaned toilets. Although he described the whole spectrum of public attitudes towards Turkish guest workers, the overall impression remained one of popular contempt and xenophobia. He described some of the highly offensive remarks about Turks that he encountered among Germans. He had also captured the working conditions and exploitation of guest workers on film, and it was perhaps here that his work had its biggest impact. In one passage he explained how an unscrupulous German boss was prepared to employ Turkish workers on a job at a nuclear power plant where they would be exposed to radiation; because they would shortly be returning to Turkey, the manager thought there would be no repercussions.[14]

Wallraff's sensational book sold 3 million copies in less than two years. He claimed to have taught his fellow Germans a lesson—not only about Turkish guest workers but about German society, which he said spoke of democracy but practised a kind of 'apartheid'. He explained in the preface to his book: 'Of course, I wasn't really a Turk, but had dressed like one in order to unmask society.... Now I know what the foreigner has to put up with.' He added, 'There's a kind of apartheid in our "democracy".' After winning a number of lawsuits brought by the companies he targeted, Wallraff claimed to have improved work conditions at Thyssen and elsewhere. Nevertheless, *Ganz Unten* could also be accused of perpetuating a stereotype about ill-educated and slow-witted Turks and of reinforcing the view that guest workers were passive victims of the economic system, rather than members of society who could speak for themselves.[15]

Filmmakers, meanwhile, ventured from the shop floor into more intimate territory. In *Angst Essen Seele Auf* (Fear eats the soul, 1974), Rainer Werner Fassbinder offered a powerful story of the developing relationship between Ali, a young Moroccan immigrant working as a mechanic, played by El Hedi ben Salem, and a much older woman, Mrs Kurowski (Brigitte Mira), the German widow of a Polish man who had been a forced labourer. Her background subtly makes a point about the complex history of migration in Germany. The opening scene takes place in a bar frequented by other migrants, where Kurowski, rather than Ali, emerges as the 'foreigner'. As the relationship develops, Kurowski's children refuse to have anything to do with Ali. Ali suffers physically as well as emotionally: the film ends with him in great pain from a stomach ulcer, brought on (a doctor tells him) by the different kinds of stress to which migrants were exposed.[16]

So-called minority literature gave first-generation migrants a voice of their own. This applied to Italians as well as to Turks. The Italian German writer Franco Biondi moved to Germany as a metalworker before becoming a social worker and founder of the Associazione Letteraria Facoltá Artistiche (ALFA, Literary Association of the Art Faculties), although its members disagreed as to whether authors should write about everyday experience or highlight bigger social and political issues. Those taking the latter view created the Polynationaler Literatur- und Kunstverein (PoLiKunst, Polynational Literature and Art Association) in 1980, with Franco Biondi, Gino Chiellino, and others, including authors from the Middle East, united around a critique of capitalism and dedicated to giving working-class writers a forum for their literary output. The question

remained: Could there be an internationalist and cosmopolitan literature, or was 'minority literature' the best that one could hope for?[17]

The protagonist of Tevfik Başer's film *10qm Deutschland* (40 sq. m
Germany, 1986) was 'Turna', a migrant who is first seen arriving in Hamburg to join her husband, Dursun. He refuses to let her out of their apartment, out of a concern to protect her, as he sees it, from the dangers of the
outside world. She manages to escape from this domestic 'cage' when her
husband unexpectedly dies from an epileptic fit. Ironically, because he
prevented her from making other contacts or negotiating the labyrinth of
officialdom, she is unable to summon help for him when he needs it.
German critics rushed to condemn Dursun's backward and outdated attitudes towards women and to make the broader point that integration had
made little progress. But they missed the point that Turna eventually does
make a success of life on her own in the film.[18]

Given the opportunity, ordinary migrants were perfectly able to voice
their own opinions. The singer Yüksel Özkasap, who arrived in Cologne
in 1966, sang (in Turkish) of the guest worker as Germany's 'beast of burden' (*Packesel*). A joke circulating in the 1970s and 1980s told of three
workers, one Turkish, one Greek, and one Italian, who are employed in a
small factory. Because the Turk works the hardest, the other two are dismissed, and he works all three machines himself. The Turk has to use his
hands and feet to maintain the pace of work: 'One day the owner comes
in and is surprised to see the Turkish worker with a broomstick thrust into
his anus. When asked about it, the Turk replies that his anus was the only
part of his body not working for the boss. Now, while running from
machine to machine he can also sweep the floor.'[19]

Migrants also reflected on the tribulations of domestic life. One man,
Memed Akkaya, told the anthropologist Werner Schiffauer of his determination to make a decent life for himself and to 'get ahead' by leaving his
Turkish village. In 1972, at the age of twenty-eight, Memed had travelled
to Germany on a tourist visa. There, he had worked as a farm labourer,
but without a regular income or legal protection. Four years of backbreaking work left him exhausted but did not lessen his determination to succeed. Within a short while he met and married an eighteen-year-old
German woman, Monika, against the wishes of their parents and friends,

who told them they were making a big mistake. For months they worked different shifts in a factory in Wuppertal and could spend little time together. Memed's marriage collapsed. After that, he had an unhappy relationship with a Turkish woman, but he eventually managed to establish a successful small business. Reflecting on this roller-coaster life, Memed adopted a philosophical attitude: 'I've seen it all', he said, adding, 'I am myself and no other.'[20]

Migrant lives were far from solitary. Turkish guest workers kept in touch with news from Turkey by listening to Turkish broadcasts on transistor radios. By 1964, they were also able to listen to Turkish-language programmes on German radio stations. Music cassettes made a star of the Turkish singer Asik Metin Türköz, whose popularity soared during the 1960s and 1970s. But this brought complaints from German neighbours that Turkish guest workers kept their windows open with the radio blaring.[21]

Political organisations and trade unions, along with churches and mosques, played a vital role in sustaining migrants and providing for the education of children, including Muslim children. Political associations helped foster continued interest in the politics of the homeland, and this included oppositional activity. They also brought to light tensions within what was sometimes assumed to be a single community. An ethnographic investigation of Turkish 'colonies' in Bamberg and Colmar revealed divisions between Alevi and Sunni Muslims, which became more entrenched during the 1980s. Alevi children came home from school to tell of the taunts they suffered from their Sunni classmates.[22]

The politicisation of migrants became a source of concern within the German establishment as well as in Turkey. Turkish politics were partly conducted on German soil, with the creation in the 1970s of German branches of conservative political parties, such as the Milliyetçi Hareket Partisi (Nationalist Movement Party) and the Milli Selamet Partisi (National Salvation Party) as well as groups dedicated to the establishment of an Islamic state in Turkey. In their German incarnation they advocated improved instruction in the Qur'an, and much of their anger was directed at liberal elements in the German media. They denounced the film *Shirins Hochzeit* (Shirin's wedding), directed by Helma Sanders-

Brahms and shown on West German television in 1976. It portrays the distressing life of a young woman who travels from Anatolia to Cologne, where she works as a cleaner. She is raped and forced into prostitution. Turkish conservatives organised protests outside the TV studio, and Ayten Erten, the actress who portrayed Shirin, had to go into hiding. Turkish newspapers kept up a barrage of complaints about single Turkish women becoming too independent for their own good.[23]

As a new generation of imams arrived from Turkey later on, Islamic fundamentalism became a force to be reckoned with by Turks and Germans alike. In the 1970s and 1980s, however, Turkish migrants regarded Islam as a guide to good conduct, not as the path to politicisation. They took pride in Islam and relied on their faith, although the law in Germany sometimes imposed restrictions on some cultural norms, much to the dismay of the head of one Turkish household, who complained that 'here you're not even allowed to hit your children'. He insisted that Turks should not 'throw their customs away'.[24]

Relations between residents and newcomers were at least as challenging in France as they were in West Germany. Migrants had to negotiate deep-rooted social and cultural stereotypes. As the author Françoise Ega, who was from Martinique, caustically suggested, 'the French government and society perceive all Polish people as agricultural workers, all Algerians as unskilled construction workers, and all Antillean women as maids'. Even when France placed a high value on foreigners, as it did when they achieved fame in athletics, it was difficult to avoid reinforcing stereotypes. The French press lauded the integration of foreign footballers, but they reserved greater praise for Yugoslav players than for those from Francophone Africa. Whereas the latter tended to attract favourable comment for their prowess on the pitch, Yugoslav stars were applauded for learning French, sending their children to French schools, and indulging in admirable pastimes, such as 'frequenting second-hand bookshops'.[25]

How did migrants negotiate this minefield of assumptions and expectations, replete as they were with deeply engrained racial prejudice? There was not much joy to be had from working-class solidarity. Migrants struggled to gain the backing of both union officials and rank-and-file members. Nor did other migrants provide much support: in the Parisian suburbs, the older generation of migrants from Italy and Spain tended to ignore the younger cohort. Another option lay in extracting as much material benefit as possible from the French state. In 1981, France inaugurated a law of associations for foreigners. The plan was that these associations would bring together young migrants from different ethnic backgrounds to foster improved local relations. Unfortunately, the government was reluctant to let go of the purse strings, and the main result was a series of well-meaning but largely ineffectual cultural activities.[26]

In October 1983, following a series of racist attacks and incidents involving police brutality, a 'Marche pour l'égalité et contre le racisme' (March for equality and against racism) brought 100,000 second-generation North Africans from the south of France to Paris, where they secured an audience with President François Mitterrand. Further marches took place in 1984 and 1985, with the newly formed antiracist organisation SOS Racisme playing a prominent role. Against this backdrop, the Moroccan French author Tahar Ben Jelloun published a sharp critique in 1984 under the sarcastic title *Hospitalité française: Racisme et immigration maghrébine* (published in English translation as *French Hospitality: Racism and North African Immigrants*). He acknowledged that France remained in principle a country of asylum, but he also observed the growing tide of racist animosity towards people from North Africa or of North African descent. Already in June 1980, a young actor, Saïd Hamani Ali, who had been born in Nanterre, had set fire to himself at the Gare Saint-Lazare to protest his imminent deportation.[27]

The immediate pretext for writing *French Hospitality* was the murder on 9 July 1983 of an eleven-year-old boy, Taoufik Ouannès, at the '4000' housing complex at La Courneuve on the outskirts of Paris. Taoufik had been born in Clichy-sur-Bois to immigrant parents. What, Ben Jelloun asked, had prompted someone to kill a little boy merely because he was playing football in a boisterous manner? This was not an isolated instance: eleven days later, a Portuguese father of five shot and killed Ahmed Benkhidi, a seventeen-year-old Algerian boy, simply for 'keeping him awake'. Ben Jelloun compiled a long list of racist murders and other attacks committed on North Africans between May 1982 and October

1983. They included a firebomb attack on SONACOTRAL hostels in Massy, Corbeil, and Colombes that left four people dead. Another hostel in Marseille was bombed in August 1983.[28]

Ben Jelloun detected in these and earlier racist murders a denial of French republican values against a general backdrop of economic slow-down. The generation of youths who in 1968 had been radicalised by argu-ments about neocolonialism and Third World struggles had grown up to become indifferent or overtly hostile to immigrants, who were the very people who had helped turn France into a more prosperous country.

Needless to say, by no means had all the political leaders in France shared in the excitement of 1968; nor did all of them now adhere to a traditionally conservative line. However, in an extraordinary intervention following the murder of Taoufik Ouannès, Jacques Chirac wrote in the French newspaper *Le Monde* that 'the threshold of tolerance has been crossed'. He went on to propose 'a bold and lucid policy to try to interrupt the flow of people arriving, some of whom are criminal types'. His state-ment thus appeased racist opinion rather than taking the opportunity to apologise to the family of the murdered boy's family. Not one to beat around the racist bush, the far-right politician Jean-Marie Le Pen lam-basted 'armed and organised foreign minorities' who threatened 'the French people'.[29]

Ben Jelloun was at pains to point out that instances of racist abuse and murder were part of a broader problem in mainstream French society. Elsewhere in *French Hospitality*, he chronicled a training session he had run in the late 1970s on behalf of the management of Renault, on the topic of 'Islam and cultural differences'. Some managers and executives had made it clear that they disliked Algerians, thought all Tunisians were 'obsequious', but looked upon Moroccans as 'reliable': 'except when they go sick'. A company doctor complained that North Africans were 'shirk-ers' who wanted free medical treatment. 'I prefer the Asians', said a nurse: 'They're straightforward, don't make a fuss.' No one accepted Ben Jel-loun's comment that this was racist talk, and he lamented the extent to which racism had become second nature to educated professionals as well as to political parties on both the right and the left.[30]

'Yet France is where I live', Ben Jelloun concluded. Ultimately, he decided that bridges had to be built. Simply affirming the 'right to be different' did not lead anywhere, in his view. It reinforced 'the herding together of immigrants in transit centres, hostels and insalubrious districts'. What mattered was the pursuit of real social and political equality and the need to call out the prejudice and discrimination to which migrants of colour were exposed at every turn, even if he himself sometimes escaped its worst manifestations. As one Renault executive told him, 'No one would ever think you were an Arab.'[31]

The written word described racism and discrimination in France in the 1980s, but music became the chief form of art for self-expression, particularly for second-generation migrants, who asserted pride in their background and their contribution to French society. The most famous rock group in France was undoubtedly Zebda, a group that originated in Toulouse in 1985, taking its name from *zibdah*, the Arabic word for butter. This was a play on the French word *beur*, a slang term referring to French citizens of Maghrebian origin. Politically aware, Zebda rapidly gained a large following on account of its campaign for social justice. Its 1995 album, *Le Bruit et l'odeur* (Noise and smell) alluded to a notorious remark by President Chirac, who had complained about the conditions in the overcrowded *banlieus*, or suburbs. The lyrics of this and other songs deliberately drew upon 'nonstandard' French to emphasise the vitality and legitimacy of the Maghrebian vernacular, which their schoolteachers had tried to suppress. Zebda's lead singer, Magyd Cherfi, said, 'I want my city [Toulouse] to be an example of a society of mixed races [*société à la métisse*] where everyone can be himself…a kind of model utopia that can become the envy of Paris.' Interviewed in 2004, one young French Parisian said that Zebda was 'the voice of my generation'; a nineteen-year-old, Mina, said the group embodied her hopes for a brighter future: 'the tears that smile'.[32]

There was nevertheless a long way to go. Yamina Benguigui (who had been born in Lille to Algerian parents) produced a documentary, *Mémoires d'immigrés: l'héritage maghrébin* (Memoirs of immigrants: the Maghreb heritage, 1997), which drew upon more than 350 interviews with North African migrants in France. One interviewee said he resented that French officials and employers treated him like a child. Women from the Maghreb detailed the material deprivations and miserable living conditions in the bidonvilles. A man, Khémais Dabous, spoke of his love of the French language and French literature and his strong attachment to the workplace, which was so great that he 'fell in love with Renault'. He added, 'I think Renault fell in love with me too, and I began to feel worthwhile.' But the France of his imagination failed to live up to reality.[33]

Things were not much better in the Netherlands. Moluccans from Indonesia lived isolated lives in remote neighbourhoods. One Moluccan recalled that Dutch landlords refused to lease property to 'unsavoury people'. Migrants struggled to interact with their fellow workers. When they did interact with the Dutch, on the street or in the supermarket, they felt that they were being patronised: 'Dutch people love to go to the Moluccan church, although it is only to look at the monkeys', said one, referring to a racist taunt, 'and then eat all our lovely food. Because that is the image Dutch people have of Moluccans.' This looked like a new form of colonialism, with Moluccans as an 'exotic' presence in the Netherlands. Moluccan activists were accused of sustaining their cultural distinctiveness because they rejected integration and intended to return to Indonesia.[34]

Surinamese arrived in the Netherlands in large numbers during the 1970s, but their arrival highlighted differences between the new cohort of mainly lower-class migrants and the more highly educated students and professionals who had already established a foothold during the colonial era. Working-class Surinamese suffered disproportionately from the decline in jobs in the 1970s, and they faced significant hostility from mainstream Dutch society. But the picture was certainly more nuanced than this. A study of their position in Dutch society found that first-generation migrants from an Afro-Caribbean (Creole) background did better than their Indo-Surinamese counterparts, because the latter had been concentrated predominantly in agricultural occupations in Surinam, and their lower level of skill translated into economic disadvantage when they reached the Netherlands. Creole migrants spoke better Dutch and were more easily able to make their way in metropolitan society, where women, in particular, found jobs in health care and welfare.

Fluency in the language gave both groups a head start over other migrants, such as Turkish and Moroccan newcomers.[35]

Moroccans who had arrived in the Netherlands in the 1960s recalled knowing little of the country: 'I knew nothing about the Netherlands, except milk and cows and that they built their country on the sea. So you expect that there are hills and valleys. But if you come here, where was the sea? Everything is flat.' 'Soccer! That is what the second generation will say, Gullit and Rijkaard. Butter! Flowers! And the beautiful women! Democracy, freedom of speech. But work... it was a country of hard work [in return for] milk, cheese, potatoes and a lot of services.' Others spoke of the opportunity for adventure: 'I received the keys to paradise, my green passport. Who ever thought that I would get it? My mother complained, "My son will go to a country full of Christians!" I left my country.... And now I work to become rich, to have a car, to get girls. I work on Saturdays and Sundays, Friday and New Year's Eve. I work the whole day, I come back late. My dinner is gross. I eat vegetables without spices.'[36]

Moroccans in the Netherlands spoke of having to conduct themselves in an 'appropriate' fashion: 'You are always conscious of being Moroccan, especially at work', one said. 'I always try to distinguish myself by being quiet and friendly. Recently, when I was in a hurry and I needed a photocopy, the copier faltered. I really wanted to scream and shout, but I did not. You say to yourself, everybody will think: "you see, a real Moroccan".'[37]

Of their encounters with local Dutch people, one Moroccan migrant had the following to say:

> I remember that when I came to the Netherlands and had to work in the mines—I spoke a little Dutch, but mostly we spoke French. Somebody asked me if we had cars. I thought, why ask me that, we do not come from another planet! So I said no, only because I just thought he was dumb! Do you have streetcars? Also, no. Do you have a bicycle? No. But how did you come over here? Yes, he was really stupid, so I said: 'With a camel!...' I really thought, are the people here stupid or clever? We also have cars, cycles and streetcars! But they did not know a lot about our country.[38]

Another was prepared to confront prejudice even more assertively:

One time I heard people talking about me. The man said to the woman: 'My opinion is that you cannot walk on the streets like that, with those clothes.' I said: 'Sir, you can say that to my face.' He did not expect my reaction, because he turned bright red. Then I said: 'Sir, one thing that we cannot do is to categorize people. Nobody is a group. I am myself and you are you. One time you wear green socks, the next time red. I do that because I have my reasons for that. So if you want to know why, just ask me.'[39]

There was a broad consensus in the 1970s that it was important for Moroccan migrants, and, by extension, others in the Netherlands, to be able to retain their cultural identity, as a means of enabling guest workers to cope with the rigours of migration and to ensure that their eventual return to their homeland would not be too much of a shock. The connection with the homeland was thought to be an indispensable element in making life tolerable for the migrants as well as for those they left behind.

Earning and spending money exemplified this dual affiliation. A Moroccan student in the Netherlands reported on his spending habits as follows:

The net monthly salary that we received included housing and so we received 600 guilders or thereabouts. For me this was enough. I did not spend much money. I sent money home each month, around 100 guilders. Yes, the first thing I bought was a moped. And new clothes. I always wore western clothes: in Marrakech in the city we wore the same. But I bought some more hip clothes to fit into the group... pants with wide legs and shirts with pointed collars.

Consumer goods also conferred prestige back home. A Moroccan guest worker said, 'When you went back (to Morocco) in the holidays you had to bring some presents for your mother and sister. Our mother preferred a mixer for the kitchen, all that nonsense. Yes, and when I came back two years later it was still in the box! She thought it was wonderful, but she did not know how to use these devices.'[40]

In this way, migrants moved between two worlds. But why should they not have a foot in both places? In any case, the state in the country of origin sought to keep tabs on its migrants. Turkey did this in relation to its guest workers in Germany, and the Dutch government referred to 'Morocco's long arm' to describe the same phenomenon, which hampered efforts at integrating migrants and contributed to their exclusion. An added and more serious complication was that the migrant could be the conduit for political interference by a foreign power. The Dutch government became concerned about heavily subsidised groups operating in the Netherlands that harassed the opponents of the authoritarian regime in Morocco and hampered the formation of independent associations.[41]

For some migrants in later twentieth-century Europe, what mattered was a sense of attachment to a much larger community, a diaspora. Diaspora implied that a particular ethnic group had been dispersed to different places, yet remained bound together by a collective identity. Diasporic organisations cultivated a sense of community among migrants, enabling them to sustain an attachment to their homeland, or, as in the case of the extensive Kurdish population, to support the creation of a state of their own. To be sure, there was evidence of division—and divisiveness—within each migrant population: migrants from the same ethnic background experienced the host society in different ways, depending on their social class, their social capital (such as their level of education and the contacts available to them), and their political affiliation. Nevertheless, the stakes could be very high for migrants, since the greater their sense of being part of a larger diaspora, the more they raised questions for the host state about belonging and integration.[42]

Whatever means they devised, migrants faced significant obstacles in coming to terms with their displacement. One option was simply to stick close together, even if this risked the formation of urban ghettoes. Where they lived close to nonmigrant neighbours, the consequences could be unsettling and even terrifying. The nonmigrant neighbours drew associations between migrants and cultural difference, and this way of thinking manifested itself in complaints—for example, by German neighbours about guest workers who played the radio on full volume, or the Parisian who murdered young Taoufik Ouannès over a boisterous football game.

It did not take much for the seemingly petty problems of everyday life to manifest themselves as deep antagonisms between migrants and the host population. Social interaction became something of a minefield. Caught up in disputes with neighbours, having to deal with bosses and bureaucrats, responding to these challenges by seeking safety in their own numbers, and risking the accusation that they were isolating themselves in deprived communities, migrants sometimes felt they could get nothing right. A migrant from the Caribbean island of Montserrat who arrived in Britain in the 1950s spoke for many other newcomers when he reflected on how often he was made to feel more like a criminal than a respected member of British society: 'You never know when you are a trespasser in another man's country.'[43]

PART 4

Reordering Europe and Managing Migration

1989–2008

CHAPTER 15

The End of Communism: Picking Up the Pieces

It was widely anticipated that the end of communist rule would unleash a colossal exodus on the part of people who had been denied the opportunity to leave. In a preposterous but not untypical intervention, the chair of the US Foreign Relations Committee predicted that the collapse of the Soviet Union in 1991 would unleash something akin to the barbarian invasions that 'destroyed the Roman Empire'. Relatively prosperous countries in Central Europe, such as Czechoslovakia, envisaged a sudden influx of Russian 'tourists' who intended to stay for good. The rhetoric in Western European capitals around dreams of freedom and the favourable publicity given to dramas of 'escape' in the 1950s seemed to be a distant memory, now replaced by apprehension about the potential weight of numbers.[1]

Although this apocalypse never came to pass, nevertheless the fallout from the collapse of communism had profound social, economic, and political consequences, some of which hardly registered on the barometer of international public opinion. Eastern Europeans took the opportunity to move more freely. A popular joke in Sofia had three Bulgarians dressed as samurai warriors. Puzzled onlookers asked them to explain: 'We are the seven samurai and we want to make this country a better place.' 'But why are there only three of you?' 'Because only three of us stayed, the rest are all abroad.'[2]

The end of communist rule had dramatic results within the USSR as well as in Soviet-dominated Eastern Europe. In the late Soviet era, people could move without legal hindrance between the fifteen different constituent republics of the USSR. But in 1991 each republic declared its independence. The consequence was that widespread internal migration within unified Soviet territory came to an end. Internal borders within the Soviet Union became international frontiers. As a mark of its sovereignty, each state issued its own passports and appointed border guards. Controls on entry had immediate implications for anyone who relied hitherto on regular migration between former Soviet republics, whether to find work, to engage in trade, to access water and other resources (vital in Central Asia), or simply to visit family and friends. The challenges of adjustment would be considerable to those who previously criss-crossed borders. They, too, had to pick up the pieces of the collapse of communism.[3]

This is not to say that migration ran smoothly in the latter years of the Soviet Union. Tens of thousands of migrants from the Caucasus and Central Asia had arrived in Russian cities from the 1960s onwards. They sold fruit, nuts, and flowers at railway stations and city bazaars, where tourists remarked on the 'colour' and vibrancy they contributed to cities such as Moscow and Leningrad. In truth, they lived drab lives in communal dormitories, and faced regular harassment from the local police and Russian inhabitants, who regarded them as little more than criminal. On the other hand, they were Soviet citizens. Nevertheless, the Slavic residents of major cities such as Moscow and Leningrad often looked down on non-white migrants from the Caucasus and Central Asia, whose reputation suffered from the activities of a handful of corrupt officials and entrepreneurs from the Caucasus who operated in the extensive Soviet informal economy. Partly for this reason, but also because of their skin colour, these migrant traders often faced discrimination and demeaning treatment at the hands of locals who called them 'black snouts' or who asked, with a touch of menace, 'Where are you from?' Patronising remarks, such as saying, 'Your Russian is very good', concealed more than a hint of menace and made them feel like outsiders in their own country.[4]

No matter how significant in domestic terms, little of this internal migration registered outside the USSR, even when it was connected to momentous events. In Ukraine, the disaster that occurred at the Chernobyl nuclear reactor in Pripyat, close to the neighbouring republic of Belarus, was followed by the mass evacuation of civilians from the surrounding area, but the story of these 'refugees' (as they styled themselves) was lost in the midst of the worldwide publicity given to the subsequent radioactive fallout and the measures taken to cover the nuclear reactor in a concrete sarcophagus.[5]

In international diplomacy, one fundamental issue concerned the barriers to exit that were regarded as a touchstone of Soviet disregard for human rights. Although the Soviet law code did not ban emigration, the Communist Party of the Soviet Union had made it extremely difficult for people to emigrate. In practice, only four specified groups could legally apply to emigrate: Jews, Germans, Armenians, and Greeks, for whom the law provided for the reunification of family members. But the Soviet state hounded those who did apply, and this had a significant deterrent effect on the numbers who left.

Under the leadership of Mikhail Gorbachev, the policies of *perestroika* (restructuring) and *glasnost* (openness) changed the rules of the game. Perestroika lifted restrictions on emigration: around 1 million people left the Soviet Union between 1987 and 1991. Glasnost made it possible to criticise expressions of socialist internationalism, particularly where it had resulted in Soviet invasion and occupation—in Hungary in 1956, in Czechoslovakia in 1968, and in Afghanistan in 1980.

After the collapse of Soviet rule in 1991, the pace of emigration did not let up, although millions of Russians, Ukrainians, and others stayed put. Ethnic Germans emigrated in the hundreds of thousands in the wake of a rapid decline in living standards along with uncertainty about their future status in the newly independent successor states formed from the wreckage of the Soviet Union—and because of the prospect of being offered greater security in Germany. Jews took advantage of the lifting of restrictions on emigration to move to Israel. Others who expressed an interest in moving to another country made exploratory visits to the United States and to Germany before reaching a decision about where to resettle. With less fanfare, the dissolution of the USSR also culminated in the repatriation of Soviet troops from Eastern Europe and Afghanistan.[6]

The bigger news concerned the upheavals taking place in the former USSR. Soviet citizenship evaporated. Although questions were asked about the status of non-Russians who ran their businesses from towns and cities in the new Russian Federation, the main issue concerned Russians living in what was known as the 'near abroad'. At the moment of Soviet collapse, 25.3 million ethnic Russians were living outside the Russian republic (RSFSR), more than half of them in non-Slavic parts of the Soviet Union. The final Soviet census, conducted in 1989, recorded 11.4 million Russians in Ukraine (22 percent of its total population), 6.2 million in Kazakhstan (38 percent of its total), 1.7 million in Uzbekistan, and 1.3 million in Belarus. Russians made up 34 percent of the population of both Latvia and Estonia. In addition, some 11 million Russian speakers living outside the Russian Federation were believed to have a close cultural affinity to Russia. Russians had already begun to return from Central Asia and the Caucasus in the 1970s and 1980s, although Russians continued to migrate to Ukraine and the Baltic republics until the end of the Soviet period.[7]

Non-Russian majorities in newly independent states made it clear that Russians would occupy a subordinate position, reversing decades of what some politicians argued had been concerted Russification and the promotion of ethnic Russians to positions of responsibility in government and economic administration. Baltic governments adopted policies to sustain a 'national renaissance' and to counter Russian influence. Many Russians were disenfranchised and treated with barely disguised contempt as the embodiment of Soviet power or Russian imperialism: 'Go back to your Russia', one Russian migrant was told. Another said that he 'felt like a leper'. Some Russians chose to remain, whether it was because of an affinity with their heritage or because they did not want to lose touch with friends and family. Others opted to migrate to Russia, some in order to safeguard the future of their children, others in search of what they hoped would be greater economic security. Some Russians escaped from persecution in Tajikistan and Kyrgyzstan to deserted villages in distant Belarus that had been abruptly evacuated in the aftermath of the Chernobyl disaster. Their decision to settle in Belarus, which maintained close ties with Russia, offered a respite from violence in their homelands, but it did not alleviate the pain of displacement and deprivation. An unnamed Tajik woman lamented the fact that 'we lost two motherlands at once: our Tajikistan and the Soviet Union'. Lena M., who arrived in Belarus from Kyrgyzstan, added, 'Our country doesn't exist, but we still exist'.[8]

Several million people moved to Russia from the other post-Soviet successor states between 1991 and 2001, either under duress or, more commonly, because they feared their Russian ethnicity would put them at a disadvantage. Official figures put the number of displaced Russians and Russian-speaking groups at 1.5 million, but underreporting and irregular migration meant that the real total may have been five or six times higher. (There was also significant migration in the opposite direction.) At first glance, their situation was not unlike that of the settlers and officials who 'returned' to Western Europe after colonial rule came to an end in Africa and Asia. As one Russian put it, reflecting on the fact that the borders moved while he had not, 'we suddenly found ourselves to be immigrants within our own country'. He added that he still felt part of a larger political entity—the USSR—even though it had now vanished. The status of Russian as a lingua franca was also diminished, as the new successor states adopted the language of the titular majority.[9]

Unable to take their rights for granted in the newly independent states that emerged from the rubble of the Soviet Union, and deciding to relocate to Russia, these Russian repatriates initially had no guaranteed rights in the Russian 'homeland'; nor could they count on being accepted by other Russians with whom they had no direct connection, even if they shared a common language. They had to negotiate a new political landscape, but without being assured of a warm welcome.[10]

Legislation that came into force in 1993 distinguished between 'forced migrants' and refugees. A forced migrant was someone with Russian Federation citizenship who was deemed to have left or intended to leave 'his or her place of residence on the territory of another state or on the territory of the Russian Federation as a result of violence or other form of persecution towards him- or herself or members of his or her family'. A refugee was someone who did not have Russian citizenship, such as an

Azeri or a Tajik fleeing violence in his or her own state. Persecution meant being threatened on grounds of race, religion, language, or membership of a particular social group or political persuasion—provisions that echoed the 1951 UN Refugee Convention—but it also included being the target of threats 'in connection with the conducting of hostile campaigns towards individuals or groups of individuals, mass violations of public order or other circumstances significantly restricting human rights'. This neat legal formulation and the recognition of citizenship rights had little meaning for migrants who encountered bureaucratic indifference. Worse, the Russian Federation began to prioritise domestic 'security' and the regulation of migration over practical assistance to those who arrived. Further legislation in 1995 and 2002 was designed to encourage Russians to stay in the 'near abroad' by tightening up the rules on citizenship.[11]

Russian migrants who moved to the Russian Federation from newly independent (former Soviet) states hoped to secure decent living arrangements, but instead they had to make do with poor accommodation. Their plight was alleviated by various self-help strategies, such as relying on family and other personal connections. But they could do nothing about local resentment towards their presence, which was compounded by the severe economic decline in the Russian Federation during the 1990s. Some government officials regarded the newcomers as a resource helping to offset the consequences of the declining birth rate in Russia. Russian migrants sometimes maintained that they contributed something else, too, claiming that they belonged to a 'higher cultural level' than that of Russians who had lived their lives within the Russian Federation. One middle-aged migrant in Samara, in 1999, said: 'It is highly qualified, cultured, intellectual, well brought up people who have arrived. They want to bring their culture and strong labour potential to the economy and culture of Russia.' Migrants thus drew a distinction between other Russians and themselves, seeing themselves as custodians of the 'real Russia'. This stance, a deliberate strategy to elicit more government support, did little to improve relations between the two communities. Longtime residents might discount expressions of cultural superiority on the part of newcomers, but they certainly resented what they took (misleadingly) to be the newcomers' relative wealth. In this context, it perhaps comes as no surprise to learn that locals were wont to refer to them as 'refugees' and even 'black assholes'.[12]

Russian nationalists exploited the situation, expressing alarm at the discrimination suffered by ethnic Russians living in the successor states. But, rather than encourage their resettlement in the Russian Federation, or their integration into the newly independent states, Russia's far right called instead for the 'reunification of the Russian nation' through territorial revision. As things stand, and with the notable exception of the reappropriation of Crimea and the ongoing and (as of 2019) unresolved conflict in eastern Ukraine, no such revision has taken place. Ethnic Russians did not join 'homeland societies' along the lines of ethnic German expellees in West Germany during the 1950s. Many of them retained a 'Soviet' perspective rather than developing a Russian nationalist outlook: 'We lived normally', said an elderly Russian who arrived in Novosibirsk in 1994. 'Then, when it all started, how do you call it, that nationalism. I don't understand where it came from. We lived all our lives there, we studied together, friends of mine got married to Kazakhs, and everything was OK. Why did it all happen?'[13]

Nationalist programmes gained ground elsewhere in the former Soviet Union. Kazakhstan, for instance, embarked on an ambitious and generous 'repatriation' programme, supporting the relocation of ethnic Kazakhs from neighbouring states, including Russia, China, and Mongolia, where they had lived for generations. This helped to compensate for the loss of ethnic Germans, whose numbers declined from around 1 million in 1989 (some 6 percent of the population of Kazakhstan) to 350,000 a decade later, and to 180,000 by 2012, most of them having left for Germany, although a significant number migrated to the Russian Federation. From 1991 onwards, Kazakhstan financed the resettlement of around 950,000 Kazakhs from a dozen countries, 640,000 of them from former Soviet republics and 110,000 from Mongolia. This was a controlled programme, with an annual admission quota. The so-called repatriates were attracted by the opportunities in the rapidly expanding Kazakh economy. In addition to relatively high wages, they received generous housing benefits, free health care, and pensions. In 1997, they became entitled to citizenship. They knew the Kazakh language and could demonstrate a familiarity with Kazakh traditions. Yet this linguistic competence did not ensure a warm welcome from local Kazakhs, who resented the preferential treatment given to the repatriates, whom they called 'Mongolians' or 'Chinese'. The repatriates were unable to converse in Russian as the lingua franca, which was widely spoken in the towns and cities of Kazakhstan as a result of sustained Soviet rule. In other words, although officially they were welcomed as exemplary Kazakhs, they experienced relocation as disruptive and demeaning. These migrants did not feel—and were not made to feel—'at home'. Subsequently, some of them opted to return to China and Mongolia. It was another sign of the painful dislocation associated with the Soviet collapse and post-Soviet state formation as well as yet another demonstration that a common ethnicity was no guarantee of acceptance.[14]

The death throes and the dissolution of the Soviet state also had implications for national minorities who had suffered persecution and deportation at the height of the Stalinist terror. Crimean Tatars, who had been brutally deported in 1944 by Stalin's secret police on trumped-up charges of treason, could 'return' to their homeland from Central Asia. Around 250,000 Crimean Tatar deportees and their descendants eventually returned to Ukraine. But repatriation posed legal and material difficulties. In 1999 the Ukrainian government insisted that those who resettled in Ukraine had to renounce their Uzbek citizenship. They tried but failed to establish an autonomous republic or to have their 'national assembly' (*Mejlis*) recognised officially. Caught, so to speak, in the midst of an intense and still unresolved Russian-Ukrainian rivalry, Crimean Tatars insisted on the right to be recognised as indigenous inhabitants of Crimea. They either squatted on vacant land or conducted frustrating and often distressing negotiations with competing (non-Tatar) claimants and the city authorities. Some family members opted to remain in Central Asia, where housing conditions were more tolerable. Others spoke of feeling 'at home' in neither place.[15]

Another group suffered even more drastically from Stalinist persecution and then from the imminent Soviet collapse. These were Meskhetian Turks, Muslims who had been deported from Georgia in the later stages of the Second World War and scattered across Kazakhstan, Uzbekistan, and Kyrgyzstan. On the eve of the Soviet collapse, their numbers stood at around 200,000. In 1989, Uzbeks in the Ferghana Valley turned on them and drove them from their homes, the second time in half a century that they had been forcibly expelled. Most of them ended up in Azerbaijan or in the southern Russian region of Krasnodar. Thousands were subsequently admitted to the United States.[16]

Continuing conflicts in the Caucasus forced people to flee their homes. Serious clashes took place in Georgia, Armenia, and Azerbaijan. More than 1 million Azeris and Armenians were displaced from the late 1980s onwards. Thanks to a combination of political and economic uncertainty, Soviet Armenia witnessed the emigration of 1 million Armenians, mostly labour migrants, to the Russian Federation and Ukraine, which together accounted for around 80 percent of the total. This migration partly followed the pattern in other former Soviet republics, namely, a response to deteriorating economic conditions, but it was also driven by the conflict between Armenia and Azerbaijan over the long-disputed enclave of Nagorno-Karabagh that erupted during the Gorbachev era.[17]

Other Armenians migrated to the United States, France, and other countries, where they linked up with the diaspora. Several hundred fled from the Caucasus to the Czech Republic and were granted leave to remain after lodging claims in Brno and spending months in refugee camps, such as in Zastávka. One woman spoke of her family's decision to leave Erevan in 1998: 'In Armenia only those who were invalid, old, stayed; those who had an opportunity to escape escaped; those who were in bad conditions so that they could not afford to take the journey had to stay, not that they wanted to stay but they had to stay.' A middle-aged man described leaving Armenia in the hope of getting a job in Germany. He only made it as far as Prague: 'They told us fairy tales that you will get 20, 30 marks per an hour, plenty of work. [But] here? No work, no such miracles existed, you know, I spent all I had in my pocket and then I saw that to be able to stay you had to go to a camp.' In a situation of considerable uncertainty, the decision to remain was mainly governed by the fact that his children were now accustomed to life in the Czech Republic. With no jobs appropriate to their qualifications, Armenian migrants worked in retailing, which enabled them to send modest amounts of money back to relatives in Armenia, who persisted in the belief that the West offered plentiful opportunities.[18]

The separatist war that broke out in 1992 between Russia and Georgia over rival claims to Abkhazia forced 200,000 people to leave their homes. Ten thousand people took shelter in the abandoned Soviet-era sanatorium in Tskaltubo, Georgia, where hundreds of them were still living with their children and grandchildren more than twenty-five years later. Particularly unsettling was the protracted war in Chechnya. At one stage, more than half a million people were thought to have been displaced, either within Chechnya or in adjacent regions. By 2000, around 140,000 refugees had sought sanctuary in neighbouring Ingushetia, where they were forced to live in tents, railway carriages, and abandoned cars until they deemed it safe to return to their homes.[19]

Not everything was about interethnic confrontation and bloodshed. One little-known episode concerned the descendants of Pontic Greeks, farmers and merchants who originally settled on the shores of the Black Sea in the eighteenth and nineteenth centuries, and who eventually chose the option of 'returning' to Greece. Their history in the post-Soviet era disclosed broader themes: not just the many crosscurrents of migration in the twentieth century, but the impetus given to migration by the hopes invested in economic progress, by the appeal of national identity, and by the prospects opened up by political upheaval.

Pontic Greeks left for Greece in relatively small numbers in the late 1950s and 1960s, but they had to circumvent Soviet bureaucratic obstacles. Their chequered history in the twentieth century is neatly encapsulated in the life story of Polychronis Boubouridis. Boubouridis was born in 1920 in the coastal town of Sukhumi. He trained as a doctor and served in the Red Army during the Second World War. His life and those of many other Greeks was turned upside-down in 1949, when they were deported to Kazakhstan. Boubouridis got a job as a neurologist in a city hospital and was then elected to the regional parliament. In 1954, he and his wife, together with their two young children, were permitted to return to Sukhumi. He went back to his old job, and his wife taught in the local music school. Life took a turn for the worse in the perestroika years, when antagonism flared up between Abkhazians and Georgians. In 1987 Boubouridis decided to sell his property and take his entire family to Greece. Since he was only allowed to take a few rubles with him when he left, he travelled around Russia and bought up goods that he could sell when he arrived in Greece. In old age, he joined a local association of Pontic Greeks and dedicated himself to making their history better known. The topsy-turvy post-Soviet world also registered in the lives of those who stayed behind. As one Greek living in Kazakhstan put it plaintively, when confronted by the departure of his neighbours to Greece, 'we are like the Etruscans here, we will soon disappear and no one will know that we have ever lived in Central Asia'. He lamented for a lost world in which it was possible to be both Soviet and Greek.[20]

Like Polychronis, most of them joined the exodus either just before or just after the collapse of the Soviet Union. By the early 1990s, the annual total stood at more than 10,000, and by the end of the millennium at least 70,000 former Pontic Greeks were living in Greece, mainly in or around Athens. They spoke Russian and a distinct Greek dialect; they had to learn a new language in order to be understood in Greece. The Greek government welcomed their 'return' because it made possible the settlement of depopulated regions, such as Thrace. Start-up loans were part of the package. Pontic Greeks were treated as Greek nationals and given full citizenship. However, the government refused to recognise the qualifications they had gained in the USSR. More troubling was the tendency of local Greeks to look upon the migrants as aliens ('Russians') and as 'lazy' people who wanted to milk the system. This history demonstrates the kind of divisive discourse that can emerge around who 'belongs'—in this instance, who is and who is not entitled to be 'Greek'. Such claims were reinforced by the belief that the later generation of Pontic Greeks were economic migrants who had little in common with those who had struggled to leave the USSR. Only the latter were perceived as having demonstrated a genuine attachment to the Greek nation. The claims of a common national identity were insufficient to enable the integration of the newcomers in Greece.[21]

Elsewhere in Eastern Europe, political and territorial upheavals created enticing prospects for people who looked westwards. This observation needs to be set in a broader chronological context. Among Polish workers, for example, the economic crisis following the declaration of martial law in December 1981 intensified labour migration and petty trade, whilst at the same time it put a stop to officially sanctioned emigration. Not surprisingly, around 150,000 Poles who were in the West chose not to return to Poland. As the economy continued to decline, irregular migration flourished; Poles applied for tourist visas and overstayed. They mostly took menial jobs on German farms, on French vineyards, or in British bars, where they could earn in a few weeks the equivalent of several months or even years of work back home. According to the Polish census in 1988, more than 600,000 people were 'temporarily absent'. When the walls tumbled down, many Poles who had been working illegally in Western Europe took steps to acquire legal status.[22]

The migration was not all one-way: Poland became a country of immigration, not just emigration. The expanding service sector recruited Ukrainian workers, so-called economic migrants (*zarobitchany*) who took up jobs in Warsaw and other major cities. Yet migration between countries in the former Soviet bloc sometimes made for uncomfortable encounters as the new generation came face to face with an older cohort. Among Ukrainians, for example, victims of the orchestrated expulsions that took place in the late 1940s had made a life for themselves in communist-era Poland. They had little in common with Ukrainian migrants who ventured to Poland in search of work in the 1990s. As a Ukrainian priest whose family had been resettled under the notorious 1947 *Akcja Wisła* described his long-standing parishioners, 'maybe they feel they are better than someone who comes here to clean and cook'. There was a strong whiff here of wanting to differentiate oneself as a forced migrant from those who exploited new market opportunities to make a fast buck.[23]

Negotiating economic opportunities was only one facet of the transformation of Eastern Europe. Another was the precarious position of ethnic minorities in the countries of the former Soviet bloc. These included groups that had retained a foothold in states dominated by members of a titular majority. Germans and Hungarians living in Romania were a case in point. The relatively small number of ethnic Germans who remained in Romania when most others had been expelled after 1945 thought of themselves, not without reason, as an embattled minority in a communist state, tarred with the brush of collective guilt. Communist leader Nicolae Ceauşescu's emphasis on Romanian 'national communism' in the 1980s made their lives even more difficult. In a cynical ploy, Ceauşescu required Germans who sought permission to emigrate to sell their homes to the state, which handed over their property to newcomers from Moldova, whose loyalty he wished to cultivate.[24]

Meanwhile, the long-standing persecution by the Romanian security services of the Hungarian minority in Transylvania (around 8 percent of the country's population) came to an end when Ceauşescu lifted the ban on emigration. As a result, during the 1980s, around 50,000 Transylvanian Hungarians left Romania. They were not necessarily given a warm reception in Hungary. Hungary's first post-communist leader, József Antall, proudly proclaimed that he was prime minister not of 10 million but 15 million Magyars, meaning also those who lived outside Hungary. He was content for them to stay where they were rather than become a charge on the Hungarian state. It was another sign of the complex and potentially fractious relationship between demography and politics in Eastern Europe.[25]

One extraordinary episode was the mass departure of some 300,000 ethnic Turks from Bulgaria when the border with Turkey opened in 1989, reportedly to escape the assimilationist policies of the Bulgarian state that compelled ethnic Turks to change their names and forbade them to use their own language. A renowned weightlifter, Naim Süleymanoğlu, 'the pocket Hercules', evaded his Bulgarian minders when he competed at the world championships in Melbourne in 1986, under his imposed name of 'Naum Shalamanov'. The Turkish government arranged for him to be flown to Istanbul. He competed for Turkey in the Seoul Olympics in 1988 (where he won a gold medal), but only after the government agreed to pay Bulgaria $1 million, an acknowledgement that Naim's success owed something to his Bulgarian coach.[26]

The emigration of Turks from Bulgaria was not without precedent, but, as happened in 1950 and 1968, the newcomers received a muted welcome. In an ironic inversion of their lives in Bulgaria, which deemed them to be 'Turkish', Turkish society looked upon them as 'Bulgarian'. This did not stem further migration—some 30,000 Turks arrived, on average, each year between 1990 and 1997—but the new arrivals were uncertain as to whether they really belonged in the new 'motherland' or could participate fully in Turkish society, since locals continued to refer to them as 'the migrants'. With the added difficulty of finding work in Turkey, as many as one in three migrants decided to return to Bulgaria. One middle-aged woman described the challenges that these migrants faced in settling down: 'My brother came to Turkey with us and swore that he would never go back to Bulgaria. He even took "Dönmez" (which means "never returns" in Turkish) as his surname. But his family pressured him continuously, and he couldn't stand against their will. Therefore, they went back to Bulgaria a few months after coming here.' Unfortunately, the only jobs available to them were in low-wage branches of the Bulgarian economy.[27]

Migration was not only about job opportunities. From her vantage point in Bulgaria, the historian Theodora Dragostinova offered personal reflections about not only the prospects but also the familiar travails of migrant families who moved to Greece as part of the 'generation of democracy':

> I constantly heard stories of personal triumph, family sacrifice, disappointment, accommodation, and perseverance. Greece was full of illegal Bulgarian labour migrants, and, on the long bus rides home during my breaks, I listened to their stories of risky border crossings, long hours of hard work, tense encounters with authorities, misunderstandings with employers, and the lingering desire to see their families and simply 'go home'. In addition to heart-breaking personal tragedies, there were also accounts of successful adaptation, financial gain, and the resourceful handling of difficult circumstances.

Dragostinova perfectly captured the emotional dimension of migration in a rapidly changing country. She described how, 'back in Bulgaria', she 'paid attention to the situation of other "others"; Turks, Bulgarian Muslims, Roma, and foreigners from all corners of the world all offered moving insights on being treated as "strangers within".' Migration asked questions about national identity in a rapidly changing continent.[28]

Something of the same willingness to challenge nationalist claims and expectations emerged in the accounts of East European migrants, such as those who could now travel much more easily to and from Germany than had been possible under communist rule. They weighed up the options before deciding whether or not to give up seasonal work abroad and look for permanent employment instead. Interviewed in 2015, thirty-year-old Kasia described what prompted her to leave Poland and make her home in Berlin:

> Had I stayed in Poland, my life would had [*sic*] been completely different; here you are thrown into the deep end and you're on your own, and during the swim you're alone; you have to motivate yourself, and when you begin getting along with people you have to make choices about what you are prepared to take. For me this is normal, I live here, I was a child when I lived in Poland. Here is my job, my life....I feel free here.[29]

Iliena, a Romanian migrant farmworker in Andalusia, neatly encapsulated the mixture of estrangement and opportunity that took her compatriots all over Europe. 'You cannot be integrated here: Spaniards don't want foreigners to settle here, they just want us to work. But it fits what we want, we don't want to stay here, we don't care about Spain.' Iliena was quite prepared to move somewhere else, 'everywhere there is something to do....I have friends all over Europe.' What looked like alienation on a distant Spanish farm—something that was not helped by rivalry with Moroccan migrants—translated into a sense of cosmopolitan possibilities in other parts of the continent.[30]

Not everyone had such a positive assessment of the new opportunities that opened up in the 1990s and 2000s. The vagaries of the market economy dictated the choices available to prospective East European migrants. Elderly and well-educated Ukrainians moved to Germany on tourist visas and took jobs as caregivers, cleaners, and caterers in order to boost the prospects of family members back home. Alongside a significant group of high-earning Polish professionals, the majority found that only low-wage jobs were on offer. By 2005, the number of Ukrainian migrants in Italy stood at around 200,000. Portugal and Spain counted 115,000 and

100,000 Ukrainians, respectively, and there were an additional 125,000 in Greece. Around half a million Ukrainians were more or less equally divided between Poland and the Czech Republic.[31]

In Italy, Polish migrants were recruited for seasonal work on the vast Capitanata Plain in Puglia, where they harvested tomatoes alongside migrants from Bulgaria, Romania, and other parts of Italy. At the peak of the summer, the total labour force exceeded 100,000, two-fifths of whom were foreign workers. They were poorly paid for the work they did, and vulnerable to abuse and exploitation. Others found temporary work in Norway and performed backbreaking work, but they learned to stick together to protect their wages from being undercut by Sikh and Vietnamese migrant workers.[32]

Everything was in flux: in Poland itself, for example, Vietnamese guest workers who had been working for many years were laid off, but meanwhile, the more entrepreneurially minded quickly started small businesses making clothes and electronic items, something many of them had already done in the shadow economy of socialism. Other governments took a hard-nosed approach to labour migration. Hungary imposed strict controls on foreign workers through a system of work permits, as a ploy to secure electoral support at a time of rising unemployment during the transition to capitalism. Most of the permits went to people working in specialist occupations, such as Ukrainian needlewomen, Romanian glassblowers and shoemakers, and foreign-language teachers.[33]

Economic uncertainty was compounded by a more hostile environment in Western Europe. Polish citizens had extensive experience of crossing the border into Austria and Germany in order to supplement their income through trading, but by the late 1980s their presence in the markets of Vienna and Berlin had caused resentment and outright hostility towards 'Polish vermin' (*Polacken-Pack*). Although the authorities in Vienna took a lenient view of Polish traders, the right-wing politician Jörg Haider worked to whip up anti-foreigner sentiment; in September 1990, he celebrated the government's decision to end visa-free travel for Poles and Romanians. Although the European Union agreed on visa-free travel with Poland in April 1991, alarm bells sounded as Eastern Europe began to send workers to the West. In the words of Roland Issen, a leading German white-collar trade unionist, 'We can't just open the floodgates.' The image of impending disaster was difficult to dispel, although it flew in the face of evidence that migrants had a great deal to offer Western European economies that cried out for both skilled and unskilled workers.[34]

The Iron Curtain was both symbolic and real. It cut Europe in two and imposed tough restrictions on migration between East and West. Nevertheless, it bears repeating that not everything was about confinement, particularly within the communist orbit. Two decades on from the collapse of communism, it is easy to forget the vision of planned economic transformation, economic integration, and socialist internationalism in the Soviet bloc, even though this sometimes took a very brutal form, as Hungarians in 1956, Czechs and Slovaks in 1968, and Afghans in 1979 understood all too well. Soviet socialist planning had allowed for and encouraged migration within a single political space, whether by moving from country to town or by settling in distant corners of one's homeland. Once upon a time, these utopian aspirations were celebrated, and indeed, they were in part realised, through the movement of Soviet people within an area that stretched from the Baltic to the Pacific.

The collapse of communism throughout Eastern Europe created uncertainty and instability. Nationalist views gained ground, and politicians adopted nationalism as a legitimate means of governing the new successor states. The Soviet bloc fragmented. Former communist countries in East-Central Europe explored the possibilities of a closer economic and political relationship with the West, leaving Russia isolated. These upheavals had profound significance for migration and migrants. The new European order removed constraints on freedom of expression, enterprise, and foreign travel. Migrants had opportunities to work abroad. But they also faced discrimination and disadvantage. Migration was therefore a mixed blessing. Although it was now possible to get out, this did not mean that it was easy to get ahead.

CHAPTER 16

Reunification, Migration, and German Society

GERMANY'S PAST WEIGHED HEAVILY on migration and migration policy after 1945. West German politicians renounced discrimination and denounced persecution on grounds of racial difference, thereby demonstrating that Germany had rejected the core element of Nazi doctrine. Being open to newcomers was one hallmark of a democratic state. And although political leaders and journalists often repeated the mantra that Germany was 'not a country of immigration', statistics told a different story. According to the Federal Statistical Office (Statistisches Bundesamt), by the second decade of the new millennium, 16 million people, one in five of the total population, had an immigrant background. This group included 'all persons who [had] immigrated into the territory of today's Federal Republic of Germany after 1949, and of all foreigners born in Germany and all persons born in Germany who have at least one parent who immigrated into the country or was born in as a foreigner in Germany'.[1]

Not all migration ran along the same lines, and 'background' meant different things to different migrants. Everyone could agree, however, that the reunification of Germany was a turning point in the history of modern Europe. With no border between the two halves of Germany, the stage was set for the internal migration of several million German workers who moved from the former German Democratic Republic or commuted from their homes there to better-paid jobs in the West. It was not an easy transition. As a cabaret joke in former East Germany had it, 'things were better in the old days—at least we could escape'. This comment exposed the changes in the political climate. A younger generation could not be expected to recall how West Germany had taken in millions of ethnic German expellees after 1945. But for anyone who did remember this mass influx, there was another important lesson to be learned from the recent past: whatever the scale of the influx, Germany managed to cope.[2]

Reunification coincided with political upheavals in Eastern Europe. Here, too, the result was a relaxation of constraints on migration. Close to 1.5 million Germans had left the USSR and Eastern European countries between 1949 and 1987, an annual average of 37,000. Most of them arrived from Poland and Romania; only around 5 percent were from the Soviet Union. But in the following decade an average of around 220,000 ethnic German *Aussiedler* (emigrants) entered Germany each year, most of them from the former Soviet Union. Between 1989 and 1993, the same number of ethnic Germans (1.4 million) arrived in Germany as had arrived in the previous forty years. In 1993, the government decided to close the *Aussiedler* programme to all but ethnic Germans from the former Soviet Union. Every one of them who arrived had the right under the 1949 Basic Law to settle and be granted citizenship in the 'homeland'.[3]

The political significance of welcoming ethnic German migrants could hardly be exaggerated. In a 1998 speech, Chancellor Helmut Kohl welcomed them 'home' by telling them 'you are all a profit to our German fatherland'. But his speech was remarkable less for these warm words than for the thoughts he chose not to share with his audience. Kohl said nothing about the fact that their arrival held out the possibility of offsetting the low birth rate of ethnic Germans at a time when nationalists expressed concern about the high number of births to women of Turkish heritage. Here was yet another indication of the legacy of German migration policy: the perceived dilemmas in the corridors of power as to how to manage the demographic and social consequences of the recruitment of Turkish guest workers in the 1960s and early 1970s.[4]

Reunification posed a challenge because it coincided with the arrival of large numbers of non-German migrants. Germany became once more the magnet for migrants and asylum seekers from outside the European Economic Community (EEC). The annual number of asylum seekers in Germany increased from 35,000 in 1984 to 103,000 in 1988, and then to 256,000 in 1991. In the following year, the total reached 438,000, far eclipsing the record in other countries. Between 1990 and 1993, Germany processed around 1.2 million applications for asylum. Here, too, the past history of migration helped to determine the course of the applications, insofar as many refugees seeking sanctuary from the terrible conflicts in the former Yugoslavia had a prior connection with Germany, by virtue of having been guest workers in Germany or having personal contacts of some kind within the country.[5]

The ramifications of reunification, combined with the decision of the German government to accept asylum seekers, spread far and wide. These upheavals had a pronounced effect on debates in Germany, inviting discussion as to whether Germany should become a more pluralistic society, and if so, to what degree. According to *Der Spiegel*, in 1992 around three-quarters of adult Germans held the view that non-Germans 'abuse our social system [and] heighten the housing shortage'. Six out of ten believed that foreigners exacerbated unemployment and 'pose a danger on the streets'. Added to this was a growing consensus that most asylum seekers had not actually suffered persecution and were instead filing claims in order to improve their economic prospects, and that those whose claims were not accepted then sought to 'exploit the system' by remaining in Germany for months, or even years, while their claims were reconsidered.[6]

After the Berlin Wall came down in November 1989, the proportion of West Germans who rated asylum and immigration as their greatest concern increased from 10 percent to 70 percent. Germans living in the former GDR tended to be more dismissive towards foreigners than their West German counterparts. Refugees, in particular, faced difficulty being accepted. The most distressing manifestation of this xenophobic atmosphere was a succession of murders in the early 1990s motivated by racism; these coincided with parliamentary debates about placing new restrictions on asylum under revisions to the Basic Law. The argument in favour of the restrictions echoed debates in Britain and elsewhere: proponents said that without the limits, public anger would intensify and the risks to all migrants would increase. Mere mention of the need for greater restriction, however, served only to inflame public opinion. It seemed as if the image of a more tolerant and welcoming German society had been badly tarnished—except that the image had only borne a tenuous relationship to reality in the first place, as many Turkish migrants would have been the first to point out.[7]

New political freedoms in Eastern Europe changed the prospects for ethnic Germans who had settled in the tsarist empire during the eighteenth and nineteenth centuries. They had survived persecution and deportation during both world wars. A pressure group in postwar West Germany lobbied on their behalf without having much to show for its efforts, although in 1981, on the occasion of an official visit by Soviet leader Leonid Brezhnev, it organised a demonstration in Bonn under the slogan 'Freie Ausreise statt Verfolgung und Gefängnis' (Free emigration instead of persecution and prison). A combination of poverty and political uncertainty encouraged many ethnic Germans to seek permission to leave, but communist governments made departure difficult. Moreover, the Federal Republic required prospective migrants to have an invitation from a relative already living in Germany. The West German government did not automatically accept all applicants, although it was a good deal easier to leave Poland and Romania than elsewhere, provided the applicant could demonstrate that he or she had been persecuted on grounds of being a member of a distinctly German minority. Nevertheless, relatively few ethnic Germans reached the West in the 1980s.[8]

As the obstacles were removed, so the numbers of those choosing to exit increased. In 1989 alone, around 110,000 ethnic Germans left the disintegrating communist regime in Ceaușescu's Romania; some of those who stayed behind hedged their bets by holding onto their new German passports. They then had to negotiate the terms of admission in Germany. In her semiautobiographical novel *Reisende auf einem Bein* (*Traveling on One Leg*), the Nobel Prize–winning author Herta Müller describes her protagonist's encounter with the *Sacharbeiter*, the official case workers whose job it was to decide whether she was an ethnic German or a 'political refugee'. Even more stressful, as the novel points out, was being expected to show gratitude towards Germany, something that reminds the protagonist of the expectations to conform that she had endured back in Romania.[9]

German reunification and the collapse of the Soviet Union made the situation of ethnic German newcomers deeply unsettling. After being processed at the reception centre in Friedland, they were dispersed to their final destination. However, local German authorities complained of being given no time to prepare for their arrival, let alone for their integration. German social workers attributed relatively high rates of depression and alcoholism among the newcomers to the unsympathetic reception they were given. According to one unnamed Russian German migrant, 'there we were the fascist pigs; here we are the Russians'. Another said simply, 'It could be worse', hardly a ringing endorsement of the host society. It all seemed very reminiscent of the problems that German expellees had encountered four decades earlier.[10]

German churches led the way in urging Germans to be good hosts to people who were 'our own countrymen'. Many of the *Aussiedler* from the former Soviet Union had a poor or nonexistent grasp of German. They were entitled to German language classes, and the government created a special fund in 1988 to support their integration. But funding for these initiatives declined after 1993. Besides, many of the newcomers, including their children, preferred to continue communicating in Russian, much to the chagrin of their schoolteachers. The recession in the early 1990s also hit them hard: female *Aussiedler* in particular bore the brunt. Their qualifications made them a poor 'fit' in the German economy— that is to say, they were overqualified. German employers wanted construction workers and nursing auxiliaries and had little use for engineers and physicians. The migrants were twice as likely as other Germans to be unemployed. As already indicated, xenophobia was quite widespread. Resident Germans complained that the newcomers preferred to keep together, such as in the Berlin suburb of Marzahn. Faced with these difficulties, some of the *Aussiedler* from Kazakhstan chose to return there. But the majority decided to stick it out.[11]

New arrivals had extraordinary stories to tell. Erich Kludt, born in 1918, had spent time in the Gulag. His father, a pastor, had been shot by the Soviets in 1935, leaving a widow with six children. But Erich attained an engineering degree after being released, and in 1961 this took him to Kazakhstan, where he managed several construction projects. He and his wife, Nelli, had two children, and they lived a reasonably comfortable life. His narrative includes wistful remarks about the fruit that grew in the garden of his dacha outside Almaty. His work brought him into close contact with Russians, Jews, Tatars, and Kazakhs, who all got along until Kazakhstan declared independence. At that time, he said, they 'feared that history would repeat itself'. In 1995 the entire family decided to leave for Germany, and they managed to sell their apartment and dacha for a few thousand dollars. It helped that his younger son would be able to find a job in the IT sector, although the older son decided to stay in Almaty to look after his successful computer business. Erich and Nelli settled in Hamburg, part of a country that he now regards as 'beautiful and well cared for' (*gepflegt*). His only complaint—apart from the fact that Chancellor Gerhard Schröder had married for the fifth time and Foreign Minister Joschka Fischer had 'a new wife every other year'—was the marked social inequalities he observed in Germany. In later years, he still felt himself to be something of an outsider.[12]

Emma Neumann spoke of having 'two homelands': one the small village of Friedental, close to Cheliabinsk in the southern Urals, the other Hamburg-Bergedorf, where she had lived since 1996. She described life in Russia as a mixed blessing: although she had an unhappy marriage to a hard-drinking Russian, she had a fulfilling job in a factory. Interviewed in the late 1990s, she took pride in retaining her German identity—'a German from Russia, not a *Russlanddeutsche*' with merely a German name, as she put it. The deterioration in her living standards under perestroika in the later years of the Soviet Union convinced her to emigrate. Many of the former residents of Friedental moved to Kamen, a town close to Dortmund, whilst Friedental itself (in her account) now became home to Kazakhs, Chechens, and Armenians, and was 'quite unrecognisable'. Neumann herself took a while to get used to Hamburg, where 'every face was unfamiliar, no one greeted me as they would have done in Cheliabinsk.... I felt myself in a foreign country.' It took time to negotiate the German bureaucracy. What helped were the new friendships she made through her church and her growing confidence in speaking German.[13]

From a later generation, Sophie Wagner described a family history in which deportation figured prominently. Her native village, Rosowka in Kazakhstan, had been filled with deported Chechens during the Second World War; her own father had been sent into exile there. Her mother longed to migrate to Germany, but her children felt at home in the Soviet Union until its disintegration. When the family arrived in Hamburg, surrounded by other former inhabitants of Rosowka, Wagner described being overwhelmed and offended by 'so much sex and so many adverts on TV'. Although she hoped that her baby grandson would be named Erich, her daughter overruled her, claiming that everyone associated the name with Erich Honecker, the former leader of the GDR. Wagner took advantage of opportunities to travel the length and breadth of Europe: she ventured that 'Turkey reminded me of Kazakhstan', a place that was associated with good times as well as bad.[14]

Maria was born in 1976 in a small town close to the Arctic Circle. It had been built as a Soviet-Bulgarian venture, in order to export timber to Bulgaria; Maria described it as 'not much older than me'. Most of the town's inhabitants originated from Bulgaria, and the school she attended there, she said, had a cosmopolitan character. Russian, Bulgarian, and Komi festivals were celebrated at the school, and in the town, intermarriage was common. Maria had a long family history of migration and deportation—her ancestors had left Germany for Moldova in the early nineteenth century; the Wehrmacht had deported her grandparents to Łódź (Lodz) in 1941; and then the Red Army sent them to the Far North in the late 1940s, to work as forced labourers. When her parents took her with them to visit relatives in Erfurt in 1990 and decided not to return to Russia, she was devastated by having to leave her birthplace. Maria's first taste of life in West Germany was the refugee reception centre in Friedland. In due course, she made friends with people from different backgrounds—it was 'so much simpler', she said, than befriending other Germans, 'since we share a common experience' [i.e., of displacement]. She concluded her narrative by asserting: 'I feel like a European, living in Germany, with Russian roots', of which she was very proud.[15]

It is important to acknowledge that not all ethnic Germans decided to leave the countries they had adopted. Even those who did depart were keen to emphasise how emotionally wrenching it was to leave their homes in Russia and Kazakhstan, places they associated with friendship and intimacy. They had generally acquired a decent education in these places. Others explained their reasons for staying put. A Kazakh German businessman who bought and sold German cars said he wished to live in the city of Taldykorgan rather than in 'such a stupid country' as Germany. Another man preferred to live in a country rich in beautiful landscapes that were accessible to everyone, whereas in Germany, he said, 'one needs permission to fish'.[16]

Ethnic affinity did not equate to assimilation. A revealing anecdote told how an *Aussiedler* man and his Russian wife invited a friend to sample one of their homemade pancakes (*blini*), something they had 'learned from the Russians'. The visitor was encouraged to eat the blini in the Russian style, folded over, dipped in sour cream, as finger food. At that moment, the doorbell rang and a German pastor came in to see how the couple were getting on. Seeing the pancake, he announced: 'Ah, crêpes suzette! You eat them like this.' He unfolded them, totally unaware of the offence he had caused to the newcomers.[17]

Something of the complex outcome of the migration of ethnic Germans to Germany was reflected in the writings of Richard Wagner. Wagner, a political dissident who left Romania in 1987 along with 14,000 of his fellow *Aussiedler*, described being a Banat Swabian, a minority group in southwestern Romania. Speaking German 'with an accent', he admitted that he remained an outsider in the Federal Republic of Germany: 'It's one thing knowing a lot about a country and another actually living in this country.' His response was to identify as neither German nor Romanian, but as someone from the Banat and a Central European: 'the only concept that represents the great diversity which there is in Eastern Europe'. It shouldn't matter how one ate pancakes, or whether one called them blini or crêpes suzette. In Wagner's view, Germany should be big enough, and strong enough, to accommodate difference.[18]

What about non-Germans in the new Germany? A Foreigners' Law (*Ausländergesetz*) in 1990 gave Turkish workers and other foreigners the right to apply for a permanent residency permit after eight years of living in the country, and to claim naturalisation after ten years' residency.

Those born in Germany to Turkish parents were not allowed to claim dual German and Turkish citizenship, but had to declare their preference on reaching the age of eighteen. In 2000, a new Citizenship Law came into effect that enabled people born outside of Germany to acquire German citizenship. Children born in Germany to parents of Turkish origin were allowed to maintain dual citizenship, but when they reached the age of twenty-three they would have to choose between German citizenship or citizenship in their parents' country of birth. The children of guest workers, in other words, were ultimately expected to decide where their loyalty lay.[19]

Other established communities looked uneasily at the newcomers who arrived in Germany after the fall of the Berlin Wall. One bleak element of the political transformation was a series of violent, racially motivated attacks on 'migrants' and 'foreigners'. German skinheads, in one case, pulled a young Polish tourist into the bushes at a park and cut out part of his tongue. The blame for the assault was pinned on East Germans (the *Ossies*). A vicious attack on a hostel for Vietnamese and Mozambican migrant workers in Hoyerswerda (Saxony) in September 1991 was the first of other similar attacks. In August 1992, a right-wing mob attacked the Central Refugee Shelter (Zentrale Aufnahmestelle für Asylbewerber) in Lichtenagen, Rostock, housing mainly Roma migrants, and an apartment block housing more than 100 Vietnamese migrants. The attackers threw Molotov cocktails and shouted, 'Foreigners out: they are not people, they are pigs.' Although there was no loss of life in that incident, the riot shocked the migrants, who found they were unable to count on police protection.[20]

The brunt of the racist attacks continued to be borne by Turkish Germans. Two German youths beat a teenager, Mete Ekşi, to death with a baseball bat in the Berlin suburb of Kreuzberg in October 1991. In November 1992, two young cousins, Yeliz and Ayse Aslan, and their grandmother, Bahide, were murdered by far-right extremists in an arson attack in Mölln. In a notorious attack in May 1993, in the famous cutlery-making town of Solingen in North Rhine–Westphalia, skinheads committed arson, setting a house on fire. A large Turkish family lived there, and five of them died: Gürsün İnce (twenty-eight years old), Hatice Genç (eighteen), Gülüstan Öztürk (twelve), Hülya Genç (nine), and Saime Genç (five). Others suffered serious injuries. Locals complained that the police only arrived on the scene when the 'Nazis' had already fled. The Turkish government, blaming the fire on the right-wing racists who had set it, absolved the German authorities of any blame. Liberal Germans blamed East Germans for the attacks—a reflection of the complexity of migration in modern Germany. Local Turks took to the streets, but were threatened with deportation if they continued to protest. The perpetrators received lengthy prison sentences. The German president, Richard von Weizsäcker, invited his fellow Germans to think of the victims: 'Think of ten-year-old Yeliz Aslan, she was born among us and had never lived anywhere else.' The bodies of the victims in the Mölln attack were returned to Mercimek, close to Adana in southern Turkey.[21]

Weizsäcker's intervention did not stem the rising tide of right-wing nationalism in the later 1990s, typified by the popularity of the Deutsche Volksunion (German People's Union). Interviewed shortly after the Solingen attack, one elderly Turkish German resident who had lived there for thirty years spoke of her fear of walking down the street, adding that she always carried a small knife to defend herself in case of an attack; another kept an axe in the wake of the unrest following the fire. Others described the animosity they encountered from locals when they managed to buy a small house in the town—neighbours called the police whenever the new owners made repairs to their home, complaining that 'the Turks' were a nuisance. At the same time, the arson attacks and murders led to organised solidarity marches. Hundreds of thousands of citizens took part in these, notably in Munich, where participants denounced neo-Nazism in a candlelight vigil. German footballers became involved in the antiracist campaigns: the 1993 season ended with them wearing shirts carrying the slogan 'Mein Freund ist Ausländer' (My friend is a foreigner).[22]

There were further straws in the wind when the prominent German historian Hans-Ulrich Wehler gave an interview in 2002 in which he maintained—in the wake of the attack on the Twin Towers in the United States—that 'the Federal Republic doesn't have a foreigner problem. It has a Turk problem.' He added that the government should 'impose strict controls.... [O]ne should not accept explosive materials into the country

297

voluntarily.' Wehler chose not to say that Germany had a 'problem' with far-right groups that literally had an 'explosive' purpose. Members of the self-styled Nationalsozialistischer Untergrund (National Socialist Underground) went on a killing spree beginning with the murder of a Nuremberg businessman by the name of Enver Şimşek in September 2000. They chose their victims simply because they were of Turkish origin. Sections of the German security services may have been indirectly involved, although it was widely believed that the murders had been ordered by members of the Turkish mafia. Certainly, terrorist attacks on German soil in later years inflamed anti-foreigner opinion among moderate members of the German public, but Nazi-inspired beliefs retained their power to inspire homegrown atrocities on German soil.[23]

Minority Turkish German leaders retorted that 'the Wall fell on us' (*duvar bizim üstümüze düştü*), by which they meant increased competition in the labour market from unemployed East Germans as well as the more intense xenophobia even among liberals. Turkish Germans described themselves as being better 'integrated' than the German newcomers from the former Soviet Union. A German civil servant, commenting in 2004 on the stance taken by Turkish Germans, said the newcomers 'had a German passport, but barely understood *our* language', whereas 'The Turks, who have no German citizenship, spoke good German and said "Send the foreigners home!".'[24]

A joke that circulated among West Germans after reunification captured something of the trials and tribulations of ethnic Germans, not the *Aussiedler* from Eastern Europe, but those who migrated from the former East Germany to the West. It began with several *Ossies* packed into the supermarket in search of bargain items: 'A Turk is standing on line at Aldi behind two Ossies[.] One Ossie complains to the other, "Look at this line. We've been waiting here for hours. I don't know why we came here. It's no different from where we were." The Turk then turns to them and says, "We didn't ask you to come."' In another version, the Turk corrects their German grammar.[25]

Germany continued to explore other avenues of labour recruitment. The government encouraged seasonal migration from Poland, Romania, and other countries in order to build the labour force in agriculture, construction, and catering. Poles crossed the border without formal permission, either as traders or day labourers. In 1990 the government also announced that it would admit up to 2,000 Russian guest workers per year. Later on, in a revival of the earlier guest worker system, additional workers were recruited from Eastern Europe through new bilateral agreements.[26]

More of a break with tradition was the decision at the turn of the century to recruit highly skilled workers. A new green-card scheme in 2000 enabled German firms to recruit up to 20,000 professionals from outside the European Union. Without what he described as a 'cosmopolitan' approach, Chancellor Gerhard Schröder warned that German firms would flounder in the global marketplace for want of labour. Initially opposed to allowing workers to bring in family members, Schröder had to concede their right to do so, lest it weaken the incentive to sign up. These measures provided further proof that Germany was undoubtedly a country of immigration. It also contributed to a sense that Germany's priorities had shifted in favour of those of higher net worth.[27]

The *Aussiedler* families of renowned (and well-paid) German footballers, such as Polish-born Lukas Podolski and Miroslav Klose, embodied something of this complicated history. Podolski, who spoke of 'two hearts beating in one chest', established a charitable foundation to support disadvantaged children in Germany and Poland. The national team's success in the 2010 World Cup and in Euro 2012 was celebrated as an example of the diversity of German society. In a qualifying match against Turkey in 2012, the midfielder Mesut Özil contributed to an emphatic victory for Germany. The significance of his contribution lay partly in the fact that he had been born in Gelsenkirchen (like his teammate Ilkay Gündoğan) and is third-generation Turkish German. The event seemed to mark a turning point in public attitudes compared to the situation just a few years earlier, when the shortcomings of the team had been attributed to its surfeit of 'foreign' players, such as the Ghanaian-born Gerald Asamoah, whom right-wingers insulted by holding up placards saying, 'You are not Germany, you are the FRG', a reference to the preunification government's decision to grant him German citizenship in 2001 and an indication that this did not make him 'German'.[28]

Appearances, however, were deceptive. Although neither Podolski nor Klose had a particularly easy time in German football, they experienced nothing like the aggression directed at Özil during the World Cup campaign in 2018. The treatment he received prompted him to announce his retirement from international football shortly after Germany's elimination from the competition. Özil cited disrespectful comments from the president of the country's football association, and ruefully noted that the German media tended to portray him as 'German when we win, and an immigrant when we lose'. It hardly helped that he posed for a photograph with the Turkish president, Recep Tayyip Erdoğan; although he explained this as a simple courtesy to a visiting dignitary, it was inevitable that it would rile sports fans and others on the both the right and the left of the political spectrum. Whatever considerations drove Özil to pose with Erdoğan, his experiences pointed to the fragility of 'integration', which no amount of success on the football field was likely to offset. Integration was regarded in mainstream German society as a one-way ticket, but the experiences of footballers indicated how difficult the passage to integration could be.[29]

All the same, no one could seriously doubt that Germany had become a 'country of immigration': it was now home to several million people of non-German ethnicity. Virtual museums reinforced the point for the post-reunification generation: the Documentation Centre and Museum of Migration in Germany (DOMiD) sponsors online exhibitions as part of its mission 'to make migration something normal'.[30]

Refugees were nevertheless perceived as a 'problem'. As with migration policy more broadly, debates around asylum made reference to the Nazi past, albeit in ways that suggested that different inferences should be drawn from German history. One notable example occurred several years prior to the political transformation in 1989, but the shock waves continued long afterwards. On 30 August 1983, twenty-three-year-old Kemal Altun threw himself from the window of a courthouse in West Berlin in order to avoid being deported to Turkey, where, as a left-wing activist, he had incurred the wrath of the military dictatorship. He had sought asylum in West Germany two years earlier, having made his way there via Bulgaria, Romania, Hungary, Czechoslovakia, and the GDR. Despite support for his cause from the newly created Green Party, from the Social Democratic Party, and from church leaders and NGOs, the Turkish government demanded his extradition on the grounds that he had incited others to murder a government minister in 1980. Against the backdrop of government support for 'friendly' relations with an ally from the North Atlantic Treaty Organization (NATO), a German court allowed the extradition request, arguing that it could proceed even though his application for asylum had not yet been heard.

In a speech at the graveside, Altun's lawyer, Wolfgang Wieland, said, 'There should never be fascism in Germany again. This also means that German rulers never work again with fascists, never work again with generals, never work again with dictators at the expense of tortured people.' His voice was drowned out by an editorial in the *Bild* newspaper, which proclaimed, apropos to Altun's death, that 'now the Federal Republic of Germany is a constitutional state, but it must not become the collecting camp for everyone in the world who expects a good life here'.[31]

In the wake of Altun's suicide, some in the media continued to speak of the 'tide' of asylum seekers, especially against the backdrop of increases in applications from Tamils from Sri Lanka, Kurds, and others. During the election campaign of 1992–1993, the Christian Democratic Union of Germany and the Christian Social Union in Bavaria (known as the CDU/CSU) attacked the Social Democratic Party for failing to support measures to deal with the 'asylum problem' at a time when applications were running at 100,000 annually. More than 1 million applications for asylum were lodged in Germany between 1990 and 1993. Although most applications failed, some asylum seekers were allowed to remain, particularly if they had been forced out of Bosnia and Kosovo.[32]

One minority refugee population, the Roma, faced an especially hostile reception. Indeed, Roma refugees from Eastern Europe complained that little had changed since the 1950s, when they had found it impossible to obtain a hearing in German courts, which insisted on treating them as 'nomads' and a social 'menace'. There was only a thin line between discretion and outright discrimination. In 1994, a readmission agreement between Germany and Romania affected the situation of 100,000 Roma asylum seekers in Germany. Between 1993 and 1995, Germany paid 120 million deutschmarks to Romania for resettlement costs, and in those years around 25,000 Roma were returned to Romania.[33]

Broader policy changes were afoot. In 1993, the government amended the Basic Law by insisting that asylum seekers should apply in the first safe country they entered. The Welfare Act for Asylum Seekers (*Asylbewerberleistungsgesetz*) preserved the principle of asylum, but there was no longer any constitutional right to asylum. Two changes in processing claims had particular implications for asylum claimants. First, an applicant who had already reached Germany, having passed through a safe third country, could now be forced to return to that third country. Since all of Germany's neighbours were deemed to fall into this category, this severely curtailed the number of migrants able to make asylum claims in Germany. Second, 'a new streamlined and simplified recognition procedure would be introduced that would allow the authorities to reject immediately claims for asylum from individuals deemed to be from countries that did not persecute their citizens'. Other important provisions related to work and mobility. Asylum seekers were not allowed to take paid work, and instead had to rely on welfare payments in kind. The legislation set the maximum value of benefits at 80 percent of the minimum standard of living for other residents, as specified in the Federal Social Assistance Act (*Bundessozialhilfegesetz*). This made it all but impossible for them to find reasonable housing and forced many into low-grade accommodation. They relied on German charitable assistance to get by. Accompanying these changes were restrictions on asylum seekers who hoped to move from one district to another.[34]

Driving these changes was the official view, clearly expressed by the Federal Ministry of the Interior, that the original Article 16(2) of the Basic Law had 'become a vehicle for uncontrolled migration to Germany', and that 'only a few of the foreigners seeking asylum were actually persecuted on political grounds'. The result was a significant decline in applications and, predictably, an increase in undocumented entry to circumvent the new legislation. One journalist wittily remarked that, 'if you think about it, there is really only one ideal asylum seeker as far as German authorities are concerned. His name is E.T.... E.T. has two things going for him. He wants to go home, and is not interested in becoming a permanent burden on the German taxpayer or taking away a job.' He added that the 1993 legislation would lead to asylum seekers being passed from one state to another until 'at some point, the refugee will end up in North Korea, a secure third state bordering on the Russian Federation'.[35]

Other changes followed. A new Immigration Act in 2005 made it even easier for the government to turn down claims to asylum. It provided three-year temporary residency permits to recognised refugees, but the government undertook to use that window to check whether grounds for asylum still existed. It also reserved the right to 're-examine the grounds for asylum at any later time'. Many German politicians took the view that the 1949 constitution, which recognised 'every politically persecuted person' as having the right to asylum, no longer corresponded to developments in the post–Cold War era. Exceptions would still be made, but in practice, this meant that countries such as Iraq, Serbia, and Montenegro were deemed to be safe places, and that it would now be assumed that returning refugees to them would not put Germany in breach of the Refugee Convention. The decision on Iraqi refugees, in particular, was widely condemned by other EU member states. History appeared to have lost its power to hold Germany to account for the crimes carried out by the Nazi state. It was time, so to speak, for everyone to move on.[36]

CHAPTER 17

Together in Disharmony:
The Death of Yugoslavia

IN THE FINAL DECADE of the twentieth century, closer integration was on the lips of many West European politicians. The situation in Yugoslavia could not have been more different. The country's disintegration marked a distinctive episode in Europe's postwar history. Disintegration went hand in hand with forced migration. The scale of population displacement beggared belief. By 1995, one person in ten of the population of Croatia had been displaced; in Bosnia-Herzegovina, every second person was a refugee. Further conflict and turmoil ensued at the end of the decade, when a combination of Serbian intervention in Kosovo and the bombing campaign launched by NATO member states unleashed further displacement.

What could be reassembled from the wreckage, and by whom? What did the post-Yugoslav successor states offer to those displaced by war? How would the migrants cope, whether they were internally displaced or refugees who had moved to another state?

Before the war, Yugoslavia had been a stable, relatively prosperous, and ethnically diverse political entity in which migration was a normal feature of everyday life. It had been built on ethno-territorial foundations and held together by the Communist Party. The country appeared to be stable, although the existence of constituent republics had always made it possible for national groups to assert themselves.[1]

Prewar Yugoslavia enabled and encouraged internal migration. Belgrade became a magnet attracting large numbers of migrants from other parts of Serbia and from farther afield. By 1981, Serbia was home to 110,000 Bosnians, an equivalent number from Croatia, 50,000 from Macedonia, and so on. But public reactions to migrants began to take on more insidious connotations. In the 1970s and 1980s, and particularly after 1989, internal migration fed into complaints that the Serb population of Kosovo had shrunk catastrophically, leading to an increase in the relative size of its ethnically Albanian population. Meanwhile, amidst declining economic growth in the 1980s, unemployment and inflation were unevenly spread, and deprived regions elsewhere in Yugoslavia resented the relative wealth held in Serbia. This development contributed to the outbreak of war. Political and cultural divisions further complicated the situation. Serbs, especially those living outside of Serbia proper, felt increasingly exposed. They demanded the right to use their own language and to set up autonomous cultural organisations. Ominously, by the mid-1980s, Serbian politicians were complaining that the authorities in Kosovo were engaged in a policy of 'ethnic cleansing'. In fact, Serbs mainly left in order to move from an economically more backward part of the country to regions with greater job opportunities. But the damage to residual ethnic harmony was already done.[2]

Long-distance migration was nothing new for Yugoslavia. Young Yugoslav men and women had travelled to Western Europe throughout the 1960s and until the 1980s to earn money, to experience a different way of life, and for more matter-of-fact reasons. A thirty-three-year-old Serbian interviewee explained to the sociologist Gayle Munro many years later that he had been 'running away' from his parents: 'That was my main motivation to be honest, anywhere as far away from them as possible.' He decided not to return when war broke out. A young woman spoke of coming to Britain as an au pair, 'but then when it all kicked off over there I didn't have much choice but to stay. I didn't want to actually, I was all up for going back but my parents said absolutely no way. . . . It was all hell by the sound of it.'[3]

The war all but obliterated the history of peacetime migration. In June 1991, Yugoslavia descended into chaos. First, Slovenia and Croatia declared independence from the Yugoslav federation. Members of the large Serb minority in Croatia protested that their own rights were in jeopardy. Serbs in the Krajina region of Croatia declared their independence, and this led to mass movements of Croats from Krajina and of Serbs from other parts of Croatia. Young Croat men fled into the interior of Croatia or made their way to Bosnia-Herzegovina, and even Hungary, in order to avoid being conscripted into the army of Serbia. Croatian forces retook Krajina in 1995, prompting another exodus of up to 350,000 Serbs. In 2001, Serbs made up less than 5 percent of the population of Croatia, down from 12 percent ten years earlier. Similar upheavals occurred in the ethnically mixed region of Slavonia, whose status as a constituent part of Croatia was finally resolved in 1998, but not before its Serbian inhabitants left for good. Elsewhere in Croatia, the breakup of Yugoslavia led to hastily arranged deals, such as when Croats who had been driven out of Vojvodina—a place familiar with forced migration ever since Germans had to abandon their homes and businesses at the end of the Second World War—'exchanged' their homes with Serbs who had left Zagreb. The verb suggests a degree of organisation and mutual agreement that did not usually correspond to the messy reality of displacement.[4]

The situation was different in Bosnia-Herzegovina, a still more ethnically mixed republic that was torn apart with far greater loss of life and displacement than in Serbia. In 1992, following a referendum that was boycotted by the Serb population, the government declared independence. In the bitter war that lasted until 1995, 2.5 million people were forced from their homes, roughly half of them displaced internally. At the outset, non-Serb and non-Croat minorities were expelled from those parts of the country dominated by Serbs and Croats, and congregated in Bosnian Muslim areas across agreed demarcation lines. Between 150,000 and 200,000 people were killed or perished during the war in Bosnia-Herzegovina. Forces loyal to the Bosnian Serb leader Radovan Karadžić were directed by paramilitary leaders such as the notorious Željko Ražnatović (Arkan) to rape, torture, and murder Bosnian Muslims (Bosniaks) in a systematic fashion. The UNHCR lacked the wherewithal to prevent attacks on Muslim enclaves in so-called safe havens. Surviving villagers, mainly women, children, and elderly men, were made to endure forced marches from Serb-held territory. Civilians in the besieged cities of Sarajevo and Tuzla experienced the war not as displacement but as a trap, although some managed to escape. The bombardment of the market in Sarajevo in February 1994 caused international outrage, exceeded only by the Serb massacre of Bosnian Muslim refugees in Srebrenica in July 1995.[5]

More than half a million displaced people remained in the territory of Bosnia-Herzegovina itself, but its economic collapse deprived refugees of adequate assistance. Eventually, as a result of international intervention, the Dayton Accords, in December 1995, led to the formation of two ethnically defined polities, one Bosnian and the other Serb, the Republika Srpska. The agreement, signed by Slobodan Milošević, Franjo Tuđman, and Alija Izetbegović, provided for people to move to their own countries, an assumption that took no account of mixed marriages. Nor did it satisfy those who felt an attachment to Yugoslavia and thought of themselves (as one refugee put it) as 'an endangered species'.[6]

Bosnian refugees scattered far and wide. Gordana Ibrović, a forty-one-year-old Bosnian Muslim from Sarajevo, described her odyssey from the city of her birth ('the most beautiful city in the world') to the Croatian city of Split, where she joined relatives—a reminder that prewar Yugoslavia knew no internal barriers to migration—before buying plane tickets for her and her children to Istanbul, leaving her husband behind in Sarajevo. She spent most of 1993 with other relatives in Turkey, but they could not grasp the dangerous circumstances that had compelled her to leave Bosnia. There were other challenges in trying to adjust to Turkish society. As Ibrović said, 'their mentality and way of life are completely different from ours in Bosnia'. Bosnian Muslims, she said, 'lean towards the West'. Every member of her family worked a twelve-hour day in the clothing trade, but eventually her relatives made it clear that they had to leave. Deciding against going to a refugee camp, they moved to Prague ('it reminded us a lot of Sarajevo'), where her husband had an aunt. When the aunt, too, turned against them, Ibrović had no option but to take her children to a Red Cross refugee camp some 70 kilometres north of Prague. This kind of odyssey was not unusual. It highlighted how being a refugee often entailed recurrent mobility, brought about by the uncertain ties of kinship as much as by the obstacles created by government bureaucracy.[7]

Some 500,000 people fled Bosnia for neighbouring Croatia and Slovenia. An additional 700,000 people found refuge in Germany, Austria, Sweden, and elsewhere. Germany admitted almost half of this total by the end of 1996. In accepting around 90,000 refugees, Austria acknowledged that many of them had long-standing ties already, by virtue of chains of peacetime migration of guest workers. The same was true of Slovenia, where thousands ended up in the third-largest town, Celje. Sweden was more generous than most, granting permanent residency to around 60,000 Bosniaks. Germany and Austria provided refugees with what was termed 'temporary protection', the argument being that offering permanent residency was tantamount to accepting that they would not be repatriated. Very few of them were recognised as refugees under the 1951 Geneva Convention. They enjoyed minimal welfare benefits. The Austrian government made accommodation available, but rather than give cash to refugees directly, the money was instead transferred to housing providers. Since they were not legally allowed to look for work, the refugees had little choice but to find jobs in the black-market economy. Besim, a thirty-eight-year-old refugee, told Barbara Franz, 'One year Zlata [his nine-year-old daughter] needed a typewriter for school and I went to work illegally in the fields of the farmers to earn the money. Next year she needed a computer and I worked illegally as a lumberjack to earn the money.' Women found low-paid work as maids and cleaners or took other menial jobs. Their income and contacts sometimes gave them a route into the legal labour market, which ended their temporary status. Besim himself became the manager of several supermarkets.[8]

This was not, in the main, a story of Western humanitarianism. Many refugees relied upon friends and family, and sometimes on the kindness of strangers. International cooperation to assist the refugees did not amount to much. France ultimately admitted only 15,000 refugees from Bosnia-Herzegovina, although members of the public had offered to take in 400,000 on their own account. Britain refused to take more than a relatively small number, on the grounds that providing permanent refugee status gave tacit recognition to Serb policies of ethnic cleansing.[9]

A study of refugee resettlement in Rome and Amsterdam by the anthropologist Maja Korac contrasted the government-backed system in the

Netherlands with the more ad hoc arrangements in Italy. The Netherlands accepted 22,000 refugees and, in 1993, allowed them to stay permanently, with corresponding access to social welfare and education as well as to the Dutch labour market. Refugees were placed in temporary reception centres; if their application for asylum succeeded, it was the responsibility of the municipal authority in Amsterdam to provide them with housing. The Dutch government enforced integration: 'I do what I am told to do, and everything is going according to "integration" rules that we "refugees" have to follow', said Boris, a thirty-five-year-old man from Bosnia-Herzegovina living in Amsterdam in 2001. 'We didn't have to integrate really, you see, we just had to do what we were told.' Other comments point to a kind of cosmopolitanism. Kemo, age twenty-three, speaking in 2000, by which time he had become a Dutch citizen, said: 'There were people from different countries there [in the reception centre] and I was happy to have the opportunity to get to know people from other parts of the world. We communicated in English, which I knew a little at the time, but during the three months we were there my spoken English improved; that was an unexpected gain from these contacts too.' All the same, refugees struggled to establish some kind of contact with the Dutch. Miro, a twenty-seven-year-old Bosnian Serb man working as an intern for a Dutch firm, described feeling 'invisible among my colleagues at work.... They behave as if I am not there'. The formal welcome did not enable refugees to overcome a sense of social isolation, and they suffered disproportionately from unemployment in the 1990s in comparison to the host population.[10]

Bosnian refugees also found it difficult to forge much of a common cause with migrants who had arrived in the Netherlands years previously. The earlier migrants had come in search of work, not because they feared for their lives. The newcomers portrayed themselves as highly educated compared to the guest workers, many of whom aligned themselves with their nationalist counterparts as Yugoslavia broke apart. By the late 1990s, however, ethnic rather than class divisions began to assert themselves. The aforementioned Miro expressed his disappointment that he had been made to 'feel like a stranger' in the different associations—Bosnian, Croatian, and Serbian—that he visited in search of company. It was as if there were no escape from the long reach of nationalist sentiment.[11]

Italy assumed that existing migrant and refugee support networks would take responsibility for refugees from the former Yugoslavia—in fact, this was justified as a means of promoting self-reliance. The involvement of NGOs also came much later in Italy than in the Netherlands, and the Catholic Church played an important but somewhat patchy role. Consequently, refugees who reached Italy had to improvise, and they initially did so by sticking together, whatever their ethnic identity. Mirsad, a twenty-five-year-old Bosniak living in Rome, explained that he initially socialised with refugees from Yugoslavia whatever their ethnic origin: 'We were pretty united in these years, we stuck together [but] later as people managed to attain some economic security, we started growing apart.' Nevertheless, as another refugee, Bojana, put it, 'I was a Yugoslav and to this day, when someone asks me where I'm from, I say from Yugoslavia, though it doesn't exist anymore. I believed in that country.' For her, forced migration had exposed the pain of leaving her home behind and of having to come to terms with the end of ethnic coexistence.[12]

Since government relief programmes were less well developed in Italy than in the Netherlands, refugees spoke of forging new friendships with local Italians. Women, in particular, found work as domestic servants (work for which they were often overqualified) and developed friendships with their employers. Forty-seven-year-old Milan added that 'socialising with our people and talking about our problems and politics would only give me a headache. It's better to be with Italians.' Marko, a thirty-year-old computer specialist, observed: 'I don't have a general impression of Italians, because I'm aware of what happened to us [people from war-torn Yugoslavia] when we started looking at people in general. There are wonderful people and there are bad people. There is no general Italian characteristic that I'm specifically fond of or that drives me crazy. Every person's got characteristics of their own.' Some refugees adopted the view that they could learn from their hosts, or that their hosts could also learn from them. One of Maja Korac's informants, Vera, then a student in Rome, remarked of her Italian hosts, for example, 'We must find what we have in common with them, although we're different. Many Italians managed to learn a great deal from us too, especially those who work with our people. We are more precise, for example, we're some kind of "Germans" to Italians. Perhaps we've changed them a bit too.'[13]

Struggling to make ends meet, Bosnian refugees were also capable of taking something positive from the upheaval. One mother told a visiting researcher why she encouraged her children to learn Slovenian: 'I would like my children to get the most out of the surroundings they live in. Every culture has its good sides and can offer opportunities for learning. I wish that they would integrate the new patterns with the old Bosnian ones.' But her willingness to embrace hybridity remained a minority view. Usually displacement reinforced feelings of incomprehension, combined with a sense of national victimhood and staunch proclamations of an eventual homecoming.[14]

In Kosovo, the conflict took the form of a bitter struggle between ethnic Albanians and Serbs that had already manifested itself in the communist era but was intensified by the discriminatory policies Serbian authorities pursued after 1989, which produced a mass exodus of Albanians from Kosovo. Albanians now mobilised on behalf of their remaining kin in Kosovo. The exodus helped Milošević to make good on his promise, in a 1987 speech, that Serbs had the right to stay in Kosovo: 'You should stay here', he said, 'because of your ancestors and your heirs'. In his view, Serbian bones lay buried in Kosovo, and they should not be forsaken; for Serbs to leave now would be a sign of their weakness. As far as the Serbs were concerned, Kosovar Albanian emigration was testament to Serbia's victory. The Serbian presence was further strengthened by Milošević's decision to settle ethnic Serb refugees from the wars in Croatia and Bosnia on Kosovar territory. Between 1995 and 1997, EU member states dealt with around 100,000 applications for asylum from Kosovar Albanians.[15]

Confrontation and conflict in 1998 produced another refugee crisis. It resulted from NATO's decision in March 1999 to launch a bombing campaign to destabilise the Milošević regime in Belgrade. Justified internationally as a 'humanitarian war', it only served to intensify civilian suffering on both sides. Around 400,000 Kosovar refugees had already begun to flee from Kosovo before the NATO air strikes began. Most of them made their way to other parts of former Yugoslavia. But according to the International Organization for Migration, some refugees used smugglers to get into Western Europe, traveling first to Hungary via Italy, and then to Germany via Slovakia and the Czech Republic. Germany apprehended and detained them. The same happened to those who entered Switzerland illegally by crossing the border with Italy. They included Kosovar Albanians, who 'replaced the Tamils as the publicly pilloried "problem group"'. At the end of March, Greece decided to boost security along the country's northern borders with Albania and Macedonia to head off an expected wave of refugees in the wake of NATO's military intervention.[16]

An additional 800,000 Kosovar refugees fled to Albania (which accepted 450,000 of them, equivalent to 10 percent of its total population), Montenegro, Bosnia, and the ethnically Albanian region of western Macedonia. None of these countries were willing or able to provide much assistance to the refugees, however, and indeed, Macedonia closed its border and deported Kosovar refugees to Albania, Greece, and Turkey in order to press the international community to commit more resources to supporting the refugees. American officials entertained the possibility of transferring an undisclosed number of refugees to the US military base at Guantanamo Bay. The UK accommodated 100 Kosovar refugees in Stockport, Greater Manchester, part of its strategy to disperse refugees. Politicians and local residents gave them a good welcome, but public opinion turned against them within a few months, once it became clear that they were reluctant to return to Kosovo: 'There must surely be a part of their country where they would be accepted', said one of their neighbours in 2000.[17]

As many as 600,000 people were internally displaced in the fledgling state of Kosovo itself. Where possible, they managed to find accommodation with friends and family members in Pristina, the capital city, which had not been badly damaged by the war. Pristina's population grew even more rapidly after the war, because of the effect the war had on the rural economy. Relations between the newcomers from the rural areas and the city's prewar population quickly deteriorated. Villagers were accused of being country bumpkins who, according to one longtime resident of Pristina, 'don't know the rules.... You can recognise them from the way they walk, from the way they are dressed, and how they talk.' This dismissive attitude exposed cultural differences that complicated the process of accommodating the refugees.[18]

Other refugees, notably Roma living in the former Yugoslavia, were largely hidden from public view. Those who fled abroad ended up in makeshift camps near Florence, Italy. One Roma asylum seeker protested, 'We are second- or third-class refugees, while Kosovars were first category [refugees]. . . . Why doesn't NATO intervene for us and for all the other ethnic minorities that the Albanians are expelling from Kosovo?' His question went unanswered.[19]

The number of people displaced by the war may be in dispute, but here was incontrovertible evidence of another refugee crisis in the territory of a hitherto stable, albeit impoverished, European state. Some refugees returned to their homes, but others described a never-ending journey in search of security: one refugee, Ćamka, who fled to Slovenia, said, 'We walked a long way on foot, but you've reached some kind of freedom, so you keep on walking.' The decision to flee had huge emotional and psychological costs, as in the case of Agim, a young Kosovar Albanian who sent his family abroad, but then reluctantly decided to join them, leaving behind in Pristina the woman he loved, who urged him to escape while he could: 'I felt the need to scream like a wild animal when you said goodbye', he wrote to her. These were the hidden injuries of displacement. A Kosovar woman told her interviewer: 'Well, you cannot describe it. It is awful, very hard to be like that. The name can show you, you know, R.E.F.U.G.E. is like the worst thing in the world, so it is something that you cannot describe. You don't have any power and you don't have anything but your soul, your body and nothing else.' Her only crumb of comfort was that she was able to secure a job with an international aid agency in Kosovo.[20]

Nor did Serbian civilians escape unscathed from the war. A thirty-five-year-old Serb who fled Bosnia and took refuge in Belgrade spoke of the years he had lost to war, saying: 'I was born at the wrong time.' When Serbian troops withdrew from Kosovo, NATO and the UNHCR stood by while the Kosovo Liberation Army (KLA) and ethnic Albanians targeted the remaining Serb population, occupying their homes to force them to leave. Surviving Serbs were now confined to enclaves in the interior of Kosovo, including the northern half of the divided city of Mitrovica, where they felt beleaguered and abandoned. Meanwhile, Serbs who fled to Serbia encountered hostility from the local population, who complained that these 'peasants' were enjoying unearned privileges. Refugees described the toll taken on families living in makeshift accommodation outside Belgrade, pointing out that 'we left houses one thousand times better than here'. They expressed sorrow at having had to abandon Orthodox monasteries and churches as well as having been forced to forfeit their homes in Kosovo. Nationalist politicians reinforced this stance by recalling Serbia's humiliation during the First World War and recycling memoirs of the 1915 'Golgotha' (the wartime retreat of the Serbian army) for a modern Serb audience.[21]

The repatriation of Bosnians began in earnest following the Dayton Accords, under which all refugees and internally displaced persons were entitled to return and reclaim their homes. International relief organisations arranged 'go and see visits' to help refugees decide if they wished to go back permanently. Many displaced people favoured repatriation in principle—elderly refugees, for example, had no wish to die and be buried in a foreign country—but most of them would consider returning only if political and social conditions permitted. They wanted not just access to jobs and housing, but also greater political security and the prospect of not being victimised. Although thousands opted to remain in Western Europe, or resettled in the United States or Australia, more than 1 million people displaced by the war in Bosnia-Herzegovina decided to return, half of them to areas where they remained ethnically a minority. Germany hastened to repatriate some 330,000 refugees to Bosnia-Herzegovina, on the grounds that they no longer needed protection.[22]

Those who went back voluntarily had a very different outlook upon their homecoming than those who were told that they had outstayed their welcome. According to one Bosnian returnee, speaking in 2001, 'What I missed most [living as a refugee in Germany] was my family and friends, the language and the whole environment, sociality (*druzenje*) and most of all the easy-going way of life.' He went on to say that 'it was very demanding to speak in German. I'm much more relaxed when I speak my own language.' He was unable to resist returning to Bosnia: 'I missed to live where I'm born [sic]. I missed to be "under my own sky" [*podneblje*].' He explained that what finally convinced him to return was a visceral attachment to the Bosnian landscape: 'It's a different matter that everything else is destroyed, but the beauty of the country has brought me back and that's what I'm enjoying at the moment.'[23]

For most returnees, this kind of emotional pull did not compensate for a bleak economic situation caused by a lack of job opportunities after the closure of many state-owned enterprises. As if finding work were not enough of a challenge, repatriation was beset by other difficulties, such as having to cope with damage to housing and infrastructure, and poor provision of education and health care. One Bosniak family returned to Banja Luka (the capital of the new Republika Srpska) hoping that peace would enable them to recover a way of life that included not having to lock their door at night. But this prospect seemed a long way off. Other returnees—such as Bosniaks who had fled to Croatia, and opted to live there after the war—reclaimed their houses but sublet them in order to maintain a kind of transnational existence.[24]

Refugees who did return were portrayed as having had an easy time of it in Western Europe—returning with 'deutschmarks and Mercedes', in one popular version—as if having spent several years as a refugee had been a luxury compared with the tribulations and dangers of life in the besieged Bosnian city of Sarajevo or in small towns and villages across Bosnia. Those who had remained behind called them *pobjeglice*, 'deserters', implying they had fled in order to save their skins. The term *izbeglice* was reserved for 'real refugees', those who had demonstrated bravery rather than cowardice. Some people wore T-shirts saying, 'I was here from 1992–1995. Where were you?' In these circumstances, one woman, Alma, who repatriated from Germany, said perhaps the best (and most charitable thing) one could say was: 'We have all changed.'[25]

Serbs who had fled Croatia during the war in 1991–1995 faced an uphill struggle to return, not least because the government of Franjo Tuđman maintained that Croats should be given priority in the allocation of scarce resources. As he put it, 'we have established a state and now we will decide who are its citizens'. Most Serb refugees opted to resettle in

Serbia, or else remained in a kind of limbo. In Kosovo, where repatriation took place within a matter of months in 1999–2000, the challenges were equally daunting, given the lack of a functioning civil administration and the ever-present danger from land mines.[26]

Refugees often negotiated the difficulties of return in an imaginative fashion. In Croatia, the self-styled 'Community of Displaced and Exiled Croats from Vojvodina', a support group, required refugees who arrived in Zagreb in 1991 and 1992 to complete a questionnaire before being allowed to join. According to the anthropologist Nives Ritig-Beljak, who conducted her research in 1994, 'the brevity and stiffness of the forms had a positive psychological effect, because it channelled strong emotions and helped the exiles to accept the fact that they were not alone in this experience, and that their departure had been inevitable'. The questionnaires provided a wealth of documentation on this community. But here, too, the process of return posed great difficulties. The old state no longer existed, and much of the basic infrastructure had been damaged. Younger refugees with educational qualifications, who had acquired or improved their knowledge of a foreign language while displaced, had better chances in the job market when they returned. Their parents were not so lucky. All the same, displacement could be turned to political advantage. It at least gave people a sense that the country needed to be rebuilt. It was a new and sovereign nation-state.[27]

Inevitably, things were still complicated. The cultural consequences of displacement emerged in many different settings. Refugees from the region of Srijem in eastern Croatia who had moved to Vitrovica in 1991, for example — sometimes leaving family members behind — lamented the loss of farms they had occupied for generations. In Vitrovica, they portrayed themselves not as victims, however, but as hardworking, enterprising people from a socially and economically advanced region who could teach the 'backward' locals how to improve their methods of work, as well as what religious, linguistic, and musical traditions should be kept alive. The residents of Vitrovica were not necessarily disposed to listen. A typical remark was, 'We are not going to get accustomed to them, they have to accustom themselves to this area.' This was a pointed reminder that cultural differences might be expressed by members of the same ethnic group—in this case, there were two groups asserting rival claims to being 'authentically Croat'. As we saw earlier, the same kind of uneasy coexistence happened in Kosovo too.[28]

Material objects could have the capacity to trigger powerful recollections of displacement. Hajrija, a Muslim refugee from Donji Vakuf in Bosnia-Herzegovina who had settled in Islamabad, described her anxiety that her children would forget the town where they were born:

> My husband made a model of our town to keep the memory alive....It takes a long time to build a town because it isn't easy to find the right materials here [in Pakistan]. We had to have red roofs on the houses and lots of green for the trees. The green was particularly hard to find. My husband was very determined. He looked and looked and finally we found some branches that we could cut to look like small trees. We must tend the model all the time because the green turns yellow.

But the model was more than a sentimental object: it asserted a political claim. The inscription on this carefully crafted model town read: 'These are our houses, on the land inhabited by our forefathers. We are going back there no matter when and in such a way that we'll be so powerful that no one will be able to force us to leave our land again.'[29]

Long-term residents of Sarajevo complained that the city changed out of all recognition, not just because of the war but because of the influx of Bosniaks from the countryside, whether displaced or not. According to the anthropologist Anders Stefansson, many of its original inhabitants described Sarajevo as 'one big village', on account of newcomers who imported 'village manners'. The implication was that they transformed the formerly sophisticated cosmopolitan city of Sarajevo into a place 'plagued by garbage, mafia-style criminality, corruption, nepotism, Muslim nationalism, cultural primitivism, improper language and so on'. But the distinction that long-term residents drew between themselves and the 'uncultured' peasants belonged to a well-established tradition that claimed urban superiority.[30]

The conflict in Yugoslavia increased the size of the diaspora from the region. Indeed, the post-Yugoslav diaspora was a complex entity. Some refugees who arrived in Western Europe in the 1990s retained an affinity with the entity of Yugoslavia, the country of their birth and the place where they had been educated (although this was not the case for Kosovar refugees, who associated Yugoslavia with oppression). The diaspora was divided along ideological, political, and class lines, with generational divisions particularly in evidence. Serbian migrants who arrived in the UK in the 1980s as students and professionals had denounced the earlier generation of migrants, from the post–Second World War era, as 'collaborators' and 'fascists'. Now, like-minded migrants from the 1980s supported new arrivals in negotiating officialdom and finding work and a place to live. Refugees who had fled the wars in Yugoslavia took gifts to family members on their periodic return visits to Sarajevo or Pristina, but they felt more at ease keeping their distance. One of them said: 'Sometimes after I come back [to England] I live on baked beans for a week or two, because all my money has been spent on taking back bottles of single malt. I have a lot of uncles.' Those who came bearing gifts might also be berated or attacked for having deserted the homeland in its time of need. They were less likely to face such accusations in their new location.[31]

Some in the diaspora forged in the 1990s resisted the label 'refugee', because it reminded them of a painful rupture in their lives. It also brought to mind the difficulties they had encountered in the country of asylum. Some of those who settled in Europe or beyond called themselves 'Bosnian expatriate nationals'. One young Bosnian man remarked that he would rather be considered 'an exile [which] makes it sound more like an intellectual decision, one made over the freedom of a cup of coffee with a cigarette, instead of over a second bottle of rakija and a half-packed suitcase'. This was not true of everyone. Some saw no reason not to use the term 'refugee'. At a distance of some two decades from the events, a Bosnian woman who left for Britain in her early twenties said, 'pretending that I am not a refugee is like saying that never happened. I am proud of what I am. I have had to struggle and fight so hard for everything.' Although some of those who were displaced associated the term with diminished status and powerlessness, her attitude testified to her determination and sense of achievement.[32]

The wars in Yugoslavia associated with the battle to forge new nation-states demonstrated the connection between self-determination and displacement. Nationalism carried the hopes of millions of former Yugoslavs for a state of their own. But the price of carving up one state to create new ethno-territorial entities was paid by minority groups who were deemed not to belong. The situation was complicated by internal differences in new polities such as Croatia and Kosovo, caused by tensions between those who had fled and those who remained behind, and between villagers and urban residents. Economic hardship and the difficult process of repatriation only hindered peacemaking. The resulting upheaval took years to resolve and created difficult legacies.

But that was not all. The route out of the Balkans for hundreds of thousands of citizens of the former Yugoslavia had by the second decade of the new millennium become the route for refugees from the Middle East. The camps in which Yugoslav refugees had found emergency shelter were repurposed to house Syrian refugees. One ordeal gave way to another, with consequences that continued to play out across Europe.

CHAPTER 18

Managing Migration and Asylum in the New European Union

THE COLLAPSE OF COMMUNISM appeared to herald the 'end of ideology' and a new kind of Europe, characterised by the spread of democratic forms of government and an increased role for supranational institutions such as the European Union. Added to this, much was made of the suggestion that globalisation had contributed to the weakening of the frontiers of national sovereignty. Capital, goods, and services, and people, too, appeared to be more mobile than at any time in the past. Borders were thought to have become more permeable.

Although overall migration slowed somewhat during the 1990s and into the new millennium, it did not judder to a halt. Indeed, net migration, the difference between people arriving and leaving, accounted for much of the overall growth in Europe's population, as distinct from the natural increase in the population, the difference between births and deaths. In addition to migrants who had more or less conventional reasons for seeking admission, European governments were confronted with growing numbers of asylum seekers from outside the European Union. One factor contributing to the migration was the impact of the refugee crisis in the former Yugoslavia, together with continuing conflicts in Afghanistan, Sri Lanka, and elsewhere that persisted into the early 2000s.

From the mid-1990s until the economic crash in 2008, sustained economic growth in most European countries created a demand for migrant labour, both highly skilled and less skilled. Governments made it easier for skilled professionals and students to consider a move to Europe, but less-skilled migrants continued to arrive, often through temporary or seasonal contracts, as well as by irregular routes, in order to fill gaps in the labour market. Between 2000 and 2005, the number of migrants in Spain rose by nearly 200 percent to reach 4.8 million. In Italy, the corresponding increase was 54 percent, taking the total number of migrants to 2.5 million, just under 0.9 million having arrived in a short space of time. France was home to 6.5 million migrants in 2005, followed by the UK with 5.4 million. Ireland, for example, experienced a huge upturn in new arrivals, such that by 2011 close on one-fifth of the population of the 'Celtic Tiger' was foreign-born, including EU citizens such as Poles and Lithuanians.[1]

Migration commentators and migrants themselves continued to ask questions: What and where was 'Europe'? Put another way, what did this apparent liberalisation imply in the first instance for migrants from 'new Europe', citizens of former communist countries who wanted to take advantage of newfound freedoms? They formulated their own view about the transformation of Europe. Sometimes they expressed genuine surprise at the prospects and possibilities. Challenged to say, 'What is Europe for you?', Ana, a young Bulgarian migrant to Italy, found this a perplexing question to answer: 'Oh, you're killing me with this question.' She was not the only person to feel confused. Other women who moved from Hungary and Bulgaria to Italy and the Netherlands, and who were interviewed by the historian Luisa Passerini and her colleagues in 2002, reacted in similar ways. The question puzzled them, because it implied that Bulgaria and Hungary only became part of Europe (or rejoined Europe) after the end of communist rule. Ana concluded that one aspect of being 'European' now meant being free to travel back and forth between Bulgaria and Italy.[2]

All the same, the idea of a golden age of globalisation and mobility stretched credulity, particularly in view of parallel attempts to restrict the options for people seeking asylum, as discussed below. The freedom implied by the upheavals in 1989–1991 was neither unconditional nor unalloyed. Rhetoric and reality did not coincide.

Migration management was partly a matter reserved to individual states, but it increasingly involved their relationship with the European Union. The extension and deepening of the European Economic Community took place with the Single European Act in 1986 and the 1992 Treaty on European Union, known simply as Maastricht. Together with the Schengen Convention, which came into force in 1990, these documents marked a milestone in endorsing unrestricted movement across national frontiers by the citizens of signatory states. Maastricht explicitly provided (in Article 18) that every EU citizen, whether gainfully employed or not, had the right to move and reside freely within the territory of member states. In the medium term, 'inactive citizens' (such as pensioners and people unable to work) had to demonstrate that they had adequate health insurance and sufficient means of support, and no one in this category could make a claim on the country's welfare system during the first three months of residence. After five years, any EU citizen living outside his or her country of birth was entitled to welfare benefits. Another important provision, with obvious implications for migration, entitled migrant workers to be joined by family members.[3]

Further agreements followed at the end of the decade. EU member states signed the Treaty of Amsterdam in 1997, which entered into force on 1 May 1999, formally incorporating Schengen into EU law. It abolished identity checks on the frontiers of member states except at the borders of the UK and Ireland, both of which opted out of Schengen. Amsterdam provided for harmonisation of visa rules and supported 'minimum standards' in the reception of asylum seekers. It laid the foundations for a much greater role for EU institutions, notably the European Commission and the European Court of Justice. Not everyone was convinced by its coherence: the distinguished international lawyer Philip Allott, for example, commented acerbically that it sustained a mishmash of different economic and legal systems, constituting 'a sort of nightmare resurrection of the Holy Roman Empire'.[4]

At the same time, Schengen exposed the position of large numbers of so-called third-country nationals (TCNs) who lacked the nationalities of the member states in which they legally resided. Whilst EU nationals benefited from enhanced opportunities for mobility, separate and more restricted provision was made for these non-EU citizens. In this sense, as the migration scholar Andrew Geddes put it, the vision of an integrated 'people's Europe' was realised only by discounting the interests of some 12 million other people who were already living there.[5]

The European Union was itself a dynamic entity, with new members joining in 2004 and 2007. EU enlargement meant that the borders between EU member states and nonmember states altered accordingly. Changes to membership of the European Union had major implications for migration and migration policy. With the admission of Portugal and Spain, for example, Portuguese and Spanish migrants in France were transformed into EU citizens in 1992, along with their counterparts in Germany, where the number of Portuguese nationals nearly doubled between 1985 and 1998, from 77,000 to at least 133,000. Ten more countries joined the European Union on 1 May 2004: the Czech Republic, Estonia, Hungary, Latvia, Lithuania, Poland, and Slovakia and Slovenia (the so-called A8), together with Cyprus and Malta. Romania and Bulgaria joined on 1 January 2007, bringing the combined membership of the European Union to twenty-seven member states. (Croatia joined in 2013.) The accession of these former Soviet bloc countries imposed requirements not only to sign up to the principle of free movement within the European Union but also to tighten controls on eastern borders.[6]

The new member states were not granted immediate access to Europe's labour markets, with the important exception of the UK, Ireland, and Sweden. In the 1990s, Britain had already begun allowing Polish migrants to enter the country without visas, thereby providing them with a route into the informal economy. Germany, under Chancellor Helmut Kohl, imposed a seven-year transitional period, although this did not prevent informal arrangements facilitating migration across the Polish-German border or the unauthorised recruitment of workers from Romania.[7]

One priority among member states was to encourage the idea of Europe as a 'filter' rather than a 'fortress'. According to the Treaty of Lisbon, which was finally ratified in 2009, but which had been subject to negotiation for most of the previous decade—and in line with what had been agreed at Amsterdam—the European Union aimed to become 'the most competitive and dynamic knowledge-based economy in the world'; it would accordingly support 'measures to attract and retain highly qualified Third Country workers as part of an approach based on the needs of Member States'. But the Lisbon treaty also restated the need for 'solidarity and fair sharing of responsibility' over migration, including refugees. The European Commission emphasised that this objective could only be realised if Europe 'speaks with one voice'. There was certainly plenty of dissent, and Ireland and the Netherlands rejected the agreement.[8]

The policies and practices of European states reflected the new borders created by the enlargement of the European Union. Hence the corollary of internal freedom of movement within an enlarged union was an agreement to strengthen its external frontiers. A key development here was the creation in 2004 of a European Border and Coast Guard Agency, commonly known as Frontex (from the French term *Frontières extérieures*). One of its functions was to ensure that each EU member state attained common standards of border management by training border guards. According to its website, Frontex had the following functions: planning and coordinating joint operations and rapid border interventions using EU countries' staff and equipment at external borders (sea, land, and air); coordinating joint operations for the return of foreign nationals staying illegally in EU and Schengen countries and refusing to leave voluntarily; carrying out risk analyses (with a view to improving the integrated management of the European Union's external borders); assisting Schengen countries requiring increased technical and operational assistance at external borders (such as humanitarian emergencies and rescue at sea, or when they faced disproportionate pressures on their borders); and developing a rapid response capability involving EU Border Guard Teams as well as a database of available equipment and resources to be deployed in the event of a crisis situation.[9]

Notwithstanding the reference to Border Guard Teams, Frontex did not amount to the kind of unified European border police force that some member states, notably France and Italy, had advocated. The UK, in particular, expressed strong reservations about what it deemed to be an unwarranted centralisation of authority and a dilution in the power vested in national border forces. In the end, Frontex was limited to operational cooperation. Frontex officials acknowledged that it could not be considered 'a European panacea for all border related issues'. Instead, the agency would concentrate on gathering intelligence and assisting with training and operations that remained the primary responsibility of individual states.[10]

EU policy-makers identified 'irregular migration' as another pressing issue. Indeed, the benefits and costs of irregular migration became a hot topic in the 1990s precisely because it was thought to be spiralling out of control, threatening the vision—some would say fantasy—of migration management. The European Union sought to curb irregular migration by imposing sanctions on employers who failed to verify the identities of the workers they took on, but internal disagreements between member states turned this into a dead letter. Migrants took jobs at low wages but continued to move if it seemed likely that they could earn more somewhere else. Firms benefited from hiring them because by doing so they could avoid the costs associated with social insurance. Small and medium enterprises could be flexible about hiring and firing workers, and governments did not have to finance extensive and costly regulations. On the other hand, these workers were vulnerable to exploitation and abuse, both by traffickers and by unscrupulous employers.[11]

The influx from outside the European Union did not stop, of course. The statistics told a story of sustained migration. Spain, for example, was by the turn of the century home to 1.6 million foreigners with legal residence, and two-thirds of them were from outside the European Union. According to a Spanish official, 'other EU member states talk about the need for a zero immigration policy, but this is completely unrealistic for Spain. We want them to recognise Spain's objective need for foreign labour. Spaniards won't do certain kinds of jobs, and we need to channel foreign labour to meet those needs.'[12]

The experience of Italy threw a bright light on national migration policies. Italy adopted the term *extracomunitari*, literally those 'outside the community' (that is, the EEC), to distinguish them from those who 'belonged'. In 1991, according to official estimates, they numbered around 410,000, but as many again were thought to be illegal immigrants, *clandestinos*, putting the total at 800,000, or between 1.3 and 1.4 percent of Italy's population. They were made up of 176 different nationalities, with Moroccan, Tunisian, Somali, Senegalese, Ghanaian, and Filipino among the largest groups, together with Eritreans, who had traditionally migrated to Italy because of links stretching back to the colonial era.[13]

However, Italy's late twentieth-century 'migration crisis' was caused by developments much closer to home. Albania was an ex-communist state, and not a member state of the European Union, but the European Union was easily accessible to anyone who took a boat across to Italy. The collapse of communism had dramatic consequences in Albania and indirectly in Italy, which lay just a short boat ride away. To all intents and purposes a closed society, Albania was now exposed to the challenges of negotiating with the outside world.

In the three short years between 1991 and 1993, around 300,000 Albanians seized opportunities to migrate to Italy and Greece. Italy was an attractive destination for thousands of Albanian asylum seekers who made the short journey to Apulia, Italy, in 1991 on small fishing vessels, reaching safety in Otranto, Brindisi, and Bari. The Italian prime minister, Giulio Andreotti, spoke of them as 'our Albanian brethren'. But his fine words did not translate into official policy. They were given a three-month period in which to find work, but were then liable to be sent home. Their presence exacerbated tensions between central and local government. In a foretaste of things to come, the residents of Brindisi complained that the central government took insufficient steps to alleviate the strain on the city's budget. The government in Rome dispersed some Albanians to other parts of Italy, but this only inflamed opinion elsewhere. In a sop to his critics, the minister for immigration announced that Albanians were no longer entitled to be considered for refugee status, because the new government in Tirana had not persecuted them. This was a pretext to be rid of them.[14]

All hell broke loose in August 1991, when some 20,000 Albanians clambered aboard the *Vlora*, a barely seaworthy vessel bound for Italy. When they reached Bari, the local police held them in the football stadium on orders from Rome, and prevented them from leaving. Their treatment caused an outcry. One Italian journalist likened the stadium to a zoo, and lambasted the authorities for failing to arrange even basic care: 'The dream of the Albanians has dissolved, but so too has that of the Italians.' Local residents, many of them suffering hardship of their own, donated food to the migrants, who were living in the open air. The filmmaker Gianni Amelio, among others, expressed solidarity with Albanian migrants. Amelio's film *Lamerica* (1994) tells of two fictional Italian conmen who travel to Albania to set up a shoe factory (in reality it's a shell company designed to draw in government subsidies). To make money off the scam, they need to enlist a gullible Albanian as a front man; instead they become caught up in the lives of the Albanians in unexpected ways and begin to understand the misery driving so many of them from their homeland. *Lamerica* indirectly pointed the finger at the Italians who despised Albanian migrants.[15]

Others were far less sympathetic, describing the migrants as heralding a potential 'flood'. Refusing to recognise the migration as a humanitarian issue, the government handed responsibility over to the police and the military. The Italian president, Francesco Cossiga, described the situation as an attack on Italy's sovereignty. The government ordered warships to patrol Albanian waters to intercept and return migrants, offering Tirana economic aid in return for an assurance that Albania would deter people from leaving. These measures went down well with the Italian public.[16]

Tragically, the new patrols in the Strait of Otranto between the Balkan Peninsula and the Italian mainland culminated in the sinking by an Italian warship of the Soviet-built *Kater i Radës* on Good Friday 1997, resulting in the death of eighty-one Albanian migrants. (The boat was originally built for a crew of just ten.) They included Albanians who were trying to return to Italy where they already had jobs, but they were travelling as 'irregulars' following a visit home, because the Albanian government had suddenly closed its ports and airports. They feared they would lose their jobs and residence permits if they did not return in a hurry. No longer heroic 'victims of communism', the survivors were put in detention centres.[17]

Beyond the immediate repercussions for Albanian migration, refugee policy in Italy fluctuated in the 1990s and early 2000s. A shift towards a more generous approach began in 1990 in the wake of the murder of the

South African Jerry Masslo (see Chapter 12), whose claim for asylum had been turned down because Italy had refused to rescind the terms on which it signed the UN Refugee Convention (restricting recognition to refugees from Europe). Masslo's murder produced a public outcry. The Martelli Law, named after the deputy prime minister of Italy from 1989 to 1992, Claudio Martelli, passed in 1990. It regularised the status of many 'illegal' migrants and rescinded the restriction on asylum claims. Asylum seekers were henceforth also provided with a modest allowance for up to forty-five days whilst their claims were being processed.[18]

However, these more generous provisions did not last. The Albanian question deterred refugees from the former Yugoslavia from lodging asylum claims in Italy: at a time when Germany received 329,000 applications from Yugoslavs, Italy processed just 332. Even this did not go far enough for some. With the increase in asylum claims from non-European countries, the controversial far-right politician Umberto Bossi, whose leadership helped the Northern League to obtain 10 percent of the popular vote in Italy in 1996, launched an attack on government policy. He had already, at the time of Masslo's murder, proclaimed that 'Whites and Blacks do not integrate'. Then, in 2002, he announced: 'I want to hear the sound of cannons[;] otherwise this story will never end.' He gave his name to the Bossi-Fini Law, passed in 2002, which was designed to make it more difficult for migrants to regularise their status. It also criminalised anyone caught entering the country illegally or who returned after being expelled. It imposed harsh conditions on asylum seekers that were contrary to international human rights law. Italy's national daily newspaper *La Repubblica* reported in September that, in response to accusations that the proposed fingerprinting of suspected 'illegal' migrants was unduly harsh, the mayor of Treviso, Giancarlo Gentilini, had asked: 'What's the problem? I think we should take prints of their feet and noses too.'[19]

Debates in the Italian Parliament sparked mass street protests. One migrant carried a banner that read 'Immigrants of the World Unite', and the Italian president himself called upon Italians to remember their own history of migration and asylum. NGOs organised a 'Fingerprint Day' and flooded government offices with hundreds of documents to mock the law and to demand the same rights for all migrants as for Italian citizens.[20]

Migration to Italy did not stall. By 2003, some 2 million foreigners legally resided in Italy, most of them third-country nationals from outside the European Union, one-third of them from Africa. Another 1 million were believed to be undocumented. Three years later, an estimated 2.7 million foreigners were living in Italy, the majority of them from outside the European Union. Half of the increase was accounted for by the regularisation of the status of migrants already living in Italy.[21]

Meanwhile, one significant group remained hidden from view but suffered at least as much heartbreak as the other migrants. This was the population collectively known as the Roma. One common response on the part of governments, Italy included, was to treat them as 'nomads'. The consequences could be pernicious. In 1999, 10,000 Roma arrived in Italy to escape the war in Kosovo, only to be told that they did not qualify for protection because they were nomads who wanted to take advantage of Italian 'generosity'. Demonised as 'bogus refugees', a term that had no meaning in international law, but whose vernacular meaning seemed to go down well in some quarters, they were held for long periods of time in camps in Florence and other cities.[22]

Policies towards the Roma in Italy as elsewhere were influenced by the belief that they constituted a single community, whereas the evidence pointed instead to a plethora of groups based around family networks and the villages from which different Roma originate. Those who moved to Western Europe in the new millennium were often treated with contempt. In Manchester, local authorities made strenuous efforts to confront stereotypes about Roma, such as about 'child marriage' or their supposed 'disengagement' from the education system, and to institute measures to build confidence and respect. But this was a rare glimmer of hope. In Paris, the municipal authorities demolished the shantytowns which some Roma had built, even though they had become thriving and well-ordered settlements. There was a long way to go before this vulnerable migrant population gained the rights they were due.[23]

Unlike policies towards Roma, which left much to be desired, there were signs in France in the 1990s that migrants were more frequently being portrayed as having something to contribute. In 1992 the socialist historian Émile Temime launched a series of books under the title *Français d'ailleurs: Peuple d'ici* (France from elsewhere: People here). It included firsthand accounts by prominent migrants from different backgrounds, including Russians and Turks in Paris, people of Algerian descent in Lyon, and others.

Temime created a valuable legacy, but it did not alter the course or conduct of mainstream politics. In 1993, with the victory of the right, the government adopted the recommendations of a report on French nationality by a leading civil servant, Marceau Long. Under the new regulations, children born in France to immigrants could not automatically become citizens at the age of eighteen, but would instead have to apply. The police cracked down on protests, and the new laws went into effect. They gave the police the power to carry out random identity checks on anyone suspected of being in France illegally.[24]

The demonisation of migrants of colour came to a head in the summer of 1996, when a group of African men and women, mainly from Mali and Senegal, decided to protest government policies. Events culminated with 324 migrants occupying the Church of Saint Bernard in the 18th arrondissement; a small number of them embarked on a hunger strike. The actions of these undocumented migrants (*sans-papiers*, those 'without papers') increased public awareness of their plight and lack of status, and French TV highlighted their living conditions and their struggle to avoid deportation. On 23 August, the government ordered the police to break down the doors to the church. President Jacques Chirac authorised a case-by-case review of the occupiers. By the beginning of 1997, 100 of them had received papers, but most of the others were still fighting for recognition. Nineteen were deported, and one had died of cancer. Key figures in the wider support network included Madjiguène Cissé and Ababacar Diop, who had contributed to Temime's *Français d'ailleurs: Peuple d'ici*. Cissé subsequently returned to Dakar and published her own account of the movement, particularly the part played by women. She argued that the root causes of migration were connected to neocolonialism and to 'structural adjustment' policies that created mass impoverishment. (Diop became a successful businessman.) More to the point, thanks to the impact of the mass protest, the French government eventually agreed to regularise the status of some 80,000 *sans-papiers*. Perhaps, as their manifesto put it, they could now 'come out of the shadows'.[25]

These improvements were hard won, but the greater prize was the assurance of migrants' rights. The migrants themselves tried to convey the importance of this objective in their public utterances. As Madjiguène Cissé said on behalf of the *sans-papiers* in France: 'The fact that we've been seen on TV, that we've been interviewed in the press, I think that has helped people to understand that we've been here for years, that we haven't killed anyone, and that we are simply demanding the piece of paper which is our right, so that we can live decent lives.'[26]

The success of the *sans-papiers* produced a backlash at the end of the century, when Prime Minister Lionel Jospin put himself at the head of a political campaign to 'defend the republic'. This campaign chimed neatly with arguments about the multiple 'menace' of globalisation, 'criminal' immigration networks, 'communitarianism', and multiculturalism. Immigrants who 'went home', he said, did the right thing by the French republic. A much more extreme manifestation of the hostile atmosphere at this point was the publication of a fierce critique in *Le Figaro* by the notorious author Jean Raspail, under the title 'La patrie trahie par la république' (The fatherland betrayed by the republic). Fortunately for him, a charge of incitement to racial hatred was dropped.[27]

Hard on the heels of these developments were measures taken by Nicolas Sarkozy, who was minister of the interior at the time, but would later become president. Sarkozy insisted on more stringent policing in districts that were home to large numbers of migrants. His tough stance led to riots in 2005 that provoked yet more punitive measures. The Immigration and Integration Law he promoted, adopted in 2006, restructured immigration policy. Selection would be based on 'economic criteria', and long-term residents would have to obtain mandatory 'integration contracts' (*contrats d'accueil et d'integration*). The law also introduced 'co-development', which meant the targeted use of French foreign aid to discourage migrants from the global South from seeking a better life in Europe. Sarkozy tapped a groundswell of popular support among the French electorate, which contributed to his election as president in 2007, but neither the new legislation nor his rhetoric prevented fresh protests from deprived migrant communities from breaking out.[28]

Other manifestations of the connection between hospitality and hostility emerged in political movements led by European politicians who insisted that being hospitable to existing migrants meant being tough in relation to prospective newcomers, particularly those of Muslim faith. Others were less circumspect. In the Netherlands, a right-wing politician, Pim Fortuyn, rallied popular support in 2001 around the slogan of 'backward Islam', insisting that he had nothing against migrants per se, but that Muslims could never be fully integrated in Dutch society. He opposed any further migration from Muslim countries. His assassination by an animal-rights activist, in May 2002, inflamed the political scene still further, as did the murder of the filmmaker Theo van Gogh by a Muslim extremist in 2004. These developments stirred a toxic mix of far-right populism, anti-Islam sentiment, and anti-immigration attitudes. The mantle of the far right was then assumed by Geert Wilders, the leader of the Dutch nationalist party Partij voor de Vrijheid (Party for Freedom), who lambasted the Dutch left for having done nothing to curb the migration of Turks and Moroccans in the previous quarter century.[29]

The often intolerant politics in individual states towards migrants had its counterparts in attitudes and practices towards refugees, of whom there were a large number. By the beginning of the new millennium, the European Union and its member states had adopted policies designed to deter people from seeking asylum. Like the mantra of 'migration management', these policies were partly designed to assure voters that government could be trusted to look after their interests.

The unforeseen events in Yugoslavia had pointed to the impact of state collapse and civil war on mass population displacement. European states reacted cautiously. The conflict coincided with an upturn in the global number of refugees from the continuing war in Afghanistan and from political upheavals and violence in sub-Saharan Africa, including Rwanda, Sudan, and the Horn of Africa. Governments then adopted even more restrictive policies, including making it more difficult for forced migrants to claim refugee status, lest this open the door to large numbers of migrants from the global South. Medium- and long-term actions were required to fully protect refugees—what the UNHCR called 'durable solutions'—but no European government embraced refugee resettlement with any enthusiasm. Instead, policy makers developed strategies of containment and encouraged repatriation where it was 'safe' to carry out. Containment meant offering packages of aid to countries in the global South. Repatriation could be sold to European voters as a humanitarian (and cheaper) option. But the main purpose of both was to nip in the bud any suggestion that refugees should be resettled in the West. By 1992, EU governments were maintaining that 'intercontinental movements of asylum seekers are seldom necessary for protection reasons'.[30]

Asylum policy remained the preserve of national governments, but this did not discourage steps to coordinate asylum practices. In 1990, the Dublin Regulations, which were extended by 'Dublin II' in 1997, stipulated that an asylum application lodged in one EU country could not then be considered by another. The member state responsible for processing an asylum claim was normally expected to be the one through which an asylum seeker first entered the territory of the European Union. The purpose was to prevent 'asylum shopping', an aim reaffirmed in subsequent discussions and agreements. According to one legal scholar, 'if Schengen was the "open Europe" then Dublin was the means by which to close it to the rest of the global South'. It was accompanied by yet another intergovernmental agreement, the European Data Archive Convention (Eurodac), whereby asylum seekers over the age of fourteen would be fingerprinted, and the fingerprints held on a central European database. Described by the European Union as 'a very important tool', the new database was launched in 2003 as part of what was termed the Common European Asylum System.[31]

By the time of an EU special summit on justice and home affairs in Tampere, Finland, in 1999, the talk was of a 'balanced and comprehensive approach' to migration. This meeting rehashed the arguments in favour of promoting economic development in sending countries in order to address the root causes, notably poverty, of migration. It was thought, in any case, that these measures would restrict 'uncontrolled' and 'illegal' migration. Over the next few years, EU member states increasingly sent the discussion of asylum and refugees to high-level meetings of foreign ministers, emphasising the importance of prevention and containment as well as cooperation.[32]

Linked to this stance was the decision to identify 'safe countries' that offered supposedly guaranteed protection for refugees, and from which asylum claims would therefore not be entertained by EU member states. This approach helped sustain the view that asylum seekers who reached Europe might 'safely' be returned to such countries without breaching the 1951 Refugee Convention, and specifically, its rules on non-refoulement. The trend toward taking this route began with a series of decisions relating to countries in the former Soviet bloc. The Cold War had ended: there could no longer be any 'escapees' from communism. Practically speaking, policy makers in EU member states did not think these countries would still be funnelling new asylum claimants their way. Germany, for example, stipulated that it could no longer be claimed that Romania and Bulgaria persecuted their citizens; this change reduced the number of asylum seekers from Romania from 100,000 in 1992 to a few thousand in 1995.

The repercussions of these various decisions—in particular, those whereby EU states reached agreements with former communist countries and supported repatriation to 'safe' countries—were considerable. In 1992, the fifteen EU member states received more than 670,000 applications for asylum; in 2000, however, the number was only 407,000, and in 2005 it stood at 235,000. At the same time, member states were not shy about using the EU agenda to their advantage. Their decisions did not bode well for those seeking asylum.[33]

The British government regularly restated its 'tradition of welcome' even as it put more obstacles in the way of asylum seekers. The 1988 Immigration Act introduced a requirement that dependents of immigrants should have a sponsor who would support them in order to avoid having 'recourse to public funds'. This presaged a growing tendency to diminish the entitlement of 'persons from abroad' to welfare, a policy designed to allay the concern of many constituents that migrants were 'scroungers' or 'benefit cheats'. In November 1995, the British home secretary, Michael Howard, insisted that the UK should be 'a haven, not a honeypot'. In 1996, Britain withdrew benefits from asylum seekers who did not immediately claim asylum on arrival in the UK, which meant that they became a charge on local authority budgets. Three years later, the new Immigration and Asylum Act restored central government responsibility for the maintenance of asylum seekers, but replaced cash payments with vouchers. In 2002, the Labour government under Tony Blair secured parliamentary approval for a new Nationality, Immigration and Asylum Act to tighten controls on entry and restrict access to welfare provision and jobs for those already in the UK, under the broad mantra of 'tackling abuse'. The government extended its list of countries deemed to be 'safe' and from which asylum claims would not be recognised. The Home Office minister, Beverley Hughes, was able to tell the House of Commons a year later that the act had halved the number of claimants; she assured the MPs that 'removals are at record levels'. The legislation was designed to demonstrate that the Labour government could not be accused (as a hostile press put it) of being 'soft' on immigration and asylum.[34]

In line with these provisions, the Blair government recommended that applications for asylum should be processed outside the European Union, such as in Turkey and Iran in the case of Iraqi asylum seekers, rather than in EU member states. Other transit processing centres were to be established in Albania, Bulgaria, and Romania. The government also reached an agreement with the Czech government to station UK immigration officers at the airport in Prague, to screen Roma asylum seekers who intended to travel from there to Britain. For EU member states, the idea of externalising responsibility for scrutinising claims by asylum seekers was attractive, and these proposals gained traction.[35]

The uncertain status of one such group of refugees emerged in a bizarre fashion in Cyprus: bizarre, that is, for the casual reader, but terrifying in its uncertainty for the people most directly affected. The history of the ordeal began in 1998, when a small group of refugees left Lebanon bound for Italy on a fishing boat badly in need of repair. They eventually became stranded on a part of Cyprus that had remained a British sovereign territory since independence in 1960. But before they arrived in Cyprus, a baby, Layali Ibrahim, was born on the open deck of the boat. Most of the seventy-four migrants were Iraqi and Syrian Kurds, members of a persecuted minority who had given their life savings to people-smugglers to transport them. When the boat's engine failed, the Lebanese crew fled in a dinghy. The group was picked up by an RAF helicopter that took them to the British airbase at Akrotiri. British officials claimed they were the responsibility of Cyprus, not the UK: 'Britannia waives the rules', the *Cyprus Mail* observed caustically. The migrants were transferred from Akrotiri to Dhekelia (another UK base) several months later and housed in former quarters for British service families that were scheduled for demolition. They received a weekly allowance. These new 'boat people' remained in Richmond Village, part of the Sovereign Base Area (SBA), because Britain claimed that granting them refugee status would lead other asylum seekers to see its Cyprus bases as a way to get into the UK from the Middle East and North Africa.

After Cyprus joined the European Union in 2004, the SBA reached a verbal agreement with the Cypriot authorities whereby the refugees would be allowed to live and work in Cyprus and would be given access to its schools and hospitals. But the Richmond Village residents opposed a permanent move to Cyprus. Layali grew up in the makeshift village. When she turned sixteen, she said: 'I never see my school friends outside class.' There were British teenagers living nearby, but she did not socialise with them. An SBA official stated that 'as failed asylum seekers, they cannot expect to remain on a British military base for ever.' Layali's parents worried, but she still hoped to become a doctor in Britain someday. She said, 'They can't just kick us out after all we've suffered here for 16 years. The only way we'll leave Richmond Village is when they tell us we can go to England.' In December 2018, the British government finally relented, allowing six families to come to the UK.[36]

Given the numbers involved, and the fact that international attention was focused on the Cypriots displaced during the 1974 war, Richmond Village attracted almost no international attention. The same could not be said of the notorious camp at Sangatte, a small town in northern France. Sangatte lay close to the Eurotunnel entrance and thus held out the prospect of relatively easy access to the UK (which had, of course, opted out of Schengen), provided that refugees could find a way to evade detection. In 1999, the French Red Cross opened what was expected to be a short-term facility (the Centre d'Hébergement et d'Accueil d'Urgence Humanitaire, or Humanitarian Emergency Housing and Reception Centre) in a disused warehouse to support a few hundred refugees who had arrived in nearby Calais. Within a few months, Sangatte housed around 2,000 refugees—in a town that numbered only 4,000 inhabitants. The refugee population was truly international: the largest group consisted of families fleeing the conflict in Kosovo, but there were also refugees from Afghanistan, Iraq, Eritrea, Sudan, and Sri Lanka. Within weeks, journalists descended on Sangatte to report on the dogged efforts of 'bogus' asylum seekers to breach the costly security measures that had been put in place by the Eurotunnel, as well as the equally resolute determination of the British authorities to prevent them from doing so.[37]

The refugees were trapped in what turned into a stalemate between the British and French governments. In the space of three years, close on 70,000 refugees passed through the Sangatte facility. Britain wanted the centre to be closed, on the grounds that it had become a 'magnet' for refugees attempting to cross the English Channel with the help of people-smugglers; the French, said the British, should process the asylum applications faster. France insisted that Britain should allow some refugees into the UK, in order to alleviate overcrowding and minimise risks to public health, as well as to reduce tensions between rival ethnic groups. In 2002, President Sarkozy agreed to close the camp. He refused permission for any more refugees to be accommodated in Sangatte and dispersed most of its residents across France. Britain agreed to admit a few hundred Afghan and Iraqi refugees, coupling this with the crackdown on asylum described above. But media references to a 'siege' and to 'consignments of illegal immigrants' showed how easy it was to compound refugees' original vulnerability.[38]

Other camps, meanwhile, garnered much less attention, partly because the numbers of refugees were smaller, but also because it served the interests of European governments to keep them out of the spotlight. Whatever the differences in size or location, camps increasingly took on common characteristics: a trapped population of refugees, supporting one another and helped by overstretched aid workers, and 'protected' by security guards, fences, razor wire, and video cameras.

The intense scrutiny and incarceration of refugees revealed the impossibility of delivering on the promise to control migration. In an endless loop, governments asserted the need to impose ever tighter restrictions as part of a package of deterrence. This went beyond the 'refugee problem'. Policing the new frontiers in Eastern Europe and in the Mediterranean formed one element in a broader process of managing migration. Another element was the 'remote control' of migration by the European Union, with the aim of deterring and excluding refugees. The camp at Sangatte demonstrated how asylum exposed tensions between member states, but its closure did nothing to reduce those tensions, let alone to provide refugees with a viable alternative.

As the archipelago of camps and detention centres spread across the continent and farther afield, the founding fathers of closer European integration—many of them having had direct experience of Nazi persecution before and during the Second World War—would surely have turned in their graves at what their successors had done in the name of Europe.

CHAPTER 19

Privileged Lives, Precarious Lives

ONE WAY OF THINKING of migration in Europe is that it operated along a spectrum. At one end stood migrants who lived precarious lives, uncertain of their status and exposed to exploitation. At the other were those who travelled without hindrance and who enjoyed the advantages of wealth and security. The political scientist Adrian Favell called the latter 'Eurostars': citizens who lived in one country but worked in another, commuting back and forth. They included well-heeled migrants, bankers, IT specialists, and other mobile professionals who accumulated large savings and established useful contacts to be activated if needed. If they were made redundant, they were likely to find work elsewhere.[1]

Although they were often under stress by virtue of high-pressure jobs and the strain imposed on family and other relationships, privileged migrants benefited from the cosmopolitan lifestyle evident in Europe's capital cities and business centres. However, even the Eurostars were not immune from complaints about their presence. In Switzerland, for example, where in the new millennium around 270,000 foreign workers arrived on Monday and left on Friday, the Swiss National Party (Partei National Orientierter Schweizer) argued that they took jobs from Swiss workers and put an intolerable pressure on the country's infrastructure. But this campaign, which culminated in 2014 in the government's decision to introduce quotas on the number of non-Swiss workers allowed to work in the country, was not primarily directed at scientists or UN employees who lived in France, Italy, or Germany. Its main target was migrants in low-wage jobs.[2]

Some of the members of this privileged group were Europeans who went to another country to settle permanently, rather than commuting. They included a sizeable British expatriate population in Spain and Italy, sometimes described as diaspora living in 'Eldorado' and 'Chiantishire'. The UN estimated that in the new millennium around 1.2 million Britons were living in EU countries outside of the UK.[3]

Ironically, in view of the widespread concern about 'illegal migrants', this migration was largely undocumented and unregulated, because expats were regarded as harmless newcomers who would keep to themselves. British migration to Spain, Italy, and France accelerated in the last quarter of the century. By 2016, close on 300,000 British citizens had been living in Spain for more than twelve months (indeed, the number moving to Spain had remained stable since 2008). At any one time, at least twice that number were living and sometimes working in Spain. Only one-third of them were over the age of sixty-five, undermining the assumption that all these expats were elderly. Many expats had visited as tourists and fallen in love with the country, and then had done careful research before buying property. Others moved to Spain and other countries because they had been made redundant in the 1980s, or had personal reasons for moving abroad, such as being bereaved or starting a new relationship. Retirement to Spain, Portugal, France, or Italy reflected longer life expectancy and a wish to spend one's remaining years in a warmer climate, returning to the UK periodically to visit relatives or to use the National Health Service. In general, therefore, this group can be thought of as a mixed diasporic population that included 'sunset migrants' as well as people who wanted to work. From time to time, British newspapers added spice to the mix by describing the efforts of criminals and gangsters to use Spain as a bolt-hole.[4]

France was a favourite destination, partly because of its proximity to the UK, but also because, as one elderly expat put it, 'it's very much like 50s–60s England....France represents something we've lost.' He specifically mentioned respect for older people such as himself. But this nostalgia did not make for a very convincing justification. Portugal was another destination of choice. Barry, a property developer, arrived in the Algarve in 1964 together with his Portuguese wife: 'There was a great opportunity here. The place was totally undeveloped with no hotels and no airport.... It was a unique opportunity for me, plus I had a built-in translator with my wife. Her parents, who came from Estoril, were appalled that I was bringing her to the Algarve, which they regarded as Africa!' Raymond Flower, a long-term British resident of Tuscany, described leaving Egypt after the Suez Crisis and being surrounded by financiers: 'You'd go into the little bar in Castellina—there were no telephones in those days—and you'd find Oliver Poole who was chairman of Lazard's, and he was trying to get through to London, having a coffee while he was waiting, to arrange the merger between Leyland and the British Motor Corporation! So yes, I suppose there was a sort of Chiantishire feel about the place in those days.' But Barry insisted that most British expats he knew in the Algarve 'are not the colonial type now of course, mostly they're professional or small company businessmen'.[5]

Expats, particularly those with second homes in Spain, maintained ties with the UK, although, unlike the classic diaspora, they did not 'long for home'. One expat referred to those who spoke in terms of returning to England as 'wimps'. British expats tended not to mix with Spanish locals, and those who worked in the leisure and hospitality sector mostly provided services to other expats. Attempts to integrate were often rebuffed in any case. In the 1990s, a retired British engineer living in Mijas Pueblo in Spain said: 'If things were to change dramatically, we would probably go back but we'll burn that bridge when we get to it!' One factor, he said, was local resentment, which periodically expressed itself in the formulation 'España en venta' (Spain for sale), a reference to the spread of apartment blocks along the coast and the impact on the local environment. An added complication would emerge in 2016, the result of uncertainty following the referendum on Britain's membership in the European Union. Having kept a foot in both camps, as it were, these people found the prospect of Britain's exit from the European Union unsettling, as it forced them to confront uncomfortable choices about their future.[6]

Affluence mobility also extended to Germans. Some 61,000 Germans, for example, were living in Spain in 2008, a fourfold increase since the 1990s. Most lived in gated communities, called *urbanizaciones*, where they—along with their Swiss neighbours—made do with German-language newspapers. Yet some German and Swiss expats saw themselves as contributing to a more cosmopolitan Europe that transcended borders. Some of them flew the flag of the European Union in front of their homes.[7]

It is important to acknowledge privileged migration of this kind, which supported the findings of specialist scholars that migration was 'mixed'. Nevertheless, the lives of the 'Eurostars' and of expats in general rarely intersected with the lives of precarious migrants, except when the former briefly encountered the latter as cleaners, waiters, or receptionists.

Faced with tougher controls on entry of the kind that never stood in the way of privileged migrants, lower-skilled non-European migrants explored semilegal or illegal options in order to gain access to European countries. Hence, the international news media became increasingly familiar with the 'people-smuggler' or 'human trafficker'. Unlike earlier rescuers who had facilitated the escape of individuals from communism or right-wing dictatorships, the new generation of smugglers attracted opprobrium, because they operated lucrative schemes that threatened, rather than secured, the lives of the people they promised to help flee violence or poverty. The criticism overlooked the fact that people-smugglers only remained in business by virtue of the obstacles to legal entry to Europe.

Only a minority of migrants travelled huge distances to Europe, but this made the journeys of migrants from sub-Saharan Africa and the Far East all the more remarkable. Migration was partly driven by persecution and violence, but it was also driven by economic insecurity and the prospect of making a better living. Putting themselves in the hands of people who promised to ferry them to Europe by circumventing the normal points of entry only compounded the migrants' sense of insecurity and vulnerability.

Migrants frequently lived under the radar of official scrutiny. No one knew with any precision how many migrants were trafficked or forced into bondage, marriage, child labour, or 'sexual servitude', in the terminology of the International Labour Organization. The United Nations deplored the trafficking of women, but distinguished it from prostitution, since women were trafficked for all kinds of purposes, including working in slave-like conditions. In 2000, the United Nations replaced the 1949 Convention for the Suppression of the Traffic in Persons with a UN Protocol to Prevent, Suppress and Punish Trafficking in Persons, Especially Women and Children, putting this problem on par with other criminal activities, such as drug trafficking. Crucially, however, the signatories did not agree on the right of trafficked persons to stay in the destination country, and most states took steps to deport them. In one notorious case, Nigerian women who in 2000 were deported from Italy as undocumented migrants and sex workers faced being paraded in public and humiliated on their return.[8]

Europe's news media regularly carried stories about the insidious activities of people-traffickers. Journalists portrayed migrants as victims who were trafficked to work in conditions akin to slavery, such as young Vietnamese men and women who worked in nail parlours on the British high street in the hope of earning enough to send remittances back to family members in Vietnam. The uncertain status of many non-European migrants found its expression in discrimination and exploitation, and sometimes in tragedy. No more distressing story emerged at the turn of the twenty-first century than the discovery by UK immigration officers in June 2000 of the bodies of fifty-eight illegal Chinese immigrants who had suffocated in the back of a lorry bound for the port of Dover from Zeebrugge in Belgium. Most British newspapers pointed the blame directly at organised criminal gangs, although *The Guardian* pointed out that, had the migrants survived, 'there would have been nothing but condemnation for the "bogus asylum seekers" and calls from both left and right for their deportation as quickly as possible'.[9]

Four years later, in February 2004, the risks run by migrants were again exposed, this time by the deaths of twenty-three cockle pickers in Morecambe Bay in the northwest of England. All of them were undocumented workers who had been smuggled to Europe from the impoverished Chinese province of Fujian; they had been given false national insurance numbers to avoid scrutiny. Prior to arriving in Britain, some of them had been taken on by farmers in East Anglia. The gangmaster responsible for their employment paid them a pittance, ferrying them from a run-down boardinghouse in Liverpool to the sands of the bay to gather cockles, an edible shellfish. At Morecambe Bay, it is crucial to keep track of the tide tables. But the gangmaster had failed to do this, and during a nighttime session, the workers got caught in an incoming tide. One man, the father of two children, used his mobile phone to call his family in China: 'The water is up to my chest', he said. 'The bosses got the time wrong. I can't get back in time.' He asked his relatives to pray for him, but to no avail. He and most of the others drowned.[10]

As a result of this tragedy, members of the British trade union movement lobbied Parliament for statutory licensing of gangmasters. (The Conservative government had abandoned licensing arrangements a decade earlier.) In a parliamentary debate on a private member's bill, the Labour MP Jim Sheridan suggested that at least 3,000 gangmasters operated in the agricultural, shellfish, food processing, and packaging sectors, employing as many as 100,000 workers. Chinese restaurants in London admitted to hiring undocumented workers by these means, a reminder that British consumers helped to keep the system going by demanding value for their money when they ate out. Meanwhile, the families of the dead cockle pickers were left to pay off their debts to the traffickers, who had reportedly received up to £20,000 (around $15,000) for each person's transit to the UK. People-traffickers continued to profit.[11]

Artists expressed the sense of loss more profoundly than any news report or scholarly analysis could, as in Nick Broomfield's 2006 film, *Ghosts*, and Isaac Julien's 2010 film installation, *Ten Thousand Waves*. Broomfield chose to employ migrants from Fujian to play the part of those who had lost their lives in at Morecambe Bay. *Ten Thousand Waves* incorporated classics of Chinese cinema, photography, music, poetry, and calligraphy to suggest that the spirits of the drowned cockle pickers might be returned to the Middle Kingdom with the assistance of the sea goddess. Equally poignant was the tea service created by the ceramicist Paul Scott in 2007. His choice of a Willow pattern simultaneously evoked the background of the cockle pickers and the long-standing connections between China and Europe that have been forged through migration. Although each of these artists interpreted migration differently, they all dramatised the perils faced by undocumented migrants. More than this, they insisted on the need to portray migration in a multidimensional and sometimes oblique fashion. These portraits made an indelible impression on anyone who saw them and offered a necessary counterpoint to the accounts in the news. They also supplemented social-scientific accounts and legal analyses, which spoke in abstract terms of globalisation, cheap labour, and low standards of protection.[12]

Other films and works of art conveyed the human stories behind similarly distressing operations. Fernando León de Aranoa's film *Princesas* (Princesses, 2005) introduces Zulema, a fictional undocumented sex worker from the Dominican Republic working in Spain, and portrays her friendship with Caye, a Spanish prostitute. The film invites the viewer to engage with the aspirations of migrants and to reflect on the fact that contemporary migration in Spain is only the latest chapter in a long history of migration to and from that nation. *Dirty Pretty Things* (directed by Stephen Frears, 2002) tells the story of undocumented migrants working in a London hotel. The lead character is a hotel night clerk, Okwe (Chiwetel Ejiofor), who works by day as a taxi driver, but has qualified as a doctor in Nigeria. At one point, a guest asks him, 'How come I've never seen you before?', to which Okwe replies, 'Because we are the people you never see'. The hotel setting provides Frears with the opportunity to explore the lives of other migrants as well, such as Senay (Audrey Tautou), a Turkish asylum seeker working as a hotel chambermaid. The drama centres on the underground trade in human organs. Pressed to become a kidney donor, Senay tells the dealer to 'go to hell', and he replies that 'this is hell'.[13]

A different kind of exploitation figures in a novel by the Moroccan-born author Mahi Binebine, *Welcome to Paradise* (1999). Binebine paints a vivid portrait of a small group of people—Algerian, Moroccan, and Malian—who gather on a deserted beach in North Africa. They are waiting for the signal to be given by a smuggler that it is safe to take a boat out to sea, and thence to board a trawler that will take them to Spain. The smuggler reassures them that many others have made the journey already:

345

'It's not a trip to the moon!' The characters reflect on their proximity to Europe and the hazards of the journey. One prospective passenger says, 'If paradise were that close, I'd have swum there by now!' They are told to bury their identification papers in the sand to conceal their identity. One person proclaims that he needs to become 'a nobody, another shadow, a stray dog, a lowly earthworm, or even a cockroach. That's it, yes, learn to be a cockroach.' Binebine explores the backstory of each of the passengers—the young cousins who resolutely stick together, the young woman who wants to introduce her baby to the father, who she thinks is working in France, the tough and talismanic Malian man who exudes confidence and optimism. He portrays the migrants as flesh-and-blood people with dreams of freedom.[14]

La traversée (The crossing, 2006), shot by the Algerian-born filmmaker Elisabeth Leuvrey, is a powerful documentary about the passengers aboard *L'Ile de beauté* (The island of beauty), a boat plying the seas between Marseille and Algiers. She focuses mainly on Algerians who made the crossing at least once a year. The film introduces the audience to each part of the boat—not just the cabins, but also the communal areas and corridors—and contrasts the claustrophobia of these spaces with the open sea. It was an uncomfortable journey in more ways than one, although it carried no great physical risk. The film points to the fact that the Mediterranean is witness to journeys that are made in different registers. Dedicated to Abdelmalek Sayad, *La traversée* was filmed entirely on the actual boat. Leuvrey's informants speak of finding it 'impossible to lead a whole life', and of living an 'in-between' life. A young Algerian girl born in France describes being mocked by Algerians as 'the immigrant'. Leuvrey explores how children grew up being separated from their fathers when they left Algeria to find work in France. They were accustomed to making return visits, but these were emotionally draining. One of the migrants says: 'Algeria is like a sick old aunt that you go and visit, but you stay for the weekend and then on Sunday evening you clear off because otherwise you'd kill yourself. But when you get back home to your little studio in Neuilly or wherever, you feel ashamed at having left your aunt in such a hurry...you quickly organise your next visit. It's a permanent indecision.' Other migrants recount the difficulties of securing an entry visa.[15]

Surprisingly, perhaps, illegality could also be a source of humour. A sense of playfulness suffuses a short novel by Didier van Cauwelaert. *Un aller simple* (in translation called *One-Way*) was published in 1994 in the wake of the Pasqua Laws, which overturned migrants' rights dating back to the 1700s. Winner of the prestigious Prix Goncourt, it tells the story of Aziz, an illegal immigrant who is deported to Morocco in the company of a French 'humanitarian attaché', Schneider. Schneider aims to help Aziz get his life back together in the village of his birth. The scenario is absurd: the village has never existed, as it turns out, having been invented by the person who originally forged Aziz's passport. The absurdity is compounded by Schneider's realisation that Aziz was born in France, but could not prove it. His parents had been killed in a car accident, leaving him to be adopted by a family of Roma. Schneider is himself a victim of his superior, who wishes to get rid of him in order to sleep with his wife.[16]

One tragic episode in real life occurred in 1996, although it only hit the headlines several years later. An overcrowded boat, codenamed F174, carrying more than 300 passengers (nearly four times its capacity), sank in stormy seas off the coast of Sicily in December 1996. Local fishermen from Portopalo began to find corpses, body parts, and personal belongings in their nets, but they kept this information from the authorities for fear of disrupting their livelihood. The story only emerged thanks to one fisherman who broke ranks and contacted an Italian investigative journalist, Giovanni Maria Bellu, who published *The Ghosts of Portopalo* in 2004. It emerged that many of the migrants were from India and Pakistan; some were Tamils fleeing the civil war in Sri Lanka. They had been transported to Cairo and Alexandria before being taken to a freighter to begin their fateful journey. They were later transferred to the F174, where the captain was drunk, and reportedly armed and aggressive. Not everyone onboard died: the survivors and their families became determined to ensure that those responsible were held to account, and it fell to journalists to investigate. The whole saga pointed to widespread public indifference towards clandestine migrants, although there is now a small monument in Syracuse to commemorate the catastrophe.[17]

A popular but dangerous passage from West Africa to Spain lay via the Canary Islands. In the 1990s, the Spanish news media barely reported the loss of life when boats capsized. The popularity of this route increased in 2006, when it became more difficult to access the Spanish enclave of Ceuta. Following the arrival of more than 30,000 migrants from Senegal and Mauritania, there was a surge in media interest, and the Spanish government built an immigration detention centre, the Centro de internamiento de extranjeros (Centre for the Internment of Foreigners). It also engaged Frontex—the European Union's border patrol force—to guard the border. Speaking in 2007 in front of the camera, the head of a Red Cross emergency team sympathised with their ordeal: 'They've spent several days on the high seas in cold temperatures, rough seas, darkness and silence, and when they land they get the feeling that they've made it, that it's over. It's very stressful.'[18]

Their odyssey was dramatised in a film by Moussa Touré, *La Pirogue* (2012). It portrays a group of Senegalese fishermen who reach the Canary Islands with the help of intermediaries before being detained and then deported. Those who eventually succeed in reaching the Spanish mainland speak of the difficulty of making a decent living: 'I would rather be fishing in Senegal than collecting waste in Barcelona.' This comment would seem like music to the ears of European government officials seeking to control migration. But the more they fashioned new restrictions, the more the opportunities increased for Europe's expanding security industry and the people-smugglers. Spain's response was to invest in aid projects in Senegal and other sub-Saharan countries of origin, in order to discourage young men from attempting the journey in the first place.[19]

The desperation of people living in precarious conditions also emerged in two Spanish enclaves, Ceuta and Melilla, which, located on the North African coast, form the only land border between the European Union and the African continent. Ceuta, which shares a border with Morocco, lies just fourteen kilometres south of Gibraltar. A Spanish possession for centuries, it remained under Spanish rule when Morocco gained independence in 1956. A tourist guidebook comments that its small territory (about eighteen square kilometres) offers 'a compact dose of fantastic architecture, interesting museums, excellent food, a relaxing maritime park and bracing nature walks' and that 'the city is particularly beautiful at night'.[20]

But there was another Ceuta, the site of numerous attempts by African migrants to gain a foothold in the European Union by clambering over the high-security fence built in 1993 and regularly strengthened thereafter. An association in support of the friends and victims of clandestine migration counted 3,286 deaths at the border between 1997 and 2001. Following the sinking in 2003 of a boat carrying migrants, a Spanish journalist, Eduardo del Campo Cortés, described the graveyard in Barbate, Andalusia, where locals buried unnamed migrants who drowned at sea:

> Gravestone number 6 contains the corpse of a pregnant girl, probably from Nigeria. Number 4 has the corpse of a Moroccan boy. Most are from Sub-Saharan Africa. They drowned the previous day on the coast of Barbate, after their Zodiac boat sank. A nun thinks that the eldest was 24 years of age. There are no names or other information about these people. The corpses will be interred in the village cemetery. Mayor Manuel de Jesús says: 'Today we bury seven dreams.'[21]

There is something poignant in the contrast between the determination of migrants and sympathetic locals, on the one hand, and the attitude of the Spanish authorities, on the other. In response to further concerted attempts by migrants in 2015 to storm the fence, the Spanish government established a Sistema integrado de vigilancia exterior (SIVE, System of Border Surveillance) with the aim of deterring more 'invaders', especially migrants from Senegal and Mali. Money poured into efforts to track their movement: not just barbed wire, spotlights, and guard dogs, but high-technology thermal-image cameras and sensors. The government spared no expense on the latest weaponry of war against unauthorised migration.[22]

Melilla, another autonomous Spanish enclave, lies adjacent to the Moroccan port of Nador. Less than twelve square kilometres in area, it has a population of around 300,000; until 1995, it formed part of the mainland province of Málaga. Like Ceuta, Melilla served as a base in the colonial period for Spanish attempts to keep Berber raiders at bay. When Spain finally joined the EEC in 1986, the government devised special arrangements for Moroccans who worked in Melilla, including strict controls and barriers to ensure they could not gain access to the European

Union. Migrants who did make it across to the mainland faced other hazards. In February 2000, a group of local men in the Spanish province of Almería set upon farmworkers from North Africa in a rampage (*caza del moro*, literally 'hunting the Moor') that lasted four days, injuring hundreds of people and destroying homes. Even this did not deter others from attempting the journey. In 2005, when hundreds of migrants crossed into Melilla, Spain reinforced the border with Morocco by constructing a razor-wire fence and forcing migrants back into Morocco.[23]

Melilla was a deadly destination. Joseph (nicknamed 'Yopo Joe') was a Cameroonian man around thirty years old who had studied hotel hospitality. He died in 2005 after jumping the fence, reportedly after having been beaten up by Spanish guards. Of those Africans who died trying to cross through Melilla and Ceuta in that year, his was the only body to be identified. Cortés, the Spanish journalist, managed to contact Joseph's sister, who worked for Cameroon Airlines. She obtained a travel visa for Melilla and visited the rubbish dump where her brother had searched for scraps of food. After weeks of delay, a Spanish NGO offered to pay for the repatriation of Joseph's body and his funeral expenses.[24]

Others survived, but with contrasting fortunes. Albert Yaka, who had been trained as an economist in his native Cameroon, left as a young man to make enough money to buy himself a recording kit. He told Cortés of his years travelling through Africa, when he became involved in the counterfeit passport business. In 1994, he flew to Poland on a fake passport, with the aim of getting into Germany, but changed his plans and went to the Czech Republic instead. Homesickness drove him back to North Africa, first to Algeria and then to Morocco. From there he bribed a guard into letting him cross the border to Melilla. He spent nearly a year sleeping rough but eventually became the leader of a group of fellow African migrants, leading two hunger strikes to demand better conditions. In 1996, he finally secured a legal permit to migrate to Málaga before settling in Cádiz, where he continued to help other migrants. He set up a studio to record the songs he had composed during his long trip. Another man, Antoine, an art student in Kinshasa, left the Democratic Republic of Congo in June 2004 for political reasons. He described a more difficult odyssey. He took a plane from Brazzaville to Casablanca before crossing the border with Ceuta as part of a group. 'We didn't want to force the border fence like this, but we were exhausted', he said. 'We only wanted to find refuge in Spain.' Cortés asked if he thought the trip had been worth it: 'No, it was not worth [it]. Look, I have lost two toes.' He did not know anyone in Europe.[25]

Migrants who gave up, or who were deported from the Canary Islands, expressed a sense of shame: 'I've missed my big chance', said Okale, a Senegalese migrant. 'I'm ashamed to face my family. I can't even tell you how bad I feel. My father is an old man, my mother is a very brave woman.... They sold everything to help the family.' A sense of personal failure and humiliation also belongs in the ledger of migration.[26]

Migrants from sub-Saharan Africa who reached Morocco continued to seek access to the Spanish enclave of Ceuta, despite the obstacles put in their way. The mayor of Barbate, a destination for many migrants who made it to the mainland, put this into perspective: 'We've had more arrivals than ever this year [2018], about 2,500 so far. There's an increase on other years but the people of Barbate are, as ever, showing their solidarity with these people who've made long journeys, some of which have lasted years.' Some officials, at least, were unwilling to turn a problem into a crisis.[27]

Another side of the coin of illegality was that astute civic leaders actually offered inducements to migrants to come. This kind of locally managed migration was exemplified in Spain, where, in the late 1990s, Luis Bricio, the mayor of the small town of Aguaviva, between Madrid and Zaragoza, launched an initiative to stem the tide of depopulation by advertising opportunities for Argentinians and Uruguayans of Spanish descent to move to Spain. Faced with a decline in the birth rate, Bricio and others founded the Asociación española de municipios frente a la despoblación (Spanish Association of Municipalities Against Depopulation), which sponsored resettlement and integration. The local authority provided housing and jobs and supported relocation costs so long as applicants undertook to stay for at least five years. Bricio wanted to encourage people with 'the capacity to integrate and adapt to our customs'; 'the natural candidates', he said, 'should be the descendants of Spaniards'. By 2000, more than 5,000 families had applied. Bricio subsequently extended

the opportunity to Romania. By 2005, the number of school-aged children had doubled in Aguaviva. Despite the fanfare, however, the scheme
had mixed results, as only modest numbers of applicants had been
accepted. Many of the newcomers from South America disliked the jobs
assigned to them and felt that the housing did not live up to the promises
they had been given. Locals compared them unfavourably to the hard-
working Romanians, who did not complain. Somewhat ruefully, Bricio
concluded that 'what really matters is the work ethic'.[28]

An estimated 1 million undocumented migrants lived in Spain by the
end of 2003. Two-thirds of them were from outside the European Union,
mainly from the global South. Men predominated among the migrant
population from West Africa, but women made up a significant proportion of those from the Philippines, Peru, the Dominican Republic, and
the Cape Verde islands. According to the legal scholar Kitty Calavita, 'permanent resident status and eventually citizenship are available for those
who can piece together years of uninterrupted temporary legal residency,
but the difficulties of achieving this are legion'. Many workers who lacked
the necessary papers were reluctant to approach medical professionals
when they were ill for fear of being exposed to the authorities. Migrants
also had to bear the risks of unforeseen events, such as the hailstorms in
Catalonia in the summer of 2002, which ruined the fruit harvest and
inflicted hunger and homelessness on thousands of farmworkers.[29]

The aspirations and prospects of other migrants in southern Europe
emerged in interviews in the late twentieth century. Senegalese migrants
in the southern Italian port city of Bari, for example, entered as tourists
but stayed on to work as itinerant street pedlars (*ambulanti*). Most of these
young men hoped to make some money and return to Senegal. But to
think of them simply as 'economic migrants' is to miss the point. They
looked on their sojourn as a passage to manhood and an opportunity to
gain greater knowledge of the world beyond West Africa. One said: 'You
suffer a little bit, but when you return to your country, you know how to
live.' As they saw it, this experience provided an informal education. They
felt they even had an advantage over the Italians, whom they regarded as
materialistic; indeed, they felt that by hurling racist epithets at them, the
Italians only seemed ignorant. As one man, 'Philippe', put it, 'I like to

travel. A lot. For me it's normal. It is necessary to know. Until you leave you're in ignorance—it's dangerous. You'll meet someone in Bari who's 100 years old and has never been to Rome.' Mamadou, working in Rimini, echoed these sentiments: 'Italians think that, being black, I am a wild person who lives with animals…and then you discover that you have experienced much more than them and travelled more than them.' Colonial attitudes also persisted, as in the depiction of Eritreans, who were deemed by employers to be reliable, honest, and 'docile'—and, one might add, liable to be exploited. It was important for these men to accumulate sufficient funds in order to demonstrate to their parents that they had not wasted their time: saving money meant saving face. But they also accumulated valuable cultural capital.[30]

Border officers and asylum tribunals were interested only in having the barest outline of the circumstances that had driven people from their homes, on the basis of which they would decide on the merits of the individual case and determine whether to grant refugee status. Only gradually, and thanks to the efforts of support workers, aid organisations, and sympathetic journalists, would more finely textured details emerge.

When the author Caroline Moorehead met him a few years later, Tesfay, an Eritrean teacher and political activist who had escaped in 1995 to avoid becoming involved in the lengthy conflict between Eritrea and Ethiopia, described his flight and his attempts to make a new life. He had enlisted the help of a people-smuggler to flee to Sudan, hoping to reach the UK. This was only the start of a miserable existence. He said: 'At home I always felt safe. I was respected, popular, I had friends. Here I knew no one. I dreaded having to tell my story again and again, to lawyers, to the doctor, to the Home Office. The only place I could find to live was the past….Whenever I talk about it, my chest becomes too tight to speak.' Tesfay explained how the Eritrean community in London—and one woman in particular, who knew his village and had herself fled persecution—had helped him gain asylum and made his life bearable. Nevertheless, he added, 'days went by when I did not speak to anyone'. This is only one fragment from one refugee's testimony. There were many others in the same vein, pointing to the extent to which refugees bore emotional as well as physical scars.[31]

One story, told at length by the Iranian-born Shahram Khosravi, sheds powerful light on what it means to find a place of safety. Trained as an engineer, Khosravi became an anthropologist in Sweden, where he wrote what he described as an 'auto-ethnography', entitled *'Illegal' Traveller*. It incorporated elements of his own experience as well as the experiences of other migrants who had negotiated the borders beyond and within Europe. In his words, 'I collect stories of the "illegals": stateless people, failed asylum seekers, undocumented and unregistered people, those who are hidden and clandestine.' But his own story was perhaps the most remarkable of all.[32]

Khosravi, who is from a 'tribal' (Bakhtiari) background, described his family's marginalisation in Iranian society. In 1986, at the height of the Iran-Iraq War, he was summoned to serve in the army, a prospect that appalled him. After some soul-searching, he opted to hide on the family farm rather than enlisting. His first attempt to leave Iran ended in his arrest, but he was released after ten days. Eventually a trusted Afghani contact in Iran helped him to cross the border into Pakistan, where he came across thousands of Afghan refugees. Khosravi decided to pass himself off as an Afghani who had lived for several years in Iran. He failed in his attempt to gain refugee status: UNHCR officials deemed his fear of being killed in a 'horrible war' to be insufficient grounds to qualify as a refugee, and he gained little sympathy from exiled Iranian dissidents. He did not mention that his father had been persecuted, or that he himself had been flogged by the Iranian police for buying illicit alcohol. Other Iranians told him to wear poor clothes and to look 'sad and profound' when he recounted his ordeal. Be inconsistent, and one's testimony was rejected; remember too many details, and one was equally implausible. Despite the lack of official recognition, he managed to board a flight to Karachi, thanks to a sympathetic UNHCR official who signed the necessary papers. His family was able to supply him with enough money to get by, including paying numerous fees and bribes.[33]

Khosravi's subsequent journey took him to Delhi on a false passport (for which he paid several thousand dollars), but with a genuine visa. In Delhi, he found the UNHCR more receptive, and he was issued with a refugee card and a small allowance, but no offer of resettlement. After several months he caught a flight to London's Heathrow Airport. He reached Sweden in 1988 on a forged Greek passport that gave him the identity of a student returning from holiday in India. After a spell in detention and the threat of being deported to Turkey, he was sent to a refugee camp in Kiruna, Sweden's northernmost city.[34]

His vivid account was full of twists and turns. At times of what appeared to be insuperable obstacles, a bribe or two could get him out of a tight corner. Khosravi's odyssey enriched his vocabulary by giving him the words for 'smuggler', 'undocumented migrant', 'fake passport', and 'journey'. He insisted that those who might otherwise be demonised as people-smugglers could be indispensable. He also pointed out that presenting oneself at the border is largely about 'performance'—about giving a convincing impersonation of the person one is pretending to be, rather than the person one really is. He felt ashamed at being categorised as 'illegal'. But by telling his story, and the stories of others living in the shadows, Khosravi portrayed the human face of migration.[35]

In 1991, three years after his arrival in Sweden, Khosravi was shot in the face by an unknown assailant, later identified as Johan Ausonius, who deliberately targeted immigrants of non-European origin. By the time he was caught, Ausonius had killed one man and left many others paralysed. Khosravi tells how Ausonius was the son of a Swiss father and a German mother, both of them immigrants. As a child he had been bullied on account of his black hair and non-Swedish name. His murderous modus operandi earned him the nickname 'Lasermannen' (Laser Man); after he was captured and tried, he was sentenced to life imprisonment. From jail he wrote to Khosravi ten years after the attempted murder to say that the attack was not meant 'personally': it was an attack, he said, on Swedish immigration policy (although a Swedish policeman told Khosravi that he should feel responsible for being shot).

When interviewing Khosravi, a Swedish journalist changed his name into 'Ali' to make it sound more 'Muslim'. His story was featured in a TV series that appropriated it for the purpose of mass entertainment. When he was able to travel back and forth to Iran in the late 1990s (on the first occasion, he was arrested for having left Iran illegally), acquaintances asked why he had become an anthropologist rather than a doctor or engineer: 'What good is "knowing the people" to us?' asked one of his father's elderly associates, referring to the Persian word for 'anthropology', which literally means 'knowing the people' (*mardomshenas*). It was a loaded question. But Khosravi's profession contributed valuable expertise by showing just what it meant to live a precarious life.[36]

PART 5

Whither Europe, Whither Migrants?

2008 to the Present

CHAPTER 20

Europe, Nation-States, and Migrants Since 2008

A SHADOW DESCENDED OVER Europe in 2008 as a result of the global financial crash and the ensuing slump. Although, as in 1973, the recession did little to discourage migration as a whole, the recession imposed uncertainty on migrants just as it did on everyone else. The pursuit of austerity, together with broader misgivings about globalisation, reinforced a sense that governments were neglecting the interests of ordinary citizens and contributing to their deprivation. It became difficult to distinguish attitudes towards migrants, including undocumented migrants and asylum seekers, from a more general sense of unease with the political process. This environment helped feed the appetite of mainly right-wing politicians who were wedded to the idea of a self-evident national identity and core 'national values', which they deemed to be threatened by mass migration. Although the most extreme xenophobes did not become part of the political mainstream in most European countries, nevertheless the political atmosphere became more rancid. This was not all. Unlike the oil crisis of 1973, the prolonged economic downturn was soon followed by enormous political upheavals, notably in the Middle East, turning the worlds of millions of people upside-down and forcing them from their homes.[1]

Once again, migration was bound up closely with arguments about Europe, the European Union, and the border between the union and its neighbours. Collectively and individually, the leaders of EU member states viewed migration as a major challenge. They struggled to formulate a collective response to what quickly became known as the 'migrant crisis' or the 'refugee crisis'. The terms were often used interchangeably, contributing to a sense that, whatever its mainsprings, migration had spiralled out of control. Numbers formed one component of the crisis: net migration to EU countries reached 1.9 million in 2015, the highest level since records began in 1961. Misgivings about the scale of migration also arose from a perception that the official figures significantly understated the total size of the migrant population—for example, because an unknown number of visitors and students remained after their original permits had expired, and were now working in the shadow economy. British politicians, in particular, made a great deal of this issue, such as when referring to migrants from East-Central Europe.[2]

But a good deal more was at stake. Unscrupulous politicians persuaded people on low incomes or who were unemployed that 'uncontrolled' migration had damaged their job prospects and undermined their access to public services. Journalists looking for a cheap headline stoked fears of migrants, including 'bogus asylum seekers' who 'jumped the queue'. Questions around migration at large extended to issues of identity, citizenship, belonging, and values, topics that became more provocative as a result of enhanced concerns about security and terrorism. Migration probed the limits of Europe's willingness to admit newcomers, and migrants became an easy target in what the historian Leo Lucassen called a 'perfect storm'.[3]

The crisis became an amalgam of ordinary and extraordinary migration: that is to say, the movement of men and women from countries in Eastern Europe to Western Europe, together with continued migration from the global South, alongside the migration of refugees from war-torn Syria and conflict zones in Afghanistan, Iraq, and parts of sub-Saharan Africa. The great crash of 2008 made everything more difficult. Complaints about the financial crisis and the impacts of austerity were displaced onto migrants. In France, Germany, and elsewhere, Muslims and Jews became victims of

Uzbek cotton picker, Kazakhstan, 2009. © *Carolyn Drake / Magnum Photos.*

Uzbek construction workers travel to seek work in Russia, 2009.
© *Carolyn Drake / Magnum Photos.*

Occupation of a church by *sans-papiers*, Paris, France, 1996. *Gamma-Rapho / Getty Images.*

Members of Bulgaria's Turkish minority leave for Turkey, 1999.
© *John Vink / Magnum Photos.*

Kosovar civilians take refuge in Kukës, Albania, 1999.
© *John Vink / Magnum Photos.*

Kosovar refugees board a flight from Macedonia to Germany, 1999. *Georgi Licovski / DPA / PA Images.*

Kosovar refugees arrive in Yorkshire, England, 1999. *John Giles / PA Images.*

Bosnian Muslim refugee near Srebrenica, Bosnia-Herzegovina, 2002. *Damir Sagolj / Reuters.*

Turkish victims of an arson attack, Solingen, Germany, 1993.
K-H Kreifelts / AP / Shutterstock.

Demonstration in Bern, Switzerland, 2011. *Reuben Sprich / Reuters.*

Demonstration in Dover, England, 2016. © *Jerome Sessini / Magnum Photos.*

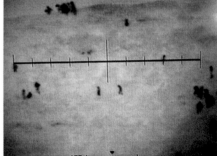

Thermal image of migrants, Chios, Greece, c. 2015. © *Enri Canaj / Magnum Photos.*

Memorial event for dead migrants, staged by the Bochum State Theatre Company, Germany, 2015. © *Thomas Dworzak / Magnum Photos.*

Tent of a Sudanese migrant in the 'Calais Jungle', France, 2016.
Carl Court / Getty Images.

Migrants hoping to reach Germany from Bihać, Bosnia, 2018.
Slavko Midzor / Pixsell / PA Images.

Top: *Porta di Lampedusa—Porta d'Europa,* by Mimmo Paladino, Lampedusa, Italy, 2008. *Guelfo.* Middle: Life jackets discarded by migrants from Turkey in Lesvos, Greece, 2016. © *Chien-Chi Chang / Magnum Photos.*
Bottom: Handprints left by migrants detained at Ventimiglia, Italy, 2015. *Valery Hache / AFP / Getty Images.*

everyday hate crimes by perpetrators who maintained that they did not belong. In Britain, Muslims who owned small businesses, such as take-aways, newsagents, and corner shops, and who worked as self-employed taxi drivers, were exposed to members of the public, many of whom had little or no knowledge of their history, religion, and culture, but were persuaded that their very presence constituted a danger.[4]

In the UK, conspicuous and well-placed commentators, such as Douglas Murray, together with lobby groups such as Migration Watch, proposed stricter controls on immigration in order to maintain 'British values' in the face of newcomers with allegedly irreconcilable cultures. These proposals coincided with promises by the Conservative government to reduce annual net migration to below 100,000, a number plucked out of the air and a promise on which it conspicuously failed to deliver. At times, the debate echoed Enoch Powell's notorious 'Rivers of Blood' speech in 1968, when he said, 'At this moment 20 or 30 additional immigrant children are arriving from overseas in Wolverhampton alone every week.' The implication was that they were transforming what he regarded as hitherto stable white communities for the worse. In a hard-hitting and widely read book, *The Road to Somewhere*, David Goodhart emphasised the social transformation wrought by migration in postwar Britain. He advocated controls on migration and measures to support concerted assimilation in order to maintain the existing social fabric rather than risk allowing it to be torn apart.[5]

These arguments reinforced a distinction between 'us' and 'them'. If migrants represented 'them', their presence could easily be portrayed as being at odds with 'us', meaning, in the words of the sociologist Bridget Anderson, 'a community of value, composed of people who share common ideals and (exemplary) patterns of behaviour expressed through ethnicity, religion, culture, or language'. The effect of such attitudes for migrants was not difficult to grasp, since they imposed on them a responsibility to adapt or risk remaining forever a group apart. For someone like Murray, this was self-explanatory, whereas Anderson, for example, found the distinction deeply divisive.[6]

Elsewhere, too, journalists and politicians who regarded themselves as politically and socially progressive (as did Goodhart) expressed similar sentiments. In 2010, the German Social Democratic Party politician Thilo Sarrazin published a book with the incendiary title *Deutschland schafft sich ab* (Germany abolishes itself), which berated Turks in Germany for their 'failure' to integrate whilst drawing state benefits. Sarrazin maintained that three-quarters of them 'deny the legitimacy of the very state that provides that welfare'. The Turk, he said, 'refuses to care for the education of his children and constantly produces new little headscarf-girls'. Sarrazin advocated tighter restrictions on immigration. By 2018, his book had already gone through thirteen editions, and although it did not appear to have hardened public attitudes towards all migration, it did nothing to alleviate the fear of German Turks. It seemed that they could do nothing right.[7]

France's leaders likewise framed migration as a question of national integrity. One of President Nicolas Sarkozy's first actions was to establish a Ministry of Immigration, Integration, National Identity and Mutual Development, thus linking national identity to the 'problem' of immigration. In 2009, the first occupant of this office, the Moroccan-born Eric Besson, initiated a debate on national identity ('What does it mean to be French?') in the light of what he argued was the disturbing spread of *communautarisme*, a perceived lack of integration as migrant communities adhered to separate cultural practices and identities.[8]

An added factor souring European politics derived from the threat of terrorism by Muslim extremists, although, in fractious times, it was sometimes forgotten that terrorist attacks were also perpetrated by white nationalists. The problem here was that no amount of restriction on the admission of migrants could prevent attacks from being carried out by people who had been born and who had grown up on domestic soil. This was not a new anxiety: in the wake of the terrorist attacks in London in 2005, then prime minister Tony Blair had spoken of 'home-grown' terrorism that had to be countered by vigilance and programmes of de-radicalisation directed at Islamic fundamentalism. Other politicians followed suit in the wake of the terrorist attack in Paris in November 2015 perpetrated by gunmen from the Brussels suburb of Molenbeek. Molenbeek, home to an established community of Moroccan and Turkish migrants, became a byword for radical Islam. The attack took place in several locations and resulted in the deaths of 130 people as well as injuries to hundreds of others. It came hard on the heels of January 2015, when terrorists stormed the Paris offices of the French satirical magazine *Charlie Hebdo*, killing twelve people, many of them cartoonists, and injuring eleven others. Responding to this atrocity, the Dutch politician Geert Wilders argued that Europe was 'at war': 'We have to close our borders, reinstate border controls, get rid of political correctness, introduce administrative detention and stop immigration from Islamic countries.' This language encouraged more mainstream politicians to follow suit: in the 2017 election campaign, the Dutch prime minister, Mark Rutte, instructed migrants to 'be normal or be gone'.[9]

The febrile atmosphere extended to Central Europe, where political leaders in new EU member states also struck a nationalist pose. Poland, for example, resolutely refused to make jobs available to asylum seekers such as Chechens, whose 'culture and psyche make it impossible for them to adapt to life in European society', a sign of the country's growing resistance to the admission of those of Muslim faith.[10]

Elsewhere, ironically, the distinction between 'us' and 'them'—one can think of this instead as the crystallisation of a hard-nosed ethno-national politics—had odd results. As we have seen in other instances, a shared ethnicity might offer no protection against being regarded as 'foreign'. Hungarian politicians regarded ethnic Hungarians living in Transylvania as Hungarian, but preferred that they stay in Romania. Not everyone did: there was an extensive migration of Transylvanians to Hungary in search of work. Their status as undocumented migrants placed them in a precarious position, and they reported suspicion and hostility towards them on the part of resident Hungarians. 'It was like you were Afghan, or something', reported one migrant worker. Another worker, who helped himself to cherries from a tree, was accused of being 'a filthy Romanian Wallachian thief'. Being ethnically Hungarian did not translate into a sense of affinity in any practical sense. If anything, despite many years of propaganda about the unity of Magyardom, putting all Hungarians in the same ethnic category, growing numbers of Hungarians now sustained the belief that Transylvanian Hungarian workers were in practice culturally distinct.[11]

Yet there was also clear evidence to suggest that public attitudes towards immigration in some areas were softening rather than hardening, particularly in Sweden, Ireland, and the UK, where a majority now regarded immigration as more of an opportunity than a problem, something that might be born of a realisation that Europe faced a reduction in its number of citizens of working age, and thus that a demographic 'crisis' loomed in Europe to which migration seemed to provide an answer. Perhaps this explains why, 'perfect storm' notwithstanding, public hostility towards migrants did not grow out of all proportion. Reports suggested that Europeans in general were becoming more rather than less favourably disposed towards migrants: the European Social Survey found that in nine out of fifteen countries, the views of citizens softened between 2014 and 2016, and only in Austria and Poland did public opinion become more negative: moreover, of the fourteen countries whose citizens had been surveyed since 2002, ten had become more favourable. Europe, unsurprisingly, did not speak with a single voice.[12]

Nevertheless, protracted austerity made life more difficult for most people. Countries such as Greece were badly hit by the recession, which coincided with an upsurge in undocumented migration by people who were prepared to take their chances or had nowhere else to go. Some people decided to leave: for example, recession drove men and women from Spain and Portugal in search of work in Morocco, Brazil, and Angola, countries where they could at least capitalise on historical colonial ties and where they spoke a common language. But their place was taken in turn by other migrant workers, such as in the Spanish region of Aragón, where 10 percent of the population was foreign-born in 2008, compared to just 1 percent in 2000. Romania contributed one-third of all immigrants in Spain, where many of them worked as low-paid fruit and vegetable pickers. In Andalusia, too, the industrialisation of farming led employers to recruit undocumented workers from Morocco and Romania. So, not everything was about austerity: technological changes also played a part in changing the pattern of migration.[13]

Thus the economic crisis did not stem the inflow of migrants to and within Europe. As in the past, employers looked to migrants to perform backbreaking work and to take on 'dirty jobs'. The new *helots*, as the German journalist Günter Wallraff described them in an interview in 2005, referring to the term for a slave class of ancient Greece, were now from Eastern Europe. Turkish guest workers had given way to Romanians, Poles, Russians, and the long-term unemployed from the former East Germany, whose economic situation compared unfavourably with Turkish workers, who had been paid around six deutschmarks (around four dollars) per hour. Wallraff found that the new migrants were getting around two euros (or two and a half dollars) per hour. Amidst widespread austerity, migrants were generally at the bottom of the ladder.[14]

In the UK, Polish and Romanian migrants continued to find work as seasonal agricultural labourers or as workers in care homes, where demand increased as a result of the ageing population. From the migrant's point of view, however, this was physically and emotionally demanding work, and a step down from the work for which they were qualified. A Polish woman in Britain explained the emotional costs of working as a hospital cleaner: 'I'd come all this way—such a big decision leaving my job and my family to get a better life.... [I]t was just awful.' Supporting a point made throughout this book—namely, that contingency and personal connections played as large a part in the movement of populations as managed or organised migration—she added, 'Then the sister of my friend[,] she got me an interview for this job, teaching English, and then I was OK.' Others spoke of doing the job even if it 'gets you down', because 'this time next year I'll not be here [but] doing something different'.[15]

Migrants coped with the social and economic upheavals in their countries of origin and in their host countries as best they could. The sociologist Anne White found that two in five of the Polish people she interviewed in the UK left Poland in the new millennium because they felt their living standards had fallen in the interval between the collapse of communism and its imminent accession to the European Union. Fewer than one in five noticed a perceptible improvement in Poland, where unemployment stood at 20 percent in 2003. After working in the UK for several years, their personal prospects had improved. They had been able to save for the future and send money back home. It was relatively easy to keep in touch with family and friends at home, so the emotional roller coaster was less turbulent than they had anticipated. Furthermore, they felt they had made a contribution to British society. Migration had benefited everyone.[16]

Some Polish migrants expected to return to their countries of origin, but others kept their options open. A twenty-six-year-old student named Malina spoke of returning to Poland one day: 'I would like to return some day. But I would also like to return when things are a little better in Poland. And I don't know if there's any sense in waiting for that because it might appear that we'll wait till we die! I don't know.' Even in an uncertain world there were more advantages to staying put than returning to Poland for good. Abroad, these migrants lived a more or less normal life. Another informant commented: 'It is obvious that the UK and Ireland are not gold mines anymore as they used to be and it is difficult to get a good job[,] but it is a fact that life is easier and less stressful over there than in our country.' Post-communist migrants, like many of those who had migrated during the communist years, hedged their bets. Something of these considerations made their way into a novel by Rose Tremain, *The Road Home* (2007), which paints a vivid picture of her protagonist's decisions. This character, Lev, finally goes back to Poland to set up as a chef; there, he puts into practice the lessons he learned in a fancy London restaurant.[17]

We also have to allow for the willingness of migrants from farther afield to regard migration as a chance to see the world, and to see the world differently. Interviewed by the anthropologist Karen Fog Olwig in 2011, a young man from the Caribbean who settled in Denmark expressed his migration as a kind of cosmopolitanism: 'I was tired of [the Caribbean], and I decided to travel the world', he said. Although he was interested in Denmark on the recommendation of Caribbean friends, he travelled first to Cuba and then to Russia. Once in Denmark, he applied for residency. From there he seems to have talked his way into receiving the permit:

And they [said], 'you know, the law is like that and so on', and I said, 'But, you know, the world is globalizing'. I just say them things like that and, 'of course, there's not much Caribbean or Rasta here, and we have to . . . want to open, to make the globalizing process a good one'. And the guy said, 'What you say makes sense'. And I said, 'If you will give me residency, I will get a job'. It's not like I lied. I'm a guy who likes to work. And they give me one year, like a work permit for one year.[18]

He married a Danish woman and on that basis was given permission to stay. It would be wrong to dismiss his comments as flippant. They read more like a statement of triumph, an indication that he would let nothing stop him in his tracks.

At the same time, the insatiable demand for labour contributed to a widespread belief that European economies relied upon reserves of undocumented or 'illegal' migration. Illegal migration was portrayed in the mass media as exploitative in a dual sense: people-traffickers and unscrupulous employers exploited migrants, but migrants also exploited loopholes in the system in order to gain a toehold in Europe. Illegality exposed migrants to multiple kinds of exploitation, and it had to be deterred by imposing fines on traffickers and detaining those found to be without documents.

Missing from these broad condemnations of illegal migration were the stories of migrants themselves. Many undocumented migrants who managed to reach the Spanish enclaves of Ceuta and Melilla in 2005 were held before being released and sent on to Spain, where they found insecure jobs. By 2010, however, the Spanish economy had less need of them, and new migrants were detained in these enclaves for months on end. They depended on welfare payments and spent the time in conditions of utter boredom. One detainee, Emmanuel, tried to put a brave face on it, saying, 'We're adventurers, we're used to struggling for survival [but] here it's like staying with mummy and daddy.' It did not take long for protests to erupt, led by Cameroonian migrants, who were quickly deported. Other inmates insisted that they had a better time of it than those who ended up in Madrid, where work was hard to come by. Aid workers pointed to the irony of this illegal migration: it was better to be incarcerated than to be free.[19]

No less disconcerting was the question of people who were suddenly 'found' to be living illegally. In the UK, for example, the rhetoric around 'illegal immigration' created personal anguish and could lead to the abrogation of rights, as happened to migrants who had arrived from the

Caribbean in the 1950s and 1960s, but decades later were expected to be able to provide abundant documentation to prove they had citizenship. In May 2018, the UK Home Office admitted to having shredded the landing cards of migrants who had arrived in Britain from the Caribbean, making it virtually impossible for them to demonstrate continuous residence. Dozens of people who had worked in the UK virtually their whole lives were deported. They were victims of successive British government attempts to target undocumented migrants, as well as of bureaucratic indifference. A journalist for *The Guardian*, Nesrine Malik, wrote of a visit to the passport office in Croydon, outside London, where 'the waiting room was a holding pen of quiet individual tragedies, full of people whose personal and professional lives had been thrown into turmoil by loss of documents, technical glitches and glacial incompetence'.[20]

Setting aside this scandal, European political leaders collectively agreed that they had a responsibility to control the borders of the European Union and to curb 'illegal' immigration. Combatting illegality enabled governments to demonstrate a commitment to border control whilst claiming the moral high ground by arguing that illegal migrants were victims of people-smugglers who treated them like slaves. However, this claim failed to acknowledge that most undocumented migration was not the result of people-smuggling; indeed, most 'illegal' migrants had arrived legally but outstayed their visas. The attempt to address illegal immigration did not bring stability to the lives of migrants; on the contrary, they lived in fear that something would happen once more to turn everything upside-down.

In the second decade of the new millennium, EU member states enlisted more IT specialists and others in programmes to control their borders. This development speaks to the securitisation of migration. Frontex continued to play an important role in what its website described as the compilation and analysis of the 'European situational picture', meaning that it assessed recent events at the borders of certain EU countries to detect changing routes or new methods being used by 'criminal networks'. It coordinated its operations with the European Police Office (Europol, formed in 1998 to combat organised crime and terrorism), with the European Asylum Support Office (created in 2010 to 'facilitate improved protection for asylum seekers and coordination between member states'), with various governmental authorities outside the European Union, and with the UNHCR and the International Organisation for Migration. Border guards from EU member states provided expertise in different areas of border management, including border checks, land and sea border surveillance, identification of false documents, and identification of irregular migrants' nationalities. One of the aims was to identify non-EU migrants whose visas had expired, the 'overstayers'.[21]

In 2013, the European Parliament approved the creation of a European Border Surveillance System (Eurosur). Eurosur was a high-tech system ostensibly designed to monitor seaborne traffic so that search-and-rescue operations could be carried out more effectively. In essence, this was an arrangement to deter 'smugglers' by intercepting vessels before they reached European shores. This information-exchange framework was designed to improve the management of the European Union's external borders. It supported EU countries by increasing their awareness and reaction capability in combating cross-border crime, tackling irregular migration, and preventing the loss of migrants' lives at sea. To complete the picture, identification procedures at the European level were entrusted to the European Data Archive Convention, Eurodac, which now began to fingerprint children as young as six. All of this surveillance, buttressed by new biometric technologies, such as facial recognition, amounted to an impressive remit and an enlargement of the scope and scale of border control. And no one blinked at the financial cost.[22]

Institutional and technological innovation was all very well, but it did nothing to resolve the question of responsibility for the refugees who were detected. Individual states were easily induced by a sense of mounting panic into adopting measures that were ad hoc in nature and contrary to EU principles and agreements. Restrictions and temporary border controls challenged the fundamental principles of Schengen, given that its purpose was to support unrestricted movement across borders. A particular manifestation of the problems between EU neighbours was the decision by the French government to close its frontier with Italy at Ventimiglia in April 2011, in order to stem the migration of Tunisian migrants who had crossed the Mediterranean in the wake of political chaos in their country. France argued that its decision was entirely in line with the Dublin Regulations, which required migrants to apply for asylum in the country where they first entered the European Union, and with Schengen, which made provision for a signatory state to close its border if it identified an imminent threat to public order. But it hardly spoke of the spirit of EU solidarity and put it at odds with a neighbouring member state.[23]

In practice, therefore, 'migration management' increasingly emphasised the need for deterrence, especially policies to prevent non-European asylum seekers from finding refuge in Europe. This meant a fondness for measures such as 'search and rescue', repatriation, and refoulement, as well as aid packages to countries in the global South where most of the world's refugees were housed. Hence, too, the rigorous denial of asylum claims: in 2013, EU member states recognised fewer than 15 percent of asylum claims from the Middle East, Afghanistan, and the Horn of Africa.[24]

The route for mainly, but not exclusively, African migrants took them across the Mediterranean to Spain, Malta, and Italy. Malta insisted that it would not be a 'pushover' (in the words of Prime Minister Joseph Muscat) and was perfectly happy that people rescued in its waters should be sent to the nearest available port, which happened to be the Italian island of Lampedusa.

Lampedusa became a symbol both for the ordeal of refugees and for the frantic efforts of the Italian government and local authorities to cope. In 2007, a small, isolated reception centre served as the point from which migrants were relocated to the Italian mainland or else repatriated or deported to countries such as Tunisia and Libya where they had first embarked. The arrival in 2008 of Tunisian migrants, whose domestic prospects were damaged by the local economic turmoil, led to massive overcrowding in the reception centre. Everything was then suddenly turned upside-down by the political upheaval in Tunisia in 2011. Thousands of Tunisians lodged asylum applications. Italy's minister of the interior, Roberto Maroni, was accused of holding them virtually hostage on Lampedusa, in order (as one EU diplomat put it) 'to send a message to its neighbouring countries and to the whole of Europe that it was not able to cope, and that Europe should act and share the burden'.[25]

The refugees faced overwhelming odds. The local people offered what support they could, but they, too, complained that they had been abandoned, both by the regional government in Sicily and by the central government in Rome. The arrival of large numbers of migrants became a touchstone for long-standing resentment. In March 2011, partly in response to a stage-managed visit by the Italian prime minister, Silvio Berlusconi, hundreds of male migrants were evacuated to hastily erected tent cities on an abandoned air force base in a remote part of Apulia, close to Manduria. They held signs that read, 'We did not come here to eat, but for liberty and dignity.' But their rights were the last thing on Berlusconi's mind.[26]

Humanitarian concern—the offer of temporary shelter and something to eat—emerged in the narrative of rescue. One notable example was the Oscar-nominated documentary *Fire at Sea* (directed by Gianfranco Rosi, 2016), which interwove shots of rescue efforts off the coast of Lampedusa with the daily routines of the island's residents. But it provided them, rather than the migrants, with an opportunity to speak about their lives, leaving the audience with the overwhelming impression of a faceless mass of desperate migrants from unidentified countries in sub-Saharan Africa. Other documentaries, less familiar to international audiences, included *Brûle La Mer* (Burn the sea, directed by Nathalie Nambot and Maki Berchache, 2014), which covered Berchache's efforts to flee Tunisia in order to reach the European mainland, and *On the Bride's Side* (directed by Gabriele Del Grande, 2014). Unlike Rosi's film, *On the Bride's Side* attempted to put migrants at the heart of the story. In explaining how he came to make the film, Del Grande said he and a friend decided to assist five undocumented Syrian migrants to travel from Italy to Sweden. The migrants had made the difficult crossing to Lampedusa, but were being held by Italian police. Del Grande and his friend decided to fake a wedding party ('You know who the border guards would never stop? The police would never check a bride's documents!'). To top it off, they would film the entire escapade as a documentary. It was a huge risk; the penalty, if they were found out, could involve jail time. One admiring critic said that the film 'reveals an unknown side of Europe—a transnational, supportive and irreverent Europe that ridicules the laws and restrictions of the so-called "Fortress Europe" in a kind of farcical masquerade'. Unfortunately, the fortress remained intact, and its defenders treated its security with utmost seriousness.[27]

Lampedusa continued to grab headlines in the second decade of the new millennium. When Colonel Muammar al-Gaddafi's grasp on power weakened in Libya—and particularly after his death in October 2011— the exodus from Libya gathered pace. When Italian newspapers and politicians whipped up public concern, other EU governments pointed to Italy's obligations under the Dublin Regulations, asking why a country of 60 million people could not absorb a few thousand Libyans. At the same time, migrants in Libya—Eritreans, Ethiopians, Somali, and Sudanese— faced the wrath of local rebels, who attacked and robbed them. Many of them were stranded, unable to return home and unable to cross the Mediterranean to Italy. Those who did manage to board boats soon entered a Kafkaesque realm in which Italy and Malta vied with one another to disclaim responsibility for offering asylum. Keen as ever to grab the headlines, in July 2011, Silvio Berlusconi, whose term by then had ended, likened migration to a 'human tsunami'. The question for the European Union, and Italy in particular, now became how to stop refugees from getting to Lampedusa in the first place.[28]

Italy took the lead in combining humanitarianism with deterrence. In 2013, the Italian government launched Operation Mare Nostrum, a 'military and humanitarian' programme that used Italian warships to search for migrants and come to their rescue before their fragile and overcrowded boats capsized. Mare nostrum in Latin means 'our sea', but the name of the operation was also a reference to Mussolini's grand vision of Italian supremacy in the Mediterranean. In any case, the teams rescued around 150,000 people in the year that followed, but thousands of others died. Several boats carrying refugees from Eritrea, Somalia, Afghanistan, and Palestine were shipwrecked in October 2013 alone, the same month the operation began. The authorities promised a state funeral; simultaneously, the survivors were arrested and threatened with fines as 'illegal immigrants'. The irony of granting the dead retrospective citizenship whilst detaining the living was not lost on those who wanted the government to safeguard the rights of refugees.[29]

Critics argued that Mare Nostrum served as 'a state-owned ferry line for migrants, a pull factor', and suggested that people-smugglers crammed too many people onto boats to maximise their profits, knowing that they had a fair chance of being rescued. A more perceptive observation came from an officer in the Italian armed forces, who was well aware of the consequences for refugees: 'We want to save them in Libya by bombing Tripoli, but once hundreds manage to leave they are abandoned. We want to save them in Libya and we let them die in the sea?'[30]

In late 2014, EU member states signed an agreement to implement Operation Triton, a multilateral effort devised by Frontex to deter migration from North Africa through 'humanitarian' action, including the use of warships. Previously, individual governments had been busy pursuing options of their own, such as Mare Nostrum; now the European Union appeared to be taking back control, or, in the language favoured by the European Commission, 'stepping up operations'. The European Union, for its part, insisted that Triton was intended 'to support the Italian efforts, and does not replace or substitute Italian obligations in monitoring and surveying the Schengen external borders and in guaranteeing full respect of EU and international obligations, in particular when it comes to search and rescue at sea'. There was nothing here about protecting vulnerable refugees once they had been rescued.[31]

The package of measures to manage the crisis included a decision to process the claims of asylum seekers on territories beyond the borders of the European Union. This approach was called 'externalisation'. Frontex played a key role in negotiating agreements with non-EU countries, such as Albania, Tunisia, Egypt, and Libya, which were offered EU funds to establish detention centres. These centres kept refugees and migrants out of the spotlight and exposed them to degradation and abuse, particularly in Libya.[32]

Nor did the collapse of Libya make it possible for Libya to act as an effective gatekeeper. The Italian government was accused of bribing tribal leaders in the south of Libya to convince them to abandon people-trafficking. But the claim stoked political discontent among the Italian electorate rather than encouraging a more appropriate response to migrants and asylum seekers in Libya, fewer than 5 percent of whom ended up in Italy or Malta.[33]

What about refugees who followed other routes? In 2011 and 2012, many refugees from the Middle East, including Afghans, Iraqis, Kurds, Pakistanis, Syrians, and others, went to Greece via the Evros River. Greece promptly introduced deterrent measures—extra fencing, more border guards, more Frontex personnel, and the use of force to push the refugees back into Turkey (contrary to international refugee law). Greece also resorted to detention in innocuous-sounding 'reception and identification centres', but the conditions were particularly dangerous for women. Refugees nevertheless continued to use this route.[34]

Some refugees made it to northern Europe, where the 'Calais Jungle' became a tangible expression of the determination among refugees trying to enter the UK. Many of them were trying to join family and friends who were already living there. Although there were other camps in northern France, such as at Loon-Plage and Téteghem near Dunkirk, the Calais Jungle achieved notoriety, both for the activists who supported refugees there and for those who opposed their presence.

The Jungle came into being in 2006, following the closure of the camp at Sangatte. Although an informal space, it boasted an elaborate infrastructure: refugees, many of them highly qualified people, created mosques and shops. They siphoned off water and electricity in order to survive. Different ethnic groups demarcated separate spaces, such as the 'Pashtun Jungle' and the 'Kurdish Jungle'. Calais offered an alternative to the accommodation provided by the British and French, which was heavily policed and afforded less privacy. At its peak, the new camp reportedly had 10,000 people living in it; they were supported by myriad volunteers attached to Médecins sans Frontières (MSF, Doctors Without Borders), France Terre d'Asile (France land of asylum), and other aid organisations.[35]

The French authorities razed the Jungle, however, in 2009, blaming gangs of traffickers for roaming the camp freely and engaging in smuggling operations. The French immigration minister, Eric Besson, said that, 'on the territory of this nation, the law of the jungle cannot endure'. But the main aim was to disperse refugees and make it more difficult for them to act in concert. Confronted by all these measures to manage migration and deter asylum seekers, the steps taken by individual refugees seem all the more remarkable.[36]

The complicated journeys undertaken by refugees who were looking for a place of safety in Europe emerged in a powerful account by one refugee who wrote under the pseudonym Ali Hassan. Hassan described his escape as a young boy in 1983 from violence in the capital of Somalia, Mogadishu, and his mother's decision to take him and his siblings to the northern coastal town of Bosaso. To escape the ongoing civil war, the family left on an overcrowded boat for Yemen, where they were held in a refugee camp in Aden. Hassan spent the following decade in Aden, but he studied English and eventually got a job with Médecins sans Frontières as a translator and subsequently as a social worker. In January 2011, following the uprising in Yemen, he took a flight to Damascus, and from there he made his way to the Turkish border with help of Kurdish smugglers. In Antalya, hoping to reach Ankara, he was detained in a military camp in Adana, before being released and finding a factory job ('Work like a dog, or die from hunger', he said).

In September 2011, Hassan decided to try his luck in Istanbul and then to take a minibus to Greece. He reached Athens and caught the train to Thessaloniki, but he was arrested at the Macedonian border and sent back to Thessaloniki. He succeeded on his third attempt, taking a bus to Skopje and then to Lojane, near Macedonia's border with Serbia. After managing to enter Serbia, he was arrested; this time he was tortured and then told to return to Lojane. Nevertheless, he subsequently made it to Losanisa and then went on to Subotica on the Serbian-Hungarian border, where he was arrested yet again and held in another camp before being deported back to Macedonia. Hassan spent six months in a Sutka detention centre in Skopje. In May 2012, he succeeded in reaching Belgrade, and from there he was able to cross the Drina River into Bosnia-Herzegovina. He then went to Croatia, where he was again held, this time in a camp in Kutina. On the next leg of his journey he crossed into Slovenia before making his way to Italy, only to be deported to Croatia. From there he was smuggled to Trieste. He took the train to Milan and bought an airline ticket to Copenhagen on a fake passport. From Denmark he walked across the Øresund Bridge to Sweden. Eventually, in November 2012, Hassan obtained refugee status in Sweden. He began to learn Swedish and moved to the north of the country to work as a counsellor.[37]

Ali Hassan's odyssey illustrates the many hazards refugees encounter on their unique journeys. In his case, and in many others, relatives helped out with money, an indication of the ties binding migrants to family and to home.

Hassan's ordeal stood in sharp contrast to the insouciant manner in which EU member states handed out residence permits to wealthy non-EU citizens who were prepared to stump up hundreds of thousands of dollars. Malta and Bulgaria, Greece and Spain, all got in on the act. In a further indication of EU inventiveness, in 2011, most EU member states (with the exception of the UK, Ireland, and Denmark) signed up to a new 'Blue Card' scheme, offering fast-track admission to professional people earning a salary at least 50 percent higher than the average.[38]

Where non-EU migration was concerned, whether one was a person with high earnings potential or a refugee paying a people-smuggler, it was clear that money talked.

CHAPTER 21

Another Europe: Borders, Routes, Migrant Lives

Beyond the European Union, migrants continued to negotiate new frontiers and to face fresh challenges. The Soviet Union had been dismantled in 1991, giving way to sovereign states. Whereas previously there were no obstacles to movement within the USSR, newly independent successor states now exercised control on whom to admit. One immediate consequence of the imposition of border controls was to interrupt, or at least to hamper, the regular movement of people crossing the borders in search of temporary work or to trade in goods. In most corridors of power in Europe, this was of little account, but it mattered a great deal on the borders between Russia and Ukraine, as well as in the Caucasus and in Central Asia. Maintaining the integrity of the country's borders, without jeopardising the prospects of migrants who wanted to make a living, remained a challenge for governments in the new millennium. The situation in Russia was complicated by the ethnic Russians living beyond the borders of the Russian Federation. In the twenty-first century, this legacy manifested itself in the insistence by Russian nationalists of the need to protect Slavic 'culture'. Here, as in Western Europe, migration raised troubling issues of identity.[1]

An added difficulty was that the borders of former communist states rubbed up against member states of the European Union. The European

Union expanded in May 2004, with the accession of Estonia, Hungary, Latvia, Lithuania, Poland, Slovakia, and Slovenia. In becoming member states of the European Union, and thus members of a bloc committed to internal freedom of movement of goods, services, and people, these countries now had hard borders with Russia, Ukraine, Belarus, Romania, Croatia, and Serbia. Romania joined the European Union in 2007, but neighbouring Moldova remained outside. Croatia joined in 2013. There were complications for migrants who customarily crossed borders, such as the one between Ukraine and Poland. The story here was about the barriers to ordinary migration and how migrants might be able to circumvent them.

The post-communist reconfiguration of the USSR and Eastern Europe thus required countries to consider where they belonged in Europe. Migration posed a challenge for new EU member states and for non-EU outliers alike. The challenge was particularly acute given the legacy of violent conflicts in the former Yugoslavia and in parts of the former Soviet Union, as well as the outbreak of war between Russia and Ukraine in 2014. These conflicts wrought havoc on the lives of civilians, whether they contemplated returning to their homes or were newly uprooted, and whether they had crossed an international border or were internally displaced.

Not everything was about territorial dissolution and reconfiguration. Turkey was notable by virtue of retaining its territorial integrity, but this came under closer scrutiny for several reasons. One concerned the ongoing conflict between the Turkish state and the Kurdish minority, and the political activities of Kurdish activists in Western Europe. Another dimension to the 'Turkish question' was the presence of a numerically significant Turkish diaspora, whose relationship with the Turkish nation-state continued to exercise Turkey's political leaders. These problems were dwarfed by the presence of several million refugees on Turkish soil, mainly Syrians seeking protection after being displaced by the country's civil war.

Hence, there were other borders as well as other migrations. Issues were raised about state sovereignty and about the contours of migration at a time of political uncertainty. Virtually everywhere, emotionally charged debates raged about the nation-state and its borders, and about citizens and noncitizens. Nationalist politicians complained about the low birth rate among citizens and the high birth rates among migrant groups.

Migrants in this other Europe navigated customary channels of migration, but fresh obstacles were put in their way. For refugees, the question was one of finding a place of safety. Powerful states, such as Russia and Turkey, exerted influence in their own right on the prospects and circumstances of migrants. Refugees from many different countries of origin — including Afghanistan, Iraq, Somalia, Sudan, and Syria — used Russia, Belarus, and Moldova as points of transit, hoping to reach the European Union, but they were frequently trapped for months or years at a time.[2]

Ukraine, for example, which signed the UN Refugee Convention in 1996, imposed tough and unrealistic obligations on people claiming asylum. Many of them originated from sub-Saharan Africa, Iran, and Afghanistan. People-traffickers dumped them in Ukraine, having duped them into believing they were in Germany. A Sudanese asylum seeker had this to say about his experiences in Kyiv, where he had been detained by the police on nine separate occasions and attacked by racist gangs: 'I can't live here. It's too dangerous for me to live here. If I go to the store, I could be murdered for being a "n—r". This country is not for Africans.' Like others, he hoped to leave at the earliest possible opportunity to avoid prejudice and further persecution. NGOs in Ukraine did their best to support refugees, such as those from Somalia who in 2009 sought protection in Vinnytsia; for these migrants, getting to Ukraine had involved securing fake documents or student visas and then paying for airline tickets to travel to the United Arab Emirates. Once in Ukraine, they were exploited and abused: 'We don't come to Somalia, so don't come to Ukraine', was a common response from Ukrainian locals. By 2017, most of them had found a way to get from Ukraine to Western Europe, leaving charities and aid workers to deal with refugees from the war between Ukraine and Russia.[3]

Arguments about migration and security became part of the political discourse outside the European Union as well as inside. Following the coordinated terrorist attacks in Brussels on 22 March 2016, in which thirty-two civilians died, with hundreds more injured, Russian officials did not hesitate to link migration and terrorism. According to one government source, 'Europeans have failed to realise what millions of migrants mean. Now they have paid the price for being reckless.' There were other borders and other routes, as well as stories that did not necessarily correspond to those in the European Union but which might be turned into political capital by those who advocated tougher restrictions on migration.[4]

It makes sense to begin with the borders between EU member states and their neighbours. The events of 1989 gave rise to a new division, with Europe's 'Wild East' on one side and the European Union on the other. Migrants now had a fresh set of obstacles to negotiate. In the words of the anthropologist Karolina Follis, 'Not unlike the Iron Curtain that divided the continent sixty years earlier, the new border seals, legitimates and solidifies the vague and shifting frontier between Europe's West and East.' Ukrainians suggested that the Iron Curtain had been replaced by a 'velvet drape' (*firanka*) between East and West, a barrier in effect shielding the European Union from without. New pressure points emerged.[5]

More than a decade after the collapse of communism in the Soviet Union and Eastern Europe, the author Yuri Andrukhovych, writing from a vantage point in the West Ukrainian town of Ivano-Frankivsk, bemoaned the restrictions on his freedom of travel between Ukraine and Poland when the latter became a member state of the European Union in 2004. 'It's like this with the border', he said: 'When I'm being told that I cannot just go whenever I want to Vienna, Warsaw or Berlin, it feels the same way as if someone locked me out of the rooms in my own house.' The border was a physical fixture but could also be traced on one's mental map, changing an individual's subjective perception of the world.

Political upheaval altered the landscape of migration. New hierarchies emerged, with some migrants being deemed legal and others illegal. For example, changes to EU membership directly affected Ukrainian migrant workers who had worked in the construction sector and in a range of service industries since the fall of communism in Eastern Europe. Ukrainian workers found jobs in neighbouring Poland as well as farther afield: around half a million of them found jobs in Italy, and an additional 400,000 were evenly distributed between Portugal and Greece. However, with the accession of Poland to the European Union, the border between Ukraine and its neighbour was transformed. There was now an external EU border separating the two states, imposing a new requirement on travellers to have a visa.

This made life very much more complicated for migrants such as Anna, who originally trained as a hair stylist in Ukraine, but worked as a fruit-picker and then as a cleaning lady in Warsaw, where she shared a run-down apartment with two female friends:

> Everyone in Warsaw has their *Ukrainka* to do the work they don't want to do. Polish women work in nice offices, wear nice clothes, they don't have time to clean and cook. So what are these visas for? Everybody knows that we're going to come anyway. If we have to pay [bribes] we pay. If we have to lie [to officials] we lie.... They [border guards] are not so stupid to think that we are coming on vacation. They know why we are here. They must check the visa[,] we must show the visa. And what? It changes nothing.

Anna, like some of her family members, found few decent job opportunities in western Ukraine, and opted instead, along with thousands of other Ukrainians, for the 'grey economy' in Poland, where estimates of the total number of Ukrainian migrants ranged from 300,000 to half a million. They spoke of paying bribes to border guards, whether to persuade them to turn a blind eye to visa irregularities or to overlook the wads of cash they took back to Ukraine. They paid close and cautious attention to men who patrolled the border trying to recruit younger women to work in 'prestigious' nightclubs.[6]

Ukrainian migrants peddled goods such as cigarettes and alcohol. In Poland they were colloquially known as 'ants' (*mrówki*), not because they were hardworking, but because they were everywhere. They described themselves as 'shuttles' (*chovnyky*), moving back and forth, and perhaps suggesting something of their monotonous life. Of their aptitude for circumventing the rules, there was little doubt. Oksana, a Ukrainian who had worked in a variety of temporary jobs in Poland, ranging from fruit-picking and cleaning homes to selling clothes and cosmetics on the cheap, described how she negotiated the new visa arrangements between Ukraine and Poland by 'losing' her passport in Warsaw, so that she could give herself a clean slate when it came to registering with the authorities in Poland.[7]

In the Russian Federation, migration took on a different meaning, partly because Russia needed to retain rather than lose workers, and partly because of the status of ethnic Russians who lived beyond its borders, the legacy of Soviet-era migration to non-Russian republics whose new leadership framed them as intruders. From Moscow's point of view, these Russians in the 'near abroad' seemed to be living on borrowed time.

Russian president Vladimir Putin took steps to support these so-called compatriots by instituting a State Programme for Voluntary Resettlement to the Russian Federation of Compatriots Abroad. Launched in 2006, it acknowledged that Russia faced a demographic deficit, and in particular a decline in the number of people of working age. As in the late Soviet period, remote regions in the Far East and Siberia were desperately short of labour. Qualified workers were also needed to fill positions in rural Russia and help stem the tide of rural depopulation. Without migrant workers, Moscow and other cities would struggle to fill jobs in the construction and service sectors.[8]

In 2007, the government took steps to attract migrants from other post-Soviet states, but with limited success: a policy projected to bring in roughly 300,000 skilled labourers per year attracted only a tenth of that number between 2007 and 2010. There was a familiar ring to the reception of those who did arrive: migrant workers were thought to be taking jobs from Russian workers. Concerns were expressed about 'illegal' migration. Russia's Federal Migration Service struggled to control undocumented immigration, inflaming public anxieties about its extent and reinforcing perceptions about corrupt officials who took bribes. At the same time, Putin was keen to limit what he termed 'ethno-cultural risks'. The solution, in addition to promoting highly qualified foreign workers, lay in facilitating the migration of Russians to the Russian Federation. The talk was of 'our culture and our values'. Relaunched in 2012, the programme was subsequently extended to Russian-speaking Ukrainians fleeing the conflict in eastern Ukraine. By 2015, in a sop to what was felt to be widespread public concern, before being granted a work permit prospective migrants were expected to demonstrate a good working knowledge of Russian and Russian history in order, as one Russian sociologist put it, 'to annoy his neighbours less'. The emphasis, according to the head of the Federal Migration Service, was on 'quality, not quantity'. Although an exception was made for migrants from Armenia, Belarus, Kazakhstan, and Kyrgyzstan, whose leaders joined a new Eurasian Economic Union (EEU) with Russia in 2015, the overall goal of Russian policy was to ensure that migrants embraced 'Russian values'.[9]

At this stage, Russia recorded between 10 million and 15 million migrant workers, who collectively generated between 5 and 10 percent of gross domestic product (GDP). Russia's Federal Migration Service arrived at this figure by estimating that there were at least 3 million undocumented migrants in the country. Many of the migrants came from outside the EEU, and particularly from Central Asia, especially Uzbekistan and Tajikistan; indeed, two in every five of the Uzbek and Tajik people between the ages of eighteen and thirty were working abroad. Many others were from Moldova, Georgia, and Azerbaijan. By 2018, there were reportedly between 1 million and 2 million Azeri migrants, popularly known as 'guest workers' (*gastarbeitery*) in Russia, including as many as 800,000 in Moscow alone. Those who failed the Russian language test simply vanished into the informal economy.[10]

Russian officials reserved the word 'migrant' for non-Russians. Life for many of them—usually temporary or undocumented migrants—continued to be insecure. This was partly because of the fraught economic situation in their home countries, where the rupture of close economic ties with neighbouring states had contributed to a decline in output and employment. But the insecurity was also a function of the obstacles that were put in their way by the Russian state. Migrants were caught in the midst of rivalries between the Ministry of Labour, which was keen to ensure that firms got the workers they needed, and the Interior Ministry and regional governors, who wanted to regulate migration in order to ensure that Russian voters felt less 'threatened' by non-Russians. Obtaining a 'guest worker permit' was very difficult. Citizens of the Commonwealth of Independent States (CIS) were expected to pay 2,000 rubles (equivalent to $60) for a work permit, but most ended up paying $600 to $700 to intermediaries and as bribes to government officials.[11]

Popular attitudes did not deter migrants, but they nevertheless created a hostile environment. Inside Russia, there were clear signs of antipathy towards people of non-Slavic origin. A survey conducted in September 2013 threw up some shocking findings: 43 percent of Russians wanted foreigners to be sent home (the percentage was higher in Moscow), and 20 percent believed that migrants deserved to be beaten up. Four out of five people were in favour of Cossack street patrols to maintain order. However, other polls and focus groups suggested that Russians were more concerned about issues such as drug abuse, corruption, unemployment, pensions, and inequality, as well as Russia's poor health service, all problems that were not directly linked to the presence of migrants.[12]

Russian nationalists continued to insist that they had been left high and dry by the collapse of the Soviet Union. They drew strength from the Russian government, which regarded Russians in Abkhazia, South Ossetia, and Ukraine as disenfranchised people whose interests needed to be safeguarded. Stories circulated of unemployed Russians who had been given tickets to work in the Caucasus but who ended up being sold into slavery. Members of the far right mobilised under the slogan of 'Russia for Russians'. They organised street demonstrations in Moscow in December 2010 that targeted migrants in the wake of the murder of a Muscovite by a Caucasian assailant; in the ensuing protests, a Kyrgyz migrant was stabbed to death. In Pugachev, a small town close to Saratov on the River Volga, the murder of a former paratrooper by a Chechen youth led to demonstrations calling for the deportation of people from the North Caucasus. In October 2013, hundreds of Russians descended on the economically depressed suburb of Biriulovo, on the southern outskirts of Moscow, chanting 'Russia for Russians' and 'white power'. This was in response to a murder committed by an immigrant from Azerbaijan. In each instance, police forces stood by without intervening to protect migrants. In Moscow, the police failed to crack down on neo-Nazi gangs and instead took migrants from the Caucasus into custody.[13]

The situation was complicated by the fact that migrants of Slavic origin typically survived on a shoestring. In the new millennium, most migrant workers—at least those who arrived in Moscow—earned poor wages, between $300 and $600 per month. In addition to economic hardship, they faced challenges from Russian racist gangs and the police. Liudmila X, a thirty-four-year-old woman from Odessa, replied to an Internet advert for a shop assistant in Moscow. When she arrived, a man took away her papers and instructed her to beg on the Moscow metro. Wearing ragged clothes, she presented herself to the local police, who promptly kicked her out because of her appearance. It took the intervention of volunteer charity workers to come to her rescue.[14]

Non-Russian migrants especially did not find it easy to adjust. Living as a non-Russian in the Russian Federation meant negotiating administrative barriers and public attitudes ranging from indifference to outright hostility. Much of their time was spent in the shadows. Men were recruited to work on construction projects or to take jobs in the retail sector, but then went unpaid: for example, Uzbek builders were told that their wages had been 'temporarily delayed'. Having surrendered their documents, they were stranded. A Moscow-based NGO called the Angel Coalition eventually came to their aid. Other migrants found shelter in makeshift hostels built out of containers that were regularly raided by Moscow police in search of undocumented migrants. Local residents claimed that these guest workers were living in unsanitary conditions and that they attracted drug dealers.[15]

Certainly, not all migrants were destitute or lived in fear of being attacked and deported. Some migrants from Central Asia began to make a reasonable life as shopkeepers and car mechanics; they were able to raise families and became accepted by local Russians because they provided essential services. When Russia hosted the World Cup in the summer of 2018, the authorities were happy to employ Kazakh and Uzbek workers if they spoke enough English to communicate with tourists. But this did not compensate for underlying discrimination and hostility, or a fundamental sense that Russia would continue to prioritise Russian culture.[16]

Russia and the successor states of the former Soviet Union were portrayed as a jungle in which organised trafficking was being allowed to flourish. A flurry of news reports in Russia sustained a standard narrative in which unscrupulous agents scoured villages in the Caucasus and Central Asia to recruit domestic servants and sex workers. Typically, a 'friend' or acquaintance would promise to lift a young woman (less often, a man) and her family out of poverty by promising a well-paid job in the West. When she reached her destination, the victim was forced to hand over her passport and work as a prostitute until she paid off the 'debt' that she incurred. Threats of violence against her family back home reinforced the sense that she was at the mercy of the trafficker and the pimp, who conducted this 'trade in people' (*torgovlia liud'mi*). *Argumenty i fakty* (Arguments and facts), a leading Russian weekly, regularly carried stories in this vein, such as one about Vera X from Astrakhan, who was abducted from public transport on her way to Turkey and trafficked to Belgrade and then Kosovo. She eventually escaped, but not before witnessing the murder of her friend. Similar stories surfaced in Ukraine, where underage girls and young women were reportedly trafficked to Turkey, part of an estimated 400,000 between 1988 and 1998. The media emphasis on deception helped counteract the view of some police officers that 'they are just prostitutes', implying they did not deserve sympathy. Other stories flagged the widespread and growing demand for sex workers in Europe—Germany and the Netherlands were singled out as 'magnets'—to make the point that there would be no supply without demand.[17]

There were several dimensions to these narratives. One highlighted a post-Soviet realm of lawlessness and corruption that facilitated undocumented migration and exploitation, notwithstanding new legislation in 2003 that criminalised human trafficking. Another pointed to the decadence of Western Europe that sustained the sex trade. Neither view captured more than a small element of truth, but migration served as a means to define cultural and political differences between East and West.[18]

First-person accounts told of the heroic struggle to retain some control over one's life. 'Larisa' (not her real name), described the difficulties in navigating the post-Soviet bureaucratic labyrinth. She had been born in 1968 to Russian and Ukrainian parents who had moved from Moscow to Pavlodar, Kazakhstan, when she was still a child. Her elderly parents spoke of Kazakhstan as their home, but Larisa's situation was very different from theirs: she had fallen in love with and married a Colombian student whom she met at university in Moscow. After they got divorced, in 1995, she sought permission to stay in Russia, and was told to return to Kazakhstan, but the Kazakh authorities deemed her to be stateless. With no other option, she went back to Moscow as an 'illegal' migrant, and then decided to use her knowledge of Spanish to make contact with a Spaniard in Málaga, pinning her hopes on making a new life for herself in Spain by marrying him for the purpose of obtaining residency. He agreed to the arrangement. Reassuring her parents, who feared that she would be forced to work in a brothel, she declared that 'it won't happen, Spain is a European country'. Nevertheless, her prospective husband refused to keep his side of the bargain. By the early 2000s, she was still in limbo, dividing her time between Málaga and Pavlodar, where her parents still lived. Larisa regarded her life as a struggle with officialdom and with the men who abandoned her. She was left to ponder where she belonged in Europe.[19]

Other migrants faced a harsh reality when war broke out between Russia and Ukraine. The tension caused another refugee crisis. Conflict between the two countries generated forced migration on a large scale. Russia's occupation of territory in eastern Ukraine in 2014 displaced as many as 1.2 million civilians on both sides. According to Russia's Federal Migration Service, by 2015 there were around 900,000 refugees from Ukraine on Russian soil, most of them ethnically Russian. Firms in Russia reportedly swapped their workforce of Central Asian migrants for refugees, but this did not prevent refugees from being exploited or treated as interlopers. Others tried to leave Ukraine but were prevented by the Ukrainian authorities from doing so. In other words, refugees became a source of cheap labour and also pawns in a bitter diplomatic and military tug-of-war.[20]

In Ukraine, thousands of civilians moved farther west in search of safety, but the Ukrainian government discouraged others from leaving, in order to minimise the burden on hard-pressed local authorities elsewhere in the country. (The figures were hard to verify, because not all displaced persons registered.) By 2018, the conflict had largely faded from the international headlines. However, the UNHCR reckoned that 600,000 people in the contested region of Donbas were suffering from impoverishment and unemployment; moreover, they faced harassment from Ukrainian and Russian troops and paramilitaries as well as the dangers posed by unexploded land mines and periodic artillery bombardment. With restrictions imposed by the Ukrainian authorities on their freedom of movement, many civilians were trapped: 'Nobody wants us', was a common refrain in eastern Ukraine, where residents contrasted their situation with the more favourable reaction to refugees from Crimea, who fled to Ukraine following the Russian annexation.[21]

Nevertheless, the magnitude of suffering, death, and displacement in the Donbas was nothing like the scale of the catastrophe during the wars in the former Yugoslavia. In the states that emerged out of the wreckage of the 1990s, civilians continued to pick up the threads after the end of hostilities. As we saw earlier, many refugees returned to their homes but faced considerable problems of adjustment. Others divided their time between their birthplace and the country in which they had taken refuge. A woman who fled to Britain from Croatia described the pain of abrupt leave-taking and her ongoing torment as she recalled the moment of departure: 'It is something that absolutely haunts me, that moment. I have been back plenty of times, there have been many departures, but that one when I didn't know if I was going to see any of them again. . . . And I knew then that was it for us, our lives were wrecked even if by some chance we were all going to be OK.' The pain was not lessened by her subsequent shuttling to and from the UK.[22]

In the new millennium, the citizens of the former Yugoslavia had to negotiate other fundamental changes. The successor states diverged in key respects. Slovenia joined the European Union in 2004, but Croatia was only admitted in 2013—although other member states were entitled to regulate the admission of Croatian nationals to their labour markets. Citizens of Bosnia-Herzegovina and Serbia needed a visa to enter EU member states. They had swapped the 'red passport' of Yugoslavia for a new passport that made travel much less straightforward. Hitherto, a Yugoslav passport had 'opened the world'. But the days of the Yugoslav guest worker or the tourist who went to Trieste on shopping trips were long gone.[23]

In the case of Kosovo, everything was made more complicated by a severe economic recession. The rate of unemployment in Kosovo reached

33 percent in 2014, and was twice as high among young people as among older ones. Men and women of working age hoped to find work in the European Union in order to improve their prospects 'for the sake of the children'. But the only realistic option was to travel as unauthorised migrants. Kosovar migrants could travel to Serbia, using just their national identification cards, and then take the bus to Subotica, a small town on the border with Hungary. But getting into the EU member state required the help of people-smugglers, whom they paid with money they had borrowed or earned by selling what assets they had. If they claimed asylum (more than 20,000 did so in 2014), the Hungarian authorities promptly deported them on the grounds that they did not qualify as refugees. It thus made more sense to work in the informal economy, with all the attendant risks of exploitation and abuse, than to try going the official route. Meanwhile, EU officials made it clear to the government of Kosovo that if the country wanted to enjoy closer cooperation with Brussels and EU member states, it should clamp down on illegal migration. Kosovo, however, looked to protect its own interests: the country relied heavily on remittances from men and women working abroad. The stakes of migration were high for prospective migrants and for the state.[24]

As the situation in Kosovo indicated, the European Commission was very happy to lecture other countries about their responsibilities towards migrants and refugees. It coupled these efforts with lofty expressions of shared European values: at the turn of the millennium, for example, the commission insisted that 'the European Union is by its very nature a pluralistic society... [which] brings with it a number of responsibilities for all of its members be they nationals or migrants'. It was incumbent on all migrants to integrate into the host society.[25]

The European Union repeated this line with neighbouring Albania, urging the government to adopt a 'holistic' migration policy that would enable it to profit from the diaspora in terms of new ideas, not just from migrants' remittances. However, these patronising statements minimised or even overlooked the difficulties Albania had wrestled with since the early 1990s. After a flurry of departures in the immediate aftermath of the overthrow of communist rule, the exodus from Albania revived in 1996–1997 as a consequence of the deteriorating economic situation and the collapse of the banking system. Migrants at this stage were predominantly young men, whereas in the new millennium, migration tended to involve entire households, partly as a result of family reunification. Although thousands of Albanians were given refugee status, many others lived a fragile and even dangerous existence. In 2001, for example, the residents of Salandra in southern Italy attacked an orphanage for Albanian children, crying 'Lynch the Albanians'.[26]

The most obvious implication for the Albanian government was the enormous scale of migration itself: according to the World Bank, the number of Albanians living abroad in 2010, mainly in Italy or Greece, stood at more than 1.4 million, close to half the country's total population. Albania itself remained impoverished, notwithstanding the upsurge in remittances from the diaspora. The European Union charged the Albanian government with the task of trying to stem the outflow in order to relieve pressure on Italy, indicating that the priority was to look after the interests of member states.[27]

The European Union also dictated how Albania should conduct itself in relation to those refugees and undocumented migrants who used Albania as a point of transit. The European Commission dangled the prospect of Albania's eventual accession when it instructed the government to be more aggressive in dealing with people-trafficking, which it deemed to be antithetical to 'EU values'. The Albanian government duly fell into line, by agreeing to formulate what it termed a comprehensive policy to combat illegal migration, to promote economic development through 'managed migration', and to protect Albanians living abroad. In making these pledges, it expressed a readiness to move towards closer alignment with the European Union.[28]

If Albania had relatively little leverage with the European Union, the same could not be said of a powerful state such as Turkey. But the relationship between Turkey and the European Union was a complicated one. Turkey's economic elites and intelligentsia favoured a closer relationship with the union. For their part, EU member states treated that aspiration with some disdain, partly for political reasons (the authoritarianism of successive regimes in Ankara and the repression of Kurds), and partly because accession would enable unrestricted entry of Turkish migrants to EU countries. Guest workers arrived in Western Europe through controlled programmes of admission, but full EU membership would create new rules. As the historian Tony Judt pointed out, Turkey's application to join the European Union also faced hurdles because the country's population was predominantly Muslim. Germany's Christian Democrats firmly opposed Turkey's admission, pointing to the problems of integrating even more Turkish migrants. So a number of obstacles stood in the way of Turkey's accession.[29]

Turkey, of course, was historically an important labour-exporting country. The statistics made for impressive reading. Around 5 million Turkish citizens are thought to live outside Turkey, 4 million of them in Europe. This figure equates to around 6 percent of Turkey's total population. As in the past, remittances played a large part in cementing the relationship between the diaspora and the country of origin. In 2010, remittances to Turkey amounted to close on $1 billion, including $640 million from Germany alone. These figures only take account of formal means for sending cash back home, and therefore underestimate the real figure. They also disguise the fact that the Turkish diaspora includes a significant Kurdish component (of which more below).

All the same, by the second decade of the twenty-first century, Turkey had become a country of net immigration and the world's largest refugee host state. Both developments are hugely significant. The sociologist Franck Düvell has pointed out that visitors to Istanbul, Antalya, and other major cities in Turkey encounter a multifarious migrant population consisting of 'German, Dutch, British or Swedish retirees, Russian and Ukrainian businessmen and women, Georgian construction workers, Armenian nannies, Moldovan domestic workers and caretakers, Uzbeks and Kirgiz workers, Nigerian street vendors, African football players, Syrian gardeners, Afghans, Egyptian and Somali shop owners or Azerbaijani and other students'. Although Turkish men and women have continued to look for work abroad, in Russia, North Africa, and the Gulf States, the traditional pattern of emigration has been reversed.[30]

Although the situation in Turkey made it difficult for political exiles to consider returning, significant numbers of ethnic Turkish migrants who had lived for many years in Germany, France, or the Netherlands described feeling homesick and deciding to return to Turkey. They kept a foot in both camps, spending several months in Turkey and visiting their children who stayed in Western Europe, but continued to regard Turkey as their homeland. One German-born Turkish man, who returned to Turkey in 2011, put it like this:

> Lately, we have invested in Turkey more, the trade opportunities have increased in Turkey, we had to return due to work-related reasons and it became an opportunity. Life in Turkey is different. It is different in terms of warmth, the view of people, warmer and intimate, more understanding, we have the same culture, same language, there are mosques here, for example. There are one thousand people in a prayer here and it is a different atmosphere and mysticism. Although I was born there, here is different.[31]

This economic and emotional commitment was music to the ears of Turkey's leadership.

None of this corresponded to the situation of minority groups, in particular the Kurds, whom the government in Ankara saw as a thorn in the flesh of the Turkish body politic. Faced with a repressive regime, Kurdish pro-independence activists continued the freedom struggle in exile. Ordinary Kurds, too, sought to escape. Whether as a respite from economic marginalisation or to escape political persecution, Kurds often had to count upon people-smugglers to gain a foothold abroad in cities such as Milan. As one explained, 'I come from a very poor family. We decided to migrate because of not having any alternatives....[G]overnments do not invest deliberately where we lived. If they did we would not be here.' However, their options were limited: whereas those who arrived in the 1990s found low-paid jobs in manufacturing, the later arrivals worked in construction or sold kebabs; firms had outsourced jobs to other countries, including Turkey. Another Kurdish migrant compared his situation to that of Italians who had moved to the north of the country years earlier: 'There are many who do not like us [but] they too came here as migrants.' An added complication was the failed coup in 2016. Along with the intense state repression that followed (government officials bandied about endless accusations of 'terrorism'), thousands more political opponents of the Erdoğan regime fled Turkey.[32]

Deterrence and efforts to forestall migration increasingly found favour with governments. Thanks to the European Union, Turkey, Albania, Tunisia, and other states were being paid to contain refugees before they even got close to Europe. In deathly bureaucratic prose, EU heads of state in October 2013 resolved to 'improve access to self-reliance for refugees in third countries [as] a key precursor to a durable solution'. This other Europe played a key role in this strategy.[33]

Thus, EU leaders concluded that Syrian refugees were best 'contained' in Turkey, and accordingly struck a deal with the Turkish government in March 2016 to deter unauthorised migration and support Turkey in providing 'temporary protection' for Syrians in refugee camps. Meanwhile, the European Union would send aid to Turkey and to two other major refugee-hosting states, Jordan and Lebanon. Under this deal, Turkey promised to hold Syrian and other refugees in situ in exchange for the prospect of greater access to Europe for its citizens. Human rights organisations were quick to condemn the arrangement: Amnesty International protested that, 'in their desperation to seal their borders, EU leaders have wilfully ignored the simplest of facts. Turkey is not a safe country for Syrian refugees and is getting less safe by the day'. But this was not the point. Rather, the European Union welcomed the agreement as a sign of its commitment to manage migration. For its part, Turkey argued that in fulfilling its share of the bargain, by providing refugees with emergency assistance, free health checks, and education, it should be allowed to restart the stalled negotiations over its admission to the European Union.[34]

EU member states sought to reassure their citizens that government policies were designed to keep them safe. The European Commission continued to adhere to the principle of controls at the border with non-EU countries. In 2018, member states adopted a new 'Entry/Exit System' for registering the comings and goings of non-EU nationals, 'in order to strengthen and protect the external borders of the Schengen area, and to safeguard and increase the security for its citizens'. Deliberately or not, this focus on security exposed large numbers of migrants to insecurity. Migrants, particularly where they were unauthorised, remained vulnerable to exploitation by unscrupulous employers. Human trafficking proved difficult to curb. The situation in Russia and Eastern Europe offered a bleak illustration of that fact. Migrant workers regularly had to negotiate manifestations of extreme nationalism that were tolerated and even encouraged by the government.[35]

The consequences could be even more devastating for asylum seekers. In Croatia, border forces used a variety of tactics, including beatings, pepper spray, and police dogs, to keep non-European refugees at bay, rather than enabling them to seek asylum. In late 2017, a family of Afghan refugees, including four children under the age of ten, crossed into Croatia from Serbia, but they were quickly intercepted and ordered to return to Serbia, which does not belong to the European Union. In the process, six-year-old Madina Hussiny was killed by a train. Croatia disclaimed responsibility, maintaining that the family never actually set foot in the country. The circumstances of her preventable death and the response of politicians and bureaucrats epitomised the new arrangements across the continent.[36]

CHAPTER 22

Belief, Bodies, and Behaviour

THE SOCIOLOGIST YASMIN GUNARATNAM devoted her career to understanding how postwar migrants to the UK negotiated death and dying. One of her interviewees was an elderly Chinese man, Feng Dai. She observed how he sat facing his doctor in a clinic at a London teaching hospital, to be told that his cancer was no longer treatable: 'Before he gets up to leave, Mr Dai asks for a pen and writes a single word on a small scrap of paper. He tells the doctor that he will look the word up in his dictionary later at home. The word? "Terminal".'[1]

Like everyone else, Feng was confronted by illness and the infirmities of old age. Migrants faced particular challenges as they reached the end of their lives, such as having to come to terms with the decisions they had made or that were made on their behalf. These included where to be buried. The writer Colin Grant described attending West Indian christenings, weddings, and funerals in 1970s Luton in England: 'You'd inevitably overhear snatches of the same mantra: "Bwoi, this country too cold to bury. Don't mek me bury here". Men and women voiced a version of the same desire to turn back towards the West Indies, to "wheel and come again" as Jamaicans say. And when the time came, their burial back home would be done with style: "Yes, man, pure excitement!"'[2]

Imminent death forces migrants to confront questions about their final journey and resting place. Questions arise, in many cases, about the circumstances leading to premature loss of life, and about the status of the dead body. Practices surrounding handling of the body illustrate some of the fundamental issues of migration: where one 'belongs', for example, and what kind of control migrants (and their next of kin) exercise over death and burial. A related issue concerns the manner of one's death: Often separated from family members, migrants might be unable to see their loved ones before they die. Where they can exercise a degree of choice, how do the dying say farewell to those who stay behind? Where it is impossible to say goodbye, and particularly where the body is missing, bereaved relatives suffer even more than they might in other circumstances.

The appropriate conduct of funerals matters for migrants and their loved ones. Sometimes, a funeral becomes an occasion for an exile to make a political point. In Sweden, for example, the politically charged funerals of leading exiles might provide an opportunity for refugees to come together and—at least temporarily—set aside their factional divisions. This was the case, for example, for Chilean exiles in Sweden in the 1980s who attended the funeral of a prominent political activist and spoke of a double bereavement caused by the death of the loved one, and by their enforced separation from the homeland. The ceremony itself combined secular, Protestant, and Catholic elements, together with political songs and speeches. Following the cremation, the ashes were returned to the family in Chile. But the ceremony made an important point about the intense feelings exiles had towards the Pinochet regime and about their hopes of eventually returning when democracy was restored.[3]

Funerals involving migrants can be more public than the conventional, private affair that is typical in the West. However, migrants are perhaps understandably sensitive about being too conspicuous in mourning the deaths of friends and relatives. A study of a funeral of a Tamil refugee in 2000, following a tragic accident in a Norwegian fish processing plant in the village of Finnmark, provided locals with the opportunity to acknowledge the efforts of Tamil workers in keeping the community afloat. But the Tamils wanted to avoid having a 'funeral which the Norwegians will turn their heads to look at. We do not want to be exotic'. Unlike in the Chilean example, politics did not intrude directly. Nevertheless, a statement was made about the importance of observing religious faith far from home and about the need to respect religious difference — something the Norwegians appeared to understand.[4]

Scholars have also explored more general questions as to where and how migrants are given a final resting place. The decision is often invested with profound meaning about migration and 'home'. According to the historian Anu Mai Köll, the daughter of Estonian refugees who were given sanctuary in Sweden, many migrants requested that, following their cremation, their ashes be taken to Estonia and the urn placed in ancestral family plots, something that only became possible in the wake of Estonian independence. An elderly Bosnian man, Ibro Sušić, who was born in the village of Brdo and witnessed the massacre of his male relatives at the hands of Serb soldiers in 1992, managed to make his way to Austria later that year. When he died, in 1997, he left instructions that his remains should be returned to his native village.[5]

Consider, too, the decisions made by the families of harkis, the Algerians who fought alongside the French colonial forces in the Algerian war and who were 'repatriated' to France in order to escape retribution at the hands of the National Liberation Front (FLN). The well-known harki leader Saïd Boualam insisted on being buried in the settlement he founded in the Camargue. Other first-generation harkis regretted that they could not be buried in the country of their birth because of the legacy of mutual hostility between themselves and the Algerian state; their children and grandchildren, however, had no wish to be buried in Algeria. Most distressing of all, the harkis recalled that the French officials who ran the internment camps in the early 1960s 'hurriedly buried the scores of babies who had died in the harsh winter conditions in unmarked graves'. The choice facing migrants was nicely captured in the remarks of a young Algerian man who described being afraid of being buried in Algeria: 'Because I don't feel that I am clean. I'm afraid of the elders. If ever they gave me a spot between my uncle, my father and everyone, I'm scared they would spend their death bothering me and reproaching me for not have [sic] led a pure life.' Conversely, others described a sense of shame—to the point of deserving punishment—at being obliged to bury their relatives in France rather than in the land of their birth. They felt this was the price they paid for having 'abandoned' Algeria.[6]

Sometimes painful decisions have to be made. Ibrahim, a refugee from Ghana who lay dying in a London hospice, was acutely aware that he would be leaving a young son behind in the UK. He hoped to be buried in Ghana so his son could visit his grave there: 'I want my son to… one day not just melt away into this society, but think of a place where he comes from and one day, or once in a while go back there, and when he goes there and then there's this gravestone standing there and say "Oh that's your Dad lying down there" just gives him some kind of attachment to a place which I will cherish…yeah.' Ibrahim wanted his son to remember him and feel a connection to the place of his father's birth, even though Ibrahim himself had left because he felt excluded and persecuted. Ibrahim's partner could not afford the costs of repatriation and burial in Ghana, so his wishes went unfulfilled.[7]

Pakistani migrants to the UK created funeral associations ('death committees') to help cover the high cost of returning the bodies of deceased persons to Pakistan to be buried in the villages of their birth. The relatives of deceased Bangladeshis likewise arranged for the bodies to be flown back, in this case to Sylhet. This allowed local kin to see their loved ones' bodies for the last time and to pay their respects at a shrine in their 'own land'.[8]

Italian migrants were more likely to be buried in Italy than in Germany, Belgium, France, or Switzerland, and they set aside money accordingly. The bodies of migrants who died prematurely were also taken back to the villages where they were born, although in some parts of the country cemeteries were extended to accommodate the migrants who wished to be buried in the place they now called home. Elsewhere, too, burial grounds were located in the host country. In Romford, Essex, the Victorian cemetery of Woodgrange Park, having been neglected for many years, got a new lease on life (so to speak) when the local Bangladeshi Muslim population acquired part of the grounds for Muslim burials and put time and effort into its care and maintenance. Polish migrants also helped.[9]

Graves and graveyards thus disclose the afterlives of migration. A study of a cemetery in Kviberg (near Göteborg in Sweden) found that graves that seemed at first sight to be identical to familiar Swedish graves were in fact the final resting place of Chinese, Iranian, Lebanese, Serbian, and other migrants. Their headstones were marked with inscriptions in their native languages indicating where they were born. Some incorporated images of flowers and birds together with lamps typical of Swedish graves, indicating a connection with the culture of the host country and suggesting that the cemetery became a place where people from different backgrounds were able to express a close affinity with Sweden.[10]

Specific issues have been raised by tragedies affecting large numbers of people, as with the thousands of migrants who have drowned in the Mediterranean in recent years. The poignant consequences are apparent, for example, in the continual replenishment of the graveyard at Barbate in Spain. In January 2017, the body of four-year-old Samuel Kabamba from the Democratic Republic of Congo washed up on the nearby beach. He was one of a group of 223 people who drowned off the coast of Cádiz while attempting to enter Spain. His mother had been seeking treatment for cancer and spent eight months in Morocco before managing to secure a place on a small inflatable boat. Rescuers subsequently found her body off the coast of Algeria.[11]

Locals on Lampedusa, on Greece's border with Turkey, and on the Greek Islands demonstrated solidarity with refugees by assisting with burials or with repatriation of the bodies of those who had drowned at sea. They helped identify the bodies and contacted relatives, and even took part in funeral services. Events were held to commemorate the loss of life. Since 2013, the members of Youth Without Borders, an organisation of refugees who obtained asylum in Germany, have regularly returned to Lesvos in Greece, which they once set foot on during their escape from violence, 'to give back what we had ourselves received: the solidarity of local people to newcomers'. They provide practical help to those who are making the journey, but they also grieve those who do not make it: 'We want to mourn all those who had been senselessly dying in the sea and cannot be with us', they wrote in a report on the trips.[12]

These deaths were unforeseen, but others have been self-inflicted. In April 2011, a thirty-six-year-old Iranian man, Kambiz Roustayi, doused himself with petrol in the centre of Amsterdam after having been denied a permanent place of safety. He had been in the Netherlands for eleven years and expected to be deported, but he feared for his life in Iran. His requests for asylum had failed every time. Roustayi had announced that he was planning to commit suicide, but no one took him seriously and he received no help. The suicide of others who are held in refugee camps and detention centres are occasionally reported, but usually without any explanation of the circumstances that lead refugees to take their own lives.[13]

Migrant newcomers often maintain a strong attachment to the religious tradition in which they were brought up. In many cases, a religious background helps them to negotiate new surroundings, whether this means finding spiritual solace or drawing on material support among faith-based networks. As the sociologist John Rex put it, 'migrants will combine with their fellows to establish familiar forms of prayer and worship in their new environments, and the religious organisation of the homeland will take active steps to ensure the continued adherence and faithfulness of their migrating members'. The presence of devout (or ostensibly devout) migrants underlined the contrast with a perceived growth of secularism in Europe. In the mid-1950s, Stella, a young wife and mother who came from Jamaica to join her husband in Britain in 1951, observed that 'the hundredth psalm say make a joyful noise unto the Lord. But English people, they do not understand the hundredth psalm.' Her interviewer, Joyce Egginton, went on to describe the growth of West Indian sects in the UK, including a raucous service conducted by a preacher by the name of Elder Francis in Camden Town. He used a book called *Redemption Songs*, suggesting that new kinds of worship had the potential to make the established Anglican Church less starchy.[14]

The host state occupies a crucial role, since it often enables faith communities to draw upon public or government resources. The French, for example, provided for the spiritual needs of Italian and Polish migrants in the late 1940s and 1950s, appointing chaplains who conducted Catholic Mass in their native language as a means of supporting 'their integration into local religious life'. But the state was, of course, only one actor among many. Irish migrants to the UK in the same period were each equipped by the Catholic Church with a *Catholic Handbook for Irish Men and Women*, instructing them to guard their faith and resist temptation. Although its patronising tone probably appealed only to a minority who left Ireland, many Irish were nevertheless devout. Outside the workplace, life revolved around Catholic schools and social clubs.[15]

Religious self-expression does not belong in a political vacuum. Greek nationalists maintained that Muslim migration posed a challenge to 'national purity'; the consequences of this unrelenting rhetoric were felt predominantly by the Muslim residents of Athens. A study of working-class Pakistani migrants who settled in the northern suburb of Nea Ionia in the 1990s highlighted the suburb's origins as a chosen location for refugees arriving from Asia Minor during the 1920s. These migrants lived cheek by jowl—but not always harmoniously—with the descendants of Muslims from Thrace and Egyptian immigrants. All of them had to negotiate the portrayal of Islam as a threat to Greek Orthodoxy, particularly when the authorities refused to approve the construction of a mosque in Athens. Their situation was further complicated by ongoing tensions between Greece and Turkey. Following the attack on the Twin Towers in New York and the Pentagon in Washington, DC, on 11 September 2001, Turkish migrants were described increasingly in terms of their religion rather than their ethnicity, and this, in turn, affected their identity and politicisation. They protested vigorously when the Qur'an was publicly defaced in Athens in 2009. The demonstrators objected to other injustices during the same event: as one Pakistani said, 'they went there to protest on behalf of the Qur'an, but they were holding placards saying: "No more unemployment".' The same happened in Germany. As the political theorist Etienne Balibar suggested, 'in a situation of pauperisation, discrimination, and the crisis of identities connected to work, education, and traditional culture, the reference to religion functions as a refuge and substitute for social recognition'.[16]

Social recognition, of course, works both ways. There have sometimes been encouraging signs of good neighbourliness between residents who profess different faiths. In Nordbahnhof, for instance, local schools in a predominantly working-class suburb of Stuttgart provided a forum for Muslim and non-Muslim families to get to know each other better. Nordbahnhof had been a migrant hub for several decades: railway and postal workers arrived there from Bavaria between the two world wars, and they were followed by refugees and expellees from the East, and subsequently by Catholic guest workers from Portugal and Muslim migrants from Turkey. From the 1990s, they were joined by refugees from Yugoslavia, Afghanistan, and Iraq. Differences of religious observance over such things as the appropriate attire for school swimming lessons, or over the food and drink served at cultural festivals, were accommodated within a framework that allowed everyone to be a 'Stuttgarter'. With a modicum of goodwill and common sense, and a minimum of fuss, people managed to coexist.[17]

Meanwhile, migrants got on with their lives. There were decisions to be made about how one presented oneself in public. Society has always manifested and enforced boundaries of class, race, gender, and sexuality through dress and fashion. But attitudes are often polarised when migration is added to the mix. Migrants contribute as consumers to the host economy to keep up appearances and to participate in cultural events, such as carnivals and religious festivals. Something of this emerged in a 2015 exhibition at the Museum of Liverpool under the banner 'H.A.I.R.' (Heritage, Attitude, Identity, Respect). The exhibition documented the history of Liverpool's black barbers and hairdressing salons. But consumption has commanded much less attention than ideas around integration. Dress and hair covering issues in particular have drawn attention to religious and cultural differences, sometimes becoming the means of making broader points about migration and its implications.[18]

Headwear has become a touchstone of behaviour and cultural attitudes, particularly in France. However, the controversies around head coverings originated not in France but in the UK, where Sikhs waged a famous campaign in 1967–1969 on behalf of the right of Sikh bus conductors to wear turbans. The campaign began in the Midlands. In Wolverhampton, the local trade union for the bus drivers agreed with the Sikhs, recommending to a local committee that the regulations against turbans be removed. The committee agreed, with one committee member saying, 'In the interests of race relations we have taken the decision to relax the rule.' (In another landmark decision, the House of Lords ruled in 1983 that Sikh schoolboys could wear turbans at school.) In the early 1970s, Sikhs also protested the British law that obliged all motorcyclists to wear a helmet for safety on the road. One of the leading figures in this campaign was Jaginder Singh Brar, who arrived in Southall from Malaysia and worked as a taxi driver. His words touched a nerve when he said, 'This is the turban that fought the last two world wars without the helmet; no one cared back then, so why now?' Conservative politicians supported him on the helmets, but they insisted on the need to maintain immigration controls, which in their view helped their constituents tolerate cultural difference. The Sikhs got their way with passage of the Motorcycle Crash Helmets (Religious Exemption) Act in 1976.[19]

Controversies surrounding the headscarf and the veil erupted in Germany and France during the 1980s, and later in Denmark, where debates focused on Muslims as potential citizens. Local authorities in Odense, Aarhus, and Copenhagen objected to the veils worn by Muslim women. In West Germany, at least to begin with, the headscarf had less to do with the social changes brought about by Turkish guest workers than with domestic politics in Turkey, where wearing the veil became a means of expressing opposition to the military regime in the 1980s. It did not take long for the debates to become transposed into German politics. For the German right, the headscarf pointed to the 'inability to integrate', although there was also grudging respect for Islam's 'family values'. For those on the political left, however, it symbolised the oppression of women: removing the headscarf became a precondition of their assimilation. In a statement issued in 2001, the Islamic Council (the smaller of two umbrella organisations in Germany) insisted that wearing the headscarf 'must be accepted and tolerated' as a basic right.[20]

Turkish residents in Europe maintained that there was no need to wear a headscarf in Turkey, but every reason to do so in Germany, in order to proclaim the Muslim faith abroad. Second-generation migrant girls did not always abide by their parents' instructions about dress, or indeed other expectations, but they came under pressure from an older generation to conform. A series of interviews in 2000 with Turkish and Kurdish migrant women who settled in Marxloh, a deprived German suburb of Duisburg with a large foreign-born population, indicated as much. According to younger migrants, restrictions were indeed greater in Germany than in Turkey. Sibel, for example, complained that she had moved from a progressive middle-class home in Istanbul to a more circumscribed environment in Marxloh where Turkish men had turned the teahouse into a male-only space. Another young woman, Ebru, seemed at first sight to conform to the stereotype of a headscarf-wearing woman, but in fact she was suing her adulterous husband for divorce: 'I started wearing the headscarf when I married my husband. He wanted it like that. I didn't wear a headscarf before, before our marriage. I would really prefer not to wear it any longer. But I can't do that right now. Then people will say, "Oh, look, she's getting divorced, now she's getting rid of the headscarf. All she wants is to catch a new man".' It was difficult to escape the feeling that hair coverings had become heavily politicised in all quarters.[21]

The relationship between migration and faith assumed particular significance in France. When women from North Africa settled in France in the 1960s and 1970s, their headscarves did not cause a political outcry. By the late twentieth century, however, the headscarf came to embody 'a surprising range of France's problems, including anti-Semitism, Islamic fundamentalism, growing ghettoisation in the poor suburbs, and the breakdown of order in the classroom', wrote the anthropologist John R. Bowen. This was a far more serious set of problems than those confronting Muslim migrants in France in the 1960s.[22]

It is important to note that France has a long history of becoming involved in the religious affairs of French citizens, notwithstanding the importance attached to secularism. That is to say, the government has helped Muslims build mosques, has set aside space for Muslim burials, and has supported private Islamic schools. This was consistent with the 1905 French law on the separation of church and state. This law ensures freedom of conscience and freedom of religion but permits the state to contribute to the construction and maintenance of places of worship. By 'bringing Islam into the light', the state could both support Muslims, by offering a space for worship and education, and also require them to accept the principles of the republic. So it is misleading to suggest that France has only lately 'woken up' to the place of religion in French society. The point is that France went out of its way to avoid creating distinct ethno-religious groups that would sustain 'communalism' (*communautarisme*), the kind of fragmented society that was anathema to orthodox French policy-makers.[23]

The vexing questions around headscarves crystallised in 1989, the year of the bicentenary of the French Revolution, which provided an opportunity to reflect on its significance for contemporary France. A series of debates took place as to whether the French 'traditions' of *laïcité* (usually translated as secularism) and republicanism trumped the right of Muslim schoolgirls to wear the headscarf. Matters came to a head in September 1989, when three schoolgirls living in Creil were expelled from their public school for attending in Islamic dress. Before long, the French media inflamed the issue by speaking of religious 'fanaticism' (this followed in the wake of Ayatollah Khomeini's *fatwa* against Salman Rushdie). Eventually, two of the girls decided to remove their scarves in school, and the matter formally ended with the understanding that no general principle was at stake: girls could choose to wear scarves or not, so long as they were in regular attendance. Significantly, however, the school's head teacher had also crossed swords with a local Jewish organisation that regularly took children out of school on the Sabbath for religious instruction.[24]

Elsewhere, students mobilised on behalf of their fellow Muslim classmates. When French secondary school students in Grenoble organised a sit-in in February 1994 to protest the decision to exclude a fellow student from physical education lessons unless she removed her headscarf, most of those who supported her were white, a sign that attempts by the far right to turn this into an issue of race, and by those on the left to warn against 'ghettoisation', did not always succeed. They took their school to court, although they lost their case when the school argued that the children had 'disobeyed' rules of conduct—such as by not attending gym classes because they refused to remove the scarf. The students' measured approach offered a firm rebuff to self-appointed arbiters of French culture, including the leading intellectual André Glucksmann, who called the headscarf 'a terrorist emblem'.[25]

The *affaire des foulards,* or headscarf affair, was not just about the headscarf (hijab), which was in any case worn by only a small minority of Muslim women in France. The headscarf issue raised questions about Islam—often portrayed in public debate as a homogeneous set of beliefs and practices—but even more about France and French society. Left and right united in opposing the scarf, the former because it was a hallmark of women's subordination, the latter because it pointed to the failure of Muslims to assimilate. For their part, second-generation Muslims, conscious of the marginal position of their parents in French society, began to identify not only as *beurs*, or Arabs, but first and foremost as adherents of Islam. Wearing the headscarf became an important part of this religious identity.[26]

Conservative figures, including Nicolas Sarkozy, urged non-Muslims to act cautiously in response to the mood among many French Muslims, and not to 'humiliate' them by forcing them into a corner from which they might emerge more radicalised. Nevertheless, legislation seemed to satisfy the urge of French public opinion, influenced by the rise of the far-right Front National under the leadership of Jean-Marie Le Pen, to 'do something'. In September 2004, following months of discussion, France banned students from wearing clothing to school that drew attention to their religion. This ban included the Christian cross as well as the Muslim headscarf.[27]

In 2010, six years after Sarkozy's support for a ban on headscarves in public schools, France banned wearing the full-face veil, or *niqab*, in public. (So, too, did the Netherlands, where the place of Islam in Dutch society had become contentious following the murder of Theo van Gogh in 2004 by a Dutch Muslim of Moroccan descent.) In 2016, the mayor of Cannes imposed a ban on women wearing the *burkini* on the beach. His decision was copied elsewhere, notably in Nice, the site of a terrorist atrocity in July 2016. To justify his decision, the mayor said that the full-body swimsuit 'overtly manifests adherence to a religion at a time when France and places of worship are the target of terrorist attacks'. Prime Minister Manuel Valls agreed that the burkini was 'not compatible with the values of France'. But it was difficult to avoid the conclusion that, as the government-appointed 'mediator for headscarf cases' put it, 'underneath all the talk about *laïcité* there is racism'. Racism was connected in right-wing opinion with a sense of a Muslim 'menace'. In a striking comment on what it meant to be Muslim in France, Fariba, a young woman who was born in France in 1978, but grew up in Algeria before returning to study history in France, said, 'When I lived in Algeria before wearing the *voile* I was Fariba, and after I began to wear it [in France] I was *L'Islam*.' She added, 'I function as a barometer of the popularity of Muslims.'[28]

Food, like religious belief, became a barometer of migration and of views about what was and what was not acceptable about migration. Migrants often had to change their practices around food preparation and consumption in the host country, but there were other dimensions, too. For many migrants, memories of the journey from a place of familiarity to a strange place were indelibly associated with food—including its cultivation and preparation—and sometimes with hunger rather than with a full stomach. Home evoked memories of abundance, the pleasure of cultivating one's own plot of land, feeding one's family, and tasting favourite dishes. Migrants often held fast to their traditional meals when possible. They searched out familiar products and rejected new ones ('you can hardly eat the bread here'). They drank more beer and less wine (too expensive). Single men inevitably had to get used to cooking and eating on their own. Workers came back from Italy with their favourite cheeses and olive oil—one migrant worker kept a live eel in his bathtub to save for a special occasion.[29]

Food also helped to introduce migrants to the societies in which they settled. At a distance of sixty years, German women who found work in Sweden in the early 1950s recollected their first taste of Swedish food: 'Meatballs with lingonberries—that was an experience! We thought it was some kind of strange marmalade.' Plentiful and different, food became a shared experience in the new society just as it had been in the old.[30]

This kind of culinary adventure was strongly associated with consumption and changing tastes in the host society. Italian migrants brought the ice-cream parlour and the pizzeria to other parts of Europe (and to North

America) before the First World War. Several famous Indian restaurants were established in London in the interwar years. This diversification of eating habits accelerated after 1945. In Germany, Portuguese migrants soon multiplied the number of Portuguese restaurants in Hamburg. Italians had the same impact in Munich. Later on, ethnic niches, such as 'little Istanbul' in the Kreuzberg district of Berlin, or Chinatown and 'curry mile' in Manchester, or the Quartier Asiatique in the 13th arrondissement in Paris, and other localities became popular tourist destinations and municipal money-spinners. The transformation of the restaurant scene created jobs and developed supply chains. In Germany and elsewhere, the manufacture and distribution of canned ravioli, frozen pizza, and other convenience foods was big business.[31]

The kebab, couscous, and chicken tikka masala, like pizza in earlier years, became part of the high street and helped shape each host society's view of the 'newcomers'. The first *döner kebab* was reportedly sold as street food in Germany in the late 1960s, and gained an appeal because it was cheap and convenient. Customers paid for this fast food with no more than a superficial acknowledgement of the people who cooked and served the dishes: 'Going for an Indian', in the famous British phrase, was popularised by the expansion of curry houses made possible by Bangladeshis who arrived in the UK, mainly from Sylhet, after the 1971 war. They helped turn tikka into mainstream British food by adding a creamy, spicy sauce. As the historian Elizabeth Buettner put it, 'while encounters with Asians, the "smell of curry", and multiculturalism as official policy in mixed neighbourhoods, at work, and at school had been—and often continued to be—widely resented and undertaken involuntarily, curry house cuisine gradually became accepted, appreciated, and ultimately celebrated.'[32]

For their owners, the café, restaurant, ice-cream outlet, and other businesses offered a route out of (or more usually an alternative to) low-paid jobs in Germany. Waiters and chefs did not make much money unless they became owners. Establishing a restaurant in Germany was not straightforward, however. Applications to open a kebab stand were subjected to an 'examination of need' (*Bedürfnisprüfung*), whereby the authorities needed to be satisfied that a specific local demand could be met before granting a foreigner permission to open a business. Notwithstanding these bureaucratic obstacles, by 1990 there were more outlets selling kebabs in Berlin than there were in Istanbul. One in four restaurants across the country was run by a non-German restaurateur, a phenomenon providing a route whereby family members could join those who had preceded them into Germany. Each café and restaurant in turn provided German suppliers with a stream of income. As Chancellor Helmut Kohl acknowledged in 1993, German Turks created nearly 90,000 businesses and paid far more in taxes and other deductions than they cost the state.[33]

The proliferation of Chinese restaurants in the Netherlands, Germany, and Britain during the 1960s encouraged the arrival of a heterogeneous migrant population from the Pearl River Delta and Hong Kong, together with ethnic Chinese from the Dutch East Indies and Vietnam. In the Netherlands, where the number of Chinese restaurants grew from just 10 in 1945 to more than 1,800 in 1987, these outlets satisfied a demand on the part of colonial repatriates for familiar food. Chinese restaurant owners in Germany became very successful and imported Chinese staff from other European countries as well as from Hong Kong. In most instances, they adapted their cuisine for the European market. Success in business did not mean that the children of restaurant owners followed in their parents' footsteps—on the contrary, there was a tendency for the children to enter more prestigious professions with shorter working hours and fewer ethnic stereotypes.[34]

This discussion would not be complete without mentioning coffee, a big business that relies in large part on the availability of migrant labour to work in coffee shops. The overall number grew from 4,700 in the UK in 1997 to nearly 16,000 within the space of fifteen years. Virtually all the baristas employed by Caffè Nero in London in the late 1990s were non-British. They had taken advantage of the freedom of movement made possible by Maastricht to support a coffee culture that was no longer associated with just Italian (or Italian American) style, but had become appropriated as part of modern Britain.[35]

Food was also bound up with identity and politics. Migrants and migration altered the consumption habits of the host society for good, but maintaining the injunctions of their faith imposed difficulties on migrants concerning food. Turkish Germans who had to abstain from pork went in search of butchers and restaurants that could guarantee the ability to supply halal meat, in the process creating another important subset of food-related businesses.[36]

The politics of food sometimes emerged in stories about the hostility between those who favoured and those who opposed migration and multiculturalism. In 2018, Vittorio Castellani, a leading chef and food journalist in Italy, decided to leave the food programme he presented, claiming that the public broadcaster, RAI, had told him to drop foreign recipes, such as Mexican tortillas and Keralan curries, from the show. In a blog post that was disputed by RAI, he said, 'It's as if learning about other cultures is something to fear. I think we are becoming hostages of the xenophobic hate generated by certain politics, which is steering Italians towards racism and convincing them that the country's problems are linked to foreigners.' It hardly helped that RAI's president had links to the right-wing deputy prime minister, Matteo Salvini.[37]

Food and clothing have revealed a spectrum of opinion about migration and migrants as well as about the meanings invested in cultural practices. The transmission of ideas about food preparation and consumption has offered a way of thinking not only about the contributions made by migrants but also about the toleration or otherwise of social and cultural difference. Eating 'foreign' food can be enticing or unpleasant, depending on personal taste and one's general attitude about the presence of migrants. It might be appropriated by the host society, as in the case of 'British' chicken tikka masala, thus serving as a symbol of a more 'multicultural' society. But the consumption of food—whether the humble 'curry' or more 'authentic' dishes—offers only a superficial glimpse into the culture of newcomers and the decisions that lead them to migrate in the first place.

Much more so than food, the migrant's body and clothing have become a site of anxiety, disturbing what was fondly imagined as a stable cultural realm. Sometimes this has been a relatively straightforward matter of personal self-expression: as a young Polish woman living in Barcelona put it, 'you can go out in your pyjamas and nobody would pay attention'. On a more serious level, discussions of Sikh turbans and Muslim headscarves and burkas point to fundamental disquiet on the part of majority populations. In the new millennium, anti-Muslim commentators have regularly insisted that Europe's cities are full of 'no-go areas'. What they refuse to acknowledge is that women who wear the burka are often fearful of going out in public: they know from firsthand experience exactly what is meant by a 'no-go' area.[38]

CHAPTER 23

Owning the Past: Migration, Memory, Museum

OLGA, A TWENTY-EIGHT-YEAR-OLD RUSSIAN woman who had settled in the northern Italian city of Reggio Emilia, spoke enthusiastically of a municipal project in 2010 to encourage a mixed group of foreign residents—from Bulgaria, Burkina Faso, China, Egypt, Georgia, Nigeria, Sri Lanka, and other countries—to take a closer look at its history, in particular the migrant workers who arrived in the 1960s: 'I think it is right that Reggio Emilia offers this kind of opportunity to get to know the history of this place. After this initiative I went home and talked to my housemates, they didn't know anything about these stories. I mean I was the one who—as a foreigner—was telling them the history of their own home place!' The initiative exposed big gaps in the knowledge of people who had lived their entire lives in the city. It took a newcomer to explain that history, and by extension, to point out that the prosperity of Reggio Emilia relied in part on migrant labour. The city's heritage could not be fully appreciated without understanding migration.[1]

Obviously, this was a very specific initiative, albeit one that made a valiant effort to understand what brought migrants to a destination in Europe. Far more ambitious attempts have been made to cement the history of migration into the history of the nation-state. States that invested in migration can also invest in its commemoration. Whether they have taken that opportunity—and if so, what form it took, and whose interests it served—has largely depended on the politicians holding the purse strings. Without money or influence, migrants have had to rely on other means if they wanted to lay claim to their own past and challenge the top-down approach taken by the state.

Public museums act as powerful custodians of what is deemed to be national heritage, but they are more than just passive repositories of arte-facts. Museums help to shape public understanding of the nation and its place in the world. In his influential book on the nation as an 'imagined community', Benedict Anderson, a political scientist and historian, argued that the museum was central to the formation of the modern nation-state. Taking this insight in a fresh direction, the cultural critic Stuart Hall maintained that 'what the nation "means" is an on-going project, under constant reconstruction. We come to know its meaning partly *through* the objects and artefacts which have been made to stand for and symbolise its essential values.' This is a helpful concept for thinking about museums and migration.[2]

There is an emerging consensus among museologists that the museum is less 'about something' and more 'for somebody', yet little agreement as to where the history of migration and migrants belongs in the modern museum. Several museums are entirely devoted to migration—in Rome, Hamburg, and Bremerhaven, not to mention the famous Ellis Island Immigration Museum in New York and an impressive museum in Melbourne. But should migration be regarded as a separate element in the nation's collections? Alternatively, the history of migration can be inte-grated into mainstream museums, but this risks portraying migration as a sideshow. Whatever decision is reached, there remains the difficulty that a collection of material objects—photographs, maps, clothes, the means of transport, and so on—convey an anodyne message, telling the visitor little of the political and economic context in which migration took place, the motives of migrants, and the challenges they faced.[3]

Probably the most impressive museum in Europe dedicated to migra-tion is the Musée national de l'histoire de l'immigration (National Museum of the History of Immigration) in Paris, housed at the Palais de la Porte Dorée, an imposing edifice built in 1931 for the International

Colonial Exhibition. The building had a chequered history as a museum of 'France overseas' before closing its doors in 2003 and reopening in 2007 after lengthy preparations. The decision to use the Palais was significant, because it drew attention to France's colonial past as a key factor in contemporary migration. The organisers wanted to avoid what they felt to be the stultifying description of 'museum', preferring instead to describe it as a 'heritage space' that would provide a forum to debate migration. It was implicitly a slap in the face to the Front National, which had scored notable electoral gains in 2002. President Nicolas Sarkozy chose not to attend the opening ceremony despite being himself from an immigrant family, and the museum was only officially inaugurated in 2014, by Sarkozy's successor, François Hollande. With relatively little political impetus, it is not surprising to learn that the museum struggles to generate large visitor numbers compared to other major attractions in the French capital.[4]

Numbers are not everything, however. The museum made an important political statement. It advertised its purpose with the phrase 'leur histoire est notre histoire' (their history is our history), implicitly acknowledging a link between migrants and citizens. It spoke of a mission to 'construire le patrimoine de l'immigration' (build the heritage of immigration) under the banner 'la France arc-en-ciel' (France the rainbow). Permanent exhibitions advertise the contributions that immigrants have made to French society, such as their role in the success of the national football team, although inevitably, this positive narrative does little to celebrate the contributions of those who are not stellar or exemplary figures. The museum made a further political statement by accepting donations of items from migrant families and placing them in the permanent collections. One visitor found among the items on display a photo of the primary school he had attended in Mali; it had been funded by previous cohorts of migrant workers in France. Such displays reinforced the point that migration was part of the collective national heritage of France and that immigrants should no longer be 'invisible'.[5]

In 2010, the museum unexpectedly found itself at the centre of politics in a more tangible way. In the autumn of that year, a group of 500 so-called illegals (sans-papiers), mainly workers from Mali, occupied the building to protest the lengthy delays in the issuance of residents' permits even for those who had worked and paid taxes for many years. Their occupation of the building, which had the support of the powerful French trade union leadership of the Confédération générale du travail (CGT, General Confederation of Labour), lasted four months; it only came to an end when the government promised to speed up the processing of documents. The museum, seizing on the opportunity to incorporate this episode into its permanent collection, now displays the 'Bonzini'-style table football game (called 'foosball' in the United States) on which the occupiers whiled away the time. It did not go unnoticed that the game table was manufactured by a firm founded by Italian migrants. The whole episode demonstrated that museums are clearly more than their holdings: they can be a forum to assert migrants' rights, and even a site of resistance.[6]

Italy, like France, took steps to highlight the role of migration in the nation's history. The Museo nazionale dell'emigrazione italiana (National Museum of Italian Emigration) opened in 2009 in the heart of Rome. Its publicity materials said that 'migration has for many years been part and parcel of our everyday life, but it is still seen as a temporary phenomenon and arouses feelings of rejection'. The new museum aimed to do more than rehearse the well-known history of transatlantic departures from Italy:

> People all too easily forget how much the history of our country was shaped by emigration. . . . We must bow to the evidence — the great majority of immigrants are legally settled in Italy and well established in their working environment. Their children, often born in our country, attend Italian state schools. We must accept the fact that we are now, amidst many difficulties, a multiethnic and multicultural society: a colourful, though still very complex, society.

Critics complained about the comparisons between virtuous Italian emigrants and the newcomers who were seeking 'illegal' access to Italy in the new millennium. The Museo nazionale dell'emigrazione italiana closed in 2016, but it is scheduled to reopen in Genoa in 2020 as a permanent site. This did not deter other curators from documenting the history of migration, as in the permanent exhibition *MeM—Memoria e Migrazioni* (MEM—memory and migration), in the Galata Museo del Mare (Galata Maritime Museum), which suggested that migrants from North Africa had much in common with Italian guest workers in Switzerland and Belgium. But it was a reminder that any museum that makes a powerful political statement can easily court controversy.[7]

The political stakes in creating museums of migration were also evident in Germany, where the oft-repeated assertion that Germany was 'not a country of immigration' made it difficult to incorporate migrants' experiences in museums, let alone to get a dedicated migration museum off the ground. The topic of German expellees was an exception. The Federal Expellees Law in 1953 required the government and federal states to preserve the culture of the former eastern regions by supporting *Heimat* (Homeland) museums, with the emphasis on folklore and the German presence in territory since ceded to Poland and Czechoslovakia. Nevertheless, the long-term result was to cultivate a kind of cosmopolitan record: for example, the Silesian Museum in Görlitz, on the border with Poland, highlighted the history of the Silesian borderlands as a multiethnic region in which Germans, Poles, and Czechs coexisted for generations until the Second World War turned everything upside-down. A joint exhibition with the museum in Zgorzelec, the Polish town on the opposite side of the River Neisse, provided an opportunity to include other stories, too, including those of Polish settlers and the Greeks and Macedonians who arrived in the GDR during the Greek Civil War. If anything, the modern museum advertised diversity rather than a singular German cultural presence.[8]

In the late 1990s, the historian Klaus Bade and colleagues took things a step further, by devising a travelling exhibition around the theme of 'Foreigners in Germany, Germans Abroad' ('Fremde in Deutschland, Deutsche in der Fremde'). Their objective was to demonstrate that Germany's history of migration could be traced back to the late Middle Ages. Although the exhibition drew attention to the history of expulsion after the Second World War, it also emphasised the migration of guest workers and asylum seekers and their contributions to German society. Another initiative belonged to the Essen municipal museum and the Documentation Centre and Museum of Migration in Germany (DOMiD), founded in 1990 as the Documentation Centre and Museum of Migration from Turkey (DOMiT), a remarkable joint initiative that assembled an exhibition in 1998 under the banner of *Fremde Heimat* (Foreign home). The aim was to allow Turkish guest workers to speak of their experiences, but the broader purpose was to show that Turks were now fully accepted rather than merely tolerated in German society. Virtual museums are likely to become more prominent in cultural life as well. This is already becoming apparent in Germany, where DOMiD sponsors online exhibitions as part of its mission 'to make migration something normal' for a country of 80 million people, around 16 million of whom have a migrant background.[9]

Official initiatives can struggle to avoid blandness. In 2016, the fiftieth anniversary of the bilateral agreement between Austria and Yugoslavia on guest workers was an occasion for the Austrian political establishment to praise the 'contributions' of Yugoslav workers to the national economy and their successful 'integration'. But the exhibit with its happy ending made little of the original emphasis on rotating guest workers; still less did it address the arduous labour they undertook or their modest pay, their difficult living conditions, or the challenges of learning a new language. Nor did it really come to grips with contemporary migration: as one critic pointed out, 'not one of the displayed works scratched the surface of the correlations between those working conditions and today's "economic" migration or how the state tries to deal with it'. There was a missed opportunity to explain how, in relation to both guest workers and contemporary asylum seekers, the state controlled the terms of their admission and frequently left them to their own devices.[10]

Even more insipid is the small Musée Européen Schengen (European Museum Schengen) that opened in 2010. This museum, in Luxembourg, is devoted to supplying 'facts and meaning' in relation to the freedom of movement in the European Union. The museum's website asks, 'Who led the way? Which countries are participating? Historical photos and videos show the development of this idea.' Visitors are invited to 'learn more about the conditions and visa procedures for travellers from different countries'. In asking 'What is Schengen really?', the website answers that the town itself is 'a wine growing village [that] lives the European idea every day. Schengen welcomes you!' Visitors are encouraged to create their own 'Schengen passports' as souvenirs. Whether one regards the museum as an impressive statement about 'European values' or as a faintly absurd gesture, the fact remains that hardly anyone knows of its existence.[11]

Like the French museum that became the site of protest for *sans-papiers*, museums in Germany have sometimes provided a forum for activism, rather than just being sites to display inert objects. 'Crossing Munich' was an initiative of artists and ethnographers in 2009 who invited audiences to reflect on the significance of the city's main railway station as the point of arrival for hundreds of thousands of guest workers as well as the place from which buses departed to take them home. Another Munich-based project, 'GUESTures', described itself as 'a situative community curating'. Its objective was to enable migrant women from different generations and backgrounds to enjoy 'an event of encounters, joint-readings from the archive, and a discussion about history and the contemporaneity of lived migration'. The focus on women was especially noteworthy because it highlighted their specific experiences of being marginalised and exploited.[12]

A small museum of migration that foregrounds refugees is in the provincial town of Friedland in North Rhine–Westphalia. Friedland has served as the main transit centre (*Durchlandslager*) for successive generations of refugees and asylum seekers since 1945, when it stood at the intersection of the British, American, and Soviet zones of occupation. Some 4 million people have passed through the refugee camp there since the end of the Second World War, the majority of them ethnic German refugees from Eastern Europe, including current *Spätaussiedler* (recent resettlers) from the former Soviet Union. Friedland is also the transit point for Syrian refugees who arrive from Turkey under the terms of the deal struck between Turkey and the European Union. Small numbers of refugees from Afghanistan, Iraq, Eritrea, and Somalia also pass through on their way to being resettled in Germany. In 2015, Friedland housed 3,000 refugees, more than three times its normal capacity. The camp is not closed, and members of the public who wish to visit will often encounter refugees.

Among the purpose-built housing and other facilities is a replica Nissan hut (a Quonset hut for military use). Its somewhat incongruous presence is a reminder of the connection between past and present. The museum itself is located in the former railway station and houses a permanent exhibition, *Fluchtpunkt Friedland* (Friedland, place of refuge), providing a brief account of the camp as part of German, European, and global contemporary history. Among the photos of Friedland and its refugees, and their personal items—such as dolls, suitcases, and name tags—there are video interviews with people who passed through the town and newspaper clippings assembled by successive camp administrators. There are ambitious plans for a fully equipped learning centre. It is difficult to think of anything else in Europe of equivalent importance for the history of forced migration.[13]

Pro-refugee activists have resorted to other means to advertise the struggles of refugees to gain recognition. Reenactment is a favourite device to commemorate refugees' journeys that ended in disaster. For example, in 2010, pro-migrant Greek activists transformed the former refugee camp at Pagani on Lesvos into a temporary museum, titling the exhibition 'Traces from Lesvos through Europe'. In 2015, the German Zentrum für Politische Schönheit (ZPS, Centre for Political Beauty) created a more challenging installation in the heart of Berlin in the form of a 'burial of refugee bodies' outside the Reichstag. The ZPS describes itself as 'an assault team that establishes moral beauty, political poetry and human greatness while aiming to preserve humanitarianism. It engages in the most innovative forms of political performance art.' These dramatic and compelling initiatives clearly have made a political point, but in doing so they have appropriated the experiences of refugees rather than allowing refugees to speak for themselves. Refugees thus figured as mute victims.[14]

Obviously, refugees and other migrants do not usually command the resources to establish museums. Refugees, in particular, have more pressing issues to address. Many of them nevertheless have left traces on the landscape. Consider the example of Karelian refugees forced to leave their homes during the Second World War by the Soviet occupation. Following the collapse of the USSR in 1991, some of the adults who were evacuated to Finland as children in 1944 made pilgrimages to their former homes. One such group made its way to Inkilä (now Zaitseva) in 1997. As well as locating roads, fields, and buildings they had heard about from their parents, the group commented on the lack of attention the current residents devoted to their property. In 2006, several hundred elderly survivors began to retrace the steps they had taken half a century earlier; a freshly laid 'trail of the displaced' aimed to 'reawaken' memories and share them with the younger generation, who were expected to dress for the part to participate in the fifteen-kilometre walk. The reenactment insisted on 'authenticity', reproducing the emotional and bodily impact of displacement.[15]

The Catholic Church has sponsored regular pilgrimages of pieds-noirs, former French settlers, to their place of birth in Algeria, but there are even more numerous participants to shrines in France itself, such as the church of Notre Dame d'Afrique in Carnoux, home to an annual procession and vigil. As a recent study put it, 'the situation is marked by a mix between a certain level of control by those bent on maintaining the memory of crucial aspects of a shared history and emotional outpourings in which the sufferings of the past fuse with the joys of reunion'. The leaders of the pieds-noirs continually remind the French public of their displacement and of the public indifference they encountered in the years following Algerian independence. They called upon French newspapers, for example, to correct the assertion that the refugee crisis in Kosovo in the 1990s constituted the largest crisis of displacement since the Second World War, because that statement had overlooked the history of the pieds-noirs. Some politically active harkis, Algerian families that supported the French cause during the Algerian war for independence in 1954–1962, formed a 'community of memory' in which the divisions between Arabs and Berbers have been subsumed into a common 'experience' of displacement, underpinned also by an insistence that France betrayed and then abandoned them.[16]

Another way that migrants and refugees have commemorated their experience is through the creation of memory books. These become a tangible reminder of the places they left behind. Memory books have typically been created, preserved, and consulted privately, circulating among migrants and their descendants rather than more widely. A familiar feature of the testimony of Palestinian refugees and Holocaust survivors, they also figure in more recent upheavals. A memory book reconstructs a history of the village of origin, enumerates its former inhabitants and their dwelling places, and establishes an association between the displaced and their homes. Books compiled by Greek Cypriot refugees after the 1974 war in Cyprus, and by Bosnian refugees in the 1990s, are not mere gazetteers, but texts that associate place with sensory perceptions—the smell of the sea breeze, the taste of lemons, or the sight of a familiar shop. Like the keys to abandoned properties, memory books assert a claim to land that has been forfeited but might yet be restored. One such book commemorates the Bosnian Muslim town of Foča-on-Drina, whose sixteenth-century mosque was dynamited and turned into a car park in 1992. In 2014, work began on its restoration, with financial support from Turkey. In Finland, the former villagers of Inkilä published a memory book in 1982 titled *Muistojen Inkilä* (Memories of Inkilä). Family members had carefully retained documents that gave them the original title to their land in Karelia. They had taken a few sticks of rhubarb, some potatoes, and tomato seeds with them on their journey, and these now provide a steady crop and are much admired for their taste. This kind of memory work shows the trauma of forced migration and the emotional pull that 'home' can exert even after a long interval.[17]

It was not necessary to create memory books, however, to connect one generation of migrants to the next. First-generation Irish migrants to the UK began in the 1970s to look to the past in order to reflect on the meaning of being Irish. They wanted their children to take pride in their heritage. Like many Afro-Caribbean migrants, they did this because the British school curriculum failed to provide an adequate account of their history. Second-generation migrants asked what had made their parents venture in search of a new life and to reflect on what they found upon arrival. The children of Italian migrants who came to France in the 1950s organised an annual Italian film festival in Meurthe-et-Moselle. But this was anything but a sentimental endeavour. Instead, they regarded films about migration as an expression of 'cultural fury', an event to draw attention to the humiliation their parents had endured.[18]

At times, migration is also about silence and forgetting. Politics, for example, determined what it was possible to commemorate under communism, when Soviet censorship imposed a blanket ban on public discussion of forced migration. Under Soviet rule, discussion about the pain of deportation took place largely within a family setting where discretion could be more or less assured. But the end of communist rule provided an opportunity for Crimean Tatars to publicly commemorate the *kara gün*, or 'black day', marked by the arrival of government detachments in their villages with instructions to deport entire families to Central Asia. Latvian parents protected their children by telling them to keep quiet about having been forcibly uprooted in the late Stalin era. One woman, Anna (b. 1945), recalled that following the family's expulsion from Latvia in 1949, her parents told her, 'You mustn't speak about it.' Yet even when the political constraints were lifted in 1991, she added, 'I didn't bother to tell anyone, it seemed to me that there wasn't anything to boast about', a sign that keeping quiet was not necessarily linked to politics.[19]

Elsewhere, too, children bore the brunt of parental injunctions to say nothing. In Italy, in the wake of terrible floods in Calabria in 1951 and 1953, children were sent to the north of the country according to the political persuasion of their parents. The Italian Communist Party placed the children of communist couples with like-minded families, whilst the Catholic Church found homes for the offspring of devout parents. Sometimes the children were snatched from their homes for these evacuations at a moment's notice, and spent months or even years separated from their parents. The youngsters were expected to hold their tongues and not to discuss their experiences. One elderly informant, Maria, told an anthropologist, Stavroula Pipyrou, 'We couldn't speak about our experiences of relocation, my parents felt ashamed and so did we. We just had to deal with it internally.' In these circumstances, it seemed better to keep quiet about one's status in order to minimise social embarrassment. But the families remembered with some bitterness that the Italian state had failed to deliver on its promises of better housing and services in the impoverished south.[20]

The lifting of constraints on remembrance also emerged in Greece, where the legacy of war and civil war in the 1940s became etched on private memories and public consciousness. Here, even more than in Italy, rival political factions used children as ideological capital, a process known as *paidomazoma*, literally the 'gathering of children'. The children who were despatched by the Greek Communist Party to countries in Eastern Europe grew up with ambivalent feelings towards their places of birth. Having spent their formative years in Hungary, East Germany, or Yugoslavia, where they acquired a new language and received an education in what they described as a 'second homeland', many of them returned to Greece to face discrimination at the hands of the right-wing government. Villagers and family members gave them a frosty reception: 'Polonka', or 'Polish kid', was one of the generic nicknames for the returnees from Eastern Europe. Stefanos Gikas (a pseudonym) who was born in the early 1940s and evacuated to Budapest before returning to Greece in 1958, recalled an early childhood dominated not by political rivalries but by relentless poverty. When he went back home, he was dismayed by the persistent backwardness of his village: 'All they had was milk.'[21]

As the Italian case suggests, democratic states were equally capable of cultivating amnesia for political purposes. The Moroccan-born author Tahar Ben Jelloun told his readers that 'there are some memories that France likes to forget'. He justified his blistering account of racism in France by saying that he wrote it 'not to make a whole society feel guilty, but simply to bear witness to an era with its inconsistencies, mistakes and silences—an era and three players in it: the French state, the countries of the Maghreb, and the great mute never-consulted mass of immigrants'. He added that the responsibility for bearing witness, 'though most of it is usually attributed to France and the French, belongs to all concerned'. The issue was complicated by the assumption of the host society that in earlier times there had been no migration to disturb the status quo. The contemporary resonance of Ben Jelloun's claims emerged in 2018 in the story of a seventeen-year-old, Mathilde Edey Gamassou, the daughter of a Beninese father and Polish mother, who was chosen to play the part of Joan of Arc in the annual spring festivities in Orléans. No sooner had her name been announced than she was targeted on social media by the Front National as being an inappropriate choice on grounds of her migrant background and skin colour. The committee that selected her defended its decision: 'This girl was chosen for who she is; an interesting person and a lively spirit [who] responds to our four criteria: a resident of Orléans for ten years, a student in an Orléans high school, and a Catholic who also gives her time to others. She will deliver our French history to everyone, as have previous Joans before her.' The festival went ahead as planned, and the French prime minister, Édouard Philippe, made a point of greeting her in person as an illustration of *'l'intégration'*.[22]

The question remains as to how to commemorate recent disasters in which refugees have lost their lives. One compelling installation can be found in the Strait of Otranto, the site of the sinking of the *Kater i Radës* in 1997 that led to the death of eighty-one Albanians. Their remains were transferred to a cemetery in the Albanian port city of Vlorë, whilst the wrecked ship itself was abandoned in Brindisi, Italy, the Albanian government having refused to pay for its return. Fourteen years later, in 2011, a local NGO led by an Albanian woman persuaded the town council of Otranto to incorporate the wrecked ship in an installation entitled *L'approdo: Opera all'umanità migrante* (The landing: A monument to migrant humanity). The local authority saw the event as an opportunity to advertise Otranto as the 'point where peoples and cultures meet'. Promoting the installation, it drew attention to the tradition of Italian generosity and hospitality, even though the boat had sunk as a result of the actions of an Italian warship. A Greek sculptor, Costas Varotsos, cloaked the hull with sheets of translucent glass to give the appearance of ocean waves. The effect he wanted to create was of a boat that 'emerges and sails once again'. However, the aesthetic purpose did not include any discussion of how the migrants lost their lives, and moreover, there was not even a plaque to explain why it was there and what it stood for, let alone any indication of the names of the people who drowned. By 2014, unloved, it had become dilapidated.[23]

Other artists were drawn to the image of the boat as well, however. In 2017, a British sculptor, Kalliopi Lemos, created an installation that she called 'Pledges'. It took the form of a small sailing boat of the kind typically used by migrants to cross the Mediterranean. Lemos chose to cover the boat with hundreds of small metallic votive objects to evoke the hopes of migrants for a better life and their appeal for protection from the elements and other dangers. It stood for several months at the entrance to the Musée national de l'histoire de l'immigration in Paris and made an impressive statement.[24]

Lampedusa, the site of so many arrivals before and after 2015, now boasts a migration museum as well, Museo delle migrazioni (Museum of Migration), housing the belongings of migrants who never made it to a place of safety: toys, religious objects, shoes, and life vests. It was conceived as a *museo diffuso*, a 'conceptual museum', that drew attention to migrants' journeys and to the efforts of those who came to their rescue or who counted the bodies of victims. The symbolic purpose was to emphasise that the saved and the drowned, the rescuers and the bystanders, all belong to *Mare Nostrum*, 'Our Sea'. This striking image nevertheless failed to address the obvious point that crossing the sea posed a much greater risk for refugees than it did for ordinary travellers. The sea did not treat everyone equally.[25]

Lampedusa also came to London. In his final act of acquisition, the departing director of the British Museum, Neil MacGregor, decided to purchase a cross for the museum. It is described in 'Curator's comments' on the museum website:

> This cross is made from pieces of a boat that was wrecked on 11 October 2013 off the coast of Lampedusa. 311 Eritrean and Somali refugees were drowned en route from Libya to Europe. Inhabitants of Lampedusa helped to save the lives of 155 others. After meeting some of the survivors who are Eritrean Christians in the church on Lampedusa, Mr Tuccio, the island's carpenter, was moved by their plight but felt frustrated that he could not make a difference to their situation. The best he could do was to use his skills as a carpenter to fashion each of them a cross from the wreckage of the boat as a reflection on their salvation from the sea and hope for the future.... Mr Tuccio kindly made this piece for the British Museum to mark an extraordinary moment in European history and the fate of Eritrean Christians. It also stands witness to the kindness of the people of the small island of Lampedusa who have done what they can for the refugees and migrants who arrive on their shores.[26]

Here, a simple object with profound significance for those of Christian faith provided visitors to the museum with an opportunity to reflect on the humanity of refugees and those who came to their rescue on Lampedusa, even if—like so many objects in public museums—it fell short of explaining the motives that compelled refugees to embark on their dangerous journey.

One final installation also takes us to Lampedusa. *Porta d'Europa* (The gateway to Europe), a five-metre-high ceramic memorial designed by Mimmo Paladino, was built with funds donated by local people. The gateway looks out across the Mediterranean towards Tunisia. Unveiled in 2008, it gained greater publicity following a visit by UNHCR goodwill ambassador Angelina Jolie in 2011. Paladino attached various items to the sculpture to highlight the objects that refugees had abandoned or that had washed up on the shore, but like the numerous memorials to the dead of the two world wars, its main purpose was to commemorate the victims rather than to apportion responsibility for their death.[27]

The gateway is an appropriate vantage point from which visitors can contemplate whether the door to Europe remains open or is closed.

CHAPTER 24

Arab Spring, European Winter

MIGRANTS AND REFUGEES FROM Africa and the Middle East had been crossing the Mediterranean in large numbers since the 1990s, but the scale and pattern of migration changed dramatically following the turmoil of the 'Arab Spring' revolutions across North Africa in 2011. Established routes and destinations became more dangerous. Libya, for example, had long encouraged and supported a large number of migrant workers from Egypt, Tunisia, Nigeria, Chad, Eritrea, and other countries, but amidst the violence and political instability that followed the NATO bombing campaign and the overthrow of Muammar al-Gaddafi in October 2011, their situation changed overnight. Migrants were no longer welcome. Although European politicians and the mass media portrayed this as an issue affecting Europe, many migrants in Libya decided to go back home rather than make their way across the Mediterranean to Italy, even though returning to their country of origin held few attractions.[1]

The colossal upheavals in North Africa and in the Middle East took their toll not on Europe but on the Middle East, above all in Syria, where the civil war that flared up after 2011 displaced an estimated 5 million people. In the corridors of power in Brussels and elsewhere, this, too, was misleadingly portrayed as a European crisis. By 2015, some 3.5 million Syrians had crossed into Turkey, since this was realistically the only viable means of escaping Syria. Istanbul, a city of 20 million inhabitants, became home to some 600,000 Syrian refugees escaping from a combination of violence, persecution, and impoverishment. Others fled to Lebanon and Jordan. Many people were displaced within the borders of Syria itself. Relatively few Syrians made it to Europe: the total number of Syrian asylum seekers in Europe in 2015–2016 represented less than one-tenth of 1 percent of the total population of Europe.[2]

In fact, there were multiple drivers of global migration. Many asylum seekers were escaping from violence, but not only from civil war and the threat of being targeted by paramilitary groups: some were leaving because of the less visible but equally insidious persecution of ethnic minorities, or for reasons of religion or sexual orientation. These movements of people encompassed Rohingya refugees in Bangladesh, for example, as well as people caught up in the ongoing conflict in South Sudan. Most refugees never showed up anywhere near Europe but instead eked out an uncertain and risky existence in refugee camps or in impoverished settlements. Those who did make it to Europe, such as Kurdish refugees from Iraq, described the terror imposed by the rule of the Islamic State, including the fierce restrictions on women. Refugees from Eritrea cited different motives, including the likelihood of being conscripted at a young age with no prospect of a return to normal life. Rarely did outside observers acknowledge that forced migrants were resourceful and often highly educated. They opted to migrate in order to avoid drastic threats to their livelihoods, such as from extortion or conscription by governments or paramilitary groups, or as a result of unforeseen calamities for which they could not be held accountable. Migration offered a prospective route out of poverty for individual migrants as well as for family members left behind, who were unable to join them but counted on their remittances of cash to survive.[3]

Not all migrants regarded themselves as refugees, and not all of them regarded Europe as a final destination. Interviewed in Sicily in 2015, a migrant from the Ivory Coast explained that he had hoped to find a better life on the African continent, not in Europe:

My idea was not to reach Italy. I didn't know Italy if not for the football. I never thought to come in Europe, because here I have not family. My family is only in Ivory Coast and Burkina. But is my family who pushed me to go to Mali. In Mali there was a war, then I moved to Algeria, otherwise I would have stayed there. I wasn't lucky enough to stay in Algeria, if not I would have to stay there. I didn't want to go in Libya, the situation is too crazy to go there. It…[was] really hard to stay in Libya…all these circumstances pushed me to reach here. I went in Algeria and I failed. I went in Libya and there was the death.[4]

In the same vein, a Syrian refugee spoke in 2015 of his original aim: 'I just wanted to leave Syria. I wasn't thinking of going to Europe.' He found a job as a waiter in Istanbul but worked long hours for a pittance. He had no recognised refugee status in Turkey. When his young daughter fell ill, he could not take her to hospital 'because we were illegal'. At that point he and his pregnant wife decided to leave Turkey in the hope of finding a more secure life in Sweden.[5]

The experiences of migrants who followed complicated and hazardous routes were flattened by news reports that portrayed them as a 'wave' or 'flood'. The Arab Spring produced a wintry response in Europe, although the drama was given added urgency by the numbers of people arriving on European shores, particularly Greece, Italy, and Malta—or dying in the attempt. Between January 2014 and March 2018, around 1.8 million migrants entered EU countries via Mediterranean crossing points, with 16,000 reported as dead or missing. It became something of a cliché to describe this as an 'unprecedented' crisis that necessitated an emergency response. In truth, there were precedents in European history, most recently when Yugoslavia disintegrated. But 'crisis' helped induce a sense of panic among European voters. The discourse of 'emergency' encouraged a demand for action by governments without necessarily requiring anyone to think through the implications.

The prevailing atmosphere in Europe also had the disturbing consequence of effacing much of the experience of refugees in favour of the perspectives of the European Union and its individual member states. Where refugees emerged as an object of sympathy, it was as nameless victims rather than as real human beings. The brief but widespread attention given to the death of a three-year-old Syrian boy, Aylan Kurdi, whose body had washed up on a Turkish beach in September 2015 after his family attempted to cross to Greece in a small dinghy, became a humanitarian rallying cry. But the photographs of Aylan's lifeless body, taken by the journalist Nilüfer Demir, only contributed to a belief among European politicians that they should do more to deter people from attempting to leave Turkey, rather than convincing them to provide a safe passage for those who wished to do so. The blame for Aylan's death was laid at the hands of people-smugglers, a trick to disguise the lack of attention policy makers were giving to the root causes of forced migration.[6]

The European Union focused its attention on broad policy issues. One was the need to secure the external borders of the European Union whilst preserving freedom of movement between member states. Another was the need to address emerging divisions within the European Union. Maintaining the principles of Schengen was a key priority. In a speech at an EU summit in Malta in November 2015, the president of the European Council, Donald Tusk, described 'a race against time' to save the principle of freedom of movement, in the face of actions by member states to check the documents of people crossing from one EU country to another, lest African or Syrian migrants make their way unhindered, as Sweden claimed was happening on ferries from Germany. Denmark and Norway suspended Schengen for three months, citing 'a big influx of persons seeking international protection'. At the same summit, Hungary accused the German government of returning asylum seekers to the Hungarian border, although a strict interpretation of the provisions of the Dublin Regulations entitled it to act in this way.[7]

In January 2016, several European ministers with responsibility for home affairs urged the suspension of the Schengen Agreement in order to prevent refugees from leaving Greece. The Greek minister responsible for EU affairs called this a 'hysterical' suggestion, which to his mind implied the return of an 'Iron Curtain' mentality in European diplomacy. 'This isn't EU integration, this is EU fragmentation', he declared. But his appeal to EU solidarity was really a defence of Greece's own interests in offloading refugees.[8]

Securing the borders of the European Union was not a new policy priority, but it garnered greater attention when governments in late 2016 began increasingly to link migration to terror, specifically attacks being prepared by the Islamic State. The European Counter Terrorism Centre issued a press release to this effect, along with a report on the Islamic State's tactics of radicalising Syrian refugees and sending its own fighters to Europe with fake refugee papers. No matter how small the scale of these tactics, nothing was better calculated to inflame attitudes towards migrants from the Middle East or North Africa. Their stigmatisation was complete.[9]

Divisions within the European Union were exposed most clearly by geography. Greece and Italy became known as 'frontline' states, as they had to deal with the immediate consequences of people claiming asylum, particularly in the Greek islands close to Turkey or on Lampedusa. A pledge by EU member states in September 2015 to relocate 160,000 asylum seekers, including 106,000 from Greece and Italy, produced meagre results.[10]

Faced with more and more people seeking asylum, European governments responded in an ad hoc fashion. In 2015, asylum seekers who crossed from Serbia into Hungary demanded the right to board trains heading west, but were prevented from doing so by the refusal of Austria and Germany to admit them, on the grounds that they were the responsibility of Hungary. Thousands of migrants—Afghans, Bangladeshis, Iranians, Iraqis, Pakistanis, and Syrians—congregated at Budapest's main railway station, where, undeterred by overcrowding and unsanitary conditions, they hoped to leave Hungary, since the alternative was to accept incarceration in one of Hungary's proliferating refugee centres. The so-called March of Hope to the Austrian border took place in September 2015, following the discovery in the previous month of a refrigerated lorry in a car park in Vienna that contained the decomposing bodies of seventy-one people, mainly Syrian and Iraqi, who had suffocated in the sealed compartment. The marchers encountered a variety of reactions. Neo-Nazis, ironically but not surprisingly, supported their demands, in order to be rid of them. Hungarian Jews adopted an ambivalent attitude: some referred to the Holocaust and expressed sympathy, and even solidarity, with people who were in desperate straits, while others took the view that Muslim asylum seekers represented a kind of existential threat to their way of life.[11]

The limited extent of EU solidarity was exposed by the leaders of other member states who ramped up the rhetoric of national self-interest. EU proposals for a mandatory organised redistribution of refugees came unstuck when Hungary, Poland, and the Czech Republic announced that they would not participate in any agreement to share the burden, challenging the proposal in the European Court of Justice. The resistance to burden-sharing was led by chorus master Viktor Orbán, the Hungarian prime minister. Dialling up the volume of rhetoric, he insisted: 'If we want to stop this mass migration, we must first of all curb Brussels. The main danger to Europe's future does not come from those who want to come here, but from Brussels' fanatics of internationalism.' He denounced what he regarded as the European Union's interference in Hungary's affairs in relation to migration, specifically, any proposal for mandatory quotas for asylum seekers. He also went ahead and built a fence between Hungary and Serbia. In a speech delivered on Independence Day, 15 March 2016, he invoked the history of Hungary's struggle for freedom, first from the Habsburg Empire and then from Soviet domination. Orbán ended with a call to assert the country's sovereignty in the face of what he took to be the intolerable imposition of political demands by the European Union, hence the reference to 'Brussels'.[12]

In the autumn of 2017, Hungary's challenge failed in the ECJ. The Hungarian foreign minister, Péter Szijjártó, condemned the court for 'jeopardising the security and future of all of Europe'. Ratcheting up the rhetoric, he added that 'politics has raped European law and values'. His outlandish statement sat oddly with the relatively modest number of asylum seekers who lodged claims in Hungary. A group of artists told their fellow citizens that they were more likely to see UFOs in their lifetime than migrants. Perhaps this explained why Orbán's referendum to ask for public endorsement of his stance was something of a fiasco: 90 percent of those who voted supported his position, but most people either abstained or deliberately spoiled their ballot papers.[13]

Nevertheless, Orbán weathered the storm and eventually got his way. At the end of 2017, Donald Tusk, the European Council president, acknowledged that mandatory quotas to accept refugees were 'divisive and ineffective'. In addition to placating the governments that refused to take in any refugees, Tusk recommended spending more on schemes to keep Syrian refugees in Turkey and to deter African refugees from attempting the Mediterranean crossing from Libya. Refugees paid the price for the failure of EU member states to agree on reasonable measures to protect and resettle them.[14]

All the while, the situation in the frontline states continued to deteriorate. Officials on the Greek islands of Chios, Kos, Leros, Lesvos, and Samos, which were close to Turkish shores, reported that they were 'overwhelmed'. This was partly the result of an influx of more migrants and the refusal of others to leave the islands until their asylum claims had been processed. In November 2016, fires broke out in heavily congested refugee camps, such as at Moria on Lesvos, where an Iraqi Kurdish woman and her six-year-old grandson were burnt to death when a cooking gas canister exploded in their tent. According to an aid worker, Fotini Rantsiou, fires were a regular hazard, the result of migrants trying to keep warm or cook in their tents; some were started deliberately in protest at the EU-Turkey deal struck earlier that year, which envisaged that most refugees would be processed and returned to Turkey. Refugees often asked her the same question: 'Will this help open the borders?' Some asylum seekers went on hunger strikes; others literally sewed their lips together to protest being held in disused army barracks and old industrial sites. Women routinely suffered attacks. Unaccompanied minors were sometimes registered as adults and placed in detention. The only thing to be said in favour of these makeshift camps was that they fostered an impressive degree of solidarity on the part of refugees.[15]

Owing to a lack of staff, asylum interviews took months to schedule. This suited the Greek government, which hoped that claimants would become impatient and return to their countries of origin. The government also expelled asylum seekers to Turkey, where they faced being returned home before their claims for asylum could be heard. A survey carried out at the end of 2015 found that most of the refugees from Afghanistan, Iran, Iraq, Pakistan, and Syria who had arrived in Greece wanted to move on because of the poor living conditions they endured. They hoped to make their way to Sweden or Germany—although this predated Angela Merkel's 'open-door' policy.[16]

The situation in Greece was truly alarming. At the height of the so-called refugee crisis, the Greek government was immersed in bailout negotiations designed to stabilise the economy. The financial problems made it especially difficult to find the resources to coordinate its response to what appeared to be the unstoppable arrival of refugees in the eastern Mediterranean. Far-right politicians argued that Greece should 'flood' the European Union with asylum seekers unless the European Commission backed down over its demand that Greece tackle its budget deficit. The racist 'Golden Dawn' party harked back to an imagined past in which Greece 'belonged' exclusively to ethnic Greeks. Ironically, it found allies among Albanian migrants who had endured racist attacks in the 1990s, but who now vented their anger on newly arrived asylum seekers from the Middle East.[17]

Against this fractious and shifting backdrop, locals complained that government funds were being diverted to support asylum seekers rather than to help Greek citizens: according to Lenio Capsaskis, who researched access to the Greek health-care system for refugees and migrants, the challenges facing refugees were 'similar to those faced by poorer Greeks'. It did not help that some of the international organisations that descended on Greece with large budgets treated hard-pressed local Greek aid workers in a high-handed manner. Those representing the international organisations urged the local workers to accelerate their attempts to process refugees' claims for asylum and deport those who did not qualify. Close observers of the scene, such as on the island of Samos, described conditions as chaotic.[18]

Stories also surfaced of the suffering and taunts that refugees received at the hands of unsympathetic Greeks. Nicos Georgoulis, the editor of the island's daily paper, maintained that Chios—which is a short boat ride away from Turkey, and at various times has had its national ownership contested between the two states—could not afford to allow a Muslim minority to settle on the island. He believed that the refugees would be used by Turkey's president, Recep Tayyip Erdoğan, as 'a fifth column and a pretext for seizing the island'. He added that 'Pakistani boys have been seen holding hands with local girls and in the future half the kindergarten will be blacks and children of migrants'. It did not take much to transform understandable concerns about a shortage of resources into a divisive and racist rhetoric.[19]

The same kind of language circulated among conservative and far-right Italian politicians, who described their country as the 'soft underbelly' and a 'magnet' for prospective migrants, particularly those from sub-Saharan Africa and the Horn of Africa. They complained about the unequal 'burden' that Italy was being asked to bear, particularly as a result of the Dublin Regulations. The increasingly powerful Movimento 5 Stelle (M5S, Five Star Movement), an Italian political party generally described as 'anti-establishment' and 'anti-immigration', demanded the complete overhaul of the rules so that asylum seekers could be distributed across the European Union instead of being obliged to stay in the country where they first arrived. It was indicative of the heightened diplomatic stakes that Italy insisted its frontiers were 'European, not merely Italian', and that other EU states should share responsibility for assisting people claiming asylum.[20]

Here, too, policy was governed less by humanitarian considerations than by a desire to keep migrants at bay. Frontex representatives were on hand in Italy to interview new arrivals, in order to establish who was a 'refugee' and who was an 'economic migrant'. The line of questioning created confusion in the minds of the people subject to interrogation, who answered yes when they were asked if they hoped to work in Italy. A young man from the Ivory Coast who sought asylum was caught out and told to leave Italy immediately, although it appeared that his response reflected a sense of gratitude and a wish to contribute to a country in which he felt safe at last.[21]

Torment found its most extreme expression in stories of the struggle to simply survive rather than drown in the attempt to gain a foothold on Europe's shores. Migrants from Syria, Afghanistan, and sub-Saharan Africa had put themselves in the hands of people-smugglers and embarked upon dangerous journeys across the Mediterranean or the Aegean Sea or via land routes. The ordeal of migration took many forms. Malick Jeng, a nineteen-year-old from Gambia, told a harrowing story of being ferried across the desert in Mali inside an oil tank, where he almost suffocated. On arriving in Libya, he was held prisoner, and escaped only when his family back home paid a ransom. Malick managed to survive the boat crossing. He was transferred to Catania in March 2016 and later to Biella, a city in the north of Italy, where he settled in a temporary reception centre called Hotel Colibri, the hotel itself having closed down ten years ago. Mamadouba, a boy from Guinea, made it to a reception centre in France, where he testified to an arduous journey and the hope he invested in being allowed to stay: 'Italy and France are two hearts with one lung: Italy rescued me from the sea, France has given me the hope to live', he wrote.[22]

Efforts to deter migrants by strengthening the Libyan coast guard, providing its forces with extra boats and training, had little impact, at least not of the kind intended. In 2015, the European Union's Operation Sophia, designed to intercept migrant boats in the open waters of the Mediterranean, ended up putting money in the pockets of the very people-smugglers whose networks it was supposed to disrupt, and who were reportedly in league with the Libyan coast guard. In June 2017, the Italian government reported fresh measures to block the arrival of boats carrying migrants from ports in North Africa after around 72,000 migrants arrived in Italy by sea in the first half of that year, a 20 percent increase on the same period in 2016. More than 2,000 people died in the attempt. In line with its commitment to deterrence, and in order to appease domestic public opinion, Italy signed an agreement in 2017 with the provisional government in Libya to turn back boats, even if they were found outside Libyan territorial waters. The Italian view, shared by politicians in the UK and elsewhere, was that search-and-rescue missions simply acted as a 'pull factor' and encouraged people-smugglers. The UNHCR had a decade earlier criticised the Italian government's actions as contrary to the 1951 Refugee Convention, which forbade the return of asylum seekers whose claims had not been properly adjudicated, and these concerns now resurfaced. Some NGOs went along with the new code of conduct, including the Migrant Offshore Aid Station (MOAS), which rescued over 35,000 migrants in the Mediterranean in 2017. MOAS used drones to track migrants and took them aboard its own vessels before transporting them to Italy for temporary assistance. Other NGOs, such as Médecins sans Frontières, refused to sign on the grounds that the code flouted international refugee law and contravened the law of the sea. MOAS then quickly reversed its earlier policy, telling its supporters that 'we cannot in good conscience take part in a process that will actively send the vulnerable people we rescue back into harm's way'.[23]

In 2018, a newly formed Italian government created an impasse when it refused the French NGO SOS Méditerranée permission to dock its sponsored vessel *Aquarius* after it had saved people from drowning. Malta had likewise turned the vessel away. Indeed, only a humanitarian gesture from Spain provided a way out. But here, too, right-wing politicians tapped into growing public antipathy: 'We need to control our external borders if we want to travel around Europe without a passport', said Albert Rivera, the leader of Spain's Citizens' Party, Ciudadanos, in July 2018. This statement echoed the remarks of the new interior minister in Italy, Matteo Salvini, who cultivated his reputation as a strongman who would make life difficult for asylum seekers and refuse rescue boats permission to land in Italy. By the end of 2018, he had clamped down on asylum seekers by restricting 'humanitarian protection', making it more likely that they would be evicted from the accommodation made available by government. The result was a standoff with civic leaders who objected to an abuse of human rights.[24]

Lost in all these discussions were the views of refugees themselves. Syrian refugees wishing to leave Turkey had two main options: either to access one of the Greek islands by boat, or to take the overland route into Greece, which entailed crossing the Evros River by inflatable dinghy. Both options carried risks of capture or capsizing. Those who made it across the Evros were often pushed back, as had happened before, in 2012. Nineteen-year-old Linda (not her real name), a Syrian refugee who hoped to join her fiancé in Denmark, was one of the unlucky ones who was returned to Istanbul. She gave up hope of making another attempt to cross into Greece and being detained at the border: 'I started being afraid because of the things I saw', she told a reporter in October 2018.[25]

Hundreds of thousands of refugees continued in their determined quest to reach Europe. A Syrian-born law student, Ghaith, for example, was in Damascus when the political opposition to the Assad regime turned into a brutal civil war in 2012. The prospect of being conscripted into the Syrian army convinced him that it was time to get out and attempt to join his brother in Sweden. He eventually succeeded, having travelled via Lebanon, Turkey, Greece, Macedonia, Serbia, Hungary, Austria, and Germany, but this litany of countries hardly begins to do justice to the obstacles, peril, and humiliation he went through, not to mention his enforced reliance on people-smugglers. Ghaith described how asylum seekers who did not want to be trapped in the first EU member state they reached (as per the Dublin Regulations) would burn their fingertips to avoid being registered. Ghaith's testimony also drew attention to the profile of Syrian refugees: many of them were students or professionals, such as doctors, dentists, lawyers, and engineers. In that sense, they were not unlike Jewish refugees from Nazi Germany or the Hungarian refugees who fled their country in 1956.[26]

Refugees who reached Europe shared the view of the governments in Italy and Greece that they should be allowed to move on. The difficulty here was that the European Union had already established the principle that 'genuine' refugees would lodge a claim for asylum in the first country of entry—and would continue to adhere to it. For many refugees from Syria and Afghanistan, this preferred procedure meant claiming asylum in Greece and being registered, fingerprinted, and required to hand over biometric information to Eurodac, the main EU database. If they made a claim anywhere else in the European Union, they would automatically be returned to Greece in accordance with the Dublin Regulations. This outcome did not appeal to them, given the economic situation in Greece and the hostile atmosphere to which they were exposed. Reem, a twenty-nine-year-old Syrian refugee, fled Syria with her family in September 2013. They travelled to Sweden via Jordan, Libya, and Italy, using her savings to pay smugglers and to buy airline tickets. They were unaware that the Dublin Regulations made her ineligible to stay in Sweden, where she had family and friends. In 2016, the family was sent back to Italy: 'Here [in Rome] we are alone. We do not know anyone. We hope that God gives us the strength to start again.'[27]

In 2018, EU leaders collectively took further steps to shift responsibility 'upstream' by adopting more rigorous measures to externalise the adjudication of claims for asylum so that migrants would not turn up on Europe's doorstep without an invitation. There was talk of 'regional disembarkation platforms' and 'joint processing centres' offshore. This ghastly terminology was dreamt up to suggest that migration was under control.

European politicians now appeared to be playing a game of leapfrog to decide which of them could carry off the prize of chief gatekeeper. The Austrian chancellor, Sebastian Kurz, proposed that migrants should be sent back from the European Union's external border to 'safe zones' in Africa, without considering their claims for refugee status, a proposal that flew in the face of international refugee law. His Danish counterpart, Lars Løkke Rasmussen, favoured relocating failed asylum seekers outside the European Union, in 'undesirable' parts of Europe.[28]

The war on refugees continued. Already in February 2016, the Danish government had announced its intention to confiscate personal items from newly arrived asylum seekers, including any cash and valuables amounting to more than 10,000 kroner (equivalent to £1,000, or approximately US$1,400), in order to cover the costs of their accommodation. This formed part of a raft of deterrent or punitive measures, including the provision that asylum seekers would have to wait for up to three years before they could apply to be joined by family members. To put this in context, Denmark processed just 20,000 asylum applications in 2015. It would be difficult to find a more blatant disregard for the human rights of people who feared being persecuted in their country of origin. At the end of 2018, the Danish immigration minister, Inger Støjberg, announced plans—agreeing with the far-right Dansk Folkeparti (Danish People's Party), whose support the government needed in order to pass its budget— to relocate failed asylum seekers to a remote island that houses a research centre into contagious animal diseases.[29]

Germany appeared to buck the trend. Between 2012 and 2015, Germany took in 230,000 Syrian refugees. Angela Merkel, herself a 'migrant' from former East Germany, welcomed them with a famous phrase designed to reassure both the electorate and the refugees: 'Wir schaffen das' (We'll manage). Her words echoed the remarks of German politicians who, coming face to face with expellees, sought to reassure them that Germany would be able to cope. Germany's president, Joachim Gauck (who, like Merkel, had been born in East Germany, and thus was familiar with the costs of political upheaval), remarked in June 2015 that Germans were themselves refugees in 1945: 'Let us remember what a great part refugees and forced migrants played in successfully rebuilding Germany.' He did so against the backdrop of rising anti-migration sentiment. Gauck invoked the past to suggest that the country had a moral duty to assist refugees.[30]

But there were limits to German generosity. The federal government imposed restrictions on freedom of movement and on employment, at least until claims had been assessed. Emergency aid took the form of assistance in-kind rather than cash payments, partly in order to deter migrants from staying on. Syrian refugees were housed in former US Army bases, such as the one in Mannheim, known as Benjamin Franklin Village. By late 2015, the purpose of German policy was to make life uncomfortable for asylum seekers. Following a series of sexual assaults, including by foreign nationals, in Cologne and Hamburg on New Year's Eve, public opinion shifted further to the right. More than 1,000 attacks on refugee settlements were reported in early 2016. The rise of Alternative für Deutschland (AfD) was an important political factor. The AfD took every opportunity to express anti-immigration sentiment in ways calculated to detach itself radically from mainstream political opinion, as with the slogan, for example, 'Der Islam ist nicht Teil von Deutschland' (Islam is not a part of Germany). These opinions went hand in hand with an uncompromising critique of EU policy. Perhaps not surprisingly, the AfD split in 2015, when some members rejected its overtly anti-immigration stance on the grounds that it was bad for business.[31]

Not everything went in the direction of restriction and deterrence. A key development was the expansion of the Bundesamt für Migration und Flüchtlinge (BAMF, Federal Office for Migration and Refugees) from a staff of 2,800 in the spring of 2015 to 10,000 at the end of 2016. The BAMF implemented a series of regulations that formed part of the new Integration Act. The government encouraged recognised refugees to take up training opportunities, and it assigned them a place to live. The BAMF required refugees to enrol in German language classes, along with orientation classes to learn about German history and culture. But refugees who failed to comply lost some of their government benefits, and it was significant that the 'integration' pages of the BAMF website, stressing the need to acquire a working knowledge of the German language, were only available in German. Commercial firms also became involved. The *Wir Zusammen* (We Together) initiative, launched in 2016 by the Internet entrepreneur Ralph Dommermuth, committed members to assist refugees through apprenticeships, internships, and mentoring schemes to facilitate their integration. More than thirty-six companies, including Bosch, Lufthansa, Thyssen-Krupp, and Volkswagen, participated. This was a public relations exercise, but the initiative boasted success stories, and corporate giants talked about the responsibilities they felt they had towards refugees. As one executive said: 'Refugees, helpers, these are not categories—we are all people, and as such we can present the common face of Germany.'[32]

In a notable literary intervention, a novel by Jenny Erpenbeck, *Gehen, Ging, Gegangen* (*Go, Went, Gone*), tells of a retired classics professor, Richard, in Berlin. Seeing a group of refugees in the midst of a hunger strike in a large plaza in the city, his compassion is aroused. He later befriends them, listening to their stories and becoming involved in their lives, including fighting in their corner when they encounter an obdurate bureaucracy. Richard himself was displaced twice earlier in life, first in 1945 and again after 1989. Ultimately, however, he recognises that there is only so much that one person can do: 'When did he turn from a man filled with great hopes for mankind into an almsgiver?' Erpenbeck's novel drew on current events. Asylum seekers did indeed begin to use public spaces not only as somewhere to live but also to draw attention to their plight. They set up tent cities in Berlin in 2015, for example, to protest poor living conditions and restrictions on their ability to work. These actions were also accompanied by demonstrations organised by the far right, denouncing government inaction.[33]

Responding to internal divisions within her cabinet—and in order to stem the advance of the far right—Angela Merkel agreed in July 2018 to close the Bavarian border to asylum seekers arriving from Austria who had already lodged claims for asylum in other countries. Her government proposed new 'anchor centres' to process existing claims as quickly as possible and to deport anyone without a valid claim. In a compound outside

Ingolstadt housing more than 1,000 migrants from the Balkans, Ukraine, Nigeria, and Afghanistan whose claims for asylum were being considered, one Nigerian, Raphael, described being in a 'prison' in which crime was rife. According to an aid worker with the Catholic charity Caritas, 'these transit centres are like black boxes; the local population isn't allowed to go inside, so they project all their greatest fears into what is going on inside. Three years ago, Germany was globally admired for its welcoming culture. What has happened to that culture? Now there is only fear of refugees.'[34]

Elsewhere, too, public opinion turned against migrants. The Italian city of Pistoia, for example, prided itself on its left-wing political tradition and had welcomed Albanian migrants two decades earlier, but public opinion shifted by 2016. According to a local councillor, Italy's centre-left leaders were 'paying for their top-down, elitist approach to migration'. A proposed reception centre faced mounting opposition: 'We have a lot of young people who are going to the United States or somewhere else because there's no work', said a member of a local group. 'And here you have people who have no education, no qualifications. What are they going to do here?' Near the proposed site, a local politician ran a community centre tied to a left-wing local organisation and agreed that 'migration makes the town richer'. But, in the face of economic difficulties, he agreed that 'people looking for a job ought to be able to find one in their own countries, rather than looking for them in countries like ours, where we struggle to find places for our own people'. Across Italy, local leaders continued to insist that they had been abandoned by politicians who controlled the purse strings. Nationalist politicians, in turn, competed to demonise 'illegal' migrants and to propose a network of new detention centres in lieu of unofficial camps.[35]

The mood was no better in other countries. More than half of those polled in early 2018 in Bulgaria, Hungary, Malta, and Slovakia thought immigration was a problem. 'Bulgaria doesn't need uneducated refugees', said Valeri Simeonov, leader of the United Patriots, an anti-immigrant party. He also had no interest in attracting educated and skilled foreign workers, who, in his words, 'have a different culture, different religion, even different daily habits. Thank God, Bulgaria so far is one of the most well defended countries from Europe's immigrant influx'. Countries whose citizens were less likely to come into contact with immigrants tended to be the ones where the public was most sceptical about their value to society, although this did not explain public opinion in Greece and Italy, where attitudes hardened in response to events in the Mediterranean.[36]

In France and Britain, political debate was consumed by the so-called migration crisis, with northern France once more the focal point. Calais remained a node for migrants hopeful of getting to the UK. In October 2016, when the Calais camp was once more demolished, its residents were scattered across France. They left behind a brand new wall that the British government built at great expense to deter refugees from accessing trucks travelling on the main road to Calais. Demolishing the 'Jungle' signalled a paralysis of policy. As historian Jessica Reinisch put it, 'the debate between proponents of a humanitarian idea to help vulnerable people in need, and those who argue that perceived and actual harshness in their treatment can deter new arrivals, is as paralysing as it has always been'.[37]

Under a relocation scheme devised by Alf Dubs, a member of the House of Lords who had been rescued from Nazi-occupied Czechoslovakia as part of the Kindertransport, the British government agreed to accept 3,000 unaccompanied child refugees as an amendment to its new Immigration Bill, but it ended up admitting only a tenth of that number. The Home Office offered no explanation for refusing individual applications, but its general line was that the admission of unaccompanied children could encourage their parents to apply subsequently, on grounds of family reunion. Children deemed ineligible for consideration either repeated their attempts to cross from Calais into the UK without authorisation or simply disappeared from view. The whole sorry saga was yet another depressing manifestation of the failure of policy makers to think beyond deterrence.[38]

There were plenty of other camps elsewhere in Europe. All too often, supposedly temporary measures to accommodate migrants who applied for asylum turned into long-term facilities—refugee camps in all but name. In Serbia, Iranians who entered on tourist visas in 2019, claiming asylum on grounds of political opinion, religion, or sexual orientation, were held in 'asylum centres', such as the Miksalište refugee centre in Belgrade. On the other side of the continent, the Irish government set aside places in what it called a 'Direct Provision Centre' in Mosney, County Meath, originally the first Butlin's holiday camp outside the UK. By 2017 it housed more than 700 asylum seekers from 39 different countries. Prevented from seeking paid work and receiving only a modest cash allowance, they felt humiliated and marginalised.[39]

To be sure, there were isolated examples of local action that offered something other than the usual combination of apathy and hostility, as when refugees were resettled in depopulated villages in places such as Sutera, Sicily, indicating that the survival of the one could contribute to the revival of the other. Gaetano Nicastro, the son of Sicilian emigrants, sees a neat symmetry in the programme: 'Here we have been dealing with integration for 2,000 years, and if then Sutera was the "salvation" for many foreigners, well, guess what? Today, the true salvation of Sutera is the refugees.'[40]

But the default position was deterrence, detention, and deportation. Resourceful migrants were not deterred, but they were liable to be incarcerated and sent back. In the winter of 2018–2019, human rights organisations and the Office of the UN High Commissioner for Human Rights issued devastating reports on the situation in Libya, where migrants were being held in abysmal conditions. For those in Libya, the situation in which migrants found themselves beggared belief. As refugees sought sanctuary, and camps dotted the landscape as they did in 1945, it seemed as if Europe had come full circle. Today's refugee camps, along with detention centres and other bureaucratic facilities, are reminiscent of the arrangements devised for refugees in the aftermath of the Second World War. Then, as now, refugees were held in transit spaces prior to their repatriation. But today's leaders take steps to slam the door in the face of migrants who are compelled to adopt the riskiest courses of action in order to achieve their aims. One Tunisian migrant detained in Italy in 2012 argued that 'the Earth belongs to everyone. If I want to breathe the oxygen of Italy, I breathe the oxygen of Italy.' Unhappily for him, this meant the air inside a detention centre.[41]

Conclusion

In the summer of 2018, Walpurga Sternad, who runs a restaurant with her husband near the highway connecting Austria and Slovenia, recollected the events of October 2015, when, following the closure of Hungary's border with Austria, around 6,000 migrants crossed from Slovenia into Austria at the crossing point in Spielfeld: 'So many people. They kept coming. They should just close all the borders in Europe, go back to what we used to have.' A group of friends nodded in approval. They made no effort to understand the motives of the migrants, many of them refugees from conflict zones in Syria and Afghanistan. Instead, Sternad added, 'It was scary', not stopping to acknowledge that the migrants themselves were scared, and for good reason. Harking back to a time of imagined stability and security, she seemed to have forgotten everything that had happened in Europe since the Second World War: the dramatic shifts of borders and people, the restrictions imposed by the Cold War, and the refugee crisis on her doorstep when Yugoslavia broke apart, forcing 3 million people from their homes.[1]

In this book I have sought to explain why I see things differently. I have shown that the history of migration in and to Europe is multilayered and open-ended: it provides many examples of political division and disagreement but also of cooperation between states. As well as examining the aims and policies of politicians and others in positions of influence, and the depiction of migration by writers and filmmakers, I have also been attentive to the motives, aspirations, and experiences of migrants. Their history cannot be forced into a single mould: the ordinary movement of people takes place alongside the extraordinary and the unexpected. In thinking about how migrants have negotiated the obstacles and opportunities, I cannot improve on the point made by the renowned Canadian historian Natalie Zemon Davis: 'We can take heart from the fact that no matter how dire the situation, some will find means to resist, some will find means to cope, and some will remember and tell stories about what happened.' She adds, 'I have wanted to be a historian of hope.'[2]

Like many of its migrants, Europe has travelled a great distance since 1945, from being a continent wracked by violence and political division to becoming a more peaceful and prosperous place. Europe was devastated by the Second World War. Fresh disruption was unleashed afterwards and the ground shifted beneath the feet of millions of people: compulsory population transfers and territorial realignments in the wake of war told a story of Europeans forcing other Europeans from their homes. The prolonged division of Europe along Cold War lines separated families. Refugees took life-changing decisions to flee to the West, and escapees from communism risked their lives to cross the Iron Curtain.

By the early 1950s, Europe had recovered and began to embark on two decades of sustained economic growth. Whether they crossed international borders or moved as internal migrants from the countryside to the city, migrants played a full part in this transformation. They responded to government schemes of organised recruitment or made their own way to new destinations in search of economic betterment, sometimes in clandestine fashion, to escape authoritarian rule of the kind imposed by dictators such as Franco in Spain and Salazar in Portugal. The positive results became apparent throughout Western and Eastern Europe. Economically backward regions and countries gained from the remittances that migrants sent back home. Although the economic miracle did not last, many guest workers and other migrants decided to stay on in Western Europe. In creating new households, they helped make Europe a more diverse place.

When the bitter schism of the Cold War finally ended in 1989, migration was again an integral part of the transformation, opening up opportunities for people to move between East and West with far less hindrance. To be sure, this was not a straightforward trajectory. Although there is certainly a positive story to tell about the scope for freedom of movement in Eastern Europe, particularly when several ex–Soviet bloc countries joined the European Union in 2004, migrants faced fresh obstacles. For example, Ukrainians who could previously move across the Polish border with relative ease were now confronted with a new and harder border.

The current 'migration crisis' ought to be understood as part of this convoluted history. From a standpoint in 2019, the nation-state seems to be a resurgent force, placing greater emphasis on the need to protect its borders, and, in the process, unsettling migrants through policies of deterrence and detention. The momentum of European integration with its emphasis on freedom of movement appears to have stalled, typified by the new fence built on the border between Austria and Slovenia, both of them belonging to the Schengen area. In the second decade of the new millennium, parliamentary elections across Europe have generated a renewed sense of anger about the presence of migrants and the changes they have sometimes made to host communities. In 2016, the Brexit vote in the UK turned in large part on a suspicion that migrant workers were taking jobs from British workers and putting an intolerable strain on public services. Those in favour of Brexit argued that it provided an opportunity to avert, in the words of the demographer David Coleman, 'a further source of inflow' of migrants from Eastern Europe. Missing from much of the public debate was any recognition of the contribution that migrant workers made to the public purse, for example, or the fact that Latvians, Poles, Ukrainians, and Italians had participated in the economic reconstruction of the UK after 1945. The same blind spots formed part of election campaigns in Austria, Germany, Italy, the Netherlands, and other European countries whose wealth was also founded in part on migrant labour. The heightened political temperature confronts migrants once more with the painful reality of prejudice and suspicion.[3]

Contemporary discussions of migration are imbued with apprehension around numbers and security. The presence of undocumented migrants has fuelled anxiety that migration to Europe has spun out of control. Surveillance and control have been sustained by new technologies, such as biometric passports, and the imposition of sanctions on airlines, ferry companies, and other businesses that have failed to check travel documents. Insofar as migrants have succeeded in circumventing these controls, sometimes with the help of unscrupulous employers and people-smugglers, their actions feed a sense of panic. In today's contentious political atmosphere, the news media feeds paranoia, particularly around Islam. At its most extreme, opponents of migration invoke the spectre of Islamic fundamentalism and a permanent terror threat.[4]

Europe's preoccupation with 'terror' has discounted the persecution from which many migrants have sought to escape. The terror they face can come in various guises, most obviously by being embroiled in war and finding oneself on the defeated side. This was true of thousands of Moluccans of Muslim faith who were exposed to violence in Indonesia and sought sanctuary in the Netherlands in 1951, and of Algerian harkis who fled to France at the moment of Algerian independence in July 1962. In more recent times, the war in the former Yugoslavia terrorised Bosnian Muslims who ended up being scattered far and wide. It is not disrespectful to the victims of Islamist terrorist attacks in Europe to point out that great violence has also been done to Muslims in and beyond Europe.

There has always been a strong emotional element to debates over migration. Apprehension about migration and migrants is not new. It has taken a variety of forms throughout history. Migrants have been called 'backward', as happened to Turkish guest workers in Germany who were assumed to be unfamiliar with Western plumbing and telephones. Irish and West Indian newcomers in postwar Britain were accused of adding to urban overcrowding and noise. Migrants have often been the first to be suspected of criminal activity, although they were much more likely to be the victims than the perpetrators of crime. Migrants have been accused of importing infectious disease, but again, the bigger story is about the risks to which they have been exposed, such as industrial accidents, substandard housing, and the stress of being separated from loved ones and being subjected to racial abuse.

Certainly, it is unwise to generalise about public opinion in Europe: attitudes can be quite volatile and contradictory. But migrants are constantly confronted with three fundamental questions by a suspicious host society: Who are you, what are you doing here, and whose side are you on? In his famous book on the experiences of guest workers, John Berger suggested that a migrant 'is seen differently and sees differently'. Decades later, his observation remains as pertinent as ever.[5]

Where does this leave policy making in 2019? In particular, is it possible to contemplate a politics that is different from what the political scientist Ivan Krastev calls a 'barricaded continent'? Attempts by the European Union to formulate a collective response to the repercussions of war and deprivation in parts of the Middle East and North Africa have foundered, and governments instead have adopted a series of ad hoc measures to protect their borders and to reassert national sovereignty. The EU ideal of freedom of movement was badly tarnished by the decision to reinstate border controls. The Dublin Regulations on asylum all but broke down in 2011 amidst the surge in applications in Italy, Greece, and Spain, and to a lesser extent in Malta, the points at which migrants reached Europe via the Mediterranean. However, EU governments agreed on one thing, namely, the need to relocate 'Europe' by externalising its borders to prevent asylum seekers from entering the legal jurisdiction of destination countries, whether or not their claim to refugee status had merit.[6]

There were earlier kinds of barricades, too, in the form of detention camps in which asylum seekers were held for months, or even years, whilst their claims were considered, as in the Spanish enclaves of Ceuta and Melilla in North Africa during the 1990s. Historically, camps served a short-term purpose, as in the case of the refugees and escapees from Eastern Europe in the late 1940s and early 1950s, the Algerian harkis and pieds-noirs who were hurriedly transported to metropolitan France in 1962, or the Ugandan Asians who arrived in Britain virtually overnight in 1972. But the camps never went away, and they continue to keep migrants in limbo, as they had been in the 'Calais Jungle'. Migration and incarceration have always worked in tandem as authorities struggle to determine who will be eligible for admission and who will be deemed unworthy.

Nor does the image of the barricade tell the whole story. It fails to consider the cautious and self-serving policies of individual states that have favoured the filter over the fortress. Today's leaders discriminate between 'desirable' and 'less desirable' migrants, just as Western Europe's postwar governments chose workers who were thought most likely to contribute to economic growth and rejected others. But the filter has been modified. Nowadays, European governments discriminate by privileging so-called high-net-worth individuals, who can cross international borders with relative ease. By contrast, in the wake of the Second World War, Western governments scoured the Displaced Persons camps and competed with one another for physically fit manual workers who could do backbreaking work: the bricklayer, not the banker, was the desirable migrant.

The history of Europe and its migrants draws attention to the ways in which governments have facilitated migration as much as they have worked to curb it. This happened on both sides of the Iron Curtain. Rebuilding Eastern Europe involved internal migration on a massive scale, as in Nikita Khrushchev's Virgin Lands Campaign in the USSR in the 1950s. That effort was touted as being of historic importance to the Soviet Union because it would transform the country's agriculture through extensive Russian settlement in Central Asia. As in Western Europe, reconstruction also required urban planning as migrants poured from the countryside into factory towns. However, not everything could be planned: the informal Soviet economy offered a route for migrants to make money, but many migrants, as well as those people left behind in the 'dying village', had to bear the social and emotional costs themselves, with a minimum level of support. No one (and nowhere) escaped the associated upheaval.

In Portugal, as in France, Italy, the Netherlands, and the UK, the history of migration was closely associated with decolonisation. Decolonisation brought *retornados* to the metropolis of Lisbon and attracted generations of nonwhite workers from Mozambique, Cape Verde, and other former colonial possessions. The political scientist Mahmood Mamdani, who was forced to leave Uganda in 1972 and seek refuge in the UK, captured the essence of these connections very well: 'The colonial child had come to the motherland. And he had brought with him England's colonial past. Past had become present.' Likewise, migration to and from and within postwar Italy demonstrated the many crosscurrents of migration; it was driven not only by uneven regional opportunities and by demand from Italy's economically more buoyant neighbours, but also by the subsequent arrival of migrants from Albania, Eritrea, and Libya, countries that were formerly part of Mussolini's empire. When a Turin newspaper commented in 1989 that 'Italy is changing its skin', it acknowledged that past colonial ties exerted a continuing influence on the pattern of migration.[7]

Where do other nation-states fit in? In Poland and Hungary, for example, escape from the domination of the Soviet state expressed itself in the assertion of national sovereignty. By the second decade of the twenty-first century, the leaders of these countries were unwilling to take lessons from anyone else, least of all from the European Union. Hungary is a member state of the European Union, but the country's leaders have refused to subscribe unconditionally to the EU's core values. In the words of Hungarian prime minister Viktor Orbán in March 2016: 'It is forbidden to say that the masses of people coming from different civilisations pose a threat to our way of life, our culture, our customs, and our Christian traditions. It is forbidden to say that the purpose of settling these people here is to redraw the religious and cultural map of Europe and to reconfigure its ethnic foundations, thereby eliminating nation-states.' This rhetoric was deliberately intended to outrage liberals in Hungary, a country that had provided sanctuary to Bosnian Muslims two decades earlier. It was no accident that he spoke of the nation-state as in peril, underscoring his belief that its foundations rested on ethnic homogeneity. This implied that migration, unless it be the migration of Hungarians, was a curse — and even the 'return' of Hungarians to Hungary had its downside, according to many locals.[8]

It would be interesting to know what Orbán would make of the elderly German who had been expelled from Hungary after the Second World War and who told his interviewer, 'When I am in Hungary, I often say: "I am going home to Germany". And when I am in Germany: "I am going home to Hungary". But I would not say I am Hungarian and neither would I say I am German....Some say we are European, but it does not feel right to me to narrow it down like that. So [I say]: "I am human".[9]

The stories of other individual migrants suggest that their experiences are rarely straightforward. Many migrants have escaped from peril—powerful firsthand accounts by Modris Eksteins, Dulce Maria Cardoso, Zahia Rahmani, Shahram Khosravi, Ali Hassan, and others testify to the urgent necessity to flee from state violence. But what about those who have escaped from an oppressive family situation? Migration is often determined not by government action but by migrants themselves, who activate personal connections and kinship ties in pursuit of new opportunities. Sometimes migration is a matter of pure chance. A family crisis might require a member to migrate, to stay behind, or to return home. A migrant might decide to follow a partner to another country, a reminder that migration can be about love as well as hate.

What is remembered, and by whom, and what has been forgotten in relation to migration? Migration might be commemorated or forgotten, depending on what has suited the interests of political and civic leaders. Migrants have been expected to yield to the claims of the nation-state to arbitrate as to what belongs in its museums, where migrants themselves have usually been neither seen nor heard. Nevertheless, this has not prevented them from articulating their experiences on behalf of their own communities, and indeed, from using their own resources to challenge the state's monopoly on the nation's past. We can see this in the personal accounts of migrants as well as in their attempts to get museums to represent the history of migration more adequately: in the contested terrain of history, migrants demand that the history of their forebears be given proper public recognition. But they again run up against the gatekeepers of the nation-state.

What lessons can we draw about migration in and to Europe? The first and most obvious one derives from the fact that in the second part of the twentieth century the continent as a whole became much richer than it had been in 1945. Migrants supported this economic growth and prosperity in Eastern and Western Europe alike as workers, savers, taxpayers, and spenders, even if the precise impact remains a matter of dispute. Although opponents of immigration focus on migrants taking jobs, in reality migrants often create new jobs, particularly in the service sector. They have made an indispensable contribution to European prosperity, but—unless they were internal migrants—have not been expected to extract their full share of the gains in production or the benefits of social welfare.

A second lesson can be drawn from the fact that migration runs along different channels. Migrants are correspondingly assigned different names: 'economic migrants', 'refugees', 'illegals', and so on. Although states classify migrants in this way and might aim to control the channels of migration, either on their own or in collaboration with partners, such as happened with guest worker programmes, this can be a fruitless pursuit and one that is sometimes derailed. Governments in the twentieth and early twenty-first centuries have sometimes been confronted by unexpected events beyond Europe, such as wars and other catastrophes, that gave non-European refugees powerful inducements to seek admission, particularly when the alternative was to stay put and risk persecution or worse. The refugees have been caught in the middle: forced to leave their homes, required to demonstrate that they had suffered persecution, but uncertain of effective protection in the place where they sought sanctuary. Their lives are put on hold. Recent events in Europe expose fresh divisions over how to manage those who wait at the gate: nation-states continue to assert their sovereignty, undermining efforts to find common ground to address the 'refugee crisis' and seeking to shift responsibility for managing asylum seekers onto countries outside Europe. Contrary to the impression created by much of the European news media, the vast majority of refugees never show up on the doorstep of Europe in the first place.

A third lesson concerns the role of nation-states in creating and perpetuating migration crises. The nation-state responds to crisis, but it can itself be the source of crisis. Newly formed nation-states have asserted their sovereignty by determining who belonged to the nation and who did not. Doing this has sometimes taken a very violent turn. This lesson takes us back to 1945, and to the persecutions and expulsions of ethnic minorities in East-Central Europe in the pursuit of greater ethnic homogeneity. Fast-forward to 1991, when the disintegration of the Soviet Union, and even more, the dramatic collapse of Yugoslavia, contributed to the mass displacement of people who faced an uncertain future. We can read the legacy of decolonisation in the same light. Colonial settlers and other elites in the newly independent states of the global South were made unwelcome: this happened in places as far apart as Indonesia, Algeria, and Uganda, with the result that European states had to manage unexpected crises of migration.

The uneasy adjustment brought about by the formation of new states was compounded by hostility, sometimes from unexpected quarters—think, for example, of the difficulties that ethnic German expellees faced from fellow Germans in postwar West Germany; of pieds-noirs from Algeria who were mistreated by mainland French; and of Kazakhs who returned to independent Kazakhstan to a chorus of disapproval. These and other migrants, such as the Karelians who moved to Finland, the Pontic Greeks who moved from Russia to Greece, and the Bulgarian Turks who resettled in Turkey, were marginalised and sometimes demonised, even when they felt that their common ethnicity with those among whom they settled entitled them to a claim to be recognised and supported in their hour of need. This is not about the numbers of migrants involved, but about host societies that magnified cultural differences in order to protect an imagined national community and, so to speak, to keep migrants in their place.

History also points to a fourth, related lesson—the fact that issues of identity are never far from the surface where migrants are concerned. Migrants frequently link identity to their place of birth and to their ethnicity, both as a source of pride and as a means of security in the face of uncertainty or hostility. Governments rarely consult migrants as to their wishes and needs when drafting policy. In these circumstances, it is hardly surprising that collective associations of migrants have enabled them to navigate an unfamiliar environment. Host societies might look at this activity as a refusal to 'assimilate', but how else could migrants make a reasonable life for themselves? Time and again they have demonstrated a capacity for self-help and resourcefulness, either individually or collectively through migrant or diaspora associations, to cushion the consequences of living far from home and in order to improve their prospects. In joint efforts they have sought to be allowed to participate as fully as possible in social and political life and for acceptance of cultural and religious differences — in short, to be given basic rights.

I began this book with the image of boats, and it is to this image that I return. Boats carrying migrants across the Mediterranean sometimes capsize, with tragic consequences. The capsizing boat makes me think about 'upset', which is another way of thinking about migration in post-1945 Europe. Migration can be unsettling, in the sense of severing personal ties and having to forge new relationships, and upsetting, in its psychological effects on the people who migrate and those who are left behind. It can also unsettle the society where they arrive.

A different image, that of the bridge, suggests an alternative perspective. Bridges invite us to think about the possibility of connecting people and places, enabling migrants to maintain contact and to move back and forth individually or in groups between their place of origin and their destinations. If all goes well, the bridge will be secure, well built, and carefully maintained. But there are risks. Bridges might topple for lack of proper investment, or be blockaded or torn down, as a result of xenophobia. But without bridges to connect different places and people, to enable new economic opportunities and facilitate new cultural encounters, and to make it possible for at least some refugees to seek sanctuary, Europe's history would have looked very different. The continent as a whole would have been much impoverished: less unsettled, perhaps, but greatly diminished.

Notes

Introduction: A European Retrospective

1. John Brown, *The Un-melting Pot: An English Town and Its Immigrants* (London: Macmillan, 1970), 47.
2. Vincent Crapanzano, *The Harkis: The Wound That Never Heals* (Chicago: Chicago University Press, 2011), 113.
3. Irial Glynn, *Asylum Policy, Boat People and Political Discourse: Boats, Votes and Asylum in Australia and Italy* (Basingstoke: Palgrave Macmillan, 2016); Lynda Mannik, ed., *Migration by Boat: Discourses of Trauma, Exclusion and Survival* (New York: Berghahn, 2016).
4. On the pre-1945 history of Western Europe, see Leslie Page Moch, *Moving Europeans: Migration in Western Europe Since 1650*, 2nd ed. (Bloomington: Indiana University Press, 2003); Saskia Sassen, *Guests and Aliens* (New York: New Press, 1999).
5. Sam Selvon, *The Lonely Londoners* (London: Alan Wingate, 1956), reissued by Penguin Modern Classics in 2006.
6. Jennifer A. Miller, 'On Track for West Germany: Turkish "Guest Worker" Rail Transportation to West Germany in the Post-War Period', *German History* 30, no. 4 (2012): 570.
7. Caroline Roux, 'Ingvar Kamprad Obituary: Swedish Business Magnate Who Founded IKEA', *The Guardian*, 28 January 2018, https://www.theguardian.com/business/2018/jan/28/ingvar-kamprad-obituary.
8. World Council of Churches (WCC hereafter) Archives, Geneva, File 425.1.043, 'Human Interest Stories'. I have omitted his full name.
9. Georges Rochau, 'Intra-European Migration in the Last Three Years', *Migration News*, no. 1 (1965): 6–11.
10. Philipp Ther, *Europe Since 1989: A History* (Princeton, NJ: Princeton University Press, 2016).

11. Eugene M. Kulischer, *Europe on the Move: War and Population Changes, 1917–1947* (New York: Columbia University Press, 1948), 289.

12. Sarah Dyer, Linda McDowell, and Adina Banitzky, 'The Impact of Migration on the Gendering of Service Work: The Case of a West London Hotel', *Gender, Work and Organization* 17, no. 6 (2010): 635–657; Wolf R. Böhning, 'International Migration in Western Europe: Reflections on the Past Five Years', *International Labour Review* 118, no. 4 (1979): 401–414.

13. Vijf Eeuwen Migratie (Five Centuries of Migration), www.vijfeeuwenmigratie.nl /sites/default/files/bronnen/Deel%20I%20Molukkers.pdf; quotation on 27, courtesy of Hans Wallage.

14. Richard Black, Godfried Engbersen, Marek Okólski, and Cristina Panţîru, eds., *A Continent Moving West? EU Enlargement and Labour Migration from Central and Eastern Europe* (Amsterdam: Amsterdam University Press, 2010), 7.

15. John Berger, *Into Their Labours: Pig Earth, Once in Europa, and Lilac and Flag. A Trilogy* (London: Granta Books, 1992), 25.

16. Jon Holbrook, 'Time to Tear Up the Refugee Convention', 15 September 2015, available at https://www.spiked-online.com/2015/09/15/time-to-tear-up-the-refugee-con vention.

17. 'Germany Remembers Racist 1992 Firebombing', Deutsche Welle, 23 November 2012, www.dw.com/en/germany-remembers-racist-1992-firebombing/a-16402637.

18. Quoted in Nicholas De Genova, introduction to De Genova, ed., *The Borders of 'Europe': Autonomy of Migration, Tactics of Bordering* (Durham, NC: Duke University Press, 2017), 1.

19. Walter Laqueur terms them 'foreign communities'. He is particularly exercised by nonwhite 'delinquent youth'. Walter Laqueur, *The Last Days of Europe: Epitaph for an Old Continent* (New York: St Martin's Press, 2007), 15, 35; Douglas Murray, *The Strange Death of Europe: Immigration, Identity, Islam* (London: Bloomsbury Continuum, 2018).

20. Gary Freeman, *Immigrant Labor and Racial Conflict in Industrial Societies: The French and British Experience, 1945–1975* (Princeton, NJ: Princeton University Press, 1979); Christian Joppke, *Immigration and the Nation-State: The United States, Germany, and the UK* (Oxford: Oxford University Press, 1999); Hein De Haas, Mathias Czaika, Marie-Laurence Flahaux, Edo Mahendra, Katharina Natter, Simona Vezzoli, and María Villares-Varela, *International Migration: Trends, Determinants and Policy Effects*, IMI Working Paper no. 141 (2018).

21. According to the European Commission report, 'Results of Special Eurobarometer on Integration of Immigrants in the European Union', 13 April 2018, https://ec.europa .eu/home-affairs/news/results-special-eurobarometer-integration-immigrants -european-union_en.

Chapter 1: Forced Migration in Europe: Changing Places

1. G. Daniel Cohen, *In War's Wake: Europe's Displaced Persons in the Post-War Order* (New York: Oxford University Press, 2012), 21.

2. Keith Lowe, *Savage Continent: Europe in the Aftermath of World War II* (London: Penguin, 2013), 27–33, 212–248.

3. Modris Eksteins, *Walking Since Daybreak: A Story of Eastern Europe, World War 2, and the Heart of Our Century* (Boston: Houghton Mifflin, 1999), x.

4. Tadeusz Borowski, *This Way for the Gas, Ladies and Gentlemen* (Harmondsworth: Penguin, 1992), 164; Lowe, *Savage Continent*, 28.

5. Agate Nesaule, *A Woman in Amber: Healing the Trauma of War and Exile* (New York: Penguin, 1997). As it happens, her parents had already been forced from their home in Latvia during the First World War before returning to newly independent Latvia.

6. Hans-Ulrich Treichel, *Lost* (New York: Vintage, 2000).

7. Janics Kálman, *Czechoslovak Policy and the Hungarian Minority, 1945–1948* (New York: Columbia University Press, 1982), 152.

8. Speech to House of Commons, 15 December 1944, cited in Philipp Ther and Ana Siljak, eds., *Redrawing Nations: Ethnic Cleansing in East-Central Europe, 1944–1948* (Oxford: Rowman and Littlefield, 2001), 78; Gomułka quoted in Norman Naimark, *Fires of Hatred: Ethnic Cleansing in Twentieth-Century Europe* (Cambridge, MA: Harvard University Press, 2001), 124.

9. Elizabeth Wiskemann, *Germany's Eastern Neighbours: Problems Relating to the Oder-Neisse Line and the Czech Frontier Regions* (London: Oxford University Press, 1956), 67; Eagle Glassheim, *Cleansing the Czechoslovak Borderlands: Migration, Environment, and Health in the Former Sudetenland* (Pittsburgh: University of Pittsburgh Press, 2017), 11, 42.

10. Joseph B. Schechtman, *Postwar Population Transfers in Europe, 1945–1955* (Philadelphia: University of Pennsylvania Press, 1962), 67; Glassheim, *Cleansing the Czechoslovak Borderlands*, 49; Jacques Vernant, *The Refugee in the Post-War World* (London: Allen and Unwin, 1953), 95–96. This figure does not take account of Germans who were deported to the Soviet Union; nor does it include the arrival of ethnic Germans in Austria. Tara Zahra, *The Great Departure: Mass Migration from Eastern Europe and the Making of the Free World* (New York: Norton, 2016), 198–204.

11. 'Gebiet und Bevölkerung', in *Statistisches Jahrbuch für die Bundesrepublik Deutschland*, 1952, courtesy of Anna Holian; Michael Schwartz, 'Refugees and Expellees in the Soviet Zone of Germany: Political and Social Problems of Their Integration, 1945–50', *Journal of Communist Studies and Transition Politics* 16, nos. 1–2 (2000): 148.

12. Catherine Gousseff, *Échanger les peuples: Le déplacement des minorités aux confins polono-soviétiques, 1944–1947* (Paris: Fayard, 2015).

13. Timothy Snyder, *The Reconstruction of Nations: Poland, Ukraine, Lithuania, Belarus, 1569–1999* (New Haven, CT: Yale University Press, 2003), 193; Orest Subtelny, 'Expulsion, Resettlement, Civil Strife: The Fate of Poland's Ukrainians, 1944–1947', in Ther and Siljak, eds., *Redrawing Nations*, 166–168.

14. Theodore R. Weeks, 'Repopulating Vilnius, 1939–49', in Tomas Balkelis and Violete Davoliūtė, eds., *Population Displacement in Lithuania in the Twentieth Century: Experiences, Identities, Legacies* (Leiden: Brill, 2016), 135–159.

15. Eugene M. Kulischer, *Europe on the Move: War and Population Changes, 1917–1947* (New York: Columbia University Press, 1948), 288–289; Schechtman, *Postwar Population Transfers*, 141–142; Kálman, *Czechoslovak Policy*, 152–172.

16. Kulischer, *Europe on the Move*, 288; Schechtman, *Postwar Population Transfers*, 44–47.

17. Schechtman, *Postwar Population Transfers*, 351–352. The Turkish government refused to admit Roma from Bulgaria.

18. Huey L. Kostanick, *Turkish Resettlement of Bulgarian Turks, 1950–1953* (Berkeley: University of California Press, 1957); Schechtman, *Postwar Population Transfers*, 358.

19. Under this agreement, Finland ceded Karelia, Samia, and Petsamo to the Soviet Union.

20. I owe this point to Seija Jalagin.

21. Heikki Waris, *Siirtoväen sopeutuminen: Tutkimus Suomen Karjalaisen siirtoväen sosiaalisesta sopeutumisesta* (Helsinki: Otava, 1952); Matti Sarvimäki, 'The Unexpected Consequences of Forced Migration', *CentrePiece*, Autumn 2009, 24–26.

22. Schechtman, *European Population Transfers*, 399; Cecilia Notini Burch, *A Cold War Pursuit: Soviet Refugees in Sweden, 1945–54* (Stockholm: Santérus Academic Press, 2014), 167; information about their return after the Soviet collapse courtesy of Seija Jalagin.

23. Toini Gustafsson, *Från adresslapp till guldmedalj* (Stockholm: Bonnier, 1969), 18; Annu Edvardsen, *Det får inte hända igen: Finska krigsbarn, 1939–1945* (Stockholm: Askild and Kärnekull, 1977), 11–12; Ann-Maj Danielsen, *Att inte höra till: Ett finskt krigsbarn berättar* (Falun: B. Wahlströms, 2000), 35–36; Jean Cronstedt, *Krigsbarn Gymnasist Läkare: Mitt liv i fyra världsdelar* (Trelleborg: Eget Förlag, 2001), 36.

24. Aira Bengtson, *Kabblekor* (Örby: self-published, 2010), 224.

25. Johan Svanberg, 'The Contrasts of Migration Narratives: From Germany to the Swedish Garment Industry During the 1950s', *Journal of Migration History* 3, no. 1 (2017): 145.

26. Glenda Sluga, *The Problem of Trieste and the Italo-Yugoslav Border: Difference, Identity, and Sovereignty in Twentieth-Century Europe* (Albany: State University of New York Press, 2001), 90; Pamela Ballinger, 'At the Borders of Force: Violence, Refugees and the Reconfiguration of the Yugoslav and Italian States', *Past and Present*, suppl. 6 (2011): 158–176.

27. Silvia Salvatici, 'Between National and International Mandates: Displaced Persons and Refugees in Post-War Italy', *Journal of Contemporary History* 49, no. 4 (2014): 514–536; Ballinger, 'At the Borders of Force', 170–172; Gloria Nemec, 'The Redefinition of Gender Roles and Family Structures Among Istrian Peasant Families in Trieste, 1954–64', *Modern Italy* 9, no. 1 (2004): 35–46.

28. Pamela Ballinger, *History in Exile: Memory and Identity at the Borders of the Balkans* (Princeton, NJ: Princeton University Press, 2003), 13; Pamela Ballinger, ' "Entangled" or "Extruded" Histories? Displacement, National Refugees, and Repatriation After the Second World War', *Journal of Refugee Studies* 25, no. 3 (2012): 366–386.

29. Theodora Dragostinova, *Between Two Motherlands: Nationality and Emigration Among the Greeks of Bulgaria, 1900–1949* (Ithaca, NY: Cornell University Press, 2011), 255–256; Stefan Troebst, 'Evacuation to a Cold Country: Child Refugees from the Greek Civil War in the German Democratic Republic, 1949–1989', *Nationalities Papers* 32, no. 3 (2004): 675–691.

30. From an interview conducted with Danilo Sarenac in Pančevo, Serbia, 11 September 2016, quoted with the permission of interviewee and interviewer; Loring M. Danforth and Riki van Boeschoten, *Children of the Greek Civil War: Refugees and the Politics of Memory* (Chicago: Chicago University Press, 2011), 137–146, 194; Milan

Ristovic, *A Long Journey Home: Greek Refugee Children in Yugoslavia, 1948–1960* (Thessaloniki: Institute for Balkan Studies, 2000); Mando Dalianis and Mark Mazower, 'Children in Turmoil During the Civil War: Today's Adults', in Mark Mazower, ed., *After the War Was Over: Reconstructing the Family, Nation, and States in Greece, 1943–1960* (Princeton, NJ: Princeton University Press, 2000), 91–104. Greece and Bulgaria did not resume diplomatic relations until 1964.

31. Bálint András Varga, *Conversations with Iannis Xenakis* (London: Faber and Faber, 1996), 47.
32. Matthew Frank, *Expelling the Germans: British Opinion and Post-1945 Population Transfer in Context* (Oxford: Oxford University Press, 2007).
33. 'The Refugee Problem Today' (August 1948), WCC Archives, File 425.2.010 ICA and Refugee Division.

Chapter 2: Migrants in Limbo: Displaced Persons in Postwar Europe

1. Courtesy of Kasia Nowak.
2. Jessica Reinisch, '"We Shall Rebuild Anew a Powerful Nation": UNRRA, Internationalism and National Reconstruction in Poland', *Journal of Contemporary History* 43, no. 3 (2008): 451–476; Mark Wyman, *DPs: Europe's Displaced Persons, 1945–1951* (Ithaca, NY: Cornell University Press, 1998), 40; Ben Shephard, *The Long Road Home: The Aftermath of the Second World War* (London: Bodley Head, 2010); Malcolm J. Proudfoot, *European Refugees, 1939–1952: A Study in Forced Population Movement* (London: Faber and Faber, 1957), 197; Shephard, *Long Road Home*, 72.
3. Proudfoot, *European Refugees*, 190, 219.
4. Seth Bernstein, 'Ambiguous Homecoming: Retribution, Exploitation and the Return of Repatriates to the USSR, 1944–46', *Past and Present* 242, no. 1 (2019): 201.
5. Iu. A. Arzamaskin, *Zalozhniki vtoroi mirovoi voiny: Repatriatsiia sovetskikh grazhdan v 1944–1953 gg* (Moscow: Stanitsa, 2001), 10–12, 54, 64–65; Nick Baron, 'Remaking Soviet Society: The Filtration of Returnees from Nazi Germany', in Peter Gatrell and Nick Baron, eds., *Warlands: Population Resettlement and State Reconstruction in the Soviet–East European Borderlands, 1945–1950* (Basingstoke: Palgrave Macmillan, 2009), 89–116; Sheila Fitzpatrick, 'The Motherland Calls: "Soft" Repatriation of Soviet Citizens from Europe, 1945–1953', *Journal of Modern History* 90, no. 2 (2018): 323–350; Bernstein, 'Ambiguous Homecoming', 215.
6. John Gibson, quoted in Linda McDowell, *Hard Labour: The Hidden Voices of Latvian Migrant 'Volunteer' Workers* (London: UCL Press, 2005), 38; *International Migration, 1945–1957* (Geneva: International Labour Organisation, 1959), 44–45.
7. Laura J. Hilton, 'Who Was "Worthy"? How Empathy Drove Policy Decisions About the Uprooted in Occupied Germany, 1945–1948', *Holocaust and Genocide Studies* 32, no. 1 (2018): 13; Arzamaskin, *Zalozhniki vtoroi mirovoi voiny*, 92–93; Marta Dyczok, *The Grand Alliance and Ukrainian Refugees* (Basingstoke: Macmillan, 2000), 131.
8. Proudfoot, *European Refugees*, 238–239; Statement by M. Langer, chief of the Polish repatriation mission, 25 June 1946, courtesy of Kasia Nowak.
9. Laura J. Hilton, 'Pawns on a Chessboard? Polish DPs and Repatriation from the US Zone of Occupation of Germany, 1945–49', in Johannes-Dieter Steinert and Inge Weber-Newth, eds., *Beyond Camps and Forced Labour* (Osnabrück: Secolo Verlag, 2005), 90–102; Shephard, *Long Road Home*, 239–240.

10. G. Daniel Cohen, *In War's Wake: Europe's Displaced Persons in the Post-War Order* (New York: Oxford University Press, 2012), 6, 15, 37; Mark Edele, Sheila Fitzpatrick, and Atina Grossmann, eds., *Shelter from the Holocaust: Rethinking Jewish Survival in the Soviet Union* (Detroit: Wayne State University Press, 2017).

11. Colonel C.A. Nelson, quoted in William Hitchcock, *Liberation: The Bitter Road to Freedom, Europe 1944–1945* (London: Faber and Faber, 2009), 332, 327.

12. Proudfoot, *European Refugees*, 225; Shephard, *Long Road Home*, 78–82; John Corsellis, *Slovenia 1945: Memories of Death and Survival After World War 2* (London: I. B. Tauris, 2005).

13. Dyczok, *Grand Alliance*, 129.

14. My thanks to Laure Humbert for confirming this point; see also Laure Humbert, 'French Politics of Relief and International Aid: France, UNRRA and the Rescue of Eastern European Displaced Persons in Post-War Germany, 1945–47', *Journal of Contemporary History* 51, no. 3 (2016): 606–634. I am grateful to Kasia Nowak for information from the files of the International Tracing Service. See also Cohen, *In War's Wake*, 39–40.

15. Proudfoot, *European Refugees*, 302.

16. Modris Eksteins, *Walking Since Daybreak: A Story of Eastern Europe, World War 2, and the Heart of Our Century* (Boston: Houghton Mifflin, 1999), 164.

17. Edward A. Shils, 'Social and Psychological Aspects of Displacement and Repatriation', *Journal of Social Issues* 2, no. 3 (1946): 3–18; Tara Zahra, *The Lost Children: Reconstructing Europe's Families After World War II* (Cambridge, MA: Harvard University Press, 2011); Silvia Salvatici, 'From Displaced Persons to Labourers: Allied Employment Policies in Post-War West Germany', in Jessica Reinisch and Elizabeth White, eds., *The Disentanglement of Populations: Migration, Expulsion and Displacement in Postwar Europe, 1944–49* (Basingstoke: Palgrave Macmillan, 2011), 210–228.

18. Dyczok, *Grand Alliance*, 129; Wolfgang Jacobmeyer, *Vom Zwangsarbeiter zum Heimatlosen Ausländer: Die Displaced Persons in Westdeutschland, 1945–1951* (Göttingen: Vandenhoeck and Ruprecht, 1985), 46–50; Jacobmeyer, 'The "Displaced Persons" in West Germany, 1945–1951', in Göran Rystad, ed., *The Uprooted: Forced Migration as an International Problem in the Post-War Era* (Lund: Lund University Press, 1990), 271–288; Eksteins, *Walking Since Daybreak*, 119, 237.

19. Dyczok, *Grand Alliance*, 157–158.

20. Newsletter, 19 April 1954, in WCC Archives, Geneva, Box 79, Commission of the Churches on International Affairs, 1951–1957, Folder 4.

21. Jennifer Carson, 'The Quaker Internationalist Tradition in DP Camps, 1945–48', in Gatrell and Baron, eds., *Warlands*, 67–86.

22. Anna Holian, 'Anticommunism in the Streets: Refugee Politics in Cold War Germany', *Journal of Contemporary History* 45, no. 1 (2010): 134–161. My thanks to Kasia Nowak for advice on this point.

23. Roman Ilnytzkyj, 'A Survey of Ukrainian Camp Periodicals, 1945–50', in Wsevolod Isajiw, Yury Boshyk, and Roman Senkus, *The Refugee Experience: Ukrainian Displaced Persons After World War 2* (Edmonton: Canadian Institute of Ukrainian Studies Press, 1992), 287–288.

24. Natascha Wodin, *Die gläserne Stadt: Eine Erzählung* (1983), quoted in Máiréad Nic Craith, *Narratives of Place, Belonging and Language: An Intercultural Perspective* (Basingstoke: Palgrave Macmillan, 2012), 3, 11, 140.
25. Roberto Rossellini, 'Stromboli', Criterion Collection, n.d., https://www.criterion.com/films/28082-stromboli.
26. 'The Baltic Tragedy', International Historic Films, n.d., https://ihffilm.com/22023.html; Sharif Gemie and Louise Rees, 'Representing and Reconstructing Identities in the Post-War World: Refugees, UNRRA, and Fred Zinnemann's Film, *The Search* (1948)', *International Review of Social History* 56, no. 3 (2011): 441–473; Edward Rothstein, 'Jarmila Novotna Is Dead at 86; Soprano of Aristocratic Bearing', *New York Times*, 10 February 1994, https://www.nytimes.com/1994/02/10/obituaries/jarmila-novotna-is-dead-at-86-soprano-of-aristocratic-bearing.html.
27. Proudfoot, *European Refugees*, 419, 427. Around 132,000 Jews went to Israel under IRO auspices.
28. Cohen, *In War's Wake*, 104, 111.
29. Dyczok, *Grand Alliance*, 133; Cohen, *In War's Wake*, 105, 108.
30. Cohen, *In War's Wake*, 112–113.
31. Quoted in Tomas Balkelis, 'Living in the Displaced Persons Camp: Lithuanian War Refugees in the West, 1944–1954', in Gatrell and Baron, eds., *Warlands*, 43.
32. Bristol (and West) Council for Aid to Refugees, Annual Report, 1952–53, Bristol Record Office file 27155 (2).
33. Cohen, *In War's Wake*, 100; J. Donald Kingsley, quoted in Cohen, *In War's Wake*, 101.
34. Proudfoot, *European Refugees*, 430; Ruth Balint, 'Children Left Behind: Family, Refugees and Immigration in Postwar Europe', *History Workshop Journal* 82, no. 1 (2016): 151–172.
35. Cohen, *In War's Wake*, 54–55; Michael L. Hoffman, 'Europe's Barriers Add to Manpower Problems: "Offered for Adoption"', *New York Times*, 9 December 1951.

Chapter 3: People Adrift: Expellees and Refugees

1. Henry Carter, *The Refugee Problem in Europe and the Middle East* (London: Epworth Press, 1949), foreword; G. J. van H. Goedhart, 'People Adrift', *Journal of International Affairs* 7, no. 1 (1953): 7–29.
2. Minutes of the Third Meeting of the Joint Executive Committee of the Ecumenical Refugee Commission, Geneva, 30–31 January 1947, Burke Library and Archives, Union Theological Seminary, New York, WCC Records, Box 69, Reconstruction, Inter-Church Aid and Service to Refugees, 1947–1953, Folder 3.
3. Ian D. Connor, *Refugees and Expellees in Post-War Germany* (Manchester: Manchester University Press, 2007), 19.
4. Volker Ackermann, ' "*Homo Barackensis*"—Westdeutsche Flüchtlingslager in den 1950er Jahre', in Ackermann, ed., *Anknüpfungen: Kulturgeschichte, Landesgeschichte, Zeitgeschichte. Gedenkschrift für Peter Hüttenberge* (Essen: Klartext, 1995), 330–346; Connor, *Refugees and Expellees*, 30–34, 142–143.
5. Connor, *Refugees and Expellees*, 38–47, 147.
6. Ibid., 27–28; Andreas Kossert, *Kalte Heimat: Die Geschichte der deutschen Vertriebenen nach 1945* (München: Siedler, 2010); Joyce Mushaben, *The Changing Faces*

of Citizenship: Social Integration and Political Mobilization Among Ethnic Minorities in Germany (New York: Berghahn, 2008), 94; Richard W. Solberg, As Between Brothers: The Story of Lutheran Response to World Need (Minneapolis: Augsburg, 1957).

7. Quoted in Connor, *Refugees and Expellees*, 65; Volker Ackermann, *Der 'echte' Flüchtling: Deutsche Vetriebene und Flüchtlinge aus der DDR, 1945–1961* (Osnabrück: Universitätsverlag Rasch, 1995), 67.

8. Rainer Schulze, 'The Struggle of Past and Present in Individuals: The Case of German Refugees and Expellees from the East', in David Rock and Stefan Wolff, eds., *Coming Home to Germany? The Integration of Ethnic Germans from Central and Eastern Europe in the Federal Republic* (Oxford: Berghahn, 2002), 38–55; Connor, *Refugees and Expellees*, 60, 78.

9. Ackermann, *Der 'echte' Flüchtling*, 71; R. M. Douglas, *Orderly and Humane: The Expulsion of the Germans After the Second World War* (New Haven, CT: Yale University Press, 2012), 309, 314–317.

10. Pertti Ahonen, *After the Expulsion: West Germany and Eastern Europe, 1945–1990* (Oxford: Oxford University Press, 2003); Ahonen, 'The German Expellee Organisations: Unity, Division and Function', in Manuel Borutta and Jan C. Jansen, eds., *Vertriebene and Pieds-Noirs in Postwar Germany and France: Comparative Perspectives* (Houndmills: Palgrave Macmillan, 2016), 115–132.

11. Thomas Bauer, Sebastian Braun, and Michael Kvasnick, 'The Economic Integration of Forced Migrants: Evidence for Post-War Germany', *Economic Journal* 123, no. 571 (2013): 998–1024.

12. Philipp Ther, 'The Integration of Expellees in Germany and Poland After World War II: A Historical Reassessment', *Slavic Review* 55, no. 4 (1996): 779–805; Michael Schwartz, 'Refugees and Expellees in the Soviet Zone of Germany: Political and Social Problems of Their Integration, 1945–50', *Journal of Communist Studies and Transition Politics* 16, nos. 1–2 (2000): 155–156.

13. Schwartz, 'Refugees and Expellees', 149, 167.

14. Manfred Wille, 'Compelling the Assimilation of Expellees in the Soviet Zone of Occupation and the GDR', in Philipp Ther and Ana Siljak, eds., *Redrawing Nations: Ethnic Cleansing in East-Central Europe, 1944–1948* (Oxford: Rowman and Littlefield, 2001), 263–283.

15. Arnd Bauerkämper, 'Social Conflict and Social Transformation in the Integration of Expellees into Rural Brandenburg, 1945–52', in Ther and Siljak, eds., *Redrawing Nations*, 285–305.

16. Michael Schwartz, 'Assimilation Versus Incorporation: Expellee Integration Policies in East and West Germany After 1945', in Borutta and Jansen, eds., *Vertriebene and Pieds-Noirs*, 73–94.

17. Ackermann, *Der 'echte' Flüchtling*, 130–131.

18. Volker Ackermann, 'Flucht und Vertreibung: Das Problem physischer und psychischer Folgen am Beispiel von Nordrhein-Westfalen 1945–1955', *Medizinhistorisches Journal* 29, no. 4 (1994): 379–395.

19. Jacques Vernant, *The Refugee in the Post-War World* (London: Allen and Unwin, 1953), 149–150; Schulze, 'Struggle of Past and Present', 43; Ned Richardson-Little, 'Of Walls and Victims: Berlin Refugees Then and Now', *Superfluous Answers to Nec-*

essary Questions, 24 August 2015, https://historynedblog.wordpress.com/2015/08/24/of-walls-and-victims-berlin-refugees-then-and-now.

20. Video footage from the press conference in the Aufnahmeheim Schönebeck, German Democratic Republic, 4 November 1958, exhibited in the Notaufnahmelager Marienfelde, Berlin, May 2017. See also Bernd Stöver, *Zuflucht DDR: Spione und andere Übersiedler* (Munich: Beck, 2009).

21. Vernant, *Refugee in the Post-War World*, 238–242.

22. *International Migration, 1945–1957* (Geneva: International Labour Organization, 1959), 60–61.

23. Vernant, *Refugee in the Post-War World*, 5.

24. Quoted in Anthony T. Bouscaren, *International Migrations Since 1945* (New York: Praeger, 1963), 54 (emphasis in original).

25. Ibid., 15; Susan L. Carruthers, 'Between Camps: Eastern Bloc "Escapees" and Cold War Borderlands', *American Quarterly* 57, no. 3 (2005): 911–942.

26. Harry S. Truman, 'Special Message to the Congress on Aid for Refugees and Displaced Persons', 24 March 1952, American Presidency Project, University of California, Santa Barbara, https://www.presidency.ucsb.edu/documents/special-message-the-congress-aid-for-refugees-and-displaced-persons.

27. Richard R. Brown, 'Sixth Anniversary of the USEP', *Migration News* 7 (May–June 1958): 12–17.

28. WCC Archives, File 425.1.043, 'Human Interest Stories'. I have omitted their full names.

29. Tycho Walaardt, 'The Trojan Horse: Outsider and Insider Influence on Obtaining Asylum in the Netherlands in the First Decade After the Second World War', *Tijdschrift voor Sociale en Economische Geschiedenis* 6, no. 2 (2009): 63–93; Carruthers, 'Between Camps', 913, 919.

30. Carruthers, 'Between Camps', 931.

31. In March 1997, two former East German guards, Rolf Friedrich and Erich Schreiber, received prison sentences after being found guilty of manslaughter. For an up-to-date account see Pertti Ahonen, *Death at the Berlin Wall* (Oxford: Oxford University Press, 2010).

32. Memorandum on the 'Eligibility Under the [1951] Convention of Refugees Who Left Hungary Because of the Events of 1956', 2 September 1959; P. Weis to M. Pagès, 9 January 1957, UNHCR Records and Archives, Geneva, Fond UNHCR 11, Subfonds 1, file 6/1/1 HUN—Protection—General—Hungarian refugees.

33. Brigitta Zierer, 'Willkommene Ungarnflüchtlinge 1956?', in Gernot Heiss and Oliver Rathkolb, eds., *Asylland wider Willen: Flüchtlinge in Österreich im europäischen Kontext seit 1914* (Vienna: Jugend und Volk, 1995), 157–171.

34. *Migration News* 7, no. 1 (1958); Zierer, 'Willkommene Ungarnflüchtlinge 1956?', 169–170.

35. Karel Norsky, 'The Forgotten Refugees: Concerted Policy Needed', *Manchester Guardian*, 24 April 1959.

36. Christian Aid Archives, SOAS, University of London, CA/I/6/7, Aid to European Refugees, Official Information Bulletin, January 1957; Beryl Oliver, *The British Red Cross in Action* (London: Faber and Faber, 1966), 531.

37. Political and Economic Planning, *Refugees in Britain: Hungarians and Anglo-Egyptians* (London: PEP, 1958), 32.
38. Ari Joskowicz, 'Romani Refugees and the Postwar Order', *Journal of Contemporary History* 51, no. 4 (2015): 782–783.
39. For example, the monthly *AFSC Bulletin*, issued by the American Friends Service Committee, March 1950.
40. Peter Gatrell, *Free World? The Campaign to Save the World's Refugees, 1956–1963* (Cambridge: Cambridge University Press, 2011), 53.

Chapter 4: Rebuilding Western Europe: Adventures in Migration

1. Linda McDowell, *Hard Labour: The Hidden Voices of Latvian Migrant 'Volunteer' Workers* (London: UCL Press, 2005), 112. McDowell changed her informants' names to preserve their anonymity.
2. Clarence Senior and Douglas Manley, 'British Experience of Immigration', *Migration News*, no. 2 (1956): 3–10; Attila Lajos, 'From Contract Workers to Political Refugees', in Mikael Byström and Pär Frohnert, eds., *Reaching a State of Hope: Refugees, Immigrants and the Swedish Welfare State, 1930–2000* (Lund: Nordic Academic Press, 2013), 175–189.
3. Charles P. Kindleberger, *Europe's Postwar Growth: The Role of Labour Supply* (Cambridge, MA: Harvard University Press, 1967), 18, 30, on elasticity of supply.
4. McDowell, *Hard Labour*, 91.
5. Diana Kay and Robert Miles, *Refugees or Migrant Workers? European Volunteer Workers in Britain, 1946–1951* (London: Routledge, 1992), 48.
6. Ibid., 49–52; John A. Tannahill, *European Volunteer Workers in Britain* (Manchester: Manchester University Press, 1958), 133.
7. McDowell, *Hard Labour*, 4, 19, 89–99, 109–110; Kay and Miles, *Refugees or Migrant Workers?*, 50.
8. John Brown, *The Un-melting Pot: An English Town and Its Immigrants* (London: Macmillan, 1970), 48–49.
9. Kay and Miles, *Refugees or Migrant Workers?*, 116–117.
10. McDowell, *Hard Labour*, 113.
11. Jerzy Zubrzycki, *Polish Immigrants in Britain: A Study of Adjustment* (The Hague: M. Nijhoff, 1956), 212.
12. Agata Błaszczyk, 'The Resettlement of Polish Refugees After the Second World War', *Forced Migration Review* 54 (2017): 71–73.
13. Tannahill, *European Volunteer Workers in Britain*, 24; Alex J. Robertson, *The Bleak Midwinter, 1947* (Manchester: Manchester University Press, 1987), 52.
14. Keith Sword, ed., *The Formation of the Polish Community in Great Britain, 1939–1950* (London: School of Slavonic and East European Studies, 1989), 280, 443.
15. Quoted in Wendy Webster, *Englishness and Empire, 1939–1965* (Oxford: Oxford University Press, 2005), 156.
16. Quoted in Johan Svanberg, 'Ethnic Encounters, Narratives and Counter-Narratives', in Byström and Frohnert, eds., *Reaching a State of Hope*, 200.
17. Pierre Legendre, 'Work of Rural Settlement in France', *Migration News*, no. 4 (1956): 19–20; Herrick Chapman, *France's Long Reconstruction: In Search of the Modern Republic* (Cambridge, MA: Harvard University Press, 2018), 50–52.

18. Chapman, *France's Long Reconstruction*, 57; James F. Hollifield, *Immigrants, Markets, and States: The Political Economy of Postwar Europe* (Cambridge, MA: Harvard University Press, 1992), 55–58; Patrick Weil, *How to Be French: Nationality in the Making Since 1789* (Durham NC: Duke University Press, 2008), 134–135; Chapman, *France's Long Reconstruction*, 59; Anthony T. Bouscaren, *International Migrations Since 1945* (New York: Praeger, 1963), 81 (opinion poll).

19. Anne Morelli, 'L'appel à la main d'oeuvre italienne pour les charbonnages et sa prise en charge à son arrivée en Belgique dans l'immédiat après-guerre', *Revue Belge d'Histoire Contemporaine* 19, nos. 1–2 (1988): 83–130; Jerzy Zubrzycki, 'Across the Frontiers of Europe', in Wilfred Borrie, ed., *The Cultural Integration of Immigrants* (Paris: UNESCO, 1959), 179; Marina M. Clayton, ' "Communists of the Stomach": Italian Migration and International Relations in the Cold War Era', *Studi emigrazione* 41, no. 155 (2004): 585.

20. Sandro Rinauro, 'Social Research on Italian Emigration During the Reconstruction Years', *Studi emigrazione* 41, no. 155 (2004): 522.

21. Clayton, ' "Communists of the Stomach" ', 590–591, quoting De Gasperi and finance minister Giuseppe Pella. Clayton attributes the phrase itself to Harry S. Truman. See also Bouscaren, *International Migrations*, 73–78.

22. Chapman, *France's Long Reconstruction*, 65; Felice Dassetto and Michel Dumoulin, *Marcinelle, 8 Août 1956* (Louvain: CIACO, 1985). A newsreel clip is available at Mineurs du Monde, http://fresques.ina.fr/memoires-de-mines/accueil; quoted in Maurizio Albahari, *Crimes of Peace: Mediterranean Migrations at the World's Deadliest Border* (Philadelphia: University of Pennsylvania Press, 2015), 170.

23. Anne O'Grady, *Irish Migration to London in the 1940s and 1950s* (London: PNL Press, 1988), 8; Enda Delaney, 'Transnationalism, Networks and Emigration from Post-War Ireland', *Immigrants and Minorities* 23, nos. 2–3 (2005): 426.

24. Enda Delaney, *The Irish in Post-War Britain* (Oxford: Oxford University Press, 2013), 23, 24–29; Enda Delaney, *Demography, State and Society: Irish Migration to Britain, 1921 to 1971* (Liverpool: Liverpool University Press, 2000), 183.

25. Quoted in G. Daniel Cohen, *In War's Wake: Europe's Displaced Persons in the Post-War Order* (New York: Oxford University Press, 2012), 122; 'Migration and Re-adaptation in the European Coal and Steel Community', *Migration News*, no. 3 (1957): 7–12.

26. David E. Christian, 'Resistance to International Worker Mobility: A Barrier to European Unity', *Industrial and Labor Relations Review* 8, no. 3 (1955): 389.

27. Wolf R. Böhning, *The Migration of Workers in the United Kingdom and the European Community* (London: Oxford University Press, for the Institute of Race Relations, 1972), 4.

28. Andrew Geddes, *Immigration and European Integration: Beyond Fortress Europe?*, 2nd ed. (Manchester: Manchester University Press, 2008), 44–45; Lionello Levi-Sandri, quoted in Böhning, *Migration of Workers*, 10. A further refinement followed in 1964, when the principle of freedom of movement was extended to seasonal workers (Regulation 38/64). Henceforth, workers in EEC countries had the right to take up an offer of work in another member state. In addition, a worker was entitled to be joined by any close dependents, not just a spouse and children under the age of twenty-one. Dependents did not have to be nationals of a member state.

29. Bouscaren, *International Migrations*, 32–36.
30. Edward O'Connor, 'The Brussels Conference', *Social Service Review* 26, no. 4 (1952): 399–404; Bouscaren, *International Migrations*, 37.
31. Richard Russell, report on World Refugee Year, Christian Aid Archives, London, CA/I/6/7 Aid to European Refugees: correspondence and bulletins 1956–66. In an unfortunate aside, Russell suggested that it would take no more than 3 million pounds to devise a 'final solution' to the refugee problem in Europe.
32. Peter Gatrell, *Free World? The Campaign to Save the World's Refugees, 1956–1963* (Cambridge: Cambridge University Press, 2011).
33. Report by Peter Kirchner, Chief Immigration Officer, British Refugee Selection Team, 7 June 1960, UK National Archives, HO 352/135; Gatrell, *Free World?*, 214.
34. *Return to Life*, documentary directed by John Krish, 1960, available at BFI Player, https://player.bfi.org.uk/free/film/watch-return-to-life-1960-online. A series of interviews with John Krish, conducted in 1994 by Rodney Giesler for the British Entertainment History Project, is archived at https://historyproject.org.uk/interview/john-krish.
35. Werner Dankwort, speech to Fourteenth Session of the Ad Hoc Committee on WRY, UN General Assembly, 10 December 1959, Bundesarchiv Koblenz, Bundesministerium für Vertriebene, Flüchtlinge und Kriegsgeschädigte, B150/6312, vol. 2.
36. File on the official opening of WRY, UK National Archives, FO 371/145387.
37. Mrs Tom Barry to Auguste Lindt, 19 October 1959, United Nations Office at Geneva (UNOG) Archives, World Refugee Year, ARR 55/0088 File Box No. 087.
38. Report of seminar, 27 April to 7 May 1960, Sigtuna, Sweden, UNOG Archives, World Refugee Year, 55/0088, File 064, Newsletter file.

Chapter 5: Building Communism in Eastern Europe

1. Article 47 of the Albanian Criminal Code in 1968 banned all travel abroad, except on official business. See *Human Rights in the People's Socialist Republic of Albania* (Minneapolis: Minnesota Lawyers International Human Rights Committee, 1990); Tara Zahra, *The Great Departure: Mass Migration from Eastern Europe and the Making of the Free World* (New York: Norton, 2016), 220, 225–226.
2. Anush Petrosyan, 'Horst Howler: Former War Prisoner of Kirovakan Camp', Mediamax 30 March 2015, www.mediamax.am/en/news/interviews/13672.
3. Lewis H. Siegelbaum and Leslie Page Moch, *Broad Is My Native Land: Repertoires and Regimes of Migration in Russia's Twentieth Century* (Ithaca, NY: Cornell University Press, 2014), 86, 143; G. A. Dokuchaev, *Rabochii klass Sibiri i Dal'nego Vostoka v poslevoennye gody, 1946–1950* (Novosibirsk: Nauka, 1972).
4. Miriam Dobson, *Khrushchev's Cold Summer: Gulag Returnees, Crime, and the Fate of Reform After Stalin* (Ithaca, NY: Cornell University Press, 2009).
5. Hill Kulu, 'Post-War Immigration to Estonia: A Comparative Perspective', in Rainer Ohliger, Karen Schönwälder, and Triadafilos Triadafilopoulos, eds., *European Encounters: Migrants, Migration and European Societies Since 1945* (Aldershot: Ashgate, 2003), 38–52; Romuald Misiunas and Rein Taagepera, *The Baltic States: Years of Dependence, 1940–1990* (London: Hurst, 1993), 99, 111–112.
6. Bohdan Krawchenko, *Social Change and National Consciousness in Twentieth-Century Ukraine* (New York: St Martin's Press, 1985), 174, 183.

7. Eugene M. Kulischer, *Europe on the Move: War and Population Changes, 1917–1947* (New York: Columbia University Press, 1948), 296, 300; Seija Jalagin, personal information.

8. Bruce Adams, 'Re-emigration from Western China to the USSR, 1954–1962', in Cynthia J. Buckley and Blair A. Ruble, eds., *Migration, Homeland and Belonging in Eurasia* (Washington, DC: Woodrow Wilson Center Press, 2008), 183–201.

9. Farid Shafiyev, *Resettling the Borderlands: State Relocations and Ethnic Conflict in the South Caucasus* (Montreal: McGill–Queen's University Press, 2018), 185.

10. Joanne Laycock, 'Armenian Homelands and Homecomings, 1945–49: The Repatriation of Diaspora Armenians to the Soviet Union', *Cultural and Social History* 9, no. 1 (2012): 103–123; Rebecca Manley, *To the Tashkent Station: Evacuation and Survival in the Soviet Union at War* (Ithaca, NY: Cornell University Press, 2009), 238–269; Shafiyev, *Resettling the Borderlands*, 199.

11. Martha Brill Olcott, *The Kazakhs* (Stanford: Stanford University Press, 1987), 224–246.

12. Nikita Khrushchev, 'On Further Increasing the Country's Grain Production and Putting Virgin and Idle Lands into Cultivation', *Current Digest of the Soviet Press* 6, no. 12 (1954): 12–13.

13. I. M. Volkov, ed., *Velikii podvig partii i naroda: Massovoe osvoenie tselinnykh zemel' v Kazakhstane* (Moscow: Nauka, 1979); Michaela Pohl, 'The "Planet of One Hundred Languages": Ethnic Relations and Soviet Identity in the Virgin Lands', in Nicholas B. Breyfogle, Abby Schrader, and Willard Sunderland, eds., *Peopling the Russian Periphery: Borderland Colonization in Eurasian History* (London: Routledge, 2007), 242.

14. Pohl, '"Planet"', 238–261.

15. Ibid., 245, 257; Michaela Pohl, '"It Cannot Be That Our Graves Will Be Here": The Survival of Chechen and Ingush Deportees in Kazakhstan, 1944–1957', *Journal of Genocide Research* 4, no. 3 (2002): 401–430.

16. Gregor Thum, *Uprooted: How Breslau Became Wrocław During the Century of Expulsions* (Princeton, NJ: Princeton University Press, 2011), 246; Beata Halicka, *Polens Wilder Westen: Erzwungene Migration und die kulturelle Aneignung des Oderraumes, 1945–1948* (Paderborn: Ferdinand Schöningh Verlag, 2013), 264–265.

17. Marta Grzechnik, '"Recovering" Territories: The Use of History in the Integration of the New Polish Western Borderland After World War 2', *Europe-Asia Studies* 69, no. 4 (2017): 678; Beata Halicka, *'Mein Haus an der Oder': Erinnerungen polnischer Neusiedler in Westpolen nach 1945* (Paderborn: Ferdinand Schöningh Verlag, 2014), 226; Edyta Materka, *Dystopia's Provocateurs: Peasants, State and Informality in the Polish Borderlands* (Bloomington: Indiana University Press, 2017), 83.

18. Anita J. Prażmowska, *Civil War in Poland, 1942–1948* (Basingstoke: Palgrave, 2004), 180–181; Thum, *Uprooted*, 71, 80–81; John J. Kulczycki, *Belonging to the Nation: Inclusion and Exclusion in the Polish-German Borderlands, 1939–1951* (Cambridge, MA: Harvard University Press, 2016), 87, 221, 89, 230; Bernard Linek, '"De-Germanisation" and "Re-Polonisation" in Upper Silesia, 1945–50', in Philipp Ther and Ana Siljak, eds., *Redrawing Nations: Ethnic Cleansing in East-Central Europe, 1944–1948* (Oxford: Rowman and Littlefield, 2001), 121–134; Prażmowska, *Civil War in Poland*, 180, 182.

19. Thum, *Uprooted*, 77, 98–104, 187.
20. Zdzisław Mach, *Niechciane miasta: Migracja i tożsamość społeczna* (Kraków: TAi-WPN Universitas, 1998), 123, 130, courtesy of Kasia Nowak.
21. Thum, *Uprooted*, 118–126; Halicka, *Polens Wilder Westen*, 170–174.
22. Halicka, '*Mein Haus an der Oder*', 13; Halicka, *Polens Wilder Westen*, 153–154, 169; Mach, *Niechciane miasta*; Sascha O. Becker, Irena Grosfeld, Pauline Grosjean, Nico Voigtländer, and Ekaterina Zhuravskaya, 'Forced Migration and Human Capital: Evidence from Post-WWII Population Transfers', NBER Working Paper no. 27404 (Cambridge, MA: National Bureau of Economic Research, 2018), 44.
23. My thanks to Kasia Nowak for this information.
24. Mach, *Niechciane miasta*, 92–93; Halicka, *Polens Wilder Westen*, 300; Dietlind Hüchter, 'Space, Time, and History in the Polish People's Republic', *European Review of History* 25, no. 6 (2018): 868–885.
25. Kulischer, *Europe on the Move*, 286–287; Andreas Wiedemann, '*Komm mit uns das Grenzland aufbauen!': Ansiedlung und neue Strukturen in den ehemaligen Sudetenge-bieten, 1945–1952* (Essen: Klartext, 2007).
26. Quoted in Joseph B. Schechtman, *Postwar Population Transfers in Europe, 1945–1955* (Philadelphia: University of Pennsylvania Press, 1962), 125.
27. Kelly Hignett, '"We Had to Become Criminals to Survive Under Communism!" Testimonies of Petty Criminality and Everyday Morality in Late Socialist Central Europe', in Kelly Hignett, Melanie Ilic, Dalia Leinarte, and Corina Snitar, eds., *Women's Experiences of Repression in the Soviet Union and Eastern Europe* (London: Routledge, 2018), 117–119.
28. Sándor Horváth, *Stalinism Reloaded: Everyday Life in Stalin-City, Hungary* (Bloomington: Indiana University Press, 2017), 93–98.
29. Katherine Lebow, *Unfinished Utopia: Nowa Huta, Stalinism, and Polish Society, 1949–1956* (Ithaca, NY: Cornell University Press, 2013), 45, 80; Kinga Pozniak, *Nowa Huta: Generations of Change in a Model Socialist Town* (Pittsburgh: Pittsburgh University Press, 2014).
30. Lebow, *Unfinished Utopia*, 60.
31. Thanks to Kasia Nowak for her translation.
32. Eagle Glassheim, *Cleansing the Czechoslovak Borderlands: Migration, Environment, and Health in the Former Sudetenland* (Pittsburgh: University of Pittsburgh Press, 2017), 123–147.
33. Celia Donert, *The Rights of the Roma: The Struggle for Citizenship in Postwar Czechoslovakia* (Cambridge: Cambridge University Press, 2017), 130.
34. Lejla Voloder, 'Secular Citizenship and Muslim Belonging in Turkey: Migrant Perspectives', *Ethnic and Racial Studies* 36, no. 5 (2013): 838–856.

Chapter 6: Migrants of Decolonisation

1. Jordanna Bailkin, *The Afterlife of Empire* (Berkeley: University of California Press, 2012), 24. See also Ceri Peach, 'Post-War Migration to Europe: Reflux, Influx, Refuge', *Social Science Quarterly* 78, no. 2 (1997): 269–283.
2. Gert Oostindie, *Postcolonial Netherlands: Sixty-Five Years of Forgetting, Commemorating, Silencing* (Amsterdam: Amsterdam University Press, 2011), 8; Ricardo E. Ovalle-Bahamón, 'The Wrinkles of Decolonisation and Nationness: White Angolans

as *Retornados* in Portugal', in Andrea L. Smith, ed., *Europe's Invisible Migrants* (Amsterdam: Amsterdam University Press, 2003), 153.

3. Jean-Louis Miège and Colette Dubois, eds., *L'Europe retrouvée: Les migrations de la décolonisation* (Paris: L'Harmattan, 1994), 18.

4. Pamela Ballinger, 'Beyond the Italies: Italy as a Mobile Subject?', in Ruth Ben-Ghiat and Stephanie Malia Hom, eds., *Italian Mobilities* (London: Routledge, 2016), 20–45.

5. I am grateful to Pamela Ballinger for sharing with me her book manuscript *The World Refugees Made: Decolonization and the Formation of Postwar Italy, 1945–1960*. See also Pamela Ballinger, 'Colonial Twilight: Italian Settlers and the Long Decolonization of Libya', *Journal of Contemporary History* 51, no. 4 (2016): 813–838.

6. Pamela Ballinger, 'Borders of the Nation, Borders of Citizenship: Italian Repatriation and the Redefinition of National Identity After World War II', *Comparative Studies in Society and History* 40, no. 3 (2007): 713–741; Ballinger, 'Beyond the Italies', 33.

7. Hans van Amersfoort and Mies van Niekerk, 'Immigration as a Colonial Inheritance: Post-Colonial Immigrants in the Netherlands, 1945–2002', *Journal of Ethnic and Migration Studies* 32, no. 3 (2006): 328.

8. J. H. Kraak, 'The Repatriation of the Dutch from Indonesia', *REMP Bulletin* 6, no. 2 (1958): 27–39; Oostindie, *Postcolonial Netherlands*, 52, 109.

9. AFSC Archives, Philadelphia, Refugee and Migration Services, Closed Cases, Box 12, WCC Immigration Forms. I have disguised the family name.

10. As above, Box 19, Memo from WCC immigration officer, 5 March 1959, requesting the family's admission to the United States under PL 85-892. See also Joost Coté, 'The Indisch Dutch in Post-War Australia', *Tijdschrift voor Sociale en Economische Geschiedenis* 7, no. 2 (2010): 103–125.

11. Oostindie, *Postcolonial Netherlands*, 28.

12. Yvon Muskita, *Snijden en stikken* (Haarlem: In de Knipscheer, 2008), 86, 108. My thanks to Hans Wallage for this reference.

13. Interview with Wim Manuhutu, director of the Moluccan Historical Museum in Utrecht, available at 'Molukkers in Nederland: Een interview met Wim Manuhutu over interculturele communicatie', n.d., http://fwillems.antenna.nl/nl/extra/ede.htm, translation courtesy of Hans Wallage; Paul Doolan, 'A Moluccan Victory in a Dutch Court', Imperial and Global Forum, Centre for Imperial and Global History, University of Exeter, 13 March 2017, https://imperialglobalexeter.com/2017/03/1.3/a-moluccan-victory-in-a-dutch-court.

14. Sabrina Marchetti, 'Migrant Domestic Work Through the Lens of "Coloniality": Narratives from Eritrean Afro-Surinamese Women', in Dirk Hoerder, Elise van Nederveen Meerkerk, and Silke Neunsinger, eds., *Towards a Global History of Domestic and Caregiving Workers* (Leiden: Brill, 2015), 380; Oostindie, *Postcolonial Netherlands*, 61–63.

15. Van Amersfoort and van Niekerk, 'Immigration'; Elizabeth Buettner, *Europe After Empire: Decolonization, Society, and Culture* (Cambridge: Cambridge University Press, 2016), 273–283.

16. Daniel Boffey, 'Belgium Comes to Terms with "Human Zoos" of Its Colonial Past', *The Guardian*, 16 April 2018, https://www.theguardian.com/world/2018/apr/16/belgium-comes-to-terms-with-human-zoos-of-its-colonial-past.

17. Buettner, *Europe After Empire*, 233; Pierre Salmon, 'Les retours en Belgique induits par la décolonisation', in Miège and Dubois, eds., *L'Europe retrouvée*, 191–212.
18. Buettner, *Europe After Empire*, 230.
19. John Solomos and Stephen Woodhams, 'The Politics of Cypriot Migration to Britain', *Immigrants and Minorities* 14, no. 3 (1995): 231–256; 'Child Migrant Stories', Queen Mary University of London, https://childmigrantstories.com/films/life-is-a-destiny; Ibrahim Sirkeci, Tuncay Builecen, Yakup Çoştu, Saniye Dedeoglu, M. Rauf Kesici, B. Dilara Şeker, Fethiye Tilbe, K. Onur Unutulmaz, *Little Turkey in Great Britain* (London: Transnational Press, 2016); Kathy Burrell, *Moving Lives: Narratives of Nation and Migration Among Europeans in Post-War Britain* (London: Routledge, 2006), 34.
20. World Council of Churches, *Workbook of Projects for the WRY* (unpublished, limited circulation, Geneva, 1959), copy in WCC Archives, Geneva.
21. Buettner, *Europe After Empire*, 224, 226.
22. 'Home from the Hill', 1987, www.bfi.org.uk/films-tv-people/4ce2b71ab1738; Bill Schwarz, 'The Only White Man in There: The Re-Racialisation of England, 1956–1968', *Race and Class* 38, no. 1 (1996): 65–78.
23. Daniel Branch, 'The Enemy Within: Loyalists and the War Against Mau Mau in Kenya', *Journal of African History* 48, no. 2 (2007): 291–315.
24. Quoted in Wendy Webster, *Englishness and Empire, 1939–1965* (Oxford: Oxford University Press, 2005), 123.
25. Stuart Hall, 'Old and New Identities, Old and New Ethnicities', in Anthony D. King, ed., *Globalisation and the World System* (London: Macmillan Educational, 1991), 42–68.
26. Smith remained in Zimbabwe until his death in 2007.
27. Ngwabe Bhebhe, Harare, 11 April 2010, quoted in JoAnn McGregor, 'Locating Exile: Decolonization, Anti-Imperial Spaces and Zimbabwean Students in Britain, 1965–1980', *Journal of Historical Geography* 57, no. 3 (2017): 67.
28. Buettner, *Europe After Empire*, 227; Anthony Kirk-Greene, 'Decolonization: The Ultimate Diaspora', *Journal of Contemporary History* 36, no. 1 (2001): 133–151; Russell King, Tony Warnes, and Allan Williams, *Sunset Lives: British Retirement Migration to the Mediterranean* (Oxford: Oxford University Press, 2000), 63–65, 84–86.
29. Portugal did not recognise the incorporation of Goa into India until the Salazar dictatorship came to an end in 1974.
30. Buettner, *Europe After Empire*, 306.
31. Dulce Maria Cardoso, *The Return* (London: Maclehose Press, 2016), first published in Portuguese in 2011, quotation on 78.
32. Ovalle-Bahamón, 'The Wrinkles of Decolonisation', 163.
33. M. Margarida Marques, 'Postcolonial Portugal: Between Scylla and Charbydis', in Ulbe Bosma, Jan Lucassen, and Gert Oostindie, eds., *Postcolonial Migrants and Identity Politics: Europe, Russia, Japan and the United States in Comparison* (New York: Berghahn, 2012), 127–154; Stephen C. Lubkemann, 'Race, Class, and Kin in the Negotiation of "Internal Strangerhood" Among Portuguese Retornados, 1975–2000', in Smith, ed., *Europe's Invisible Migrants*, 75–94.
34. Cardoso, *Return*, 191.
35. Luis Batalha, *The Cape Verdean Diaspora in Portugal: Colonial Subjects in a Postcolonial World* (Lanham, MD: Lexington Books, 2004), 31; Jørgen Carling, 'Emigra-

tion, Return and Development in Cape Verde: The Impact of Closing Borders', *Population, Space and Place* 10, no. 2 (2004): 116.

36. Pierre Lanfranchi and Matthew Taylor, *Moving with the Ball: The Migration of Professional Footballers* (Oxford: Berg, 2001), 180–181.

37. Vicente Gozálvez Pérez, 'Décolonisation et migrations à partir de l'Afrique espagnole, 1956–1975', in Miège and Dubois, eds., *L'Europe retrouvée*, 135–190.

Chapter 7: French Revolution: Decolonisation, Migration, Modernisation

1. Quoted in Félix Germain, *Decolonizing the Republic: African and Caribbean Migrants in Post-War Paris, 1946–1974* (East Lansing: Michigan State University Press, 2016), xv.

2. Neil MacMaster, *Colonial Migrants and Racism: Algerians in France, 1900–62* (Basingstoke: Palgrave Macmillan, 1997).

3. Todd Shepard, *The Invention of Decolonization: The Algerian War and the Remaking of France* (Ithaca, NY: Cornell University Press, 2006).

4. Leslie Page Moch, 'France', in Klaus Bade, Pieter C. Emmer, Leo Lucassen, and Jochen Oltmer, eds., *The Encyclopedia of European Migration and Minorities from the Seventeenth Century to the Present* (Cambridge: Cambridge University Press, 2011), 52–62.

5. Robert Debré and Alfred Sauvy, *Des Français pour la France: Le problème de la population* (Paris: Gallimard, 1946), 9, 93, 227–278, with thanks to Laure Humbert for alerting me to this text.

6. Ida Simon-Barouh, 'Vietnamese Colonial and Postcolonial Immigrants in France Since World War 1', in Bade et al., eds., *Encyclopedia of European Migration*, 729–731; 'Noyant-d'Allier, Village asiatique', Allier Auvergne, https://www.allier-auvergne -tourisme.com/culture-patrimoine/villes-villages/noyant-d-allier-5756-1.html.

7. Elizabeth Buettner, *Europe After Empire: Decolonization, Society, and Culture* (Cambridge: Cambridge University Press, 2016), 236.

8. Peter Gatrell, *Free World? The Campaign to Save the World's Refugees, 1956–1963* (Cambridge: Cambridge University Press, 2011), 69; Alexander Clarkson, *Fragmented Fatherland: Immigration and Cold War Conflict in the Federal Republic of Germany, 1945–1980* (Oxford: Berghahn, 2013), 91. By 1961 around 10,000 Algerians were living in the FRG.

9. Jim House and Neil MacMaster, *Paris 1961: Algerians, State Terror, and Memory* (Oxford: Oxford University Press, 2006). See also the film *Ici on noie les Algériens* (directed by Yasmina Adi, Agat Films, 2011).

10. Claire Eldridge, *From Empire to Exile: History and Memory Within the Pied-Noir and Harki Communities, 1962–2012* (Manchester: Manchester University Press, 2016); Maxim Silverman, *Deconstructing the Nation: Immigration, Racism and Citizenship in Modern France* (London: Routledge, 1992), 41; Buettner, *Europe After Empire*, 236.

11. Yann Scioldo-Zürcher, *Devenir métropolitan: Politique d'intégration et parcours des rapatriés d'Algérie en métropole, 1954–2005* (Paris: Editions de l'Ecole des hautes études en sciences sociales, 2010).

12. Shepard, *Invention of Decolonization*, 224.

13. Minayo Nasiali, *Native to the Republic: Empire, Social Citizenship, and Everyday Life in Marseille Since 1945* (Ithaca, NY: Cornell University Press, 2016), 89–90;

Joseph B. Schechtman, *The Refugee in the World: Displacement and Integration* (New York: A. S. Barnes and Company, 1963), 82–85.

14. Schechtman, *Refugee in the World*, 78; Yann Scioldo-Zürcher, 'The Postcolonial Repatriations of the French of Algeria in 1962: An Emblematic Case of a Public Integration Policy', in Manuel Borutta and Jan C. Jansen, eds., *Vertriebene and Pieds-Noirs in Postwar Germany and France: Comparative Perspectives* (Houndmills: Palgrave Macmillan, 2016), 95–112; Jean-Jacques Jordi, *De l'exode à l'exil: Rapatriés et pieds-noirs en France. L'exemple marseillais, 1954–1992* (Paris: 1993).

15. Eldridge, *From Empire to Exile*, 53–66; Émile Chabal, 'Managing the Postcolony: Minority Politics in Montpellier, c. 1960–c. 2010', *Contemporary European History* 23, no. 2 (2014): 237–258; Claire Eldridge, 'Unity Above All: Relationships and Rivalries Within the Pieds-Noir Community', in Borutta and Jansen, eds., *Vertriebene and Pieds-Noirs*, 145. There is a sympathetic obituary of Roseau by Douglas Johnson in *The Independent*, 9 March 1993, https://www.independent.co.uk/news/people/obituary-jacques-roseau-1496575.html.

16. Chabal, 'Managing the Postcolony', 242–243.

17. Ibid., 243.

18. Andrea L. Smith, *Colonial Memory and Post-Colonial Europe: Maltese Settlers in Algeria and France* (Bloomington: Indiana University Press, 2006), 160.

19. Quoted in Eldridge, 'Unity Above All', 135; Jean-Jacques Jordi, 'Les Pieds-Noirs: Constructions identitaires et reinvention des origines', *Hommes et migrations* 1236 (2002): 14–25.

20. Scioldo-Zürcher, *Devenir métropolitan*, 388, 389–390; William B. Cohen, 'Pied-Noir Memory, History, and the Algerian War', in Andrea L. Smith, ed., *Europe's Invisible Migrants* (Amsterdam: Amsterdam University Press, 2003), 129–145.

21. Question posed by a female harki, quoted in Vincent Crapanzano, *The Harkis: The Wound That Never Heals* (Chicago: Chicago University Press, 2011), 114; Eldridge, *From Empire to Exile*, 71; Todd Shepard, 'Excluding the Harkis from Repatriate Status, Excluding Muslim Algerians from French Identity', in Hafid Gafaïti, Patricia Lorcin, and David Troyansky, eds., *Transnational Spaces and Identities in the Francophone World* (Lincoln: University of Nebraska Press, 2009), 97.

22. Joan Wallach Scott, *The Politics of the Veil* (Princeton, NJ: Princeton University Press, 2007), 61. See also 'Charles de Gaulle: "Colombey-les-Deux-Mosquées"', *LesObservateurs*, 28 September 2015, https://lesobservateurs.ch/2015/09/28/charles-de-gaulle-colombey-les-deux-mosquees.

23. Crapanzano, *Harkis*, 120.

24. Jeannette E. Miller, 'A Camp for Foreigners and "Aliens": The Harkis' Exile at the Rivesaltes Camp, 1962–1964', *French Politics, Culture and Society* 31, no. 2 (2013): 21–44; Eldridge, *From Empire to Exile*, 73; Crapanzano, *Harkis*, 124–125.

25. Eldridge, *From Empire to Exile*, 72–78.

26. Ibid., 86–89.

27. See the brief life history of Noura, reported by Crapanzano, *Harkis*, 190. In fairness, I should add that she managed to get her daughters through school and into good jobs—and, she emphasised, with partners who were not 'Arab'; Eldridge, *From Empire to Exile*, 80–82.

28. Zahia Rahmani, *France: Story of a Childhood* (New Haven, CT: Yale University Press, 2016), 92, 115–116, 176, 120; Crapanzano, *Harkis*, 174.

29. Crapanzano, *Harkis*, 108, 143, 147, 116.

30. Ibid., 8, 9; Eldridge, *From Empire to Exile*, 279–281.

31. Laurence Brown, 'Afro-Caribbean Migrants in France and the UK', in Leo Lucassen, David Feldman, and Jochen Oltmer, eds., *Paths of Integration: Migrants in Western Europe, 1880–2004* (Amsterdam: Amsterdam University Press, 2006), 177–197; Germain, *Decolonizing the Republic*, 80–89, 121, 177. In the 1980s, BUMIDOM became *L'Agence Nationale pour l'Insertion et la Promotion des Travailleurs de Outre-Mer* (National Agency for the Insertion and Promotion of Overseas Workers), hiring Caribbean personnel and identifying job opportunities in the West Indies.

32. Germain, *Decolonizing the Republic*, 117–140.

33. Neil MacMaster, 'Shantytown Republics: Algerian Migrants and the Culture of Space in the *Bidonvilles*', in Gafaïti et al., eds., *Transnational Spaces*, 73–93.

34. Nasiali, *Native to the Republic*, 79–82; Amelia H. Lyons, *The Civilizing Mission in the Metropole: Algerian Families and the French Welfare State During Decolonization* (Stanford: Stanford University Press, 2013).

35. 'North African Workers in France', *Migration News*, no. 3 (1966): 11–15; MacMaster, 'Shantytown Republics', 85; Melissa K. Byrnes, 'Liberating the Land or Absorbing a Community: Managing North African Migration and the *Bidonvilles* in Paris's *Banlieus*', *French Politics, Culture and Society* 31, no. 3 (2013): 1–20.

36. Gérard Noiriel, *The French Melting Pot* (Minneapolis: University of Minnesota Press, 1996), originally published as *Le creuset français: Histoire de l'immigration XIX–XX siècle* (Paris: Editions du Seuil, 1988), 287 (English ed.); Germain, *Decolonizing the Republic*, 122–123.

37. Claire Etcherelli, *Élise ou la vraie vie* (Paris: Denoël, 1967); Germain, *Decolonizing the Republic*, 49; 'Black Girl (1966 Film)', Wikipedia, https://en.wikipedia.org/wiki/Black_Girl_(1966_film).

38. Crapanzano, *Harkis*, 138–139.

39. Eldridge, *From Empire to Exile*, 77–78.

40. Germain, *Decolonizing the Republic*, 58.

Chapter 8: Guest Workers in West Germany: Migration, Miracles, and Missing Out

1. 'The Verona Bottleneck', *Der Spiegel*, 27 April 1960, quoted in Deniz Göktürk, David Gramling, and Anton Kaes, eds., *Germany in Transit: Nation and Migration, 1955–2005* (Berkeley: University of California Press, 2007 [1973]), 29.

2. Mark J. Miller, *Foreign Workers in Western Europe: An Emerging Political Force* (New York: Praeger, 1981), 10; Hans-Joachim Hoffman-Nowotny and Martin Killias, 'Switzerland', in Ronald E. Krane, ed., *International Labor Migration in Europe* (New York: Praeger, 1979), 45–62.

3. John Berger, *A Seventh Man: A Book of Images and Words About the Experiences of Migrant Workers in Europe* (Harmondsworth: Penguin, 1975); Caroline Brettell, *Men Who Migrate, Women Who Wait: Population and History in a Portuguese Parish* (Princeton, NJ: Princeton University Press, 1986); Sarah Baumann, ... *Und es kamen*

auch Frauen: Engagement italienischer Migrantinnen in Politik und Gesellschaft der Nachkriegsschweiz (Zürich: Seismo, 2014).

4. In German, the full quotation reads: 'Ein kleines Herrenvolk sieht sich in Gefahr: man hat Arbeitskräfte gerufen, und es kommen Menschen. Sie fressen den Wohlstand nicht auf, im Gegenteil, sie sind für den Wohlstand unerlässlich.' For background, see Rudolf Braun, *Sozio-kulturelle Probleme der Eingliederung italienischer Arbeitskräfte in der Schweiz* (Erlenbach-Zurich: Eugen Rentsch Verlag, 1970).

5. Klaus Bade, *Auslander, Aussiedler, Asyl: Eine Bestandsaufnahme* (Munchen: C. H. Beck, 1994), 54; Rita Chin, *The Guest Worker Question in Postwar Germany* (New York: Cambridge University Press, 2007), 62.

6. Quoted in Rita Chin and Heide Fehrenbach, 'German Democracy and the Question of Difference, 1945–1995', in Rita Chin, Heide Fehrenbach, Geoff Eley, and Atina Grossmann, eds., *After the Nazi Racial State* (Ann Arbor: University of Michigan Press, 2009), 107; Miller, *Foreign Workers in Western Europe*, 9.

7. Johannes-Dieter Steinert, 'Migration and Migration Policy: West Germany and the Recruitment of Foreign Labour, 1945–61', *Journal of Contemporary History* 49, no. 1 (2014): 421–435.

8. Ulrich Herbert, *A History of Foreign Labor in Germany, 1880–1980: Seasonal Workers, Forced Laborers, Guest Workers* (Ann Arbor: University of Michigan Press, 1990), 205–206.

9. Göktürk et al., *Germany in Transit*, 26–28.

10. Herbert, *History of Foreign Labor*, 209–210; Simon Goeke, 'The Multinational Working Class? Political Activism and Labour Migration in West Germany During the 1960s and 1970s', *Journal of Contemporary History* 49, no. 1 (2014): 160–182.

11. Christoph Rass, 'Temporary Labour Migration and State-Run Recruitment of Foreign Workers in Europe, 1919–1975: A New Migration Regime?', *International Review of Social History* 57 (2012): 191–224.

12. Jennifer A. Miller, 'On Track for West Germany: Turkish "Guest Worker" Rail Transportation to West Germany in the Post-War Period', *German History* 30, no. 4 (2012): 568–569; Monika Mattes, *'Gastarbeiterinnen' in der Bundesrepublik: Anwerbepolitik, Migration und Geschlecht in den 50er bis 70er Jahren* (Frankfurt am Main: Campus, 2005), 72–82.

13. Alexander Clarkson, *Fragmented Fatherland: Immigration and Cold War Conflict in the Federal Republic of Germany, 1945–1980* (Oxford: Berghahn, 2013), 10; Karin Hunn, *'Nächstes Jahr kehren wir zurück...': Die Geschichte der türkischen 'Gastarbeiter' in der Bundesrepublik* (Göttingen: Wallstein, 2005), 203.

14. Chin and Fehrenbach, 'German Democracy', 107.

15. Hunn, *'Nächstes Jahr kehren wir zurück...'*, 72–77; Leo Lucassen, *The Immigrant Threat: The Integration of Old and New Migrants in Western Europe Since 1850* (Urbana: University of Illinois Press, 2005), 147; Ulrich Herbert and Karin Hunn, 'Guest Workers and Policy on Guest Workers in the Federal Republic', in Hanna Schissler, ed., *The Miracle Years: A Cultural History of West Germany, 1949–1968* (Princeton, NJ: Princeton University Press, 2001), 187–218.

16. Nermin Abadan-Unat, ed., *Turkish Workers in Europe, 1960–1975: A Socio-Economic Appraisal* (Leiden: Brill, 1976); Mattes, *'Gastarbeiterinnen'*; Hunn, *'Nächstes Jahr kehren wir zurück...'*, 78.

17. Tadeusz Stark, 'The Economic Desirability of Migration', *International Migration Review* 1, no. 2 (1967): 3–22. See the remarks of a Protestant minister quoted in Mattes, '*Gastarbeiterinnen*', 279.

18. Miller, 'On Track for West Germany', 555; Nikola Baković, 'Tending the "Oasis of Socialism": Transnational Political Mobilization of Yugoslav Economic Migrants in the FRG in the Late 1960s and 1970s', *Nationalities Papers* 42, no. 4 (2014): 674–690.

19. Yvonne Rieker, '*Ein Stück Heimat findet man ja immer*': *Die italienische Einwanderung in die Bundesrepublik* (Essen: Klartext, 2003), 83.

20. Paul Ginsborg, A *History of Contemporary Italy* (Harmondsworth: Penguin, 1990), 217–218, referring to works by Ugo Ascoli and Goffredo Fofi; Miller, 'On Track for West Germany', 557, citing DOMiT interviews.

21. Herbert, *History of Foreign Labor*, 208–209; Aytaç Eryılmaz and Mathilde Jamin, eds., *Fremde Heimat: Eine Geschichte der Einwanderung aus der Türkei* (Essen: Klartext, 1998), 182, photo by Manfred Vollmer, Essen.

22. Simon Green, *The Politics of Exclusion: Institutions and Immigration Policy in Contemporary Germany* (Manchester: Manchester University Press, 2004), 34–35.

23. Herbert, *History of Foreign Labor*, 214–215.

24. Carl Föhl, 'Stabilisierung und Wachstum beim Einsatz von Gastarbeitern', *Kyklos* 20 (1967): 119–146.

25. Rass, 'Temporary Labour Migration'.

26. Werner Schiffauer, *Die Migranten aus Subay: Türken in Deutschland, eine Ethnographie* (Stuttgart: Klett-Cotta, 1991), 254; Ewa Kolinsky, *Deutsch und Türkisch leben: Bild und Selbstbild der türkischen Minderheit in Deutschland* (Oxford: Peter Lang, 2000); Hunn, '*Nächstes Jahr kehren wir zurück…*', 415; Mübeccel B. Kiray, 'The Family of the Immigrant Worker', in Abadan-Unat, ed., *Turkish Workers in Europe*, 226–229.

27. Hunn, '*Nächstes Jahr kehren wir zurück…*', 416; Mattes, '*Gastarbeiterinnen*', 260–275.

28. Tadeusz Stark, 'Should the Migrant Workers in Europe Be Encouraged to Return to Their Home Countries?', *Migration News*, no. 2 (1967): 5–13; Maturi is quoted in Göktürk et al., *Germany in Transit*, 33.

29. Eryılmaz and Jamin, eds., *Fremde Heimat*, with an illustration from 1963 on 175; Herbert, *History of Foreign Labor*, 218–220; Chin, *Guest Worker Question*, 95.

30. Otto Langels, 'Ein Moped für Armando Rodrigues de Sá', Deutschlandfunk, 11 September 2014, www.deutschlandfunk.de/millionster-gastarbeiter-vor-50-jahren-ein-moped-fuer.871.de.html?dram:article_id=296998; Chin, *Guest Worker Question*, 2. Rodrigues developed cancer and eventually returned to Portugal, where he died in 1979, aged just fifty-seven.

31. Eryılmaz and Jamin, eds., *Fremde Heimat*, 166–167; quoted in Ulf Brunnbauer, ed., *Transnational Societies, Transterritorial Politics: Migrations in the (Post-)Yugoslav Region, 19th–21st Centuries* (Munich: R. Oldenbourg Verlag, 2009), 7.

32. Barbara Le Normand, 'The Gastarbajters as a Transnational Yugoslav Working Class', in Paul Stubbs, Igor Duda, and Rory Archer, eds., *Social Inequalities and Discontent in Yugoslav Socialism* (Abingdon: Routledge, 2016), 38–57.

33. 'How the Turkish Worker Should Behave' (pamphlet issued by the Turkish Institute for Labour and Labour Placement), 1963, in Göktürk et al., *Germany in Transit*, 34–36; Hunn, '*Nächstes Jahr kehren wir zurück…*', 174, 316.

34. Nermin Abadan-Unat, 'Turkish Migration to Europe', in Abadan-Unat, ed., *Turkish Workers in Europe*, 24; Hunn, '*Nächstes Jahr kehren wir zurück…*', 160–178.

35. Mattes, '*Gastarbeiterinnen*', 149–159; Anne von Oswald, Karen Schönwälder, and Barbara Sonnenberger, '"*Einwanderungsland Deutschland*": A New Look at Its Post-War History', in Rainer Ohliger, Karen Schönwälder, and Triadafilos Triadafilopoulos, eds., *European Encounters: Migrants, Migration and European Societies Since 1945* (Aldershot: Ashgate, 2003), 27–28; Charles P. Kindleberger, *Europe's Postwar Growth: The Role of Labour Supply* (Cambridge, MA: Harvard University Press, 1967), 50, 197.

36. Green, *Politics of Exclusion*, 17.

37. Delia Castelnuovo-Frigessi, *La condition immigrée: Les ouvriers italiens en Suisse* (Lausanne: Editions d'en bas, 1978), 312–314; Goeke, 'Multinational Working Class?', 170; Stephen Castles and Godula Kosack, *Immigrant Workers and Class Structure in Western Europe* (London: Oxford University Press, 1973), 152–175.

38. Mark J. Miller, *Foreign Workers in Western Europe: An Emerging Political Force* (New York: Praeger, 1981), 6; von Oswald et al., '"*Einwanderungsland Deutschland*"', 31–32; Castles and Kosack, *Immigrant Workers*, 158; Mattes, '*Gastarbeiterinnen*', 285–311.

39. Hunn, '*Nächstes Jahr kehren wir zurück…*', 137; Chin, *Guest Worker Question*, 62; Göktürk et al., *Germany in Transit*, 110–111.

40. Eryılmaz and Jamin, eds., *Fremde Heimat*, 195, 269 (photo of man with bra, Bollinger/Stern, Picture Press, 1970s), 228 (photo by Thomas Scharnhorst, Essen); Nermin Abadan-Unat, 'The Socio-Economic Aspects of Return Migration to Turkey', *Migration* 3 (1988): 29–59.

41. Abadan-Unat, *Turkish Workers in Europe*, 266–267.

42. Karen Schönwälder, 'Migration, Refugees and Ethnic Plurality as Issues of Public and Political Debates in (West) Germany', in David Cesarani and Mary Fulbrook, eds., *Citizenship, Nationality and Migration in Europe* (London: Routledge, 1996), 164; Maren Möhring, 'Food for Thought: Rethinking the History of Migration to West Germany Through the Migrant Restaurant Business', *Journal of Contemporary History* 49, no. 1 (2014): 227.

Chapter 9: Unsettling the European Periphery: Migration to the UK

1. Joyce Egginton, *They Seek a Living* (London: Hutchinson, 1957), 63–65; Kennetta Hammond Perry, *London Is the Place for Me: Black Britons, Citizenship and the Politics of Race* (New York: Oxford University Press, 2016), 2–3. Ironically, in the light of his most famous song, Lord Kitchener chose to make his home in Manchester before returning to Trinidad in 1962.

2. Laurence Brown, 'Afro-Caribbean Migrants in France and the UK', in Leo Lucassen, David Feldman, and Jochen Oltmer, eds., *Paths of Integration: Migrants in Western Europe, 1880–2004* (Amsterdam: Amsterdam University Press, 2006), 94; Colin Grant, 'Windrush Tales: My Parents Were Caught Between Nostalgia and an Inability to Return', *The Guardian*, 23 July 2018, https://www.theguardian.com/books/2018/jul/23/a-new-chapter-in-windrush-the-authors-who-echoed-my-parents-journey-.

3. Kathy Burrell, 'Stories from "The World in One City": Migrant Lives in Liverpool', *North-West Geography* 17, no. 1 (2017): 12–18.

4. Sheila Patterson, *Dark Strangers: Sociological Study of the Absorption of a Recent West Indian Migrant Group in Brixton, South London* (London: Tavistock, 1963); Michael Banton, 'Patterson (née Caffyn), Sheila (1918–1998)', www.oxforddnb.com /view/10.1093/ref:odnb/9780198614128.001.0001/odnb-9780198614128-e-70183. See also Wendy Webster, *Englishness and Empire, 1939–1965* (Oxford: Oxford University Press, 2005), 149–181; Chris Waters, '"Dark Strangers in Our Midst": The Discourse of Race Relations, 1947–1963', *Journal of British Studies* 36, no. 2 (1997): 207–238; Kevin Myers, *Struggles for a Past: Irish and Afro-Caribbean Histories in England, 1951–2000* (Manchester: Manchester University Press, 2015); Perry, *London Is the Place for Me*, 86.

5. Wolf R. Böhning, *The Migration of Workers in the United Kingdom and the European Community* (London: Oxford University Press, for the Institute of Race Relations, 1972), 50; Clair Wills, *Lovers and Strangers: An Immigrant History of Post-War Britain* (London: Allen Lane, 2017), 52–53.

6. John Brown, *The Un-melting Pot: An English Town and Its Immigrants* (London: Macmillan, 1970), 82–97.

7. Kathy Burrell, *Moving Lives: Narratives of Nation and Migration Among Europeans in Post-War Britain* (London: Routledge, 2006), 27, 29; Anne-Marie Fortier, 'Historicity and Communality: Narratives About the Origins of the Italian "Community" in Britain', in John R. Campbell and Alan Rew, eds., *Identity and Affect: Experiences of Identity in a Globalising World* (London: Pluto Press, 1999), 199–226.

8. Guido, quoted in Burrell, *Moving Lives*, 29.

9. Sean O'Hagan, 'Romano Cagnoni Obituary', *The Guardian*, 8 March 2018, https://www .theguardian.com/artanddesign/2018/mar/08/romano-cagnoni-obituary; Perry, *London Is the Place for Me*, 78.

10. Enda Delaney, *The Irish in Post-War Britain* (Oxford: Oxford University Press, 2013), 12–13, 17.

11. Mark Duguid, *The Colony* (1964), British Film Institute, Screenonline, www.screenonline.org.uk/tv/id/439126/index.html. See also Timothy O'Grady and Steve Pyke, *I Could Read the Sky* (London: Harvill, 1998).

12. Delaney, *Irish in Post-War Britain*, 93; Patrick Joyce, 'The Journey West', *Field Day Review*, 2014, available at www.patrickjoyce.info/wp-content/files/Journey_West_ FINAL.pdf.

13. Delaney, *Irish in Post-War Britain*, 66; Enda Delaney, *Demography, State and Society: Irish Migration to Britain, 1921 to 1971* (Liverpool: Liverpool University Press, 2000), 175; Margaret Ó hÓrgartaigh, 'Irish Nurses in Britain Since WW2', in Klaus Bade, Pieter C. Emmer, Leo Lucassen, and Jochen Oltmer, eds., *The Encyclopedia of European Migration and Minorities from the Seventeenth Century to the Present* (Cambridge: Cambridge University Press, 2011), 494–496; Mary Daniels, 'Exile or Opportunity? Irish Nurses and Midwives in Britain', *Irish Studies Review* 2, no. 5 (1993): 4–8.

14. Quoted in Myers, *Struggles for a Past*, 46; Debate on the Commonwealth Immigrants Bill, House of Commons Debates, 16 November 1961, vol. 641, col. 756, http:// hansard.millbanksystems.com/commons/1961/nov/16/commonwealth -immigrants-bill.

15. Webster, *Englishness and Empire*, 172; Brown, 'Afro-Caribbean Migrants', 179.

16. Nancy Foner, *Jamaica Farewell: Jamaican Migrants in London* (London: Routledge and Kegan Paul, 1979), 13; Colin Holmes, *John Bull's Island: Immigration and British Society* (London: Macmillan, 1988), 221 (adding that a similar deal was done with Trinidad and Jamaica in 1966); 'Strong Is Doing the Right Thing, Not the Easy Thing', London Metropolitan Police, https://www.met.police.uk/police-forces /metropolitan-police/areas/campaigns/2018/celebrating-100-years-of-women -policing-in-london/100-years-strong/sislin-fay-allen.

17. Katherine Hassell, interview with Levi Roots, *The Guardian*, 21 July 2017, https://www. theguardian.com/lifeandstyle/2017/jul/21/levi-roots-my-parents-moved-to -britain-when-i-was-four-i-didnt-see-them-again-until-i-was-11; Egginton, *They Seek a Living*, 180.

18. Sarah Hackett, *Foreigners, Minorities and Integration: The Muslim Immigrant Experience in Britain and Germany* (Manchester: Manchester University Press, 2013), 38–48; Roger Ballard, 'Indian, Pakistani and Bangladeshi Migrants in Great Britain Since 1947', in Bade et al., eds., *Encyclopedia of European Migration*, 483–487.

19. Karen Schönwälder, *Einwanderung und ethnische Pluralität: Politische Entscheidungen und öffentliche Debatten in Grossbritannien und der Bundesrepublik von der 50-er bis zu den 1970er Jahren* (Essen: Klartext, 2001), 100–101; Bill Schwarz, 'The Only White Man in There: The Re-Racialisation of England, 1956–1968', *Race and Class* 38, no. 1 (1996): 73; Political and Economic Planning, *Refugees in Britain: Hungarians and Anglo-Egyptians* (London: PEP, 1958); Jordanna Bailkin, *Unsettled: Refugee Camps and the Making of Multicultural Britain* (Oxford: Oxford University Press, 2018), 55, 100–105.

20. Roberta Bivins, *Contagious Communities: Medicine, Migration, and the NHS in Post-War Britain* (Oxford: Oxford University Press, 2015), 13, 43–47, 53–57, 82.

21. Perry, *London Is the Place for Me*, 82, for the quotation and analysis.

22. Elizabeth Jones, 'The Bristol Bus Boycott of 1963', *Black History Month*, 7 October 2018, www.blackhistorymonth.org.uk/article/section/bhm-heroes/the-bristol-bus -boycott-of-1963. In 1992 Stephenson helped set up the Bristol Black Archives Partnership to promote the history of African-Caribbean people in Bristol. See also Eggington, *They Seek a Living*, 92–103; Wills, *Lovers and Strangers*, 116–117.

23. Sheila Patterson, *Immigrants in Industry* (London: Oxford University Press, 1968), 101.

24. Robert Miles, 'The Riots of 1958: The Ideological Construction of "Race Relations" as a Political Issue in Britain', *Immigrants and Minorities* 3, no. 3 (1984): 252–275; Raphael Rowe, 'Who Killed Kelso Cochrane?' BBC, 7 April 2006, http://news.bbc .co.uk/1/hi/programmes/4871898.stm; Richard Davenport-Hines, 'Rachman, Peter (1920?–1962)', *Oxford Dictionary of National Biography*, Oxford University Press, 2004, online edition, September 2010, www.oxforddnb.com/view/article/53680; Wills, *Lovers and Strangers*, 248–250; Perry, *London Is the Place for Me*, 126–152.

25. Mica Nava, 'Sometimes Antagonistic, Sometimes Ardently Sympathetic: Contradictory Responses to Migrants in Postwar Britain', *Ethnicities* 14, no. 3 (2014): 458–480.

26. J. Fares, 'Moslems in Britain—Manchester (1961)', https://player.bfi.org.uk/free /film/watch-moslems-in-britain-manchester-1961-online; 'Filmmakers Capture Life in Cardiff Docks', Wales Online, 31 March 2013, www.walesonline.co.uk/news

/ales-news/film-makers-capture-life-cardiff-2390433; Ceri Jackson, '#towerlives: Rise of Towers and Fall of Tiger Bay', BBC News, 11 April 2016, www.bbc.co.uk/news /uk-wales-35997410; 'The Story of the Cairo Café', BBC2, 29 September 2011, www .bbc.co.uk/programmes/p00krrq7.

27. Randall Hansen, *Citizenship and Immigration in Post-War Britain: The Institutional Origins of a Multicultural Nation* (Oxford: Oxford University Press, 2000), 90.

28. John Solomos and Stephen Woodhams, 'The Politics of Cypriot Migration to Britain', *Immigrants and Minorities* 14, no. 3 (1995): 240; Webster, *Englishness and Empire*, 155.

29. Briefing paper prepared for the UK delegation to the ICEM, 14 November 1958, UK National Archives, HO 352/133.

30. Bivins, *Contagious Communities*, 145.

31. Hansard, 17 February 1961, cited in Bivins, *Contagious Communities*, 116; Hansen, *Citizenship and Immigration*, 83, 108; Bivins, *Contagious Communities*, 120; copy of speeches of 2 February 1960, in Christian Aid Archives, CA/I/6/7, Aid to European Refugees: correspondence and bulletins 1956–66. Gaitskell is reported in Hansard, 5 December 1961.

32. House of Commons, 19 July 1962, cols. 635–641, https://api.parliament.uk/historic -hansard/commons/1962/jul/19/miss-carmen-bryan-deportation-order #S5CV0663P0_19620719_HOC_236; Wills, *Lovers and Strangers*, 107–122.

33. Foner, *Jamaica Farewell*, 14; Waters, '"Dark Strangers in Our Midst"', 234; Robert Pearce, 'Osborne, Sir Cyril (1898–1969)', *Oxford Dictionary of National Biography*, Oxford University Press, 2004, online edition, January 2011, www.oxforddnb.com /view/article/40643; Anthony T. Bouscaren, *International Migrations Since 1945* (New York: Praeger, 1963), 72.

34. Foner, *Jamaica Farewell*, 67.

35. See the short biography of Boscoe Holder, written by his son, available at www .christianholder.com/boscoe-holder (he returned to Trinidad in 1970); Stephen Bourne, 'Atwell, (Una) Winifred (c. 1913–1983)', *Oxford Dictionary of National Biography*, Oxford University Press, 2004, online edition, January 2011, www .oxforddnb.com/view/article/58882.

36. Duguid, *The Colony*, quotation at 17 minutes; Webster, *Englishness and Empire*, 163–164.

37. Hansen, *Citizenship and Immigration*, 161.

38. Evan Smith and Marinella Marmo, 'The Myth of Sovereignty: British Immigration Control in Policy and Practice in the Nineteen-Seventies', *Historical Research* 87, no. 236 (2014): 344–369.

39. Wills, *Lovers and Strangers*, 328–330. For an account of the reverberations of Powell's speech, particularly in Wolverhampton, see Shirin Hirsch, *In the Shadow of Enoch Powell: Race, Locality and Resistance* (Manchester: Manchester University Press, 2018).

40. Dee Lahiri, '"I Don't Think I Can Die Before I Find Out What Happened to My Son"', *The Guardian*, 15 May 2001, https://www.theguardian.com/world/2001/may/15 /race.london.

41. Böhning, *Migration of Workers*, 6–7.

42. Ibid., 154, 158.

43. Ibid., 145–147.

Chapter 10: Migrants Under Communism

1. Ivan T. Berend, *Central and Eastern Europe, 1944–1993* (Cambridge: Cambridge University Press, 1996), 186–187.
2. Robert J. Kaiser, *The Geography of Nationalism in Russia and the USSR* (Princeton, NJ: Princeton University Press, 1994), 166–168.
3. Lewis H. Siegelbaum and Leslie Page Moch, *Broad Is My Native Land: Repertoires and Regimes of Migration in Russia's Twentieth Century* (Ithaca, NY: Cornell University Press, 2014), 141–144.
4. Cynthia Buckley, 'The Myth of Managed Migration: Migration Control and Market in the Soviet Period', *Slavic Review* 54, no. 4 (1995): 896–916.
5. Viktor I. Perevedentsev, *Sovremennaia migratsiia naseleniia Zapadnoi Sibiri* (Novosibirsk: Zapadno-Sibirskoe knizhnoe izdatel'stvo, 1965).
6. Vladimir V. Onikienko and Valerii A. Popovkin, *Kompleksnoe issledovanie migratsionnykh protsessov: Analiz migratsii naseleniia USSR* (Moscow: Statistika, 1973), 12; Pierre Sorlin, *The Soviet People and Their Society* (London: Pall Mall, 1969), 229; Siegelbaum and Moch, *Broad Is My Native Land*, 127.
7. Liubov N. Denisova, *Ischezaiushchaia derevnia Rossii: Nechernozem'e v 1960–1980e gody* (Moscow: RAN, 1996), 136; quoted in Siegelbaum and Moch, *Broad Is My Native Land*, 124; Onikienko and Popovkin, *Kompleksnoe issledovanie*, 98–99.
8. Martha Brill Olcott, *The Kazakhs* (Stanford: Stanford University Press, 1987), 232; Judith Pallot, 'Rural Depopulation and the Restoration of the Russian Village Under Gorbachev', *Soviet Studies* 42, no. 4 (1990): 655–674; Denisova, *Ischezaiushchaia derevnia*, 124; Siegelbaum and Moch, *Broad Is My Native Land*, 139–140.
9. Geoffrey Hosking, 'The Russian Peasant Rediscovered: "Village Prose" of the 1960s', *Slavic Review* 32, no. 4 (1973): 705–724; Aleksandr S. Seniavskii, *Rossiiskii gorod v 1960-e—80-e gody* (Moscow: Institut rossiiskoi istorii, 1995).
10. Denisova, *Ischezaiushchaia derevnia*, 132, 134, 141, translated by Jane Gatrell.
11. Romuald Misiunas and Rein Taagepera, *The Baltic States: Years of Dependence, 1940–1990* (London: Hurst, 1993), 192–193, 195, 197.
12. Siegelbaum and Moch, *Broad Is My Native Land*, 137–138; Mervyn Matthews, *The Passport Society: Controlling Movement in Russia and the USSR* (Boulder: Westview, 1993), 50; Emily Elliott, 'Soviet Socialist Stars and Neoliberal Losers: Young Labour Migrants in Moscow, 1971–1991', *Journal of Migration History* 3, no. 2 (2017): 274–300.
13. Siegelbaum and Moch, *Broad Is My Native Land*, 88; Kateryna Burkush, 'On the Forest Front: Labour Relations and Seasonal Migration in 1960s–80s' *Labor History* 59, no. 3 (2018): 295–315.
14. Siegelbaum and Moch, *Broad Is My Native Land*, 89; Hans Oversloot, 'Soviet Construction Workers (*shabashniki*) Since the 1950s', in Klaus Bade, Pieter C. Emmer, Leo Lucassen, and Jochen Oltmer, eds., *The Encyclopedia of European Migration and Minorities from the Seventeenth Century to the Present* (Cambridge: Cambridge University Press, 2011), 687–689.
15. Siegelbaum and Moch, *Broad Is My Native Land*, 93–95; Viktor Gal'chenko, 'Zhitie odnogo shabashnika', *EKO: Ekonomika i organizatsiia promyshlennogo proizvodstva* 153, no. 3 (1987): 101–136; N. Alekseenko, 'Shabashniki: Stereotipy i real'nost', *Sotsiologicheskie issledovaniia* 6 (1987): 89–94.

16. Stephen Lovell, *Summerfolk: A History of the Dacha, 1710–2000* (Ithaca, NY: Cornell University Press, 2003); Chris Leslie and Jonathan Charley, 'The Wrecking Ball Swings at Moscow: A Photo Essay', *The Guardian*, 31 October 2017, https://www.theguardian.com/cities/2017/oct/31/moscow-residents-vote-russia-demolition-rehousing.

17. Donald J. Raleigh, *Soviet Baby Boomers: An Oral History of Russia's Cold War Generation* (New York: Oxford University Press, 2012), 224–227.

18. Christopher J. Ward, *Brezhnev's Folly: The Building of BAM and Late Soviet Socialism* (Pittsburgh: Pittsburgh University Press, 2009), 112. For a Soviet-era view, complete with diaries and photographs, see L. P. Kaminskaia, *BAM—doroga druzhby: Dokumental'no-khudozhestvennyi sbornik* (Irkutsk: Vostochno-Sibirskoe knizhnoe izd-vo, 1984).

19. Christopher J. Ward, 'Far from Home: Soviet and Non-Soviet Railway Workers' Experiences During the Construction of the Baikal-Amur Mainline Railway (BAM), 1974–1984', in Andrea Walke, Jan Musekamp, and Nicole Svobodny, eds., *Migration and Mobility in the Modern Age: Refugees, Travelers, and Traffickers in Europe and Eurasia* (Bloomington: Indiana University Press, 2016), 209–234.

20. Dariusz Stola, 'Opening a Non-exit State: The Passport Policy of Communist Poland, 1949–1980', *East European Politics and Societies* 29, no. 1 (2015): 96–119; Dariusz Stola, *Kraj bez wyjścia? Migracje z Polski 1949–1989* (Warsaw: Instytut Studiów Politycznych PAN, 2010). According to Stola, bilateral agreements between 1949 and 1951 led to the emigration of 76,000 Germans and 29,000 Jews. Stola, *Kraj bez wyjścia?*, 473.

21. Jonathan Zatlin, 'Scarcity and Resentment: Economic Sources of Xenophobia in the GDR, 1971–1989', *Central European History* 40, no. 4 (2007): 683–684; Stola, *Kraj bez wyjścia?*, 473. For the Soviet history, see Anne E. Gorsuch, *All This Is Your World: Soviet Tourism at Home and Abroad After Stalin* (Oxford: Oxford University Press, 2011).

22. Stola, *Kraj bez wyjścia?*, 474.

23. Karolina S. Follis, *Building Fortress Europe: The Polish-Ukrainian Frontier* (Philadelphia: University of Pennsylvania Press, 2012), 39; Kapka Kassabova, *Border: A Journey to the Edge of Europe* (London: Granta, 2017), 49–50, 93.

24. Elidor Mëhilli, 'Socialist Encounters: Albania and the Transnational Eastern Bloc in the 1950s', in Patryk Babiracki and Kenyon Zimmer, eds., *Cold War Crossings: International Travel and Exchange Across the Soviet Bloc, 1940s–1960s* (Arlington TX: Texas A&M Press, 2014), 118.

25. I draw here upon an unpublished paper by Peter Apor.

26. Alena Alamgir, 'Recalcitrant Women: Internationalism and the Redefinition of Welfare Limits in the Czechoslovak-Vietnamese Labor Exchange Program', *Slavic Review* 73, no. 1 (2014): 133–155; Adéla Souralová, 'Mutual Emotional Relations in Caregiving Work: Vietnamese Families and Czech Nannies', in Dirk Hoerder, Elise van Nederveen Meerkerk, and Silke Neunsinger, eds., *Towards a Global History of Domestic and Caregiving Workers* (Leiden: Brill, 2015), 182–201.

27. Zatlin, 'Scarcity and Resentment', 717; Johannes D. Enstad, 'Neo-Nazis Behind the Iron Curtain', *The Restless Russianist*, 26 February 2018, https://restlessrussianist.com/2018/02/26/first.

28. Constantin Katsakioris, 'Burden or Allies? Third World Students and Internationalist Duty Through Soviet Eyes', *Kritika: Explorations in Russian and Eurasian History* 18, no. 3 (2017): 539–567.

29. Julie Hessler, 'Death of an African Student in Moscow: Race, Politics, and the Cold War', *Cahiers du monde russe* 47, no. 1 (2006): 33–63.

30. Karolina Novinšćak, 'Auf den Spuren von Brandts Ostpolitik und Titos Sonderweg: Deutsch-jugoslawische Migrationsbeziehungen in den 1960er und 1970er Jahren', in Jochen Oltmer, Axel Kreienbrink, and Carlos Sanz Diaz, eds., *Das 'Gastarbeiter'-System: Arbeitsmigration und ihre Folgen in der Bundesrepublik Deutschland und Westeuropa* (Oldenbourg: Wissenschaftsverlag, 2012), 133–148; Pierre Lanfranchi and Matthew Taylor, *Moving with the Ball: The Migration of Professional Footballers* (Oxford: Berg, 2001), 117–118; Christian Molnar, 'Imagining Yugoslavs: Migration and the Cold War in Postwar West Germany', *Central European History* 47, no. 1 (2014): 138–169; Othmar N. Haberl, *Die Abwanderung von Arbeitskräften aus Jugoslawien: Zur Problematik ihrer Auslandsbeschäftigung und Rückführung* (München: Oldenbourg, 1978), 129. I have seen both lower and higher figures quoted for workers in Yugoslavia. Yugoslavia's total population in 1971 was around 20 million. I thank Yaron Matras for the information about Roma migrants. In 1957, Bernard Vukas became the first Yugoslav footballer to sign for a foreign team; others followed in his footsteps in the 1960s.

31. Barbara Le Normand, 'The Gastarbajters as a Transnational Yugoslav Working Class', in Paul Stubbs, Igor Duda, and Rory Archer, eds., *Social Inequalities and Discontent in Yugoslav Socialism* (Abingdon: Routledge, 2016), 51.

32. Le Normand, 'Gastarbajters', 47; Haberl, *Die Abwanderung von Arbeitskräften aus Jugoslawien*, 73, for Tito's speech in 1965, and 117, for reports of strike-breaking in France.

33. Le Normand, 'Gastarbajters', 51.

34. Johan Svanberg, 'Labour Migration and the Swedish Labour Market Model: A Case Study of Recruitment of Yugoslav Workers to Svenska Fläktfabriken in Växjö, 1969–1970', *Scandinavian Journal of History* 36, no. 1 (2011): 91–113.

35. Jane Kramer, *Unsettling Europe* (New York: Random House, 1980), 89; Richard Milne, 'Sweden Immigration: Don't Look Back', *Financial Times*, 5 October 2015, https://www.ft.com/content/a8573532-65bf-11e5-97e9-7f0bf5e7177b.

36. Novinšćak, 'Auf den Spuren', 140–141.

Chapter 11: A Dual Challenge: Recession and Asylum in Europe

1. For background, see Myron Weiner, *The Global Migration Crisis: Challenges to States and Human Rights* (New York: HarperCollins, 1995); Saskia Sassen, *Guests and Aliens* (New York: New Press, 1999); Göran Therborn, *European Modernity and Beyond: The Trajectory of European Societies, 1945–2000* (London: Sage, 1995).

2. Anthony Messina, *The Logics and Politics of Post-WWII Migration to Western Europe* (Cambridge: Cambridge University Press, 1997), 25, 31.

3. Ulrich Herbert, *A History of Foreign Labor in Germany, 1880–1980: Seasonal Workers, Forced Laborers, Guest Workers* (Ann Arbor: University of Michigan Press, 1990), 234; Czarina Wilpert, 'Identity Issues in the History of the Post-War Migration from Turkey to Germany', *German Politics and Society* 31, no. 2 (2013): 115.

4. Karen Schönwälder, 'Migration, Refugees and Ethnic Plurality as Issues of Public and Political Debates in (West) Germany', in David Cesarani and Mary Fulbrook, eds., *Citizenship, Nationality and Migration in Europe* (London: Routledge, 1996), 167; Karin Hunn, *'Nächstes Jahr kehren wir zurück…': Die Geschichte der türkischen 'Gastarbeiter' in der Bundesrepublik* (Göttingen: Wallstein, 2005), 204; Klaus Bade and Jochen Oltmer, 'Germany', in Klaus Bade, Pieter C. Emmer, Leo Lucassen, and Jochen Oltmer, eds., *Encyclopedia of European Migration and Minorities from the Seventeenth Century to the Present* (Cambridge: Cambridge University Press, 2011), 76. Some restrictions predated the oil crisis. Nigel Harris, *The New Untouchables: Immigration and the New World Worker* (Harmondsworth: Penguin, 1986), 107.

5. Tomas Hammar, 'Sweden', in Hammar, ed., *European Immigration Policy: A Comparative Study* (Cambridge: Cambridge University Press, 1985), 29; Allan Pred, *Even in Sweden: Racisms, Racialized Spaces, and the Popular Geographical Imagination* (Berkeley: University of California Press, 2000), 34.

6. This emerges strongly in the work of Gérard Noiriel, *The French Melting Pot* (Minneapolis: University of Minnesota Press, 1996), originally published as *Le creuset français: Histoire de l'immigration XIX–XX siècle* (Paris: Editions du Seuil, 1988).

7. Robert Gildea, *France Since 1945* (Oxford: Oxford University Press, 2002), 173; Minayo Nasiali, *Native to the Republic: Empire, Social Citizenship, and Everyday Life in Marseille Since 1945* (Ithaca, NY: Cornell University Press, 2016), 101.

8. Pred, *Even in Sweden*, 6; Maxim Silverman, *Deconstructing the Nation: Immigration, Racism and Citizenship in Modern France* (London: Routledge, 1992), 64–65; Institute of Race Relations, European Race Audit, 2010, available at www.irr.org.uk/app/uploads/2016/12/ERA_BriefingPaper2.pdf.

9. James F. Hollifield, *Immigrants, Markets, and States: The Political Economy of Postwar Europe* (Cambridge, MA: Harvard University Press, 1992).

10. Wolf R. Böhning, 'International Migration in Western Europe: Reflections on the Past Five Years', *International Labour Review* 118, no. 4 (1979): 401–414. Compare Manuel Castells, 'Immigrant Workers and Class Struggles in Advanced Capitalism: The Western European Experience', *Politics and Society* 5, no. 1 (1975): 33–66.

11. Deniz Göktürk, David Gramling, and Anton Kaes, eds., *Germany in Transit: Nation and Migration, 1955–2005* (Berkeley: University of California Press, 2007 [1973]), 247–249; Hollifield, *Immigrants, Markets, and States*; Joseph Carens, *The Ethics of Immigration* (New York: Oxford University Press, 2013), 260–262.

12. Wolf R. Böhning, *The Migration of Workers in the United Kingdom and the European Community* (London: Oxford University Press, for the Institute of Race Relations, 1972), 18; Andrew Geddes, *Immigration and European Integration: Beyond Fortress Europe?*, 2nd ed. (Manchester: Manchester University Press, 2008), 49.

13. Christina Boswell and Andrew Geddes, *Migration and Mobility in the European Union* (Basingstoke: Palgrave Macmillan, 2011), 58–61.

14. Geddes, *Immigration and European Integration*, 88–110; 'Temporary Reintroduction of Border Controls', European Commission, Migration and Home Affairs, https://ec.europa.eu/home-affairs/what-we-do/policies/borders-and-visas/schengen/reintroduction-border-control.

15. Stephan Scheel, '"The Secret Is to Look Good on Paper": Appropriating Mobility Within and Against a Machine of Illegalisation', in Nicholas De Genova, ed., *The*

Borders of 'Europe': Autonomy of Migration, Tactics of Bordering (Durham, NC: Duke University Press, 2017), 42.

16. Margaret Thatcher, speech delivered at the College of Europe, Bruges, 20 September 1988.

17. Quoted in Donald M. Carter, *States of Grace: Senegalese in Italy and the New European Immigration* (Minnesota: University of Minnesota Press, 1997), 167.

18. Christian Joppke, *Immigration and the Nation-State: The United States, Germany, and the UK* (Oxford: Oxford University Press, 1999), 66; Patrice Poutrus, 'Asylum in Post-War Germany: Refugee Admission Policies and Their Practical Implementation in the Federal Republic and the GDR Between the Late 1940s and the Mid-1970s', *Journal of Contemporary History* 49, no. 1 (2014): 115–133.

19. Hunn, '*Nächstes Jahr kehren wir zurück…*', 455; Olaf Beuchling, 'Vietnamese Refugees in Western, Central, and Northern Europe Since the 1970s: The Examples of France, Great Britain, and Germany', in Bade et al., eds., *Encyclopedia of European Migration*, 730–734; Frank Bösch, 'Über die Aufnahme vietnamischer "Boat People" in der Bundesrepublik', *Zeithistorische Forschungen*, Heft 1 (2017), online access at www.zeithistorische-forschungen.de/1-2017/id%3D5447.

20. Rita Chin, *The Guest Worker Question in Postwar Germany* (New York: Cambridge University Press, 2007), 146–147.

21. Anke Schwarzer, 'Die vergessenen Morde von Billbrook', *Die Zeit*, 22 August 2014, www.zeit.de/hamburg/politik-wirtschaft/2014-08/halskestrasse-gedenken; Chin, *Guest Worker Question*, 147; Matthew Gibney, *The Ethics and Politics of Asylum: Liberal Democracy and the Response to Refugees* (Cambridge: Cambridge University Press, 2004), 100–103.

22. Tycho Walaardt, 'From Heroes to Vulnerable Victims: Labelling Christian Turks as Genuine Refugees in the 1970s', *Ethnic and Racial Studies* 36, no. 7 (2013): 1199–1218.

23. Mikael Byström, 'When the State Stepped into the Arena': The Swedish Welfare State, Refugees and Immigrants, 1930s–50s', *Journal of Contemporary History* 49, no. 3 (2014): 610.

24. Magdalena Jaakkola, 'Informal Networks and Formal Associations of Finnish Immigrants in Sweden', in John Rex, Daniele Joly, and Czarina Wilpert, eds., *Immigrant Associations in Europe* (Aldershot: Gower, 1986), 201–218; Hammar, 'Sweden', in Hammar, ed., *European Immigration Policy*, 17–49; Mikael Byström and Pär Frohnert, 'Introduction IV', in Mikael Byström and Pär Frohnert, eds., *Reaching a State of Hope: Refugees, Immigrants and the Swedish Welfare State, 1930–2000* (Lund: Nordic Academic Press, 2013), 228.

25. Admir Skodo, 'The Long and Short Arms of the State: Swedish Multidirectional Controls of Afghan Asylum Seekers During the Cold War', courtesy of the author; Pred, *Even in Sweden*, 37–49. The quote from Franzén appears on p. 50.

26. Laura Jeffery, *Chagos Islanders in Mauritius and the UK: Forced Displacement and Onward Migration* (Manchester: Manchester University Press, 2016), 115. In February 2019 the International Court of Justice in The Hague ordered the British government to return the Chagos Islands to Mauritius, thereby reopening the debate concerning the status of the displaced Chagossians. See Owen Bowcott, 'UN Court Rejects UK's Claim of Sovereignty over Chagos Islands', *The Guardian*, 25 February 2019, https://www.theguardian.com /world/2019/feb/25/un-court-rejects-uk-claim-to-sovereignty-over-chagos-islands.

27. Quoted in Jordanna Bailkin, *Unsettled: Refugee Camps and the Making of Multicultural Britain* (Oxford: Oxford University Press, 2018), 105.

28. Mahmood Mamdani, *From Citizen to Refugee: Ugandan Asians Come to Britain* (London: Pinter, 2011 [1973]), 55, 66; Becky Taylor, 'Good Citizens? Ugandan Asians, Volunteers and "Race" Relations in 1970s Britain', *History Workshop Journal* 85 (2018): 120–141; Bailkin, *Unsettled*, 56–64.

29. Sara Cosemans, 'The Politics of Dispersal: Turning Ugandan Colonial Subjects into Postcolonial Refugees (1967–76)', *Migration Studies* 6, no. 1 (2018): 99–119; Charles Westin and Catarina Nyberg, 'Three Generations of Ugandan Asian Diaspora in Sweden', in Peter Waxman and Val Colic-Peisker, eds., *Homeland Wanted: Interdisciplinary Perspectives on Refugee Resettlement in the West* (New York: Nova Science Publishers, 2005), 147–164; Rina Valeny, 'From Pariah to Paragon: The Social Mobility of Ugandan Asian Refugees in Britain' (PhD thesis, University of Wales, 1998), 220.

30. Tony Kushner and Katharine Knox, *Refugees in an Age of Genocide: Global, National and Local Perspectives during the Twentieth Century* (London: Frank Cass, 1999), 310–311.

31. Peter R. Jones, *Vietnamese Refugees: A Study of Their Reception and Resettlement in the United Kingdom* (London: Research and Planning Unit, 1982); Bailkin, *Unsettled*, 20–21.

32. Frank Bösch, 'Über die Aufnahme vietnamischer "Boat People" in der Bundesrepublik', *Zeithistorische Forschungen*, Heft 1 (2017), www.zeithistorische-forschungen .de/1-2017/id%3D5447.

33. Chris McCreal, 'Vietnamese Boat People: Living to Tell the Tale', *The Guardian*, 20 March 2016, www.theguardian.com/global/2016/mar/20/vietnamese-boat-people -survivors-families.

34. 'Cap Anamur: About Us', Cap Anamur, German Emergency Doctors, n.d., https:// www.cap-anamur.org/en/ueber-uns.

35. Information courtesy of Kasia Nowak.

36. Ioanna Laliotou, '"I Want to See the World": Mobility and Subjectivity in the European Context', in Luisa Passerini, Dawn Lyon, Enrica Capussotti, and Ioanna Laliotou, eds., *Women Migrants from East to West: Gender, Mobility and Belonging in Contemporary Europe* (Oxford: Berghahn, 2007), 61–62.

Chapter 12: Unsettling Southern Europe

1. Fernando Collantes Gutiérrez and Vicente Pinilla, *Peaceful Surrender: The Depopulation of Rural Spain in the Twentieth Century* (Newcastle: Cambridge Scholars, 2011).

2. Donald M. Carter, *States of Grace: Senegalese in Italy and the New European Immigration* (Minnesota: University of Minnesota Press, 1997), 32; Ilaria Favretto, 'Rough Music and Factory Protest in Post-1945 Italy', *Past and Present* 228, no. 1 (2015): 207–247; Nicola Pizzolato, '"I Terroni in Città": Revisiting Southern Migrants' Militancy in Turin's "Hot Autumn"', *Contemporary European History* 21, no. 4 (2012): 619–634.

3. Michele Alacevich, 'Planning Peace: The European Roots of the Post-War Global Development Challenge', *Past and Present* 239 (2018): 219–264; Yvonne Rieker,

'Ein Stück Heimat findet man ja immer': *Die italienische Einwanderung in die Bundesrepublik* (Essen: Klartext, 2003), 123.

4. John Foot, 'Southern Italian Workers in Northern Italy, 1945–75', in Klaus Bade, Pieter C. Emmer, Leo Lucassen, and Jochen Oltmer, eds., *Encyclopedia of European Migration and Minorities from the Seventeenth Century to the Present* (Cambridge: Cambridge University Press, 2011), 684–687.

5. Paul Ginsborg, *A History of Contemporary Italy* (Harmondsworth: Penguin, 1990), 217–218.

6. Favretto, 'Rough Music', 225; Ginsborg, *History of Contemporary Italy*, 321.

7. Ginsborg, *History of Contemporary Italy*, 225–226; Chiellino is quoted in Máiréad Nic Craith, *Narratives of Place, Belonging and Language: An Intercultural Perspective* (Basingstoke: Palgrave Macmillan, 2012), 82.

8. 'Bitter Rice (1949)', https://www.imdb.com/title/tt0040737/?ref_=nmbio_mbio; 'Rocco and His Brothers (1960)', https://www.imdb.com/title/tt0054248.

9. Inbal Ofer, *Claiming the City and Contesting the State: Squatting, Community Formation and Democratization in Spain, 1955–1986* (London: Routledge, 2017), 43; Karen O'Reilly, *The British on the Costa del Sol: Transnational Identities and Local Communities* (London: Routledge, 2000), 151.

10. Ofer, *Claiming the City*, 62–69.

11. Tony Judt, *Postwar: A History of Europe Since 1945* (London: William Heinemann, 2005), 513; Pedro Ramos Pinto, *Lisbon Rising: Urban Social Movements in the Portuguese Revolution, 1974–75* (Manchester: Manchester University Press, 2013).

12. Anthony T. Bouscaren, *International Migrations Since 1945* (New York: Praeger, 1963), 41; Yvonne Rieker, 'Italian Labour Migrants in Northern, Central and Western Europe Since the End of World War 2', in Bade et al., eds., *Encyclopedia of European Migration*, 507–511; Umberto Cassinis, 'Intra-European Movements of Italian Workers', *Migration News*, no. 4 (1956): 1–6; Sarah Baumann,…*Und es kamen auch Frauen: Engagement italienischer Migrantinnen in Politik und Gesellschaft der Nachkriegsschweiz* (Zürich: Seismo, 2014), 10. The post-1990 decline was partly explained by naturalisation (as in Belgium), the decision to look for opportunities elsewhere (Switzerland), and return migration.

13. Massimo Livi-Bacci, *The Demographic and Social Pattern of Emigration from the Southern European Countries* (Florence: University of Florence, 1972), 17, 22.

14. Rudolf Braun, *Sozio-kulturelle Probleme der Eingliederung italienischer Arbeitskräfte in der Schweiz* (Erlenbach-Zurich: Eugen Rentsch Verlag, 1970), 253, 258.

15. Livi-Bacci, *Demographic and Social Pattern of Emigration*, 117, 122.

16. Judt, *Postwar*, 334; Marion Bernitt, *Die Rückwanderung spanischer Gastarbeiter: Der Fall Andalusien* (Königstein: Hanstein, 1981), 16, 31.

17. Tycho Walaardt, 'New Refugees? Manly War Resisters Prevent an Asylum Crisis in the Netherlands, 1968–1973', in Marlou Schrover and Deirdre Moloney, eds., *Gender, Migration and Categorisation: Making Distinctions Between Migrants in Western Countries, 1945–2010* (Amsterdam: Amsterdam University Press, 2013), 75–104.

18. Marie-Antoinette Hily and Michel Poinard, 'Portuguese Associations in France', in John Rex, Daniele Joly, and Czarina Wilpert, eds., *Immigrant Associations in Europe* (Aldershot: Gower, 1986), 134; Christian de Chalonge, 'O Salto', synopsis in French, www.memoria-viva.fr/christian-de-chalonge-o-salto-1967.

19. Victor Pereira, 'L'état portugais et les portugais en France de 1958 à 1974', *Lusotopie*, no. 2 (2002): 9–27.
20. John Berger, *A Seventh Man: A Book of Images and Words About the Experiences of Migrant Workers in Europe* (Harmondsworth: Penguin, 1975), 45, 214.
21. Françoise Rembauville-Nicolle, *Guide bilingue ménager à l'usage des employées de maison espagnoles* (Paris: Les Presses de la Cité, 1964); Raquel Vega-Durán, *Emigrant Dreams, Immigrant Borders: Migrants, Transnational Encounters, and Identity in Spain* (Lewisburg, PA: Bucknell University Press, 2016), 26–27.
22. Demetrios Papademetriou, 'Greece', in Ronald E. Krane, ed., *International Labor Migration in Europe* (New York: Praeger, 1979), 187–200.
23. Hinrich-Matthias Geck, *Die griechische Arbeitsmigration: Eine Analyse ihrer Ursachen und Wirkungen* (Königstein: Hallstein, 1979), 40–41.
24. Theodoros Lagaris, 'Greek Refugees in Europe During the Military Dictatorship, 1967–1974', in Bade et al., eds., *Encyclopedia of European Migration*, 466–468.
25. Bernitt, *Die Rückwanderung*, 235–240.
26. Luis Batalha, *The Cape Verdean Diaspora in Portugal: Colonial Subjects in a Postcolonial World* (Lanham, MD: Lexington Books, 2004), 138.
27. A minority reported more positive experiences. Batalha, *Cape Verdean Diaspora*, 136–140.
28. Ibid., 144–150.
29. Hily and Poinard, 'Portuguese Associations in France', 153.
30. Batalha, *Cape Verdean Diaspora*, 222–226.
31. Ibid., 216.
32. Nayade Anido and Freire Rubens, *L'émigration portugaise: Présent et avenir* (Paris: Presses universitaires de France, 1978), 133; Andrea Klimt, '"Returning Home": Portuguese Migrant Notions of Temporariness, Permanence, and Commitment', *New German Critique* 46 (1989): 47–70; Andrea Klimt, 'Do National Narratives Matter? Identity Formation Among Portuguese Migrants in France and Germany', in Rainer Ohliger, Karen Schönwälder, and Triadafilos Triadafilopoulos, eds., *European Encounters: Migrants, Migration and European Societies Since 1945* (Aldershot: Ashgate, 2003), 262; Bernitt, *Die Rückwanderung*, 162.
33. Cármen Maciel, 'Angolan and Mozambican Labour Migrants in Portugal Since the 1970s', in Bade et al., eds., *Encyclopedia of European Migration*, 233–235.
34. Kitty Calavita, 'Gender, Migration, and Law: Crossing Borders and Bridging Disciplines', *International Migration Review* 40, no. 1 (2006): 117; David Forgacs, 'Pummarò and the Limits of Vicarious Representation', in Russell King and Nancy Wood, eds., *Media and Migration: Constructions of Mobility and Difference* (London: Routledge, 2001), 83–94. See the brief account issued by the European Federation of Food, Agriculture and Tourism Trade Unions in October 2014, '25 Years After Jerry Masslo's Death, FLAI CGIL Continues the Fight for Equal Treatment of Migrant Workers', available at www.effat.org/en/node/13636.
35. Eftihia Voutira, 'Post-Soviet Diaspora Politics: The Case of the Soviet Greeks', *Journal of Modern Greek Studies* 24, no. 2 (2006): 379–414; Christopher Lawrence, *Blood and Oranges: Immigrant Labour and European Markets in Rural Greece* (Oxford: Berghahn, 2007), 61, 70, a study of the rural township of Midea in Argolid; Anna Triandafyllidou, 'Mediterranean Migrations: Problems and Prospects for

Greece and Italy in the Twenty-First Century', *Mediterranean Politics* 12, no. 1 (2007): 79–86.

36. Lawrence, *Blood and Oranges*, 62–63.

37. Ibid., 84–86, 66, 74.

38. Peter Loizos, *The Heart Grown Bitter: A Chronicle of Cypriot War Refugees* (Cambridge: Cambridge University Press, 1981), 105.

39. Rebecca Bryant, 'Partitions of Memory: Wounds and Witnessing in Cyprus', *Contemporary Studies in Society and History* 54, no. 2 (2012): 332–360; interview with Markos M., aged seventy-two, conducted in July 2011 by Andrea Papaioannou, cited with permission.

40. Yael Navaro-Yashin, *The Make-Believe Space: Affective Geography in a Postwar Polity* (Durham NC: Duke University Press, 2012), 57–60.

41. Lisa Dikomitis, 'A Moving Field: Greek Cypriot Refugees Returning "Home"', *Durham Anthropology Journal* 12, no. 1 (2004): 7–20; Roger Zetter, 'Reconceptualizing the Myth of Return: Continuity and Transition Amongst the Greek-Cypriot Refugees of 1974', *Journal of Refugee Studies* 12, no. 1 (1999): 1–22; Nergis Canefe, 'From Ethnicity to Nationalism: Intricacies of Turkish Cypriot Identity in the Diaspora', *Rethinking History* 6, no. 1 (2002): 57–76; Peter Loizos, *Iron in the Soul: Displacement, Livelihood and Health in Cyprus* (Oxford: Berghahn, 2008), 111.

Chapter 13: 'Melting Pot' or 'Salad Bowl'? Public Opinion and Government Policy

1. Isabel Hollis-Touré, *From North Africa to France: Family Migration in Text and Film* (London: IGRS Books, 2015), 54. The film, *Mémoires d'immigrés*, is discussed briefly in the following chapter.

2. Leo Lucassen and Jan Lucassen, 'The Strange Death of Dutch Tolerance: The Timing and Nature of the Pessimist Turn in the Dutch Migration Debate', *Journal of Modern History* 87, no. 1 (2015): 72–101.

3. Ibid., 84–85.

4. Quoted in Christian Joppke, *Immigration and the Nation-State: The United States, Germany, and the UK* (Oxford: Oxford University Press, 1999), 225; Woodrow Wyatt, *The Journals of Woodrow Wyatt* (London: Pan, 2000), 2:530. Joppke argued that the government's main priority was the maintenance of public order.

5. Leo Lucassen, *The Immigrant Threat: The Integration of Old and New Migrants in Western Europe Since 1850* (Urbana: University of Illinois Press, 2005), 18–20.

6. Karen Fog Olwig, 'The Duplicity of Diversity: Caribbean Immigrants in Denmark', *Ethnic and Racial Studies* 38, no. 7 (2015): 1104–1119.

7. Rita Chin, *The Crisis of Multiculturalism in Europe: A History* (Princeton, NJ: Princeton University Press, 2017), 112.

8. Jerzy Zubrzycki, 'Across the Frontiers of Europe', in Wilfred Borrie, ed., *The Cultural Integration of Immigrants* (Paris: UNESCO, 1959), 174–175.

9. Ralph Grillo, *Ideologies and Institutions in Urban France: The Representation of Immigrants* (Cambridge: Cambridge University Press, 1985), 123–124, 133–137.

10. 'The Very Sad Story of Salah Bougrine', in Bruce Chatwin, *What Am I Doing Here?* (London: Cape, 1989 [1974]), 241–262.

11. Tahar Ben Jelloun, *French Hospitality: Racism and North African Immigrants* (New York: Columbia University Press, 2000 [1984]), 37, 39, 75.

12. Sarah Jones, 'The Notorious Book That Ties the Right to the Far Right', *New Republic*, 2 February 2018, https://newrepublic.com/article/146925/notorious-book-ties -right-far-right. The British author Douglas Murray recently described Raspail's book as prophetic. Douglas Murray, *The Strange Death of Europe: Immigration, Identity, Islam* (London: Bloomsbury Continuum, 2018), 115–122.

13. Gérard Noiriel, *The French Melting Pot* (Minneapolis: University of Minnesota Press, 1996), 29; Minayo Nasiali, *Native to the Republic: Empire, Social Citizenship, and Everyday Life in Marseille Since 1945* (Ithaca, NY: Cornell University Press, 2016), 102–106, citing INED, *L'immigration étrangère en France, 1946–1973* (Paris: PUF, 1975).

14. Ben Jelloun, *French Hospitality*, 81.

15. Nasiali, *Native to the Republic*, 97–98.

16. Ben Jelloun, *French Hospitality*, 37.

17. Charles P. Kindleberger, *Europe's Postwar Growth: The Role of Labour Supply* (Cambridge, MA: Harvard University Press, 1967), 43, 46.

18. Rudolf Braun, *Sozio-kulturelle Probleme der Eingliederung italienischer Arbeitskräfte in der Schweiz* (Erlenbach-Zurich: Eugen Rentsch Verlag, 1970), 378–436, especially 395, 397; Myron Weiner, *The Global Migration Crisis: Challenges to States and Human Rights* (New York: HarperCollins, 1995), 98–99.

19. Allan Pred, *Even in Sweden: Racisms, Racialized Spaces, and the Popular Geographical Imagination* (Berkeley: University of California Press, 2000), 34.

20. Hans van Amersfoort and Mies van Niekerk, 'Immigration as a Colonial Inheritance: Post-Colonial Immigrants in the Netherlands, 1945–2002', *Journal of Ethnic and Migration Studies* 32, no. 3 (2006): 332; Elizabeth Buettner, *Europe After Empire: Decolonization, Society, and Culture* (Cambridge: Cambridge University Press, 2016), 272; Gert Oostindie, *Postcolonial Netherlands: Sixty-Five Years of Forgetting, Commemorating, Silencing* (Amsterdam: Amsterdam University Press, 2011), 111–112.

21. Nadia Bouras, *Het land van herkomst: Perspectieven op verbondenheid met Marokko, 1960–2010* (Hilversum: Uitgeverij Verloren, 2012), 85, 89; Saskia Sassen, *Guests and Aliens* (New York: New Press, 1999), 122; Pieter Scholten, 'Constructing Dutch Immigrant Policy: Research-Policy Relations and Immigrant Integration Policy-Making in the Netherlands', *British Journal of Politics and International Relations* 13, no. 1 (2011): 75–92.

22. Bouras, *Het land van herkomst*, 78, 97.

23. Quoted in Joppke, *Immigration and the Nation-State*, 287 (emphasis mine); Simon Green, *The Politics of Exclusion: Institutions and Immigration Policy in Contemporary Germany* (Manchester: Manchester University Press, 2004), 40; Joppke, *Immigration and the Nation-State*, 64.

24. Joppke, *Immigration and the Nation-State*, 67–68.

25. Ibid., 82–84.

26. Rita Chin, *The Guest Worker Question in Postwar Germany* (New York: Cambridge University Press, 2007), 97–105; Joppke, *Immigration and the Nation-State*, 210.

27. Deniz Göktürk, David Gramling, and Anton Kaes, eds., *Germany in Transit: Nation and Migration, 1955–2005* (Berkeley: University of California Press, 2007 [1973]), 111–113; Chin, *Crisis of Multiculturalism*, 162–166.

28. Göktürk et al., eds., *Germany in Transit*, 113.
29. Sarah Hackett, *Foreigners, Minorities and Integration: The Muslim Immigrant Experience in Britain and Germany* (Manchester: Manchester University Press, 2013), 157.
30. Ibid., 193.
31. Karin Hunn, *'Nächstes Jahr kehren wir zurück...': Die Geschichte der türkischen 'Gastarbeiter' in der Bundesrepublik* (Göttingen: Wallstein, 2005), 417; Grillo, *Ideologies and Institutions*, 152–159.
32. Máiréad Nic Craith, *Narratives of Place, Belonging and Language: An Intercultural Perspective* (Basingstoke: Palgrave Macmillan, 2012), 103; Yvonne Rieker, *'Ein Stück Heimat findet man ja immer': Die italienische Einwanderung in die Bundesrepublik* (Essen: Klartext, 2003), 86.
33. Jenny B. White, 'Turks in the New Germany', *American Anthropologist* 99, no. 1 (1997): 754–769.
34. Braun, *Sozio-kulturelle Probleme*, 360; Yvonne Rieker, 'Italian Labour Migrants in Northern, Central and Western Europe Since the End of World War 2', in Bade et al., eds., *Encyclopedia of European Migration*, 507–511.
35. Gajendra Verma, ed., *Education for All: A Landmark in Pluralism* (London: Falmer Press, 1989); Hackett, *Foreigners, Minorities and Integration*, 175–186; Lucassen, *Immigrant Threat*, 204–205; Kitty Calavita, *Immigrants at the Margins: Law, Race, and Exclusion in Southern Europe* (Cambridge: Cambridge University Press, 2005), 102–103.
36. Braun, *Sozio-kulturelle Probleme*, 340.
37. Oostindie, *Postcolonial Netherlands*, 166.
38. Hunn, *'Nächstes Jahr kehren wir zurück...'*, 408; Rieker, *'Ein Stück Heimat findet man ja immer'*.
39. Marion Bernitt, *Die Rückwanderung spanischer Gastarbeiter: Der Fall Andalusien* (Königstein: Hanstein, 1981); Barbara Wolbert, *Der getötete Pass: Rückkehr in die Türkei. Eine ethnologische Migrationsstudie* (Berlin: Akademie Verlag, 1995), 65, 72.
40. Madjiguène Cissé, *The Sans-Papiers: A Woman Draws the First Lessons* (London: Crossroads Women's Centre, 1997), 23; Braun, *Sozio-kulturelle Probleme*, 424.

Chapter 14: Migrants in Western Europe: Living in a Cold Climate

1. Abdelmalek Sayad, *The Suffering of the Immigrant* (Cambridge: Polity, 2004), 296, 300.
2. Allan Pred, *Even in Sweden: Racisms, Racialized Spaces, and the Popular Geographical Imagination* (Berkeley: University of California Press, 2000), 56; 'Gavin Jantjes', *Black Artists & Modernism*, www.blackartistsmodernism.co.uk/dossier/gavin-jantjes.
3. Saskia Sassen, *Guests and Aliens* (New York: New Press, 1999), 145.
4. John Brown, *The Un-melting Pot: An English Town and Its Immigrants* (London: Macmillan, 1970), 211.
5. Maren Möhring, 'Staging and Consuming the Italian Lifestyle: The Gelateria and the Pizzeria-Ristorante in Post-War Germany', *Food and History* 7, no. 2 (2009): 181–202; Jozefien de Bock, 'Guest Workers, Entrepreneurs and the Role of Ethnicity in Immigrant Business', *Journal of Belgian History* 44, no. 4 (2014): 36–66.
6. See Karin Hunn, *'Nächstes Jahr kehren wir zurück...': Die Geschichte der türkischen 'Gastarbeiter' in der Bundesrepublik* (Göttingen: Wallstein, 2005), 237–261, for the fullest account.

7. Quoted in Hunn, '*Nächstes Jahr kehren wir zurück…*', 249; Friedrich Kurylo, 'The Turks Rehearsed the Uprising', in Deniz Göktürk, David Gramling, and Anton Kaes, eds., *Germany in Transit: Nation and Migration, 1955–2005* (Berkeley: University of California Press, 2007 [1973]), 43.

8. Miller, *Foreign Workers in Western Europe*, 59, 106–110; Rita Chin, *The Guest Worker Question in Postwar Germany* (New York: Cambridge University Press, 2007), 59; Riva Kastoryano, *Negotiating Identities: States and Immigrants in France and Germany* (Princeton, NJ: Princeton University Press, 2002), 71–72.

9. Chin, *Guest Worker Question*, 65, 70–73.

10. Hunn, '*Nächstes Jahr kehren wir zurück…*', 365, 395; Ann Brooks and Ruth Simpson, *Emotions in Transmigration: Transformation, Movement and Identity* (Basingstoke: Palgrave Macmillan, 2013), 65.

11. Hunn, '*Nächstes Jahr kehren wir zurück…*', 318–319, 514.

12. Ruth Mandel, *Cosmopolitan Anxieties: Turkish Challenges to Citizenship and Belonging in Germany* (Durham, NC: Duke University Press, 2008), 189, 224–225; Rudolf Braun, *Sozio-kulturelle Probleme der Eingliederung italienischer Arbeitskräfte in der Schweiz* (Erlenbach-Zurich: Eugen Rentsch Verlag, 1970), 287–331; *Der Spiegel*, 28 January 1980, quoted in Hunn, '*Nächstes Jahr kehren wir zurück…*', 514.

13. See 'Ausländer sucht Drecksarbeit, auch für wenig Geld', Spiegel Online, 19 October 2015, www.spiegel.de/einestages/ganz-unten-autor-guenter-wallraff-ueber-rassismus -und-ausbeutung-a-1058088.html.

14. Günter Wallraff, *Ganz Unten*, translated as *Lowest of the Low* (London: Methuen, 1988). A documentary film accompanied the German publication. See 'Günter Wallraff Ganz Unten', YouTube, posted 2 April 2015, https://www.youtube.com /watch?v=VxMkXcypdUc.

15. Wallraff, *Ganz Unten*, preface; Anna K. Kuhn, 'Bourgeois Ideology and the (Mis)Reading of Günter Wallraff's *Ganz Unten*', *New German Critique* 46 (1989): 191–202.

16. 'Katzelmacher (1969)', www.imdb.com/title/tt0064536. Compare Memed Akkaya's recollection of meeting the relatives of his young German wife in the early 1970s, in Werner Schiffauer, *Die Migranten aus Subay: Türken in Deutschland, eine Ethnographie* (Stuttgart: Klett-Cotta, 1991), 274–276.

17. Chin, *Guest Worker Question*, 113–116. PoLiKunst and its successor, *Südwind*, ceased activity in 1987.

18. Chin, *Guest Worker Question*, 173–190.

19. Metin Gür and Alaverdi Turhan, *Die Solingen-Akte* (Düsseldorf: Patmos Verlag, 1996), 23; Mandel, *Cosmopolitan Anxieties*, 57.

20. Schiffauer, *Die Migranten aus Subay*, 263–291, quotation on 277.

21. Aytaç Eryılmaz and Mathilde Jamin, eds., *Fremde Heimat: Eine Geschichte der Einwanderung aus der Türkei* (Essen: Klartext, 1998), 194, 203; Hunn, '*Nächstes Jahr kehren wir zurück…*', 142–143.

22. Martin Sökefeld, *Struggling for Recognition: The Alevi Movement in Germany and in Transnational Space* (New York: Berghahn, 2008).

23. Hunn, '*Nächstes Jahr kehren wir zurück…*', 429–431.

24. Quoted in Christian Joppke, *Immigration and the Nation-State: The United States, Germany, and the UK* (Oxford: Oxford University Press, 1999), 215.

25. Félix Germain, *Decolonizing the Republic: African and Caribbean Migrants in Post-War Paris, 1946–1974* (East Lansing: Michigan State University Press, 2016), 75, 88; Pierre Lanfranchi and Matthew Taylor, *Moving with the Ball: The Migration of Professional Footballers* (Oxford: Berg, 2001), 126–127.

26. Francis Hallé, 'A Pilot Inquiry Among the Immigrant Families in the Suburbs of Paris', *Migration News*, no. 5 (1966): 4–10; Kastoryano, *Negotiating Identities*, 80–81.

27. Stéphane Beaud and Olivier Masclet, 'Des "marcheurs" de 1983 aux "émeutiers" de 2005: Deux générations sociales d'enfants d'immigrés', *Annales*, no. 4 (2006): 809–843; 'Á la gare Saint-Lazare à Paris', *Le Monde*, 21 June 1980, www.lemonde.fr /archives/article/1980/06/21/a-la-gare-saint-lazare-a-paris-une-tentative-de-suicide -par-le-feu-au-milieu-de-la-foule-une-dizaine-de-personnes-blessees_307 2050_1819218.html.

28. Tahar Ben Jelloun, *French Hospitality: Racism and North African Immigrants* (New York: Columbia University Press, 2000 [1984]), 19, 39, 44, 47–51; Mireille Rosello, *Postcolonial Hospitality: The Immigrant as Guest* (Stanford: Stanford University Press, 2002).

29. Ben Jelloun, *French Hospitality*, 56.

30. Ibid., 63–66.

31. Ibid., 87–89, 131.

32. Danielle Marx-Scouras, *La France de Zebda, 1981–2004: Faire de la musique un acte politique* (Paris: Les Editions Autrement, 2005), 26, 30, 55, 100.

33. Isabel Hollis-Touré, *From North Africa to France: Family Migration in Text and Film* (London: IGRS Books, 2015), 48, 61. In 2012 President Hollande appointed Yamina Benguigui to the post of junior minister for French nationals abroad and relations with *La Francophonie*.

34. Interview with Wim Manuhutu, available at http://fwillems.antenna.nl/nl/extra/ede .htm; Vijf Eeuwen Migratie (Five Centuries of Migration), www.vijfeeuwen migratie.nl/sites/default/files/bronnen/Deel%20I%20Molukkers.pdf, courtesy of Hans Wallage.

35. Mies van Niekerk, 'Afro-Caribbeans and Indo-Caribbeans in the Netherlands: Premigration Legacies and Social Mobility', *International Migration Review* 38, no. 7 (2004): 158–183.

36. Aniek Smit, '*Mijn vader had een Afro!' Hoe Marokkaanse migranten in Nederland zich kleden sinds de jaren zestig* (Amsterdam: Amsterdam University Press, 2011), 57; Nadia Bouras, *Het land van herkomst: Perspectieven op verbondenheid met Marokko, 1960–2010* (Hilversum: Uitgeverij Verloren, 2012), 42.

37. Machteld de Jong, *Ik ben die Marokkaan niet: Onderzoek naar identiteitsvorming van Marokkaans-Nederlandse hbo-studenten* (Amsterdam: VU University Press, 2012), 67.

38. Smit, '*Mijn vader had een Afro!*', 58.

39. Ibid., 40.

40. Ibid., 64, 66.

41. Nadia Bouras, 'Shifting Perspectives on Transnationalism: Analysing Dutch Political Discourse on Moroccan Migrants' Transnational Ties, 1960–2010', *Ethnic and Racial Studies* 36, no. 7 (2013): 1219–1231.

42. Eva Østergaard-Nielsen, *Transnational Politics: The Case of Turks and Kurds in Germany* (London: Routledge, 2003); Alexander Clarkson, *Fragmented Fatherland:*

Immigration and Cold War Conflict in the Federal Republic of Germany, 1945–1980 (Oxford: Berghahn, 2013), 3–4, 18, and passim.

43. Quoted in Laurence Brown, 'Afro-Caribbean Migrants in France and the UK', in Leo Lucassen, David Feldman, and Jochen Oltmer, eds., *Paths of Integration: Migrants in Western Europe, 1880–2004* (Amsterdam: Amsterdam University Press, 2006), 194.

Chapter 15: The End of Communism: Picking Up the Pieces

1. Peter Jankowitsch, cited in Rogers Brubaker, *Ethnicity Without Groups* (Cambridge, MA: Harvard University Press, 2004), 154; Saskia Sassen, *Guests and Aliens* (New York: New Press, 1999), 113.
2. Ivan Krastev, *After Europe* (Philadelphia: University of Pennsylvania Press, 2017), 51.
3. Madeleine Reeves, *Border Work: Spatial Lives of the State in Rural Central Asia* (Ithaca, NY: Cornell University Press, 2014).
4. Jeff Sahadeo, '"Black Snouts Go Home!" Migration and Race in Late Soviet Leningrad and Moscow', *Journal of Modern History* 88, no. 4 (2016): 797–826; Erik R. Scott, *Familiar Strangers: The Georgian Diaspora and the Evolution of Soviet Empire* (New York: Oxford University Press, 2016), 157–169.
5. Svetlana Alexievich, *Chernobyl Prayer: A Chronicle of the Future* (Harmondsworth: Penguin, 2016), 28.
6. Judith Kessler, *Jüdische Migration aus der ehemaligen Sowjetunion seit 1990: Beispiel Berlin* (Berlin: Eigenverlag, 1997), available at haGalil, www.berlin-judentum.de /gemeinde/migration-1.htm.
7. Timothy Heleniak, 'An Overview of Migration in the Post-Soviet Space', in Cynthia J. Buckley and Blair A. Ruble, eds., *Migration, Homeland, and Belonging in Eurasia* (Washington, DC: Woodrow Wilson Center Press, 2008), 44–45; Moya Flynn, *Migrant Resettlement in the Russian Federation: Reconstructing Homes and Homelands* (London: Anthem Press, 2004), 13–15.
8. Romuald Misiunas and Rein Taagepera, *The Baltic States: Years of Dependence, 1940–1990* (London: Hurst, 1993), 303; Flynn, *Migrant Resettlement*, 62–67; Lewis H. Siegelbaum and Leslie Page Moch, *Broad Is My Native Land: Repertoires and Regimes of Migration in Russia's Twentieth Century* (Ithaca, NY: Cornell University Press, 2014), 271–272; Alexievich, *Chernobyl Prayer*, 71, 72.
9. Flynn, *Migrant Resettlement*, 70.
10. Ibid., 1, 16.
11. Hilary Pilkington, *Migration, Displacement and Identity in Post-Soviet Russia* (London: Routledge, 1998), 37; Flynn, *Migrant Resettlement*, 48, 89.
12. Flynn, *Migrant Resettlement*, 133–135, 52, 73, 136; Siegelbaum and Moch, *Broad Is My Native Land*, 273.
13. Vera Tolz, 'Conflicting "Homeland Myths" and Nation-State Building in Post-Communist Russia', *Slavic Review* 57, no. 2 (1998): 267–294; Flynn, *Migrant Resettlement*, 61.
14. Rita Sanders, *Staying at Home: Identities, Memories and Social Networks of Kazakhstani Germans* (Oxford: Berghahn, 2016), 3, 168–169; Cynthia A. Werner, Celia Emmelhainz, and Holly Barcus, 'Privileged Exclusion in Post-Soviet Kazakhstan: Ethnic Return Migration, Citizenship, and the Politics of (Not) Belonging', *Europe-Asia Studies* 69, no. 10 (2017): 1557–1583.

15. Greta L. Uehling, *Beyond Memory: The Crimean Tatars' Deportation and Return* (Houndmills: Palgrave, 2004), 115.

16. Malika Mirkhanova, 'People in Exile: The Oral History of Meskhetian Turks (*Akhyskha Turkleri*)', *Journal of Muslim Minority Affairs* 26, no. 1 (2006): 33–44.

17. Annett Fleischer, 'Armenian Returnees from Russia: Struggles Between Reintegration and Re-emigration', in Konrad Siekierski and Stefan Troebst, eds., *Armenians in Post-Socialist Europe* (Köln: Böhlau, 2016), 54–68.

18. Radka Klvaňová, 'Moving Through Social Networks: The Case of Armenian Migrants in the Czech Republic', *International Migration* 48, no. 2 (2010): 113–114.

19. Ryan Koopmans, 'Sanatorium', https://www.ryankoopmans.com/projects; Flynn, *Migrant Resettlement*, 186; Siegelbaum and Moch, *Broad Is My Native Land*, 273.

20. Fani Keramida, 'The Way to the Homeland: A "Repatriated" Migrant's Life Story', *Oral History* 27, no. 1 (1999): 75–85; Eftihia Voutira, 'Post-Soviet Diaspora Politics: The Case of the Soviet Greeks', *Journal of Modern Greek Studies* 24, no. 2 (2006): 386.

21. Violetta Hionidou, '"Abroad I Was Greek and in Greece I Am a Foreigner": Pontic Greeks from Former Soviet Union in Greece', *Journal of Modern Greek Studies* 30, no. 1 (2012): 103–127; Ioannis Zelepos, 'Greek Settlers from the Black Sea Region and Pontic Greeks Since the End of World War 2', in Klaus Bade, Pieter C. Emmer, Leo Lucassen, and Jochen Oltmer, eds., *Encyclopedia of European Migration and Minorities from the Seventeenth Century to the Present* (Cambridge: Cambridge University Press, 2011), 468–471.

22. Dariusz Stola, *Kraj bez wyjścia? Migracje z Polski 1949–1989* (Warsaw: Instytut Studiów Politycznych PAN, 2010).

23. Richard Black, Godfried Engbersen, Marek Okólski, and Cristina Panţîru, eds., *A Continent Moving West? EU Enlargement and Labour Migration from Central and Eastern Europe* (Amsterdam: Amsterdam University Press, 2010), 11; Karolina S. Follis, *Building Fortress Europe: The Polish-Ukrainian Frontier* (Philadelphia: University of Pennsylvania Press, 2012), 62, 189.

24. Cited in John J. White, 'A Romanian German in Germany: The Challenge of Ethnic and Ideological Identity in Herta Müller's Literary Work', in David Rock and Stefan Wolff, eds., *Coming Home to Germany? The Integration of Ethnic Germans from Central and Eastern Europe in the Federal Republic* (Oxford: Berghahn, 2002), 172.

25. Stefano Bottoni, 'Finding the Enemy: Ethnicized State Violence and Population Control in Ceauşescu's Romania', *Journal of Cold War Studies* 19, no. 4 (2017): 113–136.

26. Brian Oliver, 'Naim Süleymanoğlu Obituary', *The Guardian*, 3 December 2017, https://www.theguardian.com/sport/2017/dec/03/naim-suleymanoglu-obituary.

27. Cem Dişbudak and Semra Purkis, 'Forced Migrants or Voluntary Exiles: Ethnic Turks of Bulgaria in Turkey', *Journal of International Migration and Integration* 17, no. 2 (2016): 376, interview conducted in 2011; Ayse Parla, 'Irregular Workers or Ethnic Kin? Post-1990s Labour Migration from Bulgaria to Turkey', *International Migration* 45, no. 3 (2007): 157–181.

28. Theodora Dragostinova, *Between Two Motherlands: Nationality and Emigration Among the Greeks of Bulgaria, 1900–1949* (Ithaca, NY: Cornell University Press, 2011), x.

29. Izabella Main, 'Motivations for Mobility and Settlement of Polish Female Migrants in Barcelona and Berlin', *Social Identities* 22, no. 1 (2015): 63.

30. Swanie Potot, 'Strategies of Visibility and Invisibility: Rumanians and Moroccans in El Ejido, Spain', in Stef Jansen and Staffan Löfving, eds., *Struggles for Home: Violence, Hope and the Movement of People* (New York: Berghahn, 2009), 122.

31. Greta Uehling, 'Irregular and Illegal Migration Through Ukraine', *International Migration* 42, no. 3 (2004): 77–109.

32. Evelina Gambino, 'The "Gran Ghettò": Migrant Labour and Militant Research in Southern Italy', in Nicholas De Genova, ed., *The Borders of 'Europe': Autonomy of Migration, Tactics of Bordering* (Durham, NC: Duke University Press, 2017), 255–282; Edyta Materka, *Dystopia's Provocateurs: Peasants, State and Informality in the Polish Borderlands* (Bloomington: Indiana University Press, 2017), 21.

33. Alena Alamgir, 'Recalcitrant Women: Internationalism and the Redefinition of Welfare Limits in the Czechoslovak-Vietnamese Labor Exchange Program', *Slavic Review* 73, no. 1 (2014): 155; István Balcsók and László Dancs, 'Patterns of Legal and Illegal Employment of Foreigners Along the Hungarian-Ukrainian Border', in James W. Scott, ed., *EU Enlargement, Region Building and Shifting Borders of Inclusion and Exclusion* (London: Routledge, 2006), 171–176.

34. Philipp Ther, *Europe Since 1989: A History* (Princeton, NJ: Princeton University Press, 2016), 306, 309.

Chapter 16: Reunification, Migration, and German Society

1. 'Persons with a Migration Background', Federal Statistical Office of Germany (Statistisches Bundesamt, Destatis), archived at Wayback Machine, http://web.archive.org/web/20161116203146/https://www.destatis.de/EN/FactsFigures/SocietyState/Population/MigrationIntegration/Methods/MigrationBackground.html.

2. Ulrich Rosenhagen, 'From Stranger to Citizen? Germany's Refugee Dilemma', *Dissent* 64, no. 3 (2017): 134–142; Jenny B. White, 'Turks in the New Germany', *American Anthropologist* 99, no. 1 (1997): 754.

3. Philipp Ther, 'A Century of Forced Migration', in Philipp Ther and Ana Siljak, eds., *Redrawing Nations: Ethnic Cleansing in East-Central Europe, 1944–1948* (Oxford: Rowman and Littlefield, 2001), 58; Amanda Klekowski von Koppenfels, 'From Germans to Migrants: *Aussiedler* Migration to Germany', in Takeyuki Tsuda, ed., *Diasporic Homecomings: Ethnic Return Migration in Comparative Perspective* (Stanford: Stanford University Press, 2009), 108–109.

4. Matthew Gibney, *The Ethics and Politics of Asylum: Liberal Democracy and the Response to Refugees* (Cambridge: Cambridge University Press, 2004), 99; Ruth Mandel, *Cosmopolitan Anxieties: Turkish Challenges to Citizenship and Belonging in Germany* (Durham, NC: Duke University Press, 2008), 68–69.

5. Myron Weiner, *The Global Migration Crisis: Challenges to States and Human Rights* (New York: HarperCollins, 1995), 46; Alison Mountz, *Seeking Asylum: Human Smuggling and Bureaucracy at the Border* (Minneapolis: University of Minnesota Press, 2010).

6. Weiner, *Global Migration Crisis*, 56.

7. Simon Green, *The Politics of Exclusion: Institutions and Immigration Policy in Contemporary Germany* (Manchester: Manchester University Press, 2004), 5; Weiner, *Global Migration Crisis*, 56; Karen Schönwälder, 'Migration, Refugees and Ethnic Plurality as Issues of Public and Political Debates in (West) Germany', in David

Cesarani and Mary Fulbrook, eds., *Citizenship, Nationality and Migration in Europe* (London: Routledge, 1996), 160.

8. Alfred Eisfeld, *Die Russlanddeutschen* (Munich: Albert Langen, 1992), 186.

9. John J. White, 'A Romanian German in Germany: The Challenge of Ethnic and Ideological Identity in Herta Müller's Literary Work', in David Rock and Stefan Wolff, eds., *Coming Home to Germany? The Integration of Ethnic Germans from Central and Eastern Europe in the Federal Republic* (Oxford: Berghahn, 2002), 177.

10. Dorothee Wierling, ed., *Heimat finden: Lebenswege von Deutschen, die aus Russland kommen* (Hamburg: Edition-Körber Stiftung, 2004); Koppenfels, 'From Germans to Migrants', 113, 116.

11. Andreas Heinrich, 'The Integration of Ethnic Germans from the Soviet Union', in Rock and Wolff, *Coming Home to Germany?*, 77–86; Eisfeld, *Die Russlanddeutschen*, 192, citing the appeal of the Evangelical Church in Berlin-Brandenburg on 24 August 1996 to its members to 'Nehmet einander an!' (Welcome one another); Koppenfels, 'From Germans to Migrants', 111–112.

12. Wierling, ed., *Heimat finden*, 15–49.

13. Ibid., 51–77.

14. Ibid., 109–137.

15. Ibid., 78–108.

16. Rita Sanders, *Staying at Home: Identities, Memories and Social Networks of Kazakhstani Germans* (Oxford: Berghahn, 2016), 175.

17. Koppenfels, 'From Germans to Migrants', 117–118. Koppenfels was the friend in question.

18. David Rock, '"From the Periphery to the Centre and Back Again": An Introduction to the Life and Works of Richard Wagner', in Rock and Wolff, eds., *Coming Home to Germany?*, 129; '"A Form of Literature Which Was Intentionally Political": Richard Wagner in Conversation with David Rock and Stefan Wolff', in ibid., 143.

19. Czarina Wilpert, 'Identity Issues in the History of the Post-War Migration from Turkey to Germany', *German Politics and Society* 31, no. 2 (2013): 108–131.

20. '20 Years After the Rostock Riots', Deutsche Welle, 23 August 2012, https://www.you tube.com/watch?v=n7Iv5hdEqr8; Jacob Kushner, 'Revisiting Germany's Xenophobic Rostock Riots of 1992', *Al Jazeera*, 15 June 2017, www.aljazeera.com/indepth/features /2017/05/revisiting-germany-xenophobic-rostock-riots-1992-170517123148797.html; White, 'Turks in the New Germany', 762; Christoph Richter, 'Lichtenhagen Riots Continue to Haunt Many', Deutsche Welle, 26 August 2012, www.dw.com/en/lichtenhagen -riots-continue-to-haunt-many/a-16194604; Nevzat Soguk, *States and Strangers: Refugees and Displacements of Statecraft* (Minneapolis: University of Minnesota Press, 1999), 226.

21. Sigrid Averesch, 'Warum musste Mete Eksi sterben?', *Berliner Zeitung*, 10 January 1994, https://www.berliner-zeitung.de/morgen-beginnt-prozess-um-den-tod-des-tuerken -warum-musste-mete-eksi-sterben–16993392; Deniz Göktürk, David Gramling, and Anton Kaes, eds., *Germany in Transit: Nation and Migration, 1955–2005* (Berkeley: University of California Press, 2007 [1973]), 106–109, 118–120; Wilpert, 'Identity Issues', 117; Weizsäcker, quoted in Christian Joppke, *Immigration and the Nation-State: The United States, Germany, and the UK* (Oxford: Oxford University Press, 1999), 186. The survivors reportedly still live in Solingen.

22. Metin Gür and Alaverdi Turhan, *Die Solingen-Akte* (Düsseldorf: Patmos Verlag, 1996), 15–21, 163–165; Aytaç Eryılmaz and Mathilde Jamin, eds., *Fremde Heimat: Eine Geschichte der Einwanderung aus der Türkei* (Essen: Klartext, 1998), 403.

23. Göktürk et al., *Germany in Transit*, 223–226; Geoff Eley, 'The Trouble with "Race"', in Rita Chin, Heide Fehrenbach, Geoff Eley, and Atina Grossmann, eds., *After the Nazi Racial State* (Ann Arbor: University of Michigan Press, 2009), 147; Tomas Meaney and Sakia Schäfer, 'The Neo-Nazi Murder Trial Revealing Germany's Darkest Secrets', *The Guardian*, 15 December 2016, https://www.theguardian.com/world/2016/dec/15/neo-nazi-murders-revealing-germanys-darkest-secrets.

24. Mandel, *Cosmopolitan Anxieties*, 31; Koppenfels, 'From Germans to Migrants', 115.

25. White, 'Turks in the New Germany', 761.

26. Joyce Mushaben, *The Changing Faces of Citizenship: Social Integration and Political Mobilization Among Ethnic Minorities in Germany* (New York: Berghahn, 2008), 90.

27. 'Green Cards to Germany—Immigration Streamlined', Deutsche Welle, 2 October 2001, https://www.dw.com/en/green-cards-to-germany-immigration-streamlined/a-275335; James F. Hollifield, 'The Emerging Migration State', *International Migration Review* 38, no. 3 (2004): 885.

28. Udo Merkel, 'German Football Culture in the New Millennium: Ethnic Diversity, Flair and Youth On and Off the Pitch', *Soccer and Society* 15, no. 2 (2014): 241–255.

29. Matt Pearson, 'Mesut Özil Quits Germany over Erdogan Controversy', Deutsche Welle, 22 July 2018, https://www.dw.com/en/mesut-%C3%B6zil-quits-germany-over-erdogan-controversy/a-44777380.

30. 'Weiterer Meilenstein in unserer Geschichte', Dokumentationszentrum und Museum über die Migration in Deutschland (Documentation Centre and Museum of Migration in Germany), www.domid.org/de/weiterer-meilenstein-unserer-geschichte.

31. 'Flucht-Exil-Verfolgung' (Flight, Exile, Persecution), https://flucht-exil-verfolgung.de/en/ort/cemal-kemal-altun.

32. Schönwälder, 'Migration, Refugees and Ethnic Plurality', 167.

33. Ari Joskowicz, 'Romani Refugees and the Postwar Order', *Journal of Contemporary History* 51, no. 4 (2015): 760–787; Rainer Münz and Ralf Ulrich, 'Germany and Its Immigrants: Socio-Demographic Analysis', *Journal of Ethnic and Migration Studies* 24, no. 1 (1998): 26–56.

34. Gibney, *Ethics and Politics of Asylum*, 103; Suzanna Crage, 'The More Things Change…Developments in German Practices Towards Asylum Seekers and Recognised Refugees', *German Politics* 25, no. 3 (2016): 354; Christin Hess, 'Post-Perestroika Ethnic Migration from the Former Soviet Union: Challenges Twenty Years On', *German Politics* 25, no. 3 (2016): 381–397.

35. Crage, 'The More Things Change', 353; Wolfgang Koydi, quoted in Nevzat Soguk, *States and Strangers*, 227.

36. Crage, 'The More Things Change', 358.

Chapter 17: Together in Disharmony: The Death of Yugoslavia

1. After 1952 the Communist Party of Yugoslavia became known as the League of Communists of Yugoslavia.

2. Noel Malcolm, *Kosovo: A Short History* (Basingstoke: Macmillan, 1998), 330–331; Mark Kramer, introduction to Philipp Ther and Ana Siljak, eds., *Redrawing Nations: Ethnic Cleansing in East-Central Europe, 1944–1948* (Oxford: Rowman and Little-field, 2001), 26.

3. Gayle Munro, *Transnationalism, Diaspora and Migrants from the Former Yugoslavia in Britain* (London: Routledge, 2017), 21, 25.

4. Jasna Čapo Žmegač, *Strangers Either Way: The Lives of Croatian Refugees in Their New Home* (New York: Berghahn, 2007), 78, 14–17; Pascal Goeke, 'Refugees from Former Yugoslavia in Europe Since 1991', in Klaus Bade, Pieter C. Emmer, Leo Lucassen, and Jochen Oltmer, eds., *Encyclopedia of European Migration and Minorities from the Seventeenth Century to the Present* (Cambridge: Cambridge University Press, 2011), 632; Nives Ritig-Beljak, 'Croatian Exiles from Vojvodina: Between War Memories and War Experience', in Renata Kirin and Maja Povrzanović, eds., *War, Exile, Everyday Life: Cultural Perspectives* (Zagreb: Institute of Ethnology, 1996), 173–188.

5. See the graphic accounts in Hariz Halilovich, *Places of Pain: Forced Displacement, Popular Memory, and Translocal Identities in Bosnian War-Torn Communities* (New York: Berghahn, 2013), 68–74; Ivana Maček, 'Transmission and Transformation: Memories of the Siege of Sarajevo', in Alex Dowdall and John Horne, eds., *Civilians Under Siege from Sarajevo to Troy* (Basingstoke: Palgrave Macmillan, 2018), 15–35. Arkan moved to Paris in the early 1970s, where he developed a penchant for conducting armed robberies in several European cities. He spent most of the decade either in prison or on the run before being assassinated in January 2000.

6. Ivaylo Grouev, *Bullets on the Water: Refugee Stories* (Montreal: McGill–Queen's University Press, 2000), 29, 144–151; Arthur Helton, *The Price of Indifference: Refugees and Humanitarian Action in the New Century* (Oxford: Oxford University Press, 2002), 299.

7. Julie Mertus, ed., *The Suitcase: Refugee Voices from Bosnia and Croatia* (Berkeley: University of California Press, 1997), 35–39.

8. Barbara Franz, *Uprooted and Unwanted: Bosnian Refugees in Austria and the United States* (College Station: Texas A&M University Press, 2005), 55–56.

9. Goeke, 'Refugees from Former Yugoslavia', 634.

10. Maja Korac, *Remaking Home: Reconstructing Life, Place and Identity in Rome and Amsterdam* (New York: Berghahn, 2009), 64, 66, 105.

11. Ibid., 103.

12. Ibid., 97–98, 101–102.

13. Quoted in ibid., 111, 112.

14. Natalja Vrečer, 'The Lost Way of Life: The Experience of Refugee Children in Celje from 1992–1994', in Kirin and Povrzanović, eds., *War, Exile, Everyday Life*, 133–146.

15. Joanne van Selm, ed., *Kosovo's Refugees in the European Union* (London: Pinter, 2001); Goeke, 'Refugees from Former Yugoslavia', 634.

16. Goeke, 'Refugees from Former Yugoslavia', 635; 'Kosovar Refugees', *Migration News* (May 1999), https://migration.ucdavis.edu/mn/more.php?id=1801.

17. Tony Kushner, *Remembering Refugees: Then and Now* (Manchester: Manchester University Press, 2006), 76.

18. Silvia Salvatici, 'Memory Telling: Individual and Collective Memories in Postwar Kosovo', in Natale Losi, Luisa Passerini, and Silvia Salvatici, eds., *Archives of Mem-*

ory: Supporting Traumatized Communities Through Narration and Remembrance (Geneva: International Organisation for Migration, 2001), 39; Martin Geiger, 'Mobility, Development, Protection, EU-Integration! The IOM's National Migration Strategy for Albania', in Martin Geiger and Antoine Pécoud, eds., *The Politics of International Migration Management* (Basingstoke: Palgrave, 2012), 141–159; Audit of the United Nations High Commissioner for Refugees: Operations in Albania — Note by the Secretary-General, 3 July 2001, https://www.refworld.org/docid/3cbbf 1354.html.

19. As recalled by Luisa Passerini, in 'A Passion for Memory', *History Workshop Journal* 72, no. 1 (October 2011): 241–250; see also Irial Glynn, *Asylum Policy, Boat People and Political Discourse: Boats, Votes and Asylum in Australia and Italy* (Basingstoke: Palgrave Macmillan, 2016), 117.

20. Janja Beč, *The Shattering of the Soul* (Belgrade: Helsinki Committee for Human Rights in Serbia, 1997), 59; Salvatici, 'Memory Telling', 29; Joanne van Selm, ed., *Kosovo's Refugees in the European Union* (London: Pinter, 2001); Annie Lafontaine, 'After the Exile: Displacements and Suffering in Kosovo', in Losi et al., *Archives of Memory*, 70.

21. Nicola Mai, 'The Archives of Memory: Specific Results from Serbia', in Losi et al., *Archives of Memory*, 89–90; United Nations High Commissioner for Refugees, *The State of the World's Refugees 2000: Fifty Years of Humanitarian Action*, available at https://www.unhcr.org/en-us/publications/sowr/4a4c754a9/state-worlds-refugees-2000-fifty-years-humanitarian-action.html, 234; Helton, *Price of Indifference*, 68.

22. Helton, *Price of Indifference*, 42.

23. Anders Stefansson, 'Refugee Returns to Sarajevo and Their Challenge to Contemporary Narratives of Mobility', in Lynellyn D. Long and Ellen Oxfeld, eds., *Coming Home? Refugees, Migrants, and Those Who Stayed Behind* (Philadelphia: University of Pennsylvania Press, 2004), 183 (quoting the original imperfect English).

24. Khalid Koser, Martha Walsh, and Richard Black, 'Temporary Protection and the Assisted Return of Refugees from the European Union', *International Journal of Refugee Law* 10, no. 3 (1998): 444–461; Halilovich, *Places of Pain*, 75–77.

25. Stefansson, 'Refugee Returns', 179.

26. Anders Stefansson, 'Homes in the Making: Property Restitution, Refugee Return and Senses of Belonging in a Post-War Bosnian Town', *International Migration* 44, no. 3 (2006): 115–137; Marita Eastmond, 'Transnational Returns and Reconstruction in Post-War Bosnia and Herzegovina', *International Migration* 44, no. 3 (2006): 141–166; Ellen Oxfeld and Lynellyn D. Long, 'Introduction: An Ethnography of Return', in Long and Oxfeld, eds., *Coming Home?*, 9.

27. Ritig-Beljak, 'Croatian Exiles from Vojvodina', 181.

28. Žmegač, *Strangers Either Way*, 100–104, 115; Salvatici, 'Memory Telling', 40.

29. By 1997 Hajrija had moved to Utica, New York, leaving the model town behind. Mertus, ed., *Suitcase*, 90–91.

30. Stefansson, 'Refugee Returns', 181.

31. Munro, *Transnationalism, Diaspora and Migrants*, 34, 61; Salvatici, 'Memory Telling', 38; Halilovich, *Places of Pain*, 125.

32. Munro, *Transnationalism, Diaspora and Migrants*, 63.

Chapter 18: Managing Migration and Asylum in the New European Union

1. Irial Glynn, 'Returnees, Forgotten Foreigners and New Immigrants', in Niall Whelehan, ed., *Transnational Perspectives in Modern Irish History: Beyond the Island* (London: Routledge. 2014), 224–249; Christina Boswell and Andrew Geddes, *Migration and Mobility in the European Union* (Basingstoke: Palgrave Macmillan, 2011), 4.

2. Unnamed person, quoted in Luisa Passerini, 'Gender, Subjectivity, Europe: A Constellation for the Future', in Luisa Passerini, Dawn Lyon, Enrica Capussotti, and Ioanna Laliotou, eds., *Women Migrants from East to West: Gender, Mobility and Belonging in Contemporary Europe* (Oxford: Berghahn, 2007), 255.

3. James F. Hollifield, *Immigrants, Markets, and States: The Political Economy of Postwar Europe* (Cambridge, MA: Harvard University Press, 1992), 11.

4. Andrew Geddes, *Immigration and European Integration: Beyond Fortress Europe?*, 2nd ed. (Manchester: Manchester University Press, 2008), 112; Peo Hansen and Sandy B. Hager, *The Politics of European Citizenship: Deepening Contradictions in Social Rights and Migration Policy* (New York: Berghahn, 2010), 127–161.

5. Andrew Geddes, *Immigration and European Integration: Towards Fortress Europe?*, 1st ed. (Manchester: Manchester University Press, 2000), 1, 11.

6. Andrea Klimt, 'Do National Narratives Matter? Identity Formation Among Portuguese Migrants in France and Germany', in Rainer Ohliger, Karen Schönwälder, and Triadafilos Triadafilopoulos, eds., *European Encounters: Migrants, Migration and European Societies Since 1945* (Aldershot: Ashgate, 2003), 273.

7. Philipp Ther, *Europe Since 1989: A History* (Princeton, NJ: Princeton University Press, 2016), 310–312.

8. Quoted in Georg Menz, *The Political Economy of Managed Migration: Non-State Actors, Europeanization and the Politics of Designing Migration Policies* (Oxford: Oxford University Press, 2009), vi, vii. See also Martin Geiger and Antoine Pécoud, eds., *The Politics of International Migration Management* (Basingstoke: Palgrave, 2012).

9. 'Frontex in Brief', Frontex: European Border and Coast Guard Agency, https://frontex.europa.eu.

10. Julien Jeandesboz, 'EU Border Control: Violence, Capture and Apparatus', in Yolande Jansen, Robin Celikates, and Joost de Bloois, eds., *The Irregularisation of Migration in Contemporary Europe: Detention, Deportation, and Drowning* (London: Rowman and Littlefield, 2015), 99.

11. Hansen and Hager, *Politics of European Citizenship*, 147; Stephen Castles, Hein de Haas, and Mark J. Miller, *The Age of Migration: International Population Movements in the Modern World*, 5th ed. (Basingstoke: Palgrave Macmillan, 2014), 216.

12. Kitty Calavita, *Immigrants at the Margins: Law, Race, and Exclusion in Southern Europe* (Cambridge: Cambridge University Press, 2005), 3–4; Geddes, *Immigration and European Integration*, 1st ed., 25.

13. Paul Ginsborg, *Italy and Its Discontents 1980–2001* (Harmondsworth: Penguin, 2003), 62–63.

14. Irial Glynn, *Asylum Policy, Boat People and Political Discourse: Boats, Votes and Asylum in Australia and Italy* (Basingstoke: Palgrave Macmillan, 2016), 78–82. See also Russell King, Esmeralda Uruçi, and Julie Vullnetari, 'Albanian Migration and

Its Effects in Comparative Perspective', *Journal of Balkan and Near Eastern Studies* 13, no. 3 (2011): 269–286; Julie Vullnetari, *Albania on the Move: Links Between Internal and International Migration* (Amsterdam: Amsterdam University Press, 2012).

15. Glynn, *Asylum Policy*, 85, quoting journalist Barbara Palombelli; Pamela Ballinger, 'A Sea of Difference, a History of Gaps? Migrations Between Italy and Albania, 1939–1992', *Comparative Studies in Society and History* 60, no. 1 (2018): 95–96.

16. The Benetton Group later used images of the *Vlora* for its clothing adverts. Glynn, *Asylum Policy*, 83–84, 87.

17. Daniele Salerno, 'Memorializing Boat Tragedies in the Mediterranean: The Case of the *Kater i Radës*', in Lynda Mannik, ed. *Migration by Boat: Discourses of Trauma, Exclusion and Survival* (New York: Berghahn, 2016), 136–153; Maurizio Albahari, *Crimes of Peace: Mediterranean Migrations at the World's Deadliest Border* (Philadelphia: University of Pennsylvania Press, 2015), 36–37, 54–55, 64–69. Both captains were convicted of culpability, but the court did not take evidence regarding the strategy of the Italian government.

18. Glynn, *Asylum Policy*, 75–77.

19. Ibid., 87; Andrew Geddes, '*Il Rombo dei Cannoni?* Immigration and the Centre-Right in Italy', *Journal of European Public Policy* 15, no. 3 (2008): 349–366; 'Harsh Immigration Law Passed in Italy', European Roma Rights Centre, www.errc .org/roma-rights-journal/harsh-immigration-law-passed-in-italy.

20. Calavita, *Immigrants at the Margins*, 118.

21. Kitty Calavita, 'Gender, Migration, and Law: Crossing Borders and Bridging Disciplines', *International Migration Review* 40, no. 1 (2006): 117; Geddes, *Immigration and European Integration*, 2nd ed., 47; Geddes, *Il Rombo dei Cannoni?*, 349.

22. Nando Sigona, 'How Can a Nomad Be a Refugee? Kosovo Roma and Labelling Policy in Italy', *Sociology* 37, no. 1 (2003): 69–79.

23. Grégoire Cousin, 'Life and Death of a French Shantytown', in Yaron Matras and Daniele Leggio, eds., *Open Borders, Unlocked Cultures: Romanian Roma Migrants in Western Europe* (London: Routledge, 2017), 128–150.

24. Quoted in Nigel Harris, *The New Untouchables: Immigration and the New World Worker* (Harmondsworth: Penguin, 1986), 108; Robert Gildea, *France Since 1945* (Oxford: Oxford University Press, 2002), 175.

25. Madjiguène Cissé, *The Sans-Papiers: A Woman Draws the First Lessons* (London: Crossroads Women's Centre, 1997), 25; Mireille Rosello, 'Representing Illegal Immigrants in France: From *clandestins* to *l'affaire des sans-papiers de Saint-Bernard*', *Journal of European Studies* 28, nos. 1–2 (1998): 137–151.

26. Cissé, *Sans-Papiers*, 22.

27. Etienne Balibar, *We, the People of Europe? Reflections on Transnational Citizenship* (Princeton, NJ: Princeton University Press, 2004), 31–50; *Le Figaro*, 17 June 2004.

28. Stephen Castles, 'Immigration and Asylum: Challenges to European Identities and Citizenship', in Dan Stone, ed., *The Oxford Handbook of Postwar European History* (Oxford: Oxford University Press, 2012), 217.

29. Leo Lucassen and Jan Lucassen, 'The Strange Death of Dutch Tolerance: The Timing and Nature of the Pessimist Turn in the Dutch Migration Debate', *Journal of Modern History* 87, no. 1 (2015): 74–76.

30. Jef Poppelmonde and Idesbald Goddeeris, 'The Victory of National Interest: Debates on the Belgian Forced Return Policy, 1998–2013', *Journal of Migration History* 3, no. 1 (2017): 1–21; Myron Weiner, *The Global Migration Crisis: Challenges to States and Human Rights* (New York: HarperCollins, 1995), 157–164.

31. Simon Behrman, 'Refugees and Crises of Law', *Patterns of Prejudice* 52, nos. 2–3 (2018): 117; 'Identification of Applicants (EURODAC)', European Commission, Migration and Home Affairs, https://ec.europa.eu/home-affairs/what-we-do/policies/asylum/identification-of-applicants_en.

32. Emma Haddad, *The Refugee in International Society: Between Sovereigns* (Cambridge: Cambridge University Press, 2008), 175–178.

33. 'Asylum Applicants by Citizenship Till 2007, Annual Data (rounded)', Eurostat, http://appsso.eurostat.ec.europa.eu/nui/show.do?dataset=migr_asyctz&lang=en.

34. Nevzat Soguk, *States and Strangers: Refugees and Displacements of Statecraft* (Minneapolis: University of Minnesota Press, 1999), 207; Stephen Castles, 'Guest Workers in Europe: An Obituary', *International Migration Review* 20, no. 4 (1986): 761–778; Dallal Stevens, 'The Nationality, Immigration and Asylum Act 2002: Secure Borders, Safe Haven?', *Modern Law Review* 67, no. 4 (2004): 629.

35. Hansen and Hager, *Politics of European Citizenship*, 149; Geddes, *Immigration and European Integration*, 2nd ed., 133.

36. Michael Theodoulou, '"We're in Limbo": The Families Marooned at a British Military Base for 16 Years', *The Guardian*, 21 October 2014, https://www.theguardian.com/world/2014/oct/21/refugee-families-marooned-raf-base-cyprus#comments; Owen Bowcott, 'Refugee Families Allowed to Enter UK After 20 Years at RAF and Army Bases', *The Guardian*, 3 December 2018, https://www.theguardian.com/uk-news/2018/dec/03/refugee-families-allowed-to-enter-uk-after-20-years-at-raf-base. The UK Home Office described this as an 'exceptional decision'.

37. Ralph Grillo, '"Saltdean Can't Cope": Protests Against Asylum-Seekers in an English Seaside Suburb', *Ethnic and Racial Studies* 28, no. 2 (2005): 235–260; 'Sangatte Refugee Camp', *The Guardian*, 23 May 2002, https://www.theguardian.com/uk/2002/may/23/immigration.immigrationandpublicservices1.

38. 'What's the Story? Sangatte: A Case Study of Media Coverage of Asylum and Refugee Issues', Article 19: Global Campaign for Free Expression, 2002, https://www.article19.org/data/files/pdfs/publications/refugees-what-s-the-story-case-study-.pdf; Romain Liagre and Frédéric Dumont, 'Sangatte: Vie et mort d'un centre de "réfugiés"', *Annales de Géographie* 114, no. 641 (2005): 93–112.

Chapter 19: Privileged Lives, Precarious Lives

1. Adrian Favell, *Eurostars and Eurocities: Free Movement and Mobility in an Integrating Europe* (Oxford: Blackwell, 2008); John Salt, 'Migration Processes Among the Highly Skilled', *International Migration Review* 26, no. 2 (1992): 484–505.

2. David Ralph, *Work, Family and Commuting: The Lives of Euro-Commuters* (Basingstoke: Palgrave Macmillan, 2015).

3. The expat phenomenon has a prewar history. See Brian Shelmerdine, 'The Experiences of British Holidaymakers and Expatriate Residents in Pre–Civil War Spain', *European History Quarterly* 32, no. 3 (2002): 367–390.

4. Karen O'Reilly, 'British Affluence Migrants in the Costa del Sol in the Late 20th Century', in Klaus Bade, Pieter C. Emmer, Leo Lucassen, and Jochen Oltmer, eds., *Encyclopedia of European Migration and Minorities from the Seventeenth Century to the Present* (Cambridge: Cambridge University Press, 2011), 262–265; Matthew Tree, 'For British Expats in Spain, Brexit Is a Cloud over the Sun', *The Guardian*, 30 March 2016, https://www.theguardian.com/commentisfree/2016/mar/30/british-expats-spain-brexit-europe.

5. Michaela Benson, *The British in Rural France: Lifestyle Migration and the Ongoing Quest for a Better Way of Life* (Manchester: Manchester University Press, 2011), 34; quotations in Russell King, Tony Warnes, and Allan Williams, *Sunset Lives: British Retirement Migration to the Mediterranean* (Oxford: Oxford University Press, 2000), 84–85, 154.

6. King et al., *Sunset Lives*, 109, 161.

7. Klaus Schriewer, 'German Affluence Migrants in Spain Since the Late 19th Century', in Bade et al., eds., *Encyclopedia of European Migration*, 402–404.

8. 'Protocol to Prevent, Suppress and Punish Trafficking in Persons, Especially Women and Children, Supplementing the United Nations Convention Against Transnational Organized Crime, Adopted and Opened for Signature, Ratification and Accession by General Assembly Resolution 55/25 of 15 November 2000', United Nations, Human Rights, Office of the High Commissioner, www.ohchr.org/EN/Professional Interest/Pages/ProtocolTraffickingInPersons.aspx; Kamala Kempadoo, *Trafficking and Prostitution Reconsidered: New Perspectives on Migration, Sex Work and Human Rights* (Boulder: Paradigm, 2005), xv.

9. 'An Avoidable Tragedy', *The Guardian*, 20 June 2000, https://www.theguardian.com/uk/2000/jun/20/immigration.immigrationandpublicservices4.

10. Felicity Lawrence, Hsiao Hung Pai, Vikram Dodd, Helen Carter, David Ward, and Jonathan Watts, 'Victims of the Sands and of the Snakeheads', *The Guardian*, 7 February 2004, https://www.theguardian.com/uk/2004/feb/07/china.immigration1. Twenty-one bodies were recovered quickly, but one body was only recovered in 2010, and one has never been found. Robin Cohen, 'Chinese Cockle-Pickers, the Transnational Turn and Everyday Cosmopolitanism: Reflections on the New Global Migrants', *Labour, Capital and Society* 37, nos. 1–2 (2004): 130–149.

11. Matthew Tempest and Martin Nicholls, 'Gangmasters Bill Gets Government Backing', *The Guardian*, 27 February 2004, https://www.theguardian.com/politics/2004/feb/27/immigrationpolicy.conservatives.

12. 'Ghosts', Nick Broomfield, www.nickbroomfield.com/Ghosts; 'Isaac Julien—Ten Thousand Waves', Manchester 1824, University of Manchester, The Whitworth, www.whitworth.manchester.ac.uk/whats-on/exhibitions/upcomingexhibitions/isaacjulien; Paul Scott, 'Tea Service—The Cockle Pickers Willow Pattern', 2015, http://cumbrianblues.com/wp-content/uploads/2017/05/12.CocklePickers.pdf.

13. Raquel Vega-Durán, *Emigrant Dreams, Immigrant Borders: Migrants, Transnational Encounters, and Identity in Spain* (Lewisburg, PA: Bucknell University Press, 2016), 130–135, 143–150; 'Dirty Pretty Things (2002)', https://www.imdb.com/title/tt0301199.

14. Mahi Binebine, *Welcome to Paradise* (Portland, OR: Tin House Books, 2012), 17, 72.

15. My reading draws on Isabel Hollis-Touré, *From North Africa to France: Family Migration in Text and Film* (London: IGRS Books, 2015), 42.

16. Didier van Cauwelaert, *Un aller simple* (Paris: Albin Michel, 1994).

17. Frances Kennedy, 'Fishermen Hauled Up Corpses from "Phantom Wreck"', *Independent*, 8 June 2001, https://www.independent.co.uk/news/world/europe/fishermen-hauled-up-corpses-from-phantom-wreck-5364463.html.

18. Ruben Andersson, *Illegality, Inc.: Clandestine Migration and the Business of Bordering Europe* (Berkeley: University of California Press, 2014), 27–30, 69–70, 143–147; Gregory Feldman, *The Migration Apparatus: Security, Labour, and Policymaking in the European Union* (Stanford: Stanford University Press, 2012), 80–81.

19. Papa Sow, Elina Marmer, and Jürgen Scheffran, 'En Route to Hell: Dreams of Adventure and Traumatic Experiences Among West African "Boat People" to Europe', in Lynda Mannik, ed., *Migration by Boat: Discourses of Trauma, Exclusion and Survival* (New York: Berghahn, 2016), 248; Andersson, *Illegality, Inc.*, 38–54.

20. 'Welcome to Ceuta', Lonely Planet, https://www.lonelyplanet.com/morocco/the-mediterranean-coast-and-the-rif/ceuta-sebta.

21. 'Las lápidas sin nombre del cementerio de Barbate', in Eduardo del Campo Cortés, *Odiseas: Al otro lado de la frontera. Historias de la inmigración en España* (Sevilla: n.p., 2007), 109–111, 116–118.

22. Vega-Durán, *Emigrant Dreams, Immigrant Borders*, 61–67.

23. Kitty Calavita, *Immigrants at the Margins: Law, Race, and Exclusion in Southern Europe* (Cambridge: Cambridge University Press, 2005), 1; Laia Soto Bermant, 'The Mediterranean Question: Europe and Its Predicament in the Southern Peripheries', in Nicholas De Genova, ed., *The Borders of 'Europe': Autonomy of Migration, Tactics of Bordering* (Durham, NC: Duke University Press, 2017), 120–140.

24. 'La muerte de Joseph Abunaw', in Cortés, *Odiseas*, 84–88.

25. Ibid., 89.

26. Feldman, *Migration Apparatus*, 81.

27. Sam Jones, 'Hundreds Storm Border Fence into Spain's North Africa Enclave of Ceuta', *The Guardian*, 26 July 2018, https://www.theguardian.com/world/2018/jul/26/hundreds-storm-border-fence-spanish-enclave-north-africa-ceuta-spain-migration; Sam Jones, 'Spain's Right Whips Up Fear as Migration Surge Hits Andalucian Shores', *The Guardian*, 5 August 2018, https://www.theguardian.com/world/2018/aug/05/spain-rightwing-parties-spar-immigration-surge-boats?CMP=Share_iOSApp_Other.

28. David Cook-Martin and Anahí Viladrich, 'Imagined Homecomings: The Problem with Similarity Among Ethnic Return Migrants in Spain', in Takeyuki Tsuda, ed., *Diasporic Homecomings: Ethnic Return Migration in Comparative Perspective* (Stanford: Stanford University Press, 2009), 133–158.

29. Kitty Calavita, 'Gender, Migration, and Law: Crossing Borders and Bridging Disciplines', *International Migration Review* 40, no. 1 (2006): 118; Calavita, *Immigrants at the Margins*, 102, 108.

30. Bruno Riccio, 'Following the Senegalese Migratory Path: From "Ethnic Group" to "Transnational Community"? Senegalese Migrants' Ambivalent Experiences and Multiple Trajectories', *Journal of Ethnic and Migration Studies* 27, no. 4 (2001): 120; Dorothy Louise Zinn, 'The Senegalese Immigrants in Bari: What Happens When the Africans Peer Back', in Rina Benmayor and Andor Skotnes, eds., *Migration and*

Identity (Oxford: Oxford University Press, 1994), 59, 61–62; Sabrina Marchetti, 'Migrant Domestic Work Through the Lens of "Coloniality": Narratives from Eritrean Afro-Surinamese Women', in Dirk Hoerder, Elise van Nederveen Meerkerk, and Silke Neunsinger, eds., *Towards a Global History of Domestic and Caregiving Workers* (Leiden: Brill, 2015), 366–385.

31. Caroline Moorehead, *Human Cargo: A Journey Among Refugees* (London: Chatto and Windus, 2005), 232–233.

32. Shahram Khosravi, *'Illegal' Traveller: An Auto-Ethnography* (Basingstoke: Macmillan, 2010), 6.

33. Ibid., 33.

34. Ibid., 69.

35. Ibid., 61–65.

36. Ibid., 81, 87.

Chapter 20: Europe, Nation-States, and Migrants Since 2008

1. *Eurostat Regional Yearbook*, 2017, available at Eurostat, http://ec.europa.eu/eurostat /documents/3217494/8222062/KS-HA-17-001-EN-N.pdf/eaebe7fa-0c80 -45af-ab41-0f806c433763.

2. Michał Garapich, 'The Migration Industry and Civil Society: Polish Immigrants in the UK Before and After EU Enlargement', *Journal of Ethnic and Migration Studies* 34, no. 5 (2008): 735–752.

3. Leo Lucassen, 'Peeling an Onion: The "Refugee Crisis" from a Historical Perspective', *Ethnic and Racial Studies* 41, no. 3 (2017): 383–410. The UNHCR provides regular situation reports, available at Operational Portal: Refugee Situations, 'Mediterranean Situation', UNHCR, https://data2.unhcr.org/en/situations/mediterranean.

4. Joanne Britton, 'Muslims, Racism and Violence After the Paris Attacks', *Sociological Research Online* 20, no. 3 (2015), www.socresonline.org.uk/20/3/1.html.

5. David Goodhart, *The Road to Somewhere: The Populist Revolt and the Future of Politics* (London: Hurst, 2017); Douglas Murray, *The Strange Death of Europe: Immigration, Identity, Islam* (London: Bloomsbury Continuum, 2018).

6. Bridget Anderson, *Us and Them? The Dangerous Politics of Immigration Controls* (Oxford: Oxford University Press, 2013), 2.

7. 'The Man Who Divided Germany', Spiegel Online, 6 September 2010, www.spiegel .de/international/germany/the-man-who-divided-germany-why-sarrazin-s-integration -demagoguery-has-many-followers-a-715876.html; Czarina Wilpert, 'Identity Issues in the History of the Post-War Migration from Turkey to Germany', *German Politics and Society* 31, no. 2 (2013): 120.

8. Jean-François Caron, 'Understanding and Interpreting France's National Identity: The Meanings of Being French', *National Identities* 15, no. 3 (2013): 223–237.

9. Nicholas De Genova, introduction to De Genova, ed., *The Borders of 'Europe': Autonomy of Migration, Tactics of Bordering* (Durham, NC: Duke University Press, 2017), 14; Rutte, quoted in Eureka Henrich and Julian M. Simpson, 'From the Margins of History to the Political Mainstream: Putting Migration History Centre Stage', in Henrich and Simpson, eds., *History, Historians and the Immigration Debate* (Cham: Palgrave Macmillan, 2019), 16–17.

10. Karolina S. Follis, *Building Fortress Europe: The Polish-Ukrainian Frontier* (Philadelphia: University of Pennsylvania Press, 2012), 136.

11. Jon E. Fox, 'From National Inclusion to Economic Exclusion: Transylvanian Hungarian Ethnic Return Migration to Hungary', in Takeyuki Tsuda, ed., *Diasporic Homecomings: Ethnic Return Migration in Comparative Perspective* (Stanford: Stanford University Press, 2009), 194.

12. James Dennison and Andrew Geddes, 'Are Europeans Turning Against Asylum Seekers and Refugees?', *ECRE Weekly Bulletin*, 17 November 2017, https://outlook.manchester.ac.uk/owa/#OPed.

13. Fernando Collantes Gutiérrez and Vicente Pinilla, *Peaceful Surrender: The Depopulation of Rural Spain in the Twentieth Century* (Newcastle: Cambridge Scholars, 2011), 143; Swanie Potot, 'Strategies of Visibility and Invisibility: Rumanians and Moroccans in El Ejido, Spain', in Stef Jansen and Staffan Löfving, eds., *Struggles for Home: Violence, Hope and the Movement of People* (New York: Berghahn, 2009), 109–127.

14. Stephen Castles, 'Immigration and Asylum: Challenges to European Identities and Citizenship', in Dan Stone, ed., *The Oxford Handbook of Postwar European History* (Oxford: Oxford University Press, 2012), 201–219; '"The Lowest of the Low" No More', Deutsche Welle, 21 October 2005, www.dw.com/en/the-lowest-of-the-low-no-more/a-1746801.

15. Ann Brooks and Ruth Simpson, *Emotions in Transmigration: Transformation, Movement and Identity* (Basingstoke: Palgrave Macmillan, 2013), 62, 68.

16. Derek McGhee, Sue Heath, and Paulina Trevena, 'Dignity, Happiness and Being Able to Live a "Normal Life" in the UK—An Examination of Post-Accession Polish Migrants' Transnational Autobiographical Fields', *Social Identities* 18, no. 6 (2012): 711–727; Anne White, 'Polish Migration to the UK Compared with Migration Elsewhere in Europe: A Review of the Literature', *Social Identities* 22, no. 1 (2016): 10–25; Anne White and Louise Ryan, 'Polish "Temporary" Migration: The Formation and Significance of Social Networks', *Europe-Asia Studies* 60, no. 9 (2008): 1467–1502.

17. Quotations in McGhee et al., 'Dignity, Happiness', 723; Aleksandra Galasińska, 'Leavers and Stayers Discuss Returning Home: Internet Discourse on Migration in the Context of Post-Communist Transformation', *Social Identities* 16, no. 3 (2010): 316; Anne White, 'Double Return Migration: Failed Returns to Poland Leading to Settlement Abroad and New Transnational Strategies', *International Migration* 52, no. 6 (2014): 72–84, 77.

18. Karen Fog Olwig, 'Migration as Adventure: Narrative Self-Representation Among Caribbean Migrants in Denmark', *Ethnos: Journal of Anthropology* 83, no. 1 (2016): 156–171.

19. Ruben Andersson, *Illegality, Inc.: Clandestine Migration and the Business of Bordering Europe* (Berkeley: University of California Press, 2014), 184, 191.

20. Amelia Gentleman, 'Home Office Destroyed Windrush Landing Cards, Says Ex-Staffer', *The Guardian*, 17 April 2018, https://www.theguardian.com/uk-news/2018/apr/17/home-office-destroyed-windrush-landing-cards-says-ex-staffer; Nesrine Malik, 'It's Not Just Windrush', *The Guardian*, 19 April 2018, https://www.theguardian.com/commentisfree/2018/apr/19/windrush-theresa-may-immigrants.

21. Jef Huysmans, *The Politics of Insecurity: Fear, Migration and Asylum in the EU* (London: Routledge, 2006); Gregory Feldman, *The Migration Apparatus: Security, Labour, and Policymaking in the European Union* (Stanford: Stanford University Press, 2012); Israel Butler, 'No Good Reason for a Schengen Entry/Exit System', *Open Society Foundations*, 23 April 2013, https://www.opensocietyfoundations.org/voices/no-good-reason-schengen-entryexit-system.

22. Jack Shenker, 'Mediterranean Migrant Deaths: A Litany of Largely Avoidable Loss', *The Guardian*, 3 October 2013, https://www.theguardian.com/world/2013/oct/03/mediterranean-migrant-deaths-avoidable-loss; 'Identification of Applicants (EURO-DAC)', European Commission, Migration and Home Affairs, https://ec.europa.eu/home-affairs/what-we-do/policies/asylum/identification-of-applicants_en.

23. Ruben Zaiotti, 'The Italo-French Row over Schengen: Critical Junctures and the Future of Europe's Border Regime', *Journal of Borderlands Studies* 28, no. 3 (2013): 337–354.

24. Nicholas De Genova, 'The "Migrant Crisis" as Racial Crisis: Do *Black Lives Matter* in Europe?', *Ethnic and Racial Studies* 41, no. 10 (2017): 1765–1782.

25. Maurizio Albahari, *Crimes of Peace: Mediterranean Migrations at the World's Deadliest Border* (Philadelphia: University of Pennsylvania Press, 2015), 145.

26. Ibid., 148, 150.

27. Gabriele Del Grande, 'On the Bride's Side: Filmmaker's View', *Al Jazeera*, 20 October 2015, https://www.aljazeera.com/programmes/witness/2015/10/refugees-bride-side-151020134012752.html.

28. Albahari, *Crimes of Peace*, 157, 164.

29. Kim Rygiel, 'Dying to Live: Migrant Deaths and Citizenship Politics Along European Borders: Transgressions, Disruptions, and Mobilizations', *Citizenship Studies* 20, no. 5 (2016): 550–551.

30. Albahari, *Crimes of Peace*, 161, 194; Irial Glynn, *Asylum Policy, Boat People and Political Discourse: Boats, Votes and Asylum in Australia and Italy* (Basingstoke: Palgrave Macmillan, 2016), 176–178.

31. 'Factsheet on EU Operations in the Mediterranean Sea', European Commission, updated 4 October 2016, https://ec.europa.eu/home-affairs/sites/homeaffairs/files/what-we-do/policies/securing-eu-borders/fact-sheets/docs/20161006/eu_operations_in_the_mediterranean_sea_en.pdf.

32. Albahari, *Crimes of Peace*, 169.

33. Italian Minister of the Interior Marco Minniti announced that, 'on 31 March [2017] the tribes came to my office here in Rome'; Patrick Wintour, 'Italian Minister Defends Methods That Led to 87% Drop in Migrants from Libya', *The Guardian*, 7 September 2017, https://www.theguardian.com/world/2017/sep/07/italian-minister-migrants-libya-marco-minniti.

34. Eric Reidy, 'An Open Secret: Refugee Pushbacks Across the Turkey-Greece Border', *IRIN News*, 8 October 2018, https://www.irinnews.org/special-report/2018/10/08/refugee-pushbacks-across-turkey-greece-border-Evros.

35. Jessica Reinisch, '"Forever Temporary": Migrants in Calais, Then and Now', *Political Quarterly* 86, no. 4 (2016): 515–522.

36. Kim Rygiel, 'Bordering Solidarities: Migrant Activism and the Politics of Movement and Camps at Calais', *Citizenship Studies* 15, no. 1 (2011): 1–19; Elise Sandri,

'"Volunteer Humanitarianism": Volunteers and Humanitarian Aid in the Jungle Refugee Camp of Calais', *Journal of Ethnic and Migration Studies* 44, no. 1 (2018): 65–80. For the British perspective, see House of Commons Home Affairs Committee, 'The Work of the Immigration Directorates: Calais', 17 March 2015, available at https://publications.parliament.uk/pa/cm201415/cmselect/cmhaff/902 /902.pdf.

37. Ali Hassan and Linn Biörklund, 'The Journey to Dreamland Never Ends: A Refugee's Journey from Somalia to Sweden', *Refugee Survey Quarterly* 35, no. 2 (2016): 116–136.

38. Albahari, *Crimes of Peace*, 181; 'Live and Work in the European Union!' EU Blue Card Network, https://apply.eu.

Chapter 21: Another Europe: Borders, Routes, Migrant Lives

1. Madeleine Reeves, *Border Work: Spatial Lives of the State in Rural Central Asia* (Ithaca, NY: Cornell University Press, 2014).

2. European Council on Refugees and Exiles, *Here to Stay? Refugee Voices in Belarus, Moldova, the Russian Federation and Ukraine*, 2009, https://www.refworld.org /docid/49b11be53a7.html.

3. Greta Uehling, 'Irregular and Illegal Migration Through Ukraine', *International Migration* 42, no. 3 (2004): 88–89; Daniel Trilling, *Lights in the Distance* (London: Picador, 2018), 223.

4. Iakov Kedmi, 'Evropa stoit na poroge novykh terraktov', *Izvestia*, http://izvestia.ru /news/607100.

5. Karolina S. Follis, *Building Fortress Europe: The Polish-Ukrainian Frontier* (Philadelphia: University of Pennsylvania Press, 2012), 29, 184–185.

6. Ibid., 4.

7. Ibid., 29, 48, 74–78.

8. Donna Bahry, 'Opposition to Immigration, Economic Insecurity and Individual Values: Evidence from Russia', *Europe-Asia Studies* 68, no. 5 (2016): 898.

9. Martha H. Myhre, 'The State Programme for Voluntary Resettlement of Compatriots: Ideals of Citizenship, Membership and Statehood in the Russian Federation', *Russian Review* 76, no. 4 (2017): 690–712; Matthew Kupfer and Bradley Jardine, 'For Russia's Labor Migrants, a Life on the Edge', *Moscow Times*, 4 November 2016, https://the moscowtimes.com/articles/for-labor-migrants-a-life-on-the-edge-56018; Leonid Ragozin, 'Russia Wants Immigrants the World Doesn't', Bloomberg, 14 March 2017, https://www.bloomberg.com/news/features/2017-03-14/russia-s-alternative -universe-immigrants-welcome.

10. Mary Buckley, *The Politics of Unfree Labour in Russia: Human Trafficking and Labour Migration* (Cambridge: Cambridge University Press, 2018), 194; Christos Nikas and Russell King, 'Economic Growth Through Remittances: Lessons from the Greek Experience of the 1960s Applicable to the Albanian Case', *Journal of Southern Europe and the Balkans* 7, no. 2 (2005): 235–257; Andrew MacDowall, 'Kosovo at 10: Challenges Overshadow Independence Celebrations', *The Guardian*, 16 February 2018, https://www.theguardian.com/world/2018 /feb/16/kosovo-at-10-challenges-overshadow-independence-celebrations.

11. Caress Schenk, *Why Control Immigration? Strategic Uses of Migration Management in Russia* (Toronto: University of Toronto Press, 2018).

12. Ellen Mickiewicz, *No Illusions: The Voices of Russia's Future Leaders* (New York: Oxford University Press, 2017), 215–217, quoting from a public opinion survey by the SOVA Center in September 2013; 'Public Opinion in Russia: Russians' Attitudes on Economic and Domestic Issues', Associated Press–NORC Center for Public Affairs Research, n.d., www.apnorc.org/projects/Pages/HTML%20Reports/public-opinion-in-russia-russians-attitudes-on-the-economic-and-domestic-issues-issue-brief.aspx. See 'Racism and Xenophobia', SOVA Center for Information and Analysis, https://www.sova-center.ru/en/xenophobia.

13. Buckley, *Politics of Unfree Labour*, 73; Mickiewicz, *No Illusions*, 149–150, 159–160.

14. Buckley, *Politics of Unfree Labour*, 211.

15. Ibid., 192–201.

16. Kupfer and Jardine, 'For Russia's Labor Migrants, a Life on the Edge'.

17. Uehling, 'Irregular and Illegal Migration Through Ukraine', 82; Buckley, *Politics of Unfree Labour*, 96, 103.

18. For the legal background and the implementation of the law in Russia, see Lauren A. McCarthy, *Trafficking Justice: How Russian Police Enforce New Laws, from Crime to Courtroom* (Ithaca, NY: Cornell University Press, 2015).

19. Eduardo del Campo Cortés, *Odiseas: Al otro lado de la frontera. Historias de la inmigración en España* (Sevilla: n.p., 2007), 219–239.

20. Buckley, *Politics of Unfree Labour*, 193–194; Greta Uehling, 'Everyday Life in Ukraine's War Zone', *Current History* 116 (2017): 264–270.

21. '"Nobody Wants Us": The Alienated Civilians of Eastern Ukraine', International Crisis Group, 1 October 2018, available at https://www.refworld.org/docid/5bbc61af4.html; Agnieszka Pikulicka-Wilczewska and Greta Uehling, eds., *Migration and the Ukraine Crisis* (Bristol: E-International Relations, 2017).

22. Unnamed interviewee, quoted in Gayle Munro, *Transnationalism, Diaspora and Migrants from the Former Yugoslavia in Britain* (London: Routledge, 2017), 25–26.

23. Stef Jansen, 'After the Red Passport: Towards an Anthropology of the Everyday Geopolitics of Entrapment in the EU's "Immediate Outside"', *Journal of the Royal Anthropological Institute* 15, no. 4 (2009): 822.

24. Kristen Chick, 'Thousands Flee Economic Despair in Kosovo for EU Countries, Welcome or Not', *Los Angeles Times*, 15 February 2015, www.latimes.com/world/europe/la-fg-kosovo-refugees-20150215-story.html.

25. Quoted in Peo Hansen and Sandy B. Hager, *The Politics of European Citizenship: Deepening Contradictions in Social Rights and Migration Policy* (New York: Berghahn, 2010), 134–135.

26. This terrible episode provides the dramatic opening paragraph of Kitty Calavita, *Immigrants at the Margins: Law, Race, and Exclusion in Southern Europe* (Cambridge: Cambridge University Press, 2005), 1.

27. Russell King, Esmeralda Uruçi, and Julie Vullnetari, 'Albanian Migration and Its Effects in Comparative Perspective', *Journal of Balkan and Near Eastern Studies* 13, no. 3 (2011): 269–286.

28. Martin Geiger, 'Mobility, Development, Protection, EU-Integration! The IOM's National Migration Strategy for Albania', in Martin Geiger and Antoine Pécoud, eds., *The Politics of International Migration Management* (Basingstoke: Palgrave, 2012), 141–159.

29. Tony Judt, *Postwar: A History of Europe Since 1945* (London: William Heinemann, 2005), 767; Ruth Mandel, 'Fifty Years of Migration, Fifty Years of Waiting: Turkey, Germany, and the European Union', *German Politics and Society* 31, no. 2 (2013): 66–78; Eva Østergaard-Nielsen, *Transnational Politics: The Case of Turks and Kurds in Germany* (London: Routledge, 2003).

30. Franck Düvell, 'Turkey's Transition to an Immigration Country: A Paradigm Shift', *Insight Turkey* 16, no. 4 (2014): 87–103.

31. Filiz Kunuroglu, Kutlay Yagmur, Fons van de Vijver, and Sjaak Kroon, 'Motives for Turkish Return Migration from Western Europe: Home, Sense of Belonging, Discrimination and Transnationalism', *Turkish Studies* 19, no. 3 (2018): 422–450.

32. Semra Purkis and Fatih Güngör, 'Drifting Here and There But Going Nowhere: The Case of Migrants from Turkey in Milan in the Era of Global Economic Crisis', *Journal of International Migration and Integration* 18, no. 2 (2017): 434.

33. Maurizio Albahari, *Crimes of Peace: Mediterranean Migrations at the World's Deadliest Border* (Philadelphia: University of Pennsylvania Press, 2015), 185.

34. Ege Aksu, Refik Erzan, and Murat Guray Kirdar, 'The Impact of Mass Migration of Syrians on the Turkish Labor Market', Koc University-TUSIAD Economic Research Forum, 2018; Gregory J. Goalwin, 'Population Exchange and the Politics of Ethno-Religious Fear: The EU-Turkey Agreement on Syrian Refugees in Historical Perspective', *Patterns of Prejudice* 52, nos. 2–3 (2018): 132; Daniel Howden, 'Greece: Between Deterrence and Integration', *Refugees Deeply*, May 2017, http://issues.newsdeeply.com/greece-between-deterrence-and-integration.

35. 'What is the Entry/Exit System (EES)?', Schengen Visa Info, https://www.schengenvisainfo.com/entry-exit-system-ees.

36. Emma Graham-Harrison, 'They Treated Her Like a Dog', *The Guardian*, 8 December 2017, https://www.theguardian.com/world/2017/dec/08/they-treated-her-like-a-dog-tragedy-of-the-six-year-old-killed-at-croatian-border.

Chapter 22: Belief, Bodies, and Behaviour

1. Yasmin Gunaratnam, *Death and the Migrant: Bodies, Borders and Care* (London: Bloomsbury, 2013), 1–2.

2. Colin Grant, 'Windrush Tales: My Parents Were Caught Between Nostalgia and an Inability to Return', *The Guardian*, 23 July 2018, https://www.theguardian.com/books/2018/jul/23/a-new-chapter-in-windrush-the-authors-who-echoed-my-parents-journey-.

3. Marita Eastmond, 'The Politics of Death: Rituals of Protest in a Chilean Exile Community', in Sven Cederroth, ed., *On the Meaning of Death: Essays on Mortuary Rituals and Eschatological Beliefs* (Stockholm: Almqvist and Wiksell, 1988), 82.

4. Anne Sigfrid Grønseth, 'Migrating Rituals: Negotiations of Belonging and Otherness Among Tamils in Norway', *Journal of Ethnic and Migration Studies* 44, no. 16 (2018): 2617–2633. The victim's body was sent to India for burial.

5. Anu Mai Köll, personal communication; Hariz Halilovich, *Places of Pain: Forced Displacement, Popular Memory, and Translocal Identities in Bosnian War-Torn Communities* (New York: Berghahn, 2013), 74–75.
6. Vincent Crapanzano, *The Harkis: The Wound That Never Heals* (Chicago: Chicago University Press, 2011), 117, 122, 209; quotation in Isabel Hollis-Touré, *From North Africa to France: Family Migration in Text and Film* (London: IGRS Books, 2015), 43.
7. Gunaratnam, *Death and the Migrant*, 150.
8. Katy Gardner, *Age, Narration and Migration: The Life Course and Life Histories of Bengali Elders in London* (Oxford: Berg, 2002), 195–196.
9. Giovanna Campani, Maurizio Catani, and Salvatore Palidda, 'Italian Immigrant Associations in France', in John Rex, Daniele Joly, and Czarina Wilpert, eds., *Immigrant Associations in Europe* (Aldershot: Gower, 1986), 190; Sue Bailey, 'Woodgrange Park Cemetery', London Cemeteries, 11 April 2011, http://londoncemeteries.co .uk/2011/04/11/woodgrange-park-cemetery.
10. Eva Reimers, 'Death and Identity: Graves and Funerals as Cultural Communication', *Mortality* 4, no. 2 (1999): 147–166.
11. Sam Jones, '"He Was Just a Kid": The Boy Who Became a Symbol of Spain's Migration Crisis', *The Guardian*, 26 January 2018, https://www.theguardian.com/world/2018 /jan/26/boy-symbol-spain-migration-crisis-samuel-kabamba.
12. Kim Rygiel, 'Dying to Live: Migrant Deaths and Citizenship Politics Along European Borders: Transgressions, Disruptions, and Mobilizations', *Citizenship Studies* 20, no. 5 (2016): 556, 557; 'Journey Back to Lesvos: Creating Networks of Solidarity and Struggle for Freedom of Movement,' Welcome 2 Lesvos, n.d., http://lesvos.w2eu .net/files/2014/02/Lesvos2013-Screen-DS.pdf.
13. Immigration and Asylum Minister Gerd Leers called Mr Roustayi's death 'very tragic', but insisted that official procedures had been applied properly. 'Netherlands Failed to Help Self-Immolation Victim', Radio Netherlands Worldwide, 8 April 2011, http:// immigrantdetentionwatch.blogspot.com/2011/04/netherlands-failed-to-help-self .html.
14. John Rex, introduction to Rex et al., eds., *Immigrant Associations*, 8; Joyce Egginton, *They Seek a Living* (London: Hutchinson, 1957), 27, 118.
15. Jerzy Zubrzycki, 'Across the Frontiers of Europe', in Wilfred Borrie, ed., *The Cultural Integration of Immigrants* (Paris: UNESCO, 1959), 174–175; Clair Wills, *Lovers and Strangers: An Immigrant History of Post-War Britain* (London: Allen Lane, 2017), 123–124.
16. Emilia Salvanou, 'Muslims in Athens: Narratives and Strategies of Belonging', *Journal of Modern Greek Studies* 32, no. 2 (2014): 349, 357.
17. Petra Y. Kuppinger, 'Cinderella Wears a Hijab: Neighborhoods, Islam and the Everyday Production of Multi-Ethnic Urban Cultures in Germany', *Space and Culture* 17, no. 1 (2014): 29–42.
18. 'Hair: Heritage, Attitude, Identity, Respect', Museum of Liverpool, n.d., www.liver poolmuseums.org.uk/mol/exhibitions/hair.
19. Satwant Singh Brar, 'Jaginder Singh Brar Obituary', *The Guardian*, 23 March 2018, https://www.theguardian.com/world/2018/mar/23/jaginder-singh-brar-obituary; David Feldman, 'Why the English Like Turbans: Multicultural Politics in British

History', in David Feldman and Jon Lawrence, eds., *Structures and Transformations in Modern British History* (Cambridge: Cambridge University Press, 2011), 281–302; '1969: Sikh Busmen Win Turban Fight', BBC, 'On This Day: April 9', http://news.bbc.co.uk/onthisday/hi/dates/stories/april/9/newsid_2523000/2523691.stm.

20. Rikke Andreassen, 'Take Off That Veil and Give Me Access to Your Body: An Analysis of Danish Debates About Muslim Women's Head and Body Covering', in Marlou Schrover and Deirdre Moloney, eds., *Gender, Migration and Categorisation: Making Distinctions Between Migrants in Western Countries, 1945–2010* (Amsterdam: Amsterdam University Press, 2013), 215–229; Deniz Göktürk, David Gramling, and Anton Kaes, eds., *Germany in Transit: Nation and Migration, 1955–2005* (Berkeley: University of California Press, 2007 [1973]), 185, 220.

21. Ruth Mandel, 'Turkish Headscarves and the "Foreigner Problem": Constructing Difference Through Emblems of Identity', *New German Critique* 46 (1989): 27–46; Patricia Ehrkamp, ' "I've Had It with Them!" Younger Migrant Women's Spatial Practices of Conformity and Resistance', *Gender, Place and Culture* 20, no. 1 (2013): 19–36.

22. John R. Bowen, *Why the French Don't Like Headscarves: Islam, the State, and Public Space* (Princeton, NJ: Princeton University Press, 2007), 1.

23. As one French mayor put it in 2003, 'I find it healthier that mosques be financed by public money than by foreign states'. Bowen, *Why the French Don't Like Headscarves*, 61. In the nineteenth century, the French state sought to remove the grip of the church from public life and to maintain a kind of neutrality with respect to religion, but at the same time it conceded that parents might wish to educate their children in Catholic or Jewish schools, in which case they could send them to private schools subsidised by the state. Religious belief was a private affair. For a good summary, see Émile Chabal, 'Managing the Postcolony: Minority Politics in Montpellier, c. 1960–c. 2010', *Contemporary European History* 23, no. 2 (2014): 237–258.

24. Rita Chin, *The Crisis of Multiculturalism in Europe: A History* (Princeton, NJ: Princeton University Press, 2017), 196–197.

25. Quoted in Bowen, *Why the French Don't Like Headscarves*, 90; Jacqueline Bhabha, ' "Get Back to Where You Once Belonged": Identity, Citizenship and Exclusion in Europe', *Human Rights Quarterly* 20, no. 3 (1998): 592–627.

26. John Wallach Scott, *The Politics of the Veil* (Princeton, NJ: Princeton University Press, 2007), 3.

27. Bowen, *Why the French Don't Like Headscarves*, 1, 66–67.

28. Agence France-Presse, 'Nice Becomes Latest French City to Impose Burkini Ban', *The Guardian*, 19 August 2016, https://www.theguardian.com/world/2016/aug/19/nice-becomes-latest-french-city-to-impose-burkini-ban; Bowen, *Why the French Don't Like Headscarves*, 96, 79–80.

29. Rudolf Braun, *Sozio-kulturelle Probleme der Eingliederung italienischer Arbeitskräfte in der Schweiz* (Erlenbach-Zurich: Eugen Rentsch Verlag, 1970), 225, 232; Yvonne Rieker, *'Ein Stück Heimat findet man ja immer': Die italienische Einwanderung in die Bundesrepublik* (Essen: Klartext, 2003), 121.

30. Johan Svanberg, 'The Contrasts of Migration Narratives: From Germany to the Swedish Garment Industry During the 1950s', *Journal of Migration History* 3, no. 1 (2017): 146.

31. Maren Möhring, 'Food for Thought: Rethinking the History of Migration to West Germany Through the Migrant Restaurant Business', *Journal of Contemporary History* 49, no. 1 (2014): 209–227.

32. Joyce Mushaben, *The Changing Faces of Citizenship: Social Integration and Political Mobilization Among Ethnic Minorities in Germany* (New York: Berghahn, 2008), 182; Eva Barlösius, 'Nahrung als Kommunikationsmittel', in Hans-Peter Waldhoff, Dursun Tan, and Elçin Kürşat-Ahlers, eds., *Brücken zwischen Zivilisationenen: Zur Zivilisierung etnisch-kultureller Differenzen und Machtungleichheiten. Das deutsch-türkische Beispiel* (Frankfurt: IKO, 1997), 149; Elizabeth Buettner, 'South Asian Restaurants and the Limits of Multiculturalism in Britain', *Journal of Modern History* 80, no. 4 (2008): 880.

33. Möhring, 'Food for Thought', 214; Christian Joppke, *Immigration and the Nation-State: The United States, Germany, and the UK* (Oxford: Oxford University Press, 1999), 218. This was in the wake of the Solingen atrocity, discussed in Chapter 16.

34. Flemming Christiansen and Liang Xiujing, 'Chinese Restaurant Owners in the Netherlands and Germany in the Second Half of the 20th Century', in Klaus Bade, Pieter C. Emmer, Leo Lucassen, and Jochen Oltmer, eds., *Encyclopedia of European Migration and Minorities from the Seventeenth Century to the Present* (Cambridge: Cambridge University Press, 2011), 289–291.

35. Jonathan Morris, 'Why Espresso? Explaining Changes in European Coffee Preferences from a Production of Culture Perspective', *European Review of History* 20, no. 5 (2013): 891.

36. Ruth Mandel, 'Turkish Headscarves and the "Foreigner Problem": Constructing Difference Through Emblems of Identity', *New German Critique* 46 (1989): 27–46.

37. 'Top Italian Chef Quits State TV Show "After Being Told to Drop Foreign Recipes"', *The Guardian*, 30 October 2018, https://www.theguardian.com/world/2018/oct/30/top-italian-chef-vittorio-castellani-quits-rai-state-tv-show-ready-steady-cook-after-being-told-to-drop-foreign-recipes.

38. Izabella Main, 'Motivations for Mobility and Settlement of Polish Female Migrants in Barcelona and Berlin', *Social Identities* 22, no. 1 (2015): 73.

Chapter 23: Owning the Past: Migration, Memory, Museum

1. Michelle Bellelli and Federico Zannoni, 'The Reggiani Factory and New Immigrants: Memory and Local History to Strengthen Integration', in Perla Innocenti, ed., *Migrating Heritage: Experiences of Cultural Networks and Dialogues in Europe* (Farnham: Ashgate, 2014), 238.

2. Benedict Anderson, *Imagined Communities: Reflections on the Origin and Spread of Nationalism* (London: Verso, 1983); Stuart Hall, 'Un-settling "the Heritage", Re-imagining the Post-Nation', *Third Text* 49 (1999): 5.

3. Katherine Goodnow, Jack Lohman, and Philip Marfleet, *Museums, the Media and Refugees: Stories of Crisis, Control and Compassion* (Oxford: Berghahn, 2008); Sharon Macdonald, 'Museum Europe: Negotiating Heritage', *Anthropological Journal of European Cultures* 17, no. 2 (2008): 47–65.

4. Maureen Murphy, *Un palais pour une cité: Du Musée des Colonies à la Cité Nationale de l'Histoire de l'Immigration* (Paris: RMN, 2007); Nancy L. Green, 'The Immigration History Museum', in Edward Berenson, Vincent Duclert, and Christophe

Prochasson, eds., *The French Republic: History, Values, Debates* (Ithaca, NY: Cornell University Press, 2011), 242–251; see also the remarks of Benjamin Stora, president of the executive committee, in *Libération*, 13 October 2017, https://benjaminstora .univ-paris13.fr/index.php/articlesrecents.html.

5. Mary Stevens, 'Immigrants into Citizens: Ideology and Nation-Building in the Cité Nationale de l'Histoire de l'Immigration', *Museological Review* 13 (2008): 57–73.

6. Sophia Labadi, 'The National Museum of Immigration History, Neo-colonialist Representations, Silencing, and Re-appropriation', *Journal of Social Archaeology* 13, no. 3 (2013): 310–330.

7. Alessandro Nicosia and Lorenzo Prencipe, eds., *Museo Nazionale Emigrazione Italiana* (Rome: Gangemi, 2009); Anna Chiara Cimoli, 'Identity, Complexity, Immigration: Staging the Present in Italian Migration Museums', in Christopher Whitehead, Katherine Lloyd, Susannah Eckersley, and Rhiannon Mason, eds., *Museums, Migration and Identity in Europe: Peoples, Places and Identities* (Farnham: Ashgate, 2015), 285–315. Thanks to Pam Ballinger for supplying additional information. In Turin, too, the Museum of Resistance, Deportation, and War set aside space for a special exhibition on the history of immigration, complete with videotaped interviews with migrants from Romania, Morocco, and Congo, as well as an activist from the Roma community. Guido Vaglio, '*Turin—Earth*: City and New Migrations', in Innocenti, ed., *Migrating Heritage*, 163–175.

8. Susannah Eckersley, 'Walking the Tightrope Between Memory and Diplomacy? Addressing the Post–Second World War Expulsions of Germans in German Museums', in Whitehead et al., eds., *Museums, Migration and Identity*, 112. On proposals for a museum of migration, see the press release issued by the Dokumentationszentrum und Museum über die Migration in Deutschland (DOMiD, Documentation Centre and Museum of Migration in Germany), 20 April 2015, www.domid.org/en /news/press-conference-kick-start-central-migration-museum.

9. Dietmar Osses and Katarzyna Nogueira, 'Representations of Immigration and Emigration in Germany's Historic Museums', in Cornelia Wilhelm, ed., *Migration, Memory and Diversity: Germany from 1945 to the Present* (New York: Berghahn, 2017), 158. Brief details of the exhibition, 'Fremde Heimat—Yaban, Sılan olur', are available at Dokumentationszentrum und Museum über die Migration in Deutschland (DOMiD, Documentation Centre and Museum of Migration in Germany), https://www.domid.org/de/ausstellung/fremde-heimat-%E2%80%93 -yaban-s%C4%B1lan-olur. The website of the new 'Virtual Museum' is https:// virtuelles-migrationsmuseum.org/en.

10. Jana Dolecki, '"Home, Foreign Home"—Commemorating the 50-Year Anniversary of the Signing of the Agreement on Labor Migration Between Austria and Yugoslavia', European Institute for Progressive Cultural Policies, October 2017, http://eipcp .net/transversal/1017/dolecki/en.

11. 'The Schengen Agreement—More Than a European Contract', Musée Européen Schengen, www.visitschengen.lu/en/european-museum.

12. Marion von Osten, 'Auf der Suche nach einer neuen Erzählung: Reflektionen des Ausstellungsprojekts "Projekt Migration"', in Natalie Bayer, Andrea Engl, and Sabine Hess, eds., *Crossing Munich: Beiträge zur Migration aus Kunst, Wissenschaft und Aktivismus* (Munich: Schreiber, 2009), 90–93; Osses and Nogueira,

'Representations of Immigration', 159, 162; Wolfram Kaiser, Stefan Krankenhagen, and Kerstin Poehls, *Exhibiting Europe in Museums: Transnational Networks, Collections, Narratives and Representations* (New York: Berghahn, 2014), 172; Katja Kobolt, 'How to Speak Precarious Histories from a Precarious Position?', European Institute for Progressive Cultural Policies, October 2017, http://eipcp.net/transver sal/1017/kobolt/en.

13. 'Friedland—Perspectives of Migration: The Exhibition', Museum Friedland, www .museum-friedland.de/museum/#p90; 'German Refugees Art Exhibition—Life in Camp Friedland', *Pathé*, 1960, https://www.britishpathe.com/video/german-refugees -art-exhibition-life-in-camp-friedl. Additional information courtesy of Klaus Magnus.

14. 'Pagani—Last Goodbye', Welcome to Europe, 13 September 2010, http://w2eu .net/2010/09/13/pagani-last-good-bye; Kaiser et al., *Exhibiting Europe in Museums*, 176; Centre for Political Beauty, www.politicalbeauty.com; Seth M. Holmes and Heide Castañeda, 'Representing the "European Refugee Crisis" in Germany and Beyond: Deservingness and Difference, Life and Death', *American Ethnologist* 43, no. 1 (2016): 12–24.

15. Karen Armstrong, *Remembering Karelia: A Family's Story of Displacement During and After the Finnish Wars* (New York: Berghahn, 2008), 10, 11, 56; Anna-Kaisa Kuusisto-Arponen, 'The Mobilities of Forced Displacement: Commemorating Karelian Evacuation in Finland', *Social and Cultural Geography* 10, no. 5 (2009): 545–563. See also work by Merja Paksuniemi, 'Finnish Refugee Children's Experiences of Swedish Refugee Camps During the Second World War', *Migration Letters* 12, no. 1 (2015): 28–37; Merja Paksuniemi, Tuija A. Turunen, and Pigga Keskitalo, 'Coping with Separation in Childhood—Finnish War Children's Recollections About Swedish Foster Families', *Procedia—Social and Behavioral Sciences* 185 (2015): 67–75. In 1991–1992, some 1.3 million Finns crossed the border to visit their former homes in Karelia.

16. Michèle Baussant, 'Pied-Noir Pilgrimages, Commemorative Spaces and Counter-Memory', in Manuel Borutta and Jan C. Jansen, eds., *Vertriebene and Pieds-Noirs in Postwar Germany and France: Comparative Perspectives* (Houndmills: Palgrave Macmillan, 2016), 221; Yann Scioldo-Zürcher, *Devenir métropolitan: Politique d'intégration et parcours des rapatriés d'Algérie en métropole, 1954–2005* (Paris: Editions de l'Ecole des hautes études en sciences sociales, 2010), 389; Vincent Crapanzano, *The Harkis: The Wound That Never Heals* (Chicago: Chicago University Press, 2011), 171; Claire Eldridge, 'Returning to the "Return": *Pied-Noir* Memories of 1962', *Revue Européenne des Migrations Internationales* 29, no. 3 (2013): 121–140.

17. Susan Slyomovics, *Object of Memory: Arab and Jew Narrate the Palestinian Village* (Philadelphia: University of Pennsylvania Press, 1998); 'Aladža Mosque in Foča Soon to Join Invaluable BiH Cultural Heritage', *Sarajevo Times*, 22 October 2014, www.sarajevo times.com/aladza-mosque-foca-soon-join-invaluable-bih-cultural-heritage; Anna-Kaisa Kuusisto-Arponen and Ulla Savolainen, 'The Interplay of Memory and Matter: Narratives of Former Finnish Karelian Child Evacuees', *Oral History* 44, no. 2 (2016): 59–68.

18. Kevin Myers, *Struggles for a Past: Irish and Afro-Caribbean Histories in England, 1951–2000* (Manchester: Manchester University Press, 2015), 109, 136; Laura Teulières, 'Recovering Memory Is Regaining Dignity: Collective Memory and Migration in France', in Rainer Ohliger, Karen Schönwälder, and Triadafilos Triadafilo-

poulos, eds., *European Encounters: Migrants, Migration and European Societies Since 1945* (Aldershot: Ashgate, 2003), 300–318.

19. Greta L. Uehling, *Beyond Memory: The Crimean Tatars' Deportation and Return* (Houndmills: Palgrave, 2004), 137; Vieda Skultans, *The Testimony of Lives: Memory in Post-Soviet Latvia* (London: Routledge, 1997), 51.

20. Stavroula Pipyrou, 'The Untold Story of Thousands of Italian Children Sent Away from Their Parents in the 1950s', *Independent*, 19 April 2017, https://www.independent .co.uk/life-style/health-and-families/italy-mussolini-1950s-calabrian-italian-children -a7687141.html.

21. Loring M. Danforth and Riki Van Boeschoten, *Children of the Greek Civil War: Refugees and the Politics of Memory* (Chicago: Chicago University Press, 2011), 137–146, 194.

22. Tahar Ben Jelloun, *French Hospitality: Racism and North African Immigrants* (New York: Columbia University Press, 2000 [1984]), 39; Angelique Chrisafis, 'French Far Right Attack Choice of Mixed-Race Girl for Joan of Arc Role', *The Guardian*, 23 February 2018, https://www.theguardian.com/world/2018/feb/23/french-far-right-targets -mixed-race-teen-playing-joan-of-arc.

23. Daniele Salerno, 'Memorializing Boat Tragedies in the Mediterranean: The Case of the *Kater i Radës*', in Lynda Mannik, ed. *Migration by Boat: Discourses of Trauma, Exclusion and Survival* (New York: Berghahn, 2016), 141.

24. See the artist's website at Kalliopi Lemos, http://kalliopilemos.com.

25. Maurizio Albahari, *Crimes of Peace: Mediterranean Migrations at the World's Deadliest Border* (Philadelphia: University of Pennsylvania Press, 2015), 204–205.

26. The British Museum, Collection Online, 'The Lampedusa Cross', https://www .britishmuseum.org/research/collection_online/collection_object_details.aspx? objectId=3691920&partId=1&searchText=lampedusa&page=27; see also Mark Brown, 'Lampedusa Cross Will Be British Museum Director's Final Acquisition', *The Guardian*, 17 December 2015, https://www.theguardian.com/culture/2015/dec/18/lampedusa-cross -will-be-british-museum-directors-final-aquisition.

27. Karina Horsti, 'Imagining Europe's Borders: Commemorative Art on Migrant Tragedies', in Mannik, ed., *Migration by Boat*, 83–100; Albahari, *Crimes of Peace*, 186–188.

Chapter 24: Arab Spring, European Winter

1. Hein de Haas and Nando Sigona, 'Migration and Revolution', *Forced Migration Review* 39 (2012): 4–5; Heaven Crawley, Franck Düvell, Katharine Jones, Simon McMahon, and Nando Sigona, *Unravelling Europe's 'Migration Crisis': Journeys over Land and Sea* (Bristol: Policy Press, 2018).

2. Anna Rowlands, 'Turkey, Crossroads of the Displaced', Refugee Hosts, 11 April 2018, http://refugeehosts.org/2018/04/11/turkey-crossroads-for-the-displaced.

3. Heaven Crawley and Dimitris Skleparis, 'Refugees, Migrants, Neither, Both: Categorical Fetishism and the Politics of Bounding in Europe's "Migration Crisis"', *Journal of Ethnic and Migration Studies* 44, no. 1 (2018): 48–64.

4. Vicki Squire, '"I Never Thought to Come in Europe": Unpacking the Myths of Europe's "Migration Crisis"', Open Democracy, 31 May 2017, https://www.opendemocracy.net /beyondslavery/vicki-squire/i-never-thought-to-come-in-europe-unpacking -myths-of-europe-s-migration-c.

5. Crawley et al., *Unravelling Europe's 'Migration Crisis'*, 105.

6. There is now an extensive literature on the creation and dissemination of the image of his lifeless body. See, for example, Farida Vis, and Olga Goriunova, eds., 'The Iconic Image on Social Media: A Rapid Research Response to the Death of Aylan Kurdi', Visual Social Media Lab, December 2015, https://research.gold.ac.uk/14624 /1/KURDI%20REPORT.pdf.

7. Matthew Holehouse, and Isabelle Fraser, 'Migrant Crisis: European Council President Tusk Warns Schengen on Brink of Collapse', *The Telegraph*, 13 November 2015, https://www.telegraph.co.uk/news/worldnews/europe/eu/11991098/Migrant -crisis-Donald-Tusk-warns-that-Schengen-is-on-brink-of-collapse-latest-news.html.

8. Nikos Xydakis, quoted in David Crouch and Patrick Kingsley, 'Danish Parliament Approves Plan to Seize Assets from Refugees', *The Guardian*, 26 January 2016, https:// www.theguardian.com/world/2016/jan/26/danish-parliament-approves -plan-to-seize-assets-from-refugees.

9. 'Islamic State Changing Terror Tactics to Maintain Threat in Europe', Europol, press release, 2 December 2016, https://www.europol.europa.eu/newsroom/news/islamic -state-changing-terror-tactics-to-maintain-threat-in-europe.

10. Heath Cabot, *On the Doorstep of Europe: Asylum and Citizenship in Greece* (Philadelphia: University of Pennsylvania Press, 2014), 29.

11. 'March of Hope', Moving Europe, 31 July 2016, http://moving-europe.org /march-of-hope-3; Annastiina Kallius, Daniel Monterescu, and Prem Kumar Rajaram, 'Immobilizing Mobility: Border Ethnography, Illiberal Democracy, and the Politics of the "Refugee Crisis" in Hungary', *American Ethnologist* 43, no. 1 (2016): 25–37.

12. 'Speech by Prime Minister Viktor Orbán on 15 March', Website of the Hungarian Government, 16 March 2016, www.kormany.hu/en/the-prime-minister/the-prime -minister-s-speeches/speech-by-prime-minister-viktor-orban-on-15-march.

13. Jennifer Rankin, 'EU Court Dismisses Complaints by Hungary and Slovakia over Refugee Quotas', *The Guardian*, 6 September 2017, https://www.theguardian.com /world/2017/sep/06/eu-court-dismisses-complaints-by-hungary-and-slovakia-over -refugees; Ivan Krastev, *After Europe* (Philadelphia: University of Pennsylvania Press, 2017), 47, 105.

14. Patrick Wintour, 'EU Takes Action Against Eastern States for Refusing to Take Refugees', *The Guardian*, 13 June 2017, https://www.theguardian.com/world/2017/jun/13/eu -takes-action-against-eastern-states-for-refusing-to-take-refugees; Jennifer Rankin, 'EU Could "Scrap Refugee Quota Scheme"', *The Guardian*, 11 December 2017, https:// www.theguardian.com/world/2017/dec/11/eu-may-scrap-refugee-quota -scheme-donald-tusk.

15. Helena Smith, 'Surge in Migration to Greece Fuels Misery in Refugee Camps', *The Guardian*, 29 September 2017, https://amp.theguardian.com/world/2017/sep/29 /surge-in-migration-to-greece-fuels-misery-in-refugee-camps; Cabot, *On the Doorstep of Europe*, 31, 194–197, 213–217.

16. Katie Kuschminder and Khalid Koser, 'Why Don't Refugees Just Stay in Turkey or Greece? We Asked Them', *The Conversation*, 13 December 2016, https://theconver sation.com/why-dontrefugees-just-stay-in-turkey-or-greece-we-asked-them-70257.

17. Daniel Howden and Apostolis Fotiadis, 'The Refugee Archipelago: The Inside Story of What Went Wrong in Greece', *Refugees Deeply*, 6 March 2017, https://www.news

deeply.com/refugees/articles/2017/03/06/the-refugee-archipelago-the-inside -story-of-what-went-wrong-in-greece; Cabot, *On the Doorstep of Europe*, 209.

18. Daniel Howden, 'Greece: Between Deterrence and Integration', *Refugees Deeply*, May 2017, http://issues.newsdeeply.com/greece-between-deterrence-and-integration; Crawley et al., *Unravelling Europe's 'Migration Crisis'*, 26; Helena Smith, 'Greece Races to Move Refugees from Island Likened to a "New Lesbos"', *The Guardian*, 22 February 2019, https://www.theguardian.com/global-development/2019/feb/22/greece -races-to-move-refugees-from-island-branded-new-lesbos-samos.

19. Howden, 'Greece: Between Deterrence and Integration'.

20. Maurizio Albahari, *Crimes of Peace: Mediterranean Migrations at the World's Deadliest Border* (Philadelphia: University of Pennsylvania Press, 2015), 17, 172.

21. Crawley et al., *Unravelling Europe's 'Migration Crisis'*, 119, 125.

22. César Dezfuli, 'From Gambia to Italy: A Refugee's Perilous Journey', *Al Jazeera*, 22 March 2017, www.aljazeera.com/indepth/inpictures/2017/03/gambia-italy-refugee -perilous-journey-170305105814251.html; Annalisa Camilli, 'Dodging Death Along the Alpine Migrant Passage', *Refugees Deeply*, 25 January 2018, https://www.news deeply.com/refugees/articles/2018/01/25/dodging-death-along-the-alpine -migrant-passage.

23. Zach Campbell, 'Europe's Deadly Migration Strategy', *Politico*, 1 March 2019, https:// www.politico.eu/article/europe-deadly-migration-strategy-leaked-documents; Patrick Wintour, 'Italy Considers Closing Its Ports to Boats Carrying Migrants', *The Guardian*, 28 June 2017, https://www.theguardian.com/world/2017/jun/28/italy-considers -closing-its-ports-to-ships-from-libya?CMP=share_btn_tw; 'Which NGOs Have Signed the Italian Code of Conduct?', *InfoMigrants*, 10 August 2017, www.infomi grants.net/en/post/4529/which-ngos-have-signed-the-italian-code-of-conduct; 'Italy: UNHCR Deeply Concerned About Lampedusa Deportations of Libyans', comments by UNHCR spokesperson Ron Redmond, 18 March 2005, www.unhcr.org /news/briefing/2005/3/423ab71a4/italy-unhcr-deeply-concerned-lampedusa -deportations-libyans.html; 'About MOAS', Migrant Offshore Aid Station (MOAS), https://www.moas.eu/about; Charles Heller, Lorenzo Pezzani, Itamar Mann, Violeta Moreno-Lax, and Eyal Weizman, '"It's an Act of Murder": How Europe Outsources Suffering as Migrants Drown', *New York Times*, 26 December 2018, https://www .nytimes.com/interactive/2018/12/26/opinion/europe-migrant-crisis -mediterranean-libya.html.

24. Lara Keay, 'Safe After a Week at Sea: Ships Carrying 630 African Migrants Including Pregnant Women and Children Finally Dock in Spain After Being Refused Entry to Italy and Malta', *Mail Online*, 17 June 2018, www.dailymail.co.uk/news/article -5853061/Aquarius-ship-carrying-630-African-migrants-arrives-Valencia-Spain-refused -Malta-Italy.html; Sam Jones, 'Spain's Right Whips Up Fear as Migration Surge Hits Andalucian Shores', *The Guardian*, 5 August 2018, https://www.theguardian.com /world/2018/aug/05/spain-rightwing-parties-spar-immigration-surge-boats?CMP=Share _iOSApp_Other; Lorenzo D'Agostino, 'New Italian Law Adds Unofficial Clampdown on Aid to Asylum Seekers', *IRIN News*, 7 December 2018, https://www.irinnews.org /news-feature/2018/12/07/new-italian-law-adds-unofficial-clampdown-aid-asylum -seekers.

25. Eric Reidy, 'An Open Secret: Refugee Pushbacks Across the Turkey-Greece Border', *IRIN News*, 8 October 2018, https://www.irinnews.org/special-report/2018/10/08/refugee-pushbacks-across-turkey-greece-border-Evros.

26. Nicholas Schmidle, 'Ten Borders', *The New Yorker*, 26 October 2015, https://www.newyorker.com/magazine/2015/10/26/ten-borders.

27. Kim Rygiel, 'Bordering Solidarities: Migrant Activism and the Politics of Movement and Camps at Calais', *Citizenship Studies* 15, no. 1 (2011): 8; Crawley et al., *Unravelling Europe's 'Migration Crisis'*, 127.

28. Marion MacGregor, 'Danish PM Proposes Asylum Camps Outside the EU', *InfoMigrants*, 7 June 2018, www.infomigrants.net/en/post/9763/danish-pm-proposes-asylum-camps-outside-the-eu.

29. David Crouch and Patrick Kingsley, 'Danish Parliament Approves Plan to Seize Assets from Refugees', *The Guardian*, 26 January 2016, https://www.theguardian.com/world/2016/jan/26/danish-parliament-approves-plan-to-seize-assets-from-refugees; Martin Selsoe Sorensen, 'Denmark Plans to Isolate Unwanted Migrants on a Small Island', *New York Times*, 3 December 2018, https://www.nytimes.com/2018/12/03/world/europe/denmark-migrants-island.html.

30. Gaëlle Fisher, '*Heimat* Heimstättensiedlung: Constructing Belonging in Post-War West Germany', *German History* 35, no. 4 (2017): 568–587; Pertti Ahonen, 'On Forced Migrations: Transnational Realities and National Narratives in Post-1945 (West) Germany', *German History* 32, no. 4 (2014): 599–614; speech delivered on World Refugee Day, 20 June 2015, reported at ' "Moral Duty" to Save Mediterranean Migrants, Says Gauck', Deutsche Welle, 20 June 2015, www.dw.com/en/moral-duty-to-save-mediterranean-migrants-says-gauck/a-18528520.

31. Suzanna Crage, 'The More Things Change…Developments in German Practices Towards Asylum Seekers and Recognised Refugees', *German Politics* 25, no. 3 (2016): 344–365; Florian Trauner and Jocelyn Turton, ' "Welcome Culture": The Emergence and Transformation of a Public Debate on Migration', *Austrian Journal of Political Science* 46, no. 1 (2017): 33–42. Many thanks to Margit Wunsch-Gaarmann for her recollection of life on a US Army base in Germany.

32. Ulrich Rosenhagen, 'From Stranger to Citizen? Germany's Refugee Dilemma', *Dissent* 64, no. 3 (2017): 135; Dr Karl-Thomas Neumann, chief executive of Adam Opel AG. See *Wir Zusammen* (We Together) website at https://www.wir-zusammen.de/das-netzwerk/ueber-uns.

33. Translated as Jenny Erpenbeck, *Go Went Gone* (London: Portobello Books, 2017), 175.

34. Katrin Bennhold and Melissa Eddy, 'Merkel, to Survive, Agrees to Border Camps for Migrants', *New York Times*, 2 July 2018, https://www.nytimes.com/2018/07/02/world/europe/angela-merkel-migration-coalition.html; Philip Oltermann, 'Germany to Roll Out Mass Holding Centres for Asylum Seekers', *The Guardian*, 21 May 2018, https://www.theguardian.com/world/2018/may/21/germany-to-roll-out-mass-holding-centres-for-asylum-seekers.

35. Michael Birnbaum, 'In Once-Welcoming Italy, the Tide Turns Against Migrants', *Washington Post*, 25 August 2017, https://www.washingtonpost.com/amphtml/world/europe/in-once-welcoming-italy-thetide-turns-against-migrants/2017/08/25/244ac3d4-7c39-11e7-b2b1-aeba62854dfa_story.html; Stephanie Kirschgaessner and Jennifer Rankin,

'Italy's First Black Minister Fears Far-Right Party's Government Influence', *The Guardian*, 18 May 2018, https://www.theguardian.com/world/2018/may/18/italy-government -cecile-kyenge-the-league-lega-far-right.

36. Ruth Alexander, 'Why Is Bulgaria's Population Falling Off a Cliff?', BBC News, 7 September 2017, www.bbc.co.uk/news/world-europe-41109572; Claudia Finotelli and Irene Ponzo, 'Integration in Times of Economic Decline: Migrant Inclusion in Southern European Societies, Trends and Theoretical Implications', *Journal of Ethnic and Migration Studies* 43, no. 4 (2017): 1–18; 'Results of the Special Eurobarometer Survey 469 on "Integration of Immigrants in the European Union"', European Commission, Migration and Home Affairs, 13 April 2018, https://ec.europa.eu /home-affairs/news/results-special-eurobarometer-integration-immigrants-european -union_en.

37. Matt Broomfield, 'Calais Jungle Wall Is Completed Two Months After All the Refugees Were Driven Out', *Independent*, 13 December 2016, https://www.independen dent.co.uk/news/world/europe/calais-jungle-refugee-camp-wall-completed-emptied -two-months-cleared-a7472101.html; Jessica Reinisch, ' "Forever Temporary": Migrants in Calais, Then and Now', *Political Quarterly* 86, no. 4 (2016): 519.

38. Benny Hunter, 'Young People Are Still Dying in Calais', *Huffington Post*, 2 July 2017, https://www.huffingtonpost.co.uk/benny-hunter/calais-jungle_b_14633908.html.

39. Saeed Kamali Dehghan, ' "Iran Was Like Hell": The Young Refugees Starting Life in Serbia', *The Guardian*, 28 September 2018, https://www.theguardian.com/world/2018 /sep/28/iran-refugees-europe-eu-serbia-belgrade-asylum-seekers; 'Improved Mosney Direct Provision Centre "a Template to Follow"', *RTÉ News*, 27 July 2017, https:// www.rte.ie/news/2017/0727/893288-direct-provision.

40. Lorenzo Tondo, ' "They Are Our Salvation": The Sicilian Town Revived By Refugees', *The Guardian*, 19 March 2018, https://www.theguardian.com/world/2018 /mar/19/sutera-italy-the-sicilian-town-revived-by-refugees.

41. Sandro Mezzadra, 'The Proliferation of Borders and the Right to Escape', in Yolande Jansen, Robin Celikates, and Joost de Bloois, eds., *The Irregularization of Migration in Contemporary Europe: Detention, Deportation, Drowning* (London: Rowman and Littlefield, 2015), 127; 'Desperate and Dangerous: Report on the Human Rights Situation of Migrants and Refugees in Libya', United Nations Support Mission in Libya, Office of the High Commissioner for Human Rights, 20 December 2018, https://www.ohchr .org/Documents/Countries/LY/LibyaMigrationReport.pdf; Kai Dambach, 'New Images of Tortured Migrants Emerge from Libya', *InfoMigrants*, 1 March 2019, https://www .infomigrants.net/en/post/15467/new-images-of-tortured-migrants-emerge-from-libya.

Conclusion

1. Katrin Bennhold, 'This European Border Is Still Open, But for How Long?', *New York Times*, 24 July 2018, https://www.nytimes.com/2018/07/24/world/europe/austria -slovenia-border-migrants-spielfeld-schengen.html. In the winter of 2015, Austria constructed a fence along its border with Slovenia.

2. Natalie Zemon Davis, 'How the FBI Turned Me On to Rare Books', *New York Review* -turned-me-on-to-rare-books.

3. David Coleman, 'A Demographic Rationale for Brexit', *Population and Development Review* 42, no. 4 (2016): 690.

4. See the speech that Douglas Murray gave in The Hague in September 2006, at an event in honour of the murdered Dutch politician Pim Fortuyn: 'What Are We to Do About Islam? A Speech to the Pim Fortuyn Memorial Conference on Europe and Islam', 3 March 2006, Way Back Machine, http://web.archive.org/web/20080201133647/http://www.socialaffairsunit.org.uk/blog/archives/000809.php.

5. John Berger, *A Seventh Man: A Book of Images and Words About the Experiences of Migrant Workers in Europe* (Harmondsworth: Penguin, 1975), 220.

6. Ivan Krastev, *After Europe* (Philadelphia: University of Pennsylvania Press, 2017), 108.

7. Mahmood Mamdani, *From Citizen to Refugee: Ugandan Asians Come to Britain* (London: Pinter, 2011 [1973]), 55; Turin newspaper quoted in Donald M. Carter, *States of Grace: Senegalese in Italy and the New European Immigration* (Minneapolis: University of Minnesota Press, 1997), 166; Saskia Sassen, *Guests and Aliens* (New York: New Press, 1999), 138–139.

8. 'Speech by Prime Minister Viktor Orbán on 15 March', Website of the Hungarian Government, 16 March 2016, www.kormany.hu/en/the-prime-minister/the-prime-minister-s-speeches/speech-by-prime-minister-viktor-orban-on-15-march.

9. Gaëlle Fisher, '*Heimat* Heimstättensiedlung: Constructing Belonging in Post-War West Germany', *German History* 35, no. 4 (2017): 584.

Index